The
Satisfaction

JOHN FARLEY, JR

"Amanda" is a fictional character, any similarity to a real person, living or dead is coincidental, and not intended by the author. Her purpose is to elaborate on issues, and move the story forward. She is an amalgam of many people and conversations.

Many names in this work have been changed to protect those persons and the author.

Summary: A risqué romance leads to secret courts, rogue cops, and worldwide conspiracy that threatens the foundation of society.

ISBN10--0-9674252-4-7 ISBN-13 978-0-9674252-4-5 paperback

ISBN 10-- 0-9674252-3-9 ISBN-13 978-0-9674252-3-8 ebook

Editor: Cindy Davis
Front Cover Design: Guido Henkle
Back Cover Design and Interior Book Layout: Jennifer Carson

Dedicated to all my ancestors who have made my life possible. To my family, and future relatives, yet unknown. To all those who love liberty, and sacrifice their own freedom for mine and yours. To you, dear patriot, I call you friend, hero, brother, and sister— we are related.

To Liberty and Justice for All.

Ecclesiastes: 3: 1-8

A Time For Everything

There is a time for everything,
and a season for every activity under
heaven;

a time to be born and a time to die,
a time to plant and a time to uproot,
a time to kill and a time to heal,
a time to tear down and a time to
build,

a time to weep and a time to laugh,
a time to mourn and a time to dance,
a time to scatter stones and a time to
gather them,

a time to embrace and a time to
refrain,

a time to search and a time to give
up,

a time to keep and a time to throw
away,

a time to tear and a time to mend,
a time to be silent and a time to
speak,

a time to love and a time to hate,

a time for war and a time for peace.

1

Laughter and applause! I'd just finished performing my comedy hypnosis show. A singles group brought me in to their Northern California party at a local hotel. Over 125 men and women attended the posh event.

The way the show works is that after the introductions, the hypnotist, that's me, brings 12 men and women up on stage I hypnotize them in eight minutes and then the fun begins. People want to have a good time, and lots of laughs, so that's the aim. It's a part-time gig when I'm not leading dating seminars for men only.

After the show is over, and the handshaking done, I meet Amanda. She wants to interview me for a local magazine. I recognize her from the description over the phone. She heard me interviewed on a big radio show where I talked about some controversial issues, and she wants to know more.

A tall, thin blonde with a nice figure and all smiles as she waited for me at the doorway with a laptop under her arm. Fortunately, I'm able to stay on task. It's not easy when they're that attractive, but over the years I've learned to keep myself under control - usually. That may seem trivial, but not for me. Self-control around attractive women is a big deal. The price I've paid to develop that self-control has been steep, but we'll get to that.

As we walked down the hall, I asked the questions. "Did you enjoy the show?"

"It was entertaining," she said.

Unimpressed by how I'm able to seemingly make grown men, and women do all sorts of things they would normally never do in public, she turns the tables. "Let's start at the beginning. Where were you, and what were you doing when you discovered this so-called, 'master plan for humanity?'"

That made me anxious. I stretched my neck higher to look far down the hallway. "Let's not call it that."

"What then?" she said with an edge in her voice. This was a young woman who had lived her life believing the mainstream worldview.

"Let's just say it's a conspiracy by global leaders. Writing and speaking about this topic is not something I planned or ever wanted to have happen."

"Then why now?"

I opened the glass door to the hotel's cafe and let her walk through. She walked past me without a "thank you" and I made a mental note.

"It seems it's my destiny. I tried to escape this—this nightmarish reality, but it won't leave me alone."

We found a table in the cafe and got settled. After she pulled out her computer she blurted out, "And now you're a magician?"

As if water spilled onto my lap, I responded, "No, no. Hypnotist, I'm a hypnotist. I help people change their minds, access more of their human potential—improve their lives."

"And make them do silly things," she said sarcastically.

I smiled and chuckled again hoping to break the tension. "The show's a good time for everyone. It demonstrates that hypnosis is real. In my private and exclusive bootcamps for men," I said in a serious tone, "I subconsciously program each man's mind for dating success with attractive women, *such as yourself*," I said with a slight change of voice tone and a twinkle in my eye.

Amanda stared at me as her eyes got wide and her lips parted. "You can do that?"

"Of course." I gazed back at her with a playful, devilish grin. "It's 2/3rds confidence mixed with a generous portion of personality. But then there's all the rules of dating, that when ignored, lead to massive pain."

Amanda paused to take in what I said. Meanwhile, I scanned our surroundings. "We're going to need a much more comfortable place for me to tell you my story," I said, as I pushed back from the table.

"Let's go to the hotel lobby."

Actually, it's a room just off the lobby with big, plush furniture and an all-night health bar. I'd spotted it earlier when I arrived. We picked up our things and scurried off before someone else had the same idea.

I walked fast to avoid off the cuff conversation. "It's right over here." I pointed toward the corner.

I opened the heavy door to the room. Amanda's shoulders relaxed as she took in the calm atmosphere. A gentle lavender aroma engulfed us.

She chose the couch with big cushions and I sat on the other side of the coffee table in a plush love seat. We sank into the deep, soft furniture and I asked, "How should I start, 'Once upon a time?'"

She smiled politely with her computer on her lap ready to type. "What caused you to become such an outspoken critic of this subject?"

This subject—this subject.

"I suppose, I have a sense of justice and fair play. And, truth be told, I really enjoy women. And I like children. They're an acquired taste," I chuckled.

"The women I counsel are often disillusioned about love. Men are more confused than ever about their role in society and children are paying the price as a result of all this frustration and confusion. Not to mention that God has been minimized in people's lives."

Her squint softened when she heard "God" mentioned.

"My aim is to share my experiences, and start changing things for women's sake."

Her eyes widened and fixated on me as she stopped typing. I suspect she wasn't expecting that comment, but didn't completely believe it either.

"It started years ago for me..."

1993 - Mid-morning in New York City—Barry's Fifth Avenue Apartment.

My eyes felt as if they'd glazed over when an image popped into my mind.

She haunts me like a ghost. I suppress the thought. No matter where I am or what I do, her image eventually breaches into consciousness, the way a beach ball held under the water's surface forces its way to the top.

I gazed out Barry's apartment window overlooking Central Park, oblivious to the dark clouds crying up above. Barry spoke to me. "John, it's raining. On your way out, meet Harold at the limo. He'll take you wherever you want to go. I'll call down to let him know you're on the way."

I turned around and extended my hand. "Barry, I really appreciate that, thank you. I'll see you for a workout next week. Enjoy the weekend."

"You too." Barry draped a towel around his neck to absorb the sweat from our workout. As the elevator door closed inside his apartment I stepped outside myself to view the scene.

Barry's a very rich man. How rich, we don't know and it doesn't matter. He's rich enough to have a fabulous apartment with a private elevator straight to his door overlooking Central Park on the Upper East Side, a limo and driver, a personal fitness trainer, maids, and other things that make life comfortable. Those are my clients. In the blink of an eye the elevator door opened.

Sure enough, there was a well-dressed man holding an umbrella near the stretch limousine. Harold, a tall, black man with a pleasing personality. Dressed for GQ, he happily opened the car door with his free hand.

I dodged the rain and ducked inside. "Thank you very much!"

Moments later Harold was behind the wheel. This wasn't an old limousine or one with 800 number bumper stickers on it. This machine was black, shiny and looking as sharp as Harold's suit.

"I'm John, Barry's personal trainer."

Harold glanced into the mirror. "Nice to meet you. Mr. G said to take you wherever you want to go."

I slid across the leather seats to get comfortable. Like sliding into bed after a long day, I noticed the softness immediately. This was no taxicab and certainly not a bus ride.

"I'm heading back home to West 58th."

The car glided effortlessly into traffic like a hockey puck on ice. I felt a wave of relaxation come over me.

"I must say." I looked at Harold in the rearview mirror. "I could get used to this."

Typically, I walked through the city at breakneck speed from one appointment to the next. Today, I'd be soaked without this ride. I could seriously get used to this.

Wealth was certainly important, but my ultimate aim was to do something—something, memorable. The thought of achieving that lofty ambition made me smile. Memorable. Perhaps something great. Greatness. Why else be in New York City if not to do something great?

Seriously? I don't know what that would be, but I'm working on it. A flash of frustration coursed through my body. Perhaps I should settle for getting rich. As if that's easier.

I felt snobbish just sitting there without talking. "Yes, I'm Barry's personal trainer. I work with clients at their homes. A lot of clients are from the publishing industry."

Harold drove the long vehicle easily as if sightseeing on a sunny, country road on a Sunday morning instead of managing Manhattan's mid-morning traffic.

"I could use some fitness training myself." he said with a laugh.

"Everybody could use a little help in that area." With childlike wonder I gazed out the window. New Yorkers were scrambling across the wide streets. I felt a twinge of guilt bubble up into my throat. Why should I get to ride in a stretch limousine? I glanced down at my roughed up sneakers. After all, I'm not dressed for it. I know why. I'm well connected!

As we floated along, parallel to Central Park, I noticed those outside. Regular people, like me, mostly. They walked head down in the rain, dodging puddles and rushing for buses and taxis.

Half the people held up those miniature, cheap, black umbrellas sold on every Manhattan street corner when it rains. The other half carried a sturdy umbrella or none at all. Normally, I'd be sloshing through the puddles getting as wet as a dishrag if not for this ride.

I couldn't resist rubbing my hands across the soft seats. I eased back a little more. This is better than my furniture at home, but that's not a good comparison, I reasoned.

It's not that I'd never been in a limousine, but all limousines are not the same. I felt spoiled and I liked it. I reflected on how fortunate I was. Personal fitness trainer to the wealthy and powerful. Working for myself. Bigger and better things coming soon, I'm sure of it.

I stared off into the wide sycamore trees of Central Park. As the green leaves of those odd trees flashed in front of me, my mind drifted into a memory.

Before long, the limousine rounded a corner and brought me back to the present. I noticed the famous Tavern on the Green restaurant. Overpriced, but one of those things to do in Manhattan when you visit.

I'm not sure how we got to the west side so quickly, but I was soon lost in a daydream as the rain silently slid down the windows.

Tonight would be another opportunity for a career-launching event. Personal training was my day job, but as an aspiring motivational speaker, I lead seminars. My fire-walk seminar for The Learning Annex was tonight, and *ABC's Good Morning America* would be there to film the entire event.

Firewalking was something I discovered in the mountains of California. Only a handful of instructors in the world know this skill. Once out of college I added firewalking, hypnosis, martial arts and other mind power skills to my seminar toolkit.

My secret for successful firewalks? Hypnosis. Hypnotizing my seminar attendees made firewalking easier and safer.

Soon I'd be one of only four people—and perhaps the youngest—to hold a firewalk in the middle of Manhattan. The morning television show will broadcast the highlights nationwide. It's going to be an exciting event.

Some think firewalks aren't real, but they are. The wood we'll burn tonight will be cedar—a quarter cord. The flames that flicker off the wood are real, burning at a temperature of about 1,200 degrees.

The attendees: average New Yorkers with regular jobs, who expect a life changing experience. Even if they don't think they'll walk, by the time the nearly five-hour seminar is over, nine out of ten will toss their shoes and stroll the coals.

It's not really about mind over matter. The firewalk is about meeting fear head on. It's about breaking through the limiting fears that block human potential. That's the point of walking barefoot on burning hot coals, to master fears that suppress us. To master fear we have to overcome limitations within ourselves. The firewalk makes fear and success tangible.

The limousine moved down Central Park West like a boat gliding through a lazy river. My mind continued to lull me into a reverie. At 26, I was fired up. I had to be fired up to convince a group of professionals to want to take off their shoes and socks and walk on burning hot coals in the middle of the Big Apple

John Farley, Jr.

I recalled that earlier that day, The Learning Annex had set up a conversation with me, and Bill Ritter, the co-host of *ABC's Good Morning America* program. We agreed to meet at the hotel over on Madison Avenue for a pre-seminar interview.

"How's this?" Harold rolled the big car to a stop inches from the sidewalk.

"Great. No need to get out, I can manage." Harold looked like he had every intention of staying dry in the limo.

I opened the car door to see a line of wet New Yorkers pressed against a building trying to stay dry. They looked at me as I swung my gym bag over my shoulder. Admittedly, I felt strange, guilty perhaps, for hopping out of a limousine. As if I needed to justify my good fortune.

Once inside the apartment, I changed clothes. I have plenty of time, just relax and let go.

I drew a breath, and sat in a hardback chair to collect my thoughts. I thought about my life up to this point. Images flashed though my mind. I had my own real life firewalk to contend with.

A few years ago, when I was 23, I'd met a woman nearly 15 years older than me. It was at a seminar, a seminar like the one I was now teaching. I enjoyed motivational seminars and so did she.

My mind flashed to the end of that event. A group of us stood along the street outside the hotel. We were saying our goodbyes after spending an intense seminar weekend together.

The woman approached from across the street. She walked right up and wrapped her arms around me, kissed me squarely on the lips and placed a piece of paper in my hand. "Call me," she said still looking at me as she turned and walked away.

Stunned, I glanced at the paper. Whoa, what was that?

Soon afterwards, it was a weekly rendezvous, usually near her home on Long Island. She's a doctor and doing well. One daydream melded into another.

My memories skipped forward to later that summer. I remembered taking a trip to Greece with a friend. The vacation was a chance to get clarity in my life. A chance to plan my future.

My mind drifted to a memory of sitting on a beach on a Greek island. I was in the Aegean Sea on the tiny island off Paros called Antiparos. The temperature was easily one hundred degrees with the sun brightly shining.

As I sat on the large boulders, I felt my insignificance faced with the size and power of the sea. As the waves rolled in and crashed upon the rocks, inner conflicts rolled around inside my mind. My daydream skipped again to the long flight back home.

The woman I'd dated…. Something wasn't right. She's a free spirit, a child of the 60's. Me? Clark Kent, smirking to myself. It was my college newspaper that dubbed me Superman when I led the men's basketball team in fitness conditioning exercises. They'd never seen anyone do handstand push ups against a wall, splits or some of the exercises I barked out. The comparison was flattering.

I stared out the airplane into the clouds as my thoughts clashed. Point is, we're too different. She wasn't what I needed right now in my life. I had subconscious expectations even I couldn't articulate or didn't dare to. The daydream faded as the clouds blew past the plane.

The Greek adventure had given me mental space. I'd made up my mind to give this strange relationship one last ditch effort and if a miracle didn't happen, I'd end it. A loud truck honking its horn startled me—a reminder that I'm still in my Manhattan apartment daydreaming. Then, the scene of our last date came to mind.

I'd set a movie date. It was time to tell her it was over, but in person. I wanted to leave a slight opening in my mind for second chances. If something dramatic happened on the date, I'd reconsider. Another part of me was convinced that it—we—had to end. I can't keep doing this. I wanted to end it as quickly and as painlessly as possible. Then I reconsidered. Perhaps I'm wrong and I'd feel differently when we met.

The day and time for the date had arrived. Admittedly, I was unhappy about it.

I took her to the Ziegfeld Theatre in Manhattan to see White Palace with Susan Sarandon and James Spader. The poster read, "It's the story of a younger man and a *bolder* woman." It seemed to mimic what was going on with us.

We sat in the dark theatre without touching. During the film I became agitated. The movie struck a little too close to home for me. I sat brooding. What is this relationship based on besides physical attraction?

The more I watched the picture the more uncomfortable I became. My jaw tightened, my legs twitched and my mind narrowed. I didn't know what I felt, but there was something going on with her and I couldn't understand it. My emotions were being short circuited, like pulling a lamp cord from the wall socket.

The film ended and we walked along the city streets toward my place. A painful silence grew even though the city was filled with loud sounds of car horns and crowds of people. Why doesn't she say anything? I wanted to lighten the mood, but it didn't happen. Like water spiraling down a drain, my attitude was going south.

The inner conflict rose up again. Why is this so difficult? We said nothing until we reached the tall, heavy gate to my apartment building. I looked around. Was anyone nearby to make this an embarrassing confrontation? All was clear and I forced myself to blurt out what had to be said.

"Us—dating really isn't working out. I don't want to go out with you anymore," I said, coldly and with a hint of unjustified anger. I just didn't know any other way to do it.

At first, her facial expression seemed like I'd given her a compliment. Shock, then a forced, fake smile. I hesitated, waiting for a protest, but she said nothing.

"Okay?" I said in a *take that* manner.

"Okay." She shrugged as if she didn't mind at all. I fiddled with the key in the lock. As it opened, "Okay then, bye," I said coldly as I gave her one last glimpse. I hated doing it, but I had to end it somehow.

She left for her truck and I walked up the five flights to my apartment. I was ticked off at her and with myself. She seemed unconcerned by the whole thing. I don't know if it was the right thing to do, but something was wrong. Maybe the last couple months were meaningless to her. Maybe it was meaningless to me. Who knows?

I put her out of my mind as quickly as I could, relieved it was over, yet guilt plagued me. Life went on. Time went by and I had to move forward.

She put me on her newsletter list. She had her own doctor's practice and I now received her newsletter in my mailbox each month.

The first time the letter arrived it surprised me, but I soon got used to it. I'd look the newsletter over very quickly, page by page and then get up, walk over and toss it in the trashcan. This happened month after month, time and again. Newsletter after newsletter—all of them ended that way.

Except this one.

John Farley, Jr.

2

"Explain to me the newsletter," Amanda said.

"It was back at the start of summer—1991..."

New York City

Today's Manhattan air felt somewhat clean. It's strange how New Yorkers get used to living a little like zoo animals. City dwellers settle for tight spaces, polluted air, dirty streets and subways, and then there's the noise. Soon however, one gets habituated and it feels normal.

The characteristic Big Apple electricity was palpable as I walked along 9th Avenue. I felt good and noticed a guy working at the corner newsstand. The upside down, sensational headline on a newspaper caught my eye, but it turned out to be nothing important.

That's when I noticed my roommate walking half a block up the street.

"Steve!" I called out. It took a moment for the sound of my voice to reach him.

"Hey John." Steve had recently graduated from a college in the south and now worked as an engineer at NBC studios, General Electric, really. He'd be working in Manhattan for one year before he transferred out. With his 50,000 megawatt smile, and a "Yes We Can" attitude, Steve was a descent roommate and a genuine good guy. Smart, good looking, friendly—he was likely to inherit a bright future.

We met at the corner and Steve flashed his pearly whites as if he hadn't seen me in weeks. "I'm going out tomorrow night with a group of friends. You know, we'll grab some drinks and chat. Are you up for joining us?"

"Sure," I shrugged. "Why not?"

John Farley, Jr.

"Great! I'm going to drop something off at the office. I'll see you later."

Steve took off in one direction while I headed in the other.

Back at 58th Street, I picked up the mail and bounded up the five floors to our apartment. Rifling through the mail, I saw it. She sent me another newsletter.

This particular summer was hot. All the heat from the lower levels rose to the top floor like a helium balloon, but with nowhere to go.

Inside the apartment I tossed the mail onto the kitchen table and grabbed a bathroom towel to wipe the beads of perspiration off my forehead. Back in the kitchen, I scooped up the mail again and picked though it. Ah, there's Dee Dee's newsletter. I placed it down and went to the cabinet, grabbed a tall glass and the water jug on the countertop.

The cool water went down like velvet. Again, I picked up the mail on the tabletop.

I hope there's something good in here today. I sat down, and sank back into a kitchen chair to take a load off my feet.

After I'd scanned the other envelopes I thumbed through Dee Dee's newsletter. Feeling detached, I glanced at the pages and looked for something interesting. An open house is coming up. A descent health article on the next page. Some photos of people. I flipped the pages. And, ah, a picture of a smiling woman holding a newborn baby. Babies are nice, as I turned to the back page.

Wait. What did that say? I peeled the page back.

Let's read this. The baby has Dee Dee's last name. Hmm. I kept re-reading the caption.

Oh, it's her sister's baby. She and her husband had another baby. Good for them. I'd met Dee Dee's sister. I'm glad for them, but something—something is off. Something doesn't make complete—

Wait. No, that's not right. This doesn't make sense. This says—

That's not her sister's baby. That's her baby! I planted my feet squarely on the floor under me as I straightened myself in the chair, but next thing I knew I was standing.

Wait, wait, w-a-i-t a minute. Wait, okay, okay, okay, wait, wait. Let's count, stay calm, count, let's count.

I counted on my fingers. One, two, three, four, five, six, seven, eight, nine. Oh, what? Re-count. O-n-e, t-w-o...n-i-n-e.

Okay. It's possible, but it can't be. It can't have anything to do with me. She had to be seeing someone else when I went to Greece or after we split or before. Didn't she say it was impossible for her to get pregnant? I know she did.

I inhaled until my shirt buttons nearly popped and then sat back down. I stretched out my legs and leaned back to relieve the building anxiety before I crouched forward on the table to re-read the newsletter. This is a riddle, right? Stand up.

I paced throughout the apartment to focus and understand what I'd read. I decided I'd consult my roommate later when I saw him.

Steve arrived a few hours later. Our apartment had a strange setup. When you opened the door you were met by a brick wall. It's a railroad apartment. Turn left, and you'd pass through the kitchen area into Steve's room. Turn right and you'd end up in my room at the end of the hallway.

Steve walked in wearing jeans, a purplish golf styled shirt, sneakers and sunglasses. "Hey!" he called.

I walked out of my room. Steve took off his sunglasses. "Do you mind if I listen to music?"

"I don't mind, but I want to talk with you about something, if you have a moment."

"Sure, give me a second."

He ducked into his room. Within a few minutes he'd changed into shorts, grabbed a pre-made sandwich and turned on the tube. I walked into the kitchen area with the newsletter in hand.

"Steve, do you remember I told you about that woman I dated about a year ago?"

"Was that the dentist?"

"Doctor," I said.

Steve's hand shot into the air as if answering a game show question. "Doctor, that's it!"

I spoke cautiously. "I've been getting her newsletter for months—many months—since we dated."

Steve glanced back and forth from the baseball game.

"I received her newsletter today."

Steve took a bite of his sandwich as he looked hard at me, then glanced at the television.

I pulled my chair closer and leaned in. "Her newsletter seems to say," I swallowed and focused on the floor for a moment before letting the words loose, "that she had, a—baby."

Steve stopped chewing for an instant and looked at me as a blank stare crossed his face, then he quickly recovered. "Yeah. Great."

I stared at him waiting for the light bulb to turn on.

With mild curiosity he asked, "When did you go out with her?"

My stare grew more intense. "Last summer."

He chewed a few more times, then placed the sandwich on the plate and sat with his hands on his lap for a moment before extending an arm. "Let me see the newsletter." He read the article out loud as I listened and then counted on his fingers. His chest expanded just before speaking. "I don't think it's yours," he said without hesitating. "She would have told you. I'm sure she would have told you."

We looked at each other in uncomfortable silence. Steve's the kind of guy to tell you "it's just a flesh wound," after a near fatal accident. He's optimistic that way.

"If you really want to make sure, there's a simple way to find out. Call her up and say, 'I read your newsletter and I just wanted to congratulate you on your baby,' and see what she says." Steve stood up and with a slight hesitation, pushed the newsletter at me as if it was no big deal. He grabbed his sandwich and took a bite.

After all, it's not his issue. But perhaps I worry too much.

"That makes sense. She'll probably tell me that it's someone else's or maybe she did one of those artificial arrangements. Who knows, right?"

"Right," he said. We sat facing the television, but I couldn't see anything. My mind was flooded with thoughts.

Steve was done talking about the newsletter.

"I'm going to read in my room," I told him.

The following day, when the apartment was quiet, I psyched myself up to call Dee Dee's number. I hadn't dialed it in a long time.

Was it still the same?"

I bit the bullet and went to the phone. I have to know that I at least made the call. It's the responsible thing to do. I opened my address book. There it is. I stared at each digit the way a new salesman does before his first cold call.

The phone receiver felt as heavy as a dumbbell. My heart pounded. When the phone rang, my heart raced faster and my mouth felt dry.

The phone rang and rang, but no answer. Finally, an answering machine. "Hello, Dee Dee, it's John. I received your newsletter today and I—I read something in there I wanted to speak with you about. Please give me a call."

I left my number, just in case she didn't have it any longer.

It was done. I made the effort. It was the right thing to do. If this baby has anything to do with me then Dee Dee will call me back. Better to face reality than live in denial. For all I know she's happy and with someone else. I could be imposing.

Hours later, Steve came home and started to wash dishes.

"Hey."

"Hey, so did you call her?"

"I called, but had to leave a message."

"Good!" Steve said, giving me a verbal high five. He continued as if negotiating a business deal.

"The ball is in her court now. If she has something to say she'll call you back."

There was no call back from her that day or the next day, or the next week or the next month. My mind was clear now. In fact, I never gave it another thought. She had a new life, and I had mine. I felt relieved and happy that things ended well for her.

My life continued on with graduate school at Columbia, and my small, but liberating in-home personal fitness training business. The summer passed and I soon celebrated my 25th birthday. Life was going along and I was more concerned about my career than anything.

November 1991

I'm at my apartment when the phone rang. No caller ID. "Hello?" Silence.

"Hello?"

Is it a prank call or a bad connection? Tempted as I was to hang up, I waited when suddenly a faint voice that sounded half asleep and unhappy emerged on the other end.

"It's Dee Dee. I'm returning your call."

My mind raced to put voice, name and face together. "Dee Dee. Oh. Hi! You're returning my call."

She's just being courteous.

"The call I made to you four months ago?" I said it with an attitude, but was met with silence. "Thanks. Yes, I was calling about your newsletter. I read it and I noticed you—" Suddenly I felt pressure. The same feelings that had snuck up on me months before.

"It seems from what I read—" The gravity of what I was asking hit me. "What I'm trying to say is—that from what I read in there—it seems that you…you—had—it seems, from what I read—it seems that you, had—a baby. And—well, ah, so, I was wondering..."

My heart thumped so loud I thought she might hear it. The time had come to ask the critical question I thought I'd put to rest months earlier.

Her complete silence intensified my anxiety. I stood with my feet apart to ground myself. My neck tensed. The phone was silent.

"I'm curious though—who—who, I was wondering—who—I just was wondering Who. Is. Who. Is. The. —Father?" I grimaced with eyes closed, I held my breath as I pressed the phone into my left ear with my right hand clenched, bracing for impact.

Silence. As if the phone were muted. My teeth clenched as I waited for the balloon of anxiety inside me to burst. Suddenly, the silence broke.

"We better talk," she said like an unhappy boss. My mind went blank. I wasn't ready for that answer.

What did that mean? Reflexively, while in a daze of confusion, I said, "Sure. When do you want to meet?" as if setting up a casual lunch date.

Her reply was decisive. "This weekend."

We quickly decided on the day and time and hung up. I tried to put it out of my mind, yet the upcoming date lingered like a stuck—in—your—head radio jingle.

I sat down and put the pieces together. I concluded again that I wasn't the father. I knew what it was. She and the child's father had broken up, and now she wanted me to help her, to be there for her. I'd be her shoulder to cry on.

I'll hear her out. She was probably having a difficult time without the father around. I'll comfort her and provide moral support. But I also wondered, could this be an elaborate plot to get me back?

The week crept by like a stalled subway car on a hot, humid day. The meeting with Dee Dee was coming up. Like an impending doctor's appointment, I felt anxious as the day came closer.

The weekend arrived and the appointed time approached. I headed out to get on the Long Island Railroad. During the train ride I put everything out of my mind as much as possible.

She just wants to see me. That's what this is about. I kept my expectations low. What does she want with me? What? As if struggling with a Zen koan, a riddle, it was too much for my conscious mind. I don't know, we'll see.

The train arrived in Huntington Station, Long Island. It had been nearly one and one half years since I'd been out there. I stood inches in front of the train doors and waited for them to open as I took a deep breath. Commuters huddled around the train door the way eager dogs do—ready for their daily walk. The train doors burst open. I stepped onto the platform and rushed down to the street level.

At the edge of the parking lot I scanned the sea of vehicles idling bumper to bumper. Where is her SUV-like truck? Suddenly, like the sun emerging from behind a cloud, I saw it.

Dee Dee sat in the driver's seat like a still painting. I walked to the truck with naive confidence and slight trepidation. I peered through the passenger window when our eyes met. She was different. Her hair was now much shorter, just past her shoulders. Her face was expressionless at best, timid at worst.

As I opened the passenger side door, a baby's car seat came into view inches in front of me. I looked down at the car seat to see a tiny baby in pink looking up at me. For some reason, I hadn't expected to see this baby, not here, not now.

Dee Dee's face spontaneously turned into a smile while she gazed down at her. Then, as her eyes lifted to meet mine, her smile quickly vanished. Now, she looked like she'd stolen a cookie from the cookie jar. Why? I wondered.

The tiny baby, wrapped in pink, smiled at me briefly. I realized the baby owned that front seat and she wasn't going anywhere. I squeezed my way into the back. Dee Dee started the truck and we began moving. The silence was thick. I stopped my mind from jumping to conclusions. Instead I remained in the moment, open to finding out what happened.

I leaned over the front seat. "What's her name?"

In a mournful tone, as if someone had died, rather than been born, Dee Dee spoke. "Sally." Dee Dee seemed too depressed or afraid to be a new mom. But not when she looked at that baby. Every glance at the little girl made her smile.

We arrived at Dee Dee's home as the truck came to a stop. I knew she'd lived with a man previously. He'd been very sick. Perhaps he was the father and had since passed on. I tried to figure it out.

So, here's her home. She has a baby, but she's not saying anything to me. What does all this mean? She lifted the car seat with the infant inside as we walked into her living room.

For the first time, I saw where she lived. A small, well kept place on two acres of land with a garden in a nice neighborhood. I rent an apartment, go to graduate school and work a part time business and other jobs. She's so much further along than I am. We're opposites in many ways.

I stood near the door in the living room. The baby rested in the car seat amusing herself. I had to ask the most basic question, the question that remained unanswered.

Dee Dee stood in the living room focused on the baby moving her arms and legs. The room looked nice, neat and clean. Everything in the room fit perfectly, but me.

I stood close to the door, and began to feel more certain that the father had left her high and dry. Confused at this point, I blurted out the question as I caught her glance.

"So, who is, the—father?"

Her body contorted. She burst into tears as she walked into me and forced my embrace. "I didn't know what to do," she said over sobs. "You broke up with me. I was going to tell you that night, but when you left, I decided I'd never tell you."

John Farley, Jr.

Numbness covered me like a blanket. What is she saying? I turned to the car seat. Is she telling me I'm the father? No.

Confused, shocked, in denial, "What? I'm the—" Time stood still. "Why did you tell me then?"

Her eyes briefly flashed at me. "A friend convinced me that I should tell you."

She gently pushed away and looked at Sally. "I want you to know that we're fine and that you're free to go and live your life. We don't need you to be with us."

The tears along with her closed body posture suggested something more.

My pose likely resembled a wax statue while Dee Dee smiled at the baby.

"Isn't she gorgeous? I can't hate you too much. You look just like her." she said.

"How can you tell?" I asked. Wait. "What? Hate me? Why would you hate me? Besides, she would have to look like me. I was here first."

Dee Dee glanced in my direction. "You did this to me. It's your fault. But she's so beautiful."

Before I could digest the situation, she pulled me from the living room to her bedroom and the waiting waterbed. Whatever confusion was within me was suspended for a time.

But confusion quickly returned by the time the waterbed waves settled. Eventually, it was time to leave and get back to Manhattan.

Dee Dee drove me to the train station for the hour ride home. I said goodbye to baby Sally in the car seat.

My clouded thoughts raced while I waited on the train platform.

After the locomotive roared into the station I found an isolated spot by myself. These train seats were rough, crowded and barely comfortable. Nothing like limousine seats. My life was now taking a new track.

What just happened? What—just—happened?

Alone with my thoughts, reality was sinking in fast. I am that baby's father. A father. Her father! The pressure overwhelmed my senses. Heat rushed to my face in embarrassment. Shame overwhelmed me as I sat feeling a tremor inside.

God, what did I do? This can't be real. This wasn't supposed to happen. I have plans for my life. Something, perhaps a raindrop, hit my cheek. No, it was a tear that I never felt coming. I swatted it away before anyone noticed.

My thoughts ran to my sisters, my brother, my mom, roommate, friends, relatives, clients, my karate teacher. The next thought rushed in and hit hard. How will I ever be able to do *this*?

3

May 1993

"That's how fear controls us," I said to an empty, echoing living room while I paced back and forth. I gestured with one hand and gripped notes with the other while I made imaginary eye contact with an invisible audience.

A few more hours and my firewalk seminar would start. The sod guys would arrive soon. Sod, the big, thick, strips of grass that the hot coals are placed upon, is crucial for firewalks. Two layers—not one.

One layer of sod is a big mistake. It would leave a black, smoldering mess on the Madison Avenue sidewalk. Imagine a small camp fire with burning logs. Then imagine ten campfires placed side by side. That's what the firewalk looks like before it burns down to glowing hot coals.

The phone rang, but I kept rehearsing until the last moment before, "Hello?"

"Hey, it's Trent. We have the sod, and we're waiting to cross the bridge into the city."

"Great. You'll have plenty of time—see you at the hotel." I hung up and scanned my notes. Where was I? The desk clock caught my eye. Oh, look at the time. Let's check the seminar list once more.

For some reason, my mother came to mind. Perhaps because tonight was a pressure filled event and it reminded me of another one. Oh God, I thought, remembering the day I told her about Sally.

I sat on the couch for a moment, took a deep breath and closed my eyes. The memory came back and I could see everything in full color. My mom, seventy years old and a devout Irish Catholic. I'd never even brought a girlfriend home before.

Dialing her number was tough. I was embarrassed. I could hardly remember anxiety so intense. Here I am, a young swinging bachelor, no girlfriend, calling up my mother to tell her I'm a father.

The feeling was frightening. The adrenaline rush and the anxiety reminded me of a childhood memory when mom left for the grocery store. To help out, I vacuumed the living room, but I knocked over an antique lamp with the hose. The lamp smashed into pieces in the living room. All I could think of was how irate she was going to be. I heard her coming up the porch steps when the front door opened. "Mom, I was—" But she saw the mess and burst out, "Oh my God!" It was like I'd shot the dog. She was livid over that one.

Today was different, but the feeling was the same. Now, nothing's knocked over, but someone got knocked up. Mom's phone rang. It felt like my head was held under water, waiting to surface.

I knew every inch of her home. I imagined she heard the phone ring and walked from the kitchen three rooms over. Then, the inevitable. That familiar voice answered the phone. "Hello?"

I cleared my throat one last time, "Hi Mom, it's John."

"Oh John, what a surprise. How is everything with you?"

"Mom, I need to tell you something. I'm going to tell you this, but I'm not joking around about it. I'm serious about what I'm about to say." She was used to me joking around.

Patiently she asked, "What is it John?"

"Mom, I'm— I was with a woman, and we—" I took a deep breath as I clenched my hand as I raised it to my temple to physically brace myself as I exhaled, like releasing air out of a slightly overfilled balloon. "She—she—"

Her anxiety kicked in. "What is it?"

I stuttered at first, but then I let it out, like diving into a cold pool. "She became pregnant." I said it as I waited with clenched face and hands.

She chuckled, "You're kidding with me, aren't you?"

Oh, God no. Now I have to convince her. "Mom, I'm not kidding. I need you to listen to what I'm saying. I'm serious. I got a woman pregnant." Saying it again wasn't easier, it just brought the gravity of the situation into my consciousness, and increased my shame.

The yelling started. "What? What are you— Oh My God!"

"Mom, Mom, she had a baby! I'm the father. It's a six-month-old girl. I know I—"

"Holy Mary mother of God!"

The embarrassment flooded me. "Mom. I know, I—"

"Praise the Lord! Oh My God!"

What? What did she say? Did I hear that right? She sounded giddy and kept yelling. "Oh my God! Praise the Lord!" She only yelled like that when the St. Patrick's Day parade was on television.

Mom seemed shocked, yet thrilled to have another grandchild. Until now, I thought I'd purchased a one way ticket to Hell.

A loud honking noise came from the street below jolting me into the present as my eyes popped open. I took a breath and closed my eyes again. My mind drifted to another time.

Over the last eighteen months, Dee Dee and my mom were getting emotionally closer. It was a little disturbing to me. My mother began taking Dee Dee's side on issues between us. She wrote to Dee Dee and talked on the phone with her much more than she did me.

Soon, Sally would turn two, but Dee Dee only let me see her when she wanted. I felt frustrated not seeing my own child. I felt like a rental dad or babysitter. I lived a dual life. One as Sally's part time dad and the other as a bachelor.

John Farley, Jr.

The phone rang. My eyes popped open and shocked me into the present. I stood up.

"Hello?"

It was the seminar team. "I'm heading over now."

All my gear was ready and it was time to meet up at the hotel. I left the apartment and hailed a cab. During the ride I imagined a successful event. After all, this seminar was going to air on *ABC's Good Morning America.*

The cabbie raced to the hotel street corner. "Right here!" I stuffed the cash through the slot in the thick plastic partition.

I dodged cars while hurrying across Madison Avenue and headed directly to our team's truck loaded with the sod and wood.

Trent, the one in charge of the supplies, stood at the base of the truck. A tall, lanky, blonde, Nordic type fellow, he's a hardworking laboring man.

"Hi Trent. You have everything handled?"

Trent put down the logs and turned around. He slipped off his gloves and reached for my hand. "Everything's all set." He pointed to the street corner. "The police officer is over there. The fire truck just arrived. Those firemen can't believe that people are going to pay money to walk barefoot on hot coals."

I grinned. "You know, the firewalk's a metaphor. Participants are paying to have a once in a lifetime experience of going beyond their self-imposed limitations. Sometimes you have to do something way outside your comfort zone to discover what you're really capable of."

I glanced at the firemen in all their gear as they stood watching. "Everywhere I go" I told Trent, "firemen are amazed at the firewalk seminar. People get conditioned to believe certain things about life and themselves. Those beliefs can end up limiting our lives. The firewalk is about breaking through to another dimension of possibility. It's about having faith and overcoming fear in order to live the life you dreamed possible for yourself."

34

The television crew arrived for the interview. A well dressed man approached and crossed the street. "You must be the man himself," he said.

I smiled as we shook hands. "Yes, and you must be Mr. Bill Ritter."

Bill Ritter, a sharp, savvy New Yorker and co-host of the weekend show seemed excited. "You're pretty young. What qualifies you to tell people how to improve their lives?"

I had to think quickly about that. "The firewalk's a skill. One I know how to do. Just like karate. At 17 I became a black belt. I'm qualified to teach karate and I also know how to walk on hot coals safely. So, if you want to know how, I can show you."

Ritter mulled over my answer as we started toward the hotel. "We'll interview you inside," he said as the television crew followed.

My excitement grew. I'd learned to turn my fear of public speaking into enjoyment so now an interview for one of America's biggest shows would be fun not frightening.

The crew set up the lights and cameras. Bill looked at me as we sat with bright lights in our faces. "What else do you do?"

"I'm a fitness consultant to executives."

Ritter paused. "You mean, you're a personal fitness trainer?"

With a nod and gesture, I agreed. "Yes, personal trainer and seminar leader."

The cameras weren't rolling yet and Ritter wanted to loosen me up. "You don't have any children, do you?"

I froze momentarily. Where did he get that question? I took a slow, deep breath. "Actually,—I—have a daughter." I smiled, with some embarrassment. Was that answer going to end up on national television?

Ritter followed up. "How old?" With the bright television lights in my eyes, he'd thrown me a curve ball.

"She— she's two—just turned two," I said, feeling as though my secret was out.

John Farley, Jr.

"We're ready." A crew member with headphones around his neck said. Time for the real interview. Ritter launched with questions about the seminar and everything went very well.

The attendees filled up the seminar room. Everything in the hotel room was set up including our DJ. Dance music played until it was time for me to take center stage.

I came out and got everyone involved right away. "Everybody stand up! Clap your hands. Let's get the energy up!" The seminar launched into high gear. I noticed a tall, thin, blonde haired woman at the seminar. She looked attractive for sure and seemed to have a "no make up, country girl" quality about her.

Hours passed and it was time for the secret sauce. Hypnosis was the ingredient that made my seminar complete, the way spices make a meal extra good.

The lights dimmed as we approached the hypnosis portion of the seminar.

I yelled, "Move the chairs and find a spot on the floor."

Moments later, there were bodies crowded together, lying in every direction.

I guided everyone, including Bill Ritter, into a hypnotic trance. The music reached a crescendo with *Chariots of Fire*. After the hypnosis, the lights came on and the people staggered to their feet. The cheering and clapping reached a fever pitch. Everyone followed my lead and yelled."

It's time to walk barefoot on burning hot coals. Everyone followed me outside and across the street to the fire. A crowd of spectators had gathered to see what was about to happen. The air felt cool and the sky looked dark, but television lights lit up the sidewalk.

Lead by example, I reminded myself. I took Trent's rake and plunged it into the burning coals. The rake dragged flaming coals across the sod bed. Two or three strokes and I'm forced to turn away from the heat that's nearly melting my face.

Attendees waited patiently as I raked out the coals. The coal bed sizzled and glowed in the night sky. I raked a ten foot long, three foot wide gauntlet of fire across the sod grass.

I slipped off my dress shoes, then peeled off my dark socks, and rolled my pants halfway up my legs. I feel exhilarated and nearly ready to put flesh on fire. The moment of truth arrived. I stood inches from the start of the glowing hot coal bed. I focused and let the crowd's anticipation build.

Go!

Confidently I took the first step onto the sizzling coals. As a crowd of seventy five watched and bright television lights flooded my eyes, I walked across until I reached Trent on the other side. I wiped my feet and lifted my arm in victory.

Some in the crowd reacted with cheers while others watched motionless. I walked back to the front of the line to direct the seminar attendees.

The participants lined up ready to go. The first man looked determined. He stood barefoot waiting for me. "When you're ready, go," I said.

With his suit pants rolled up high and his white shirtsleeves up past his elbows, he exhaled and walked across the coals as if it were moist grass.

Next was a young woman. Her face looked relaxed and focused. With a gentle style she crossed the coal bed.

Ritter started near the back of the line, but now it was his turn. He looked completely determined, and focused.

I told him, "When you're ready, go."

He stepped out confidently with large, commanding steps. He marched across with power. At the end he wiped his feet, pumped his fist and yelled, "Yes!"

At first he stared straight ahead as he paced in a semi-circle toward the camera. He grinned from ear to ear. His hands rubbed over his face and head in astonishment as the elation hit him full force. Then he let out the pent up anxiety. "Ha, ha, ha, ha—I did it! ...I can't believe it, I did it!"

It was a fantastic night and a big success. We did what many believe to be impossible. Thirty people walked barefoot on hot coals, unharmed. More importantly, some limiting beliefs were shattered.

One month later, when the show aired on Father's Day June 20th, 1993, Bill Ritter told the nation, "It was unbelievably exhilarating."

I decided to host a free seminar a few weeks later at the same hotel. No firewalk this time, just an informational seminar. Some of the previous firewalk participants who felt empowered came back. A few rows in was a blonde woman and a man.

They sat quietly and at the end of the presentation, they came up. I stepped away from the podium to shake hands, "Nice to see you both."

The woman asked, "Do you have a moment?"

She looked serious. I wondered for a split second if there'd been a problem since the firewalk, but her demeanor suggested something else.

"Sure," I said.

The woman handed me an ordinary-looking videotape. "We'd like it if you'd watch this video. We believe you're someone who can impact a lot of people and get the word out about this."

I looked at what appeared to be a homemade video label. This can't be for a multi-level marketing opportunity because she's not promoting hard enough.

I took the video. The guy seemed easy going, while she had a sense of mission about her.

"Sure, I'll take a look. Thank you." The man interjected, "Our phone number is on there. You can call us if you want to discuss it. We'd like to speak with you more after you've seen it."

My curiosity was piqued. Either this video is a waste of time—some shady business scheme—or hmm, I don't know. But, I'm curious now.

4

The apartment door squeaked as it shut behind me. I whipped off my jacket and tie, then my shoes. All I could think of was the video. I pulled it from my bag and crouched down at the VCR. My fingers pushed the plastic rectangle into the machine. Let's see what this is.

I sat on the edge of the couch. What could be on this video that's so important?

Immediately, the image bounced around the screen. The sound started off disjointed. The screen image fluttered and skipped. Then it settled down. Sounds became normal. Images of Bill Clinton taking the oath of office for president flashed across the screen. Images of slums, poverty and police in riot gear flickered on a bed of ominous music.

It's talking about the history of the country, the founding fathers. What's this about? Where is it going?

To my surprise there was a photo of one of my fitness clients: David Rockefeller eating a meal with dictator Fidel Castro of Cuba. What is Rockefeller doing in a film like this?

The Rockefeller family wealth is so vast, it's known as The Great Fortune. I was the exercise physiologist guiding him through his exercise program at Cardio Fitness Center at Rockefeller Center. He and I talked whenever he came in. Eventually, I worked as personal fitness trainer for Peggy, his wife, at their East Side mansion.

This video was discussing the Founding Fathers, laws, and events that happened generations—centuries—ago. Why are they talking about the banks? What is the Federal Reserve Bank? What do they mean that the Federal Reserve Bank is no more federal than Federal Express? Intriguing, but so what?

After laying out the history and the facts, the film made incredible claims:

1) The Federal Reserve is not Federal, but is a private company.

2) Income tax is based on voluntary compliance, and

3) Income tax is a fraud. All the money collected from the income tax goes to pay the national debt, which was created by the Federal Reserve Bank.

4) FEMA - The Federal Emergency Management Agency can be activated by the President of the United States to put Americans into concentration camps.

Interesting, but this has nothing to do with health, personal development, or success - does it? I leaned in closer.

This was the video they wanted me to see? That income tax is a fraud? It's a violation of the fourth and fifth amendments to the constitution? Wait a minute. This is all very interesting, but whoever made this video is trying to tell me that all the accountants, all the tax lawyers, all the college professors and all the politicians, are behind an income tax fraud or they're just not smart enough to figure this out?

This is pretty far fetched—and I have an open mind.

The video ended. I sat back on the couch to ponder what I'd seen and the folks who gave it to me. They sure seemed sincere.

When morning came around the video was still on my mind. After getting a glass of water, I strolled into the living room to find the video on the table—as if it was waiting for me.

I popped it in the machine as I stretched my legs and sat to watch it a second time. This sure is radical.

A few days later, my lawyer and friend from martial arts class, and I were on the phone talking business. I stared at the blank wall in front of me as he came on the line. "Jerry, I have to get my business taxes completed. Who can you recommend?"

"John, great to hear from you. Stella. She's excellent. I've known her for years. She'll do a great job for you."

The video was fresh in my mind. "By the way, I was given a video by folks who came to my firewalk seminar. It was all about—and I know this is going to seem outrageous—but it's about how the income tax is, well, voluntary and a fraud. It talked about the Federal Reserve being private and—"

Chuckles came through the phone. "Tax protesters! You got propaganda from tax protesters."

"Tax protesters? I don't know. There were very interesting points, I mean—"

In a loud voice, he got my attention. "John, do you know how many people have tried to get out of paying the income tax and failed? That's how they got Al Capone. Forget it." More chuckles. "I have a Master's degree in taxation." His volume lowered nearly to a whisper, "Everybody wants to put money in tax shelters—offshore bank accounts. Stay out of trouble. All those arguments used by people have been tried, and they've all failed. Tax protesters go to jail."

No doubt that Jerry knew what they taught in law school about taxes, but could there be more? "I hear you. I'm not talking about doing anything, but it raises some interesting questions. How can they make you sign something under penalty of perjury if it's not voluntary? How could anyone be forced to waive their Fifth Amendment right not to be a witness against themselves?"

The chuckles continued. "Forget it!"

"But Jerry, wait. Listen. Signing a 1040 form is signing a confession, right? They can't just put a gun to your head and make you sign it. Signing has to be voluntary. If it's voluntary, then you just have to stop volunteering, right?"

Jerry's voice became slow, soft, calm and clear. "The courts have ruled against all tax protesters for many years. With his New York/Italian accent, he continued. "Look, stay out of trouble. Stay away from tax protesters."

I drew a breath. "Okay, I'll file whatever the accountant says to file, but there's something wrong here. Something doesn't make logical sense."

"John, I always enjoy talking with you. I have to go now and meet a client."

"No problem. I have to go too. I'm doing personal fitness training at a new studio. I'll talk to you soon."

We hung up and I sat for a moment to reflect. He hadn't answered the Fifth Amendment question.

I was starting work at Biodesign a new personal training gym down on 23rd Street off Broadway. My new boss was a character. Eric was barely 22. He'd been taking voice lessons, so he spoke with a deep, full voice, which was like talking to a radio announcer. He's aggressive, optimistic, friendly and a little too confident.

There was someone else too. A young, blonde haired, blue-eyed girl worked at the studio as a personal trainer and as the self-appointed manager. Originally from California, Janet was in New York to earn a master's degree in health promotion. It turned out that putting some miles between she and her father was a side benefit of New York City.

At 23, Janet was an innocent, California girl. I wasn't trying to corrupt any innocent girls—I seemed more attracted to girls who wanted to corrupt me. Janet wore upper middle class clothes and had that all-American look to her.

After a few weeks working with each other, I decided it wouldn't hurt to talk to Janet outside of work.

"Bye!" Janet said to a client as he left the studio.

At that moment, I put my gym bag into a locker. I walked near the only desk in the place and looked through my day planner.

When the client was out of sight, Janet turned and passed by.

"Janet, what would you say about grabbing something to drink around here after work?"

She brushed the hair away from her face as she scooped a folder off the desk. "I'd go, but I need to find out about something."

Hmm. What does that mean?

While Janet made a phone call, my next client came in and we started working out on the cardio equipment. From across the small room Janet called to me. "I can do it."

Great. This will be nice.

After work, we walked outside. I looked down 23rd Street thinking about where to go. I suspect that Janet sensed my indecision. "I know a bar and restaurant around the corner." It was a warm summer night. Cars buzzed all up and down the streets. We crossed to the other side of 23rd Street. Within moments we were standing in front of a tavern.

I reached for the door and she ducked under my arm. Once the heavy wooden door closed, the city traffic noise disappeared. The dim lighting and the quiet atmosphere made the place seem intimate.

"Two?" asked the young hostess who greeted us. She led the way into the half filled restaurant.

I slid into my side of the booth once Janet got settled I noticed the solid, dark wooden walls, and table. My aunt had told me to be careful of restaurants with dark walls, they are great cover ups for an insect infestation. Not a pleasant thought, so I didn't mention it.

The waitress came over. "Hi, I'll be your server. Do you know what you'd like?"

"Ladies first." "I'll have a beer," Janet said.

The waitress sounded like an auctioneer as she listed the brands. Janet chose one. I looked at her curiously now. I examined her face—too young and innocent to order beer.

"Cranberry juice for me. Thank you." The waitress turned and left. A moment of uncomfortable silence lingered in the air. "I don't drink," I explained. "People ask me, 'are you on medication? Is there something wrong?' I tell them I just don't drink. My karate teacher never drank and frankly, I can't think of a good benefit to drinking, so I don't."

Janet smiled. "We had a lot of parties in college. I partied too much my freshman year." I noticed her blonde bangs as she gave a nervous giggle. They gave her an innocent look. "My grades weren't good that first year. My parents weren't happy so I partied less the next year."

When the drinks came, Janet drank her beer, but with some hesitation. I sensed her self-consciousness as I sipped my cranberry juice. "Did you study physical education in college?"

A hint of pretension made her straighten up at that comment. "No. Exercise physiology."

I squinted a little. "I don't know any undergraduate programs in exercise physiology. Are you sure it wasn't physical education with an exercise physiology minor?"

Janet wasn't about to be labeled a physical education teacher. "Our program was mostly exercise physiology."

"I've never seen a undergraduate degree program in exercise physiology, but anyway, that's interesting." My two fingers pinched the straw in my glass as I went to suck on it. "Is your family in California?"

"My parents and brother are, but they're originally from out here. I still have family on Long Island."

We kept talking. I sensed a little insecurity. The check came, and the waitress placed it in the middle between us.

"I'll get it." I reached into my pocket, as Janet reached for her purse. "Are you sure?" I gave her a quick smile. "Yeah."

We left and said our goodbyes. This non-date ended well. Janet was someone I felt comfortable with.

In The Fitness Studio:

Days went by and soon we were back at the studio training clients. When the last client left for the evening, Janet seemed to be hanging around a little longer than necessary.

I picked up two dumbbells and placed them on the metal rack. Janet's reflection in the wall mirrors caught my eye. "Janet, how would you like to go to a pool club on Friday?"

Looking as though she hardly heard me, she went to look at her schedule. "Friday?" There was a hesitation. Uh—oh. "Sure," she said.

From her body language I couldn't tell how interested she was. I liked her easygoing style. This would be fun. Pool's not my game, but I'm an athlete and she's a girl. I'll do fine.

Friday, after work, Janet changed her clothes. She now looked like we were going on a date in a form-fitting, black leather-like dress that ended a couple inches below the knee.

We walked into the pool club on the west side of 23rd Street. I noticed guys huddled around one table. We choose an empty table toward the back. The lights were dim. Besides the occasional loud "crack" of the cue ball slamming into the others, the place was quiet.

We got our pool sticks. Janet's skirt distracted me, but not enough to completely wreck my focus. I gave her a big smile. "Alright, here we go. You can break first."

Janet's demeanor changed. She looked serious, with a cocky attitude. She smacked the cue ball, but nothing went in. Undaunted, she focused on the table.

My turn. "Let's see what I can do." My first shot went in, but I missed the next.

Janet chalked the pool stick as she gazed across the table. She walked as if she owned the place. She bent over the table to line up her shot, as her butt caught my eye.

The stick moved fluidly between her fingers. With a quick flick, the cue ball bashed into the target ball, which rolled easily into the corner pocket. Janet grabbed the blue chalk, and rubbed it on the stick as if filing her fingernails, but without looking.

I ended up standing for several minutes while she knocked ball after ball into the pockets. Then she missed. I stretched my arms out, like I was ready to get serious. I lined up my shot and knocked the ball into the pocket. But missed the next. Janet quickly ended my agony by knocking the rest of her balls in.

John Farley, Jr.

That was humbling. "I see you're a shark and you didn't tell me."

Janet smiled, and giggled. "My dad taught me to play pool. We have a pool table at home. I used to practice a lot."

I nodded.

A pool table at home. She must have been upper middle class. I was lucky to have a bike, a basketball and a park down the street.

The night ended well and we had a good time.

After several more dates I invited Janet over to my place. She accepted. Since I had a roommate, "my place" was mostly my room. I stepped away to use the bathroom. When I came back in, Janet looked agitated, as if something was on her mind. "I want to ask you something." She looked serious, yet uncomfortable.

I prepared myself. "Yes?"

"I wasn't snooping or anything, I was just looking at the things you have on your shelf and—" I knew where this is going.

"I noticed a Father's Day card from your mom to you. Why would your mom give you a Father's Day card?" I paused and repeated the question. "That does seem odd, doesn't it?"

Oh, no, what now? Thinking quickly, but with nowhere to go, I took a breath and swallowed. "She gave me the card because I'm—I'm a—I'm a father." Janet's blue eyes widened.

Why did this have to come up? I'm not ready for this conversation. I was never ready for this conversation with anyone.

We sat down and I told her the story. Something I rarely told anyone. Surprisingly, Janet was accepting of the idea of me being a dad. I clearly struggled with this new identity. I wasn't looking for a girlfriend either. My focus was creating a successful career.

Dee Dee was happy being a mother and letting me have "play dates" with her daughter, but only when she wanted. At this point, Dee Dee treated me like a second rate babysitter. I had no say in Sally's life except when I had her. I was the daddy doll that got pulled off the shelf once in a while when Dee Dee felt like it. The more I begged to see Sally, the more Dee Dee enjoyed shafting me. With Janet in the picture, the picture frame was about to explode.

5

Dee Dee knew I was desperate to reconnect with her. She acted like a cold fish whenever we spoke. I pretended I had moved on, but she knew better. She could always sense my desperation.

Then, something changed. The last time I went to see Sally, I was more relaxed, more unconcerned and Dee Dee must have noticed something was different.

She was throwing a birthday party in celebration of Sally turning three. It was a big deal, and a big event. I was invited. The big bash was set to be held at a kid's party place on Long Island in the evening. There was only one problem: Janet had now decided to make herself my steady girlfriend. I mean, the topic never came up—she simply inserted herself into that role. I didn't object, but it wasn't something I wanted either.

One day as Janet and I stood in my living room, the birthday party came up. "Janet, Dee Dee is throwing a birthday party for Sally this weekend and I really need to go."

Janet took a few steps toward the exit and crossed her arms. She stood looking at me without saying anything. Her downtrodden expression sent a clear message.

"Janet, it's not that I want to go all the way out there, but it's for Sally." An uncomfortable silence lingered.

In a sharp, pouting tone, she said, "I want to go. I should be there with you. How much longer are you going to pretend I don't exist?"

My tone got a little whiny. "I'm not pretending you don't exist, it's—it's just not a good idea." My palm instinctively pressed against my forehead as I closed my eyes for an instant. "I mean, she's not inviting you."

Her face looked like a water damn about to bust. "Couple's go to events together!" she said with her jaw jutting forward and then her eyes watered. A guilty feeling came over me.

"You should be going to these events with your girlfriend. Dee Dee has to get used to the fact that I'm your girlfriend!"

I looked at her as my hands drifted to my hips. She was really upset about this. Is this what it will take to get her to stop nagging and crying? I rubbed my fingers into my forehead and stood there as if inspecting the wooden floor.

"Okay you can go." I finally blurted. "The focus is on Sally—it's her day—remember that."

Janet's arms slowly uncrossed, her eyes were still red and her face still scrunched up but she was getting her way.

The week went by and soon it was time to head to Long Island for the party. Janet and I arrived at the location in a friend's car. As we walked in the door, Dee Dee was moving around from guest to guest. I scanned the place. Where's Sally? There she is! And Dee Dee?

Dee Dee was wearing tight jeans, high heels and a low cut top. Her outfit was too revealing for a children's party. When she saw us arrive, she waited a few minutes then she pranced over to us and stared Janet down. Her voice shook a little when she said, "You decided to bring her to Sally's party." I could tell she was barely concealing her rage. It wasn't long before it boiled over.

Dee Dee leaned a little closer to Janet. "You see what John gave me as a gift for Christmas," showing off a sapphire necklace around her neck—thrusting it toward Janet's face. It was an attempt to start a fight. I got angry. "Cut it out Dee Dee." I reached for the necklace and got my fingers around the stone and chain.

"Leave your hands off it!" She yanked back violently.

"Give me that." I grabbed the necklace in an attempt to erase a past mistake. As I pulled, trying to rip it off her neck, she dug her nails into my thumb. "Agghh! That hurt." I let go, and held my thumb as a bubble of red blood oozed from the gash.

Kenny, Dee Dee's friend—a pot smoking, pudgy, throwback to the 60's—barged in. "Dee Dee, are you okay?"Dee Dee tried to appear calm, but was unconvincing. Her voice shook. "Yeah, Kenny, I'm okay."

Guests heard the yelling, and formed a semi-circle around us. It was getting uncomfortable, even threatening. Janet stayed quiet as I did my best to handle the scene.

"Everything's fine, Kenny. Don't butt in." He moved a little too close.

"You get outta here, you jerk!"

"You get outta here! This is my daughter's party!" I fired back.

"You don't scare me, you asshole."

I couldn't believe this pudgy, pothead was challenging me. "This party's for my daughter. You leave."

Closing the gap more and staring up at me, he shouted, "No, you leave you."

He deserved to be decked. It was now a scene. Sally's party was ruined by the adults. More verbal jabs continued. It was time for everyone to go.

What was supposed to be fun turned into an embarrassment. Everyone packed their things. Dee Dee and her guests headed for the door. Dee Dee's hands were full of presents and I followed her outside. Janet went to our car as I asked her to.

"Dee Dee, why did you do this? You picked a fight. You cut my thumb— "

Dee Dee stormed across the parking lot toward her four door sedan. "It's your fault John," she announced over her shoulder" You did this on Sally's birthday," At this point, I don't know where Sally was—it was all a whirlwind of motion.

"Dee Dee, dammit—you had no right to attack Janet like that."

Her volume was twice what it needed to be. "You're the one who brought her here to your daughter's birthday party!" She stopped at the car trunk with a stack of presents and piled them into the truck while she ignored me.

I was so furious. I pushed my hand against her ribs in frustration—nudging her and gritting my teeth. "Why did you do this?"

Her voice dripping with anger and blame. "It's your fault, John!" The second time my hand was more forceful. She felt that one.

"Ahh!" Blam! Dee Dee threw all the presents at me. The parking lot was littered with colorfully wrapped gifts. She yelled out for everyone to hear. "Don't hit me!"

A woman crying wolf is not good. The party guests heard her as they fanned out across the parking lot. I turned and walked straight to our car and got in.

Dee Dee pointed at me and a few men walked toward our car. One tried to open the locked door. "We're leaving," I told Janet. "She dug her nails into me and drew blood— you saw it."

We left before things got uglier.

6

In the Hotel with Amanda

"She dug her nails into you and you nudged or poked her in the ribs—is that correct?"

"That's a fair description. The deeper issue was that I was being played like a banjo by two women and the emotional turmoil was clouding my decision making process. That is, I was one confused guy. Dee Dee was in charge. She decided if and when I ever saw Sally."

"Most parents I know of can hardly make it through the day without seeing their children. How long were you going without seeing her?" Amanda asked.

"Months. I knew it was time to talk to a lawyer. After calling around, I made an appointment with a firm in lower Manhattan. The next day, I rode the subway and located the office address."

Lower Manhattan

The outside of the building was a throwback to the 1900's with tall, large, antique windows. I dressed casually for the meeting. In the lobby, I spotted the name of the law firm listed on the board. As I stood there, well dressed men and women were coming and going, bypassing me as if I was a lamppost.

"I stepped into the elevator. Riding up gave me a moment to ponder. I wonder what they'll tell me?

I sat in the waiting room. Soon, the receptionist came out. "Mr. Farley, they'll see you now."

She escorted me to the lawyer's office door, opened it with a quick pull and announced, "Mr. Farley is here to see you."

She turned and left as I stepped inside. The two male lawyers were busy sorting papers into a tall, metal filing cabinet behind the main desk in the middle of the room. I felt anxious. Just explaining my embarrassing situation made me uncomfortable. The lawyers were in the mid-thirties, wearing dress shirts, ties, but no jackets.

After a quick handshake, one lawyer said, "Have a seat," and sat directly across from me. As I slipped into the the hot seat the other lawyer continued putting folders away. "Tell us what happened," he said.

I told the story and the lawyers looked at each other. The second lawyer came to sit at the desk next to the other. Nearly in unison they asked, "How do you know you're the father?"

Huh? Are they kidding? I sat bewildered.

"Before you go any further you need to find out if you're the father of this child."

Are we talking about a silly technicality here? More time wasted? Is this a lawyer's ploy? "The mother said I was the father."

Both lawyers grunted and shifted in their chairs. The main lawyer became forceful in his delivery. "Maybe you are, but how do you really know? You don't want to create a relationship and pay for somebody else's child for the next couple decades, do you?"

It was hard to believe this was a real issue. "But she said—"

"You need proof. You need a paternity test. That's the most basic thing." The other lawyer slowly nodded and took a deep breath before standing. "Excuse me." He went back to the file cabinet. Meanwhile, my thoughts raced.

Dee Dee mentioned that another guy thought he was the father—that he was there for the delivery. The thought flashed through my mind how Dee Dee originally told me it was impossible for her to get pregnant. The lawyers didn't even want to discuss the case further until a paternity test was done. "We can help you with this."

"I need to think this through." The meeting ended and all the while, I kept thinking about how much time and money this court stuff was taking. I left the law offices more confused than ever. Dee Dee assured me that her getting pregnant was impossible. I just believed her. It's time to bring the matter to the Manhattan family court. After getting the basic documents filed, a court date in Summer of 1994 was set.

Manhattan Family Court

It was time for the big day.

The Manhattan family court building provoked an uneasy feeling. The atmosphere was tense. The enormous entrance line was slow moving. Once I made it to the X-ray machine for bags and the metal detector, things moved faster.

The court officers barked out orders. "Step up. Take everything out of your pockets!"

All the people obeyed. On the other side of the court officers were the elevators. Dull gray and silver—the doors opened and closed with a pop, like horse racing gates. Those elevator doors opened and closed with an unforgiving finality.

No laughter or jokes could be heard in the halls—only somber faces underneath those flickering florescent lights. I made my way into the elevator and my tension grew as our crowded car stopped at each floor.

The number for the fourth floor lit up. Here it is. "Excuse me."

Nudging my way through the motionless bodies, I squeezed myself into the hallway. To the left was a waiting area and to the right—something. The signage is terrible. Which is mine? There. I see the number.

The waiting area was filled with tension and chatter. Like a sponge, I sensed the building had collected the negative energy of tens of thousands of men, women and children who'd walked the lifeless halls and sat in the unforgiving chairs. The anticipation was as unsettling as stepping into swamp water. Court, I'd come to realize, is war without blood.

Dee Dee arrived. Dressed well and nearly on time. I wore dress clothes, but didn't overdo it. I approached the expressionless court officer, a middle-aged man who had no trouble yelling to get attention. I walked up a few feet from him while another person finished.

"Name?"

"John Farley."

"You have a lawyer?"

"No."

"Is the other party here?"

"Yes, she just got—"

"Have a seat. You'll be called when your case is up."

Dee Dee and I sat in the crowded waiting area not too far from each other, but not close enough to talk. Like a Vegas casino, clocks are nowhere to be found. The walls, chairs and floors are mostly gray. Those florescent lights drained my life energy the way a silent mosquito siphons what it wants from an unsuspecting victim.

The uncertainty of waiting became maddening. It's an out of control feeling.

Finally, the court officer yelled out, "Farley versus O'Dell."

Tension was in the air. Why do they have to say "versus?" Aren't we here for Sally?

The officer held the door open. "This way." We walked into the courtroom. Dee Dee was with her lawyer while I trailed in last.

The courtroom was silent and nearly empty. The court officer pointed to places in the round cornered room. "Respondent over here—have a seat."

We moved to our designated spots. Silence took hold throughout the room. The tension was reminiscent of parents telling children to go to their room. We sat and stared toward an empty, elevated court bench, waiting for the judge to enter.

Without warning, a door in the corner of the room opened.

"All rise!"

We stood while judge Ruth Jane Zuckerman walked through the doorway, her profile toward us. Her black robe, an ancient symbol of a dark power, draped over her.

She first reviewed papers on her desk, then looked up. "Counselor?"

Dee Dee's lawyer, a Gerry Spence type, but in a three piece suit, made a statement. "We have a case here with a child—"

"We know that. What are you asking the court to do?"

"A paternity test, your honor."

"Both sides agree?"

I managed to say that I did.

The judge looked up. "Mr. Farley will pay the $300 fee."

My eyes got wide. "What? Why do I have to pay the fee?"

"You're requesting the test!" the judge snapped back.

My thoughts raced. How come the lawyers didn't mention that little factoid?

"Your honor," her lawyer continued, "Dr. O'Dell has a busy work schedule, we'd like to have the court date on a Wednesday if it pleases the court."

The judged looked over at Dee Dee, apparently sizing her up. The judge called out a court date without asking if it was convenient for me.

"That's all," the judge said." Adjourned."

The officer barked—"Everyone out of the court room."

As I walked to the door I felt lost, as if it was my first day of grade school. The officer handed me a slip of paper with the next court date on it.

We went outside the courtroom. I felt annoyed that I had to pay for this test. A waste of time and money. Nonetheless, I resigned myself to it.

Days later, the paternity test was set up. This would give everyone peace of mind. Days went by until the day before testing. Mother, daughter and alleged father showed up at the testing facility for blood work. Another lifeless, colorless, cold, hard, building awaited. A little blood draw would be simple.

Once inside the facility, a large, white woman, wearing a hospital outfit came out. She was as empathetic looking as a brick to the head. She looked at us standing in front of her, glanced at her papers, then back at us. "You're here for a blood draw. Follow me."

We followed her into a square room. She shut the heavy door behind us. "Have a seat." We sat in chairs looking forward. One lone seat faced us. It reminded me of an executioner's chair.

The room was cold. Concrete and steel, with no outside sound leaking in. I felt slightly more comfortable in this room than if I'd walked into an empty laboratory as the door locked behind me and a man wearing a hockey mask stood up from behind a counter.

"Let's have the mother first. Come sit in this chair."

"Me?" Dee Dee said, "How about—"

"Come up here and have a seat."

Dee Dee did what she was told. Tubing was wrapped around her arm. The tech gripped a long needle. She held Dee Dee's arm and the needle was poked through her flesh. Dee Dee instantly started to cry. Her head sank into her other hand and tears streamed down her face uncontrollably.

The three-year-old reacted in my lap. "Mommy!"

The tech heard the child and looked up. "You can't cry like that! The child is going to get upset."

Her tears continued to flow. Sally mirrored her mother as I lightly bounced her on my leg to calm her. "Sally, it's okay."

The tech slid the needle out of Dee Dee's arm and it was over. Dee Dee looked shaken, with a bruised arm, but she recovered fast. The technician looked bothered by Dee Dee's outburst.

Sally was next and Dee Dee placed her in the lone chair. The tech strapped her tiny arms down. When I saw the straps, I swallowed. My eyelids stretched open and my fists clenched. Sally fought against the straps. Unable to move, she looked up toward us in fear. "Mommy! Mommy!"

The tech put a needle that seemed as large as a drinking straw toward Sally's tiny arm.

Oh God! Oh. My. God! I gnashed and gritted my teeth and clenched one fist so hard I thought I'd break a finger. The other fist went in front of my mouth. Sally squirmed twisted and began panting.

The tech forcefully held her arm down. Dee Dee was crying, helplessly watching. The tech scolded her again. I was ready to call it quits. This wasn't worth it. I felt like an accomplice to my daughter's torture.

"Mommy! No! Mommy! The child screamed. YOU'RE HURTING ME. YOU'RE HURTING ME."

My heart sank. I felt powerless. I wanted to jump out of the chair and end it. What seemed like forever, ended moments later. My jaw unclenched, but my heart kept pounding. Sally went to Dee Dee as they sat and dried their tears.

It was my turn. I sat, pretending the procedure was fun and easy. I'd show Sally that it's no big deal to have blood drawn. I'll re-focus her little mind. "Watch Sally, I'll show you. It's easy. You just relax, breathe, smile—you see." The tech strapped my arm and then inserted the needle. "You see it's no big deal you just breath…"

The room spun. The lights grew dim and suddenly—I was out cold. Yeah, it's embarrassing. My head bobbed around and dropped down. Saliva ran from my mouth. The tech grabbed my shoulder to keep me in the chair. I was unconscious for a few moments. Within seconds, I'd gone from cool to drool.

Moments later I started to sit up. The technician held on to me. My eyes opened, but my vision was blurry. The tech consoled me. "It happens. You held all the tension in and then it overwhelmed your system causing you to blackout."

That explanation helped my ego, but Dee Dee ate it up. With a big smile on her face, she chuckled. "Come on Sally, get Daddy a wet cloth."

Sally wasn't crying anymore. She had a new focus—save Daddy. She walked over with a wet cloth she got from somewhere. "Here Daddy!" she said, happy to help me regain my composure. Cold sweat came off my brow. I wiped my mouth and re-oriented myself to the room. That wasn't what I had planned.

Outside, Dee Dee continued having a laugh at my expense. I looked at her as she got Sally into her car. "That was tougher than I thought," I said.

She smiled and laughed. "John, you're the one who wanted to get this done."

That's true. I did. They drove off and I stood on the curb no longer dizzy, but still perplexed. Weeks went by.

Family Court in Manhattan

We were back in court. The judge held the results of the paternity test. She read the results into the record. It showed a 97% likelihood that I was Sally's father.

"Do you agree with the findings?" the judge asked me.

The question seemed confusing. How can I disagree with DNA? "Yes, I agree."

The judge directed me to another floor. I walked into another packed room. Why am I the only upscale looking white guy here? As the tension built, I took a deep breath and announced myself at the window. A pudgy, short-haired woman with glasses glanced up at me. "Have a seat. You'll be called."

An hour went by. An hour of anxiety, wondering when you'll be summoned. It's far worse than the DMV. A voice from the window called out, "John Farley!"

I quickly made my way to the window. The women clerks seated behind the glass were stone faced as they handed me the papers. "You'll be paying this amount every week for your support payment."

"What? Support? What is this? The mother didn't ask for support. This wasn't what the hearing was about."

With a glare she looked at me. "It's automatically provided. You're lucky you haven't had to pay since the beginning." I stood there as the line of people behind me grew more impatient. "This is unbelievable."

"You'll have to take it up with the judge. We can't do anything about it."

How can I go to court for my parental rights and end up with a weekly bill to pay Dee Dee money for the next ump—teen years? What was this all about?

Back Home

Let me call Janet. I gazed at the floor for a moment as the phone rang.

"Hello," an enthusiastic voice said.

"Hi Janet, I'm back."

"How'd it go?"

"I'm Sally's dad, as expected and I'll get visitation days, but guess what else? They gave me a child support order. I have to pay Dee Dee money every month."

"What? That's ridiculous. She's a doctor in private practice, has multiple homes and the two of you were never married. This was her doing, not yours."

"I know, it's outrageous. I can hardly believe it. I'll have to talk to a lawyer and find out how to get rid of this."

Janet was upset. "I mean, I'm a woman, but that's not fair. She did all this behind your back, and now—"

"I know. It's crazy. I have to do something about this."

Soon, we hung up. The conversation reminded me: Janet's there for me.

Feeling drained and overwhelmed, I had to lie down. By the time the next day arrived, I opened the phone book and searched for a lawyer. The previous two lawyers didn't give me a sense of compassion. After a few phone calls, I'd made an appointment just up the street and before I knew it I was at the attorney's office.

My impression over the phone was that this guy was a hardcore New York lawyer. He was on the phone and motioned for me to sit facing his desk.

Lots of papers and files were piled around.

John Farley, Jr.

"Call me back when you find out." He hung up. In his late forties perhaps. Very busy, and not wanting to waste time. He lowered his energy as he turned to me. "You called about a child support case. What can I do for you?"

I started off slowly and clearly. "I have a child support order and I don't feel—"

"Is the child yours? Did you get a paternity test?"

"Yes, I got the test. The child is mine, but this is not fair and I—"

"You have to pay it."

I swallowed, and started again. "I came here to discuss how to not pay it, because it's unfair—she should be paying me as a sperm donor."

That set him off. He was now convinced I was delusional. He looked at me straight on. "You want my advice, here it is, pay it. You're the father. I'll save you attorney fees—pay it."

I paused and started again with a gentle, clear tone. "But I was never married to her, I was never asked if I wanted a child—"

He got up from his chair and turned to his files. "It doesn't matter. You're gonna be paying it and there's nothing you can do about it and that's it."

"But I'm here to ask you about representing me to fight this. Aren't you interested in taking on a case—getting paid?"

Turning his head to me briefly. "You're not going to win this. I'm trying to save you money. Take my advice. Just pay it." He got up, turned to his filing cabinet and pulled out a folder.

"But don't you—"

"I'm very busy. I can't help you. I have to make a phone call." He closed the file as he grabbed the phone off the desk. "Good luck."

I sat for a moment. I'm not finished. I suppose he'll continue ignoring me until I leave. Moments later, frustrated, I did just that.

This fight wasn't over. Someone besides me has got to see that Family Court is unfair.

8

Time for another trip to lower Manhattan. I made an appointment to meet with a family law attorney. The solid wooden furniture in the waiting area was polished to a brilliant shine. A receptionist wearing a headset, sat behind a glass enclosed area. She answered one call, then the next and another. Then, she looked in my direction, as a cue to announce myself.

Between phone calls, she leaned toward the voice slot in the glass. "Mr. Greenbach will be with you shortly. Have a seat."

Less than five minutes later, a door opened. "John?" a man said. His black shoes shined. His light blue dress shirt and bright tie gave off an air of honesty. "Hello. I can meet with you now."

We sat face to face across his desk. I explained my story. As I spoke, he listened, but not with empathy—more like patience—with both hands clasped in front of him on the desk. He explained the court process the way a doctor explains a simple surgery.

"Our retainer's $2,500. We'll handle this for you. Anything not used is refunded. We'll start on this now. You have a court date coming up, so we need to get on this right away."

"I'll give you the retainer and you're going to handle this for me, right?"

"Yes, I'll be representing you. Our firm will handle everything for you."

I signed the paperwork and wrote out a check at his desk. That was a lot of money. But as I handed it to him, a sense of relief came over me. This lawyer was experienced and confident. He'd handled family court cases many times and he's the owner of this law firm. I left with a sense of relief that he'd go in and get everything straightened out.

John Farley, Jr.

Once I arrived home, I was got back into the swing of life and work. Stuck in my mind loomed the next court hearing.

Several weeks later I arrived at the courthouse and made it into the packed elevator. Moisture greased my palms. I felt a sense of anxiety throughout my body. My heart started to pound. Without realizing where it came from, a cold drop of perspiration fell from my armpit and splattered on my ribcage.

I really am nervous. Once out of the elevator I saw my courtroom ahead. I approached the court officer holding a clipboard. Without any pleasantries, I announced. "Farley versus O'Dell."

Hearing me, a young woman with dirty blonde hair approached. "I'm Amy with Mr. Greenbach's office. I'll be handling your case."

"Ah, oh, nice to meet you. Where's Mr. Greenbach?"

"He won't be here," she said, as she turned toward the seating area. "He has other appointments. I'm the attorney assigned to this case. Everything is set."

"But he told me he was going to represent me."

"Our firm is representing you. Everything will go fine."

I wanted to give her the benefit of the doubt. We sat on the hard, plastic chairs. A crowd of people filled the seats around us. Immediately, I sensed she wasn't focused enough. I twisted in my chair to face her, but she preferred an angled conversation.

My nerves would surely calm down if we talked court strategy. "I'm not sure what their plan is today. Dee Dee's lawyer could be up to something."

Unconcerned she hardly glanced at me. "I have your file here. It'll go fine. Did you see the football game yesterday?"

I felt my face droop as my jaw clenched. Is this young woman—perhaps hungover from some party, really, asking about a football game? My eyes noticed her naked throat for a fraction of a moment as I started to feel threatened. After a conscious breath I re-focused on her face. "Honestly, I'm not interested in talking about, or watching, football games. I want to focus on this case and what's about to happen."

Her lips tensed. "As I said, everything is set. Once we go into the courtroom, I'll explain to the judge what you want regarding visitation."

An awkwardness surfaced between us. "You and I haven't spoken about what I want."

She looked away. "I want Dee Dee to bring Sally to me once per week instead of me always having to travel to her. It takes a lot of my time and costs money. She should be willing to do that once a month."

"That's not likely to happen. The judge isn't going to go for that." "But that's what I want and I want you to tell her," I said.

"I'm not going to do that because, as I—Let's just wait until we go in." I took a deep breath. "Why would we wait to go in? We need to prepare now, before we go in."

Our conversation was going nowhere. My football loving lawyer was sure of herself, but I knew she wasn't prepared for a showdown with this judge. We sat in silence. I daydreamed of being seated on an airplane. A flight attendant whispers in my ear, "It's her first flight as captain, enjoy the ride." She winks at me before she straps on her parachute, opens the escape hatch and jumps out the plane.

A shout comes from across the waiting room. "Farley versus O'Dell!"

We made our way into the courtroom and to our respective spots. Dee Dee's lawyer stood near her. He's her friend with decades of experience. I'd tried to negotiate with him at one point, but got nowhere. He's her hired gun. At nearly sixty, he was over six feet, with shaggy, silver hair, a strong presence and a commanding voice.

After a few tense moments, judge Zuckerman came out in her black robe. She glanced at us with a scowl and took her position high above. Dee Dee's lawyer was quick on the draw stating his demands. "Your honor, my client wants—"

My lawyer opened her mouth. "Your honor, if this case—"

It all became a blur of words and activity in my mind. Legalese everywhere.

"Hold it!" The judge said. "Where are the documents for this?" At this point, my lawyer would have been more comfortable answering football stats. "I, um, that is—"

"Before you come in here, and start requesting things you have to have the proper documents." This female judge seemed to get a special sadistic thrill from giving this young, cocky, woman lawyer a hard time.

My head swam. What's happening here? More verbal jousts. Just when the hearing started, it was over.

Dee Dee's lawyer requested a day and time and the judge agreed. By the time my lawyer opened her calendar, the other side had left. I walked out of the courtroom feeling like I'd stumbled into the middle of a foreign film.

Outside, Amy and I stood against the gray wall. Her demeanor was as if we'd won a victory. "You got the court date for next time, right? I'll see you then."

"Wait a second. I can't believe this. We just had a court date and we didn't even get to say anything. It was over before it started. The judge even reprimanded you for not having the documents you needed. I told you what I wanted to have happen, I mean, this is a complete waste of time and money. I expected Greenbach to be here. That's who I am paying for."

Amy stood firm. Perhaps she remembered her football cheerleader days before law school when guys would grovel at her feet seeking approval. No longer smiling, she instead copped an attitude. "I don't know what you are talking about. I'm fully qualified to handle this case. It's been assigned to me. You'll have to take it up with Mr. Greenbach."

My frustration meter was close to overload. Time to talk to Greenbach. When I got home, I called his offices.

"Hello, Mr. Greenbach. This is John Farley. Your attorney, Amy, was at court today. I was expecting you to be there. That's what we agreed to. I want to confirm that you'll be showing up for the next court date."

Greenbach spoke in a cold and calculated tone. "Amy is highly qualified for your case. She's part of our legal team. She explained that everything went fine today. Except that you're giving her problems."

"Things went fine? I'm giving her problems? Even the judge recognized that she wasn't prepared and didn't know what she was saying."

Greenbach, shot back. "The hearing went well. Amy has explained the situation to me and that you're being very difficult."

"I'm difficult? I expect that the lawyer representing me, which should be you, will be prepared. The judge tore into her today because she wasn't. If expecting my lawyer to be ready means I'm difficult, than we do have a problem. Will you be here for me next time?"

Greenbach's volume raised slightly, "Amy's your attorney. She'll be handling the case."

I paused. "If you're not going to show up to court, then I want to terminate your services. When will the balance of the funds be sent to me?"

"The retainer fees have been used up. In fact, you owe fees for reviewing documents, and doing legal research."

"What are you talking about? If anybody owes anybody, you owe me. I'm going to sue you!"

"I wouldn't advise that."

The call ended.

I stood in my apartment with my hand on my forehead and my frustration level rising. Arrggg! If you want something done right...

In the Hotel with Amanda

"You were going to court a lot."

"I sure was. I never realized how intense court and legal matters were. Before I knew it I was back in lower Manhattan again."

Manhattan Family Court

I'd decided to get a court appointed lawyer because I was running out of money. I sat in the waiting area outside the courtrooms. The deadness of that place enveloped me the way an amoeba engulfs prey. The scene reminded me of the Port Authority bus terminal late at night—a little spooky, but more a sense of vulnerability. Instead of a few people scattered about the terminal, there're nearly one hundred packed in the court's waiting area. My anxiety, mixed with everyone else's, vibrated the room.

Dee Dee arrived with her attorney. She had on a nice white blouse with a professional jacket, dress pants, decent shoes. Her hair looked neat, but it was a show. She was a child of the 60's with all the free spirited propaganda of that time.

When lawyers—the important people—arrive, a case gets called faster than normal. I was feeling out numbered right about now. This waiting for court to start reminds me of sitting in a doctor's office—a proctologist, of course.

My mind drifted to Sally, she was the reason for all this. I remembered a recent time when I had picked her up at the Huntington, Long Island train station. At three years old, her reddish-brown hair, and her little sneakers were too adorable for me to handle.

We walked hand-in-hand through the waiting area. People sat in chairs all around the perimeter. I'd always look for at least one chair for her to sit on while we waited for the train. As the people watched us, many spontaneously smiled just seeing her walk by. Before Sally, children didn't register with me much at all. They were simply someone else's concern. After Sally, a new world of appreciation mixed with responsibility opened up.

The train pulled into the station with a roaring sound and bells dinging. "Come on, Sally. Time to get on the train." She slid from the chair, holding my hand for balance. The crowd swarmed around us going toward the exit as I picked her up, grabbed her multi-colored backpack and made our way to the train.

Inside, I found seats for us as I took off her jacket. Ideally, she'd fall asleep, but I doubted it would happen today. After trying to make small talk, looking at her doll and telling her how much fun we were going to have, I came up with something else to keep her occupied.

I'd spent the last few years learning and practicing hypnosis. Children's brain waves stay in a natural hypnotic state until about age eight. I can tell her a hypnotic story to both entertain her conscious mind while it guides her subconscious mind throughout life.

She was getting restless, so I checked my watch. We have a lot of time. "Do you want me to tell you a story?" I said with exaggerated facial expressions.

Her eyes lit up as she nearly bounced in the train seat. "Yeah. Tell me a story!"

We turned toward each other. She looked eager to absorb every word. "Once upon a time, there was this young girl, about your age. She was pretty and happy. Everyone really liked her."

Sally fixated on me. Her face changed expressions as her mind turned my words into pictures.

"This little girl was a good little girl. She made her mommy and daddy so proud. She was kind. She did well in school. She was polite. Her life was filled with happiness, and joy." Sally smiled, nearly shaking with excitement. "Then there was another little girl."

My voice tone dropped along with my countenance. "This little girl was a baaad little girl. She started smoking and drinking, and she didn't listen to her parents. She didn't do well in school and she was hanging around with bad people. She ended up with no friends and she was very sad. Her life was unhappy."

A look of dread came over Sally. "The good little girl stayed away from alcohol and smoking, and she had lots of friends. The good little girl was happy and went on to have a great life."

Sally smiled. Her eyes beamed and her cheeks perked up. Her little body started to rock in her seat. She bounced, and clapped her hands together, "Daddy! Tell me the story again about the little girls!"

"Okay, once upon a time...." I had very little idea of what I would say next. So long as the story encouraged her to be that good, happy, friendly girl, then it would be beneficial. After all, if I didn't put good things in her mind now, she might someday be prey to the alcohol commercials, the drug dealers, the fast food companies, even her well-meaning schoolteachers.

A loud voice broke into my daydream. "Next case is!" a court officer announced.

Our case was called. Moments later we were face to face with the judge who was positioned on the bench and ready to go. She looked at me. "Where's your lawyer?"

With my arms folded and resting on the exceptionally long, curved table, I leaned in a little. The first word wouldn't come out until I paused to clear my throat. "I'm no longer working with that firm. That lawyer was not the one I'd hired and she was incompetent."

The judge squirmed, sighed, and rolled her eyes.

I spoke up. "I want the court to give me a lawyer."

"You have to be indigent."

What does that mean? Dee Dee's lawyer rustled papers. Before he dominated the airtime, I blurted out, "What does indigent mean?"

With squinting eyes, the judge said, "A poor person."

Each attempt to speak felt like interrupting a college professor who hated interruptions.

It wasn't going well, but after some negotiation, the judge finally agreed. "I'm appointing Mr. Lezee."

Great. Now I have a lawyer, at no cost, who'll work with me the way I want. I was given time to meet at the lawyer's office, go over the case, and be ready to present arguments at the next court hearing.

Meeting at the lawyer's office

We met at his cluttered office one afternoon. Here he is, Mr. Lezee, balding, bearded, overweight and myopic, but mostly, disheveled. "Mr. Farley. Have a seat."

I sat in a chair at the end of his cluttered desk, in his tiny, cluttered office. Mr. Lezee opened a folder.

"Mr. Lezee, what I want is to have the child support order terminated and I want Dee Dee to bring my daughter to me once per month for my visitation time. Now, that may seem odd to you, but if you think about it, you'll see my point."

"We can't. I can't do that. The law is very clear. You get a certain amount of time with your daughter and you pay 17% of your gross income. That's the law."

"But I don't agree to that. My case is different and I just don't agree to that. We have to negotiate this hard."

Lezee heard me out, but then re-stated his position.

In this case, my free lawyer was worth every penny. I was getting nowhere and he wouldn't agree to present my case the way I wanted. As I walked from Mr. Lezee's office I pondered. Should I get another lawyer who will go through the motions, while I pay for their real world experience?

It was time for something different. What if I looked for a group of people in my situation? After searching, I found a group of non-custodial parents, the vast majority of whom were middle-aged, divorced men.

One weekday evening, I attended a Father's Rights group in an old building on 23rd street. After the presentation was over, I took aside Irwin, a middle-aged father trying to get access to his children. He pulled a chair around to a table in the middle of the room. "Let's sit here," Irwin said. He seemed like a nervous guy who carried around a backpack stuffed full with court papers, court folders and law books. He'd been studying the law for years now, all because of his divorce. Once our introductions were over, I got to my point.

"Irwin, how do I deal with the court without a lawyer? Can I even do it?"

"Yes, go in as pro per, that is, in propria persona."

"I though it was called pro se?"

"No. Pro se means you represent yourself."

"Aren't I representing myself?"

"You don't want to give the court jurisdiction over you. Make them prove they have jurisdiction. If they don't have jurisdiction they can't move forward. When a lawyer represents you in front of a court, they automatically concede jurisdiction because they're officers of the court."

I took a deep breath, and said, "Okay and…"

"Lawyer comes from the old French word atorne meaning, to turn. Attorneys turn you over to the jurisdiction of the court. They work for the court, not you. That's why judges are always telling litigants to get an attorney. It makes their job a lot easier." Irwin took off his glasses to polish them on his flannel shirt. Then he pulled a linen cloth from his pocket and blew his nose.

I leaned forward and took another deep breath. "What does this have to do with pro se?"

"Pro se means you're representing yourself. That makes you your own lawyer and subject to the court's jurisdiction. It means you're admitting jurisdiction and giving the court power over you. Instead, announce to the court that you are pro per— that is, in propria persona." Irwin stopped, and looked at my wristwatch. "What time is it?"

"Nearly 8 p.m." I said.

"I have to go!" He stuck his glasses on his face. "I'm meeting Ernest—you have to meet him sometime. Remember, without

74

an attorney, they have to be very careful with you because you don't know the law and that means they have to explain it to you, otherwise they can deprive you of your rights. With a lawyer representing you, it is assumed that the lawyer defended your rights properly, which they don't do. The system wants everyone to have a lawyer." Irwin threw his massive backpack onto his back.

"Can you help me with this?" I lifted the bulging pack until Irwin's arms were securely in place. He walked out the door while I sat back and pondered the legalese he dumped on me.

Manhattan Family Court

Once again, I was inside the Manhattan courtroom. I was ready to get some justice. Dee Dee was with her lawyer, while I was with mine.

At this point, I had already told the current lawyer that I wanted him to resign. He and I sat at the long curved table. "The judge appointed me. I'm your lawyer until the judge changes things. I'll tell the judge you want to speak," he whispered.

The judge came out, and the hearing started. Mr. Lezee got the judge's attention. "Your honor, my client wishes to address the court."

The judge glared at me. "What is it?"

I sat up and cleared my throat. "I don't want this attorney any more."

The judge slapped a folder on the desk, and turned toward the clerk. "You can't dismiss your lawyer! He was appointed to you by the court. What are you saying?"

"I don't want him anymore. I'm firing him."

She squirmed in her chair and rolled from side to side. "That's outrageous! Are you going to hire an attorney to represent you?"

"No. I don't need a lawyer. I can do a better job myself."

My attitude must have ticked her off. She placed her hand on the desk, but it made an audible slapping sound as she looked at

Dee Dee's lawyer and then at Lezee. "Oh, you can. Is that right? You know more about the law than your attorney, do you?"

"I can do—"

"Quiet! I'm still talking! When I'm done talking I'll let you know! Mr. Lezee, what do you have to say about this?"

Lezee hunched over a stack of folders. "Your honor, I have fully prepared the documents required for this case and I'm prepared to represent Mr. Farley to the court. However, Mr. Farley has expressed his desire that I be removed from this case."

The judge, looked down at us from her bench. "What's your reason for wanting to dismiss Mr. Lezee?"

With my arms folded on the table in front of me, I replied, "He's incompetent. He won't do what I ask. I can do a better job myself. I want him fired."

The judge's hands hit the desk to brace herself as if a tremor hit the building. "We're taking a recess!"

The judge got up and walked out of the court. Everyone stayed seated there and waited while the judge disappeared through her secret passageway. The time moved slowly and the tension thickened. When the judge re-entered, she took her time to make a statement. "Mr. Lezee, although you have provided adequate legal representation for Mr. Farley, you are hereby relieved from this case at the request of Mr. Farley."

"Mr. Farley will be pro se from this point on."

I raised my hand. The judge stared down. "What is this, second grade? What is it, Mr. Farley?"

"Judge, I am not pro se, I am pro per."

"What?" The judge looked toward Mr. Lezee.

Mr. Lezee stood up. "Your honor, Mr. Farley means pro se."

"No, I don't mean pro se, I mean pro per."

"Say that again." The judge leaned forward from the bench.

"PRO PER," I announced.

"Your honor, he means pro se."

"No, I don't."

"How do you spell that?" the judge asked.

"P-R-O P-E-R, pro per."

"What does that mean?"

"I don't know—but that's what I am! Proper."

Her eyes widened as she recoiled. Looking around to the lawyers in the room, she held back her amusement or outrage, I wasn't sure which. Moments later, Mr. Lezee was dismissed from the case. The judge sat back and waited. "Well, are we going to be here all day? You think you can do this so well, go ahead."

I stared wide-eyed back at her. "What am I supposed to do?"

The judge gloated as I floundered.

The court was hearing two petitions today. Mine was about Dee Dee blocking my visitation and hers was to move the child support issue to the family court in Suffolk County, Long Island.

I decided to talk. "Ms. O'Dell has stopped me from seeing my daughter and I want you to tell her she's violating the visitation order and make her follow it."

The judge seemed ticked—she rattled off legal terms and finally stated to Dee Dee's lawyer, "And your client had better follow the visitation order."

The attorney, the silver haired, baritone in his late 50's took charge of the court. Clearly, the judge respected him. "Your honor, the child, and mother are in Suffolk County, therefore, the venue should be moved there."

The judge seemed to think this was logical. She took notes. While writing, she glanced up to notice me raising my hand. "If you have something to say, you have to stand up and yell, 'I object!'"

I stood up and spoke with hesitation, "I object."

"Overruled!" she yelled back.

My hands turned up in the air. "What does that mean?"

"Mr. Farley, what do you want to say?"

Frustrated and angry I spoke up. "I live here. I'm the one that brought the visitation case here—the case should stay in Manhattan."

Her lawyer popped to his feet. "Mr. Farley has not paid the court ordered amount of child support, your honor."

The judge jumped in, "What's your occupation, Mr. Farley?"

"I'm a personal fitness trainer and I don't feel I should have to pay Ms. O'Dell anything. She should be paying me. I didn't agree to all this."

The judge spoke as if addressing an audience of dozens. "Child support is a responsibility of parents."

"I support her when I see her. I pay the rent, our travel, the food she eats, the toys, the activities. I'm paying for her when she's with me. Why should I have to pay Ms. O'Dell anything?"

"State it again, what is your occupation?"

Sitting a little straighter in the chair, "I'm a personal fitness trainer." The judge stopped taking notes, put her pen down and folded her hands.

"Why don't you find a job that pays better if that's the problem?"

"I don't want to find a different job. Why should I have to do that? I should be able to do a job that I enjoy."

The judge countered, "A person should strive to be happy in their work, but you have a responsibility to support your child."

That struck a nerve. "Am I a slave working and earning money for someone else? A wallet for Ms. O'Dell? What if I don't want to work at all? What if I want to do nothing? Don't I have a right to be a bum—a loser—if I want to be? If I want to be a bum and sleep on the streets, isn't it my God given right?"

"Order! That's enough. Who do I look like, Solomon!" The judge took a recess and once again disappeared. The court was as quiet as a wax museum while we all sat waiting.

After a tense ten minutes, the judge came back in and took the bench. "The court orders that the visitation order stay here in Manhattan and the child support order be vacated. If the mother wants to file for child support, she can file for it in Suffolk County."

Like Solomon, the judge split the requests down the middle. Now, I'd have to travel to Suffolk County for child support hearings. I left the courthouse and gathered my thoughts. Later on, I had managed to get a number for Ernest, the man Irwin had mentioned I should meet. I called and got him on the phone. "Ernest, Irwin mentioned you to me. I need some help with a Family Court case." Ernest is a laid-back, black man from the Bronx, but with a Southern style about him.

"If I had custody of my daughter, I could practically live on the street with her, and never work at all so long as I care for her needs, right? They can't make me work? If they can force me to work, then there is something wrong with that. It's not that I don't want to. It's that now that the court is involved, they're demanding I earn what they want."

Ernest patiently listened. He gave out a gentle laugh, "You have an interesting point, but the courts aren't going to buy it. You have to pay something, that's the key. You have to pay something."

I sensed an inconsistency. Something smelled rotten, and I was determined to sniff it out.

9

Amanda and I sat looking at each other in the hotel. "What year are we in?"

"Ah, let's see. December, 1994. Just before Christmas."

Amanda typed notes on her computer. "What happened next?"

Spontaneously I awoke at 5:15 a.m.
Go! I tossed the covers off, put on my karate pants, walked through the apartment and into the living room. I started stretching. The wooden floor felt solid underneath my bare feet.

"I did the martial arts movements I'd studied for so many years. The moves and the deep breathing cleared my mind.

"I'd mentally committed to Janet. She was my girlfriend."

"What was going on within you now?" Amanda asked.

"My life plans were interrupted in a big way. My natural evolution had been disrupted. Instinctually, I knew this. Normally, a young man seeks adventure before getting serious about a wife and family. If the baby comes along before he plans it, he has to curtail his life's adventures and start building his family. He has to be committed and the commitment has to be something he's agreed to.

"In my case, I didn't have a wife, or even a child who lived with me. All I had were play dates and a support bill to someone who duped me. Dee Dee was being manipulative. Sometimes she let me see Sally and other times not. I felt ripped off."

"It was early December now, right?" Amanda asked.

"Yeah, and Sunday was one of my days with Sally. I headed out to Long Island by train and stayed out there for the day. To travel back and forth would take six hours. I called my friend

Marcy to help out. Marcy's my college friend. She and I always had a nice time together. Her dark, bushy hair and engaging smile always made my day."

"Marcy, it's John. I have a favor to ask. I want to borrow your car on Sunday, if possible. You're out near Dee Dee and I have Sally for the day. If you can meet me at the train, I'll drive the car back to your place later in the day. Deal?"

She agreed.

"What were you going to do with Sally all day?" Amanda asked.

"The only thing I could think of was the mall. It was too cold to spend time at a park. Marcy met me at the train. She drove her car and one of her friends followed to take her home. She got out of the car, bushy hair and smiles.

"Hey there," she said.

"Hi!" I got a hug, and a peck on the cheek.

"Here are the keys. Drive carefully!"

With that, I got in her car. A spacious, dark colored four-door, in great shape. Minutes later, I pulled into Dee Dee's circular driveway.

Knock, knock. Dee Dee answered the door, in what seemed to be a good mood, yet impersonal.

"Hi Dee Dee, I'm here. Is Sally ready to go?"

"Almost. I'm just putting some things away."

I walked into the living room as Sally waddled in from the kitchen to see me. "Hi Sally! I picked her up and looked into her pretty eyes. "What a happy little girl!"

She was excited to see me, but after a hug and a kiss she wanted down. I placed her feet on the carpet and she scurried off while I stood waiting.

Why can't she have Sally ready to go? She knows when I'm going to be here.

I looked around the corner. A stepladder stood in the tiny hallway.

"Can you help me get something up here?"

Without giving it a second thought I started toward the hallway. "What is it?"

"Can you get that ceiling opening to close?"

Looking up, I didn't see anything. What does she mean?

"Go up for me and take a look."

I stepped up on the ladder. All I saw was a closed panel. What? "It's closed," I said.

Her voice came from below. "Close it for me."

"I don't know what you mean. It's—"

I felt her hand on my blue jeans around mid-thigh level. I swallowed hard, as my mind went nearly blank. I stopped moving as electric current surged through my body. My heart raced. I could hear it pounding. I didn't want this, but I couldn't stop it. I was flooded with feelings. Rational control was gone. Her hand went slowly to the inside and slid upwards. Her other hand joined in. Gently she pulled me back down the ladder. The adrenaline caused me to shake, but I forced the words out.

Stammering, trying to remain calm. "Dee Dee,—I'm— I'm—with—Janet—you, you know that. Stop, stop. I don't, I don't—want to do this."

She took my hand, and led me toward her room. I stopped her at the doorway. I pulled myself away, but she pulled harder. I summoned the little emotional strength I had left. "I'm here for Sally," I said unconvincingly. "Come on," she said, as she slid her hands all over me. Like kryptonite to Superman, I felt weak—defenseless.

"Have you forgotten how?" she taunted.

I was too far gone.

"No," I said, with a hint of indignation. I couldn't believe what was happening or that I couldn't stop myself.

I was mad at myself the moment I saw the waterbed. She closed the door and grabbed me. My disappointment in myself was building. My emotions were more mixed up than the bed sheets. She got what she wanted.

I hurried out of the room and searched for the reason I'd showed up in the first place. "Come on Sally, we're going now." I hoisted her up and went to the front door. "Dee Dee, we're going now."

"Wait, the car seat!" Dee Dee raced to her car as I stood with Sally.

She removed the seat from her car, walked over and put it in mine. She buckled Sally in while I gritted my teeth. All the while, thoughts flooded my brain. Without saying much, I got in the car and we left for the mall. Dee Dee acted pleased with herself.

The Christmas season was in full bloom. That meant the man in the red suit would be at the mall. I desperately tried to concentrate on spending time with my little girl. My mind stayed stuck on what had just happened.

We arrived at the mall. "Sally, we're here. Time to see Santa Claus." This was Sally's time with Dad and I wanted to make it count. I felt bad. I knew I'd been suckered—tricked. Dee Dee got me to break my commitment to Janet—pure manipulation and I let it happen.

Sally took little steps as we walked around the mall. Outwardly, I was patient, but my mind raced. We walked into a toy store. As she looked at the toys on the shelves, I pretended to be really interested. Bright colors were everywhere. I was hoping, begging my mind to focus on the here and now.

"Look Sally. Here's a nice toy." I picked up a soft doll for her to hold. She liked it for a few seconds, maybe one minute. Then it was on to the next toy.

Images of what happened kept interrupting me. She tricked me. She had no right to forcefully seduce me. It was wrong, wrong, wrong! She did it to control me.

We left the toy store and started walking down the corridor toward Santa. We stopped across the hallway from the long line of children waiting for the white bearded bearer of gifts.

All the children stood waiting their turn to tell Santa what they wanted for Christmas. I wanted Sally to have that experience. My heart pounded. I was overcome with emotion—literally, my chest was flooded with heat. My breathing quickened as I stared off into space. I can't concentrate on my daughter. I'm so angry. I—am so—angry. I have to get this straightened out right now!

I thought I could let it go. Just ignore it, but I couldn't. We'd only been at the mall about thirty minutes when I couldn't take the flooding of emotion any longer. That's it.

"Sally, we're going now." I picked her up and we went to the car. I imagined what I wanted to tell Dee Dee. Dee Dee deserved an opportunity to understand how I felt and to apologize for what she did. If she'll apologize, I'll be able to manage. If she doesn't apologize—I—I don't know.

The car pulled into her driveway and practically parked itself. "Sally, I'll be back in a moment, just sit here. I closed the car door making sure she was safe—only steps from the front door.

Knock, knock. Moments later Dee Dee opened the door and looked past me.

"Where's Sally?"

"She's fine. She's in the car. I want to talk to you." I stepped forward nudging her, moving her back into the house as I closed the door behind me.

Dee Dee's voice tensed up as she walked into me. "Where's Sally? Why is she out there?"

I stood blocking the door. "I need to talk to you a moment."

Her voice became shrill as she tried to go around me. "I want Sally right now."

"Wait a minute," I said sharply. "You put your hands on me earlier and I didn't like it."

She became demanding. "Get out of my way, I want Sally right now!"

"Not until I talk to you about what you did. Don't ever put your hands on me again."

She looked beyond me to the door as she tried to push me out of the way. "I'll put my hands on you anytime I want to. Get out of my way!"

What she said felt as if she was spitting in my face. I grabbed her by the shoulders and moved her toward the sectional couch. "You need to understand that you can't put your hands on me anymore. I'm with Janet."

My words bounced off her like a rubber ball off a brick building. She continued trying to walk around me or through me.

She yelled. "I'll put my hands on you anytime I want to. Get out of my way!"

I put my hands up to stop her. "No, you listen to me. I told you, I don't want you to touch me."

"I can touch you anytime I want to."

It all happened in a fraction of a second. The disrespect of it all. Rage overtook me.

All I could do was direct the anger and try to contain it. Adrenaline coursed through my body like lava down a volcano. My hands shook. All the deception from the beginning up until today boiled over inside—I snapped.

Grabbing her shoulders, I forced her down on the sectional couch.

"Get off me!"

I grabbed her pant leg as she crawled backing away. I smacked her in the thigh. "Ahh!" she winced. I was irate. I managed enough control not to hurt her, but give her a glorified spanking. "Don't ever put your hands on me again!"

She pulled her leg back, ready to kick me in the groin.

I stopped. "You want to kick me? You better not miss." I grabbed her leg. I smacked her in the thigh and buttocks again. Then, I stopped as the rage let up.

Fearful, but unrepentant, she sprang to her feet. "You get out of here!"

"You still didn't learn, did you, Dee Dee?"

There would be no apology from her—she'd take no responsibility for her actions. In her mind she was the victim. I got her pregnant. I forced this life on her.

She rushed to the door. I could tell she was unrepentant. "You keep your hands off me. Do you understand?" I told her.

Furious, she yelled. "I want my daughter now. Get out of my way!"

I walked out the door first and she bolted out from behind me to get Sally from the car.

"Let it go," I said, as I went to the driver's side. "Let it go, Dee Dee."

After grabbing Sally, she rushed inside and in a flash she was back with her cordless phone. "You're finished!"

"You still didn't learn, did you? Let it go, Dee Dee—we're even."

"You're finished now, buddy. You're finished!"

I got in the car and pulled away still able to hear her last insult.

"It wasn't that good either!"

I drove out of the driveway and headed to the train station. My heart raced, but this time from fear. She was probably calling the police. What did I do now? I was out of control. I've never felt so violated in my life.

I better get out of here. I'll let Marcy know the car was at the train station.

Once the car was parked I hurried aboard the waiting train. I sat still, but my hands were shaking. An hour later, the train arrived at Penn Station.

I was safe now. Back in Manhattan. What she did was wrong, but I don't know what came over me.

Janet's going to question me about the day.

I went straight to my Westside apartment. After grabbing a cup of water, I anxiously paced back and forth re-living what happened in my mind.

John Farley, Jr.

The scene played over and over. I had a bad feeling about this.

Dee Dee was angry. So was I. What I did wasn't good. I felt guilty for breaking my promise to Janet and for losing control, but justified in standing up for myself.

What if the roles were reversed? If I had forced her into the bedroom? How am I going to explain this to Janet?

Why should I? It's a non-issue.

I have to call Janet. I'm not ready, but I have to. I put the water down, picked up the phone and dialed.

"You're home already? Is Sally with you?"

"No, I took her back early."

"What happened?"

"Everything was fine. We went to the mall."

The conversation was strained. I was still thinking of what had happened.

"I decided to send Sally back early, that's all. Let's talk tomorrow." Janet probably knew I was leaving something out. We hung up shortly thereafter and I tried to block the day from my memory.

A few days later it was time to visit the gym for a long overdue workout. I hoped it would relieve the tension.

When I came home my roommate was there. "Hey John, some cops were here. They dropped papers off for you."

I stood motionless and speechless.

It had to be about family court. I picked up the papers from the kitchen table and looked them over. Whatever it said was unclear. What does this mean?

10

Amanda's mouth gaped open. She swallowed as her eyes dipped down along the carpet. She looked up at me sitting there in my suit and tie and shiny shoes. I reached for the bottle of water sitting on the table in front of me.

"You smacked her?" More of a statement than a question.

The water bottle stopped in mid-air before I slowly brought it down to rest on the couch as I closely watched her facial expressions. I paused, as if thinking about her question. "Your whole life you've been told about domestic violence. Perhaps you even grew up with it in your family. It's something that supposedly only happens to women. Well, that's not true."

Amanda's face looked curious.

Continuing, I said, "I agree. It shouldn't have happened. After all, throughout history men have been the protectors of women and children. To inflict injury on either is the opposite of what men are hardwired to do."

Her mouth closed and jaw tightened as she slowly lifted her chin and fixed her eyes on me with a relaxed gaze.

I raised the water bottle and took a sip. Could it be, as bad as smacking a woman supposedly is, that maybe, just maybe, in some cases, the woman disrespected the man so much, that he felt he was, in his mind, defending his honor, his dignity?"

She squirmed in her seat, as she took a deep breath. "Is that what you were doing?"

"Of course. She physically violated me. Plain and simple. She had no right to do it. Let's take this one step further, if you can handle it and I'm sure you can. The domestic violence laws are designed to ruin families."

"What?"

"They prevent men from exercising the leadership, and authority women crave."

"I—I mean, I've never heard that before. Where in the world did you come up with that?"

"It took me a long time to see it, but I'm not the only one to realize it. Scholars have noticed it too. The feminist agenda is to destroy the institutions of marriage and family."

She smiled, but it had a patronizing crook to it. "This just keeps getting better."

Amanda adjusted herself, rotated her wrists once in each direction, took a deep breath and exhaled slowly. She eyed at me a little too long. "What happened next?"

Long Island

A cold January breeze chilled the air. This Sunday morning was my visitation day with Sally. I got on the train to Long Island.

Sometimes visitation was Friday night through Sunday and other times it was all day Sunday. Sunday visitation made for a very long day. It was hard to take the train out to Long Island and then back to Manhattan, then back to Long Island and then back to Manhattan. Too hard, but I did it anyway. The total travel time was six hours door to door. Little energy was left over for fun.

Janet stayed home and waited for Sally and I to arrive at her place.

The train pulled into the station. The loud speaker came on. "Huntington Station." I hurried off the train and rushed to find a cabbie in the parking lot.

Being half dazed from all the sitting, the short cab ride flew by. We pulled into Dee Dee's driveway around nine. I opened the cab door. My breath froze as I carefully stepped onto the snow and ice covered driveway. "Wait here please, I'll be back in just a minute." The cabbie kept the engine running. I walked to the door and knocked.

Dee Dee opened up with the phone to her ear.

"Hi, is she ready to go?"

She walked back toward the kitchen and left the door open.

"I'm here for Sally. Is she ready to go?" Silence.

I looked for Sally as I stepped through the doorway. Sally walked out of the kitchen into the living room, happy to see her dad.

"Just a moment," Dee Dee said coldly, without any eye contact at all, still talking on the phone. I couldn't hear what she was saying.

What's the problem?

"I'm ready to go. The cab is waiting."

A sound came from outside. A car pulled into the driveway. I peered through the living room window and noticed a police car.

I looked back at Dee Dee. "What is going on?"

She walked past me as if I were invisible and went outside. She spoke to the officers on the frozen walkway. Two cops, in their thirties, listened to her as they glanced toward the front door. They stood there all puffed up from their dark vests and police gear. I felt a twinge of nervousness. Moments later they walked to the front door.

"John, we want to speak with you. You're in violation of an order of protection by being here."

"What you are talking about?"

The cop spoke in a calm, conversational tone. His partner stood next to him and looked around the room. "You're not allowed to be here."

"What are you saying? I have a court order to see my daughter today, at this time."

The lead cop was calm and direct. "There's a court order barring you from being here."

"I have a Manhattan judge's order that says I have visitation with my daughter right now."

"Do you have that order on you?"

"No. I don't carry it around with me, but Dee Dee knows I have the order, that's why I'm here. She knows this. Ask her."

"You're going to have to go back to court to straighten this out."

"Okay. I'll get it straightened out."

"You have to come with us now to the station."

"What are you talking about? For what? If my being on her property is the problem, then let's do this, I'll stand on the side of the road, off her property and she can—or you can—bring my daughter to me."

Without flinching, the officer responded. "We can't do that. You have to come with us to the station."

Incredulous, I stood my ground. "But I'm supposed to be here."

"You're going to have to come down to the station and do some paperwork."

I looked away for a moment to think. "What's going to happen there?"

"We'll do some paperwork, that's all."

"So, if I go with you, we do paperwork and am I going to have time with my daughter afterwards?"

"I can't promise that. You need to go back to court and get this straightened out."

The cab driver's car hummed in the driveway, until he switched off the motor and the silence became unsettling.

I glanced at Sally walking around inside the house. "Okay, let's go and get this over with."

The other cop pulled out cold metal handcuffs.

"What? Handcuffs? I'm not a criminal. For what?"

"We have to handcuff you, it's policy."

"Handcuff me? What's going on here? I'm just here, following a court order to see my child."

"It's policy. Turn around John, we have to handcuff you."

I looked at both cops with their guns fastened to their hips. The entire scene flashed through my mind. Did Dee Dee want this? No, she didn't realize this would happen. I sighed and turned around, embarrassed at this ludicrous scene.

Snow and ice blanketed the walkway and the driveway. With hands behind my back, one officer held my arm. Like a guide dog, he led me toward the police car.

"Watch your head," he said as he led me into the back seat.

The embarrassment matched my growing anger. How humiliated I felt.

During the short ride, I rambled on about how this was all a big mistake. The cops were quiet, not saying much at all.

They're going to do some paperwork and let me leave, but what a waste of time.

We arrived at the police station. The cops walked me toward the back room where there were long metal tables, with stools. They handcuffed my wrist to the chair.

I never experienced this in my life. "Can't you take me out of these handcuffs?"

"We can't do that." One of the cops who cuffed me, sat directly across the table. He wasn't looking at me so much as studying me. "John, I need to fill this out. You have blue eyes, right?"

"Yes."

The questions kept coming, one after another—over and over. After I'd told him everything he'd asked, he paused. "Time to get a thumb print."

"Thumb print? What for?"

"It's procedure." The officer stood up, walked around the table and unlocked the handcuffs. "Stand up and walk over here."

He brought me to the fingerprinting area a few feet away. This is what criminals have done to them, isn't it? After putting on his blue gloves, he took my thumb in his hands, and precisely rolled it onto an ink pad. Then he moved my hand, like carrying an overfilled glass of water, to special paper. This was the classic

John Farley, Jr.

criminal experience. I couldn't have felt more like a bad person than at this moment.

Afterwards, he brought me back to the table and locked the handcuffs again.

Feeling uneasy now, I pushed for specifics. "I want to make a phone call. How long am I going to be here?"

The officer stood up and looked toward the open door as other cops walked by and peeked in. "It's too late to see a judge; you'll see the judge tomorrow."

What! I didn't just hear that. "I thought you said we'd be finished shortly and I could go!"

Another officer came in smoking a cigarette just outside the room.

"John, you're going to go with this officer." This 50-something cop thinks it's okay to break the law and smoke in the building.

"Excuse me, but isn't smoking in here prohibited? Can you put that out?"

He sneered and quickly ducked out of the room. He came back moments later still with the cigarette. We weren't starting out well.

The smoking cop released the handcuffs from the table. "We're going to bring you somewhere else. Come with me."

We walked into another area as he opened a jail cell door. "Let's take the handcuffs off you."

Finally, I'm going to be let go.

He leaned toward the front of the open cell. "Step in. Step all the way in."

I took a couple steps forward. The squeaking sound of metal caused me to turn around.

He was closing the door.

My hand instinctively extended to stop it. "Wait, I'm not supposed to be in a cell!"

The cop let go of the door and sprang at me. He grabbed my arm behind my back, pushed me further in, and against the concrete wall. He pressed his forearm against my throat. He twisted hard! "You get your ass in that cell and cut the crap!"

"Okay, okay!" I said.

After he was convinced I would comply, he let go. Up until now I'd worked hard to build a good reputation—always a model citizen, doing the right thing. How could this be happening?

They lied to me. They just committed battery on top of it. They tricked me just as Dee Dee had tricked me. Now I'm ticked! "What is this? You told me I'd go to a judge. When?"

"Monday." As he slammed the heavy metal outer door to the room. I was now in a cell, which was behind a closed metal door. I became furious, but also scared. I could barely hear faint sounds far off behind the closed doors.

My face felt flushed. I panted in anger. I started yelling over and over and over again. "I want my phone call!" I kept yelling as loudly as I could. Like Achilles standing at the gates of Troy, yelling for Hector.

After what seemed like a long time, the metal door opened up. The smoking cop came back. "Yeah, you'll get you your phone call, just wait," he snapped as he shut the door.

"How long do I have to wait? I want my phone call now!" I yelled over and over again.

I was furious. Handcuffs, assault and battery—taken from my daughter.

I yelled at the metal door. "You have some nerve locking up a father for seeing his child! What the hell is wrong with you people? I WANT MY PHONE CALL. I want you to let me out of this cell. This is bullshit! I want my phone call!"

Eventually, the cop opened the door again. He brought with him a phone with a very long cord, reaching to the cell. "Who do you want to call and what's the number?"

I panted in frustration. "Janet, she's my girlfriend." I recited the phone number and composed myself. "Do you have a fax here? I want her to fax you some documents that I need for my hearing with the judge."

John Farley, Jr.

The cop looked at me. "I'll see."

When he came back, he dialed the number and handed me the phone through the metal bars. I stretched the cord away from the cell door.

It rang and Janet picked up. "Janet, it's me. I'm in jail...I know. It's a long story. Dee Dee got me thrown in jail!...I know, I know. Here's what I want you to do. Hold on. What's the fax number?"

The cop leaned against the concrete wall as if he was out on a fishing boat waiting for some action. The officer fired off the fax number.

"Janet do you have a pen? Write this down: 631–555–1212. Janet, I want you to write on a piece of paper, 'Let John out of this jail' and fax it over and over and over again until they let me out. Will you do that? Just keep faxing it over and over again for hours if you need to."

The cop popped off the wall he was leaning on and reached for my phone through the cell bars. "Hey give me that phone." He couldn't reach me so I kept talking to Janet. "Just keep faxing it." He fumbled with his keys, then opened the cell and at that moment I handed him the phone as a look of confusion crossed his face. He turned, slammed the cell door as he mumbled and cursed and then left the room in a huff.

I stood there, my posture straight, with a wry smile, gloating. Soon, the sergeant came into the area. A stocky, tough guy, in his late forties. "What do you think you're doing? She's clogging our fax line. She could be charged for that."

"Yeah, do it." I said. "You let me out of here."

The sergeant squinted at me. "You're not leaving here until tomorrow morning when you go to see the judge."

"You're a bunch of scumbag, losers. I came to see my daughter. You're a bunch of mindless robots doing what you're told. You're brainless. You're a bunch of slaves!"

His tone mellowed. "I'm not the one in a jail cell."

I glared back, "You're still a slave. You're a slave to the system."

He looked at me with disdain. "Yeah. Anyway, she better stop that, or we can have her arrested."

The sergeant turned and shook his head as he slammed the heavy metal door.

Time crept by. Later, two cops opened the metal door. From their unhappy faces, I figured the continual faxes might still be coming in. The cops decided to move me to another cell and the night was still young.

11

The sudden sound of a bolt slapping against metal startled me. The heavy door to the hallway creaked open. The smoking cop came into the area in front with another officer. They stood in their intimidating uniforms, peering in momentarily through the bars.

"We're moving you to another cell. One cop slipped a key into the lock and opened the door. "Step out."

I obeyed and must have looked unhappy. They shadow behind and guided me to another cell block a few steps away down a hallway. Cells lined the wall from one end to the other.

"Over here," one cop said. In a smooth, quick motion he unlocked the door. As he did, I caught a glimpse of men in their cages as they slept motionless on metal slabs projecting out from the concrete walls. "Stop here. Take off your shoes, your socks and your outer shirt."

I begrudgingly did what I was told.

A cop opened a cell door. "Go in."

I stepped in and the heavy metal door with steel bars slammed closed.

I'm caged again. The realization that I was stuck in a steel and concrete trap, messed with my mind. The cell was about 6 feet by 8 feet—enough space to sit and lie down. The walls were gray. The toilet was a dull metal with no seat, but attached to a sink. The bed was just a metal shelf bolted to the wall. The place was cold—very cold with florescent lights flickering down.

It's dead in here. Everything is dead. Nothing natural. Just steel, concrete, stale air, fake light. No clocks. No magazines to read or television to watch.

The cops left and closed the outer door to the hallway. The place was silent except for an occasional snore from an unseen neighbor in a cage next door.

As I sat on the cold, metal slab, seconds felt like half hours.

There's only so much stretching and meditation one can do. What's going on here? Why am I in this cell? If I escaped, where would I go? They took my coat, my shoes—it's freezing outside—ice and snow on the roads.

I thought about what Dee Dee did to me and how the cops coerced me to go along with them. It was outrageous and I was angry. The more I thought about it the angrier I became. Here I am, stuck in a cell. For what?

My inhibitions loosened as my rage boiled over. Perhaps I was becoming unhinged. I panted, and then noticed a roll of toilet paper on the sink and reached for it. I ripped off some sheets, turned the faucet and drenched the paper until it dripped.

I rolled balls of soggy toilet paper and stepped to the front of the cell. Winding up, I threw the wet wad in between the bars toward the concrete wall several feet away. SPLAT.

The wad stuck to the wall. I tore off more paper and did it again. "LET ME OUT OF HERE." I kept throwing the balls of paper. Ten times, 20 times, 30 times, 40 times. There were wads of drenched, sticky toilet paper dripping from the wall.

Eventually, a young cop opened the main door and stood slack-jawed at the dripping mess. I whizzed a wad past him, "splat."

"What the hell are you doing? Stop it right now!"

Still panting, I glared back at him. "Let me out of this cell."

"Stop throwing that!"

I stepped back away from the door. "You let me out of here."

He stepped toward the bars and held out his hand. "Give me that toilet paper right now."

I lowered my tone, ready to brawl. "Why don't you come in and get it?"

We eyed at each other until the cop broke eye contact and left without another word.

I quit throwing toilet paper and sat down. This wasn't like me, but I'd never been treated this way before.

As the hours went by I was becoming increasingly stressed. My back was hurting. It always acted up under stress. Mental tension, that is, intense emotion, caused the muscles to tighten which led to pain spasms.

"Arrgggahh!" By the late night, I was having excruciating back pain. "Arrgggghhh!" I felt crippled by it. "Help. I need help!" I yelled for 30 minutes or more, most definitely waking the other prisoners, but none said a word.

The main door opened. "What do you want now?" the young cop said.

My voice sounded weak like a dying man in the desert. "My back. My back is killing me. I need a doctor."

"You'll go in the morning."

"No. I can't wait. My back. I can't lie down. I can hardly move. I need ice for my back."

"We're not giving you ice."

"You have to do something. My back is killing me."

He left, but a few minutes later he opened the main door. "You'll have to wait an hour, and someone will take you to the hospital."

"Why so long?"

"Units are out," he said, as the door closed behind him.

At least an hour passed before two cops came to my cell. In seconds the metal door creaked open. Every inch of movement caused painful electricity to stab through my body which instantly halted my breath the way pinched nerve paralyses the muscles.

It took what seemed to be several minutes to bend down and put on my boots. Then the cops put shackles on my legs and handcuffs on my wrists and then bent my arms behind my back.

John Farley, Jr.

Each of my footsteps was cautious, as if crossing thin ice on a frozen lake. It seemed to take forever to get outside.

The slick ice covered the parking lot in the dark of night. If I slipped on the ice, with hands behind my back, I was sure to shatter bones like an ice sculpture slamming down on concrete.

Crouching into the backseat of the police car felt like getting stabbed in the back with a thin needle, followed by a long, vice-like muscle pinch. When the cop closed the car door, a sense of relief came over me and lasted for all of a few minutes.

12

The police car rolled to a stop in front of a hospital. The darkness of the night sky covered everything except for a circle of light directly shining down in front of the entrance.

Shackled, cuffed and in pain, I waited as the cops got out and opened my door. One foot strained to lift and leave the car floor. The hip flexor muscles tensed and pulled on the lower back bones with vise-like pain. The cops stood by as their breath froze in the motionless night air.

Inside, I walked down the hallway looking more like a stroke victim than a fitness professional. Each step rattled the chains from waist to ankle, as if I was the ghost of Jacob Marley.

One cop stopped me at a hallway chair. "Sit here."

As I sat, people passed by. Patients, visitors—all staring. I felt embarrassed again.

A small child walked by. She looked at the leg irons and handcuffs locked into a belt around my waist. Does she think I'm a bad person? An evil person? What if she knew I had a little girl that I was supposed to see today? I wanted to disappear. It was as if I could read minds.

What did you do? Did you murder someone?

I wanted to say, "My crime was visiting my daughter at the time and place I was ordered to."

Finally, a doctor came to see me. Late fifties, white coat, graying hair, twenty pounds to lose, downtrodden—clearly unhappy to have to deal with someone such as myself. He managed to spit a few words out as he looked down his nose at me. "What's the problem?"

My voice was weak from pain and horse from yelling. My mind was foggy from lack of sleep. "My back is killing me. I just want some ice."

The doctor gave me a quick examination, in a small room, then spoke to the cops. He came near me. "I don't find anything wrong with you."

"I'm in a lot of pain. There's something wrong."

Exasperated or annoyed, he muffled a sigh. "We can give you a pain killer."

"I just want ice. Can I get a bag of ice?"

"No, it's either the pain killer or nothing."

I didn't want drugs in my system.

We left the hospital and got back into the cop car and headed to the police station. The entire trip only served to humiliate me more.

Where did I go wrong? I graduated from college. An Ivy League university. I've been a model citizen. Been on television, radio—taught children karate and self-defense. I'm a little girl's dad. What the hell is going on?

When the jail cell door slammed behind me, I managed to sleep a few hours before the main door unlocked and opened.

"BREAKFAST."

The cops doled out metal plates with eggs, bacon and coffee to each prisoner. I passed. It's not my type of fare and frankly, I didn't trust the food or the cops.

Sometime later, more officers came in to the cell area. They had chains and belts with them. They whispered.

My back felt a little better. "Where are we going?" I called out.

"To court," a cop said without so much as a glance in my direction.

The officers opened each jail cell one at a time. "Come out," he yelled. "Stand facing the wall."

The guy in the first cell came out. He looked terrible. Long, unkempt hair, jeans, and a wrinkled T-shirt. Like a mute zombie, he lumbered to face the wall.

One by one we all lined up to be shackled, handcuffed and chained to the waist of the man in front and behind us. Minutes later, we were outside. They herded us into a van as a half dozen chains rattled and echoed inside the metal hull.

"Duck your head and keep moving back. LET'S GO." We prisoners slid down the bench and pressed against one another. This is a mistake. How can this be happening to me? The van cruised along on the roads for about thirty minutes. Without warning it stopped inside the holding facility underneath the courthouse. The front doors to the van opened, then slammed shut. The others next to me squirmed and shifted about, their chains rattling.

Something was about to happen. The back doors jerked open. "Step out of the van." The guy closest to the door moved quickly. I was third in line.

"When you get inside, walk against the right side. Keep your shoulder to the wall. Look straight ahead. NO TALKING." The cops wore blue uniforms, while the sheriffs stood like soldiers with their intimidating black garb and bright blue rubber gloves.

We were herded inside, told to face the wall. One by one, sheriffs released our chains as the giant rolling door to the outside closed down. An eerie feeling gripped me. A helpless feeling.

The sheriffs yelled, "Take off your shoes and socks. Turn your socks inside out. Put your hands on the wall. LIFT UP YOUR FOOT." They were checking for weapons hidden in socks or on the bottoms of feet.

"Pick up shoes and socks and walk straight ahead."

We walked down the long hallway and the light shining through jail cell glowed in the distance. As we arrived, doors opened.

"Step into the cell," the deputy sheriff ordered.

Going into this large cell was like a first day of school. A different world. A dozen men of various races sat watching a few of us as we made our way in.

I felt awkward, nervous, vulnerable. Don't stare at anyone and don't smile. I sat on the bench and waited. Once in awhile a conversation would start. I listened, but kept to myself. Prisoners' names were called out by a man with a pen and clipboard, who was dressed in normal clothes.

"FARLEY."

I walked to the front of the cell feeling like a school child. "Is your address..."

"Yes." His questions kept coming until I interrupted with a high pitched voice. "I was following a visitation order—a court order from Manhattan. I was just doing what I was supposed to do."

Peering up from his clipboard, he said, "Look, I have to decide what bail to recommend to the judge."

"Bail! For what? I'm a dad who was going to pick up my daughter as ordered by the judge in Manhattan Family Court. There shouldn't be any bail." He scanned my face for a few seconds, then looked down at his papers and back again.

"Okay, let me see what I can do. Have a seat. JACKSON."

All of us sat in the cell for what seemed like hours. Some guys talked a lot, while others kept quiet. I kept to myself, staring at the gray colored concrete floor. The hard metal bench, cold walls and florescent lights siphoned energy from me like a leech.

"Go to the back of the cell," a voice yelled. One by one, sheriffs called each guy out to line up against the wall to be handcuffed and shackled.

"FARLEY." I walked from the back of the cell to be fitted with cuffs. Faceless deputies called out behind us. "Keep looking straight ahead and stay next to the wall. Open ONE." We stood in a narrow space surrounded by deputies resembling border collies rounding up sheep.

"MOVE IT OUT." My chains connected to the men in front and behind me. We shuffled through several locked doors and stood outside a courtroom sealed off from the regular citizens.

"QUIET."

The deputies kept their timing of events secretive. Uncontrollable tremors nearly buckled my legs. When the door to the courtroom opened my bladder was ready to release. A deputy yelled. "WALK IN. LOOK DOWN. DON'T LOOK AT THE JUDGE. Slide all the way down the bench."

We shuffled shoulder to shoulder to the right. The loud metal chains clanked against themselves and rattled across the wooden bench confirming our lowly status.

I started to look up when I heard the judge less than ten feet away. A court officer yelled, "LOOK DOWN. DON'T LOOK AT THE JUDGE."

My heart pounded. Sweat dripped under my shirt.

Other guys were called up first. When their name was announced, an officer would unhitch them from the chain gang. Still cuffed and shackled they stood up and were moved into position.

The scene was surreal. Each prisoner had thousands of dollars in bail assessed. My heart pounded more. Oh my god, I have to focus. I have to get my message across quickly, persuasively and strongly. I've only got one chance.

Then, I heard it. "JOHN FARLEY." Time stood still.

"STAND UP," the court officer ordered.

"Judge," said a prosecutor, "the defendant is accused of violating an order of protection against Dee Dee O'Dell. We recommend $1,000 bail."

The guy with the clipboard jumped in. "Your honor, Mr. Farley followed an order out of Manhattan Family Court. We recommend he be released under his own recognizance."

Say something. "Judge, may I speak? The judge, a middle-aged man, mostly hidden by his black robe, lifted his gaze from the bench on high.

"What would you like to tell the court?"

"I showed up at the exact time and place that the Family Court order from Judge Ruth Zuckerman ordered me to. I was seeing my daughter for visitation. I was following the court order."

Fortunately, the judge recognized the inconsistency of the court orders and that I was not a danger. He agreed to release me without bail. Still, it would be another couple of hours in a cell before I'd be let go. Eventually, I made it back to the train station.

I sat on the train a changed person. The ride, which used to be ordinary, now seemed spectacular. I could move my arms and legs. The sky was in view from the window whereas before I saw only a wall. The air was cold, but fresh. People treated me with dignity, not condescension.

Indentations from the metal cuffs still marked my wrists and ankles. Those marks, while painful, would fade in time. But what about the indelible mark on my mind?

Relief came over me as I opened my apartment door. I sat on my comfortable bed. It seemed softer than I remembered. Food from the kitchen tasted better. I looked up and out the living room windows toward the sky. It seemed more vibrant than I remembered.

My mind wrestled with what happened. I was chained like a slave, lied to and humiliated. I can't believe Dee Dee did this to me. Did she really want this to happen?

I was staring off through the living room window into the pale blue sky when an idea came.

13

At the Hotel with Amanda

"How did all this impact your work and career?"

"Not well. I had to make excuses for why I was missing in action. That's never good. What would really impact my work and career was the incredible hostility that was festering inside. Many people think that the type of experience I had is easily forgotten— it's not. Often, the effects linger."

At Janet's Apartment

Janet's roommate was out, so we talked in the living room. The floral colored love seat against the back wall seemed large in the small space. The television was eight feet away against the opposite wall. Janet brought us both a glass of water.

She sat near me in the natural wood finished rocking chair. I took another sip and noticed scenes on TV with the sound muted.

She held her glass in her hands. "What are you going to do now?"

I rubbed my fingers along the glass as I attempted to focus. I sat and watched the muted screen. "Lawyers are too expensive, but going to court without knowing the law is like playing golf with a tennis racquet. I'll see if the father's rights group can help me."

We finished our water, turned off the television and put on pleasant music. We took advantage of the solitude before Janet's roommate came home.

Days later, I was back to my normal routine.

That night the father's rights meeting on West 23rd Street was held in a room that reminded me of a classroom with wooden floors and plastic chairs.

About 25 men showed up. This wasn't a business meeting. These men were dressed in plain clothes, some in old jeans and flannel shirts. This wasn't the same as the motivational seminars I'd been to where people were happy, excited and filled with hope. These men mostly looked tired, timid and reserved at best.

I was surprised that so many men in their forties and fifties were dealing with custody, and child support issues. One man stood up and went to the front of the room. He looked to be in his late fifties, clean cut, dress pants and a long sleeve shirt rolled up nearly to the elbow. He broke through the din of voices to get everyone's attention. "Let's get started. There was a ruling on a case in New Jersey impacting custody...."

I sat patiently. Anxiety caused my breathing to become shallow as the group talked about issues unrelated to mine.

The leader stopped and looked at everyone. "Let's put our chairs in a circle." The meeting quickly became an encounter group. "Introduce yourself and tell us what brought you here."

A forty-something year old man introduced himself and gave some of his story. "I'm a doctor and I've paid $400,000 to lawyers and I still don't have custody of my child." Even though I heard it, the number was too big to imagine.

Next, a thirty-something year old man in blue jeans, shared. "My ex-wife has an order of protection against me and she's using it to keep me away from my two children."

I perked up. That's like my situation.

The group leader looked toward me. "Go 'head."

I straightened up in my chair and looked at him to calm my nerves. I told my brief story to the group. Blank faces looked back as I spoke. Thirty minutes later, the meeting ended.

I took slow steps toward the guy who seemed the most knowledgeable one in the room, Bruce, the Caucasian guy.

He leads a group in New Jersey. He's smart, blue collar, loud, strong and blunt—some would say, abrasive.

A small circle of people surrounded him. I waited for my opportunity. "Bruce, can I speak to you a moment?"

Without looking at me, he continued packing his bag with court documents. "I have to leave," he said with a glance that suggested I could talk until he was done packing.

I quickly explained my story including the latest confrontation. "The cops arrested me. How can they do that? I have rights."

"You have to get that visitation order changed."

"What if I just refuse to go with the cops when they try to arrest me?"

"They have guns."

I gave a nervous chuckle. "They can't just shoot me."

Bruce stopped packing to scold me. "You're ignorant. You're really ignorant about what happens."

I pondered the comment before defending myself. "Ignorant doesn't mean stupid. I'm not stupid. Ignorant means a person doesn't know something."

Bruce grabbed another file for his bag. "What good is being right about something after they've shot you?" That possibility never occurred to me. At that moment, another man joined the conversation. That's when I met Ernest in person.

Ernest seemed to be in his 50's, perhaps 60's. He was a black man from the Bronx with a cordial personality more common in the south. He's one of the few who always had a smile, despite some missing teeth. Ernest had a gentle laugh and a kind word ready. He wore an old-time hat with a broad brim, and if you looked closely you'd notice a few holes in his clothes.

Ernest liked to talk. Looking at him, you'd think he only knew how to repair shoes, but to my surprise, I discovered that Ernest knew how to read and write legal documents. He pointed to a chair. "Let's sit down." He handed me court papers to look at. "You see, you need to modify your visitation order, like this one."

As I looked the document over, Ernest became very quiet. A few moments later, I noticed Ernest's eyes were closed and his mouth was open.

"Ernest? Ernest?" His eyes opened and he continued right where he left off. That was strange. We talked a bit longer, until it was time to leave.

Walking back to the subway station, I decided to call Dee Dee. The call would be strictly about visitation and we'd come to an agreement.

I'd made a commitment to Sally and to myself to be her dad even if it wasn't convenient, easy, cheap or fun. I'd be there for her and make sure she learned critical life lessons—that's what dads do for their children, right?

The next day I picked up the phone to call Dee Dee at home and got her answering machine—I left a message. Next, I called her office and the receptionist answered.

"Hello, may I speak to Dee Dee?"

"May I ask who's calling?"

"This is John Farley, Sally's father."

"Hold please."

Moments later, "I'm sorry, Dr. O'Dell is with patients."

"Can you ask her to call me? She has my number."

"I'll let her know."

Days went by with no return call. I called her at work again. This time the receptionist was curt and rude. "She's not available right now; she's with patients."

"Do you know who I am? I'm Sally's father. I need to speak to her now about my daughter."

"She's with patients; can I put you on hold?"

"No, don't put me—"

She put me on hold. After 5 minutes, I hung up and called back. "You had me on hold for 5 minutes."

She snapped, "Dr. O'Dell is with patients and I can't disturb her."

"Tell her this will take one minute."

"Please hold."

I waited several minutes, hung up and called back. "You had me on hold again for 5 minutes. Now, I want to speak with Dee Dee about my daughter."

"Let me check for you.... I'm sorry she's with patients. I'll tell her you called."

"Tell her I need to speak with her."

"Hold on."

Anger boiled inside me. Not only does Dee Dee disrespect me, she has her staff do it too.

I just want my child. After another five minutes on hold I hung up. This time I speed dialed her number. When it rang, I hung up and I kept doing it over and over and over again. Dozens and dozens of times. Professional, no, but I'm sure it got her attention.

Finally, during one of the speed dials, Dee Dee picked up. "John?" she asked, sounding surprised. Her voice was hushed and her tone made me feel like I'd done something inappropriate. "John, I'm with patients. I'll call you later."

Panting in frustration, I said, "When, Dee Dee? When? I have my schedule in front of me. Just tell me a time."

"John, I'm with patients right now."

"Dee Dee, what time would you like me to call you or you call me?"

"John, I can't talk right now. After work you can call."

"After 7p.m.? 7:05? Tell me the time you want me to call."

"You can call then."

We hung up and my body started to calm down. I relaxed and waited until the appointed time. Finally, she and I would talk about this visitation issue like adults and just get it handled.

The time arrived. I called and got a message machine. I left a message. Did I miss her? Is this my fault?

Time went by, but no call back. I felt frustrated. She's blocking me from my daughter. What can I do?

A few days later I picked up the mail downstairs and found a letter from the police department in Northport, Long Island. I tore it open as I walked back up the stairs. It's on official police letterhead. It says I have to appear for a court hearing in Northport. What?

Back inside I called the number on the letter and spoke to the officer in charge. "Hello. I received this letter. What is this about?"

"You have to come in here to have a court hearing."

"For what?"

"Dee Dee O'Dell filed a criminal report that you called her over 100 times in violation of a court order of protection."

Stunned and confused. "What?"

"You want me to come out to Northport court for this? This order was entered in Central Islip. Why haven't I heard from them? Why Northport?"

"The calls were made to Northport."

I tried to reason with him, but he wasn't being reasonable. In frustration, I wrote down the date for the hearing in my calendar and prepared to show up in several weeks.

This is getting ridiculous. Is this woman on a power trip or what?

Time went on. I did my best to focus on work and other aspects of life.

Days later, I received another letter in the mail from the Northport police station. It stated that the court date had been cancelled and that I didn't need to show up to the court hearing after all.

14

What a relief. It was well overdue good news. I crossed Northport off my calendar and got back to focusing on business and life.

About one week later, I was back home from working out with clients. I was sitting at my bedroom desk when the phone rang. "Hello?"

"This is Deputy Sheriff Smith calling for John Farley."

Silence. "Yeah, this is John."

"John, our office has some papers for you from family court that we need to give you. When can we come by tomorrow?"

I thought for a moment. "Why don't you put them in the mail?"

Smith responded in a relaxed, easy going voice. "We can't do that, John. We have to give them to you in person."

I felt mildly surprised. This cop has to drive all the way out here because of some legality. I looked again at the day planner on my desk. "Okay, I'll be here this time tomorrow, twelve noon."

"Okay, we'll come by at noon, but John, you're going to be there right? This is a long drive for us and we don't want to drive all the way out if you're not going to be there."

Does he think I'm irresponsible? "Yes," I said calmly. "I said I'd be here, so I'll be here."

The Next Day

The following day arrived and it was business as usual. At noon I was at my desk as I said I would be. The temperature inside was warm. I had already changed into shorts and was walking around without shoes or socks on the hardwood floor.

John Farley, Jr.

While working at my desk, the front door bell rang loudly.

That's odd. There are two locked doors before anyone can get into the building and my buzzer to unlock the doors didn't ring. I sprang to my feet and went to the door.

"Who is it?" I said, peeking through the peephole.

"John, we have papers for you."

I opened the door just enough to put my hand through the open door. "Okay, give me the papers."

The sheriff shoved his foot inside the door.

"Hey, what are you doing?" I weakly held the door closed, but within seconds the door was slowly, but forcefully, pushed open, as I jerked my bare feet away from the oncoming door.

"Hey, what are you doing?"

The first officer came through with one hand resting on his gun. This guy didn't look like much of a cop; more like Barney Fife. Behind him was a second officer, about six-foot-one with a solid build. They were dressed in their black uniforms, with badges shining and guns visible.

The first officer looked around the room. "John, we have a warrant for your arrest. You'll have to come with us."

I backed up as they kept moving forward. "What are you talking about? You can't just barge in here. I demand to see that warrant right now."

"We have a warrant for your arrest."

I moved backward from the tight hallway into the kitchen. "I demand to see it."

The shorter cop casually walked toward me looking about the room, while the second cop glared at me over his shoulder. "We'll show it to you later at the facility, but we have to go and you're coming with us."

I backed toward the bedroom. "Wait a minute. I demand to see a warrant. If you don't have a warrant you can't come in here."

The taller sheriff spoke up. "John, we have a warrant. Now, get your shoes on and let's go."

116

"My shoes are in my bedroom and I want to put long pants on. I'll be out in a few minutes."

Both deputy sheriffs, walked behind me into the bedroom.

They walked in like they owed the place. "What are you doing in my bedroom?"

The shorter one continued looking around the room. "Go ahead, get dressed, hurry up; we have to go."

"What the hell is going on here?" I turned and sat at my desk. "You say you have a warrant. I've asked to see it and you don't have it with you. How do I know you have one at all?"

The tall one blurted out, "John, we've been over this. Now, you need to get changed or we'll take you like that."

I sat with shorts on as two fully armed deputies stood in my bedroom ordering me to come with them. I placed my hands in front of me, fingertips touching like a steeple and calmly asked, "What if I refuse to go?"

The tall one snapped back. "Then we'll pepper spray you and take you with us."

"Oh, that will look really good in the papers: Cops break into man's home without a warrant, pepper spray and kidnap him."

The tall one verbally shot back. "It doesn't matter. Do you want to do this the hard way or the easy way?"

I weighed the options. "Okay, I'll go. Let me change in the bathroom."

"Leave the door open," snarled the tall one. The bathroom connects to my bedroom and with the door open there's no privacy.

I changed my clothes as they watched. With my pants on, I walked through the bedroom toward the front door.

The shorter one stopped me at the door. "John, turn around, we have to put cuffs on you."

"What? Cuffs? What for? Let me walk down the stairs without cuffs on. What are my neighbors going to think?"

"We can't do it, John."

Justified anger welled up the way a lightly shaken carbonated soda rushes out of the lid.

Once the handcuffs were on, we walked down five flights of stairs to the street to their patrol car. It'd be at least a one hour drive to Long Island. The back seat pushed the cuffs tighter against my wrist bones. The metal dug in and slowed the blood supply and numbed my hands.

"Can you loosen these a little, please?"

The tall one spoke up. "You'll be okay," as he drove the car across 7th Avenue.

We sat in silence for what seemed like thirty minutes. No one said anything until the shorter one asked a question. "John, how did all this happen to you?"

"I don't want to get into it."

"What do you do with a samurai sword, John?"

"How do you know I have a samurai sword?"

"I saw it in your closet. We're trained to notice things, you know, to observe." Now, his partner wanted in.

"Why did you violate the order of protection again?" It felt as if he was poking me. When did I ever get that order?

"Violate it how?"

"You called Dee Dee O'Dell on the phone, and you weren't supposed to."

"You mean to tell me that's what this is about? A phone call to find out if the mother would abide by the court order and let me see my daughter? That's what this is about?"

The shorter one interjected. "The police report says assault and battery, John. A court order forbids you from contacting her, even by phone."

"Yeah, where is that order? How do I see my daughter, if I can't contact the mother to make arrangements? I have a court order TOO. I have rights TOO. You guys are liars. I was honest with you. You told me you had papers from family court that had to be delivered in person and I agreed to meet with you for that purpose. You have no papers. You forced your way into my home without a warrant, as a trick to arrest me because I made a phone call to see my daughter? How do you sleep at night? Aren't there real criminals you could be going after?"

The tall one, the bad cop, smelled blood. "You're under arrest because you broke the court order!"

Smith's turn. "John, I have a relative, and he beat the hell out of his wife. That order of protection saved her life by keeping him away from her. It's wrong to beat up women, John."

"I didn't beat her up. This is all a plan, her plan. She's a doctor with a photographic memory. She's smarter than all three of us put together. This is all a con game she's running."

Suddenly, they hit a hard bump on the Long Island Expressway. "Ahh!" The cuffs dug into the flesh and bone as the car slapped back down to the road. Good cop Smith heard my reaction and turned to bad cop.

"Easy. Don't hit those bumps so hard."

Bad cop had to know I was worked up. "You broke the judge's order. You beat your ex-wife. You're behind on child support payments. What kind of father are you? I've seen plenty of guys like you. You deserve to be locked up."

My fuse was lit now. "Shut up. Just shut your mouth. You don't know what you are talking about. All you lying cops should be shot in a firing squad."

Good cop jumped in. "John, do you know what you're saying? Do you really mean that?"

I yelled. "Just shut up."

Good cop had turned around nearly facing me. "Have you ever seen a man hit by bullets? Flesh and blood flies all over. Are you serious about shooting cops?"

"You guys are putting words in my mouth. That's it. I'm not saying another word. Don't talk to me."

We arrived at the sheriff's facility within the courthouse in Central Islip, the one Christy Brinkley would eventually make famous. I wasn't going in the front doors like beautiful Brinkley. I'd be going through the back.

15

The cop car stopped. "Step out, John," Good Cop said.

Next thing I knew I was inside in a hallway surrounded by many deputies. It looked like it could be an underground military bunker.

A voice from the side barked, "Take off your shoes and socks. Turn your socks inside out."

I had been through this drill before, but it wasn't getting easier. Kidnapped by strangers with guns and taken to a secluded prison is intimidating. They got what they wanted—fear.

The space felt cold. The cement floors and walls seemed almost icy. The florescent lights high above lit the depressing space with a dull hum. I was brought into a small room with Bad Cop leading the way as Good Cop trailed behind.

I felt a mild confidence the way a child feels confident because he doesn't know what what he doesn't know.

Bad Cop spoke up, "We have to fingerprint you. Step over here."

I was ready for this. I'd been reading up on my rights. My tone was polite and firm. "Fingerprinting is a violation of my fourth amendment right to my property. So, I am declining fingerprints."

Bad Cop stopped to digest what he'd heard. "What are you talking about?" His mouth hung open as he placed his hands on his hips. "Everybody gets fingerprinted. It's not a violation of any rights."

"I disagree. My fingerprints are my property and I'm not giving them to you."

Good Cop joined in. "John, we have to fingerprint you before you go in front of the judge."

"Why? Just bring me in front of the judge. I don't get fingerprinted when I show up to court normally, so why is this different? Just bring me in front of the judge. My fingerprints are my property and the government doesn't have a right to my property. Are you going to give my fingerprints back to me?"

Looking at each other, Bad Cop started to walk away. "If that's how you want it."

I was moved to a very large cell by myself. It looked like Hannibal Lecter's cell, but with bars, not glass. I had plenty of room to move around. Even so, I sat in leg irons and handcuffs. Good Cop came by the cell, his demeanor almost submissive. Not the usual tough guy approach. Standing sideways to the cell bars, he peered in. "John, can we get those fingerprints from you now?"

I looked at him while I sat on a bench. "No," I said gently.

Moments later Bad Cop came over. "If you don't give us those prints you're going to Riverhead."

What did he mean by that? "What's so special about Riverhead?"

Good Cop turned to walk away. "Nothing really. It's just a jail."

I watched his face and body language. He seemed convincing and I shrugged it off. Time went by. The lights stayed on. No clocks, just concrete and steel. I could faintly hear sounds of other prisoners in far off cells, but couldn't see any of them.

Good Cop came by. "John, would you like a magazine to read or something to drink?" This was surprising. They never allowed me to have anything like that before. He seems very accommodating.

Something is odd. "No," I didn't want to be indebted to them for any favors.

Time crept by, like a long, lonely night. I did deep breathing exercises and meditation. They knew I was a black belt in karate and seemed intimidated, or at least uneasy by the deep breathing and meditation that I used to occupy my time.

Good Cop appeared out of nowhere in front of the cell. "Here's some food, John." He put a plate with one of those ham sandwiches into the cell. I looked at it and let it sit there. That food could be laced with something—unlikely, but possible.

Moments later, Good Cop was back, noticing the sandwich where he placed it. "John, we need you to give us those fingerprints before our shift is over. If you don't we have to take you to Riverhead."

Seemed like the pressure was on them to fingerprint me soon. "Fingerprints are mine and I'm not giving them to you."

Good Cop didn't look happy about this and left. It was getting late into the night. Within what seemed thirty minutes, both deputies appeared at the cell, opened the door, and ordered me out.

I was brought outside to a van. Bad Cop and Good Cop opened the back of the van and herded me inside. Each step was slow and precise because my ankles were bound together. I sat on the hard bench shackled and cuffed. The darkness was relieved only by a sliver of moonlight bouncing through the back window.

Suddenly, the window partition opened, and I could see and hear the deputies. Anxiety kicked in. "Where're we going?"

No answer.

The window separating us closed. The van was dark, empty and cold. The engine revved and suddenly jerked into motion. I was thrown toward the back. There was nothing to hold onto. My hands were locked together, unable to be spread apart—unable to hold myself up. It was as if I was armless.

The van took off. My heart responded, as I quickly sucked in air and swallowed reflexively. Then…

Boom! I launched for a microsecond into the air. My head smashed against the metal roof. The pain was immediate.

"Hey! You guys are going too fast!" I called to the closed window. They must be running over speed bumps at high speed.

Boom! My head hit the roof again. I tried to drop lower—to crouch. The van came to a near stop very quickly causing me to slide into the front wall. The van jerked forward, knocking me back the other way. With nothing to hold on to, I smashed into walls and ceiling. Boom! My head hit the roof. I'm afraid now. My heart pounded.

I could slam into a wall, and be seriously hurt. What if they break my nose or neck, or something else? The ride from hell seemed to last 30 minutes or more, or maybe a lot less, I couldn't tell. Then, without warning, it ended.

The van stopped. Front doors could be heard opening. Seconds later the back doors flew open. "Step out."

Relief came over me the way it does after any seriously close call. I did my best to appear calm.

I stepped out and down the van steps making sure not to trip. Am I somewhere else? Or, did they take me around the parking lot?

"Is this Riverhead?"

No response. I was taken inside a building and put in a jail cell. At first I thought it was a different place, but no, this was the same place I was just in.

The officers came to the cell. "John, this is the last opportunity to give us your fingerprints or we have to take you to Riverhead."

I was not giving in now. "No fingerprints. Let me see a judge."

Time was a blur and soon I was back into the van. The ride was perhaps an hour, uncomfortable and rough, but not as rough as the first time.

Finally, the van slowed. The deputies opened the partition between us. I could see out the front window just a little. A massive barbed razor wire on top of high fences loomed in front of us. Circles of razor wire on top of circles of razor wire. This didn't seem like just a jail. In fact, it turned out to be a combined maximum/medium security prison.

I figured it was close to midnight now. I'd been in custody for about 12 hours.

"Where are we?"

Good Cop responded, "Riverhead."

It was late night. The sky was dark. There was a bright light near an entrance.

Once outside the van, we walked toward a door, the type you might see on the side of any industrial building. I stood chained and nervous. After the deputies communicated with whoever was on the other side, it opened.

I stepped through and was met by large, scowling, brown-shirted corrections officers. These were the guys the deputies were handing me off to. They were all tall, wide and rough looking.

I looked around me. My senses were on high alert. I bet these guys had expected me.

"Turn around," one yelled. Within seconds my leg chains and arm cuffs were released.

"Stand in the middle," one of them called out.

Slowly, I walked forward, noticing Good Cop standing off to the side of the large open space—out of the way.

A wall of jail cells were directly behind me. An elevated control room was in front with a huge glass window spanning the length of the room. Around the perimeter of the space stood close to one dozen brown shirted corrections officers. One of them, a 50-something man weighing about 240 pounds sat at a desk in the upper corner to my left. I stood motionless freed from shackles and handcuffs.

He stopped writing and looked up. And after a moment's pause he spoke in a strong, commanding voice. "Come over here..."

16

I stood without shoes or socks on the cool, hard floor.

"You're going to be fingerprinted." He stood almost six feet tall and roughly two hundred forty pounds, with wide, thick forearms, he looked like a tough old bird. Many corrections officers stood silently around the perimeter, mostly out of my view.

I didn't realize I'd entered a lion's cage. I stepped my bare feet toward his desk, as I attempted to explain myself in a polite voice. "I told the other officers that I am declining fingerprints as it's a violation of my fourth amendment rights."

His posture straightened. He quickly closed the gap between us. "Oh, you're going to be printed." He grabbed my left wrist with his large, right hand.

I heard Good Cop from the back corner. "Don't do it, John."

A wrist grab. I could get out of this with a quick jerk. Instead, I brought my hand very slowly toward my chest while gently twisting my wrist making it very difficult for him to hang on. "As I mentioned, I'm declining fingerprints...."

As the officer's hand slipped from my wrist, large men from every direction grabbed me. My adrenaline surged. "GENTLEMEN, I DECLINE FINGERPRINTS! THIS IS A VIOLATION OF MY FOURTH AMENDMENT RIGHTS! LET ME GO!"

They held me in place. About ten men to my left and right grabbed me while bracing themselves against one another.

I yelled. "Let me go! This is a violation of my fourth amendment rights—" They're not allowed to harm me for asserting my rights. This is a game, a test. Let's see what happens. Slowly, like a glacier, I started to use all my force to push to my right side where only two officers were holding me.

The others were on my left or behind me all holding on, or bracing each other. The two officers to my right reacted to my slow pressure and started to push back. I continued to push harder and harder until I felt one group pushing me to the left and the others pulling me toward to the left.

Instantly, I reversed my force to the left as hard and as fast as I could. The entire line of men stumbled and nearly fell like dominos. They pushed back the other way and I again changed directions. Again, the line nearly fell over the other way. At this point, it all seemed like a game to me.

"BRING HIM OVER HERE," one officer told the mob.

With all of them grabbing my arms and body, they walked me a few steps to the front where ink and paper waited. They grabbed my right hand and I clenched my fist. They pried open my fingers, forcing my right thumb to the ink pad. They carefully lifted the freshly inked thumb to the paper in order to roll it across. I relaxed my arm. The officers loosened their grip ever so slightly. The moment the thumb touched the paper I used all my strength to slide the thumb instead of letting it roll.

"It smudged. Do it again!"

I clenched my fist again. They pried it open again and rolled the thumb on the ink pad. They held my thumb and could have easily broken it. I had to relax it or suffer a fracture. As they placed the thumb on the paper, I jerked my finger just a few millimeters, but it was enough to smudge the ink.

One guard twice my size spoke up. "I've had enough of this." He picked up the ink roller. It's smaller than a paint roller, and made of hard, dense, shiny metal with one small metal knob protruding on each end. He turned the roller sideways, holding it like a hammer, knobs out.

"Hold his hand up." The men extended my right arm straight out. I couldn't move it. The elbow was locked tight in mid air.

The angry, dark haired officer took the roller, pulling it back past his head and, as if hammering in a defiant nail, he struck the back of that hand full force. "AGHHH!" My hand flew open automatically. A tiny chunk of flesh flew off, revealing blood underneath. I yelled, but it was more like a scream, "AGHHH! PRINT THE THUMB!"

The officer pulled back, and smashed the hand again.

"AGHHH! PRINT THE THUMB!" I said.

Again he smashed the hand and again and again. I was trapped, helpless, I couldn't move. I thought for sure my hand bones would be crushed. I felt tortured. Seconds felt like hours. As the back of the hand ached in pain they again brought me to the ink pad.

Now, I was relieved to give them the thumbprint. They rolled the thumb into the ink, while the hand shook from shock.

There. They had what they wanted.

"OPEN THE CELL." They picked me up off the ground and held me like a log. They ran me toward the open cell door like a battering ram. My head was going to hit the steel bars! I turned my head to the left at the last moment before impact.

"AGHHHHH!" My shoulder. As I bounced off the immovable steel. "I'M RELAXED! I'M RELAXED! I'M RELAXED!" I continued pleading.

"Put him down!"

My body was smashed onto the cot in the middle of the cell. A six foot four officer punched down onto my lower back, again, and again, and again. He punched my spleen as hard as he could from a devastating downward angle. I yelled, "I'M RELAXED. I'M RELAXED!"

The thug in a uniform continued punching again and again. While I lay stunned and in pain, they slapped iron shackles on my legs.

Huffing, they walked out of the cell and locked the door. I realized what happened. These thugs just wanted to beat me up. They hammered my hand and could have broken bones. They smashed me into the metal bars, punched me after smashing my body and face into the metal cot. Rage came over me. I got up with my legs shackled.

"OH, I didn't know you wanted to FIGHT! Open this cell right now, you pile of horse—!"

"SHUT UP" one of them yelled.

"You want to fight? Let's go! Open up right now! I said I was relaxed and you...you F-ING ASSHOLE. You punched me!"

They walked away. Some called me names. Finally, a forty-something, balding brown shirt came over. "John," he said, making his way to the front of the cell, "we're going to get what we want. If it takes one of us or 100 of us, we're going to get what we want."

"You're a bunch of scum suckin' pigs," I yelled." You pieces of dog crap."

Why did they have to do that? Why couldn't they have explained it to me first? I was just stating my legal position.

It took hours, but I finally calmed down and fell asleep. In the middle of the night, the cell door creaked and woke me.

Three officers stood inside the cell door. I slowly put my hands behind my head and looked at them.

"What's up?"

They came in, and took the shackles off my ankles and left. Finally, morning came and so did breakfast. They had to feed prisoners, but I still wasn't eating the crap they slipped into the cell. Now that they had my fingerprints, I have to go in front of a judge in Central Islip. My hand ached and bleed slightly. My shoulder had a deep bruise while my back smarted in pain. As long as I can make it out of here alive, I'll be okay.

17

Something's happening. Prisoners came into the main area outside my cell. The sound of their chains bounced off the concrete walls. The men looked scruffy and depressed with shoulders and heads drooped. A few women, mostly black, stood next to the men in a separate line.

What am I doing here? An officer came and unlocked my cell door. "Come out."

Everyone, including me, was then chained and connected to the prisoner in front and behind. We shuffled outside to a waiting dark colored sheriff's bus. The sound of metal chains dragged and rattled while the echo bounced around. One glance at the man in front of me and then down at my own chains reminded me that we were now tainted. Armed deputies sat in front of the bus behind a locked, mesh metal door.

We sat motionless in old style school bus seats in total silence. The image of who I thought I was began falling away. I'd cultivated my public image my whole life. Now the separation between me and people I thought I had nothing in common with was blurring.

It'd been over 30 hours since being captured at my home. Adrenaline must have pumped through me as if I was hooked up to an IV. I became hyper aware of my surroundings. The round metal handcuffs rubbed against my rectangular wrist bones. The shackles pinched my ankles. Seeing men with rifles a few feet away and knowing those guns were to be used if anyone got out of line, was enough to keep everyone completely quiet.

A feeling of helplessness and guilt crept up on me like a slow approaching spider.

After what seemed about an hour, the bus arrived at the court in Central Islip. Inside the building we were searched again. My senses heightened—nerves on edge. Awareness was automatic. There was little thinking about past or future—only the moment.

They herded us into the cold, lifeless concrete hallway. As ordered, I walked barefoot, carrying my shoes along with the chain gang under the watchful eye of black uniformed deputies.

I was becoming suspicious. Subtle signs, a glance, a whisper, that I would have rationalized away were now given a second thought.

The deputies had decided to separate me from the other prisoners. Two deputies walked me to another cell. "Go in here." The door closed once I was in. I sat alone and waited for someone to let me know what was going on. It was better to be in a cell alone than with a dozen other people. Anything could happen in a small space with a bunch of cons, right?

A short time later a group of six deputies came to the cell.

"We're moving you." They opened the heavy door. They changed the handcuffs from the front to locking my hands behind me.

"Look straight ahead and walk."

"Where are we going?"

"Shut up and look straight ahead."

We walked down a hallway past other holding cells. What are they doing with me now?

"Stop here."

We reached the last prison cell. A deputy quickly put his key in the lock to open the door. "Walk inside. Go to the right. Face the wall."

I did what he said, not giving it much thought. In front of me there was a metal bench connected to the wall.

"Get on your knees on the bench."

"What?"

"Do it now! Get on your knees, face the wall and shut up!"

132

What is this all about?

One knee—ah, the metal is pressing into the shinbone—balance—stay up, now the other knee.

About five male deputies stood behind me and one woman. I stared at the concrete wall noticing the texture when—

BAM! My head was hit from the left side and my body jerked to the right as I nearly toppled over.

"What the hell was that?"

"KEEP LOOKING AT THAT WALL!"

"I AM I AM." He just hit me!

A loud, intense, husky deputy screamed at me. "What did you say to those officers?"

My eyes felt as wide as quarters as terror gripped me. "What officers? What are you talking about?"

BAM! Another blow to the side of my head, nearly knocked me off the bench.

"STAY ON THE BENCH. STAY ON THE BENCH!"

I pleaded in desperation. "I AM. I AM!"

"Turn around, face me."

The metal bench dug into my shinbones as I struggled to turn ninety degrees.

The nearly six-foot tall 225-pound deputy yelled, "YOU TOLD THOSE OFFICERS YOU WERE GONNA KILL'EM DIDN'T YA?"

The officer's arm moved. Instinctively I exhaled as hard and as fast as I could.

WHAM, my body bent over. The officer threw an uppercut body shot with full force into my mid-section.

"AGHHH!"

"WHAT DID YOU SAY TO THOSE OFFICERS?!"

My teeth clenched, as I sucked in air. "NOTHING, I didn't say anything!"

"Stick out your tongue."

"What?"

"STICK OUT YOUR TONGUE."

I opened my mouth and stuck out my tongue.

"IT'S PURPLE! YOU'RE LYING."

In a split second his arm moved. I exhaled hard and fast and, WHAM.

"AGHHHH." My body bent over as I unconsciously started to get off the bench.

The group yelled. "STAY ON THE BENCH."

In a flash. the cop's arm moved again, and loudly and forcefully I exhaled completely getting the air out of my lungs as the third gut punch landed squarely in my solar plexus.

"AGHHH!"

"YOU EVER SAY ANYTHING TO THOSE OFFICERS AGAIN AND WE'LL KILL YOU. FACE THE WALL."

I stayed kneeling and facing the wall. My heart pounded, adrenaline surged and fear flooded me. The sound of footsteps moved toward the cell door.

I heard the cell door close and lock. All their faces were hidden from view, except for the one who did the punching. I saw his face very clearly. Peering over my shoulder to find that they'd all left, I got off my knees and sat. My body shook as my mind rationalized what happened. I must be a very bad person. Did I deserve this?

Soon, two other deputies came back to the cell. "COME UP HERE."

I better make amends. I sheepishly walked to the cell door rattling my chains. Not unlike a ten year old talking to bullies on the playground, I tried to make friends.

"I want you to know that I'm sorry, I apologize and whatever you think I said to any officers I didn't mean it."

The deputy sneered. "You're an asshole. Turn around."

I did. He changed the cuffs from behind to in front and walked me down the hallway to a different cell. The shackles and cuffs were taken off and I was ordered into the cell.

I sat and waited. Time became inconsequential. There's only now. Two white deputies came to the cell and stood outside in their dark uniforms. "You have to have a strip search."

I lifted my elbows off my knees and slowly stood up before speaking politely. "What are you talking about?"

"You have to have a strip search. Take off your shirt."

I looked at them as they shined a flashlight through the cell bars into my eyes.

"What is this for?"

"Either you take off your clothes or we'll have them taken off for you."

I swallowed hard and took off my shirt.

"Turn around. Take off your pants and underwear."

I looked down— my head shook from disbelief and indignation. I can't believe this. I can't believe I'm letting this happen. I have no choice. I took off my pants and underwear.

"Turn around. Bend over and spread your butt cheeks."

"Wait a minute— this is—"

"Do it."

Is this really happening? I paused. I took a deep breath, turned around and tried to think of it as a doctor's exam.

"Turn around." He ordered me to show my genitals in full detail while a bright light nearly blinded me. I glared back wishing—hoping for revenge.

I hesitated, feeling resistance well up within me. My jaw clenched, while I looked down. I wanted to say no. I did what I was ordered to do as I looked away in shame.

The flashlight beam clicked off. "Put your clothes back on."

After I slid my pants on and put my arms through my shirtsleeves when a very tall, black deputy came to the cell door and stared at me.

I braced myself. What in the name of God does he want? He stood glaring down at me through the steel bars. I said nothing, but waited like a child whose angry father had walked into his bedroom.

John Farley, Jr.

"YOU BETTER REMEMBER—THIS IS STRONG ISLAND."

I looked down without saying a word. I finished putting my shirt on and sat still. The psychological operation against me was complete. My jailers had now dominated and humiliated me. I lost track of what happened next. All I remember was a deputy commanding me.

18

Next thing I knew I was out in the hallway looking into a cell. From behind, the deputy ordered me around like a bad dog. "Go in."

I walked into a cell filled with other prisoners. I reminded myself to look both non-threatening, yet confident. Keep to yourself. Act like you know what's going on.

I overheard conversations. The men in this cell were drunk drivers, drug users and drivers with suspended licenses. All dressed in jeans and tee shirts. "What are you in here for?" one asked me.

I spoke with calm assuredness. "They say I violated an order of protection. I just want to see my daughter and the mother is stopping me."

As we spoke, someone stood in front of the cell door. A geeky guy with the clipboard began calling people by name to the front. Through the bars, he discussed the case with each person and then decided what bail to recommend to the judge.

Those who can't pay stay in jail. I kept to myself. Nervously, I visualized what I wanted—freedom. I imagined myself persuading this guy to make me free. I blocked out everything except my goal. Fear of failure kept me motivated and focused.

He called my name and I got up and stepped toward him, mentally rehearsing what to say. The man glanced at me through the metal mesh and then his clipboard. He talked louder than needed, as if I wasn't a person, but rather a lessor human. "You've been in here before for violating the order of protection. Since you've been here before for the same thing...."

My eyes felt like they were bugging out as I swallowed before speaking. "You have to get me out of here." He kept staring at his clipboard, hardly hearing me. "You've done this before. The judge isn't…"

I became animated as my hand reached out to the mesh between us. I cut him off with a hushed, but frantic and desperate tone that sliced through the air. "Listen to me. You have to get me out of here."

He lifted his head as we locked eyes through the tiny holes in the metal door. "The recommendations are…"

"FORGET ALL THAT. Forget all that. They're trying to kill me. Do you hear me? They're trying— to—kill me. You have to get—me—out—of—here."

He paused, I suspected, because he heard a ring of truth instead of the usual excuses.

More than the others, I was desperate to be free. "Get—me out of here. Get me out—please. Please."

He looked down at his clipboard trying hard to remain detached. "I'll see what I can do." Before he called the next name on his list I whispered, "Do whatever you have to do."

Time went by slower than a stopped clock.

Then, without warning, it was time for some of us to go in front of the judge. We were brought out and lined up—left shoulders against the wall. There was no talking or moving allowed. We were cuffed, shackled and chained to each other.

When the signal came, my group was led through locked doors into a hallway. We waited for the next signal.

"Now!" an officer called out. The door to the courtroom opened. "Walk in, all the way down. Don't look at the judge."

All of us—the accused—sat next to one another with chains from waist to ankle. I listened closely as names were called out to stand before the judge.

"Don't look at the judge. Keep your head down."

"John Farley."

I have to succeed. I stood up as chains rattled against the wooden bench.

An officer ordered me. "Stand here."

The man with the clipboard spoke to the judge. The prosecutor wanted bail. The clipboard man told the judge no bail and explained my situation. My heart pounded in fear, but I interjected.

"Your Honor, I was following the court order out of Manhattan to see my daughter. If I didn't show up, I'd be in contempt of the visitation order."

Conflicting thoughts came to me. Why didn't I tell the judge that I had just been brutally battered in Riverhead and here in Central Islip? Why didn't I demand that the police come out and arrest those that had just beaten me?

"Release him on his own recognizance," the judge said.

I'm going to get out of here. Thank God.

We were led back into the hallway and into the holding cell. Repressed joy came over me. I sat in the cell relieved. It was just a matter of time and formality now. I'm going home.

Names of the other prisoners were being called for release. I listened for mine. The time dragged. I didn't want to ask what was taking so long. I kept waiting, looking at the cell's concrete wall. What a waste of time.

I started to notice all the cracks in the wall. The length, shape. Anything to occupy my mind. This was taking too long, even for the government. Something seemed wrong. The guy with the clipboard came over to the cell for someone else. I went up to the front of the cell and as soon as he finished with the other guy I interrupted. "What's going on with my case? Why are things taking so long?"

"I don't know. I'll see what I can find out." He came back a few minutes later. "There's a hold on you in Northport."

My breathing stopped. "A hold. What is that?"

He turned to leave. "I don't know anything else."

My shoulders drooped. A sigh came over me as I pressed my fingers against the bridge of my nose. I then waited all day before detectives from Northport showed up.

John Farley, Jr.

Troubling thoughts kept invading my consciousness like bugs flying in an open window. Does anyone know where I am? My family has no idea. Janet has no idea. Sally may never know what happened to her dad.

Many hours later the Northport detectives arrived. How much longer can I stay focused? What's going to happen to me now?

19

I left the cell cuffed and shackled. Two slightly overweight white men in their fifties, wearing plain clothes stood in the open area next to a couple of deputies in black uniforms. I don't remember getting in, but there I was, sitting in the back seat of an unmarked car. This time, I stayed silent. No questions were asked and none were answered. The half hour ride to the village of Northport felt like an hour. One thing remained the same, the too tight handcuffs behind my back painfully pressed into my wrist bones as I leaned against the back seat.

Don't these people know I'm a good person? I obey the law. I'm a respected karate black belt—a top fitness professional, a trained hypnotist. I'm a little girl's dad. I can't believe this is happening.

After parking in the open parking lot, the detectives got out and opened my back door. In broad daylight with chains rattling, they walked me into the police station. The embarrassment of being seen in public had shrunk my confidence from superman to Clark Kent in record time.

The chief detective, a no-nonsense guy about 55, mustache, thirty-five pounds overweight, wearing a short sleeve dress shirt, dark brown slacks and comfortable looking dress shoes, finally spoke to me. "The magistrate's coming in for this hearing."

I waited outside the room, cuffed, shackled, bruised, hungry, dehydrated and worn-out.

The one detective prepared the room for the magistrate—a judge of sorts. He's a lawyer by day and court magistrate by night. It'd been approximately thirty-six hours since my arrest. I was functioning on a few hours sleep. I hadn't bathed or even combed my hair, not to mention eaten anything since the beginning.

The chief detective came out glanced at the other guy and then me. "He's ready."

The detectives grabbed my arms, one on each side as I shuffled along the floor like slaves I'd seen in movies. The door opened to what looked like a large conference room. At the end of the room stood the judge. He stood slightly elevated above us with only his black robe and the back of his head visible from behind. At that moment I realized he was judge, jury and possibly, executioner.

My energy was drained. What does he want from me?

He stood and thumbed through a document as I was brought forward. He reminded me of a dark lord of the Sith. He rotated toward me and scowled down. "You are in violation of an order to appear in court." His words bounced through my brain as if they were a pinball I was trying to follow.

I forced my mind to focus and blurted out, "What? What are you talking about?"

"You heard me. You're accused of a serious matter. Where's your father?"

Huh, what did he just say? "My father? My father's dead! What—I—uh..."

Why in the world did he ask about my father? Do I look that young? Would having my father in my life somehow prevented this from happening?

"You were supposed to show up to court and you didn't."

What's happening? Don't panic. "I received a letter in the mail from the police station telling me the court date had been cancelled. That's why I didn't show up."

"There was no letter. You're lying. Take him away." The detectives started to pull me, but I held my ground for a split second.

"Wait. This is a mistake!"

They pulled harder as I sheepishly followed their lead, walking me down behind the offices to a row of old-time jail cells. The chief opened the cell door and unchained me. I walked in, and the detective closed and locked the door with its long, steel bars.

As the door shut making a loud clacking sound, I asked, "What happens now?"

"The judge set bail for you at $500. If you pay the bail you can go."

"Five hundred dollars. I don't have any money on me. The judge in Central Islip didn't put bail, why did this judge? How do I get bail money?"

"Do you have any relatives or friends who can get the money?"

"I live in Manhattan. It's over two hours from here by train and cab on a good day. What if I don't get the bail? You're keeping me here until when?"

"No, you can't stay here past midnight. If you don't make bail we'll take you to Riverhead."

I could feel my eyebrows reaching for my scalp. "Riverhead! No, no, no. Not Riverhead. Let me call my girlfriend."

I gave him her number to call from the office. He left, promising to call for me.

Time went by. No return call. Every minute felt like holding my breath underwater, waiting for air. All I could do was sit in the dimly lit cell and stare at the steel and concrete. My incessant thoughts became irritating to my mind the way mosquito bites aggravate the skin.

I heard hallway footsteps approaching. What's going to happen this time? The chief appeared in front of my cell door. "She called and says she'll be on her way, but if she's not here by midnight we have to take you to Riverhead."

His words sank in. It was getting late. Traveling to Northport during the week by train was the only way that made sense. It'd take thirty minutes to get to Penn Station. An hour to get to Huntington. Change trains and then another thirty minutes to Northport. Grab a cab and fifteen minutes more to the courthouse.

Images of Riverhead kept intruding over my positive thoughts.

They might kill me this time. Anything could happen. How long would I be there? Time crept by the way it does on a lonely Sunday. The difference was the fear factor. The chief and the other detective came to my cell.

Anxiously I stood up, swallowed and asked, "Is she here yet?"

"No," said the chief. "It's getting late. If she doesn't get here soon we have to take you to Riverhead." With looks of disappointment on their faces, they left back down the hallway.

Oh God, please, get me out of this situation.

Time ticked by. Images of Riverhead kept flashing through my mind. Prayer was not my usual ritual, but I prayed now.

After another thirty minutes the chief stood at my cell door. "She's not here. We have to move you to Riverhead. Let me tell my partner and we'll get ready to go."

The detective walked back down the long, narrow hallway. In desperation I called out, "But she'll be coming here with the money!"

My heart sank and my muscles started to tremble.

I'm doomed in Riverhead. I'll be at the mercy of psychotic corrections officers. What was my big crime again? It was something about following one court order and not following another conflicting order.

Suddenly, fast footsteps came down the hallway. The chief appeared and rattled a key into the cell door. He was genuinely excited. "She's here. She's here," he said.

Janet had arrived with the money. For the detective, that meant he wouldn't have to drive all the way to Riverhead. I'd never been so excited to see Janet, or anyone, in all my life. The cell door opened. My chains were released. Just like that, I was free—back on the other side of society.

We left the building and crossed the street to a waiting cab. We hugged momentarily inside the cab, but I didn't feel very huggable. Janet was filled with a mix of shock and anger. "What did they do to you?"

"It's too much to go into now—let me relax a moment." The trip was long. All I could think about was taking pictures of my bruises. We arrived back in Manhattan late into the night. My apartment was too risky. We'd go to Janet's place on the Upper East Side.

At Janet's apartment she found her camera and I took off my shirt. I had a big bruise on my shoulder from being slammed into the cell bars. There was the black and blue mark on my abdomen from the repeated punches. My hand was pocked with cuts and specs of dried blood still visible from the fingerprinting roller.

Days and weeks went by, but the nightmares kept coming. The anger, fatigue and anxiety seemed never-ending. It was nearly incapacitating. Each day, at some point, questions would burst through the door of my mind the way a geyser explodes water from the ground.

Did this really happen? Is this America? America—where the word "freedom" is tossed around like flags on the Fourth of July. Enough. Stop it. Let's get back to the real world.

20

After training sessions with my clients, I trekked from the subway station on 59th Street, and Broadway back home while I pretended everything was normal. Clients can't know about these arrests, it's bad for business.

Something's different. I'm different. Now, I noticed cops standing on the street corners. I was suspicious of everyone. Every television commercial was trying to trick me into buying their crap. Politicians, lawyers, cops—even the cute girl behind the register at the supermarket who asked if I wanted to donate to some relief fund in Africa. I didn't trust any of them. Like a traumatized dog, I was ready to bite and snap, even at well meaning hands.

Downstairs in my apartment building, I opened the mailbox. A loud noise startled me, causing my head to whip around without conscious control. The middle-aged woman who lives on the first floor had opened her creaky door. I think she noticed the fearful look in my eyes.

She talked to me as if she hadn't noticed anything. "Is the mail in?"

"Ah," I said, clearing my throat. "Yes." I'd stopped myself from saying more. It was unlike me to be so curt.

This woman, my neighbor, dresses like she lives on a farm upstate, not in Manhattan Her hair was messy. The oversized T-shirt, and sweat pants didn't match the quick mind I knew she had. "I'll see you later." I darted up the five flights of stairs with letters in my hand.

At the top, just before I reached the door, I noticed a letter from my bank. Inside the apartment I opened it and pulled out a letter. It explained how the bank had confiscated my money because of a court document they'd received. There was hardly any money in the account, but it was all of my money. Without it I couldn't eat for days until my next client paid me. What if they take that too?

Pressure built inside me like a car engine overheating. I rubbed my forehead with my eyes closed trying to keep the anxiety from making me dizzy. I had to do something about this immediately.

Within fifteen minutes I'd walked to the bank. Outside, the automated teller machine wouldn't give me any cash. I opened the heavy glass entrance door. Inside, the spacious building was as quiet as a church. I approached a teller, a young woman behind tall glass that stretched to the ceiling.

My face certainly must have appeared unhappy. "I received this letter, but I want my money, because this is not a court order."

The young woman looked at the letter and typed a few keys on the computer keyboard. "I'm sorry, but funds are on hold because of this notice."

She looked back at me with her corporate poker face. Most likely I was easy to read. Perhaps it was an involuntary twitch at the corner of my eyelid, or a grimace that made her take notice.

I spoke calmly and quietly in a measured tone. "This is not a court order." My fist clenched as my tension rose. "This is just a letter. I want my money." I'd started to regress to a less civilized, more primitive stage. "It's my money—and—I want it."

With only a moment to read my face she replied, "Let me get my manager." I took a deep breath as she scurried off. A mature looking woman in business attire came to greet me.

"Sir? Let's meet in my office." I followed behind her as if going to the principal's office. She sat behind her solid, wooden desk. "Please have a seat. I understand there was a problem on your account."

My body had tremors, and they traveled to my voice. "The problem—the problem is" I said, as I felt the heat travel up through my neck toward my face, "that you allowed someone to take, to steal, my money, my mon—ey. I. Need. My. Money and I—have to have it—right now."

My eye twitched, and the tremor in my leg muscles rose up through my body. I felt in-between realities. She looked at me first the way hard corporate types do, but then stopped. I stared right through her, and she froze for a split second. She looked away toward her computer, when I noticed her gulp.

Without looking at me she pushed her chair back from her desk. "Let's get you that money right now." She quickly stood up, and walked around the desk, past me and out toward the tellers. I followed her to the same teller as my shakes continued. "Please give Mr. Farley the money in his account."

Instantly, the tension left my body. A deep, relaxing breath happened naturally. I felt almost normal again. Friendly again. This was odd. The teller gave me fifty dollars. Fifty dollars was all the money in my account, and I knew it. But it was all the money I had at the moment and having it completely changed my personality. I took the money and left.

I'd had very little money in the past, but this experience had felt like being cast out into the cold world, broke and penniless. I left the bank, and went to the corner bookstore.

There has to be something here to teach me the secrets of money, and banks. *The Federal Mafia* by Irwin Schiff. I want that book, but not today. I'll come back later when I get paid again. It was time to re-watch the video that the man and woman from my seminar had given me.

Back at the apartment, I popped the video in. A quote came up on screen by Johann von Goethe. "None are more hopelessly enslaved than those who falsely believe they are free." My mind had changed after being abducted and beaten by those deputies.

Later that night, Janet came over. We sat in the kitchen area and sipped water before making dinner. My hands cupped my glass while Janet leaned in toward the table. "I see two worlds. I still see the world everyone else sees—Central Park, taxi cars, buildings, and businesses. But I also see another world. A wild world. A place where anyone could be taken away to jail on someone's allegation. In one world, you own your property, your fingerprints, your bank account. In the other world, you're owned. Everything can be taken from you. Possessions. Freedom. Even your life."

Janet listened and nibbled at her lip while she stared off with glassy eyes. I was becoming highly negative and my quick, wry humor was drying up. My thoughts turned obsessive—consuming me day and night.

After a swig of water, I placed the glass on the table. "Our lives are so fragile. We live on the blind trust given to strangers and government. Government is becoming more untrustworthy everyday. The average person is more suspicious of a black man running out of a grocery store, holding a bag and looking over his shoulder than they are of the IRS, the courts and the cops."

Janet nodded as I took my finger and reached toward her mouth. "Stop biting your lip." She took a breath.

"I'm going to study the income tax. Something's wrong there. If the bank could take my money, then whose money is it? What about child support? It just doesn't make sense to me." Janet stared at the wall in front and shook her head. "It's not fair."

"I agree. I'm paying—or we're paying. You know, when Sally stays with me. I'm paying for the rent, the heat, the lights, the food, the transportation and entertainment too. Why wasn't that taken into consideration by the courts? Why do I have to pay money directly to Dee Dee?"

The rest of the evening was more relaxing. Before the night was over, we hugged and kissed, but my mind was elsewhere. My heart was hardening as if it were a thin veil of water in the cold winter wind and I couldn't stop it.

As time went on, I read the income tax laws in more detail. Each spare moment I found myself studying secret information no one talked about. I discovered something interesting. To file a 1040 form, it has to be signed. It's really a confession, as one author described it. When a person signs a 1040 form they are confessing to how much "income" they received. That confession could be used against them in a criminal case. The author explained it all very clearly.

I'd had a few normal weeks go by while I anticipated the next court appearance. One weekend afternoon, Janet and I went over to the museum of modern art in mid-town. This was Janet's chance to get a culture fix while I focused on enjoying the moment and forgetting my problems. The quiet, serene and dimly lit space inside the museum gave us a chance to dial down our thoughts and anxieties.

Even inside the museum, I felt like a pot ready to boil over.

When we left, I did my best to forget government as long as possible, but within three blocks of walking along the Manhattan streets, my thoughts filled my mouth. As we waited to walk across the street, I turned to her and started talking aloud at the place where my internal dialog had left off.

"The problem is that if you were arrested and brought into a police station, they couldn't force you or threaten you with jail if you didn't sign a statement admitting to something. In fact, you have no obligation to speak to the police at all."

Janet looked over and nodded. She was getting good at keeping up with my off-the-cuff comments or pretending to.

"Think about this: The IRS claims that every year that a person has to fill out and sign a confession about his money and then hand some of it over. Or get some money back, since the IRS already took it."

The streetlight turned green and we stepped into the crosswalk. I kept talking pretty loudly, unconcerned about being overheard by the half dozen New Yorkers crossing the street all around us.

John Farley, Jr.

"If that tax form isn't 100% accurate, then the tax filer could be fined or jailed. The tax filer has to sign the form waiving his Fifth Amendment right not to be a witness against himself, but if you don't sign they won't accept it and they'll fine you."

"Yeah?" Janet said, half-listening.

"The IRS wants to tax our labor, something that the Supreme Court said over 100 years ago was unconstitutional. Income is not money received. It's increase in value. Working for your employer is an equal exchange of labor for compensation. But that's not income. Income is, for example, when a stock goes from $100 to $120. The increase in value, $20 is the income—the gain. The Gain. Businesses, for example, pay tax on profits—the gain—not on revenue before expenses are taken out."

Janet was listening, but also looking around at the sights and sounds on 57th and Sixth Avenue.

"Follow me on this. I have to work to live and eat. If I don't work I can't live, nor eat and my modern lifestyle is over. If the government could tax me 1% on my labor, which I have to do to live, then government could tax me 25% or 75% or even 100%. If the government taxed me 100% I'd be a complete slave. If the government can tax my labor 1%, then government is saying that it has a claim on my life, that it owns me and I have no way out of that slavery. Get it?"

"Okay?" she said, doing her best to follow along.

"I'm a free human being, owned by no one. If the government owns my labor, which the courts say is my property, and if they own my money and my body then they can do anything they want with me. I exist at government will and not by God-given right."

Janet continued saying, "Uh huh," while she looked around.

"That's not what this country was founded on. This country was founded on the right to life, liberty and the pursuit of happiness." My view of the world was dramatically changing, but the ride toward this new view was not smooth.

152

21

Janet and I sat on my living room couch gazing into the empty fireplace. Our non-functional fireplace, with its marble shell, stood out from the red brick wall as a remnant of a distant past. "I think I see what she's doing," Janet said. In slow motion, I turned to her.

"What is it?"

"Dee Dee will keep stopping you from getting Sally. Eventually, you'll get tired of making the four-hour train trips out and back, and then you'll stop going."

I snapped, "I won't stop going."

"She's betting that you will and if you do, she'll claim you violated the visitation order by not showing up."

"I can't go to Dee Dee's house anymore. She keeps getting me arrested."

Janet seemed restless. She grabbed a magazine from her bag and started flipping through it. "You have to tell the court."

I placed my hands to my forehead as if to brace my brain for the coming thought. "I have to change the court order. I have to get the pick up place moved. As much as I hate the idea, if she met me at the police station she couldn't make up stories."

Janet unconsciously squeezed her lips between her fingers. It's something she does when anxious. "I have to go home and get ready for tomorrow."

Traveling from West 58th to East 92nd was a solid thirty minutes by train. Moments later she was out the door and descending the stairs. I leaned over the banister. "I'll call you later."

I closed the door and turned the lock, but then examined the lock closer than ever. Until recently, that little bolt gave me a sense of security. It had kept all the burglars away. Now police concerned me, not burglars.

I went to the living room and turned on the stereo, then turned it off abruptly. Someone could hear the music from the hallway. That would be a dead giveaway that I was home. I sat and turned on the television and kept the volume barely loud enough to hear. What's going on? I'm paranoid, aren't I? But for good reason. Suspicion was crowding out my curiosity.

I glanced past the television to the photos on the mantle. Pictures of Sally looked back at me. My mind drifted to a recent time when me, Janet and Sally were all at Janet's apartment. We sat and watched a children's movie and snuggled.

Sally became entranced in movies. Her eyes got big and she leaned forward during an exciting scene. Her toddler's arm would extend toward the screen trying to touch the characters. It seemed silly, but it's those moments that make it so hard to quit.

Janet should be home by now. I picked up the phone and dialed. "Hello?"

"Hi, it's me." Click, click.

"Do you hear that?" I said.

"Yeah."

"It's really annoying and I've noticed it recently. The line constantly clicks."

"Anyway, I've been thinking about a business idea. I get this newsletter on health and nutrition and I really like it. They have great articles and it's really well done. Newsletter subscriptions could be a fabulous business."

"Okay. Sounds good." Janet liked all my bright ideas. "I was thinking of the name. We'd want a name that captures the essence of what it's all about. How do you like Vitality!"

"I like it," she said with encouragement. "But, we have so many things happening right now. Here's what I'll do," I said. "I'll map out some ideas and see what it would take to make this happen."

Janet changed the subject to family. "I spoke with my mom, and she asked how you were doing. I told her you were doing well, considering the circumstances."

"That's nice. I hope your parents are well." We talked a little more before we hung up. My mind flashed back to the first time I met Janet's parents Janet bragged about her father often. Her parents had flown in from California. They were transplants from Queens and Brooklyn and that meant her father was a tough guy and a tough businessman.

As the memory came back to me, I sat down on the couch and thought of that first meeting. The four of us met outside a New York restaurant on the Lower East Side. I arrived early, and waited on the sidewalk. Dressed in a suit and tie, I was ready for a nice dinner, but it was a little stressful. Janet had shown me photos of her family. When a cab pulled up and Janet got out, I immediately recognized her parents. Her mom's wide smile, and pretty features beamed toward me. I stood still as they approached.

Janet was all smiles and excited to introduce everyone. "John, this is my mom." I extended my hand with an enthusiastic grin. "Hi, very nice to meet you in person." Her mom was friendly, if a little reserved.

"Nice to meet you. You can call me Jane."

"This is my father." Mr. Kay, a man about my height wearing a dark, classic three-piece suit and tie. He looked at me without smiling. His face seemed confrontational.

I greeted him with, "Hi, very nice to meet you." Our hands gripped one another and he turned to Janet before separating.

"I see you didn't teach him how to tie a tie." The remark surprised me.

"I never did master that knot," I responded.

We went inside and upstairs to be seated at a large, comfortable table. We ordered and Janet and I dipped bread into the olive oil saucers as her parent's poured themselves glasses of white wine. Janet and her mother seemed unnaturally quiet.

Janet's father was seated to my right, and rarely made eye contact with me. The conversation, or lack of one, was very tense. After 20 minutes, the waiter arrived with the entrees. He placed a bowl of pasta in front of me and served the others. The large, shapely bowl made the food look expensive and appetizing.

The conversation started to trickle, but it was still strained. Somehow the spotlight turned to Janet. Her father spoke up as he gazed across the table at her. "Janet's going to graduate with a master's in public health." He glanced at his wife as a flash of pride came across his face. I guessed that the comment was directed at me.

"John graduated with a Master's from Columbia," Janet interjected.

Her father looked at me in between bites of his steak and with a commanding, fatherly tone said, "You have to go and get your Ph.D."

Twirling the pasta between my fork and spoon, I smiled, thinking this was casual conversation,, "I have no desire to get a Ph.D."

The women lowered their head's slightly. Janet's mom interjected, "Pass the salt, please."

Janet's dad stretched to grab the salt and handed it across the table. He looked directly at me as he stopped moving and delivered a sharp reply. "Why not?"

I put a fork full of food in my mouth to buy time. I sensed he didn't want to wait for me to chew before answering his question. I swallowed quickly and gave a thoughtful response. "A Ph.D. is all about research, and I don't want to do research."

The tension level in the air increased. The wine kept flowing while the conversation stalled. I could tell he was unsatisfied with my answer. The women remained oddly quiet. Somehow we made it through dinner. The meal eventually ended, and I now understood why Janet had traveled to the other side of the country for her graduate degree.

Later, when Janet and I spoke alone she played down the interaction as nothing to be concerned about. My reverie ended and I was back to the present moment in my apartment. It was time to sleep and awaken in the morning to make phone calls.

The next day I started calling lawyers to find an attorney who would take a case against the government. I waited on hold for a lawyer to pick up and as I waited, the clicking sound continued. All the law firms I called sounded like one version or another of Dewey, Cheetem & Howe.

"Yes hello. It was a warrantless arrest along with serious assault and battery. What? You're not interested?"

I couldn't understand the lack of interest from lawyers. Meanwhile, with every phone call the clicking continued. My immediate aim was to get to see my little girl. I was determined to be a decent father. The Family Court seemed to think paying child support was crucially important, but yet my visitation rights were a technicality.

After months of showing up to court only to have the case adjourned to another day, I got Dee Dee to a hearing. Part of my strategy was to make her drive into Manhattan on her day off and pay for a lawyer.

Dee Dee had a lawyer for all Manhattan court dates, but for the Suffolk County criminal she never needed a lawyer or even to show up. The People prosecuted me on her behalf. For family court she rarely needed a lawyer either.

Manhattan Family Court

I was waiting outside the courtroom for the case to be called. I was on time and Dee Dee was late. This was now the norm.

When she arrived she sat about eight feet away without looking at me. We never spoke anymore. As I anxiously waited to be called, Dee Dee turned in my direction. She hesitated for a moment while I sat surprised that she was even looking at me.

Then she started to speak. "I was thinking about something you said to me awhile ago about a project you wanted to do."

I looked at her, and wondered what exactly what she was talking about.

A devilish grin came across her face as she spoke with clarity and calmness. "You could start a newsletter. You could call it, Vitality." Her grin widened as she looked away for a moment and back again. My eyes stayed on her. What did she just say? I tried to remain calm as I forced a few words.

"Great idea." Stunned, I looked away in hopes of not giving away my astonishment.

Is she a mind reader? Who could have told her this? Was this coincidence? A chill ran down my spine. She couldn't have known what I said to Janet over the phone. Where did she get that name? This is too incredible. Could my phone be tapped? But that's illegal without a warrant. Even if the police tapped my phone, how did the information get to Dee Dee? Did she have an inside connection to the cops? Are they helping her destroy me? I can't believe that. How could that be?

How did she know about the newsletter and the name? This was getting crazier and crazier. A shout broke my trance. "O'Dell versus Farley."

I stood, but was still confused. Game on. Time to focus.

22

"All rise!"

Dee Dee, and her lawyer took their places in the courtroom as judge Ruth Zuckerman came out. In silence, the judge reviewed the paperwork on her desk. She raised her head and locked eyes with Dee Dee's lawyer, cueing him to speak.

"Your Honor, we move to dismiss this case."

My breath stopped as I raced to stand. "Objection." I wasn't sure what I was doing, but objecting made sense, and certainly couldn't hurt. The lawyer continued.

"Mr. Farley never showed up for the visitation, and his visitation rights should be re-evaluated, possibly revoked."

"That's ridiculous. Ms. O'Dell blocked me from seeing my daughter. The mother had me arrested when I called her on the phone to confirm visitation and when I came to her house to pick up my daughter."

"Your Honor, my client has an order of protection stopping Mr. Farley from contacting her by phone or showing up at her house or place of business because of a domestic violence incident."

"Wait a minute. This is ridiculous. How am I supposed to see my daughter?"

The judge looked suspiciously in my direction. Her expressionless eyes bounced from me back to the lawyer. "Where is this order of protection?"

I leaned forward across the long table in front of me. "That order is based on Ms. O'Dell's allegations. Nothing is proven."

The judge shot me a look with her squinted eyes. "I know that," she snapped. The judge seemed to be talking more for the court reporter as she lifted her chin in the air. "There has to be a reason this order was put in place."

"It's Dee Dee O'Dell's overblown story. The issue here is me seeing my daughter. I have nothing to say to Ms. O'Dell except to discuss visitation." The judge gently slapped her hand holding court documents onto the desk.

"Why do you have to call her at all? The time and place are on the order."

"Yes, but if I am going to be late, or if I can't make it or if I want to change the day and time or my daughter is sick or any other reason, I need to be able to speak to her. Doesn't this make sense?"

Her eyes softened, but included a crooked smile as she picked up the papers on the desk. The judge's face looked tense. She glanced at my opponents, took a breath and let out a frustrated sigh. A tense silence filled the courtroom. The judge stared down at the documents through her black-rimmed glasses. I pinched the fleshy part of one hand between the opposite thumb and finger to vent.

Slowly, the judge lifted her head, aimed at the lawyer. "I want both sides to discuss this, and negotiate. Come back with your plan." The judge stood up, and the bailiff ordered us out of the courtroom. Dee Dee lingered a little too long before standing. Her faced looked resolute and annoyed.

23

The judge made a decision when we returned to the courtroom. As usual, she made the announcement with an edge in her voice. "Mr. Farley has his visitation with the child and Ms. O'Dell needs to obey the order."

Just like that, this case was over. It was time to get back to day-to-day activities.

I still felt as though I was hiding something in my life. Being a once or twice a month dad, but never married is playing tricks on my self-image. It had been months since I'd last seen Sally. She recently turned four, a great age, and Sunday morning at 9 a.m. was my next visitation day.

When Sunday arrived, I left my apartment early, took the subway to Penn Station, and boarded the Long Island Railroad (LIR). I quickly found a seat on the train when a secure feeling came over me. I sat back, and watched as the people boarded the train. One hour to chill out. What will I do with Sally today?

My legs stretched as far as they could before pressing on the back of the seats in front of me. My right hand spread out across the vinyl seat. My eyelids shut for a moment only to pop open when the train bell rang and the doors closed.

It's a warm, beautiful July day. I'll bring her back on the train, and we'll get together with Janet. We'll play and go to Central Park.

Once the train went through the dark tunnel separating Manhattan from Queens, it burst into the sunlight on the other side. The thought of freedom mixed with the passing white clouds left me humbled and grateful.

John Farley, Jr.

The blue sky stretched as far as I could see. The feeling of going to see Sally instead of a judge was night and day.

The landscape had changed and I knew we were getting close. A voice over the loud speaker announced, "Huntington Station." The weekend train vibe was relaxed. No one rushed or crowded the doors when the locomotive stopped. I headed for the parking lot where a taxi waited. I opened the door to see a Caucasian man around age forty ready to start the meter.

The door shut with a secure, tight sound. "I need to go to a residence."

He looked up from his clipboard into his mirror. "What's the address?" I gave it to him, and ten minutes later we pulled into the circular driveway at Dee Dee's home. I had no intention of staying long.

"I'll be right back."

I walked with a spring in my step to the front door. Knock, knock. Moments later the door opened a few inches. I caught a glimpse of Dee Dee when she said, "Just a minute," and walked into another room.

After what seemed a minute or less I knocked again. "Dee Dee, I'm here to pick up Sally." Moments later the door opened wider. Dee Dee had the cordless phone to her ear.

"John, I'm on the phone."

"Dee Dee, I'm here for Sally, let's go, I have a cab waiting." I opened the door wider as Dee Dee walked the other way toward the kitchen. I saw Sally standing ten feet in front of me as Dee Dee passed her.

I walked in. "Hi Sally, come here little girl." I picked her up, walked out the door and carried her to the cab. I opened the door, placed her on the back seat, got in and sat beside her. I felt good, and was happy to get the show on the road.

I alerted the cabbie. "We're going to the train station." Dee Dee came out the door with the phone taking quick strides, while she talked fast. She took the phone away from her head, and spoke through the cabbie's front window.

162

"You need to stay here."

I craned my neck toward the Plexiglas partition. "Dee Dee, what are you doing?" She ignored me, and spoke only to the cab driver.

"The police are on the way. You need to stay here." She stepped back away from the car and placed the phone to her ear. What does she think she's doing?

Sally sat patiently as I leaned in toward the cab driver. "Don't listen to her. I have a court order to be here. I'm the passenger. We need to go to the train station right now."

He turned off the engine to the car. "She told me to stay."

"I'm telling you to start the car and go." With resignation he shook his head. "I can't go."

"I'm the customer, not her. I want you to take me to the train station right now."

The cabbie looked into his rearview mirror. "I can't leave if she's calling the police."

"Yes, you can leave. I'm telling you to leave. I have a court order to be here. I'm the father and I'm here at the right time on the right day. If you want to get paid, then drive me to the train station."

"If I leave, the police will arrest me to. I can't do it."

Moments later, a police car pulled into the driveway as Sally sat on my lap. "Sally, we're going soon," I said with an upbeat tone. "Just wait a little longer,"

Two officers looked into the cab and starting talking with Dee Dee just beyond earshot. A cop opened the back door of the cab. "John, this is captain Watts. We need to talk to you." I held Sally's waist between my hands as I turned to the officer.

"There's nothing to talk about. I'm the father and I have a court order to be here."

Watts kept the door partially open, and spoke briefly with the other officer. He stepped back to the car, opened the door wider, and climbed in on my left side. Watts spoke in a matter-of-fact tone. "John, there's an order of protection that you're violating. You're not allowed to be here."

The perfectly blue sky sparkled through the car window. I shook my head gently. "That's very wrong. This is exactly where I'm required to be on the third Sunday of every month at 9 a.m. Here is a copy of the court order, signed by Judge Ruth Zuckerman."

Watts looked at the order. "Dee Dee O'Dell's order of protection prohibits you from being here. You'll have to go to court, and take it up with the judge." Dee Dee came near the car and motioned to Sally. As Sally noticed her she started to wail.

"Sally, it's okay. Shhh," I said, while I gently bounced her on my knee.

"John, you're going to have to come with us."

"For what? I'm here legally," I said." In fact, this is the only place in the world I'm supposed to be right now, by court order. If I wasn't here, I'd be in violation of a court order." Sally's cries became louder, and unnerving.

"I understand what you're saying, but you have to come with us. If you don't you can be charged with resisting arrest." I heard Watts, but the cries had my attention.

"Sally, it's okay, breathe honey, breathe."

I gave Watts a hard look. "Resisting arrest. That's absurd. I should be resisting arrest because this is wrong."

Watts ignored me for a moment. "That's right breathe, Sally. John, you wouldn't hurt her, would you?"

The question struck me as odd, even insulting. I looked Watts straight in the eye with scorn. "I would *never* hurt my daughter."

"Good. That's good to know. Now, we need to leave, and you can save yourself that resisting arrest charge. Just give her to me, and I'll hand her to her mother."

My teeth clenched tighter. "This is complete crap, and you know it. I'll give her to you and then you let me leave."

"We can't do that, but we won't charge you with resisting."

"This is outrageous. How dare you get in the way of my time with my daughter? You guys disgust me."

"John, we have to go now or you'll be charged with resisting."

"So what? If I give her to you, then you let me leave."

"I can't do that?"

"What if you did?"

"This is your last chance."

I resigned myself to the inevitable. "Sally, I'm giving you to this man and you'll go to your mother, just breathe." I passed Sally to Watts, who passed her to Dee Dee, then turned back to me.

"Good, you saved yourself from that second charge."

"Who cares?" Dee Dee, with tears in her eyes, had snatched Sally from Watts as if she'd rescued her from a burning building. I stepped out from the car and a young, lone ranger cop told me to turn around as he put the handcuffs on me. This was not supposed to happen.

I sat in a cell at the Huntington police station all day and all night. In the morning I got another look at the Central Islip holding facility. The jail was cold, the metal bed painful, and the lights glowed until morning—the usual.

Some of the same deputies brought me before another judge. Soon, I'd be out of this cage.

24

At the hotel with Amanda

The ambiance in this part of the hotel was so peaceful and serene. Colorful flowers were on tables throughout, and a gentle vibration permeated the space as the wait staff periodically stopped by to check on us. Talking about this drama was a bit out of place.

"Wow, you were going through a lot of stuff just to see Sally."

"Yeah, you can say that."

"Why was Dee Dee doing this? Revenge?"

"That had to be it. She warned me that I was finished, remember?"

"Was a Northport court date coming up?"

At My Apartment:

A loud perky voice came through the receiver. "Hello!"

"Hi Janet, I'm leaving soon for Northport court. I don't expect to get home 'til close to midnight."

Janet responded as if I was going on vacation. "You have everything you need?"

"Yeah," I said, looking at my worn brown bag. I kept it exclusively for trekking documents to and from court.

"Be safe. Call me if there's a problem."

We hung up as I checked my watch. I took one last look in the mirror at my sport jacket, and dress shirt.

Minutes after 4 p.m. I'll leave now and arrive in plenty of time. After a subway ride and two Long Island railroad trains later, I entered the Northport Village courthouse. It's a wing on the tiny police station. It was still daylight when I opened the double glass doors and stepped into the open area.

I'm early, but where is everyone? Directly in front of me were big, wide, wooden, double doors leading to the courtroom. An uneasy silence gave me the willies. An emptiness permeated the space. It reminded me of going to an old church during off-hours, except to me, this was anything but church.

While I paced around the area, the courtroom door opened. It was a police officer. A fit man in his late forties.

I walked up casually to avoid startling him. "Excuse me, where do I find the assistant DA?"

The officer turned to lock the doors. "He won't see ya. He'll talk to your lawyer."

Here we go again. "I don't have a lawyer."

He turned to me and scanned my face for a moment. I felt awkward, a little intimidated, as an uncomfortable silence lingered. "Didn't the judge tell you to get a lawyer last time you were here?" The gun strapped to his waist appeared as if out of nowhere.

I softened my tone. "What if I don't want a lawyer?"

The officer put his thumbs in the front of his waistband as his posture straightened. "You got some serious charges here. You're gonna need a lawyer. The assistant DA won't talk to ya without a lawyer."

Breaking eye contact, I angled my body to a less confrontational stance. "Maybe he'll make an exception," I said as I took a smooth step backwards.

The glass doors leading outside opened, and a stocky man wearing a suit and tie came thundering in. He gripped a large briefcase dangling from his hand. With precision, he marched toward the assistant DA's office. The doorknob wouldn't turn. He put his briefcase down, and stood against the wall like a soldier at ease.

More men, all lawyers, came through the glass door. They waited in line behind the first guy. After a few, slow, minutes the assistant DA's door opened. The first man, reached down grabbed his bag, and rushed in. Within minutes he came out, looking pleased, and taking his place against another wall.

When the line to the assistant DA's office emptied, I grabbed my brown bag and headed straight into his office.

He looked to be fifty-something in formal suit, and tie as he sat in the small space. I reflexively swallowed. My stomach had butterflies. The personification of law and order sat reviewing documents. His hair cut was precise—something out of the CIA of the 1940s. Short brown hair, with a touch of gray at the ends. He wore a classic, light colored suit with a very conservative tie. He turned to look at me and immediately suspected I wasn't a lawyer.

He swiveled nervously in his chair. "Are you representing a defendant?"

"No." I started to sit down. "I am the defendant."

He leaned away. "I can't speak with you," as he stood up from his chair. "You'll have to have your attorney contact me." He reached for the doorknob to open it wider.

"There's no attorney and I'm not getting one."

His cadence picked up as he motioned out the door. "I can't speak with the defendant. You'll have to discuss this with the judge."

"I have a letter here from the police—"

His pitch, and cadence increased as he cut me off, "I can't look at evidence or anything. You'll have to speak to the judge when court starts."

I walked out of the office slightly grinding my teeth. Tempted to lean against the wall, I forced myself to stand straight, as not to get lazy in my thinking. By now, a large crowd crammed into this outside area.

Seven o'clock rolled around. The atmosphere felt like waiting to get on an overcrowded bus to grade school. The sacred church atmosphere was replaced by anxiety. The kind you feel right before you're about to do something inherently dangerous.

As the big doors opened, the crowd squeezed in. I entered with a chip on my shoulder and found a seat in the long, pew-like rows. The accused masses of people walked in. Each person's posture gave away their embarrassment or guilt. Casual was the style of dress for everyone, except for the lawyers and me.

The cop, now the bailiff, moved away from the door and toward the bench. "Let's not have any talking. If you need to talk, step outside the courtroom." The crowd instantly hushed itself to near silence.

The butterfly feeling surfaced again. Remember what you're going to say.

Then, it happened. The cop yelled out, as the secret door behind the judge's bench flew open. "All rise!" The sound of silence broke as one hundred people stood up in unison. A black robed figure took center stage. A spindly man in his early forties peered above his oversized glasses. He spoke to us the way priests address their congregation. "You may be seated."

There he is. The magistrate who accused me of lying, and asked where my father was. Will he recognize me now that I'm not in chains like a mangy dog on a leash?

"Robert Smith." the bailiff, yelled out. A lawyer stood and walked forward. He extended his arm motioning to his client to step forward the way a teacher motions to a fourth grader.

The accused stood, looking afraid and guilty. He made his way to the front as one hundred people stared. For a moment, the place was silent as if stage curtains were raised for a Broadway show. Mr. Smith dressed nicer than most. I could feel his nervousness from across the room.

The lawyer had on a nearly white suit, with one of those bolo ties you'd expect to see in the deep south. He topped off the look with a wide, brim hat.

The flamboyant attorney addressed the court. "Judge, after conferring with the assistant district attorney, my client would be happy to pay the $700 fine, and a 6 month probationary period, if it pleases the court."

The assistant DA stood, nodding as needed. Moments later, after a brief chastisement from the judge, it was over.

The defendant breathed a sign of relief. Both sides looked pleased. This scene played out with person after person. Each defendant was happy to have their guilt and shame washed away. They got their lives back for the small price of coin mixed with a dose of public humiliation.

A deal. They're making a deal. That's what this is. Lawyers are dealmakers, and judges are referees between the two lawyers who make deals.

"The court will take a short recess," yelled the bailiff.

Squeezing past the people, I made my way to the bailiff. "Excuse me, I traveled here from Manhattan. It takes me two hours to get here, and two hours back. The last train out of here is 9 p.m., which means I have to leave here by about 8:30. I'd like to be placed near the front so that I can get back home before midnight."

As I spoke, the cop scanned the courtroom watching the people exit the door. My words bounced off him like BB's off his bulletproof vest.

"We'll have to see how the docket looks tonight." His waistband and gun came into focus. How hard is it to put me near the beginning?

Court reconvened. I waited as person after person was called ahead of me. All locals.

About half-way though the docket…

"The People of Northport Village against John J. Farley."

The assistant DA blurted out, "Your honor, the defendant is accused of calling the offices of Dee Dee O'Dell 100 times and another dozen times on the following dates..."

I stood in front of the judge. Images of being brutalized flooded my mind. I was nearly snorting with anger. The waiting masses watched quietly.

The judge eyed me like bird droppings on a car window. "Where's your lawyer?" he demanded.

Fear gripped me and weakened my voice. "I don't have a lawyer," I said, voice cracking.

He spoke to me like I was a juvenile delinquent. "You have to have a lawyer. We're going to adjourn the case for you to get a lawyer."

I summoned courage and spoke-up. "It's not the law that I have to have a lawyer, is it?"

The judge squirmed in his seat and shot back, "I am requiring that you have a lawyer. We're going to adjourn this case, and I want you to come back with a lawyer."

My heart pounded like I was in serious danger. "Wait a minute. I don't have to have a lawyer." The cop and his gun were in the corner of my eye.

"When is your next court date in Central Islip?" he interrupted.

"In three weeks."

The judge turned to the woman assistant scheduling the calendar. "Put the next hearing down two months from now."

Still feeling the fear, I spoke up again. "I have to see if that date is good for me."

The woman ignored me and told the judge a date. He moved the file off his desk and looked past me. "That's enough time to get a lawyer. Next case."

The bailiff moved closer to me. "Step outside the courtroom," he demanded as he then opened the solid door for me to exit.

I walked out into the open area. All that, and what did I get? Another court date.

Within forty minutes, I was on the train back to the city. I remembered what Dee Dee said to me one time. It was after a court session in the elevator. She turned to me and said, "You know what our problem is? You care what people think of you."

Incredible. Of course I care what people think. Look at all those people tonight. They walked into court embarrassed at what they had done or were accused of doing. I care what they think, but I'm not embarrassed to stop Dee Dee from stealing my daughter from me. I won't be embarrassed to stand up for my rights.

On the way back, I did my best to let it all go. As the train entered into the tunnel between Queens and Manhattan, the pressure change plugged my ears. A quick swallow, and the pressure equalized. Moments later the train lights went dark as they always do. For a few minutes my mind enjoyed the cocoon-like feeling of freedom—of not having to be responsible for anything. Just a moment of suspended animation.

As the train pulled into the station that responsible feeling returned.

Now, I have to get a damn lawyer—on Long Island. The train doors opened. I stepped out and drew a breath. God, it's late.

I gotta do, what I gotta do. This game is on.

25

I traveled back out to Long Island for a meeting with a big time lawyer, a former prosecutor. The cab stopped at Mr. Robert's offices, a lone building off the beaten path. I dressed well, but not too well. I didn't want to give the wrong impression.

A final deep breath filled my lungs and settled my nerves before I opened the front door. Inside, the attractive receptionist was busy fielding phone calls behind a glass partition. She greeted me with a glance and a lifted chin as she told one caller after the next to "hold please."

"John Farley. I have an appointment wi— "

She raised her hand with one finger, cutting me off.

A caller won her attention, and after robotically transferring calls, she spoke to me professionally, the way a hotel concierge greets travelers. "Mr. Robert will be with you in a moment."

With a nod, I turned and sat on the functional, but comfortable couch-like chairs. Magazines were spread out on a glass table asking to be picked up, but I decided to collect my thoughts instead.

Minutes later, a side door opened. A middle-aged man walked out wearing a sharp suit, shiny shoes and glasses. He approached, and when our eyes meet, he stretched out his hand. "John. Gilbert Robert.

I took a moment to stand and give him a firm handshake accompanied by a mostly blank expression. "Nice to meet you."

He gave off a secure, easy-going style. "Right this way." We walked to his office. "Come in and have a seat." Mr. Robert glided past me and headed to his ergonomically designed chair behind his impressive mahogany desk. I was directed to the padded, wooden chair directly facing him, and several feet back. "You have documents for me to look at—let me see those—"

I pulled papers from my bag and stretched to put them on this desk. "Let's start at the beginning. Tell me the story. What happened?"

For some reason, I looked down while I leaned forward in the chair, my elbows resting on the arms. I interlocked my hands and fingers as I stayed leaning forward, as my thoughts came together. "I called the mother to set up a time to see my daughter."

Mr. Robert swiveled his chair at a slight angle to me. "Didn't you already have a time, and day for the family court order?"

"Yes, but she had been blocking me until this point. Sometimes she'd call and leave a message that Sally was unavailable for the weekend. Other times, I might travel for over an hour, take a cab, show up at her door and she'd call the cops to arrest me."

His chair swiveled, again, and he interjected. "For what? Oh, because of the order of protection."

"Yes."

"What did she claim?"

"She claims I hit her."

"Did you?"

"I'm pleading not guilty to that ridiculous charge."

His focused attention suggested that he could read my face, tone and body like a law book. He picked up the documents off his desk and flipped through them. "The Northport claim is that you called her over 100 times disrupting her business. Did you do that?"

"Sure I did."

Shifting in his chair now. "You're not allowed to call her according to the order of protection, and you called her over 100 times. This is not looking good."

"She's kidnapping my child. I'll call her 1,000 times to get my daughter. How can calling a kidnapper who stole my child and violated a family court order of visitation be a crime?"

Robert angled his chair to the other side. His gaze suggested I was an idealistic sap who needed some bad tasting medicine to straighten me out. He delivered the bad news. "You're facing jail time here. This is very serious."

His words knocked me off my soapbox. He spoke louder and faced me head on as he leaned in. "I know people in Northport. What information do you have from the prosecution?"

"The assistant district attorney won't talk to me about the case. He only wants to speak to a lawyer. The judge in Northport is stalling, waiting for Central Islip to decide the case."

He looked me in the eye like a doctor prescribing treatment. "You need a lawyer. Our firm is well respected. I can't make any promises, but we've handled large cases and been successful." He thumbed through the pages of court charges against me. "You're looking at several years in jail."

I felt my eyes get big as he delivered the diagnosis with a grim look. "Each of these offenses carries a one year sentence."

Like the sudden twinge of a pinched nerve, I reacted. "But that's ridiculous. This is about seeing my child. Everything should be dismissed."

Robert leaned back. "We can handle both Central Islip and Northport for you. Our fee for both is $25,000, and we'll take care of everything. This will end it for you and you can get on with your life. Obviously, I can't promise what the outcome will be, but we're very well connected and you'll get the best possible results."

Did I just hear what I thought I heard? If I could pay $25,000 I'd use that money to pay child support for years to come. I broke eye contact. "I can't afford $25,000," I said, feeling inadequate.

Mr. Robert looked disappointed. "What are you going to do?" "I—I'm not sure yet. I'll have to think it through some more."

John Farley, Jr.

With that, the interview ended rather quickly. I left Mr. Roberts' offices for another long, costly trip home. It was another waste of time and energy. One day I'll see justice. I just have to wait a little longer.

26

A cab let out a passenger at the Central Islip courthouse. I rushed and opened the back door. The cabbie leaned over the backseat. "I can't take you. I have another fare already. Call the cab company—they'll send another car for you."

I memorized the number on the side of the green colored cab and trotted back inside the courthouse to find a pay phone. After I hung up from the cab company, I went back outside. Twenty minutes to wait for a cab. What a waste of time. What a waste of life. Half a day wasted. For what?

The sky was typical New York, overcast gray. The air was crisp with occasional bites of bitterness.

Twenty-five minutes later, a cab arrived, and I got in. "To the train please—going to the city."

The cabbie turned on the meter and glanced at me. "Are you a lawyer?"

"No," I said with a forced grin. "Just showing up for a court date." Before all this mess happened in my life I'd mingle and chat, but now I had nothing positive to say. I felt a little uncomfortable not talking, but not uncomfortable enough to chat. As the cab pulled into the train station I reached into my pocket for the four dollar fare, and a few quarters for a tip. "Here you go."

I grabbed my bag, opened the door, "Thanks," and heard the train whistle off in the distance. I'd just missed it. Forty minutes to catch the next one.

I walked into the station waiting room. Plastic chairs, dirty floor and a junk food vending machine in the corner. One dozen people sat waiting for a train. A few white folks who looked lower middle class. Most others looked Hispanic and blue collar.

Everyone looked bored, tired and uninspired. I sat as long as I could, but soon ended up feeling the way everyone else looked.

The dull atmosphere compelled me to head out onto the train platform. Outside, I stepped closer to the edge to find out how far down the tracks I could see. Off in the distance I saw a faint light. That's it. That's the train. It took another five minutes before the train roared into the station traveling at perhaps 70 mph. The cool air it pushed hit me like ten industrial strength fans.

Minutes later, I was in a train seat by myself, daydreaming. As the train plowed down the tracks from town to town, thoughts of Sally sprang into my mind. It was a pleasant day when she and I strolled out of my apartment. The four-year-old walked with me from my place on West 58th to Janet's apartment on East 92nd.

We traveled along the sidewalks of Manhattan toward Central Park. Her hand held my fingers as we plodded along. Her small steps doubled our commute. Her little arm stretched behind me as I gently pulled her forward. My opposite shoulder carried her light backpack with clothes, and a bottle of water in it. Then I heard that little voice.

"Daddy, wait. Daddy, let's take a cab."

A cab would be one more double-digit fare I didn't want to splurge on. Besides, when I was young I biked or hoofed it a lot. "No, not this time. We're going to walk and see the park." I turned to her and with an exaggerated voice tone, wide eyes and big grin I asked, "Do you know what's in the park?"

She greeted me with a blank look. "What?"

"Big trees! A big pond with rowboats and ducks. A path with bikers and skaters and runners. We're going to see all of them!"

This was my sales pitch. I'd make the best of the late night television pitchman blush. Why not have her forget those tired legs as she walked?

Big Central Park trees were all around us. "Do you know what this tree's called?"

She shook her head. "A sycamore tree. You can remember it 'cause the bark looks sick." The big tree held her attention for a few seconds before she remembered her goal.

"Daddy, pick me up."

I gently pulled her along. "No, not now, later." I knew that once she became airborne it'd be over. "Look over there!" I pointed in the air to a far off "wonder."

We lumbered along inside the park and stopped at a bench. With my hands under her armpits, I lifted her and placed her on it. "Here you go!" For a few moments we enjoyed the birds, the sun, the trees and the people. For a few moments, she forced me into the present moment. I needed that. Without intending to, she caused me to stay present to what's important—to what's real.

"Let me tie your shoe," I said. Once a better knot was secured I pulled water out of the bag. "Here have a sip." She grabbed hold as she brought it to her mouth. I sat, and watched—absorbed by her. Not a care in her little world. She's completely dependent on me right now. It's her unwavering trust and dependence on me that makes me feel like a grown-up—a dad.

That's long enough. With my hands underneath her armpits I lifted her again. "Time to go."

Seconds after her feet touched the ground I heard, "Pick me up!" She put her arms high above her head.

"No, not now. Hold my hand." I grab hold of her little palm with my two fingers and thumb. Moments later, she ran in front of me and stopped—with her arms high in the air.

"Pick me up!"

"No, not now. Look at the trees!"

Undaunted, she ran in front again. "Pick me up!"

Who can resist a child for long? I lifted her, and noticed the contentment on her face. She got what she wanted and I was happy to give it to her. Sally thoroughly enjoyed being high in the air and hanging on for the ride. But it didn't take long before my muscles ached. "Sally, my arms are tired, I have to set you down."

Seconds after her feet touched ground... "Pick me up!"

"Not now." My dream was soon interrupted by a loudspeaker announcement as we arrived in Manhattan. I had a very important meeting the next day. Plus, Janet had to move out of her apartment unexpectedly.

27

It was a quick four-block walk from the apartment to the lawyer's office. I pulled a piece of paper out of my pocket. The address on the paper matched the brownstone apartment building in front of me. The intercom was at the top of a small set of concrete stairs. I checked my watch as I went up. Right on time. Number three it says. I pressed the buzzer and waited.

"HELLO!"

"It's John Farley. We have an appointment—"

"COME ON IN—I'M ON THE THIRD FLOOR."

The door buzzed open and I started up the creaking wooden staircase. I rounded the corner on the third floor and approached the door. As I started to knock, it opened. "JOHN?"

"Yes, hi. I'm John Farley." We shook hands.

"STEVE EDWARDS. COME ON IN, AND HAVE A SEAT."

New York's a loud place, but for some reason Steve spoke as if we were in gale force winds.

Stacks of legal folders one foot high were piled across multiple desks and around the floor space. Heavy looking chairs, couches and desks filled the room. It looked and felt cluttered.

Steve, a well-dressed Caucasian man in his late thirties, sat in his desk chair. "HAVE A SEAT. TELL ME WHAT HAPPENED."

I found a spot on the leather couch that wasn't covered with folders and sat. "As I mentioned when we spoke on the phone, I was beaten by the deputy sheriffs in Suffolk County and the guards at the Riverhead jail. They repeatedly punched me, struck me with a ink roller, strip searched me, slammed me into metal bars—I brought the photos."

Steve sat leaning to one side of his chair, hand on his chin. "Let me see," as his voice volume approached normal. Steve flipped through the photos. "YOU'RE SAYING THIS WAS FROM THOSE BEATINGS?"

Lawyers always seem to double check what appears to be true, don't they?

"Yes, that's what I'm saying. They beat me and they had no right to do it."

Edwards, leaned back in his big, soft, leather chair, "SO, WHY DID THEY DO THAT TO YOU?"

"I wouldn't give them my fingerprints."

"WHY DID THEY WANT YOUR FINGERPRINTS?"

"I don't know why, but they're mine, why should I have to give them my property? They take my other property in the jail, but they give it back when I'm released. They don't give back my fingerprints. Why should they have a right to keep them? It's a fourth amendment violation, but regardless, they beat me up."

Edwards swiveled his chair around as he listened more intently. Perhaps he thought, What a fascinating legal position. "YOU'RE SAYING THAT THEY HAVE NO RIGHT TO HAVE YOUR FINGERPRINTS. WHAT MAKES YOU SAY THAT?"

I took a deep breath and exhaled, as I was still getting used to Steve's loud voice, "I don't know exactly. I've heard it, but even if I'm wrong, they certainly don't have the right to handcuff and shackle me, hit me in the head, and punch me in the stomach and threaten to kill me!" At that moment I was having a mini-flashback.

Edwards observed me and took it all in. "TAKE ME BACK TO THE BEGINNING. HOW DID THIS START? WHAT DID THEY WANT WITH YOU ANYWAY?"

I hate re-telling this story, but here goes. "I have a child with a woman, Dee Dee O'Dell. She has an order of protection against me."

"YOU MEAN A JUDGE PROVIDED AN ORDER OF PROTECTION TO KEEP YOU AWAY FROM HER."

"Right. Not to go to her home or business or call her. Anyway, I also have a visitation order."

Steve listened as he thumbed through the court papers I'd brought over. "HOW OLD IS THE CHILD?"

"She's four."

"AND YOU'RE THE FATHER. HOW DO YOU KNOW THAT?"

He really is going to thoroughly check all assumptions, isn't he? "I had a test done."

"JOHN, DID YOU BREAK THE ORDER OF PROTECTION BY CONTACTING HER?"

"Well, that's the issue. I have a visitation order to see my daughter and to see her I have to go to the mother's home. Besides, what if I have to call her for some reason?"

"WHY WOULD YOU HAVE TO CALL HER?"

"If my daughter, Sally—her name is Sally—if she were ill, or…"

Interrupting, "JOHN, LET'S GO BACK. HOW DID YOUR EX-WIFE GET THIS ORDER OF PROTECTION—WHAT WAS HER CLAIM?"

"First…she, and I were never married. She claims I hit her.

"SHE CLAIMS YOU HIT HER. WHY WOULD SHE CLAIM THAT?"

I opened my mouth before the thought was fully formed. "Dee Dee O'Dell is—she's angry that I have a new girlfriend and this is about her getting me back. Possibly even taking my daughter away from me."

"YOU'RE SAYING THAT HER CLAIM THAT YOU HIT HER IS NOT TRUE?"

Clearly uncomfortable with where the conversation was going I spoke more slowly, "I'm saying she's exaggerating. I've pled not guilty to this. What I think is more relevant is what the deputies did to me."

John Farley, Jr.

Steve leaned forward with the photos in hand. "WHEN DID THE COP BEATING HAPPEN?"

"The date's on the paperwork."

"CAN YOU DESCRIBE THE PEOPLE, THE FACILITIES? WHAT DO YOU REMEMBER?"

I described to him the cells, the deputies, and the facilities. Edwards listened, and took notes on his yellow legal paid. "YOU REMEMBER A LOT OF DETAILS ABOUT THIS PLACE. I FIND THAT AMAZING."

He has to be testing me to see if I'm making this up. "I've been there multiple times now. Each time I went back, I made sure to remember as many details as possible."

"USUALLY PEOPLE DON'T REMEMBER SO MANY DETAILS."

"That would make sense if I had only been there once, but I was there multiple times."

We continued going over the details for about two hours—a small fortune in legal time. Steve Edwards agreed to take the case on contingency. He'd only get paid if we won. It was a risk few lawyers take.

"Let's sue them for $20 million dollars," I said. Edwards paused as his volume dropped. "That's a lot." "For what they did, they should pay it. It'll teach them a lesson so they don't do this to anyone else or they'll keep doing it to others and maybe kill someone."

Steve looked at me, perhaps rolled the number around in his head. He'd soon start the paperwork, and get the process moving. This wouldn't happen overnight. We shook hands and I left. I had to get back. Janet was nearly ready to move in.

It was done. Janet was now living in my Westside apartment. It wasn't my idea, but I agreed to it. Meanwhile, I'd filed with the Manhattan court to bring Dee Dee in for both contempt of the visitation order and to change the pick up location.

It was a nice day out. Janet and I were home. She cleaned and did housework. I was writing up some business ideas. Ring. I walked over to the desk, and picked up the phone, "Hello?" There was no one there. I hung up and went back to what I was doing.

"Who was that?" Janet asked. "No one was there. What are we going to do with Sally's toys and clothes and things?" Janet pointed to the desk against the wall. "I made a place for them under this desk. That way it'll be easy for her to get to and it'll be her space."

We sat next to each other on the couch. "How do you like the couch cover?" She'd sewn a cover for the couch that made the old thing look pretty good. I examined it more closely.

"Very nice, I like it. How did you make the puffy arms on each end?"

She glowed with pride. "I put some fabric and towels in there." I passed my hand over the fabric and then pressed down hard to feel the hard wood underneath.

"Those arms are hard. It's a good thing you put that fabric over them."

"Let's go to the other room," I said. We walked through the railroad apartment to the other side, and were standing in the kitchen when—

Bang, Bang, Bang, Bang, Bang!

My heart instantly started pounding. Janet and I were face to face only seeing each other, but listening to everything. I held my palms up to tell her to stay still. Her face looked calm, but perhaps it was more disbelief.

"Police! Open up!" Bang, Bang, Bang, Bang, Bang! We stood in the middle of the kitchen as if our feet were stuck in cement. Moments later, I heard noise on the roof of the five floor walk up. Did I really just hear that?

We stood motionless. I was hoping they'd go away. Afraid to move, or breathe, we stayed frozen. Then, all the sounds disappeared. My heart was beating so fast I could feel it in my throat. Minutes went by, but we didn't move an inch, afraid the floor would creak and give us away. I wondered if the police had given up and left.

The entire apartment was strangely quiet. As quickly as the pounding had started, it ended. Were they that dumb? I doubted it. A faint sound came from the other end of the railroad apartment that faced the street five floors below. A slight waft of air moved past my face. Outside sounds suddenly seemed more crisp.

I inched my gaze from the edge of the hallway back toward Janet. Her scared blue eyes were all I saw. A shiver ran through me making my arm hairs stand on end. I knew what was happening. I mouthed to her. "They're i-n-s-i-d-e."

It took what seemed like forever, but then I heard it. The floorboards creaked. Footsteps were inching down the hallway. We couldn't see around the corner. A false move now might cost us our lives. Visually, I locked onto the hallway corner only seven feet away.

A shadow came into view. I waited, partially shielding Janet. A figure appeared. It was Good Cop. As I recognized him, I said, "What are you doing in here?"

Another deputy behind him rushed toward us. "Hands up!" he yelled, as he pointed a can of pepper stray inches from our faces. "Put your hands up!" I raised my arms partially shielding Janet. "Easy, easy, easy!"

"Put your hands up!" The cop kept yelling.

"Leave her alone. You want me, right? Leave her alone."

"Hands behind your back!" yelled the cop with the spray can. Good Cop unlocked the front door letting in another three officers. He had a smirk on his face.

"John, I bet you didn't expect us to come up the fire escape, did you?"

I snapped back. "I was wondering what took you so long."

The other guy pushed me toward the door. "Come on, you're coming with us."

"For what? Do you have a warrant this time?" I asked. As they walked out the door with me and toward the staircase, Janet was angry now.

"You guys are in trouble. We're going to sue you!"

Good Cop chuckled. "You've been watching too many cop shows on television."

It was another humiliation for me. I wondered, what my neighbors thought was going on here. "Janet, call Edwards, and let him know," I yelled, as they brought me down in cuffs. The deputies claimed there'd been a previous violation of the order of protection. These guys somehow decided to count one of the calls to Dee Dee as a separate violation.

Apparently, they enjoyed coming into the city to taunt me. They put me in the cop car and started the 90-minute drive to Long Island. Once again, Smith was in the front seat with Bad Cop. "Don't you guys have any real criminals to raid the homes of?" This time, that was the only comment I made.

It'd be a long drive and a longer night. I didn't feel safe at home. After years of living in New York City, I realized the only people who'd broken in were cops and deputies. There was something very wrong about all this.

We arrived in Central Islip. I gave up my fingerprints without complaint. As I was moved around throughout the facility, I looked closely at everything. I noticed the cells, the walls, the floor, and the layout. Steve Edwards would want to know these details.

Locked away in a depressing, cold cell, I remembered a time with Sally. Anything to take my mind off of the emptiness of the steel and concrete. I laid on the bench, closed my eyes and had a daydream. It was early morning at my apartment. Sally was in

John Farley, Jr.

the living room sitting, watching television. I stood barefoot on the wooden floor, gently practicing martial arts moves.

"Daddy, I'm hungry," the toddler said.

I stopped my routine and noticed her slightly slumped posture on the couch. "What would you like to eat?" She shrugged her little shoulders.

"What do you have?" I chuckled.

"That's what I used to say when I was little like you. Let's go look."

We went to the kitchen and opened the refrigerator. "How about cantaloupe?" Sally nodded and watched as I took a sharp knife, and sliced open the melon. She became excited when I placed the chunks of fruit in bowls for us and then set the table.

We sat there without talking, only looking into each other's eyes and chewing. She poked her fork into a orange chunk of fruit and smiled.

"Sally and Daddy are eating melon together," she said. The scene faded from my mind. The hard bench on my backside woke me. What's next? I wondered as I rubbed my fingers against my forehead. The next day I was released again on my own recognizance and made my way back to the city. These one day kidnappings were not helping my business or personal life.

28

I was already back from my early morning clients. Janet was dressed up and ready to go to her job at the fitness center.

"Say hi to Mr. Rockefeller, if you see him," I said.

Janet smiled. She knew I was being serious and facetious at the same time. Both of us were friendly with David Rockefeller, grandson of John D. Rockefeller, Sr., the first American billionaire. Janet often interacted with the oil tycoon at the fitness center. Now in his seventies, Rockefeller appeared harmless. His family had many secrets he kept closely guarded, but Janet and I were learning how powerful his family really was.

We discovered Rockefeller founded The Trilateral Commission, a secret society designed to promote world government. Top positions in the White House often went exclusively to members of The Trilateral Commission. He chaired The Council on Foreign Relations, another breeding ground for power brokers. Rockefeller, and a dozen men like him, had been accused of being the shadow government of the United States and controlling events from outside the political arena.

Cardio Fitness Center in mid-town Manhattan is where I met the man. As an exercise physiologist, my job was to talk to the members on the exercise floor.

"Janet, do you remember how I met David Rockefeller?"

"Yeah, you told me—it was on the treadmill or...?"

"No. One time, while he was on the stationary bike, I approached him to make small talk. I said, 'Hello, Mr. Rockefeller!' He glanced over his shoulder to find me standing there. He smiled meekly and gave a weak sounding 'Hello' in his distinctive, upper crust voice. Perhaps a bit British, or simply an aristocratic flare, his voice tone was one I'd never heard before."

Janet jumped in. "You asked him about Trump."

"'Yeah,' I said, 'I'm reading a book by Mr. Trump, *The Art of the Deal*. What do you think of Mr. Trump?' He squirmed on the stationary bike as if the seat was getting hot. He raised his chin a little and lifted his shoulders after clearing his throat. 'He's a little too flamboyant for my tastes.' Perhaps he surprised himself for voicing a critical remark. Then his posture slumped ever so slightly."

Janet giggled.

"Another day I saw him alone working his thighs on a leg machine. I sat next to him ready to start a conversation. I waited until he completed his repetitions. 'Anything exciting happening?' I inquired. He looked down and away. He didn't seem comfortable having a one on one conversation with me. Perhaps it was my innocent way of asking, but he let out that he'd recently returned from Russia."

Janet shifted her weight to one leg. She liked the story, but was pressed for time.

"I asked him, 'What's going on in Russia?' Little did I know that the Rockefeller secrets would make the mob jealous."

Janet nodded as she started grabbing folders off the kitchen table.

"He spoke without saying much. It's an art to be able to say little and not appear to be avoiding the question."

Janet checked her watch. "Funny," she smiled. "I have to go." She started to walk around the apartment gathering her work bag and filling it.

At the time, I thought Rockefeller was a silver-spoon senior citizen, born into a fortune who didn't really do much anymore. I had no idea I was conversing with the leader of one of the most ruthless business families the world had ever known. Heir to what's been called "Great Fortune" Rockefeller moves invisibly like a giant octopus deep under the ocean. More colorful characters, like Trump, resemble barking seals—clearly visible and not very dangerous. Only later would I come to realize that David Rockefeller was busy manipulating world events during his global travels.

"Do you remember I told you that I was contacted by another fitness trainer to be his one and only trainer to work with his super rich clients?"

"Yeah," Janet said. "Tomorrow I'll go to work with Peggy Rockefeller at their mansion."

She paused and took it in. "No kidding? That will be interesting." After a hug and kiss, she left for work. The day flew by and when nighttime came, I was eager for a sound sleep.

Before I knew it my body clock told me to get up. Morning had arrived.

Instead of my usually nice pants and a polo shirt, Richard, the trainer I was subbing for, demanded that I be dressed differently. Dress pants, dress shirt, tie and sports jacket was the required attire for personal training the super rich. I doubled checked my tie in the bathroom.

Janet peeked in. "I can't believe you have to dress like that."

"I know, but Richard has a dress code. Time to go." I finished up in the bathroom, and headed out the door and down the street.

Before I knew it, off to my left stood the famous Plaza Hotel, a majestic structure fit for royalty. As I crossed over Fifth Avenue to the East Side, I felt as if the world had become brighter and more opulent. Perhaps it's the pristine, sky high buildings or the frequent limousine sightings—or maybe it's the people on the sidewalks who dressed to impress.

I neared Rockefeller's neighborhood. The noise level of the city became quieter and the trees seemed bigger and more green than on the west side.

"There it is."

29

The Rockefeller's three story, brick building was right there on the street as plain as day. I took a moment to psych myself up as I approached the front door of the multi-billionaire's home.

"Here I go." Up two steps, and I pressed the door buzzer. The moments after releasing the buzzer reminded me of picking up my prom date in eleventh grade—a bit tense.

The door cracked open and a tall man, mostly hidden stared back at me. "Yes?"

"Hi. I'm John Farley, here for Mrs. Rockefeller." He scanned me quickly from head to toe. "Wait here." The door closed and after what seemed minutes, opened again.

"Come in." Without so much as a smile, he pointed down to an interior room. "Have a seat over there, please." I noticed the conspicuous handgun holstered near his ribcage. The wait felt similar to job interviews I'd been on, minus the gun.

Minutes later the man came to the vestibule. "You can go up stairs now." The prom feeling returned as I ascended the spiral staircase. Paintings adorned the wall. Is that a Monet? I wanted to stop and stare, but I had a schedule to keep. What's that? Renoir?

A few more steps and I reached the top of the stairs with a few doors around me. The logical place to go was straight ahead and into an expansive room. I stepped inside, dressed better than most bankers.

The space felt enormous, decorated right out of the Gilded Age. I had a sense of being back in the 1920's, or even a century earlier. Golden sunlight poured in through expansive floor to ceiling windows that lined up across the far wall.

John Farley, Jr.

A slim figure of a woman was in the back of the room moving about. She turned around, and walked in my direction. She looked to be in her late sixties and characteristically thin with Irish features.

She called out to me directly without introductions. "Richard didn't tell me you were coming."

"Oh, I, uhmm. Hi. Well—I don't know why. Yes, he told me I'd be working with you today. I'm sure I have the right day." She continued to come closer.

"I just spoke with him. He says you're very good." Relieved, I responded.

"Thank you. Will we be in here?" She went past me, but I don't recall a formal introduction. "We'll be in the room next door."

We stepped a few feet into a much smaller, empty room. This was the exercise room? With only a rug on the 10 x 10 floor, a workout would take creativity.

Richard taught me to give a client a workout without any equipment. By using my body as resistance against theirs, all the major muscles could be trained.

As she lay on the floor, facing upward, she placed her hands against mine as I squatted over her. She knew the drill. It was a bench press against my downward pressure until she couldn't do any more. We switched to another position.

Casually, I smiled and mentioned, "I know Mr. Rockefeller. I used to work at Cardio Fitness Center. That's where he and I met." Mrs. Rockefeller's eyes widened as she stopped and listened. I'm not sure she believed me.

"Really," she said, more of a statement than a question.

"Yes. Please tell him I said hello and I hope his workouts at the center are progressing well." After a pause she replied as if I'd said something profound.

"I will mention it to him." After putting her through the paces for close to an hour, our session was over.

196

Richard, the guy who hired me, had heard that the session was great, and sent me back again a few days later. When I arrived the second time, I was ushered in and upstairs much faster to a waiting Mrs. Rockefeller.

We exercised in the same room. During a rest break, she paused with her serious expression—one that suggested she was almost surprised at what she was about to say. "I told Mr. Rockefeller that you said hello. He *does* remember you from the fitness center." Somehow I'd earned a little more respect. We soon finished our session and parted ways.

Downstairs, the tall guard closed the front door behind me as I crossed the street. I realized I might not ever get to visit here again. Already reminiscing, I turned back toward the brick mansion to take it in. The history of the Rockefeller's multi-billion dollar dynasty after more than 100 years in oil, banking and countless other stakes, had left me with a surreal feeling.

Incredible. A kid from upstate New York who became the personal fitness trainer to what some call the richest family in America. Pleasant, cordial. How could people say that the Rockefeller's are ruthless? Surely it's an exaggeration.

30

Rush hour in Manhattan. I called Janet at work. "Janet, I'm leaving to pick up Sally. Wish me luck."

"Good luck. Are you taking a book to read?"

"No. If I'm arrested, they'll take it." Less than an hour later I was on the train to Long Island. I rested back onto the vinyl headrest. With my eyes closed I visualized success and happiness. It was getting harder to do that.

Be positive. You can turn this around. If anyone has the skills, you have them. The solution to my problems was very simple. All I had to do is follow orders. Why was this so hard? Other people see their children, pay child support and all is well. Of course, I don't personally know any of these people, but that's what outsiders keep telling me. Then there's the pesky criminal charges I'm being attacked with.

Before I knew it, the hour ride was up. The train slowed. The screech of the wheels became louder, almost painful. Before the doors opened, commuters crowded around the opening the way children squeeze through the entry-way onto the playground.

The moment my foot landed on the station platform I hunted for a taxi. Most were quickly taken. There's one. I waved him over and quickly got in. "Ahh! The Huntington police station, please. I'm picking someone up. It'll be a round trip."

I sat quietly. My desire to chat and make friends was gone. Anytime I met someone new I just wanted to be quiet or even become invisible. What's the point of getting to know people? It only leads to questions I don't want to answer.

The taxi pulled off the road into a gravel parking lot. One small, lone building in the middle of the parking lot with one parked car. Joanne, the babysitter, is supposed to have Sally with her. My gut told me to stay in the backseat.

"Will you honk the horn?"

Beep, beep! The door to the building opened and Joanne came out holding Sally's hand. I opened the cab door and waited for them to come closer as I stayed alert. Joanne seemed reluctant to hand Sally over to me. She bent, hugged Sally and looked at me suspiciously.

"Hi, Joanne. I'll take Sally. Thank you."

I took my daughter by the hand. "Hi Sally! How are you?"

"Good," she said, as I noticed the green hair clip on her reddish-brown head.

Joanne handed me her kid-sized backpack and Sally and I stepped toward the open cab door. I picked her up and placed her on the backseat.

"The train station please."

Ten minutes later and we were waiting in a long line at the station. Sally didn't want to stand, but all the seats were taken. A chair opened up and I lifted her onto it as I waited in line.

Forty-five minutes later, the train pulled in. The mass of commuters getting off the train nearly collided with those getting on. The scene looked like cars merging onto a highway with traffic going in opposite directions.

"Hold on." I lifted her and held her close. "Those seats." We quickly claimed our spots. I leaned back. We're more than halfway done with this trip.

Sally looked up at me with her cream-colored cheeks and bluish eyes and asked, "Where are we going?"

"We're going to the city. When we get there we're going to see Janet and we're gonna play fun games."

Her face dropped and then, in a sad, slow, drawn-out tone. "I want my mommy." She had my full attention now. Why did she say that? What is happening? In an adult-like, comforting way I leaned into her.

"You're going to see your mommy in a couple days. Right now you're with me, Daddy."

She spoke louder this time. "I want my mommy."

I swallowed and did a quick check of the people around me. What if these people think I've kidnapped her? How would I prove she's my daughter?

She repeated the mantra again and again. I want my mommy. Now I was self-conscious. I had to distract her. "Hey! Guess what? I'm going to tell you a story. Once upon a time there was a good little girl. She was pretty and happy, and everybody loved her!"

The mantra stopped as I secured her attention. She blocked out everything but me. My tonality became ominous. "Then there was another little girl. She was a baaad little girl. She smoked and drank alcohol, and didn't listen to her dad and mom. She got in trouble in school, and she didn't have any friends."

I thought about what people might think. Of course I'm programming her subconscious mind. Better me hypnotizing her to be successful and happy than Madison Avenue brainwashing her to waste money, drink, smoke, and do drugs. The story wasn't long because I ran out of things to say. She liked that story and wasn't ready for the end.

"Daddy, tell me that story again!" She was nearly bouncing with excitement. Little did she realize that my story had a subconscious goal to make her life as joyful as it could be. Without warning, the train went dark. "We're in the tunnel! Can you say it? Can you say, 'we're in the tunnel'?"

She clapped her hands together and in a high-pitched voice called out. "We're in the tunnel!" She was in the present moment now. Minutes later we pulled into the station and the doors opened. Hand in hand, we rushed through the corridors to the subway system. Once on the subway platform we waited patiently for the subway train.

The station seemed quiet today. With Sally's backpack slung over my shoulder and she and I hand-in-hand, now I looked like a dad.

I pointed a few feet in front of us to the platform. "See the yellow line? We need to stay back here, behind it. Look. See down there! A rat. See him?" I said.

At first she didn't know what I was talking about and mindlessly gazed down on the tracks. Then, as she kept peering over the edge she saw the rodent. "There he is!" she said. The rat disappeared under a railroad tie likely because it could hear the approaching train before we could.

"Here comes the train. Ears." Ears was our cue to cover them as the train came to a long, deafening, screeching stop.

Ten minutes later, "Fifty-ninth Street," the conductor said. As we hurried to the exit, people scurried past us at double our speed. We ascended the escalator to the street level and once on the sidewalk Sally ran in front of me. "Carry me!"

"No, I can't. I have your backpack to carry." Fortunately, today's weather was fine. It wasn't raining and the temperature was mild. When it rained, it was bad. Cabs were impossible to get and we'd both be wet, even with an umbrella. I filled my lungs as we approached the gate to our building for the final ascent.

"Up the stairs we go. Take your time. Rest if you get tired." Five flights of stairs were tough on adults and her legs were little. Once at the top, we rounded the corner and Sally ran to the front door.

The moment the door unlocked she pushed it open. "Janet! We're home!" Sally was looking forward to seeing Janet who'd become her big sister and I was looking forward to a rest.

Nearly 8 p.m., and no Janet?

Looking from one end of the apartment to the other, Sally raised her eyes up at me. "Where's Janet?"

"Give me a few minutes. Play with some toys."

I called Janet's work number. "Hi, we're here. Aren't you done yet? I can't believe you're not here." She sounded odd. "I had to work late." My disappointment was obvious. "When will you be here?" "Another 30 minutes, maybe forty-five."

A sigh escaped me. "Okay. We'll see you then." Sally and I sat on the floor and played with dolls and other toys. She paused with a doll in her hand.

"When's Janet coming home?" "Forty-five minutes," I said. "What does that mean?" she said, curiously.

Explaining time was always difficult. "It means, ah, it's a long time. We have to entertain ourselves. Let's play checkers." I got out the checkers. She knew how to play because her mother had taught her. Even in the middle of what I thought was an interesting game, Sally asked, "When is Janet going to be here?"

"She'll be here in a little while. Just play the game and before you know it she'll be here."

"But when?" While preoccupied with Janet, her pieces were disappearing off the board faster than she realized.

"That's game," I said, taking her last piece. "I won. Good game."

Sally stared at the board, confused. She'd never experienced this before. "No, no I win. I have to win!"

"No, you don't have to win. I won, you lost. Maybe next time you'll win."

A pained face stared back at me as her breathing became labored. Her eyes became glassy. With a sad, whiny tone she continued. "But Mommy always lets me win!"

Now I had a smug look on my face. "I'm not Mommy, and I'm not always going to let you win."

Tears flooded her eyes. "But I'm supposed to win. Mommy always let's me win!"

"I'm your father and I'm gonna beat ya any chance I get!" I said, half teasing. She sat in disbelief, bargaining with fate.

"But I have to win!" as the tears streamed down her face. I raised my voice still half teasing.

John Farley, Jr.

"I won. Maybe next time you'll win," I said without apology. The doorknob jiggled, and instantly my smug appearance vanished. Did I remember to lock the door? The door opened as I held my breath and waited to see who our visitor was.

"HI," said Janet. "Janet!" Sally yelled as she sprang to her feet, forgot about me, and rushed toward the door. "Janet's here—"

Sally's abandonment opened up an opportunity to rest. A momentary sense of relief came over me. As always, the weekend with Sally would offer lots of joy and it's share of challenges. Before I knew it, I'd be back into my weekly routine. The problem was that my life had become anything but routine.

31

BUZZ. The door rang from below while I typed at the computer. The sound had come to represent so much more than a visitor that it caused me to freeze. Clearly, I had post-traumatic stress—I was a nervous wreck at times.

Who could that be? Should I answer it? After a big exhale I got up and tiptoed to the intercom. Here goes. "Hello?"

A clear, strong male voice answered. "Package for John J. Farley."

"Okay." I reached toward the button when my finger froze in mid-air as if preparing myself for an electric shock.

I pressed it. The buzzing sound to release the locks traveled up the stairs ever so faintly. I opened the front door to listen. It took a minute, but soon footsteps became louder as the visitor inched up one step after another. Only one flight to go and the mystery person would appear.

A man dressed in plain clothes rounded the fifth floor banister. "John Farley?"

"Yes?"

He reached into his jacket, and pulled out a white envelope. He extended his hand without taking his eyes off me. "I'm serving you with court papers."

For a split second I hesitated before taking the envelope as if I we were playing tag and I was now "it." The man turned on a dime and walked back down the stairs.

Suckered again. Dammit. What now?

The return address said, Suffolk County Family Court. I opened it as I walked back inside and back to my desk.

A child support hearing coming up on Long Island. I let out an audible and sarcastic, "Great."

John Farley, Jr.

Meanwhile, I have to go back to the Northport court soon, plus Suffolk Criminal Court. I took a deep breath, found my day planner, and scheduled the events.

Do these judges think I could ever have a regular job? How often could I ask for half the day off from work before they fired me?

By this point in time, I'd invested a lot of time researching alternative opinions to the income tax. After seeing the underground video I'd been given years ago claiming the income tax was a fraud, I felt compelled to know the truth.

Truth. The more I looked into the basic assumptions of the income tax, the more lies I found. My entire paradigm of the world was undergoing a shift.

Is anything as it seems? Could the income tax really be a fraud? Could lawyers, and judges really be covering up something almost every American believes to be true?

Interesting that Rockefeller's grandfather became rich beyond belief at a time in history when there was no income tax at all, zero. His billion dollars of over 100 years ago is estimated to be worth $300 billion now. Income tax free.

I pulled a book off the shelf and started going through it. How can anyone sign a 1040 IRS form without giving up their Fifth Amendment right. The Fifth Amendment says a person doesn't have to be a witness against himself. I don't have to answer questions from a police officer. I don't have to sign a confession, even if an officer tells me to do it.

I flipped through the book. The 1040 tax return is a voluntary confession. People fill it out without being ordered to. Once they fill it out under penalty of perjury they've given up their fifth amendment rights. Why would I have to hand over financial information in a court, unless I was ordered to do it, but I have to do it every April 15th?

Not all the tax protester information made sense, but some of the more compelling defenses included the fifth amendment.

Something about child support and the income tax smelled fishy. Something is just not adding up.

Child support payments don't make sense to me. I have to pay the income taxes on the child support payments, yet the mother gets that money tax free? I never actually receive the money at all. I work for the money, then the mother gets it, but I pay the tax on something I never received? Incredible.

The money was supposed to go for the child's upkeep, yet no one cares what the mother does with the money. She could be using it for her retirement fund or for lottery tickets. No one in the court system cares about that.

Something's wrong. I remember one of the tax guys I spoke to said it's called the tax code because it's written in *code*. We're not supposed to know what is says or means. The thousands and thousands of pages of *the code* aren't meant to be understood by average people—even tax experts can't agree what it says. Yet, the IRS expects average people to fill out tax confession forms every April 15th without mistakes? Why? Something's very fishy, isn't it?

Something's equally wrong with child support. It seems right to average folks, to lawyers, to judges—but not to me. It's politically incorrect to ever say you don't pay or believe in child support. Yet, the dirty secret is that child support is not about children, it's about something else. What, I'm not sure yet.

Something is wrong. The government doesn't get to steal my money from income taxes, child support, brutally attack me, humiliate me and then not protect my time with my daughter. NO. I just can't take it anymore. Isn't it a moral crime, if not just plain stupidity, to give money to those who will destroy you and what you hold dear?

The pressure of the legal system was never ending. My mental state bounced between anxiety and despondency. Resign yourself to it, John. Deal with it.

Time to get ready for the next battle.

32

In The Hotel

Amanda was sipping some tea as she seemed to be pondering what I'd said. "The income tax stuff has to do with child support in some way?"

"Yeah. It comes down to being ordered to hand over papers. Since when does an American citizen have to hand over financial documents to a court or prosecutor unless they've already signed away their rights?"

"I don't completely follow."

"Stay with me and we'll get to it."

Long Island

The money slipped from my hands into the cabbie's. "Receipt?"

"Sure."

He handed me a blank card to fill in on my own. I took it, while I reached for my brown bag handle on my way out the back door. The taxi pulled away and a sense of being stranded on an island with cannibals came out of nowhere and flooded me.

I stopped on the sidewalk in front of The Suffolk County Family court building. Wait. Collect yourself. After expanding my chest with air I released it, but on the way out it felt like a sigh instead of a strong preparation. The adjoining criminal court building seeped into my periphery. I'll be going back there soon enough.

I'm jittery. But it could be worse. Some guys I know throw up before court.

John Farley, Jr.

The revolving door seemed to be waiting for me. On the other side was a podium, a cop, and an x-ray machine. The line stretched 50 people out. After standing too long in a line as lifeless as the building itself, I made it to the officer. A middle-aged male with a blank expression lifted his eyes off the paper to give me a quick scan. "Name."

I hesitated. "John Farley." Giving anything to cops was difficult. With his pencil he pointed to the waiting area on his left. "Wait for your name to be called."

The waiting area was filled with poor looking immigrants. What am I doing here, really? Time crept by slower than a Sunday traffic jam.

O'Dell would have to arrive before I could go upstairs to the hearing rooms. She lived in the area, yet she was always late. I assumed it was a negotiating tactic to wear me down. After I'd resigned myself to waiting a long time, in through the revolving door she came. Her clothes looked nice, but not too nice.

After another ten minutes of sitting, an officer called out, "O'Dell and Farley!" We strode past the cops who guarded access to the elevator bank. Dee Dee took the elevator while I took the stairs. I wanted to get the blood pumped and the nerves calmed.

After bounding up the half-dozen flights and passing through the third floor door, my breathing was the loudest noise. An eerie quiet permeated the wide, sunlit hallways. There was no one in sight. Each step down the carpeted hallway increased my jitters. I turned a corner to see a few people sitting and waiting near my room, so I sat nearby. The silence was unnerving.

Dee Dee straggled twenty paces behind and sat on a bench far away and looked oddly timid. It was all an act. Every minute I waited seemed like ten. The door to the hearing room pushed open with the sound of keys dangling from the court officer's belt startled me. He held papers in his hand and passed a sheet of paper to the man and woman seated across from me.

"Fill this out," he told them sternly. He turned to me with the same document, "Fill this out." It was a form asking for assets and liabilities. The hearing examiner will look at this document to decide the amount of money to set for child support. I didn't fill it out because I don't have to.

Time went by. The door to the hearing room opened again. People came out. No one looked angry or sad or happy. Just blank faces eager to leave. The court officer, a husky Caucasian guy in his forties, went back inside and closed the door with a gentle touch.

Perhaps another ten minutes went by when the door reopened. The court officer came out, and announced strongly, "The court is taking a recess and will reconvene shortly. Don't go very far."

With that announcement he disappeared behind the locked door. More silence and empty hallways kept me company. Dee Dee sat motionless with her eyes straight ahead like she was watching television where only a blank wall was.

Perhaps she knew I was staring at her, because a slow moving, creepy smile stretched across her face. Perhaps an intimidation tactic. A mix of anxiety and dread spread through me.

The door opened again, and the officer shouted, "O'Dell versus Farley!" Instantly, butterflies in my center took flight faster than my legs could stand me up.

"Go right in," the officer said.

Dee Dee lagged behind. The officer commanded us. "Sir, sit here. Ma'am, over here."

The door shut behind us with the officer nearby, but out of sight. The administrators, three of them, sat directly in front of us at the same height. Eight feet of solid desk-like table separated us from the man in the middle—the hearing examiner.

The case had started before I knew what was happening. We were sworn in. William Rodriquez, a dark skinned, loud voiced, hearing examiner was in charge.

His tone was tinged with a touch of arrogance as his elongated words echoed off the small walls.

"Mr. Farley, the court will determine a child support order. Do you have your financial documents with you?"

Timidly I replied, "No, I don't."

While still handing papers back and forth to his clerk, he replied instantly. "Why not?"

I drooped my head toward the desk as I searched for words. I noticed my hands vibrating. "I think... I should have a lawyer," I choked out.

The hearing examiner looked to the clerk next to him and made some remarks before he looked back at me. "Are you asking for time to get a lawyer?"

I cleared my throat. "I want the court to give me a lawyer." Rodriquez nearly stepped on my words. "I'm not providing you lawyer. If you want a lawyer you'll have to retain your own private attorney. Are you asking for time to get an attorney?"

"Uh, yeah. Yes, that's what I want."

"Let the record show that Mr. Farley will return with his own attorney at the next hearing. This case is adjourned until—" Rodriquez paused and leaned over to his clerk before turning back to us. "Wait outside." The officer's voice came from behind us, "The parties will leave the courtroom."

I pushed back my chair, grabbed my bag and went out the door with Dee Dee somewhere behind and moving like cold molasses.

"Wait here for the next court date," the officer said before he ducked back into the room. A few moments later the officer came out and handed each of us a piece of paper with the date and time for the next court date. My mind couldn't register the date at that moment. Incredible. All this time and travel for what? Another court date. This hearing examiner is a bit of a jerk. I walked out the building and looked for a cab when I remembered something Janet told me.

33

Many weeks had passed. Things were calm, yet like an old farmer who smells rain on a clear day, I sensed something off in the distance. I went into the living room while deep in thought. "I have a strong feeling there's a warrant out for my arrest."

Janet folded laundry while the television flickered in the background. "Why?" She tossed a clean towel on the couch. "What now?"

I came closer. "I'll help you with that." I grabbed a shirt and folded it. "I can't put my finger on it. There were so many phone calls to Dee Dee. I have a sense that there was one more call the cops never acted on. It could also be that Dee Dee might make up a complaint. Unlikely, but it could happen."

"She would." Janet tossed a folded shirt onto a pile.

"We have to have a plan. You come with me to the police station to pick up Sally. I'll be in the taxi just in case the babysitter insists Sally's to be given only to me. If there's a problem, we'll just leave."

Friday 6:00 p.m.

Janet, and I got off the train in Huntington. It was chilly, but for December it was very mild. Once off the platform, we searched the parking lot for an open cab, which is like finding a green ball in the high grass hills of upstate New York.

Janet reached over and rubbed her hand down the sleeve of my jacket. "I like that coat on you."

My long, gray, wool dress coat looked stylish.

"There." I tapped her arm and she followed me around the parked cabs toward the middle of the lot. I grabbed the door handle signaling that I'd claimed the cab.

John Farley, Jr.

"Slide in." The door closed tightly with a secure, snug sound. Another middle-aged cab driver. Seems that's the norm here for this profession.

"We're going to the police station outlet in Huntington. We'll be picking up someone and going back to the train station." The driver nodded and we inched out toward the roadway. Janet was calm.

"It gets dark so early now, doesn't it?" she said.

I turned to the window, and focused on the bright moon. Still preoccupied, I mumbled back. "Yeah—yeah, it does." She put her hand over mine as it rested on my thigh. Her touch grounded me. Within ten minutes the cab pulled into the dirt and gravel driveway.

"You can park right here," I said. I wanted to stay away from the building, if possible.

"Just get Sally and bring her here. If there's any problem forget it and come right back."

Janet got out of the car and went to the front door of the police building that looked like a mobile home. I watched her every step until the moment she disappeared on the other side of the glass door. This should only take a minute.

The cabbie and I sat there. It was taking longer. Too long. My teeth clenched. "Let's leave," I said. The cabbie looked in the mirror waiting to see if I was serious.

"Let's leave, let's just go." He started the engine and the cab started to move, when the door to the building opened. Two cops came out and walked—nearly ran—toward the cab. "Let's go. Right now, let's go."

The cops yelled, "Stop, stop!"

Oh, no. They opened the back door as one stood towering over me. "Are you John Farley?"

"What do you want? You don't have any right to stop this cab."

The cop held the door open. "Let me see some ID now!"

"I don't have to show you ID. Let go of the door!"

The middle-aged, white cop with a beer belly yelled, "Get out of the car right now." He grabbed the arm of my wool coat.

214

The other young, dark haired cop opened the door on the other side.

"Let go of me right now—"

"Get out of the car!" The other cop came around the cab, reached in and grabbed my other arm. We struggled until I stepped out of the car.

I tried halfheartedly to pull away, but the bulky coat stopped me from moving. Each cop pulled an arm stretching me out for crucifixion.

Janet was standing far back away from the car, but in plain sight. "Janet—Janet, look at this! Look what these cops are doing. You're witnessing it."

The porky bald cop turned to Janet for a split second. "Janet, you're a witness to resisting arrest."

That fat jerk's comment irked me. The urge to kick him off me was strong, but the long coat hindered my leg from lifting into the proper position—I just couldn't kick—which would have been a bad idea anyway.

"Get down on the ground," the cop yelled. They continued to pull my arms. It was all a waste of energy.

"I'll go on the ground, but watch my glasses—" As they brought me face down into the stone gravel parking lot, I continued yelling, "Watch my glasses." Meanwhile, Sally and her babysitter, Joanne, must have heard it all from inside the station.

I learned later that Dee Dee had told the babysitter to have the police call her when I showed up so Dee Dee could tell them there was a warrant for me. Imagine.

The cops took me straight into a police car and off to the local jail. I spent the next full day in a cell, and then back to Central Islip court. I managed to get out without bail or major trauma. Still, it was another weekend without my daughter and without my liberty—and for what again? The year was ending, and I seriously hoped that something better was on the way.

34

At the Hotel

Amanda pulled out a nail file and took a quick break while I rushed off to the restroom. When I returned, she asked, "Before you left you said that you and Janet went to California to visit her family and friends."

"That's right. We flew out, were greeted by her parents, and took a ride over the Santa Cruz mountains to Monterey and the Pacific Ocean."

California

Janet drove us toward a highway. To amuse myself, I gazed out the window looking for palm trees. The sky's unusually bright blue color surprised me while the light brown of the dry grass on the far off hills presented another peculiar sight, brown hills.

I rolled the window down and sniffed the air. "You know, I always say any day outside of the city is a good day. I like it here in California."

Janet smiled. "I've always said that it's easier to be happy when the sun's shining." I paused and studied her profile for a moment as that simple statement rattled around in my analytical brain. She is cheerful. Could it be from the sun and blue skies? Maybe there's something to it. I do feel happier here in California, if only a little.

The long drive over the Santa Cruz mountains was intense. For whatever reason, I just don't do well on boats, carnival rides, or windy roads. The highway over the mountains is filled with intense curves, which means you'd better have liked your lunch, because you may taste it twice.

An hour later, we came closer to Monterey and from the highway the Pacific Ocean was visible. All at once I felt more relaxed; the giant expanse of water seemed to extend to infinity. This California coastal town, which claimed author John Steinbeck as one of its own, was already growing on me. We parked in a lot and walked to the Monterey Aquarium, perched over the sparkling Pacific Ocean.

My tension evaporated as I enjoyed the casual coastal town and absorbed the vibration of the ocean. Janet stopped an older man as he walked past. "Could you take our picture?"

"You bet." he said in a friendly, California way. "Smile." He snapped a photo of us in a happy moment. Janet's blonde hair and blue eyes sparkled. She looked very Californian. The rhythm of the ocean washed our troubles away, at least for a time. Soon, we went inside the darkened aquarium to look at the incredible sea life, from sardines to sharks.

Afterwards we had lunch at a quiet corner bistro specializing in, what else—seafood. As we left the restaurant, the smell of the salt water filled our nostrils.

It was time to head back over the mountains to Janet's parents.

35

Back home, Janet reached for the doorknob, but found it locked. She started to knock when her mom opened the door. She smiled. "How was the trip?"

"It was nice," Janet said as we walked inside. "He didn't do so well on Highway 17." Mrs. Kay gave me a quick visual assessment and commented on my slightly pale face.

"That road is windy."

I nodded and grinned. "It sure is."

Janet touched my arm. "Let me show you some things we have downstairs." I followed her down past my room as the two dogs tagged along. "You two stay out." Janet closed the door to the last room at the end of the hallway.

It's the formal dining room below the kitchen. The slight drop in room temperature was apparent. It was the only room in the house without carpeting. A musty odor was immediately noticeable. The large room was filled with objects, but it wasn't overly cluttered. A long, shiny, rectangular wooden table dominated the space, nearly filling it all by itself.

"Lately, my dad gets a lot of things from auctions." She pointed around the room. "This artwork over here, and all this antique furniture."

"You like these things?" I asked.

"Sure, look at the wood on this chair. This is oak, real oak. We polished it, and now this chair is worth ten times what Dad got it for," she said beaming.

"It's nice." But what good are all these things if they just sit in storage, unused? Janet didn't have an answer, but kept on admiring the antiques.

John Farley, Jr.

"I saw your dad has audio programs in the room I'm in. They look really interesting. Negotiating, sales, business. I'd like to listen to those."

Janet grabbed a cloth on a nearby table, and cleaned a spot off a chair leg. "I'm sure he'll let you have them. He doesn't need them anymore."

"Really? He'd let me have those?"

Janet stopped rubbing the spot, and looked up at me, surprised at my shock. "Yeah, I'll ask him later." I noticed a white chess set. "Wow, this looks nice." "It's ivory," she said.

The room was quiet, no animals or television. "Let's play a game. What do you say?" I sat in front of the chessboard. Janet set the cloth on the couch and pulled up a chair. We arranged the chess pieces and were well into the game when Mr. Kay entered the room. He stood a moment peering down at the board.

"Chess. One of my favorite games," he said loudly.

I acknowledged him with a glance and a smile although he stayed focused on the board. Janet continued to fixate on the board as well. "Chess was developed over 1,500 years ago. It was for the nobility, and a game of warfare," he said.

To recognize him I attempted eye contact, grinned and gently nodded.

I was ahead by a few pieces, and Janet and I sat in silence while I strategized.

Mr. Kay walked to Janet's side and analyzed our positions. After about a minute he said, "Janet, you should move your rook over here."

She continued to look down at the board without acknowledging what he'd said.

Did he know we're competing in a one-on-one game, not two against one? Reluctantly, Janet moved the piece he told her to move, as if it were her idea. But he wasn't done. He continued to direct her to move pieces and she reluctantly did what she was told without any visible signs of angst.

This is really odd. I'm playing against two people. If she wins, does she really win?

A vent, the size of a small television screen and mostly covered, provided a conduit for sound from the kitchen to our room down below. A voice came through the opening. It was Mrs. Kay. "Janet can you send your father up here?"

Mr. Kay reluctantly tore himself away from the chess match to go upstairs. When he left, I felt immediate relief. We continued the game without so much as a word.

Eventually Janet's king was taken. Moments afterward, Mr. Kay entered the room and stood over the board. "It's over?" he asked, looking at Janet. "Who won?"

"I did," I said, gently.

He never looked at me, and Janet had her head down with a disturbed pout on her face as she put the game pieces away. There were no congratulations to me, but only the crestfallen posture of a humiliated father.

He really wanted Janet to beat me. It was as if he was playing against me and his family honor was at stake.

"Well," I said, wanting to crawl out of the room unseen. "I'm going to rest a little and clean up before dinner." I slinked out toward my bedroom. Janet continued putting the pieces away while giving her father the silent treatment. Something was odd.

36

The Hotel

Amanda and I sat on the comfortable hotel couches. She gently tossed her hair away from her face. "What did the chess game mean to you?"

I uncrossed my legs, leaned back and reached up to stroke my chin as the thought crystallized. "At the time, it meant he was focused on his daughter. She represents him. He wanted her, his protégé, to outwit me. In retrospect I see the chess pieces as a metaphor for the stages of a man's life. Being a young guy in my late twenties, I was in a stage of manhood some call 'knight.'"

Intrigued by the metaphor, Amanda interrupted. "Knight—like the chess piece you were just playing with?"

Nodding, I continued. "Knights, more than anything, are looking for adventure. My adventures had been dating women, college, getting on television and pursuing exciting business ideas."

Amanda sat nearly motionless and absorbed by what I was saying. "What about Mr. Kay? What stage was he in?"

"Mr. Kay had reached the stage called king. All men want adventure, but during the king stage men have stronger needs. Kings are very opinionated. They want to give certain things to certain people in their lives. To provide for the people they consider to be apart of their kingdom and who they feel responsible for. A king needs admiration.

"Mr. Kay spent his life building his kingdom—his home, investments, real estate—as well as his family. He was proud of it, too proud perhaps. As for me, I wanted a mentor or even a business partner. What I didn't realize is that kings, like Mr. Kay, have already completed their careers and don't want to rebuild their kingdoms unless they're forced to. Their ambition is a lot less than a knight or a prince."

Amanda smiled. "A king and his kingdom. Did he see you as a threat to his kingdom?"I reached toward my glass on the table between us. "Hmm, at that point I didn't know." Amanda readjusted herself and fluffed up the pillows on the couch. "Are those the only stages?"

"No, there's more. Prince is the most complicated stage a man goes through between knight and king. I was really entering prince. We'll get to that later, perhaps."

Amanda sat ready to type. "What happened next?"

California

The dinner table was set downstairs at the Kay's home. Mrs. Kay called out from the kitchen, "Time to eat."

The meal looked wonderful. Bowls were spread across the long table and filled with fabulous vegetable and meat assortments. Candles flickered as the light bounced off colorful flowers spread out around the table.

Mrs. Kay sat down and smiled at me. "I made you a special vegetarian dish." I nodded. "Thank you, I'm looking forward to having that."

Steve-o wandered into the room and sat across from me, and near his father who sat at the head of the table. Janet sat between me and her mom. Mr. and Mrs. Kay faced each other down the long table.

Once a prayer was said, the bowls of food quickly moved around the table. I turned toward Mrs. Kay. "This is very good." Complimenting the chef is always a wise move.

"Have more potatoes," she encouraged. Steve-o interrupted. "Mom, pass the bread." Please."

Despite the perfect dinner table, uncomfortable silences lingered in the air. For some reason, everyone was on eggshells, including me. I figured it would pass, but it didn't.

With a giggle and a smile, Mrs. Kay directed a comment toward me. "Janet mentioned that you lived in Astoria, Queens. I grew up in Queens. Steve and I met at a dance."

I nodded, grinned and gave a muffled, "Oh," in between bites of rice. I rushed to swallow and took a sip of water.

"Yes, I lived in Astoria for one year. My first year in New York. I was there with a friend of mine, and his friend."

Mr. Kay listened as his head stayed aimed toward his plate. He rarely, if ever, asked a question. I ask questions out of curiosity and to encourage others to talk. At a previous time Janet had explained to me that to Mr. Kay, asking questions made a man look ignorant, possibly even stupid. Interestingly, Janet rarely if ever dated in high school because boys never made it past her father.

Summoning my courage, I turned to the head of the table. "Mr. Kay, you worked for companies doing sales?" Mr. Kay chewed on a piece of beef while his fork and knife extended vertically from each hand. He glanced up at me as he chewed.

In an attempt to fill the dead-airtime I reached for my water glass gingerly, as if diffusing a bomb. Mr. Kay straightened up. He started speaking with his gaze focused just past his dinner plate in front of him. No one at the table said a word. "I worked for a semi-conductor company. I was in-charge of the entire sales division." he said in a scratchy, Brooklyn accent.

With a mouth half-full of food, Steve-o blurted out, "You weren't in-charge of the whole sales division worldwide. Mom, pass the carrots…please!"

Mr. Kay seemed solid, rooted in his chair. His head still pointed down to the table, but his gaze drifted upward. "Excuse me son." His voice became clear, slow and measured with a hint of repressed hostility. "I was in charge of the California division."

With scorn, likely from a bad childhood, Steve-o fired back. "That's not the entire sales division!"

Mr. Kay stayed motionless while his tone became smoother and a little higher pitched. "No-o-o....it's the entire sales division of California."

He lifted his fork and knife and gently stabbed the slab of beef lying on his plate. The tension was obvious, but the reason for it, less so.

"Janet is doing very well at her new sales position," I said.

"Even if she's an air-headed blonde," Steve-o interjected.

"Ha, ha, very funny," Janet countered.

The comment struck me as odd. I wasn't used to the sibling insults that many families endure.

Janet focused on her plate and continued eating.

After a few more helpings and strained conversation, Steve-o was the first to leave. Without a word, he pushed his solid wooden chair away from the massive table and grabbed his plate with his good hand.

"You're done?" his mother asked.

"The game's on," he countered.

Within ten more minutes Mrs. Kay excused herself. "I'm going to clear the table."

Janet was quick to follow, "I'll help you." Within a few moments the table was cleared off. I wanted to excuse myself too, but Mr. Kay was now looking at me.

The second bottle of White Zinfandel wine was halfway gone and Mr. Kay was ready to talk. "When I worked for that company, I used to tell the president how our division would work best. One time he told me he wanted a project completed. He was getting ready to call down through the chain of command. I told him I could have it done faster than he could so we bet on it—he and I."

I smiled and nodded.

Mr. Kay went to sip his wine glass and turned it upside down in the air as the last drop fell toward his open mouth. "A few days later I walked into the president's office and held in my hands the completed project. He couldn't believe it."

"Wow," I said, very interested, but not fully impressed. "How did you do that?"

"You sure you don't want a drink?" he asked. It was almost a command more than a question.

I gave a polite, "No thank you, I don't drink." Mr. Kay was a man from tough neighborhoods in New York City. Men drank hard, smoked a lot, and settled disagreements outside. Many years ago he even directed his dentist to pull out his perfectly functioning teeth so as not to be bothered by the bony protrusions anymore. As time went on I came to believe that Mr. Kay thought I was a little too soft or at least strange.

As I sat at the table with Mr. Kay the pressure to win his approval mounted. His fingers rubbed the outside of his wine glass and I could nearly see his mind working.

"I'd built up favors throughout the company. All I needed to do was pick up the phone and talk to my guys. I'd call in favors I'd done for them in the past. Before the company president could even get started, I was finished." He tipped back the wine glass.

Hours went by. The rest of the household had gone to bed, even the dogs. I continued smiling and nodding even as my bladder was about to burst not wanting to be the first one to end the conversation. Soon, it was past midnight. I was stiff, sore and tired from hours of sitting, but to call an end to the meeting would've been seen as weak or rude, or so I thought.

He slurped the last drop of wine from his glass then finally said, "It's time for bed." Mr. Kay was calling it a night, and none too soon for me.

The next night ended the same way, and the next, and the next. Janet was nowhere to be found. She never intervened. Never tried to come to my rescue. To her, this was between her father and me.

Each night was a psychological torture that I felt obligated to endure.

John Farley, Jr.

One night, to do something different, Janet, Mom and me played Pictionary against Mr. Kay who, by that time, was half drunk. To my surprise, he always beat us—three against one—and it wasn't even a close game.

Janet explained it to me as things wrapped up. "'Steel trap,' that's what we call him. Once information goes into his mind, it stays there."

I made it through my vacation week with the Kay family. It was time to go back to the concrete jungle and face a different set of challenges.

37

Manhattan Family Court

The day I'd waited for had arrived. After many months, Dee Dee would have a contempt trial in Manhattan Family Court. Despite my effort to negotiate with her, she wouldn't compromise. She took pride in relentless stubbornness.

We sat in the packed courthouse's waiting area until the court officer called out our names. "Farley versus O'Dell."

Moments later, the officer pulled open the heavy door to the courtroom. Dee Dee and her lawyer assumed their positions while I took mine about ten feet away.

"All rise!"

The judge came out, looking as unsympathetic as always. Her tone always bordered on sarcastic. "We're having a trial today, is that right?" she asked.

The lawyer spoke up. "Yes, your Honor."

The judge motioned in my direction. "Then let's go."

On this day I wore dress pants with a dark sport coat in hopes of making a favorable impression. I stood up, glanced at my opponents and then back toward the judge. "What am I suppose to do now?"

The judge's eyes darted to all corners of the room as she took a deep breath and swiveled in her chair toward her court assistants. "Settle in, people, we're going to be here a long time." She swiveled back toward me. "Make an opening statement!"

I opened my folder to view the notes inside. The court reporter sat poised and ready to type. Everyone was still and my heart was starting to pound. I raised my head from the folder and up toward the judge.

John Farley, Jr.

"Dee Dee O'Dell is guilty of violating the order of visitation on multiple occasions. Her aim is to take my daughter away from me. That's what I'm going to show the court."

Her well dressed lawyer stood up and called out, "Objection—"

The judge called back. "Sustained."

What does that mean again? That's right, it means that she agrees with him, not me. I did a lot of talking, but mostly her lawyer kept interrupting and objecting to everything I said and the judge agreed with him. After much frustration, I finally got to call Dee Dee to the hot seat.

"I call Dee Dee O'Dell to the stand."

Once Dee Dee was in position, the court officer gave her the oath, as she raised her right hand.

I stood about fifteen feet in front and eyed her intensely, but she kept her gaze from mine. The visitation dates were written in my notes. I named a specific Friday night for her to think about. "Where were you on that day?"

After a brief exchange, her lawyer jumped to his feet. "Objection—"

The judge agreed. "Sustained."

The lawyer was really bugging me now. I'd had it with this legal game that I didn't know the rules to.

Like two kids on the playground I turned to him in a confrontational posture. "What's your problem?"

"That's enough—" the judge cautioned. "Do you want me to look at those documents you have?"

"Yes."

"Then you have to enter them into evidence."

Somehow I got the visitation order entered into evidence.

"Now," said the judge, "you can ask your questions."

"Where were you on the date in question?"

Dee Dee spoke in a low, steady, and measured tone as she refused to make eye contact with me. "I don't recall."

I decided to assist her memory. "I can tell you where you were, you were at your office. You were supposed to have Sally at the pick up spot, and you weren't there!" I yelled.

Dee Dee's lawyer shot up like a rocket. "Objection—"

The judge slapped her hand on the table. "Sustained. You can't make statements like that to the witness."

I stood there confused wondering why not. I know, I'll show that Dee Dee was faking a bad memory. "Ms. O'Dell, didn't you tell me once that you have a photographic memory?"

The lawyer hardly had time to sit down before he was back on his feet. "Objection—"

The judge turned to me. "Where is this going?"

"I want to show that Ms. O'Dell has a photographic memory, and she does remember these things."

The judge leaned forward toward Dee Dee. "Do you know what a photographic memory is?"

Dee Dee paused, and started to shrug her shoulders as if confused. "I'm not sure."

The judge swiveled to her right to get a better look at Dee Dee sitting slightly below her. "What do you normally do on Friday evenings?"

Dee Dee lifted her head as her eyes darted to the lawyer.

"You don't have to look at him, just answer the question."

"I might have been working, I don't recall," she said in the same calm manner.

"I'll help you remember. Do you normally work on Fridays?"

"Yes," she said.

"Is there any reason you wouldn't have been working on this Friday?"

She paused as a nervous smile broke through. "I don't recall," she said, with a higher pitched tone.

"It's possible you were working that evening?"

Her mouth opened as her mind scrambled for an answer. "It's possible."

The judge locked eyes with me. "Are you getting the idea?"

John Farley, Jr.

I replied, "I think I'm getting the hang of it."

Dee Dee's lawyer stood up. "Your Honor, I'd like to address the court."

I stood up and yelled, "Objection—"

The judge's face scrunched up as she turned to me. "What are you objecting to?"

"I didn't like what he said."

The judge gripped her desk with either amusement or annoyance. She made eye contact with her law clerk until the feeling subsided and her face returned to normal.

"Your Honor, I'd like Mr. Farley to get to his point." The judge recovered. Let's move on, people."

Dee Dee continued to dodge questions, but it was clear to the judge that she was trying to mislead. Finally, it was my turn to take the stand. I had no idea how the pressure of being on the witness stand would impact me, and neither did anyone else.

38

Each step toward the witness stand made my heart race faster. The court officer called for everyone to hear, "I'll remind you that you are still under oath."

I pulled out the solid wooden witness chair while nervous tension caused my hands to shake. The judge turned her chair in my direction. "State what you want to say."

I started out with a controlled voice. My focus alternated between Dee Dee, fifteen feet in front of me, and the judge. A memory came to me. "I went out on the train on the first Sunday in July. It was early in the morning. I got a cab to Dee Dee's home, just as it says in the visitation order. I arrived, and told the cabbie to wait—that I'd be back with my daughter."

My heart edged closer to my throat. My hands started to shake more. The judge listened, but she looked away from time to time. The court reporter's fingers bounced off the keyboard in rapid fire. Dee Dee's lawyer took notes as the court officer stood like a wax figure near the door. Without warning, a feeling of indignation from the memory overwhelmed me. I raised my voice. "I took Sally to the cab and told the driver to go. Dee Dee came out and stopped the driver—told him not to leave—that the police were on the way."

I became even louder. My hands seemed to gesture by themselves. The sight of her sitting there, innocently, was too much to take. I yelled, "The police came and took Sally from me, my daughter. My little three year old girl. They took her away from me. During MY time."

Fury overwhelmed me. This time, on purpose, I slapped the back of my hand into the other palm sending a shock wave of sound through the courtroom. The judge leaned away as she looked toward her assistants. I thrust my arm and finger toward Dee Dee and yelled. "YOU! It was a beautiful summer day, and YOU had me arrested—"

My yell turned to a growl as I again thrust my outstretched arm in her direction and pointed directly at her. "YOU had me arrested for nothing—for picking up my daughter."

Rage overtook me. The judge gulped. "Relax, Mr. Farley, relax."

"Relax?" I turned to see her. "You want me to relax?" I said in a higher pitched, calm tone. "I'll relax...." I pointed at Dee Dee. "You did it again and again. Over and over. You got me arrested, and I had to spend the night in jail where I'm attacked, and beaten and strip searched."

After a few more minutes my testimony was finished. It was extremely tense and I'm sure the judge knew I was being authentic to say the least.

It was time to adjourn until a verdict was ready. Upon leaving the courtroom I felt exhausted. The stress of reliving these traumatic events drained me.

***

Weeks had gone by since the trial, and we were back at the courthouse. Dee Dee and I waited to be called back into the courtroom. As I sat there, I daydreamed of a recent time with Sally when I took her downtown to see lower Manhattan. We walked underground in an area that's home to many stores. Sally's hand held mine as we walked slowly toward the giant underground escalator.

"Ready? We have to step onto the escalator. On three. One, two, three—"

I marveled at that girl. Her potential was largely my responsibility, right? She depended on me in this moment. She knew me as "Daddy" the man who could do anything. I felt the pressure to be a great dad, but I didn't feel great.

The ride up the escalator was long, but coming to an end. "We have to get off soon. On three. One, two three." We stepped off the escalator and walked hand-in-hand to the revolving door leading to the busy street.

Outside, we waited on the street corner for the light to change. As the cars went by I looked around as I scanned for danger, constantly on the alert. Sally's presence only increased my carefulness.

"Sally, let's say this building, this big one right behind us, fell. It would fall like this." I held up my forearm vertically and allowed it to fall like a tree. "If it fell toward us we'd want to run sideways, not straight out. If we ran straight out it would land on us, but if we ran to the side, we'd have a chance."

Sally, only a few years old, listened. It was an odd conversation, but I wanted to teach her every way to be safe that I could. It was the mid 1990's, but I'd remembered that a bomb exploded in that very building not long before. Little did I know that those twin towers we stood under would implode several years later. Implode. And building seven, one I'd worked in a few years ago, would come down exactly as if it was a controlled demolition.

My reverie ended when a shout echoed through the waiting area. "Farley versus O'Dell." Dee Dee, her lawyer and myself went into the courtroom. Several minutes later the judge entered. She prepared herself as everyone sat and waited for the verdict. Silence made the tension that much thicker.

The judge gave some fast legal-speak. "This court finds that Dee Dee O'Dell has violated the visitation order." Yes. This is fantastic. Finally. Justice.

The judge went on to revise the visitation order, but to my astonishment there was no punishment at all. I blurted out my shock to the court. "What?" She doesn't get punished?"

The judge rolled her eyes before fixing them on me. "And what would you have me do?" That was easy.

"Put her in jail."

"Argg!" The judge tapped her hands on the desk and shook her head. "That's ridiculous."

Sarcastically I replied. "Ohhh, but it's okay if I go to jail for following a court order, but she doesn't go to jail for breaking it?"

The judge wasn't changing her mind, but I had made my point.

Dee Dee left the courtroom minutes later. The scowl on her face suggested she thought she'd received a punishment. My symbolic victory probably bothered her more than it actually impacted her.

I was shocked and upset. All this time and effort that I put in. I win, yet I lose. It was clear. Dee Dee could break the court order anytime she wanted and face no punishment. I had to re-focus now. There were more battles to fight.

39

I knew who it was when I heard the apartment buzzer. "Hello?"

"JOHN, IT'S STEVE EDWARDS."

"I'll be right down." I released the buzzer and stepped into the bathroom, to straighten my tie and adjust my dark blue suit jacket.

I went out the downstairs gate and opened the door to Steve's modest car. "Good morning Steve." I scrunched into the passenger seat.

"GOOD MORNING."

"I'm a little nervous about today. What else do I need to know?"

Even in his small car, Edwards spoke as if we were going 80 mph in a top down convertible. "YOU'LL BE ASKED A SERIES OF QUESTIONS. IF YOU DON'T KNOW THE ANSWER YOU CAN SAY YOU DON'T RECALL. DON'T ANSWER QUESTIONS THAT AREN'T ASKED. SAY YES OR NO WHEN ASKED YES OR NO QUESTIONS."

The slow moving traffic along 58th street intensified my anxiety. "How long will it take to get there?"

"ABOUT 90 MINUTES."

"Should we go over the details of the case again?"

"ARE YOU NERVOUS?"

"I'm revved up and ready to go," I said, attempting to convince myself more than him. The thick file of papers I brought gave me something to flip through and review.

"Maybe a little nervous."

"YOU JUST WANT TO RELAX AND ANSWER THE QUESTIONS. I'LL BE THERE TO GIVE YOU SOME

GUIDANCE—YOU KNOW, MAKE SURE THE OTHER SIDE DOESN'T BREAK THE RULES."

The thought of being face to face with my jailers made me jittery. "Will the sheriffs who beat me be there?"

"NO THIS IS JUST YOU AND THE LAWYERS GOING OVER SOME DETAILS OF THE CASE."

Hmm, why is that? It was a long drive, but we arrived on time. Wide-eyed, and amped, I got out of the car. I kept he door open longer than necessary while I looked around. Adrenaline pulsed through my body, I could feel it. Game on.

"JOHN, I HAVE TO GET SOMETHING OUT OF THE TRUNK."

As I closed the car door, I could feel the brisk air and the hard pavement underneath the sole of my dress shoes. I was on high alert.

Soon we walked through the front doors of the building and stood face to face with several marshals—men in their late fifties and sixties ready to search our bags.

The building was eerily quiet, the way a church is during off-hours.

HOW ARE YOU FEELING?" Edwards glanced over as we emptied our pockets before the metal detector. He must have noticed a shift in my demeanor.

"Uh, I'm okay."

Police make me feel uneasy. Once past the marshals, we headed down the hallway to a room with a long table. Within minutes, the county attorney came in the room like a whirlwind. There she was, a tall, thin woman, with short, bushy, wavy, flaming, red hair, on top of her large head. She dressed in a masculine styled suit. To say she was high strung would be an understatement. It soon became clear that this woman was very aggressive.

"HELLO, I'M STEVE EDWARDS."

The woman lawyer stopped and planted her feet while her body nearly shook. I sensed that she interpreted Edward's volume as an intimidation tactic.

As she spoke to Steve her argumentative tone was unmistakable. She started moving around again like a film clip stuck on fast forward. "I represent Suffolk County. I need your client to sit over here. We'll begin in a few minutes."

I watched the interaction between the two lawyers. Edwards seemed just a little unsure of himself. The county attorney wasn't here to make friends or even be friendly. It was clear she came to play hardball—to win. I wondered if he knew that.

The lawyer directed me to sit near the end of a long table. The room was filled with fluorescent lights, yet it wasn't brightly lit. The lawyers were across from each other. Edwards took a chair near me. Then, as if on stage with the house lights down and the spotlight shining on me, it was game time.

"State your name for the record," the redhead demanded.

Steve interrupted. "Wait, we need to make sure this is official."

The lawyers spoke to each other in legalese. I sat and observed them the way you watch people on a foreign television channel and try to pick up their meaning through tone and body language. We started again, but one lawyer or the other would interrupt every few minutes.

Where were the pictures of the cops? This should be simple. Show me pictures of the deputies. I'll point them out and that's it. Why aren't there any pictures?

It took perhaps two hours to get through the deposition and then we left. I was all a blur, and next thing I knew we were headed back to the city.

John Farley, Jr.

During the ride I had a strange feeling. The lawyer's questions kept replaying in my mind. Edwards must know what he's doing, but I wanted to know something. "Why weren't there pictures of deputies so I could identify them?"

My lawyer seemed unfazed by the question. "NOW'S NOT THE TIME FOR THAT. THE OTHER SIDE BROUGHT UP A TECHNICAL REASON WHY PHOTOS WEREN'T AVAILABLE. WE SHOULD BE ABLE TO GET THEM."

"You mean to say that even though we know the day and place this happened, they claim they can't get the photos of their own employees who work there? That's outrageous. All they have to do is show me pictures and I'll tell you who hit me. It's that simple."

Something's wrong. It's not like we have to hunt down the perpetrators. The missing photos disturbed me.

40

In the Hotel

Amanda stopped to check her phone messages and then we continued.

"When I arrived home there was a letter that said I had to go to court for missing jury duty. I couldn't believe it."

"Did you skip jury duty?"

"No. I never got the letters they claimed they sent me. Here's the lesson that was reinforced for me. I showed up along with about 100 others including lawyers who the court said didn't show up for jury duty. Everyone was getting hit with fines up to $800."

"Ouch. That's a lot." Amanda grimaced.

"Yeah, so I noticed that any demonstration of fear or giving in was met with swift punishment by the judge—the same thing I'd noticed in other courtrooms. So, I did the opposite. I made a scene and put the judge on the defensive."

"How did that work out?"

"Ultimately, they dropped the issue and I never heard from them again. These judges thrive on intimidation. At some point a person has to stand up for themselves or suffer the consequences."

The Long Island Railroad

It was late afternoon on Friday and the train was busy. There shouldn't be any problems getting Sally.

As the Huntington locomotive rolled to a stop, I rushed out the doors the moment they popped open. I went to a new pick up place. It's a police station on a street corner that looks more like a dry cleaners.

John Farley, Jr.

The location's about a 12 minute walk from the train. More like 20 minutes with Sally. It'd be easy in the good weather, but tough in the rain and snow.

The parking lot across the street from the police station was empty. I stood there waiting. I hope she's on time or we're going to miss the train.

I told Dee Dee's lawyer I'd meet her in the parking lot, not inside the station. The last time I went into the station the cop asked for my identification. Where do these cops get off? There's no need to go inside. Dee Dee just needs to give Sally to me.

I looked at my watch, and felt a shiver run through me as the sun went down. A few minutes after six o'clock. Where is she?

She's got to be on time. At the last pick up I spoke to her. She never looks at me when I talk—just stares straight ahead. I told her that if she's late, Sally and I miss the train, then Sally has to spend an hour doing nothing, at this seedy station.

She's here. Her nice, four-door car pulled into the parking lot. I walked over and waited. Dee Dee's hands rested on the steering wheel. What is she doing?

Ah, she's talking to Sally as she sat motionless in the passenger seat gazing up at her mom. I glanced at my watch. What in the hell is she doing? I went around and opened Sally's door. "Hi Sally. We have to catch a train. Let's get your things."

I reached down in front of Sally and grabbed her blue and pink backpack. "Let's go."

Dee Dee looked at Sally with a sad face. Dee Dee looked so unhappy. Mournfully, Sally mumbled, "I don't want to go."

Why in the world wouldn't she want to go?

"Sally, you have to go. It's our time together. That's why you're here right now."

Dee Dee was up to her tricks again. Anytime she wants Sally to resist me she fills her mind with sad thoughts, or schedules fun events during our time together.

When Dee Dee wants Sally to have fun, she fills her mind with happy thoughts. I have to be really excited and positive to counter this. "Sally, we're going to have so much fun. We're going to play games, see a great movie, and go see really exciting things."

I reached into the car, picked her up, and grabbed her bag. "Wave bye to Mommy," I told her. Sally waved, as I closed the door. I set her down, then slung the backpack over my shoulder. We started to walk, but Sally kept whining, "I don't wanna go."

"Wow, we are going to have so much fun." I kept enticing her with fun activities.

We crossed the street hand in hand. "Watch for the light. We get to walk when the light is green," I told her.

No train in sight yet, that's a good sign. "We have to walk faster to make the train."

What's that sound? I knew that sound. It meant Sally's shoe came untied. I stopped, released her hand, and put the backpack on the sidewalk. "Let me tie your shoe." Sally stood there and watched while I tied her shoelaces faster than a cowboy ropes a calf.

"Let's go." Minutes later we were at the station.

"There it is." I still had to buy tickets. As we crossed the tracks, I looked at my watch—still enough time.

We rushed into the train station and lined up for tickets. We're going to make it. We inched closer to the ticket window.

"Yes?" asked the man behind the glass.

"One adult and one child to Manhattan."

"Ten fifty." He slid the tickets and change to my side of the window. "Thank you."

Moments later we were seated on the train. Sally got excited about our time together. Soon, I knew she'd be glad to be with me. The train conductor came down the aisle, so I pulled out our tickets. Sally watched as he punched other people's tickets.

With hesitation, she whispered to me, "Will you ask him for the ticket after he punches it?" Leaning over as if whispering a big secret, I said, "You ask him."

"No, you ask him," she shot back.

"No, you ask," I said, playfully.

Nearly bouncing out of her seat, she replied, "No, you ask!"

"No you." I continued. "Here he comes–you ask."

"No you...please!" she said shaking with anticipation. The conductor turned to our row.

"Okay, I'll do it, but next time you do it."

"Tickets please," the conductor said, wearing his trademark hat. "Excuse me. My daughter would really like to have the ticket when you're done, if you don't mind."

Excited at the chance to make a child happy, he became animated. "She does? Well, here you go." He handed it to her as if presenting a beautiful rose. Sally smiled as if it were a a brand new toy. Just then, I noticed a police officer walking in our direction.

41

The police officer walked down the aisle as Sally tried to talk to me. All my attention was on the cop's gun, badge, and facial expression as he got closer. My arm muscles tensed as he brushed by my right side. I had no reason to believe he wanted anything from me, but at this point all cops made me tense.

The officer strode to the back of the train and then out the doors that connected one car to the next.

"Daddy—"

I sucked in air and exhaled to release the pent up tension. "Yes?" Now that my trance was broken I noticed her hands, hair, and those adorable sneakers she had on. She grounds me to what's really important, and forces me to live in the moment. Like a Zen master, she lives in the now, not tomorrow or yesterday. Unfortunately, much of my life was spent in the past and future. Before she asked me her question, I had some of my own. "So, tell me about this guy your mother is with."

"Ezel?" Sally said.

"Is that his name? He has dreadlocks?"

"Yeah. He's nice. Mom says he's a good man."

A good man? I kept my thoughts to myself, after all, I wanted her to be kind and accepting of others. On the other hand, some guy, dreadlocks or not, is living in the same house as my daughter and I'm paying child support to pay off Dee Dee's mortgage. My molars meshed together like two metal gears. "What does he do? Ah, for work."

"I dunno." She shrugged, with an innocent expression. Of course she doesn't know.

As always, it would be a long train ride. I wanted to play with her, but I kept thinking, why is this so damn hard? What sense does this make? Traveling hours and hours to be a father to this little girl and paying Dee Dee for the privilege, is wearing me out. Is this a sick joke?

The Zen master in the seat next to me broke my trance, and forced me into the present.

"Tell me a story," she said, as she brought her face closer to mine. A story? Hmm, a story? There are stories that entertain and then there are hypnotic stories that change people. If I had to tell a story I wanted it to be a life changing story. I'd have to figure it out as I went along.

"Once upon a time, there was a little girl. I told her the story of the little girls.

Sally's face became animated as I told her this hypnotic tale with dramatic intensity.

Sally mirrored my expressions. While I paused to create the finale, she interjected. "Tell me more about the little girls, Daddy!"

She listened to every syllable as intently as any hypnosis client ever did.

"Tell me that story again," she said while pressed up against me.

My brain needed a rest. "Let's thumb wrestle." Anything to make the time go by.

Soon, the train arrived at Penn Station. Hand-in-hand, we made our way through the tunnels and subways, and the streets of the city until we made it to 58th and Ninth.

"I have to go to the bathroom," she reminded me for the fourth time. We hurried past the apartment gate and into the building.

"It's time to climb the stairs to the fifth floor." I made everything into a game, a challenge, or an adventure. Having her climb the stairs was good for her leg muscles and her heart and lungs, but not her bladder. Mostly, it was good for her mind. It would strengthen her determination and self-confidence.

She'll need determination and self-confidence throughout life a lot more than she'd need the latest doll.

When I unlocked the apartment door, Sally pushed it open and called out, "Janet. We're here!" She popped out of her jacket the way a baby chick breaks out of its shell. She rushed into the living room to find her playmate.

The moment her jacket hit the floor, I kept repeating, loud enough for her to hear, "Pick it up, pick it up, pick it up..." By the fifth time, she heard me, and turned back to retrieve the jacket and place it on a chair.

The rest of the night was peaceful and the weekend went well. We were developing a routine of play, adventure, and learning. When the weekend was over everything was fine and she was delivered back to her mother safe and sound as always.

Time was going by and I didn't realize that people in my life had their own plans for me.

42

During the following week, Janet and I went to a restaurant around the corner from our place. It was an upscale Italian place on 57th and 9th Avenue with great prices.

The waiters all wore black and white uniforms. The tables were close together—a common theme in Manhattan. With space at a premium, restaurants cram as many tables and chairs together as they can. It often feels as if you're having dinner with everybody around you, but New Yorkers have developed selective attention and are able to tune out their neighbors.

A young woman showed us to our table. We were seated for less than a minute when our waiter showed up. "Welcome to Mario's. I'll be your server this evening. Would you care to start off with the wine list?"

"No thank you," I said. "We'll have the menus."

"Certainly." He handed them to us. "I'll give you some time, and come back for your orders."

We read over the entrees as the tables around us filled up. The front wall of the restaurant is a giant window that can open up to the street. Soon it was a packed house and the energy level soared.

"I went to a networking meeting today," I said.

Janet had decided on her meal, closed her menu, and gave me her attention. "The same one you went to last week, right?"

"Yeah, same one, but this week was different."

At that moment a Latino attendant put two water glasses on the table in a flash and then nearly dumped the water and ice into them. It sounded as if metal spoons were bouncing off the cups and added to the high energy of the restaurant.

I reached for the water and took a sip. "Today two girls joined."

"Girls?" Janet said.

"Well, women, young women. You know how it is. If they are younger than me they're girls. If they're older than me, they're women. By the time I'm 110 there won't be any women left in the country."

"How did it go?"

At that moment our waiter appeared. "Folks have you decided?"

"Yes. Janet?" "I'll have the farro risotto al verde with sauteed shrimp."

"Excellent. Sir?" "I'll have this ravioli here." I pointed to the menu. The waiter bent forward. "The ravioli di magro."

"Yes. That's it." The waiter scooped up the menus and dashed off.

An attendant appeared with a bread basket and two small plates. He squirted the yellow and dark colored oils onto them with the intensity of a gunslinger.

"Anyway, I was listening to these two girls, women, and how much energy they had. They were so motivated, such go-getters. They were like, 'we did this and we did that and next time we're going to do this.' The more they talked the more I felt like a worn-out loser." Janet listened sympathetically as she dragged the warm bread through the oil.

"It was then that I decided to leave the group." Janet stopped chewing for a moment.

"Why?" I sipped my water, and pulled off a bread slice out of the basket.

"I realized I couldn't keep up. I just don't have the fire. I'm not motivated, at least not as motivated as they are. Maybe I'm depressed, but whatever it is, I realized those two women are at another level. If I stayed in the group I'd just look like I couldn't produce."

"You have a lot going on. It's not easy dealing with everything you have happening." The attendant came back and splashed water into our glasses.

"I used to be motivated. I used to make things happen. The last few years have just drained my spirit." At that moment the waiter arrived with two large, fancy, white bowls filled halfway with a colorful mixture of foods.

"Here you are. Is there anything else I can get you at this time?" Janet looked content.

"Perhaps a little more bread," I said.

"Certainly."

I have ideas. I've started writing a weight loss book. The idea of starting a distance learning college is really exciting to me. But, I dunno. Janet chewed and listened.

"I had motivation to do all sorts of things, but now I feel like all my energy is used fighting these court cases. Any leftover zest is for daily work and Sally." I poked a ravioli with my fork and took a moment to read her face. "Thanks for letting me vent."

Janet lifted her water and paused before sipping. "It's difficult. What they're doing to you is absurd. Dee Dee is, I'm sorry, but that woman is—"

"I know," I interrupted. "I have to get ready to go back to the courts on the Island this week. You never know if you'll walk out the same courthouse door you walked in."

After a nice meal, we strolled up 9th Avenue for one short block. We went back to the apartment and started to settle in for the evening. Something was bothering Janet. She was spacing out a little, her eyes looked glassy.

"What is it?" I asked.

Her voice was strained. "You and I have been going out for years—five years. I'm getting...I want to know if you and I are getting married or not." Her voice shook and her eyes watered. "You have to decide, because if we aren't then I need to move on."

This was a metaphorical two by four upside the head. I saw stars. "Ah, okay, that's …I hear where you're coming from."

What? What in the world? She's forcing me to make a decision now? "Let me—I need to think. I have a lot on my mind." She really put the pressure on me. "I need to go out. I'll be back soon. We'll discuss it more."

I went to the closet, found my jacket and left. I ended up walking around in some local market on 9th Avenue. How do I make this decision? I mindlessly looked at items on the store shelves not seeing anything.

Do I love her? Yes, I mean, she's so loyal. I don't know what I'd do without her. She's paying half the rent. Backs me when the cops and courts screw me over. Sally is very attached to her. Passion is not our strong point, but...

I decided I was better off with her than without her. Having her in my life was what I wanted. I went back to the apartment and found her in the living room. Her face was tense with a mixture of anger and sadness. She stood with her arms crossed.

"I want to say something to you." She came over. Her face cast down as her eyes looked up to mine. "I want you to know that you are very important to me. Will you marry me?"

Her face lit up. Her tears started to flow as she wrapped her arms around me. "Yes!"

I sensed that it was the happiest day of her life.

43

I stood on the cold Huntington Station platform waiting for the next train to pull in. It was coming, I could see it. The old train rounded the bend. It was shaped as if out of a 1950's movie. Loud, big and as dull blue-gray as the Long Island winter sky it rolled closer. My heavy brown bag nearly dropped from my hands as I rushed to cover my ears due to the locomotive's deafening screech.

I boarded and took a front seat. Twenty minutes later, a garbled voice came over the antiquated speaker system. "Northport station, Northport."

The rickety doors rattled and shook as they opened, and then I located a taxicab. The cabbie saw me coming. "I can't take you."

He'd been waiting for someone else. The company phone number was visible on the side of the car. I figured I'd call for my own cab. The line for the pay phones was short, but the callers were long winded. As the cold air of the coming winter blew through me, I did knee bends to generate body heat. It probably looked odd, but I didn't care.

A cab pulled up after only five minutes. Great— "Radcliff?" the cabbie yelled from his window. A woman waiting near the curb approached the cab. I felt a touch of envy as she got in. My turn was coming. The point is, just getting to court was an ordeal above and beyond the hearing itself.

Ten more minutes. My cab arrived. "The courthouse please." I wanted to make conversation with the cabbie, but couldn't bear chitchat about baseball teams, rock concerts, or other drivel.

"Here we are." We pulled to the curb. This waterfront town was quiet. Everything seemed normal, but I felt tense. "Could I get a receipt please?" I passed him the fare and a modest tip. The unassuming courthouse waited across the street. Butterflies fluttered in my stomach as I walked up the steps, and into the building.

A heavyset, fifty-something man was there. He had to be a lawyer. An armed police officer stood in front of the courtroom doors. I walked toward him with my *Don't Tread On Me* attitude. The officer looked my way, then turned to the lawyer and gestured. The lawyer bent, grabbed his massive bag and took a few steps in my direction.

"You're John Farley?" The length of my pause must have surely seemed excessive.

"And you are?"

"I'm Mr. Dominick," he said quickly like an auctioneer warming up. "I'm your court appointed attorney. We have some things to go over."

My mouth hung open for a moment. "Wait a minute. I never asked for a lawyer. In fact, I don't want a lawyer in this case." He motioned to a quiet corner away from the entrance.

"Let's talk over here for a moment." Mr. Dominick led the way to a tiny table and chairs.

His expanded waistline was most likely the result of many delicious Italian dinners. With his short, dark, greased back hair he looked to be in his mid to late fifties.

"You don't have a choice in the matter any more," he said confidently, the way all authority figures tell you that your days of free will are over. "The magistrate wants me to take this case and that's it." He reached for his legal bag. I had to summon my courage again and risk not being liked.

"No. No, that's not what I want. I get to decide if I represent myself. Not that judge."

Dominick leaned in. "Listen, you've got very serious charges here...."

"Horse crap. These charges are bogus. So what if I called her 100 times. I should have called her 1,000 times. She stole my child. Do you understand that? If someone steals your child they deserve to be called every minute for the rest of their life until they return your child."

He turned away for a moment, but kept his cool. "Okay, look. You're going to have to take a plea on this case. I've talked to the assistant DA and he says he'll offer you two misdemeanors down from four."

"No. Absolutely not. For what? I am not taking—Listen… they need to drop all charges or else we go to trial."

Mr. Dominick drew a breath, shook his head and glanced down. "John, the assistant DA is not going to drop the charges."

"That's fine. Let's go to trial. Tell him that. If you're going to talk to him on my behalf, which I don't want, but if you're going to do it anyway, then tell him I want a jury trial."

Dominick seemed frustrated at my bull headedness. He got up and walked away. After he left, I felt pulled toward the front of the lobby. I stared out the glass wall into the street and the ever-darkening night.

The doors behind me opened. Night court was about to start.

"All rise." Tension filled the room. If I didn't have a lawyer representing me I'd certainly be called last. Within the first fifteen minutes I heard it.

"John Farley—" Mr. Dominick, sprang up and started speaking to the court as he motioned for me to come forward. "Your Honor, I represent Mr. Jonathan Farley…."

That's not even my correct name. Nervousness bubbled up on cue the way a geyser begins to erupt. "I object!"

The middle-aged magistrate verbally pounced on me. "DON'T speak." His forcefulness stunned me, but my desire— my need—to be heard urged me on. "I can speak. I object to this. I never agreed to this. I don't want him as my lawyer. He's incompetent. I want him dismissed."

The judge stared squarely at me and shouted. "Enough! Don't say another word." The cop took one step toward me. His weapon seemed larger than normal. My lawyer continued talking and a side bar was called between the judge, the lawyer, and the assistant DA. "Let the record show I object to this side bar." But the three conspirators ignored me.

The judge turned to the court reporter. "We're back on the record. This hearing is being continued in two months."

The lawyer had convinced the others that they should wait for the Central Islip case to conclude, but at the same time they'd drag me back to court every few months to find out what progress was being made. Before I knew it I was out the door and on the train platform.

The Northport station was quiet. The 9 p.m. train would be along soon enough. There's nothing to do at the train station except think and pace back and forth to stay warm. The wind was mild that night and the air crisp. I strolled back and forth on the empty platform.

A vision of choking the life out of that judge, and slapping some sense into the lawyer kept my mind occupied and served as my only avenue to release my pent up anger. What a bunch of crooked, conspiring cretins.

I wanted to quit, to give in. I really did, but that wasn't an option. Quitting would lead to an even worse fate. If I had the money, I could buy my freedom. I had an idea to create big money and something even better.

44

In the Hotel with Amanda

Amanda gracefully got up from the couch making sure not to let her skirt ride up her leg. She wanted to stretch so I joined her. We migrated toward several beautiful paintings on the walls. One in particular was very nice. Our conversation continued as we took in the rich colors on the canvas.

"What was your big idea?"

The question itself got me excited. Not only did I have the idea, but we actually made it happen. I became animated as I perked up. "My first idea was to create a distance learning college."

She turned to me and waited a moment as I nodded and smiled back at her. "When you say 'college' what do you mean?"

"That's funny because nearly everyone asks that when I say the word."

"You mean you were associated with a college?"

"I mean I wanted to create a real college that gives university degrees to students who graduate."

Amanda had a hard time wrapping her mind around that concept. She talked faster and eyed me askance. "But you had no real money, and most colleges are worth tens or hundreds of millions of dollars. How do you do that?"

"That's what I didn't know and set out to discover. Long story short, Janet and I created a distance learning college through the state of California. We ran it from our New York apartment and even hired professors long distance to coach students by phone and email."

Amanda crossed her arms. "Was this a scam?"

"Not at all. I wanted to teach sports psychology and fitness, but I also wanted a business that would run itself even if I was locked up unexpectedly or otherwise unable to show up on a particular day."

She uncrossed her arms and turned back to the painting. "Interesting. How did you get students?"

"We ran small advertisements in magazines. Truth be told, this was extremely difficult to do and our dreams of big money from this venture never materialized. I really wanted to succeed big, settle all the financial issues with Dee Dee and move on."

I stepped toward the couch and Amanda followed. We found our spots and got comfortable again. "What did you do instead?"

"We kept the college going, but meanwhile there was my multi-million dollar lawsuit against Suffolk County. As the late 1990's approached, that trial was getting closer, but the government still had numerous criminal charges against me, any of which could be devastating." Amanda got her computer ready.

"What happened next?"

45

Janet hung up the phone just as I called to her from the other room.

"Let's take a walk in Central Park," I said.

"How's the temperature?" she asked. I opened the coat closet. "Chilly. Better dress in layers."

Within five minutes we were at Central Park and 59th Street. I took her hand. "Let's walk up the West side. This week I have a meeting with Steve Edwards about the Suffolk County lawsuit I have another hearing in Northport, then Suffolk criminal court, and then Suffolk family court. That's four court related events."

Janet's mouth opened and her face dropped. "That's ridiculous. I'm sorry but she's...."

"It's not all her fault. I mean, the government's pushing all this."

Janet snapped back. "But Dee Dee's behind it. She could stop it."

I gazed up at the sky. The expansiveness of it felt invigorating. "You're right. She probably could stop most of it—maybe all of it."

I took in the trees and the sky and did my best to become absorbed in the moment. An unexpected flashback took me to a lifeless, cold jail cell. Within a blink of an eye I was back in Central Park. After a deep breath I mumbled to myself.

"Thank you."

"I'm just so in awe of freedom. I feel bad for anyone who has to be locked up in jail— even real criminals. Intellectually, I know they deserve punishment, but jail is—" I closed my eyes for a moment, flared my nostrils as another jail memory caused a chill through my shoulders.

Janet pulled me toward her. "Let's walk on the trails." She led me off the road and toward the grass. We headed toward the giant pond. "What's happening with Steve Edwards?"

"Soon I'll meet with him to discuss the case. We're getting closer to either a deal or a trial date." We stood on a boulder overlooking the still water. "No boaters today," I said. "It's too chilly, but the ducks are out."

Janet stared at my forehead. She took her thumbs and pressed them between my eyebrows. "Stop squinting like that. You're getting 'eleven' lines on your forehead."

"It's from constant aggravation. I feel agitated all the time. It's the endless battle."

"Hug me." She put her arms around me and her head on my chest. I hugged her, but only with my arms—not my heart. My world was growing smaller. Life was becoming all about me. My survival. My success or failure.

The pressure of court caused frustration to drip out of me the way juice runs out of a squeezed orange. The courts, with Dee Dee's help, were doing most of the squeezing. There were other life issues too. Issues I didn't dare face. Issues that were too threatening right now.

"Let's head back. I want to do some work and prepare for all these court dates."

Before I knew it, court had arrived. It was time for battle. Court never became routine anymore than a street fight does. In court, your life, liberty and fortune are always on the line.

46

At nearly 11 a.m. the elevator door opened. The crowd I was in walked penguin-style into the elevator. I filled my lungs and visualized walking out the door a free person.

My pro bono defense attorney wanted to talk to me about something. I walked into the courtroom. Ms. Mason, my attorney, was talking to what had to be a new prosecutor near the front of the courtroom.

As she turned around, I signaled to her with my hand. She recognized me and hurried over. "Ms. Mason I—"

"I need to speak with you." She led the way out down the aisle and out of the courtroom.

Mason's a thirty-something bookworm type. She's underpaid, overworked, overweight, and nowhere near as attractive as the bombshells the DA's office hires. However, she wants to help me.

We found a spot in the hallway against a wall. Mason lowered her voice. "The prosecutors said they have a tape that's very damaging to you. They plan to submit it as evidence."

I hid any emotion and kept my face as blank as I could. "And, what's on the tape?"

She swallowed and looked uncomfortable. "They said it's your voice on Ms. O'Dells's answering machine."

"So? I probably called to see my daughter." Mason made a quick check over her shoulder probably to make sure we weren't being overheard.

"Mr. Farley, they said you made threatening statements."

"Maybe I did. I don't know. I want to hear the tape. Wouldn't any parent make threatening statements if their child had been kidnapped and the police and courts were all in on it?"

Mason glanced at her notes for a split second. Her gaze crept up my torso until our eyes met. I had the sense that she was now a lot less certain about me and our case. Perhaps an invisible noose was being slipped around my neck. "I have to speak with the judge about this," she said. "I'll let you know what the outcome is."

That was it. I left the courthouse for the city. I'd be back out to Long Island before I knew it.

Tuesday: Northport Courthouse

Mr. Dominick arrived minutes before the court hearing was to begin. He walked in the door and made eye contact with me. I'd already been waiting twenty minutes. He gripped his miniature filing cabinet, otherwise known as a briefcase, and pulled the toothpick from his mouth when he saw me.

I met him halfway—no handshake needed. "Mr. Dominick, what's happening today, please?" Dominick set his briefcase down. "Has anything progressed in Central Islip?"

I gave him a stern look. "No, and it shouldn't matter."

Dominick started to pick up his heavy attaché case. "I'll go talk to the assistant DA. Wait here."

Before Dominick could leave, I blurted out. "Tell him you want the case dropped."

Dominick released the case handle and straightened himself. "I'm not telling him that. I told you, they're not dropping the case."

"First of all, never say no for the other guy. Force him say no to your proposal—he might just accept it. You work for me and my interests. This case is complete crap and the judge is blocking me from my right to represent myself. Tell him you want to quit or that I'm firing you."

The lawyer let out a sigh. "John, I'm your last hope. The judge isn't gonna dismiss me. You're stuck with me, pal."

"This is complete... You're supposed to protect my rights not the government's interests. I'm telling you to tell the assistant DA to drop the case." This time he bent down and grabbed his briefcase. "I'm not doing that."

"Then let's go to trial." I said before he turned. Mr. Dominick noticed the line of people against the wall waiting for the assistant DA.

"They won't give you a trial until the Central Islip case is resolved."

"Why in the world am I coming back here all the time if this court's waiting for the other court. You mean to say this court is afraid to make a decision?"

"Wait here." He walked toward the front of the line. That night's court hearing would be like all the others, ending with another court date a couple months out.

Seasons at the Northport train station came and went, and so did I, every other month, one season after the next.

One time while waiting on the train platform the memory of visiting my mom in upstate New York came to me. I grew up poorer than I realized. At this particular point in life I wanted to know about her family—my family. She never spoke about her father and rarely, if ever volunteered information about her parents. My ancestors were mostly a mystery to me.

On this particular visit, the two of us sat in the dining room. We talked about various things, but the conversation was dull. Mom wore a thin, light blue sweater because she was often cold. It was buttoned at the top and draped around her shoulders like a cape. Her elbows gently stretched across the table where she sat lost in thought. A large, framed photo of Mary holding baby Jesus was centered high on the wall above the table. I knew it gave her hope and comfort, and perhaps companionship.

Mom sat still with her hands surrounding the outside of a three quarters full beer bottle. The fingertips of both hands gently touched it. On this day I saw my mother differently than I had in the past. I saw a woman in her mid-seventies who'd been through a lifetime of disappointments and struggles.

She appreciated having company over and receiving phone calls from friends and family. Any human contact was greeted with joy and excitement, but also a hint of desperation that said, "stay." I could see the despair and loneliness in her eyes and I could hear it when she'd mumble to herself.

Life had been tough for her as the last of nine Irish-American children who'd grown-up poor during The Great Depression. To top it off, she perhaps felt guilty about the choices she'd made in life—for having me out of wedlock and never telling me until I was 25 and only when I pressed her for answers.

We rarely had a deep conversation—perhaps never. There just wasn't much to talk about. Our interactions were short Q & A style mostly with an occasional story here and there. At this point in my life, I wanted to know about my family, where I'd come from and who I was. With Mom getting up in years I figured I'd better ask her while she still had the memory to tell me.

"Mom, I remember my grandmother a little bit, but that's all. Tell me about your father." Mom's eyes opened wide as an upside-down smile flashed across her face followed by a shrug of her shoulders. She stared ahead at the empty wall.

"What's to tell? My father went to work as he did every day. He was always working hard. He waited at the train station and before the train pulled into the station he had a heart attack and died. Right there on the platform."

Mom resumed her posture and stared ahead at the wall. Her fingertips had started to lightly tap the bottle. I could almost see the images breach into her consciousness for the first time in a long while. She now fully grasped the beer bottle. She lifted it and paused—a slight hesitation in front of her mouth before bringing the bottle to her lips.

That magic elixir, her friend, would wash away that memory as I'm sure it had for decades. I watched and listened with much more compassion than I ever had when I was younger. I started to make connections to my own life. Mom had lost her father at an early age and her mom, my grandmother, had nine children to raise on her own.

The memory faded as a loud horn brought me back to the present. The light of the locomotive glowed off in the distance. I felt some mental relief as a cold wind whipped up. Steve Edwards wanted to meet with me about our case against the government. I hoped he had good news.

"John, let's go over the facts again. Describe what happened when the Suffolk County deputies had you in custody—the time they beat you."

I leaned forward on the couch in Edward's office. I was looking toward the floor when the images came back to me. "They brought me and the other prisoners into the facility. There were fluorescent lights hanging down. The hallway was one long corridor of cement. We turned to face the wall when a deputy yelled out for us to take off our shoes and socks and lift up one foot at a time."

Edwards sat in his big leather chair taking notes. "What else?"

"They put me into a cell with other guys. The cell had white walls with two metal benches running front to back. Across from the cell, about 20 feet away, was a command center with glass all the way around it."

Edwards stopped writing. "John, how is it that you remember so many details? I find it very unusual for someone to recall so many details in a situation like this."

He'd commented on this before, but seemed fascinated enough to mention it again. "It would be difficult if it had only happened once, but these deputies brought me to this facility five or six times. Each time I made it a goal to remember the surroundings."

"But to remember so much—"

"If you'd been in the same place multiple times and deliberately focused on remembering the details of the place, you'd be able to recall details too, I'm sure of it."

"Let's look at the photos again." He handed me one of the snapshots.

"This is the bruise and scrape on my shoulder from getting slammed into the jail cell bars." He handed me the next one. "This photo here is of my lip after they smashed me down on the metal cot." I took the next two from him. "This one's the bruise on my hand with cuts."

"That was from the roller?" Edwards asked.

"Yeah, when they held up my hand and hammered it with the ink roller. This one's my abdomen. It's when they punched me repeatedly, full force, while my hands were cuffed behind my back, legs shackled and forced to kneel on a metal bench."

Edwards looked at me in surprise. "God, John, they did this to you?"

I looked back at him with a polite smile. It had been years since we'd gone over these details, so likely Edwards needed a refresher. "That's why I am here. They did this to me and it's wrong."

"Okay, could you recognize these sheriffs deputies if you saw them?"

I thought for a moment. "Some of them. I could certainly recognize the ones who hit and punched me. If you showed me some photos, I could have a pretty good idea. I can describe some of them right now."

Edwards looked at me while he thought. "It's been a long time since this happened. What's going on with the cases against you in Suffolk County?"

"They're still pending. They keep dragging me out to Long Island month after month. It's either criminal court or family court in Central Islip, or Northport or Manhattan family court. I have more court cases than most lawyers."

Edwards nodded in amusement. "It would be a lot better to hold off on those cases until our case goes to trial."

"I've tried to get them to do something, but they won't. They keep postponing. What about Suffolk County settling?"

Edwards leaned back in his chair. "No, they won't settle. It's going to go to trial most likely, but it takes a long time to get there. I'll let you know when the court responds to my latest motion." Steve got up, and I followed.

"Thanks for the meeting, Steve." We shook hands as he showed me out. By the time I'd reached the sidewalk I remembered something important.

47

I stepped cautiously toward the ringing phone. The caller ID came up "private." It could be the sheriffs. I'd noticed a coincidence between answering calls from private numbers and being raided by cops less than 30 minutes later. I waited patiently to see if there was a message. I stood completely still and barely breathing—an automatic reaction left over from previous police raids.

Occasional loud street noises often spooked me. When alone, I'd often keep the television low and the stereo off. Any sound coming from the apartment could tip off the cops that I was inside. In my case, the line between cautious and paranoid has blurred.

The phone message machine indicated it was Jerry my business lawyer. "John. Jerry, give me a call when you have a moment." I exhaled a big sigh of relieve and then dialed his number. "Jerry. It's John, returning your call."

"John!" he said enthusiastically, before quickly lowering his volume.

"How's business?" I smiled into the phone. "It's good, but it could be better."

"Welcome to the world of business." Again, he lowered his tone. "How is Janet doing?"

"She's very well. Thank you for asking." Jerry always has a nice word.

"She's fabulous," he continued. "I mean she's really a great person." Everyone I know agrees. Janet's a good one.

"I have a bookkeeper you can use. She's excellent. I've known her for years. Her name's Susan."

I jotted down her name and number into my day planner. "Remember that book I bought? It talks all about the federal income tax—"

Jerry interrupted with a raised voice. "Forget it. These guys make great arguments, but they all go to jail." His Brooklyn-Italian accent was clear, but just above a whisper. "Stay out of trouble."

"Well, hear me out for just a moment," I said, with a sharp inflection. "If they make great arguments, why are they going to jail? I mean, this guy's points really makes sense to me. If the government has the right to tax a person's labor at 50% or 20%—or even only 1%—what would stop them from taxing at 99% or 100%?"

Jerry jumped in. "That's the law! There are ways to reduce taxable income."

"I know, but if I have a right to my property, and if my labor is my property, as the Supreme Court has ruled, and if the fruit of my labor is my property, than how can the government take my property before I even receive it?"

"Stay away from tax protesters. Don't get caught up in that stuff," he almost whispered. "Remember, that's how they got Al Capone. Not murder. Tax evasion."

I shook my head and sighed. "It's very strange to me. There are so many inconsistencies. The tax law should be void for vagueness, shouldn't it?" I rushed to make my point. "The fact that it's called the tax code is odd. Aren't they telling us by the name that it's written in a secret code only some people understand?"

"John," he said with a long pause. "I have to go. You're a great guy. Just stay away from tax protesters."

"Alright Jerry. I'll talk to you later." As we hung up, I walked to my bookshelf. I'd collected a few hard-to-find books on the subject of the income tax from the tax honesty movement, or tax protesters, as they're known.

Why would the tax code be thousands and thousands of pages long while some countries fit their form on a postcard? Something's out of place here.

The front doorknob jiggled. I felt my eyes open wider for a moment and my breath stopped until the door opened.

"Hi," Janet said from the hallway.

"Hi," I called out.

She walked in and stood watching me as I hunched over the pile of books. "What are you reading?"

"This is fascinating information about the income tax. Remember that video that was given to me years ago? I'm starting to make the connections."

"Okay." She had her handbag over her shoulder and looked very metropolitan in her dark colored, pressed pants.

I grabbed a book from the stack as if I'd discovered a secret treasure map. "See this?" She peeked at the cover as she slipped off her shoes.

"This author went to jail for tax evasion, yet afterwards he still wrote this book, and claims he was right, and the government convicted him unfairly."

Janet started changing her shirt and ducked into the spare bathroom. "Let me make some tea," she said, still catching her breath from the five flights of stairs. I started scribbling concepts from the book onto my notepad.

Perhaps it was ten minutes later when Janet came back with her tea. She sprawled across the couch and caressed the steaming teacup with both hands. She seemed peaceful. Her hands wrapped around the cup and absorbed the warmth while a pleasant aroma filled the room.

I spoke and she sipped. "You and I talked about this before, but it's on my mind more than ever. On the one hand, this guy went to jail. On the other hand, I've experienced local government corruption. Perhaps he's right and they're wrong. Maybe there's something to this."

John Farley, Jr.

Janet slipped in a question in between sips. "What's this guy saying again?"

"He says the federal income tax is voluntary—that the IRS even admits the tax system is based on voluntary compliance. He's saying that a person just has to stop volunteering."

"How do you do that?" She lowered the cup to her lap, and crossed her legs underneath herself. I bookmarked the page and closed it. "He says you stop filing the 1040 form."

Janet set her cup on the table in front of the couch. "That's it? Just stop filing?"

I covered my mouth with my hand to reflect. "That's what's confusing. If you don't file, then you can be charged with failure to file an income tax form. That's what he got charged with and was found guilty of.

"So, he changed his approach and now claims you can file a form, but put all zeros in it stating that you have no income received. The problem with that approach, if you ask me, is that by signing and filing the form, the government can charge you with filing a false tax return or even tax evasion."

Janet looked at me the way she does when she wants attention. "Come snuggle with me."

My train of thought was interrupted, but I got up and sat next to her. We snuggled for a few minutes until I thought she'd had enough. Despite the pout on her face, I got up and went back to reading. "One argument he makes is about the fourth amendment to the US constitution." Janet recovered and decided to tidy up the room.

"I'm listening. What's the fourth amendment?"

"It says no searches or seizures without a warrant. It specifically says the people, that's us, are to be secure in their persons, houses, papers and effects. This guy says that by *papers* they're talking about personal financial records."

Excited, I held up the book even though the print was too small for her to see it from ten feet away. "But this is really interesting. He says the Fifth Amendment is key. No person…

shall be compelled in any criminal case to be a witness against himself…without due process of law."

Janet had made her way to the computer desk. "Yeah? But if this were true, I mean, there are thousands of lawyers who would have figured this out by now, right? How could this be correct? Are all the lawyers and law schools, and congressman in on it?"

Janet bit her lip as she waited for my response. I turned toward the brick wall above the fireplace to collect my thoughts.

"When I go to court and they tell me to fill out financial information for child support, I don't fill it out. Everyone else does, but I don't, because they can't make me. They can't force me to give over my financial records. They have to coerce me or trick me into believing that I have to confess to them. Everyone I've seen falls for this, but I haven't."

Janet turned around. "Oh," she said as she reached into her bag. "You have a letter here from the court. Sorry, I forgot."

She walked over with the letter in her outstretched hand. I reluctantly ripped it open and read it. "It's a reminder. The Manhattan family court date is coming up."

48

"All rise." We came to our feet as Judge Ruth Zuckerman walked out and glanced around. She appeared calm, in a good mood or more likely, a cover for how she really felt.

The court isn't supposed to move itself, that is, take action on its own, so I rushed to start the process. "Judge, this is a continuation because Ms. O'Dell violated the visitation order. She continues to try to have me arrested. I've asked for modifications to the order."

O'Dell's lawyer was already on his feet, ready to pounce. "Your Honor, we believe there's an arrest warrant for Mr. Farley, we ask the court to contact the Suffolk County law enforcement…"

No. I was afraid this could happen. No. They're cheating. My heart raced to the point of breathlessness. "See." I shouted as I reached my hand toward the judge. "THERE."

The words flew out of my mouth faster than I could think them. "DON'T let them arrest me. I came here in good faith to argue my case. You can't do this in a courtroom!"

Her lawyer shouted. "JUDGE."

I shouted over him. "DON'T let them do this. No, no. I'm here in good faith. You can't let them take me in a courtroom. This is what I've been saying. She's doin' it right NOW."

The judge's face looked panicked as she held out her hands. "Wait! Everyone hold on." Tensions rose. My heart felt ready to explode.

The judge looked shaken by the unexpected commotion. "I don't have an arrest warrant here…."

The lawyer interrupted, "But Your Honor, we can…"

"NO! DON'T LET'EM TAKE ME."

John Farley, Jr.

The judge stretched out her hands to quiet the insurrection as she spoke to the lawyer. I kept repeating my pleas for freedom while the judge spoke legalese to the lawyer. "This court is not here to find warrants. This case will be heard..."

I was wired. Images of sheriffs barging in or waiting outside to and take me away to a modern dungeon distracted me from my purpose.

"Let's get on with this case," the judge demanded.

I composed myself as fast as possible while I flipped through my folder to buy time. I tried to speak coherently as my blood pressure lowered. "Your Honor, previously in this matter, I presented the dates when Ms. O'Dell frustrated my ability to be with my daughter. The court should find her in contempt of court again for violating the order of visitation. Additionally, I've asked for modifications to the visitation order."

The lawyer was on his feet before I finished. "Your Honor, my client made the child available to Mr. Farley at all appropriate times. Mr. Farley simply didn't show up for visitation. We ask that visitation be changed to supervised visitation only."

"I object. This is outrageous. The only reason I missed visitation was because of Dee Dee O'Dell calling the police saying I violated her order of protection. She needs to be punished for this."

Evidence was presented to the judge from both sides and the clock ticked.

Scanning the papers on her desk with a scowl, the judge began, "The court will take a short recess before delivering the verdict."

We left the courtroom for the waiting area filled with one hundred people. My eyes darted from corner to corner as I checked for cops. I watched the lawyer's body language as he pulled out his cell phone to make a call.

The time seemed to creep by slower than a snake after a big meal. I kept thinking about the incredible amount of life I'd spent in courthouses. By now, years had gone by. Am I insane? Should I just flee the country? No, I can't leave Sally.

The court officer opened the door and motioned to us. Moments later we were in the courtroom with the judge seated and ready. The officer called out, "The parties will remember that they're still under oath."

The judge started out with the technical issues of the case and then announced what I'd waited for. "The court finds, based on the evidence and the testimony, that Ms. O'Dell is not in violation of the visitation order."

Stunned, as if the wind were knocked out of me, I sat motionless.

"The court has granted changes to the location for pick up and has granted Mr. Farley one week of summer vacation with the child."

Moments later it was over. The judge had saved Dee Dee and given me something in return. I don't remember leaving the building, but somehow I was on my way home.

The hard red, orange, and yellow subway car seats felt familiar. The crowded, underground tunnels were one of the few places I felt safe. Once again, Dee Dee has been allowed to violate my rights, Sally's rights, and if that weren't enough, she wants me jailed.

The trial against the deputies was about to happen. Steve and I needed to prepare our case against the county before Suffolk criminal court prosecuted me. If the criminal court convicted me of anything it would hurt my chances against the county. I've got to outlast them, but now the clock is running out.

49

"Good luck. Get those jerks." Janet gave me a hug and a kiss.

I straightened my tie. "Do I look good?"

Janet fixed my jacket and gave it a wipe with her hand. "Yes, you do." I paced back and forth. The wooden floor creaked with each step.

Janet flashed me a smile as she left for work. "I'll see you tonight."

"Okay." I stopped to watch her leave. As the door closed I faced the windows at the end of the hall. It's nearly time. I've got to make this happen.

The phone rang. Steve Edwards showed up on caller ID. "JOHN. I'M DOWN IN FRONT OF YOUR APARTMENT IN MY CAR. PLEASE COME DOWN. I'M DOUBLE PARKED."

"I'll be right down," I said and hung up.

I lifted my arms overhead and took a deep breath. Yes. I'm doing this. Moments later I was headed out to Long Island. Small talk was kept to a minimum. Years of courts and cops had conditioned me to be comfortable with silence.

After more than an hour, we arrived in the parking lot. My life and liberty we're not in jeopardy, yet I felt nervous. It'd been four long years and this was the moment of truth. Edwards and I sat in silent preparation as he turned off the engine.

He turned to me. "Are you ready to do this?"

"I'm—I'm ready. You have to do more than me. Are you ready?"

"Yeah, let's go. Let me grab things from the trunk."

I waited next to the car, felt the crisp air and looked at the courthouse. It was incredibly quiet and had as much foot traffic as a vacant building.

We entered, passed security and found the large federal courtroom, the largest courtroom I'd ever been in. The pool of jury members sat waiting for something to happen. Edwards and I took our places at the table as he prepared to speak with the judge.

The female attorney for the county was there, as wired as usual. Edwards seemed passive, intimidated perhaps, but if so, he hid it well.

The judge sat in a giant leather chair high above the floor's action. His arms occasionally rested on the massive wooden desk that stretched across half the room. Behind him, to his left, was an armed officer serving as a reminder that should words be insufficient there's always force. This federal judge sat as a king on his throne. His black robe, a traditional symbol of an ancient God, covered him from the neck down. His white head of hair, and deep voice magnified his deity status. Within his jurisdiction, his zone of power, he is God, and he most certainly knows it.

The jury sat quietly, stealing glances in my direction. Yes, it's me, the guy claiming to have been brutalized illegally. I felt that the jury was judging me at that moment. Two deputy sheriffs sat at a table. One deputy was Smith, but the other one, a big, tough, intimidating guy with a mustache and a scowl, I didn't recognize.

Edwards stood at our table and reviewed paperwork while the judge and the red haired county lawyer discussed something.

"Steve, where are the other deputies? Where are the guys who beat me?"

Edwards seemed preoccupied and had no answer for the missing deputies. Next it was time to pick the jury. The lawyers asked questions of each person during voir dire or the process of finding out which jurors should be tossed from the jury pool.

Edwards came over to me, leaned down and whispered. "What do you think about the jurors?"

He's asking me my opinion? He must trust my judgment, but I'm not a lawyer. I'd noticed a middle-aged woman who looked at me with empathy. I had a sense she would be fair, even sympathetic to my cause.

"Keep the woman close to us here in the blue." Edwards looked toward the one in question and went back in front of the jury. Moments later, Edwards instructed the judge to dismiss that same woman. My mouth hung open. What? What did he just do?

I sat wide eyed, and stunned. The woman looked over at me with a sad expression on her face as she stood up in the juror's box and made her way out. Did she think I told Edwards to reject her? I can't believe he did that.

Edwards walked over to our table. "Why did you let her go? She was the one I told you to keep."

He didn't answer, but grabbed paperwork from his folder and walked away to interact with the judge and the county's lawyer. Oh no. I can't believe he made that mistake. What happened? It's too late. I had to shake it off and keep up with the action. After some time had elapsed, the jury was chosen. The trial was on.

50

Much time had elapsed in the federal courtroom. The newly selected jurors, all well-dressed white men and women from their thirties to fifties, had re-entered and filed into the jury box. This case wasn't only me against the cops. It was New York City against Suffolk County Long Island. I was the outsider here.

The judged seemed so comfortable high up on his bench that it made me nervous. Does he know something special I don't know?

He gave instructions to the lawyers loud enough for everyone to hear. "If you have an objection, don't say anything. Don't speak. I'll address the objection."

What? That doesn't make any sense. If a lawyer doesn't object, then is the objection even on the record? The jury won't know that there was anything in question? This is already very strange.

Deputy Smith was called by the county's lawyer. He carefully walked to the stand wearing his dark police uniform. She spoke to him with reverence. "Deputy Smith, what happened when you were in John Farley's apartment on the day in question?"

The jury watched while the judge sat up above the action the way a wise owl scouts out the forest floor. Smith stayed completely calm and collected. Each word seemed carefully delivered, as in a B movie. "Mr. Farley" he paused, "I remember it very well. He was sitting in a chair in his bedroom while myself and my partner were standing just inside the doorway. He put his hands together like this," Smith placed the fingertips of both hands together, "and held them in front of his chest, like this."

Smith pressed the tips of all fingers together into prayer-like steeple. The lawyer kept her focus on the officer while speaking loud enough to reach the jurors.

"Then what happened, Deputy Smith?"

"I noticed he had weapons." The lawyer turned toward the jury.

"What kind of weapons?"

"He had a sword in the closet."

Edwards stood up and started to speak when the judge cut him off. "Ah, no objections spoken aloud. Overruled."

The redhead continued. "How did you feel at that point?"

"Concerned. I didn't know what he was going to do next."

The lawyer continued her questions all the while painting a picture of the officers being in danger and concerned for their safety and of me being capable of violence.

When there was a break in the action the judge called for a recess. Edwards and I sat at our table. I looked around the room expecting to see other deputies, the ones this trial was supposed to be about.

"Where are the guys who beat me up? Why aren't they here? Why am I having a trial against people who aren't even here?" Whatever Edwards said was unintelligible to me.

It was our turn. Edwards got up. "Your Honor, I call John Farley to the stand." As Edwards directed the action, I described how the guards grabbed me in the Riverhead jail and what was done in Central Islip. It was an intense few minutes of testimony.

This was the heart of our position. There had been no justification for that vicious attack. Edwards made our case. The county lawyer came to her feet undaunted, perhaps a little arrogant. It was time for my cross-examination. "Mr. Farley," she said with a hint of scorn. "Is this your mug shot?"

Edwards' didn't even attempt to object to the phrase, mug shot. I gave a reluctant, "Yes."

"Do you have a sword in your apartment?"

"Yes." With this question I came to life. "It's a replica, not sharp of course, but I use it for practice."

"You have other weapons in your apartment, don't you?"

"Yes." I gave more details in an almost friendly manner. She soon brought up the case in Central Islip criminal court and Northport too.

"Aren't you charged with assault and battery and violating an order of protection seven times!"

I looked to Edwards, but he couldn't help me now. I was desperate for the right words. Edwards didn't prepare me for this.

"So you're complaining about being manhandled, is that what this is all about?" she growled. A sarcastic smile spread across her face as she glanced at papers in her hand. Then she mocked me with an insulting smirk.

"Aren't you asking this jury to award you twenty million dollars?"

She made the sum seem outrageous. But my lawyer agreed that we should ask for that amount. I back peddled as a sense of unworthiness spread through me. She continued her insults. I could see where this was going.

"You're just a cry baby aren't you?"

That did it. "I'm not a cry baby. What they did to me was wrong. You don't do that to somebody. You don't do that to somebody!" I yelled.

"Hey!" the judge reprimanded. "You stop that!" The judge was now yelling at me, the one attacked. My lawyer sat helpless. I didn't want the jury to turn on me, so I repented.

"I'm sorry." I sounded like a teen whose father had scolded him. I apologized for defending myself, like a rape victim who apologized for wearing tight clothing.

"No further questions, Your Honor."

I slinked off the stand. I felt as though I'd been at the carnival dunk tank. I was the guy poised on the seat high above the water. The lawyer kept throwing balls at the target until she hit. The seat collapsed and I got dunked.

Back at our table, Edwards turned to me and whispered. "John. When she asked about the sword, ah, I wish you hadn't enjoyed the question so much."

"I didn't want them to think I was hiding something."

Edwards cross-examined Smith, but it was a waste of time. Smith wasn't there in Central Islip, only Riverhead. The county lawyer made her case all about the justification of those thugs beating me to get my fingerprints. She claimed that my argument, that the fourth amendment to the U.S. Constitution means my fingerprints are my property and therefore, I don't have to give them up, was wrong. She told the jury the corrections officers in Riverhead could "manhandle" me to get my fingerprints.

But what about the Central Islip beating? Where the hell are those officers?

This case is simple. I was wrongly, viciously attacked for no lawful reason. Fingerprints or not, you can't beat the hell out of a someone who can't defend himself because you don't like him. That's all there is to it.

The jury went out of the courtroom to deliberate. Everyone else sat and waited in silence. In less than an hour, the bailiff said something to the judge. The judge's headed lifted slightly upon hearing the news and turned to the rest of us.

"Alright. The jury is ready to deliver the verdict."

51

Edwards leaned in. "That's not a good sign."

Maybe it's not a good sign normally, but this time it is. The facts were simple a man was beaten by cops for no reason. Even if the jury thought the cops were justified for the fingerprints, it's impossible to justify the torturous cell beating.

All of us, except the judge, stood as the jurors entered the courtroom. The judge addressed the foreman, a tall, fit sharply dressed man in his late thirties. "Have you reached a verdict?"

Time slowed and I felt on edge. "We have. Your Honor, we, the jury find the defendants Not Guilty...."

Not another sound echoed through the room. My mind went blank and my breath stopped. I couldn't believe what I'd just heard. What? No. Were these people not listening? Couldn't they detect the truth? Where were the scumbag, pieces of dog dung that beat me up. I felt numb and as if twelve strangers had looked me in the eye and said, "We don't believe it, John."

The jury left the courtroom. Moments later the cops walked past our table with their shoulders back and more spring in their step then they had earlier in the day.

We made it to Edward's car when I saw the redheaded lawyer interviewing some of the jury members. She was all smiles, even chuckling. She reminded me of the Manhattan prostitutes I'd witnessed talking to passersby on 57th and 6th— whatever it takes to get the money.

The deputies were standing near her celebrating their rigged victory. I waited for Edwards to unlock the car door. My mouth hung open while I peered over at the victors the way one looks pale faced at a failed exam paper you knew you'd aced.

Once on the highway, I wanted to cry, but felt too deflated to muster up tears. Four years I'd waited for this moment. Much the way an Olympian waits four years for a shot at making history, but then loses to a cheating opponent. They get the gold and you leave with nothing.

Edwards looked straight at the road with a faint grin on his face. He seemed fine. "YOU HAD YOUR DAY IN COURT. THAT'S WHAT THE SYSTEM IS ALL ABOUT."

I could not believe my ears. Did he really believe that? We lost. We lost for a half dozen reasons, but we lost. A famous sports quote came to mind. Show me a good loser and I'll show you a loser.

I looked at him for a moment before doing a 180 to mindlessly gaze out the window and collect my thoughts. I bowed my head toward my feet before I got the words out.

"You don't understand. This means that there's nothing to stop these cops. They have proven that they can do anything they want and get away with it. They can even kill me or anyone else and there's no one to stop them."

A chill shot through my body. I hadn't felt a fear this intense since the 1995 beatings. This was "price on your head" type fear. The jury had just supported a street gang for torturing an innocent person.

The late afternoon trip to Manhattan felt longer and more uncomfortable than the morning ride. I wanted to throw up, shake sense into Edwards and scream out the window all that the same time, but instead I sat in shock, oblivious to everything except my own thoughts.

Edwards seemed detached and unconcerned or perhaps he didn't want to share his own disappointment with me. Didn't he have a lot riding on this case? He only got paid if he won, but we lost. If we had such a strong case and his salary was based on the outcome, then why wasn't he either better prepared or as upset as me?

As the car pulled up to my apartment, I struggled for what to say. I reached for the door handle and found it difficult to hold my gaze at my lawyer. The words, "I appreciate the effort," tasted bitter as they left my lips. Certainly he detected my dejection.

"I'll be in touch," he said. "There may be some papers for you to sign, you know, to wrap things up."

I nodded out of courtesy. "Sure, just let me know. Okay, thanks. Take care." I shut the door.

The apartment lights were off and the living room quiet. My mind raced as I talked out loud to myself. Four years. I struggled to get this case to court over four years. Now it's over, and I lost.

Let me get this straight. I get beat up by a gang of thugs with badges—have my visitation rights with my daughter violated over and over again by a ruthless mother and I pay her for the privilege? What the hell is this? Am I in a parallel universe where logic and morals are suspended?

Within two hours, Janet came home. As she walked through the door, I could hardly marshal the courage to tell her, but she could read it on my face. After her initial shock, we sat in the living room.

"It's unbelievable," she said, as dismayed as me. "I'll keep fighting the criminal court cases. I'll take Dee Dee back to family court if she violates the visitation order again. I'll call Ernest, and talk to him about an appeal. Edwards won't do the work for an appeal, lawyers want huge fees for appeals."

Janet was getting angrier each moment, an unnatural state for her. She had nothing good to say about any of the actors behind this drama, including Dee Dee.

"I know, but it's not all her doing at this point. The government is out of control."

Janet relieved her mounting tension by busily organizing the knickknacks in the living room. "She's behind it. She could've ended all of this and she doesn't want to. She wants you in jail and out of Sally's life forever." I weighed her words carefully.

It's an easy answer, but I'm Sally's dad. Having me out of Sally's life is just plain wrong.

"I'll contact Ernest. He'll create a plan with me to get justice."

52

The buzzer rang. "Hello?" Only the distant sounds of cars echoed in the background.

"Hello?" I held the button a little longer.

"Yeah."

It was him, Ernest. He'd traveled down from the Bronx to meet with me. Minutes later I opened my front door as he rounded the stairway corner with great effort.

"Water, Ernest?" "Please." He removed his fedora hat and wiped perspiration from his brow with a white hanky. "It's hot out there," he said with his characteristic chuckle.

I pulled out a chair at the kitchen table so he could rest his bones. "Have a seat. It's hot and you're wearing that tweed sport coat." I poured a large glass of water from a jug and was eager to get to work on the appeal, but didn't want to rush Ernest before he had a chance to catch his breath.

He drank the water in gulps while I riffled through a thick folder of court papers to find documents that Steve Edwards had given me. "I wanna appeal this case."

"What case are we talking about?" he asked, in his black, Bronx accent with a pinch of southern drawl thrown in. He and I had discussed this on the phone. Oh, I forgot, he helps lots of folks and probably doesn't remember the details.

"The case against the county for beating the hell out of me."

"Let me see the papers you got there," he said.

I pushed the documents across the table, but before he laid eyes on them, he wanted to tell me something. "You see, you have to know what the law is in order to properly sue them."

I waited for the moral of the story and shot him a grin. "That's why you're here, to help me with the legal stuff."

"Let's see," he said, as he checked things over. I waited and waited until soon, without realizing it, I was daydreaming for who knows how long. When I snapped out of my trance I glanced over and saw Ernest's head bobbing. Then, within an instant, "Zzzzz." Ernest had fallen asleep at the table with papers still in his hand.

Is he really asleep? Did he have a stroke? "Ernest, are you— are you alright?" His eyelids fluttered open and in a drowsy tone he answered, "Yeah, ah, I'm just reading this over." It bordered on funny. He continued as if nothing happened, but then moments later, "Zzzzzzz." I waited a little longer this time expecting him to wake up. Does he have narcolepsy?

I hesitated, but he stayed asleep.

"Ernest." This time his eyelids shot open the way a window shade shoots up when it's pulled and released. He stared at the page without letting on to his cat nap. "Ernest, you need to get more sleep. Perhaps you're working too hard?"

He sat up a little straighter as he continued looking at the documents. "I'm fine. Just reading these papers."

"Let me ask you," I said to him, "what is the procedure for this?"

"You're going to have to file the document I write up for you," he told me.

"File it where?" "In the appeals court in Brooklyn." I nibbled at my bottom lip. "Is this something I can pay you to file for me?"

"No, you have to go there and file it yourself. You only have a limited about of time to get it in, and then you'll have to go there again with more documents before time runs out."

I leaned in and across the table. "I could have a problem. The deputies may, that is, they might, I don't know for sure, they may have a warrant waiting for me right now."

Ernest looked surprised. "For what?"

"I don't know anymore. There's been so many. I think it was a time I called Dee Dee because the trains were running behind schedule."

Ernest's raised his eyebrows along with his voice. "So? How does that get you an arrest warrant?"

"Remember, she has an order of protection." "Still? he said with a surprised look on his face. "How long has she had that thing?"

I let out a sigh along with a forced laugh as the absurdity registered. "Four years or so. But anyway, I can't call her for any reason or she calls the police. Then the deputies get their jollies from putting me in jail."

Ernest bowed and shook his head. "Jeez, that's—okay then. Let me get this done for you, and you take it to the court." Our time was up and in unison we pushed our chairs out from the table. I pulled cash out of my pocket and gave it to him—$25. That was his price, and I trusted him as much or more than the lawyers.

"We'll do this one step at a time." He grabbed his hat with one hand and a gulp of water with the other. Within a few weeks he sent over the documents, and I was ready for court.

***

The Brooklyn subway was one I'd never been on. When I neared the courthouse I checked around outside, but I saw nothing suspicious. No cars or people were on the street or sidewalk. The place was quiet.

I walked up the massive white stone stairs that looked to be half a block long and higher than gymnasium bleachers. An eerie silence enveloped me the moment I entered the building's massive dome shaped entryway.

On the left side was the door to the office I needed. Inside, a male clerk was working behind a desk that stretched from wall to wall and separated us. I asked him to file my documents and within a few minutes I was on my way out.

Mission accomplished. The whole process was time consuming, but straight forward. Hope was rising in me again. Only one more step to complete.

53

"Heeello," Ernest said, as he answered his phone. I'd filed the notice of appeal, but now had to file the appeal itself.

"Ernest, it's John. Do you have the appeal documents done? I'm running out of time to file at the Brooklyn courthouse."

"Yes, they're done," he said, in his characteristic tone. "I told you I'd have it done for ya and it's done…" He trailed off with a chuckle.

"And I'll see you tomorrow." Whether it's memory loss, or selective memory, Ernest didn't always show up as expected. "But the day after tomorrow is the last day I can file or I automatically lose. I have to have it no later than tomorrow afternoon," I told him.

"I'll see you tomorrow at 3pm," he said.

"Great. I'll see you here tomorrow. Thank you, I appreciate it."

The next day, Ernest arrived with the legal documents and stayed long enough to drink a big glass of water and catch his breath. "Here you go. File these." He put the papers on the table as he wiped perspiration from his dark brow, "And you'll be set. That's $25."

I pulled cash from my pocket and handed it over. Ernest reached for the greenbacks and in one fluid motion, like a baseball outfielder snagging a ground ball, and throwing it to the infield. He transferred the money from hand to pocket without even looking.

It's much too late in the day to file at the courthouse. Tomorrow would be the last day and before I knew it, tomorrow was here.

***

As usual, I got up early and met with my clients. When I arrived back home the rest of Manhattan was just getting to work. I changed clothes, grabbed the court documents, and left for the subway.

After the long ride to Brooklyn, I got out, and made my way to the street. The massive, white, court building stuck out on the corner. The street was quiet. A woman walked up the courthouse steps ahead of me. No parked cars where anywhere on the street. This should only take a few minutes.

Inside, I quickly made my way to the clerk's desk. He was busy putting papers into filing cabinets. I handed the documents over and the clerk thumbed through the pages one at a time. "This is going to take about fifteen minutes," he said. "Just have a seat back there and wait."

"Alright" I said.

Behind me, against the back wall, was a row of waiting chairs with arm rests. They seemed confining. There's only one exit. For some reason I felt uncomfortable. Something about the way the clerk told me to sit and wait seemed just a little... I don't know. I nearly tiptoed out of the room, bit my bottom lip for comfort, and gazed up high at the dome ceiling.

Off to my left I noticed a very large opening to another room. Inside, the space was mostly empty and dimly lit with a majestic ambiance to it. Giant paintings of judges adorned the walls. Being hidden away in this room made me feel a little safer. I kept checking my watch waiting for time to go by. My brown bag felt heavier as it dangled at the end of my hand. Perhaps the clerk had finished by now. I've really become paranoid over the years, haven't I?

After ten minutes I walked into the silent foyer and stood there staring up at the adorned wall opposite the clerk's office. A piercing shout rang through the air, "JOHN!"

Without conscious thought my head instinctively turned to the source of the sound. Two middle-aged white men in plain clothes stood at the clerk's room entrance. The moment our eyes met they rushed over. "We're detectives," the shorter one said, "you're under arrest."

"Put the bag down," the tall one commanded.

Caught off guard. They put the cuffs on me right there and led me out of the building, down the steps, and into the unmarked car that now waited directly outside the courthouse. I made no protest at all. After all these years I'd learned to keep quiet, but these detectives had nothing to say to me anyway. It would be an hour ride of silence as the handcuffs between the backseat and my lower spine cut into my wrists.

What had happened to my life?

It would be another charge of an alleged violation of the order of protection. The cops were waiting for me at the courthouse. They'd killed two birds with one stone. They blocked my appeal and put me in jail. Thankfully, the judge would release me late the next morning without bail, and I'd find a way to the railroad—back to Manhattan.

The appellate court documents weren't filed and the deadline was missed. The cop beating case would never see justice. It was over and something I'd have to live with, forever.

Janet and I needed some enjoyment.

54

It was evening when Janet and I arrived at 30 Rockefeller Plaza. We leaned back, and peered skyward to admire the General Electric building towering above.

"It's amazing," I said to Janet as we walked from Sixth Avenue toward Fifth. "David Rockefeller's family built all this. Can you imagine the money is must have cost?"

I suspected Janet was more interested in the art and antique aspects of Rockefeller Center. "I read," she held up a thin pamphlet, "that in 1985 David commissioned a $25 million dollar restoration and expansion of the Rainbow Room. Look." She pointed over our heads toward the building's entrance. "This carving is called 'Wisdom'."

We gawked and pointed at the powerful image the way tourists do.

Behind us was the ice skating rink. We crossed over a tiny street and watched the skaters gliding around just one level below. A giant golden figure on the other side of the rink was surrounded by people, and we went over to check it out.

Janet paraphrased from her pamphlet. "That's Prometheus, a Titan, a race of old gods who reigned before Zeus and the Olympians. Prometheus means 'Forethinker' and he was blessed with the gift of prophecy. He was a clever deity, a master craftsman, and creator, but also a trickster."

I listened while examining the statue in more detail. "Interesting, isn't it, that the Rockefellers wanted a statute of Prometheus here, and not the God of the bible or Jesus. John D. was raised Baptist."

"Prometheus," Janet continued, "was thought to embody the lone genius whose efforts to improve human existence could also result in tragedy." Those words seemed to have something profound within them, but I couldn't decipher exactly what it was. We marveled a little longer, taking in the grandeur of the entire complex before I tapped her arm. "Let's go."

We went into the GE building, found the elevator bank, and headed upward to the Rainbow Room, the famous restaurant near the top of the building. When the doors opened, we took our time around a corner, and were greeted by two sharply dressed men standing behind a polished, dark wooden desk. "Welcome. Your name please."

"Farley." After a quick read down the list, he motioned to us. "Right this way, Mr. Farley." We were seated at a table overlooking an empty, but elegant dance floor. Janet seemed happy and excited judging by the grin on her face.

"I was doing some research on this place. It opened in 1934 and was originally a supper club for the elite and New York influential types. The dance floor even revolves." Our tuxedo-wearing waiter brought menus. "Good evening, I'll be your server. We have a wine list—"

"Thank you," I interrupted, "but we won't be needing the wine list. The menus will be fine."

"Certainly."

"Take your time. I'll come back for your order."

The menus were, as expected, large, sturdy, and leather-bound. Moments after ordering our meals, the house photographer came to the table. "Let's get a nice photo of the two of you." We leaned in toward the table, and smiled for the camera as he snapped away.

Janet noticed I was quiet. "What are you thinking?" I frowned a little, raised my eyebrows, and flared my nostrils to suck in more air.

"All the craziness. I just can't escape all the craziness." Janet turned toward the revolving floor. "Look they're dancing."

An older crowd of men and women started to sway as the band played tunes from the 1940's. "I don't know how to dance, but it would be nice to learn," I said.

In reality, it's a cramped place, but we enjoyed ourselves. "Are you ready?" I asked. We had fun with our tourist-type adventure. It was a nice escape. The twenty-minute walk back home was pleasant too. I used the time to get clarity on my life, which was anything but clear. Tomorrow was expected to be a new and normal day, and I for one was looking forward to that.

55

7:30am The apartment

The shower was pleasant. Warm water rushed over my head and body. I was relaxed for the first time in ages when the bathroom door burst open.

"John! John, the police are here and they want you." Her words, partially muffled by gurgling water, took a moment to register.

I whisked droplets from my eyelids, and pulled back the curtain. "What—The police are inside?"

"No, they're outside." she said, appearing upset, but not panicked. "They say they have a warrant for your arrest."

"What the hell is going on now? Don't let them in. Stall them. Tell them I'm in the shower, and I need time to get dressed."

"This is insane." Janet said as she tore out of the room.

Meanwhile, I frantically toweled off, and got dressed. Warm clothes. I need to put on a long sleeve shirt, the jail's cold. I prepared mentally for the inevitable. I took half a minute to comb my wet hair before I rushed just off to the side of the front door. "Who is it?"

"It's the deputy sheriffs and New York City police; we have a warrant for your arrest. Open the door!"

"A warrant for what?"

"Open the door, you'll find out later."

"I'm calling my lawyer first and ask him what to do."

"Open the door!" "Hold on, just hold on," I yelled. "I need to call my lawyer first. I don't know that you have a warrant."

I bounded to the phone, and punched in Edwards' number. My hands shook and my heart pounded. God, please Steve, answer the phone. Edwards answered.

"Steve! It's John Farley. Steve, right now, sheriffs are outside my door, they're demanding I let them in. They say they've got a warrant for my arrest. What do I do?"

Edwards was silent and then asked me a half dozen questions. He convinced me that I had no choice. I called to Janet down the hallway to let them in.

A moment later she opened the door and the first cop stepped through the doorway the way those professional wrestler guys enter the ring, all puffed up. Three more cops squished into the tight hallway mimicking players pouring out of a football locker room on game day. They circled my chair like wolves waiting for the alpha to give the signal while I held the phone to my ear, and my other hand motioned to wait.

"Hold on a minute," I said.

"You're coming with us. Stand up and put your hands..."

I was remarkably calm, and it seemed to have an effect on the lead cop. I spoke in professional, non-confrontational language in hopes of getting out of this mess. "This is my lawyer. Wait one second. My lawyer wants to speak to you for just a moment. He can clear this up."

The cop paused, listened, and took the phone. He spoke to Edwards and less than one minute later handed the phone back to me.

"John, you need to go with them," Edwards said.

I made an effort, but it was no use. We hung up. I spoke to the cop without pretense. "Let me walk down the stairs without handcuffs on."

"Can't do that, we gotta cuff ya," he said with attitude.

With my hands behind my back I looked down the hall past the cops to see Janet. "Not too tight," I said, more a command than a plea.

Janet stood at the other end of the hallway watching helplessly as the goon squad moved toward the exit. They led me down to the police car, and off to Suffolk County, but for what? What did Dee Dee do now? Did she claim that I called her home or office? Was this an old warrant they were just getting around to?

At the Suffolk County jail facility I went through the usual searches, and spent the night in a cold, hard cell. Before each court arraignment I prayed to be released without bail. When it was finally my time before the judge he agreed to my request. Even so, being let out of custody never happens fast. It takes hours. I was placed in a cell with many others waiting to be called.

I looked through the bars at the deputies when I noticed one from years before. There he was. The one who made me kneel on a metal bench, and punched me full force again and again and again.

Mustache, around 5 feet ten inches tall, 235 pounds—and he's walking my way.

He came over to the cell with his face up close to the bars. All of us in the cage were as cramped as a midtown subway at 6 p.m. I could hardly move. My heart started to race and my mouth felt dry.

The rogue cop came closer and fixated on me. "You," he said with a sly grin.

Pretending not to hear, I kept looking away. He came closer to the bars—inches from my face. I swallowed reflexively.

"You," he said slowly. "You look familiar to me. Do I know you?"

Summoning my courage I allowed my gaze to migrate upward to meet his sadistic, blue eyes only inches from mine. My lips pulled in, but I fought back the temptation to swallow again. The adrenaline made me breathless, but I acted calm. "I don't think so," I said, with a polite smile.

He paused to savor the moment. "Are you sure I don't know you, because you look familiar to me," he gloated.

John Farley, Jr.

This time I had to swallow, perhaps this time it was my pride. I looked straight back at him, and forced a faint smile. "I—I think you have the wrong guy," I said, waiting for him to break eye contact.

With that, he sauntered back to his buddies near the control room. With each step that he took I felt more relief. But later I was left with the same emotional sensation as if having stood by while a dog urinated on my leg in public.

Eventually, I was released, and caught a train back into Manhattan. A guardian angel must have made sure I left unharmed, and without posting bail.

During the train ride back, I realized something deep within had started to shift. I had a chance, one chance, to tell that sadistic punk what I thought of him, but instead I cowered. Not out of forgiveness, but fear. I let him take the last smoldering ember of dignity I had, and snuff it out.

On the train, I peered through the window, but without seeing anything. Instead I sat lost in memories. I kept replaying in my mind the scene in the cell. My self-esteem was lower than whale dung. Anger welled up unexpectedly from repressed conflicts in my mind, then retreated the way water goes down a partially clogged drain. Self-disappointment mixed itself with the knowledge that, based on the outcome of the Federal trial, those deputies could kill me, and get away with it. Intellectually I told myself that I'd made the right decision, but emotionally I regretted it. But I had to do it, I rationalized. A legalized mafia was tormenting me. They had ultimate force, and I was losing every battle. There was one main solution to my problem, and I was desperate for it.

56

Amanda came back from the restroom and plunked down on the couch on the other side of the coffee table. "I ordered non-alcoholic drinks from the bar—well, mine's non-alcoholic. I spiked yours," I said with a wink.

She smiled. "Why did those judges release you without bail?"

"I'm squeaky clean. I made it clear to every judge that each alleged violation of the order of protection was a mistake, a conflict between the Manhattan court's visitation order and Suffolk's order of protection."

"Squeaky clean! Didn't you have a criminal record by now?"

"No. The arrests were just that. All the criminal charges had been dragged on for four years because I wanted jury trials in Central Islip and Northport."

"That's a long time." "It sure is. Sometimes I'd go months without any court dates, but other months I'd have several at multiple courts."

Amanda kept typing, only to look up on occasion. "How was Sally doing?"

"She seemed great, but Dee Dee never encouraged Sally to go with me. Anyway, children adapt. We always had a nice time together. The change in the Manhattan court order allowed us one week in the summer when she was about eight."

"What did you do?"

"I enrolled her in ice skating classes at the famous Chelsea Piers sports complex on the Hudson River where I rented a small office for my new distance learning college and hypnosis counseling. We even took her to a giant water park on Long Island. That was a lot of fun."

"Things were calming down. I'd re-focused on my career. The solution to my problem was money. That's what the courts wanted from me, cold, hard cash, that's all they cared about."

Amanda stopped and reached for her drink. "But the money's not for the court, it's for your daughter. You have a responsibility."

"A part of me believed that too. On one hand, I didn't want to pay Dee Dee at all. I felt used and abused and besides, having Sally with me took cash, ice skating, water parks, meals, movies, toys, travel—all that dough came from me."

Amanda squinted. "The mother has to pay for lots of expenses too. What about medical costs and clothes?

"Hmm," I said with a smirk while I sipped my drink. "I know, but let's come back to that later. By now I knew that enough money could free me from the government's grip."

"Were you paying child support regularly?"

"I paid something each month. Ernest had implored me to make a payment, but I didn't always pay the amount the court had ordered."

"Why not?"

"The thought of paying Dee Dee tore me up inside. Part of it was frustration over her blocking me from Sally for months, yet being ordered to pay anyway. Then there was my gut feeling that government-run child support was somehow wrong. Plus, it was too much."

Amanda frowned, raised her eyebrows, and let out a disapproving sigh while she pecked at her keyboard. "You mentioned earlier that you and Janet were planning a wedding."

"Yeah, I had two issues with getting married. The first was that I didn't want the government licensing me."

"What do you mean licensing? Marriage license?"

"Yeah. It's a device government's use to control people and I just couldn't let myself submit to any more government oppression. Secondly, the court could try to make Janet's revenue part of my overall revenue. That would raise my support order."

"No, that doesn't seem—are you sure about that?"

"The court could claim Janet's money was an asset to me. It's possible. There's guidelines, but these courts make up what they want."

"Then you didn't get married?"

"The two of us and four friends went to another country for the wedding."

"You went to another country? Why? Which country?"

"It's a secret."

Amanda peered over her laptop. "Mexico? Canada?"

"I'm telling you a lot of secrets, but that's one nugget I'm holding on to."

Amanda stopped typing and stared for a moment.

"About ten days later we arrived in the states, marriage certificate in hand. We chose not to file any paperwork here in America. I didn't want it lodged in government records. My aim was to be invisible. We got married and I was able to kept the government away from Janet. There was only one challenge. No sooner had the plane landed back home when I had to pick up Sally the next morning for visitation."

"Did you make it?"

"Sure. I picked her up on Long Island and took her back into Manhattan were we changed clothes and had a big formal reception. My mom was there along with Janet's parents plus lots of friends and relatives."

"At the end, Janet and I said our goodbyes to everyone. Guests came up, one by one, to congratulate us. Mrs. Kay waited patiently for me to finish with a relative, and then she approached and gave me a hug and said some nice words. No sooner had we parted when Mr. Kay appeared. I expected a simple 'congratulations' or 'welcome to the family'—something like that.

He extended his hand, and we shook. That's when he leaned closer and half-whispered, *"Treat her well."* When our hands separated I froze for a moment. Embarrassed perhaps. His words rattled around in my mind the way a pinball bounces endlessly in the upper part of the machine, rolling from bumper to bumper."

Amanda looked up. "Embarrassed?"

"I knew that every decent father wanted his daughter to be treated well. Up until now I didn't feel that I had treated her as well as he expected or as well as I wanted. I didn't feel ready to get married. This was a shotgun wedding. There I was, only days before in the ceremony, tense, anxious, annoyed. Something was wrong. I shouldn't be getting married. Nonetheless, I bit the bullet and took the vows."

"You didn't want to marry her?"

"I didn't want to marry anyone. I wasn't ready to be married. Men who get married are supposed to be willing to take on certain responsibilities and the one responsibility I consciously chose, but had no choice in initially, was to spend time with Sally. Child support, courts, career—it all overloaded me. Admittedly, my life's vision was vague, but this wasn't what I had in mind."

Amanda sighed.

"Everyone had an agenda for my life, demands for me to meet. I wanted to pursue my goals and instead I was being made to meet other people's agendas."

"Your choices brought all of these events on you."

"It's more complicated than that. Now, looking back, I believe it was my destiny to confront these issues. Not just for me, but for others as well. But we're getting ahead of ourselves."

"So, the marriage?"

"The rules of courtship and marriage were unknown to me. Even worse, I know now that I'd been given the wrong rules to follow."

"Rules? What about finding your soul mate?"

"People, usually men, who get married without knowing what it takes to keep a woman in love most often end up divorced, and let's face it, women aren't blameless either."

The look on her face suggested she knew I was onto something. "What I'm saying is that our society should not be surprised that men and women are having more difficulties than ever."

"Because?"

"Because forces outside our awareness have done a great job of confusing men and women about our roles in society."

"What roles? Nowadays women can do whatever men can do." I gave her a tilted head nod, with a raise of one eyebrow to suggest a caveat. "The traditional roles of men and women have shifted within society, but not biologically."

Amanda had already stopped typing. Perhaps the conversation was getting personal. "Women still have the babies... I don't—I'm not following."

"Men are the protectors, the providers and the procreators. Not only was this simple statement not explained to me growing up, but most men have been indoctrinated to think that it doesn't matter who makes the money or who does what. Women have been trained to enter the job market and compete with men."

"What's wrong with that?"

"Men hate to compete with women, unless they've been thoroughly brainwashed to do it."

"You don't think men and women are equal?" she said with a higher pitch.

"Not—" I took a deep breath to clarify my thoughts before saying something I'd regret. "We're equal in terms of worth, but we're not the same. This is where both men and women have been led astray. The family court system has made things worse for men, women, children and families."

"You're saying all this ties in with your story?"

"Sure. What I'm saying is that women have expectations about relationships and men have different expectations. Both gender's expectations have been engineered by shadow forces over many generations. The result is confusion about core values."

"Shadow forces? What does this have to do with your story?"

I took a deep breath and let my cheeks puff up like a blowfish before exhaling. "We're getting way ahead of ourselves. Let me tell you about the surprise."

57

"Here you go." I handed cash to the cabbie in front of the Central Islip courthouse.

As the cab drove off I turned, planted my feet, and took two deep breaths.

William Rodriguez, the hearing examiner, had always seemed to get a sick joy from our previous jousts while I fended off his attacks.

On this day I arrived empty handed. They can't take papers I don't have. A hollowness in my stomach welled up before I entered the tiny chamber. Sitting, king-like was the hearing examiner with court aids nearby. The officer pointed to a chair. "Sir. Sit here."

Dee Dee trailed in moments behind and was directed to the seat on my left.

Sitting in front of me, and barricaded by eight feet of solid desks, was Hearing Examiner Rodriguez. The court staff flanked him and passed papers back and forth. After he'd announced technical details for the court reporter, he turned toward me with an intimidating stare as he spoke in spurts. "Are you— John—J.—Farley?"

Lawyers and judges are always asking questions to set a person up for a lynching later on, but this one seemed hard to dispute.

"Yes," I said, reluctantly.

"And are you, Dee Dee O'Dell?"

A meek voice responded, "Yes."

The hearing examiner asked about my finances, about payments made. He read off a tally of the payments and requested to see financial records. I sat with my hands folded on the table in front of me. "I don't have those."

"WHY NOT?" he demanded.

"Can you," I said, clearing my throat, "require me to give you my financial records? Isn't that a violation of my fourth amendment right against searches, and seizures of my property and papers?"

Rodriguez shuffled a stack of folders against the desk. He spouted off legal statutes and claimed the ability to violate my constitutional rights. He and I went back and forth debating payments, assets and other things.

Dee Dee fidgeted while Rodriquez and I batted legal issues back and forth like a pin pong ball. Rodriquez finished my interrogation before he addressed Dee Dee.

"Ms. O'Dell, do you have any questions for Mr. Farley?"

Dee Dee swallowed and cleared her throat. "Yes. I have a question."

Rodriguez looked down and started to move papers on his desk into folders. "What is your question for Mr. Farley?"

Her voice was still weak, but louder, as her words tumbled out. "I'd like you to remind him that he's under oath."

Rodriguez paused. "He KNOWS he's under oath. What is your question for Mr. Farley?"

She started again and this time the words came out smoother. "I want to know if he's married."

I lowered my chin. What—what kind of question is that? I felt instantly nervous. "I object to that question."

Rodriguez put the folders down and leaned in. "Overruled," he snapped back forcefully, but with a hint of glee. "Answer the question," he said, with a tone that suggested enjoyment, while I squirmed in my seat.

Nonetheless, I sat up taller, but to no avail. "This question is irrelevant. I object to—"

"ANSWER the question."

I hesitated and looked down searching for the right words. Anyone could tell I was dodging the interrogation. "This question is not..."

"ANSWER. THE. QUESTION."

I swallowed and clenched my teeth before resolving to answer. I took a breath, looked up and then turned my upper body directly toward her.

Cautiously, only her eyes flashed toward me momentarily. Then slowly, she turned in spurts to peer over her shoulder. Her eyes crept down along the table before her gaze glided up to meet mine. Her expression suggested an 'I got you" attitude with a hint of curiosity, yet I sensed vulnerability. A familiar feeling came over me. The one I'd had many years ago as she and I stood at the entrance to my apartment building. I braced myself to let the chips fall where they may. For the first time in along time we were eye to eye and close up. I opened my mouth and just said it.

"Yes," I paused. "I am."

And then it happened. "Gasp—" Her chest deflated as she winced. Her head slumped. I turned back to Rodriguez who stayed fixated on her for a fraction of a second longer than I would have expected.

"Anything else?" he asked with the same detached tone. Dee Dee's head stayed slumped.

"No," she mumbled. I felt guilty. Did I just hurt her? I didn't intend to rub it in her face. I wanted the whole thing kept secret. Moments later the hearing was adjourned. I left the building amazed and bewildered.

What was that? Why did she respond that way? She actually cares if I got married or not? This woman's been trying to jail me, perhaps kill me and she's hurt because I got married? Anyway, she's with somebody else.

Her response distracted me from who I should have been focusing on. Rodriquez. He was up to something.

58

Rodriquez had done something to get me in front of a Central Islip family court judge for contempt for not paying child support. I stood handcuffed behind my back and off to the left of Judge Trainor.

The judge sat high up on the bench and peered across his massive barricade. Earlier, a cop had mentioned that this judge was bad news if a guy owed child support. My legs developed a mild but uncontrollable tremor. I stole a glance upward. There he was, fat, balding, and looking bored. What did he want from me?

A conversation between the judge and some type of prosecutor happened during a sidebar. Think clearly. Think clearly. You get one shot.

"John Farley!" a court officer yelled. The cop ordered me closer to the judge.

There was no opportunity to speak. The judge barked out his order. "The amount owed in child support is $10,000. You'll be held until it's paid."

My jaw dropped as my face stretched from top to bottom. "TEN THOUSAND DOLLARS!"

"QUIET. Don't talk," the cop demanded, as two of them pulled me away.

"I don't have ten thousand dollars." I yelled before being hauled out the side door in the blink of an eye.

Moments later, I was in the bowels of the building sitting in a cell. The air was cold and the cement floor lifeless and hard. Despite only the silver metal bench and seatless toilet to keep me company. I reminded myself that I was a good dad, a good person. The fluorescent lights flickered and drained my energy.

John Farley, Jr.

"You're going to Riverhead," a deputy sheriff said through the heavy cell door. My face felt frozen. No. It's a bad dream. Not Riverhead. Not there.

***

I don't remember how I got there, but within a couple hours, I'd arrived at the prison—the one I was in four years earlier. The next thing I knew I was being questioned by guards. "Face front." A woman snapped a photo of me, a mug shot.

"Are you suicidal?" she asked from behind a partition.

"Not yet," I told her, trying to keep any sense of humor I still had. Not amused, she asked again. The smirk on my face faded. "No."

Moments later, I was brought to the showers. The black guard corralled a group of us prisoners into the multi-shower room. Shamed and fearful, I stripped down while my heart pounded. I felt my spirit and my dignity swirling down the drain as I peered into the showers filled with naked convicts.

This is prison. I'm in prison. My God, I could be in here forever if I don't pay the money they want. The big, black guard, dressed in his tan uniform, yelled from the edge of the showers. "Hurry up. Get in, and get out. You get one phone call. Make it count."

After the shower, I used the phone and reached our home recorder. I whispered, but then remembered that all calls are recorded. "Janet, it's John—I'm in the Riverhead jail. You have to get me out of here. Get hold of Mr. Dominick. Do whatever you have to do to get me out of here. Hurry. Please."

This can't be. I sued them and lost. Now they can kill me, and who's to stop them? The guards don't seem to care much who you were on the outside. As far as they're concerned, I wasn't much different from other inmates, perhaps worse, because I owed child support. When it comes to jail, convicts and guards don't like men who hurt children. Somehow, they think child support falls into that category.

318

I was brought over for fingerprinting. This is familiar, but something's different. Now a new guard sat at the same fingerprinting table I remembered four years ago. He's not combative. Not yet. He peered up from the desk. "Will you provide your thumbprint?"

What? Was this a trick question? Where were the ten guys ready to pound me? Why is he asking me this instead of telling me what to do?

"Yes," I said, fearful of the consequences of refusing. I stepped up and rolled my thumb in the ink and pressed it onto the paper. Perhaps my lawsuit did change something, however slight. Soon I was ordered down a hallway. One fence—like cell door opened to a long corridor of individual cells.

There were two cons housed with me. I don't remember much except feeling that I'd better make friends quick. They asked me dozens of questions, and while I didn't feel comfortable around them, they seemed safer than the guards. I suspected one was an undercover cop gathering information for the court.

Hours passed.

A guard appeared at the cell. "Farley! Come here." A short, stocky, mean looking guy in his forties stood at the metal mesh door.

Obediently, I walked up close. His face looked hard and unforgiving. Another guard stood far back and off to the side. The first guard's keys rattled in the lock as the tumblers turned. "Stand against the wall."

I stepped gingerly forward, but felt uneasy with him behind me. "You're a deadbeat, huh," he said, sounding like an angry dog's muffled growl. "You're a real piece of shit."

I started to turn my head ever so slightly in his direction, but stopped.

"Walk straight ahead," he ordered as he continued to egg me on. His low growl continued. "You don't take care of your children...you're a wife beater—what a pile of garbage you are."

John Farley, Jr.

My heart raced faster. *None* of this is true—all false. Is he about to jump me?

A few minutes later, I was again, semi-safe in a different jail cell.

***

A day had gone by and before I knew it, I was sent before the same judge.

This was the moment of truth; either he'd let me go or keep me in jail. I rehearsed what I wanted to say. The cops brought me in handcuffed and shackled. A prosecutor read the legalese to the judge and then a pause happened.

With maximum intensely I interjected. "JUDGE! If you'll let me go, I promise—I'm promising you—I'll have a job within two weeks making at least $25 per hour and we'll get this matter settled. I am promising you that I will have a job."

The judge looked at me askance as I held a soft stare along with my breath and awaited his next words. Only moments passed, but they felt long, as if I was standing wet and shirtless in an Arctic wind.

"All right, Mr. Farley." He glanced at the papers on his desk. "We'll set a court date four weeks from now, and we'll see if you can do what you say you will do."

Relief flooded my body, yet it was mixed with anxiety, similar to a close call on the highway and you realize that you've cheated death. The judge gave me a chance. I was sent back to Riverhead and by sunrise I was released. Janet had managed to get a cab to take me to the nearest train station. There was only one thought in my head. Get a job or go to prison.

59

Amanda's Interview

"What did you do?"

"I immediately applied for interviews at health clubs in Manhattan."

"But why did you need a job? You had a job."

"I worked for myself, but the support mafia, as I call them, wanted me to work for another company so that they could take money from my paycheck before I ever saw it. After my last stay in Riverhead, I was very motivated. I hated being forced to get a job, but I agreed, so I did. I landed a position as a personal fitness trainer in under three weeks."

"Where at?"

"Let's just say a major health club a few blocks from the apartment. That's where I met actress Laura Bundy. Laura was young a star on *ABC's The Guiding Light* and the smash hit film *Jumanji*. I gave her workout tips and we became friends."

"Oh, yeah I've heard of her. She's in musicals too, right?"

"Yes, she's very talented."

"You had a hearing in Manhattan coming up about Dee Dee violating the visitation order again, didn't you?"

"To my surprise, our judge had been moved from Manhattan to the Bronx. She kept some cases with her, and mine was one of them."

"How was the Bronx courthouse different from Manhattan?"

"Frankly, all I remember was sitting in court. It looked like a high school classroom. Dee Dee had been called to the stand by her lawyer. Everything was normal—tense, but normal. Then everything changed in an instant when her lawyer brought up the past."

John Farley, Jr.

"He said, 'Ms. O'Dell, tell the court what happened that day in December 1994.'"

"Out of nowhere, Dee Dee became more and more emotional. She went from a withdrawn flower to a dry sponge submerged in water and expanding in all directions. She started to cry, I mean loud wailing! I sat there stunned. She told the judge that I grabbed her, threatened and hit her. All the while wailing, crying, moaning in agony. I actually felt bad for her and how distraught she was. Something in my demeanor changed, I felt it. As Dee Dee wound down, judge Ruth Zuckerman shot me a glance and our eyes met. Judges read people all day long, and I knew she'd caught me in a moment of remorse."

"What did she do?"

"The judge frowned as she looked down her nose at me from her perch and said, 'You disgust me'."

"She did?"

"Yes, but I didn't feel guilty. I felt compassion for Dee Dee, despite the fact that she deserved what she got."

"But you shouldn't have—"

"Amanda. I wish I hadn't, but she violated me; it was disrespectful. Anyway. I told the judge straight out that I didn't care what she thought of me. I just wanted her to protect my rights."

"You said that?"

"The years had transformed me from Mr. Nice Guy to Mr. I don't care what you think about me, Guy. Defending my interests, my rights and my dignity, took priority over social niceties. Sometimes I came off as rude. It's hard to explain what triggered it. What I discovered that day in court sent a shiver up my spine. There was no way that I could go in front of a Long Island jury with Dee Dee crying a river of tears and expect to be found Not Guilty. I was going to have to negotiate a deal while I still could."

Early Morning

Janet and I sat in the living room while I finished writing up my idea of a new business. Janet enjoyed my passion. "What's the idea?" she asked.

"It's a way to help people, have fun, and make money. With the cash I can pay off child support and get a descent lawyer, an oxymoron, I know. We'll be able to stop Dee Dee from whatever game she's up to." I checked my watch. "Geez, I have to go to court on the island."

"When do you want me out there?" Janet asked with a long face.

"Mr. Dominick, from the Northport cases, agreed to represent me in Central Islip this one time. Show up at the courthouse at 11, please."

***

I spied the scenery out the train window while mentally rehearsing for the upcoming hearing. Things were clear now. If my criminal cases went to trial I'd be eaten alive. It would be very difficult to convince a jury, and certainly a judge, that Dee Dee's glorified spanking was defensible, even if she deserved it. The reality is that female victims attract men, while male victims repel everybody.

Today, however, was the immediate threat. Mr. Dominick and I had to show the judge that I had a job plus money in my hand for child support arrears. Before I knew it, I'd arrived at the courthouse.

My heart raced as I walked down the court hallway. The ominous silence was unnerving.

I saw the number on the outside wall. The solid, extra large, wooden doors to the courtroom were locked. I'll stand here and wait for Mr. Dominick. Seconds felt like minutes. At the other end of the long hallway I spotted him and his characteristic silhouette.

He strode with a slight sway while the toothpick in his mouth finished the look. The giant briefcase he held tilted his shoulders to one side.He greeted me without a smile. "Hi," he muttered as if it were painful.

I felt jittery. "What do we have to do, what's happening? Let's go over—"

"Stay here," he ordered. At that moment a court officer unlocked the doors. Mr. Dominick slipped inside, and left me behind. My heart pounded faster. Minutes later he came out. "The other side is here, except for Dee Dee. Where is she?"

"I don't know. Dee Dee arrives when she wants to. The court is supposed to revolve around her schedule." We waited a few more minutes, as I prayed for her to be late. The judge decided enough time had elapsed.

Dominick got the cue from the court officer. "The case is called. The judge wants to start." I swallowed hard.

Mr. Dominick and I walked in, and over to the podium on the right. Dee Dee's lawyer, a woman, stood alone at the opposite podium. I'd never seen her before. I glanced over my shoulder and to the courtroom door; no Dee Dee to be found.

The judge sat God-like on the bench looking more rotund than the last time. He called the case. The other lawyer spoke first. "Your honor, my client will be here soon."

The judge fidgeted. "We're starting. Mr. Dominick—"

Surprisingly, Dominick turned on the energy as if a corralled racehorse had just be let loose. He spoke with passion and flair. His oratory skills rivaled any carnival barker from here to Buffalo.

"Judge! My client has secured a position at a health club in Manhattan as a personal fitness trainer. We have the documentation right here. He's making a flat rate plus commission bringing his hourly rate between $20 to $40."

Mr. Dominick really turned it up now. "Your Honor, we also have here back child support payments in the amount of twelve hundred dollars in cash!" I turned to him and franticaly whispered, "Thirteen hundred, I gave you thirteen hundred."

In auctioneer style he yelled out, "Make that thirteen hundred dollars in cash today, your Honor." The other side started to speak before the judge gave the invitation.

"Your Honor, this is a pattern with Mr. Farley we are asking the court to commit him to jail for six months."

I rubbernecked around Mr. Dominick to see this woman with my own eyes as my jaw dropped, and my eyes felt bugged out.

Did I just hear what I thought I heard? She couldn't be serious? Did she not listen to what Dominick said? I have a job. Did it not register to her that I have brought $1,300 in cash for her client? What purpose would jail serve if the goal was to receive money from me? Oh my God. I could be going to jail right here, right now for six months.

The judge looked at Dee Dee's lawyer, and then turned to Mr. Dominick. The judge's face looked twice as big to me than before. My eyes zoomed in on his mouth the way a ship captain's binoculars focus on a distant iceberg. The next words the judge spoke would determine my fate. I held my breath unconsciously as I leaned over the podium.

The judge inched back just a little. "Mr. Farley has secured a job. The court sees no reason to grant that request. Case dismissed."

I exhaled as if pulled from the bottom of a swimming pool. My attorney was great, at least he was great today. As we left the courtroom he whispered, "I was trying to save you some money."

I smiled back. "You're not saving me any money. It has to go to her anyway." I was thrilled and overjoyed to be free.

Suddenly, I saw Dee Dee as she walked down the hall racing toward the courtroom. She narrowly passed on my right side, but never looked my way. I couldn't suppress my joy. I smiled as I spoke into her ear. "You're too late. It's over."

We both continued in opposite directions, and I could only imagine her disappointment at my escape. I found Janet, and we headed to the courthouse cafeteria on the same floor. We purchased a muffin, juice, and water.

"There's a table by the window." I leaned back in the chair and breathed a sigh of relief. "I'm a little nervous hanging around here. I'm never really sure what the court or cops are going to pull next. Can you believe it—six months. The lawyer wanted six months."

We each pulled apart pieces of the muffin. "Are you serious? Her lawyer wanted you in jail for six months?"

"Yeah," I said with a nod. "It doesn't make any sense at all. I just thought that maybe— maybe it was the system rolling over me. I figured she was powerless to stop it."

Janet swallowed her muffin. "I told you she was behind this." I sipped my water.

"All that stuff the courts and lawyers talk about, you know, the best interests of the child—all that crap—yet her lawyer would rather me go to jail, then have a job and pay money? The lawyer was only doing what Dee Dee asked her to do, right?"

Janet cupped her hands around her juice box. "She wants you in jail, and she wants to take Sally away from you." She had my full attention. Her words didn't slide off the side of my brain this time. Now her words soaked into my mind like fresh paint on dry wood. The light bulb came on.

"You're right. It's true. There's no other explanation. You know what else? I have to take a plea bargain in the criminal court."

"What?" she said with aggravation.

I know, but it's all a big negotiation." I scanned the cafeteria for anything suspicious and then peeked toward the exit. I felt anxiety creeping up. "Let's get out of this courthouse. I have a weird feeling."

61

In the Hotel with Amanda

Amanda and I stood up to stretch our legs. I reached overhead and twisted to get the kinks out of my back.

"Did you have any connections that could pull some strings for you?" Amanda asked, as she slipped off her shoes to relax her feet.

"No," I said, as I dropped my hands down to my sides.

"Hmm, one. David Rockefeller." By this time, I knew that the Rockefellers weren't some old relic of the Gilded Age, but a powerful dynasty that had managed to conceal their political and financial power for over 100 years."

Central Islip Criminal Courthouse

The line into the court stretched down the hallway, but moved steadily the way a conveyer belt moves products along. My scuffed shoes and worn wool sports jacket reminded me that money was tight.

Weeks ago I received a return letter from David Rockefeller's personal assistant. I had shamelessly asked if he could help get my case in Central Islip dismissed.

The reality of jail time loomed, and it was causing me extreme stress. Rockefeller had a hell of a lot of power, surely he could pull a few strings on my behalf. The letter from his secretary said in essence, that Mr. Rockefeller didn't know any judges on Long Island.

Doesn't know any judges on Long Island? This man knows the most powerful leaders around the world. His brother was vice president of the United States and his family's political and financial power extended around the globe. I'm supposed to believe that he couldn't make a few calls on my behalf? He simply doesn't want to get involved.

The line was moving. Before I knew it I was beyond the officers, in and out of the elevator and in front of the doors to the criminal courtroom.

Crowds of people brushed past me on both sides as they went in and out. I looked over the sea of heads at the lawyers in the belly of the court.

Sometimes I liked having a lawyer and other times not. Talking directly to the judge is a double-edged sword. If you're good, you can slice through all the pretense and get the judge to see you as a human being. The reality is that very few people can do that. Instead they end up cutting their own throats.

My pro bono lawyer was talking with the prosecutor, but then turned and strode up the aisle toward me. "Mr. Farley, please come outside."

We found a nook just outside the doors to have our hushed conversation. "Okay," she said, as I pressed my shoulder against the wall and listened. "The other side wants to move toward trial." I suppressed the urge to panic. Panicking never helped so I spoke with a devil may care attitude.

"I'd be willing to take a plea, but no jail time of course and one misdemeanor."

"You're willing to take a plea?" Her eyes got wide. One misdemeanor—I don't think he'll go for it—you have oh— seven charges."

"Never say no for the other guy," I said slowly as I gazed back at her.

"Wait here and I'll talk to the prosecutor." A middle-aged man got up from a hallway bench and I filled the space without missing a beat.

This is incredible. Dee Dee sexually assaults me. I smack her in the leg and butt a few times and tell her to keep her hands off, and I'm the bad guy? The cops get to take me to their private dungeon and beat the crap out of me yet never have to show up in court for their crimes? This is a sick joke.

Moments later my lawyer pushed through the heavy, wooden courtroom doors. "He wants probation, and three misdemeanors," she said, as she looked at me with eager eyes. "This is a good deal."

I took a deep breath, and pressed my teeth together in thought. "It's not a good deal. I've essentially been on probation for the last four years. I've been arrested a half-dozen times and spent nights in jail for trying to see my daughter exactly as I was ordered to do by the court."

I looked down at the floor and considered that if they won at trial—and they would win— I'd be screwed. I stared back at her. "No deal. Either one misdemeanor and no probation or let's go to trial."

Her face seemed mixed with frustration and disappointment as she held her gaze at me. "I'll ask," she said in a defeated tone.

The hallway traffic had disappeared. I stared at the floor, wondering how many more times I'd have to come back here. Minutes later my lawyer was standing in front of me with bated breath. "Okay, you got it, the prosecutor agreed. You're going to have to admit that you committed a crime."

The sound of that bothered me. "What exactly am I admitting to?"

"That you did what they're alleging." My mind raced. What were they alleging? That I hit her? Is that the big crime? We filed into the courtroom and up to the front. The judge and the lawyers called a conference as I waited near a table off to the side.

When they were done talking the judge turned to me. "Mr. Farley, your lawyer has informed the court that you will be voluntarily accepting a conviction. You understand that a conviction of this type is no different than if the jury had found you guilty…"

As I listened to the judge rebellion built inside me. I was admitting to a crime. A conviction—a conviction—the word "convict" sickens me. I am not a convict.

"Do you admit that you..."

Then he said it. He said that I had hit Dee Dee and that I now had to admit to it. I felt as if I was admitting to scratching my neighbor's car while she and her friends took baseball bats and crowbars to every inch of mine. When he was done reading the allegations I remembered what all those deputies got away with. I could barely get the words out of my mouth.

"I believe so." The judge was quick to reply.

"No. You can't believe so. Do you admit..."

Anger welled up within me along with a generous portion of embarrassment. But then I forced out the word that they wanted. "Yes." There I said it. I hated saying it, but everyone does it. People takes pleas all the time. That's how these courts and lawyers make it through the day, by getting people to take pleas.

The judge accepted it and there would be no jail time. No probation. After more than four years, I was free, never needing to return to this criminal court again. When I walked out of the courthouse I didn't feel free, I felt stained, as if I wore a Scarlet letter under my jacket. One more criminal court to go.

62

The Hotel with Amanda

Amanda kept typing when I told her of the Central Islip deal. "Dee Dee wasn't in court when you took the plea bargain?" she asked with raised eyebrows."

I sat snuggled in an oversized chair with one ankle crossed over my knee while sipping a cup of organic hot chocolate. "She never appeared at the criminal court hearings. The government prosecutors did all her dirty work. After I left the court that day, I called Mr. Dominick and told him the result and that led to another argument about a plea deal."

"What did he say?"

"The usual, that is, until I mentioned the letter I'd received years earlier from the Northport police department."

"What letter?" "Remember the typewritten note on police letterhead stated that I didn't have to show up to the Northport court for a hearing? I never questioned the letter, I just didn't show up."

"Oh, right. That was one of the times you were arrested and taken in front of a judge and he called you a liar when you mentioned the letter, and then had you drug off to a cell."

"Exactly. So, Mr. Dominick told me to put it all down in writing and mail it to him and he'd give it to the judge before my next hearing."

Night Court in Northport

I felt tired and anxious as I waited in the hallway. The rough brick wall at my back was propping me up. I dragged the callused skin of my knuckles across the red bricks and gray cement in an effort to distract my mind with the stinging sensation.

Mr. Dominick showed up just in time. He sauntered through the glass doors wearing his gangster garb. He spotted me immediately. "Hey," he said, looking distraught at the sight of me standing there. "Where are we with this case now?"

The question made me pause. Isn't he supposed to know the answer to that?

"You received my letter to the judge?"

"Oh yeah, right, I'm going to give that to the assistant DA. That should help your case," he said as he set his briefcase down.

"Help my case? That letter proves that somebody from the police station in this building sent me a document not to show up for court. The judge called me a liar, insulted me and had me taken away in chains, thrown in a cell and forced me to pay $500 in bail that I never got back—all because I never showed up to a court hearing that the police letter said was cancelled."

Mr. Dominick listened, but he seemed unconvinced.

"If that's not bad enough, the judge's been making me come out here—six hours all told—for four years. Someone committed a crime. Is the DA going to prosecute the cop that did this? I want the charges dropped, all of them."

Mr. Dominick sighed and squirmed. "He's not going to do that."

"Why not? Remember, don't say no—"

"You took a plea in Central Islip. They're going to want a plea here too."

"Tell him I want them to dismiss this case."

He looked away as he bent down to pick up his massive briefcase.

"Don't say no for the other guy," I said, before he was out of range.

He strode ahead of the non-attorneys in line, and made his way toward the assistant DA's office. I stood outside the courtroom with all the others who were waiting for the show to start. Several minutes went by when Mr. Dominick came back grinning. He practically dropped the briefcase so he could gesture with both hands. "Good news. All you have to do is take one misdemeanor and it's over and you can go home."

He was in sales mode. I could tell by the tone of his voice and the up tempo. He dangled the court's carrot close to my nose. It was tempting, but I took a moment to reflect.

The road that got me here had been a long and bumpy one. I was weary of battle. All I had to do was bend just a little, and I'd be free. He looked happy, eager, to put this case to bed, and get rid of me. Then I remembered why I was here, why I'd fought so hard for so long. What I was about to say would be difficult if not for my dignity.

"I called one hundred times to Dee Dee's office to find my daughter. I would have called her 1,000 times and I don't care about a damn court order, this is my child. Cops conspired and sent me a letter to purposefully make me miss a court date, and yet I'm the one charged with a crime."

I looked at the ceiling momentarily as my nostrils flared. "I will not take a plea. If they don't dismiss this charge I will demand a jury trial. I don't care if I have to come back here for another four years."

Mr. Dominick glanced down, grimaced, and grabbed his briefcase. He went back to the assistant DA. I waited, hoped, and prayed. A few minutes later he came out.

"They're willing to dismiss the case." It was fast, almost too fast. His posture seemed as if he was the one who had conceded, not them.

Really? I greeted him with a wide-eyed stare. They're really going to drop all the charges? Fabulous! Absolutely fabulous. I then wondered how hard he'd worked for me all this time.

Moments later we were in the courtroom and my case was called. From what I'd been told by Dominick, the court had read the letter, consulted with the prosecutor and reviewed the case.

The judge tried to maintain his composure, but he nervously fidgeted with papers. I suspected that he was shocked and dismayed that someone right under his nose conspired against me illegally. Perhaps he was embarrassed. He rattled off legal jargon to the court reporter and then, moments later, said, "Case dismissed."

Our eyes met for a brief moment as I passed in front of him with Mr. Dominick leading the way toward the door. I felt as if I'd walked out of that courtroom more respected than when I had entered.

There was no applause or cheers or congratulations. And I certainly never got any bail money back. Only a quiet sensation of liberty gripped me on the other side of the courtroom doors. I felt free, vindicated, but not happy. I beat the rap, but not the ride.

"Good job," I told Dominick in an attempt to reward his efforts, whatever they were.

"The other side finally said yes," I told him.

He checked his watch and glanced my way. "Good luck to ya," he said robotically, before walking out the door and leaving me to call a cab from the pay phone in the corner. He wasn't giving me any more than that.

His real client wasn't a father trying to see his daughter, it was the court system. He'd be doing business with the judge and the prosecutor for years to come. After all, they'd forced me to have Dominick as my lawyer in hopes that a deal would be struck in their favor, not mine.

The sky darkened, and a cab took me from the tiny courthouse to the train station. As I waited for the last time on the platform, relief enveloped my being and eased my buried agitation, the way the tiniest drop of water gives pleasure to a parched mouth if only for a fleeting moment.

My criminal court days were done, but the completion was anti-climatic in the same way that a tied baseball game leaves everyone agitated. Regardless, I'd savor the moment, and look forward to my next time with Sally.

63

With Amanda at the Hotel

We decided to stroll around the hotel. Amanda recorded our conversation on her phone. "What happened next?"

"I took the train to pick up Sally in Huntington. Janet and I decided to take her to the big sports club where Janet worked. Eventually, I'd get a job there too. The club was fabulous. One hundred eighty thousand square feet with a marble entrance on the upper west side. It was every personal fitness trainer's dream club. It was tough to get a job there, but I wanted to upgrade from where I was working."

"In a typical month Janet would meet the biggest stars from television and film."

"My club wasn't all bad. I met television and film star Laura Bundy, and the pay covered child support. Fortunately, Janet made money or I'd be close to homeless and hungry."

"Was Sally cooperating with the visitations?" Amanda asked.

"Her mood depended on how Dee Dee had manipulated her to feel. On one particular visitation day Sally was pouting. She didn't want to get out of the car."

Amanda and I walked in unison the way slow moving deer do in the forest. "Why not?"

I stopped at the railing to look out at the indoor garden a few stories below. "Dee Dee had told Sally that she was going to miss a birthday party for one of her friends by going with me." I turned toward Amanda.

Her eyes scanned my pained expression. "What did you do?"

"I pulled her by the arm out of the car and walked her through the parking lot onto the train. All the while she yelled, 'You're hurting me!'"

"Are you allowed to do that?"

I chuckled, but not because her question was funny, but because of the irony. "Am I allowed? First, I didn't hurt her. Am I allowed to be a parent? Allowed to do what I need to do? I'm constantly treated as a glorified babysitter, you know, expendable."

"Did Sally cooperate once you were on the train?"

"No, in fact she kept repeating, 'you take me home right now' and then she slammed her elbow into my upper arm."

"Wow, how did she learn that?"

"I taught her karate and now she was using the techniques on me!"

Amanda smiled, if only a little.

"I figured Sally would eventually focus on our time together, but I have to say it was the longest 90 minute trip in recent memory. Once at the apartment I picked up the phone and called Dee Dee. Sally just kept repeating 'I want my mommy' so I figured I'd let her call. The answering machine came on and Sally started talking to it in a sad tone. Within seconds Dee Dee picked up. I couldn't tell what Dee Dee was saying, but Sally's tone became worse until finally I took the phone and hung it up."

"Did she ever change her attitude?"

"At some point, things got better. The next day we went to the sports club, and she rock climbed. Overall it was fun. At the end of the weekend I took her back to her mother and figured that was the end of it."

64

Arriving from Long Island

I pushed the front door open. "Janet, I'm back." No scampering feet or a high-pitched voice accompanied me. Janet looked surprised when I stood at the living room entrance. "Where is she?" I made the announcement calmly. "Dee Dee didn't show up again. How many times am I supposed to get on a train and travel for nearly four hours and stand around for nothing? I can't believe she does this."

Janet's mouth hung open. "She doesn't even call to let you know? That's wrong."

"I know, I know. I've already filed to take her back to court." Janet motioned toward the kitchen. "You have some mail from the court on the table."

Once I had the letter in hand, I lumbered back into the living room. "You know they moved the family court back to Manhattan, right?" I said.

"I thought it was in the Bronx?" "It was, but they moved it back to Manhattan." I tore open the letter and read silently.

Janet watched me out of the corner of her eye. "What's it say?" "Ahh," I moaned before sitting down and easing into the love seat. "It says they want me to call this court worker about a meeting." Janet headed to the computer to type something. "What's that about?"

"It seems that they want to look around the apartment, and interview me about Sally."

***

When the weekend was over I called and spoke to a court worker. A day and time were set up to meet at the apartment.

On the appointed day Janet was at work, while I sat home and waited for the visitor.

"Buzz." That's her. But you can never be too careful. "Who is it?"

"CPS case worker," a woman announced. I buzzed her in and then waited and watched through the peephole to see who would arise from the mountain of stairs. It was a lone, dark skinned, pudgy woman. As she reached the door, I flicked the lock, turned the knob and lifted the door to dull the screech as I opened it.

"Hello," I said, coldly.

"Hello Mr. Farley, I'm Ms. Mayberry I've been assigned to your case."

"Okay, come in." Like vampires, they can only come in when invited, and that was my first mistake. I showed her into the living room and directed her to a seat on the couch while I planted myself in the antique rocking chair. She set her lawyer-styled bag down and pulled out her clipboard and pen. Her humorless expression put me on guard.

"What is the purpose of this again?" I asked.

"We just want to make sure that your daughter, ah—Sally," she said, checking her papers, "is being taken care of properly and so—"

"Why would you need to make sure of that?"

"We just want to check to make sure your daughter is safe."

"She's safe. Of course she's safe."

"You don't have the proper window guards on both windows," she said staring behind me.

"As you can see, the other window goes to the fire escape and the police might find window guards obstructive if they want to raid me again," I deadpanned.

"Where does she sleep when she's here?"

"She sleeps in the bedroom on a blow up bed."

"Where do you sleep?"

"I sleep in my bed," I said with a slightly condescending tone to reflect the stupidity of the question.

She kept writing. "Sally's getting older now. She needs to have her own room."

I smirked. "There's no other room. We have one bedroom—this is New York City. What about all the families that have one bedroom and multiple children?" Now my fuse was lit and short. "What are you talking about? Where am I supposed to sleep?"

She continued with her emotionless tone. "You would sleep somewhere else."

"What do you mean somewhere else? We have one bedroom, and my bed is in it. I'm not putting her all the way out in the living room. She doesn't like that. She's never complained about sleeping in the same room as us." A moment later I caught on to her meaning. "You think I should sleep out here?" I said, impatiently.

"Yes, the child should have her own space."

"I don't think you're dealing with reality. This is my apartment. I pay the rent here. There is one bedroom here, and I'm not sleeping on a couch when I have a bed to sleep on."

"How is your relationship with the child's mother?"

After all these years my anger was controlled, but constant and my inhibitions had broken down. "The mother is a law breaker. The mother has violated the visitation order more times than I can count. She should be in jail. But no, the court doesn't want to put her in jail, but it's fine if I go to jail. The mother—now listen to me closely—I'm not going to do this, but someone should do it—the mother should be beaten." I said it partially out of frustration, partially to break her robotic trance and partially because I believed it.

Her eyes got wide so I lowered my voice and articulated my words. "It's okay that I get beaten and punched and slammed into metal bars in a jail just for showing up for my court ordered visitation with my daughter, but when the mother breaks the law—breaks the court's visitation order over, and over, and over again and then steals my daughter and nothing happens—she doesn't deserve punishment?" I said, rhetorically.

"Yes, she should be beaten as punishment. That would teach her. Or put in jail–just once–so she learns not to break the law. She needs to be taught a lesson. She can't kidnap my child. Now, let me remind you, I am not the one to do this. I hope you're hearing me—not me, I never would I do this," I said as I gestured and leaned forward. "But someone needs to teach her a lesson."

The woman took notes and without much more conversation, made her way out the door.

Amanda at the Hotel

Amanda stopped typing, mouth agape. "You actually said that to her?"

I replied softly with gentle eye contact. "Yes. I did." She swallowed and seemed uncomfortable. "Doesn't that seem a bit crazy to you? I mean, come on."

I shrugged slightly. "In the Middle East, thieves get a finger or hand chopped off for stealing trinkets."

"But this isn't the Middle East," she snapped.

"Right. This is America and one night in jail or a good paddling is more than fair for stealing a man's child—that's what I think."

Amanda typed while her head shook and her jaw tightened.

"I told that government spy the unvarnished truth and hoped she'd see the logic in what I said—fat chance. Of course, I didn't realize that as the male, I always have to be calm, never threaten violence, and never raise my voice so as to appear rational, no matter what. How dare a stranger tell me where to sleep and how to live my life? Parent's outside the court system are never told where to sleep, but I am?"

"Yeah, but telling her that Dee Dee should be beaten, that's, ah, I'd say that court worker was convinced that you have a serious problem."

I chuckled and grinned. "You'd think so, but I still say I'm the normal one. Women or men who do violence against me or my child deserve to suffer the consequences. When I'm attacked, physically or legally, I have a right to defend myself. Dee Dee doesn't learn. She just doesn't learn. And why should she? She never gets punished."

Amanda looked tense, but kept typing. "When were you due in Manhattan court?"

"The court date was only a few weeks away, and it was a clear case of Dee Dee violating the visitation order. The court would hear my petition to hold her in contempt of the visitation order and there was no question that she was guilty."

65

Manhattan family court

The waiting area seats were packed. I suspected that my pale face stood out from the black and Hispanic crowd. The hard plastic seats bolted to the floor and wall added to the rigid ambiance of the room. I blocked out the people sitting to either side and squished against my arms.

Where is Dee Dee? This time we were scheduled for a different courtroom. As always, I felt tense. The florescent lights continued to drain my energy the way oil leaks from a worn out car.

Otherwise, I'm on a slight adrenaline high. I can win this. Stay focused. She'll be in big trouble this time. She's already been found in contempt. Violating the judge's order is serious. How is she going to explain this?

Then, out of nowhere, she came into view the way a small ship appears through a dense fog. Dee Dee walked over to the officer who guarded the courtroom entrance. She wore slacks and a nice blouse, but otherwise I couldn't get a read on her.

She stayed near the courtroom door. A dark haired woman showed up and they started talking. Who is she? I haven't seen her before.

A strange feeling flashed through me. But I rationalized away my paranoia. I'm the one filing the petition, not her. She's the one who violated the court order, not me.

The constant buzz of the waiting room chatter nearly distracted me. The dark haired woman had folders in her hard, and she kept walking in and out of the courtroom.

What does she have to do? No, forget that. Focus on your arguments to the judge.

The officer came out from the courtroom with a firm grip on his clipboard, while he propped open the door with his foot.

"Farley versus O'Dell!" With a deep breath I stood up and moved quickly to the entrance. Once inside I immediately looked toward the bench. A male judge. What? Who's he?

Dee Dee came in behind me followed by the dark haired woman with her arms crossed in front clutching folders to her chest. Court personnel moved about the room and things seemed chaotic.

This new judge was lanky, middle aged, dark haired and a fast talker. It was all a blur.

"Where's Judge Zuckerman?" I asked a woman court reporter.

"She's retired."

"Order in the court," the judge called.

The dark haired woman spoke. "Your Honor, I have the documents..." She talked fast and handed papers to the court officer, who passed them along to the judge. Everyone ignored me. What the hell is going on?

The dark haired woman continued. "Your Honor, based on the report received from the case worker, we recommend that Mr. Farley submit to a psychological examination at this time." I turned and locked onto her.

The judge replied, "The court agrees. Mr. Farley, this court wants you to have a psychological examination."

I couldn't believe what I heard. "I'm not having a psychological examination. That's not what this hearing is about. It's about the mother's violation of the visitation order. I'm here to have you enforce my visitation rights with my daughter."

The judge shuffled papers and folders as he looked from one side of the courtroom to the other. "If you want visitation you'll have to have a psychological examination. This case is adjourned for September..."

"What? I have a visitation order. I'm the one who brought the petition."

The court officer flung open the door. "Everyone step out of the courtroom. Right now. Everyone step out." It was as if we met in the middle of a boxing ring and while the ref talked, I was sucker punched and knocked out. A helpless feeling bubbled up in my midsection.

The court officer handed me a piece of paper on the way out. "The next court date," he said. Two more months. Dee Dee just got permission from a judge to violate my rights. On the way to the subway it was all I could do to control myself. I have to re-focus now. Think about business—business. I left the court jungle for the concrete one. I decided to think about my newest entrepreneurial venture.

I was partnering with Link, the dark skinned and muscular gymnastics instructor who was going in with me on a new project. He and I were working on what we believed could become a super successful television show. I forced my mind to think about the possibilities of success instead of the slap down I'd just endured.

I walked so fast to the subway that I was nearly jogging— anything to burn off the anger and anxiety. Arrrgh, that judge should be hung. Stop. Focus on something else. What about the project?

Working on this concept had kept me very busy. There isn't anything I can do about the court right now. I don't have the funds or the patience for these family court lawyers. When this idea of ours becomes successful, I'll be rich, famous, and in the perfect position to get Sally back. It'll happen soon enough. I rushed down the subway steps, pulled a token from my pocket, and dropped it into the turnstile before I pushed my way through.

The platform was covered with people waiting for the next train. I found a place to stand and peered down onto the tracks, and blanked my mind. A very faint light came into view before I could hear the distant rumblings. I hoped that glimmer hinted at a brighter future.

66

With Amanda at the Hotel

The reporter and I resumed our places in the lounge and sank into the soft furniture. Once settled in, I noticed her smug expression and had to comment. "What?"

Amanda couldn't hold it in any longer. "I knew something like that was going to happen in court after you said what you did to the case worker. That wasn't a very smart thing to do."

After a big inhale, I let the air slip out and nodded. "Well, sometimes I put my foot in my mouth even though I know better." I gave a shrug and raised eyebrows. "Perhaps I had post-traumatic stress disorder. I don't know. I still might. But if I detected any government exploitation, it instantly set me off. By now I felt as if I was living in a fourth dimension."

As I spoke, Amanda was inspecting her perfectly manicured pink painted fingernails. "What do you mean?"

"It was as if I lived in one reality and everyone else lived in another. The family court laws are a world unto themselves. Once the family court comes into your personal life, or more accurately, once they're invited into your life, they take over. When they get you into the system you're not protected anymore."

"Protected from what?" "Government intrusion. Tyranny."

Amanda didn't react. I couldn't tell if I got her mental wheels turning with that statement or not. She sat up, and positioned her hands on the keyboard.

"Let's continue. What was the project you were working on?"

I leaned in and gestured toward her. "Now this was exciting. It had two parts. Part one was a television show idea. Janet and

John Farley, Jr.

I were able to raise about $30,000 for our new business venture. At this time, reality television was the new thing. *Survivor* was big and I had an idea even though I didn't know much about how television deals work."

Amanda stopped to look up from her screen. "You raised money for a TV show idea?"

"Yes, and a related business as well. Link and I spent months writing a script, contacting producers and getting people we knew to be in the production. Plus, Laura Bundy, my gorgeous, blonde television soap opera star friend from the health club, agreed to be in the show. Getting her involved was huge."

"What happened then?"

"It was mid-summer, just weeks away from shooting when I felt ill. A pain started in my right side and I thought I'd get over it, but it didn't go away. It got worse and worse until, days later I was delirious, in agonizing pain and feeling like my insides were going to explode. After three days of real suffering, Janet convinced me I needed to go to the hospital. By now she was sure that I had an appendicitis."

"Appendicitis. That's an emergency. So, you went to the hospital."

"Yeah. Here's the embarrassing part. We lived right across the street from the hospital. On the third night, at 1 in the morning, even though I could barely move, we walked— one slow, painful step at a time across the road.

"What did the doctors tell you?"

"Unfortunately, because I'd waited so long to go for help and they took another nine hours before they operated, my appendix burst, infection spread and I almost died."

Amanda's face flashed a hint of genuine concern in my direction. "Wow, that's serious."

"You're telling me. It took almost a month before I was home. I should mention that even though I wasn't working, child support payments continued to rack up.

Link was anxious for me to get well and star in our pre-pilot, but the production crew we'd hired was ready to cancel our agreement and move on to other projects if we couldn't shoot in the next few weeks."

"What did you do?"

"I'd lost twenty pounds that I couldn't afford to lose and looked frail. Nonetheless, even though moving around was painful, we spent three 15-hour days shooting the pre-pilot and I had a great time."

"You haven't told me what the show was about."

"It was called, *The Body Revolution Challenge with John Farley.* We had three personal fitness trainers responsible for getting their clients into the best shape of their lives, you know, lose weight, reduce body fat and do challenges to earn points and crown a winner."

Amanda paused for a moment and then her eyes got wide. "That sounds a lot like—"

I flashed her a corny grin. "Yeah!"

"Once the show was done we sent our video to producers around the country, including my client who was a senior producer at NBC studios in New York. To our shock and surprise, NBC came out with a show called *The Biggest Loser* about three years after we produced our show."

Amanda looked up from her screen and stared across at me. "Do you think they stole it from you?"

"It sure seems that way. It was so close to ours. On top of that, a year after our show was done Discovery Health produced a show called *Body Challenge*—it was exactly the same as ours."

"Did you sue?"

"A lawyer I spoke to said we had little chance and he wouldn't pursue it for us. It was devastating. We spent all this time, effort and money and made other people rich and famous beyond imagination. It was all I could take. But I'm skipping ahead. Before all that happened I came to a new realization while I was laid up in the hospital. My near death from a burst appendicitis was a wake up call like none other. My life was being eroded away in legal battles. I decided not to go back to the Manhattan family court."

This time Amanda kept gazing at her screen but stopped typing. Her face scrunched up. "But wasn't that your petition to hold Dee Dee in contempt for violating the visitation order?"

"Yes. The court allowed her to hold Sally hostage to get me to submit to a psychological exam. I knew it was just a ploy to further violate my rights with my child so I refused. In the hospital I decided it was time to change my life. If Dee Dee had contacted me to see Sally I'd go, but otherwise I just couldn't take the torture anymore."

Amanda leaned back and looked up. "You mean, you gave up on your daughter?"

I grimaced and let out a sigh. "I gave up battling her mother in court. It was either retreat or die fighting something I wasn't going to win. Dying a martyr's death was not something I wanted nor was it something anyone would've appreciated. It was a very tough decision. In fact, I didn't realize how tough it really was."

"It seems hard to imagine you'd quit like that." We sat in silence for what seemed a long time before Amanda asked her next question. "What was the other part of the business?"

"The second part was a weight management, meal delivery program. We rented a commercial kitchen, hired chefs and created a fabulous meal program that was healthy and delicious. Our company delivered a rectangular blue bag filled with gourmet meals right to our client's doorstep by 6 a.m. in the morning. It was excellent. We knew we had a multi-million dollar idea because another company was already doing it and making a fortune. Problem was, we were nearly out of money."

"Did you tell me earlier that you had spokespersons?"

"Yeah, I had some connections. Actress Laura Bundy was a spokesperson, and so was Dara Torres, the female multi-

Olympic gold medal swimmer. Oh, but something happened before we ever started operations."

"Wait. You mean before you started the meal business?"

"Yeah. We wanted to have one night of relaxation before we started working eighteen hours per day, so Janet and I decided to have dinner and see a movie."

Amanda was typing fast to get all the information down. "By now I hadn't seen Sally for at least a year. I had lost track of time and blocked everything out of my mind except work. I was determined to become successful and get the money I needed for a good lawyer to get back into the fight without killing myself."

Amanda paused. "Is going to the theatre important to the story?"

67

Spring 2001

The film sucked us in as soon as the theatre lights went down. Johnny Depp's character is George. George is a drug smuggler. While his life is a series of ups and downs, his daughter Kristina is always in the back of his mind.

Eventually, George is caught by the FBI one last time. The Feds leave George in a room alone at a desk-like table to speak into a tape recorder that they'll pass along to his father. George looked at the tape recorder in front of him, pressed the record button and began to speak.

"Hello Dad…I remember a lifetime ago, I was about 3 and a-half feet tall, weighing all of sixty pounds, but every inch your son." George continued to describe going to work on Saturday morning with his dad—getting into his green truck—it seemed like that truck was the biggest truck in the universe… "I thought you were the strongest man in the world…. Remember the home movies with mom…us playing football in the yard…coming home with the FBI chasing me…

"And that time when you told me the money isn't real, well, old man, I'm forty-two years old, and I finally realize what you were trying to tell me, I finally understand. You're the best dad, I just wish I could have done more for ya. I wish we had more time. I love you Dad."

As he abruptly pressed the "stop button" it was clear that he'd relayed his final message to his father. The scene faded into a scene overlooking a prison yard and its green grass. Many years had gone by since George's recording to his dad.

John Farley, Jr.

George is in a garden with one knee down in the dirt while he's bent over and tending plants. A prison guard calls out, "George! George, come on. You have a visitor."

A tall, model-like woman about 20, with long brown hair stands next to the guard on the grass. She's wearing a powder blue, form-fitting dress down close to the ankles.

With her arms clasp timidly in front and her, head cast down, she walks timidly across the green grass toward George. The guard had already turned and left. George placed his palms against his thigh, and pushed himself up on both feet. The years had aged him. He walked toward the woman who approached.

They stood in front of each other. George spoke to her in a gentle tone.

"Hello sweetheart," he said.

With trepidation, she replied, "Hi, Daddy."

George smiled, reached out and caressed her arms. "You're so big," he said. He quickly confessed that he'd screwed up. She shook her head, and looked sad.

"No," she replied.

"Come here," he told her as he hugged and held her head in his hands.

"You're the only thing in my life that ever meant anything."

Suddenly, the angle changes. The scene is now looking from behind George and he's holding a young girl—the daughter he remembered—her legs in the air, wrapped around him and her arms draped around his neck and shoulders.

"Swear?" her little voice asks him.

"I swear baby. Swear. I love you, Kristina."

Then in a blink she's a young woman again hugging him.

George continues. "You're the only good thing in my life. You're the only thing that ever meant anything to me. I love you."

As they gaze at each other, they start to walk. The tension broke, and they began to talk casually while holding hands.

The prison guard called out, "George, let's go!"

Georges' daydream is broken. He realizes Kristina is gone. She was never there, but only a figment of his imagination. Confused, he looked around as he stood in the yard, alone.

I watched the screen as feelings bubbled up toward my eyes. I capped the emotion as if trying to put the top back on a shaken soda can.

The movie ended and Janet and I walked home. During the walk back to the apartment I felt tense and hardly spoke. There was nothing I could do to stop the film images from being planted like seeds in my subconscious mind. I wanted to stay in denial, but I also knew that seeds eventually sprout.

68

It was Friday, the beginning of May and Sally's birthday was coming up soon. Something urged me to go out and see her. She'd be turning ten and I hadn't seen her since she was 8 1/2.

We devised a plan and put it into action. Janet and I rented a car and drove out to Long Island. We decided to show up at her school at the end of the day. During the drive Janet asked, "Can the school do anything to you?"

"I can't imagine how, but as we've seen in the past, nothing's impossible when it comes to keeping a dad from his daughter. We have to time this just right," I said.

Appearing there without permission from some authority made me nervous, but also angry at the very thought. Meanwhile, I mentally rehearsed how I'd search for Sally.

After a one-hour drive we arrived at the school. Janet turned down a tree-lined street. "I see it." I said.

My heart pounded. Why is my heart pounding? This is my child. I'm her father. I have a legal right, a moral right, to see my child. Why the hell is this so backwards?

I swallowed hard while I leaned forward, and barked out directions. As the car rolled closer to the school I had this odd feeling I was doing something criminal.

"Okay, okay, pull up over there," I said loudly. "I'm going to get out with Sally's birthday present. I'll find her, and give it to her. Wait for me."

I got out of the car as if pulling a bank heist. I reminded myself that this is MY child.

A long line of yellow buses stretched down the crescent shaped roadway in front of the school. I have no idea which bus she's on. Which one? How do I know? The lead bus started its engine. They were getting ready to leave.

My heart pounded. I dodged children on the sidewalk as I scanned for Sally's face. I must have stood out the way a single three-story building does on a street filled with ranch houses.

A woman teacher stood on the sidewalk guarding her post when I stopped and spoke to her. "I'm looking for Sally O'Dell, I'm her dad. Which bus is she on?"

The teacher mumbled something and scurried off. While I was concerned that she was about to tattle on me, I rushed to the lead bus and kept scanning faces. Moments later a man approached. "I'm the vice principal. What can I do for you?"

I glanced at him to see if he was a threat before I continued to peer into the crowd. "I'm looking for my daughter." I poked my head into doorway of the bus in front of us. "Sally!" I yelled, but there was no reply.

"Sally's bus has already left," he said.

I gave him a quick stare to get a read on him before I turned back to the line of a dozen buses revving their engines. I offered him an unfriendly, "Thanks," and rushed back down the long sidewalk to the car where Janet waited.

"Let's go to her house. We might be able to get there before the bus," I said. A short time later, we drove down Dee Dee's highway-like road. "No sign of anything. Let's circle the block." The second time around I checked for any sign of cops or buses. Still tense, I pointed to the entrance. "Let's pull into the driveway."

Once on the circular driveway I saw Ezel, the man who'd taken my place as Sally's father. He was raking leaves in the front yard. We drove to the end of the driveway and I got out. Ezel stopped raking.

I walked toward him with Sally's gifts, but I kept my distance as not to frighten him. "Ezel?"

"John," he said quietly. He stood still.

"Sally's birthday is Monday and this is for her. Is she in the house?" He seemed calm, perhaps frightened.

"No. No, she's at school."

Is he lying? I could give the present to him to give to her, but I can't trust that—I could've mailed it. "I know school let out a while ago."

I turned, and started toward the car. "Tell Dee Dee I said hi." I said with a hint of sarcasm. I opened the car door and got in. "We might as well leave."

"Look!" Janet said.

A big, yellow school bus pulled up and stopped in front of the driveway. Moments later the bus doors opened and a girl stepped out. It was Sally—she was taller.

"Wait here." I got out of the car with my little girl only forty feet from me. She barely glanced in my direction as she walked ballerina-like with her head down. The bus waited and again I felt pressure as if I was a child predator. Ezel was gone. Is he contacting the police or Dee Dee?

I called out, "Sally!" She walked faster, ignoring me. I stepped forward. "Sally. It's me, Dad! I brought you a birthday present and a letter. I took another step and as my foot touched ground Sally started running as if scared to death. She raced around to the back porch and out of sight.

I stood frozen. Between the bus hovering over me, Ezel possibly calling the cops and the fact that I was trespassing, I did nothing, but stand there looking foolish. I dropped my chin, reflexively. It was the final blow. Embarrassed, I slinked back to the car.

"Let's go," I said as I shut the car door. "She ran away from me." The drive back to Manhattan seemed extra long. Once home, I collapsed on the bed. It was too much. I couldn't take it anymore.

I was face up on the bed, arms crossed over my chest with my eyes closed when the movie we'd seen weeks earlier flashed across my mind. Janet came in and lay next to me and put her hands on my arms. That's when the damn broke. I couldn't hold it back anymore.

Tears flooded through my closed eyelids and left my face as wet as washcloth. Like most guys, I hated crying, but I hated to admit it even more. That day crushed my spirit. There was only one straw left.

69

It was very late in the evening, but I convinced Amanda to join me in the hotel health club for a workout. The facility provided exercise clothing for guests, everything but sneakers, so we decided to do yoga together.

Once changed, we met in the yoga room off the main workout floor. I managed to get there first and started stretching. A few minutes later she opened the door and shuffled in with her computer and other gadgets under her arm. After she set it all down in the corner of the room, I checked her out. No matter how polished a businessperson looks in the corporate world, the gym levels the playing field. Unless you're talking to a gorgeous woman, that is. The short shorts she had on made up for the baggy blue t-shirt that covered her curves.

"Let's do some poses and get re-energized," I said.

She stood in front of me and started to follow along. After 40 minutes of intense poses, we grabbed our towels and bottles of water and spread out across the wall-to-wall navy blue foam flooring.

"Our weight loss-meal delivery business was hurting through August, but I was optimistic that September would improve. We worked hard all summer long, metaphorically biting our nails in wait for Labor Day to end. That's when the unthinkable happened. Our television wasn't working the week after the holiday. I remember getting a call from Janet who was on her way to lower Manhattan around 9:30 a.m.

"It was the day the world changed. To our shock and disbelief, the twin towers, along with world trade center seven, imploded and collapsed. Our business kitchen was only one mile from the destruction. Operations were crippled. We had to close for a week. When I picked up the phone to make sales calls I was literally calling people who had lost friends and relatives and it was gut wrenching. Comfort food was in favor, not weight loss."

Amanda stretched her long, legs across the floor while her head rested against her arm. "What did you do?"

"Our money was running out. Employees wanted paychecks, suppliers demanded cash and clients had to be fed. Our own bills were growing. Child support payments never let-up, not even for 9-11. We hung on for another month until we had nothing left. It was time for a painful choice. We closed the business, packed all our belongings into a moving van and left for the only place that made sense."

"California," Amanda said with a sparkle in her eye.

"Yes. California," I said, almost matching her enthusiasm.

It took one week to drive across country. Our van, with all our belongings in it, arrived across the California border on November 1st, 2001. Not a drop of water had fallen during our road trip, but when we crossed the California state line, I pointed to the windshield as the first rain drops fell and wondered if it meant anything.

Sally was now thousands of miles away, but so were the family court jails and their rogue cops. The disappointment of leaving Sally was counterbalanced against the hope of a new life. I'd had glimpses of living in California, and I really hoped it lived up to my expectations.

70

In the Hotel with Amanda

"Can I get you something?" the waiter said to us. Amanda was focused on typing.

"You go first," she said.

"Pineapple juice, please." She seemed unconcerned about the beverage.

"Same for me," she said with only a moment's hesitation. Before the waiter had time to leave, she was back on task. "I want to go back to something you said earlier about chess. Tell me more about chess."

I collected my thoughts, drew a breath and momentarily gazed at the ceiling. "The queen is the most powerful piece in chess. She starts off next to the king, and on her own color. Her moves are the most versatile. Some say she's the most valuable."

"And the king?"

It'd been a long night. I rubbed my eyes and thought about her question. "The king is the weakest piece in chess. Except during the end game when it matters most. The king's value is infinite, because it can't be captured or exchanged. What's interesting is that when a king and a queen are battling against a lone king, the endgame is near."

"What is so interesting about chess? Why not monopoly?"

"Chess is ancient. It's based on warfare. In life, girls transform from a princess into a queen. Boys progress from page, to knight, to prince and if all goes well they'll someday develop into a king, a man who knows who he is, and who the people are in his kingdom that he wants to give to. In life and in chess, a kingdom is more likely to last if it's ruled by a king and a queen. Women have so much natural power that to give them more power would create problems in the game."

Amanda cocked her head. "What kind of problems?"

"Many queens, that is, powerful women in society, have taken on the role of king in many ways. They're playing the game of life without having a king in the kingdom. Some women are proud to say that they don't need men in their lives."

Amanda perked up. "Women are more independent now and have more freedom of choice," she said. I nodded. "When society gives a woman additional political, economic or business advantages over a man, on top of her natural power, it has the effect of a pawn getting queened."

Amanda paused with a serious expression. "Is that a gay slur or some sexual innuendo?"

"No—not at all." I chuckled.

"Oh, you mean when a pawn gets promoted to queen?"

"Yes. Now, one side has two queens or even three queens. The game quickly becomes so lopsided that the other side loses fast."Amanda sat in silence as her fingers hovered over the keyboard.

"I'd say it's still a man's world."

I smiled. "That's what I'm told. In chess and in life, the king and queen make a strong kingdom. But when one of them amasses more than their natural power, a delicate balance is upset."

"Do you expect women to give up the power they've fought for? I know I wouldn't."

"If women want men, then they have to give up some political power or they'll continue to be unsatisfied. In chess, kings can't become too powerful, but in real life the balance of power is delicate." The waiter came back with our drinks."What stage of development were you in at this time?"

"I didn't know it then, but I'd say 'prince.' A prince is known for building. Typically a man is building a family or a career. For me, all I wanted was to build a successful business or career. I wanted economic freedom and I was so frustrated at not achieving it—of failing—that I felt extreme stress.

"A prince needs nurturing, patience and encouragement from the people in his life. In my case, I was eager to build my online college, but Janet had other needs and priorities that I didn't realize."

Amanda's eyes brightened. "What happened next?"

California

We drove through California and arrived at the in-laws home. As soon as I stepped out of the car Mr. Kay greeted me with a surprise hug as if I was a long, lost son. I found this strange, but nice.

Later that night, we all went out to a Mexican restaurant. Mr. Kay read over the menu while Janet and I did the same. Steve-o sat across from us fidgeting and looking around.

Mr. Kay and I had a few similar qualities. We both hung back to see where a conversation was going. Admittedly, he was better at this than me. He often sat like a spy as he listened to table conversations.

Frankly, he was intimidating. He claimed to have an IQ of 169, a high level genius and I didn't doubt it. He grew up in another age. A time of tougher men. He was focused on his objective, whether it was ordering from a menu or closing a large business deal. Smiles were rare and laughs more so. Everything to him was a competition and his number one competitor, me, was now living in the house next door. Problem was, I didn't know it was a competition.

Mrs. Kay sat near me at the table and explained our new living arrangement. "The home you and Janet will stay in temporarily was where my grandparents lived when we brought them to California from the East Coast."

The waiter came by to refill our plastic bowl with tortilla chips. Janet took the opportunity to show off her knowledge of California. She picked up a chip and tilted it against the light the way store clerks hold up bills to see if they're authentic.

"California is filled with Mexicans and the Mexican restaurants here are the best. This is real Mexican food," she said, as she crushed the chip between her white teeth and flashed me a smile.

As our meals arrived and the waiter put burritos in front of each of us, Mr. Kay broke his silence. "What you need to do is start personal fitness training." I swallowed and then re-adjusted my grip on the burrito while I glanced at Mr. Kay and then leaned in to bite off a mouthful. I chewed at half speed in order to buy time.

"Being a personal fitness trainer isn't why I traveled across the country." He stopped eating and locked onto me while I took another bite. His rusty Brooklyn accent came through loud and clear.

"Fitness is what you've been successful at. You've had success," he said with a two hand gesture. "Do what you've been successful at."

We'd just trekked across country to California. I'd left everything I've ever known—including any chance I'd see my daughter again in order to start up in a new world, to re-invent myself and I'm being told to go backwards? I would have preferred if he'd encouraged my ambitions and had some faith in me.

My tone stayed soft. "I understand what you're saying. The thing is, I didn't travel all the way across the country to be a personal fitness trainer. If I wanted that I could have stayed in New York City. Everything I'd need for personal fitness training I already had in New York. My aim for being out here is to grow the distance learning college not to do personal fitness training,"

His volume increased as his facial features changed in a bad way. Everyone else at the table chewed their food or talked quietly and pretended to ignore us. Mr. Kay became animated as he articulated every syllable. "The aim in business is TWO words: make money."

Our eyes met briefly before I looked away and went in for another bite. I felt the pressure to conform. This was his domain, his turf. Between the courts and him, living my own life was becoming increasingly difficult, but my life was too important to give up on during the first night of our arrival. After a gentle throat clearing I responded. "I'm really not interested in being a personal trainer anymore. I want to make money with the distance learning college I've started."

He looked down at his plate and I felt as if we were on the verge a full-blown argument. I wanted to deflect attention from myself and so I started to ask Janet's mother about California when Mr. Kay interjected.

"Janet says you've done some speaking." Perhaps he was curious about my speaking success? "Yes, I've spoken at corporate events, on radio shows, seminars and television."

He held a fork in one hand and a steak knife in the other as if they were microphones, but his posture resembled a warlord. "I've given a lot of speeches. One speech I've given I call the difference between a good businessman and a bad businessman. That's what I call it in public, anyway. It's really the story of the Jewish businessman and the Christian businessman."

Mr. Kay had spent his entire life working with and learning the ways of different people in business. He knew how the Jews, the Christians, the Indians, the Muslims and many others made deals and negotiated. To him business was similar to politics, civilized warfare.

"The story goes that the bad businessman was in his kitchen, opened the refrigerator, took out a carton of milk and poured himself a cup. As he turned around, he knocked the cup over and spilled the milk. He grabbed a rag, wiped up the milk and poured himself another glass."

As he paused, I took the opportunity to bite into my burrito.

"One day the good businessman was in his kitchen. He opened the refrigerator, took out a carton of milk and poured a cup. As he turned around, he knocked the cup over and spilled the milk. He grabbed another cup from the cupboard, poured the milk and set it on the counter. Then he walked into the other room, opened the screen door and brought his cat inside. The cat came over and drank the spilled milk. That's the difference between the bad businessman and the good businessman."

I nodded while he stared through me with a smug face. I was eager to digest the parable as fast as possible—faster than the burrito. He and I thought differently and I desperately wanted to glean business wisdom from him if he would share it.

The bill came and I reached for my wallet. I whispered to Janet, "I want us to contribute to this." Janet glanced across the table. "Mom, does he want—"

Mrs. Kay smiled. "It's okay, we have it." Janet's brother never flinched. I suspect he knew his meal ticket was covered.

"Thank you," I said, as Mr. Kay handed the waiter a few bills.

***

We moved in with Steve-o and another housemate directly behind the Kay's main house. We didn't realize it, but we were depressed for about six months after the September eleventh attacks. Our entire lives had turned upside down.

We spent our evenings watching lighthearted television to distance ourselves from all we had been through—the loss of our business, our lifestyle and Sally. Consciously, my "father" identity was drifting away from me faster than a loose helium balloon, but nothing replaced it.

Weeks after we arrived in California, envelopes came in the mail demanding child support payments. It was a constant reminder of what I'd left behind and a constant reminder that I had to continue to work for Dee Dee.

Time went by and my attitude was going downhill. Mr. Kay had so dominated his own children that they couldn't live their own lives and now he was attempting to control me. I had every indication to believe that he was disappointed in me. I was trapped in a double bind. On the one hand I was expected to be a success, but on the other hand he didn't want me to surpass him. He was the big lion of the family and he never liked the new cub in town. Something had to change.

71

The wall clock struck midnight and Amanda and I were still going strong. After a stretch break, we sat and sipped our warm tea. "Our marriage didn't last long when we arrived in California," I said, as I brought the teacup to my lips.

Amanda sat wide-eyed. "What happened?"

"Between the stresses of the online college, Janet's intense job, paying bills, my clashes with her father and my own demons, it all took a toll. At the heart of it was my frustration at not feeling as though I was in control of my own life."

Amanda paused. "Life's not fair. You have to take responsibility at some point." "Responsibility." I mulled over the word for a few moments. "The conflict I faced was between doing what I wanted to do professionally versus what the courts demanded me to do to pay Dee Dee."

"Dee Dee?" she asked, as she conspicuously uncrossed and re-crossed her slender calves below her tastefully short skirt. "Wasn't she out of the picture by now?"

"I was safe in California, but she hired California process servers to find me, pound on our front door, and try to serve me with court documents." Amanda's face scrunched up. "For what?"

"She wanted me held in contempt of court for not paying child support and she asked the court for an increase in my support payments."

"Were you paying?" she asked.

"A little here and there, but not as much as they wanted. I had to make sure I could survive before I gave away the little I had. Plus, it made me angry to pay her for stealing my child.

Anyway, many events happened over the course of several years."

"Like what?"

"I got a return letter from David Rockefeller's private assistant in 2003. She let me know that Mr. Rockefeller was writing his memoir and wasn't able to help out our online college. It confirmed my belief that the Rockefellers only funded big projects they controlled in order to influence society, and the world."

"The world?" She raised her eyebrows.

"I only had a vague idea about Rockefeller's involvement in world events since I'd watched that secret video way back in 1993."

"Did you have more contact with the Rockefellers after that letter?" "No, that was it. As time went by I searched for different career opportunities, but nothing paid much, if any money. Then Janet and I began constantly fighting, more than usual."

"About what?"

"Everything it seemed. Then it happened. I was on the couch while she sat in a chair across from me with tears in her eyes. That's when she let me know that she wanted a divorce. It was as if I was knocked to the ground. I never thought it would happen. At that moment, it seemed to come out of nowhere. I didn't realize that many of my problems stemmed from a misunderstanding of women, and what was expected of me as a male in society. If I'd understood more about men and women when I was younger things would've been different."

"So you got divorced."

"Not exactly. What neither of us realized is that technically we didn't need a divorce because we never filed marriage paperwork in this country. As far as the U.S. was concerned, we weren't married, but we never knew it. Perhaps I could have brought it to court and gone after her for assets, but to me that's not fair."

"So are you still married or you were never married?"

"Both I suppose. She left and suddenly I was single. We'd moved several times in the local area and now I was by myself. I remembered sitting in the living room by myself. The silence was deafening and I felt very alone."

"What did you do without Janet's help paying the bills?"

"I got serious about the online college and I started personal training to the wealthy, but the college struggled. I was broke and alone. Not a good feeling. About six months later it struck me. I had no social life and it was impacting my attitude. I decided to take a chance and visit a dance studio to learn salsa. When I started ballroom dance I was terrible—self-conscious, off beat and had no confidence while dancing."

"Dancing!" Amanda perked up. "That sounds like fun. I love to dance." "Most women do. The first thing women said was that I needed to be more confident. One woman told me she could tell a lot about a guy by the way he dances."

"Really? Like what?" "She could tell whether or not he's sensitive to her, protective and if he's a take charge kind of guy."

Amanda leaned in. "For many women," I said, as I sipped tea, "dancing is like sex and the better the man dances, the better he's expected to be in the bedroom—that's what I heard from some women."

Amanda momentarily broke eye contact and started typing. "Ballroom dance," I said, "is one of the last places in society where the man *must* take charge and the woman *must* follow his lead."

"Huh, what do you mean?" "Today, men have been so emasculated that most don't know what to do or how to act on a date."

"Hmmm?"

"Some men don't know if they should open the door for a woman, pay for lunch or how to treat her. Most wait for the woman to take the lead or give him a neon sign sized clue. The reason has to do with women demanding equality and men being brainwashed to think equality means everything is equal between men and women."

Amanda looked up at the wall clock. "It's all interesting, but I want to get back to the story."

"Sure. My mother had unexpected health trouble back East. Her illness was getting worse over time. The loss I felt when she passed away was a real wake up call. That's when I noticed that many of the white, California transplants I knew weren't very close to their families, yet my immigrant friends were close to their families and they often came to this country together. It got me thinking."

"So, at this point you were feeling a loss of family?"

"Yeah, and I was starting to see patterns. I'll come back to that."

Amanda stroked her hair. "What happened with child support?"

"They doubled it instantly when Dee Dee asked for it to be increased. Stunned and helpless all I could do was go into denial. A few years later, the case was transferred to California and the Department of Child Support Services came after me. I was running out of money and the online college was hanging on by a shoestring."

"What did you do?"

"Years had gone by and one day I realized Sally would be graduating high school—she'd be 18. An idea popped into my head. What if she's on this new thing called Facebook?"

"Was she?" Amanda said in a high pitch.

"I searched with my heart pounding in anticipation and within minutes there she was! I hadn't seen a photo of her in many years. Dee Dee never sent me anything even though I wrote and asked. My little girl had turned 18. She looked the way I remembered, but grown. I was so overwhelmed with joy, excitement, sadness, and anger. Her photo looked so good. I couldn't believe I'd found her. She was right there, yet far away. I absorbed her smile, reddish brown hair, and bright eyes."

"Did you contact her?"

"There was no phone number. After thinking through what I wanted to say, I sent her an email. I poured my heart out to her. I told her I was sorry that I couldn't have been there for her."

"Do you have a picture of her?" I pulled up her photo on my mobile phone, and leaned over as Amanda took it and smiled. "Then it hit me. All the lost years. The lost relationships between her and our family. All the frustration, the humiliation and pain—it overwhelmed me. I was a basket case."

"Did she write back?"

"To my amazement, Dee Dee sent me an email and said they got mine and were considering a trip to California. Dee Dee would let me know when a decision was made."

Amanda's expression begged for an answer."She never replied and when I called her office she hung up on me repeatedly. As for Sally, I sent hundreds of emails over several years, but no response."

Amanda paused. "How did that make you feel?"

"I felt unimportant and discarded, but mostly used and abused by her mother and bulldozed by the system. To add insult to injury, Melissa Popps, of the California Department of Child Support Services, kept calling to insult me and threaten to take my driver's license away. Anything to coerce and guilt me into paying child support to Dee Dee, even if it meant I couldn't pay my rent."

I paused a moment to clear my mind. "I kept emailing Sally and waiting for a reply."

"She never contacted you?" "No." I reached for my phone. "What I realized after many years was hard for me to come to grips with. It's the idea that Dee Dee has many psychopathic qualities."

"What. You're calling her a psychopath?"

"I looked at her behavior patterns and it became clear. She's never apologized to me or anyone I know of, not once. She justifies every malicious act she's done as not her fault and she's absolutely a pathological liar. Her emotional reactions are explosive, I'd say abnormal. Plus, she doesn't care what anyone thinks of her so long as it gets her what she wants. She seems to fit the profile of what's called a victim psychopath. They appear weak, vulnerable, even pitiful in order to garner sympathy. I always called her the master manipulator, but I never realized how right I was."

"Creepy." Amanda tapped the keyboard.

"Time passed and I did many jobs, but most weren't profitable. I had an unpaid radio show and interviewed some very famous people, including the late fitness legend and television personality, Jack Lalanne and the famous film producer, Aaron Russo. Russo produced the films *Trading Places* with Eddie Murphy and *The Rose* with Bette Midler. He and I talked about his last film, *Freedom to Fascism*."

"Was he a right-winger?" she asked with an edge in her voice.

"Russo was an American who strongly believed in freedom. He exposed the income tax and the Federal Reserve bank as complete frauds."

"Wait—Frauds?"

"Remember all my inquiries into the income tax? Well, I was right. The income tax is fundamentally unconstitutional and the Federal Reserve Bank isn't federal—it's a private banking cartel."

"Do you have proof of this? I mean, it sounds farfetched."

"It seems odd, but the Rockefeller family has been involved with banking since the Federal Reserve came into existence in 1913. Many books have been written on the Federal Reserve and some independent publishers have discussed the unconstitutionality of the income tax."

"But that stuff's not true," she insisted.

"You'll have to look into it yourself and decide. Russo and I talked about our connections to the Rockefeller family and their connections to what's called The New World Order."

"Hold on. New what?"

"New World Order. To sum it up, the mega-banks and their owners from across the globe are planning to implode the economies of countries worldwide and bring in a one world government."

Amanda's face looked pained and disappointed just before she straightened up and drew a breath. "This is what you didn't want to tell me at the start of the interview. Are you one of those conspiracy theorists who think that someone out there controls the world?" she said as her mouth hung open.

"Not someone, but the ultra rich families that have controlled the masses for many hundreds of years. They have more money than you can imagine and they're very powerful. The Rockefeller family is only one name out of many who wield enough power to shape world events, create wars and plunge world economies into depression."

Amanda fidgeted and talked rapidly. "But what does this have to do with Dee Dee and you?" "As far as I could tell then, nothing, but my viewpoint changed as I learned more. The gap between The New World Order and my life seemed unrelated, but it was connected."

"What's the connection?"

"That's where my dating life comes in. I was making the same mistakes with women in my mid 30's as I did at 22. Finally, after a particularly painful experience, I swallowed my pride and decided to do something about it."

Amanda's expression intensified.

"For my radio show I interviewed several dating experts and out of desperation I decided to make dating and relationships a formal study."

"Really? How'd you do that?" she blurted.

"I found a man I considered the dating grandmaster and studied with him for many years." A big grin spread across Amanda's face.

"A dating grandmaster," she said skeptically.

"Yeah, people made fun of me and I had my doubts about the whole thing, but what I learned was life changing."

"I can't wait to hear about this." She grinned.

"Before I forget, let me say that my child support debt was growing and growing at 9% per year interest plus the weekly bill."

"Wow. That's a hefty interest rate."

"It sure is. More than you can get anywhere else with zero risk."

"I'm confused. Are we talking about dating or child support?"

"Dating was an ongoing study. What really changed my view on child support was something else. My new girlfriend at the time took me to what sounded like a rock concert coming from inside a large church."

72

My new girlfriend and I drove into the expansive and packed parking lot.

"Here we are. We got out and gazed with wonderment at the magnificent church building.

Jasmine, a fabulous Vietnamese woman, looked great. She had on a beautiful floral dress, with heeled shoes that had little orange bow ties on the tips. Her stylish, thick, jet-black hair and fabulous smile were magnetic. She radiated class, style and virtue with a touch of sexiness.

"Wow." We walked closer to the entrance. "That's loud." Between the large building and the powerful music, I knew something was different. "It sounds like a rock concert."

Jasmine turned to me and smiled as we ascended the steps.

Volunteers, eager to shake our hands, welcomed us. Jasmine led the way into the main church with giant video screens up high and off center. The open space was filled with enough chairs to seat thousands. The live band, with dozens of choir singers, rivaled any rock concert I'd seen. My chest vibrated to the pulsating beat, while the congregation stood, clapped in unison, sang, and swayed to the beat.

An usher hurried us down to seats in front near the pulpit which is more like a stage. The Christian rock consumed me. The intensity of the sound forced me to take a deep breath. The passionate voices and the spirit-filled music shook loose my stoic exterior as I felt my eyes get moist for some reason. The band continued for at least ten more minutes.

As the music became soft and started to fade, we took our seats. I'd never experienced a church like this before. Eventually, the pastor walked up onto the stage-like altar. A tall, fit, energetic man, with a full head of white hair, he made his way to the pulpit. I noticed his expensive, well-made dark suit, classy blue tie, and a bright white shirt.

The pastor spoke gently, as the soft music trailed off in the background. "Let's look at Proverbs. The most practical book in the bible." The pastor flipped the pages of his black book. "Open to Proverbs 22:7. 'The rich rule over the poor and the borrower is servant to the lender.' Servant or you could say slave to the lender."

I pondered the passage. Servant. Slave. Borrower. Lender.

The church service went on and the pastor continued to preach, but my mind replayed the Proverbs quote.

Near the end of the service, Jasmine and hundreds more put their hands high in the air, and shouted "Amen." To my pleasant surprise, I felt renewed.

***

That evening at my condo, after Jasmine had gone home, I sat reading on my living room love seat. I found the Proverbs verse in an old bible I'd been given.

A thought interrupted me. What about the United States constitution? It mentions slavery. No slavery or involuntary servitude, right? Which amendment is that?

I closed the bible for a moment to check the computer for the U.S. constitution. There! Inspired, I grabbed the phone and dialed a friend. He's a buddy of mine, an engineer and a Stanford graduate—always open to solving problems. He had much more experience with computers than women, which made for endless hours of conversation.

No involuntary servitude. I remembered that phrase from the video I saw back in 1993. It said that the so called income tax got around the "no involuntary servitude" part of the law and the fifth amendment's protection against being a witness against oneself by making the filing of an income tax form voluntary. Voluntary compliance.

"John!" Russell said, as he answered the phone.

Once we got the usual pleasantries out of the way I got to the point. "Russell, listen to this. I've got something interesting here. It looks to me that child support is a violation of the thirteenth amendment to the constitution."

"Go on," he said, skeptically.

We talked for two hours. A few days later we talked again and then once more a few days after that. As we debated and looked at legal documents, it became clear. Child support, forcing someone to get a job to pay a debt or jailing them for not paying the debt, is debt slavery, also known as peonage or involuntary servitude, a type of slavery. That's what Proverbs warned about.

After we'd discussed the details of child support and the 13th amendment, Russell, stopped me. "John, I have to go back into work. What's next for you?"

I paced around the living room and stared out the large glass door into the wind blown palm trees. "A Department of Child Support Services agent calls me up and threatens to take my driver's license away. They've already stopped me from renewing my passport so I can't leave the country. The agent phones and insults me." I let out a big sigh. "I've had it."

"Yeah," he said in a low-pitched voice. "I have to sue 'em. How? I don't know."

"What happened to your ninja philosophy of being invisible?" "That's what I prefer, but now it's time for a samurai approach. Attack."

We hung up and I researched the internet and found some very good news.

U.S. Federal District Courthouse, San Jose, California

The elevator opened to what seemed like an airtight, desolate hallway. The sign on the wall directed me around the corner. One step beyond the wall and there it was, the legal office that offered free help for filing Federal lawsuits. The door was open, but I knocked anyway. A young woman sprang to her feet and came from around her desk. "Hello?" she said formally as she projected her voice above normal.

"I'm John Farley." I put out my hand. "Here to see Rachel."

"Yes, I'm Rachel." She grasped my palm with a firm grip, but with a hint of trepidation and frantic energy. "Yes, let's see," she said with strained precision. "I have you for an appointment starting in five minutes. Have a seat. I'll be back in just a few minutes."

"Okay." I took two steps into the cramped space and sat.

Minutes later she rushed in and plunked down at her desk. My first guess was that she'd exceeded her caffeine limit for the day. She explained how the free legal service worked and gave me papers to sign. Once signed, she then she gave me her full attention. Whatever she said suggested she was new here and wanted to do everything perfectly.

"What is it," she asked, as if pressed for time, "that you need help with?"

I'd sized her up in the first few minutes. Probably late 20's. The rock on her finger meant marriage, perhaps recently, but I didn't sense any motherly qualities coming from her. Her conservative clothes and short, precise hairstyle indicated rigid thinking and some masculine characteristics. Her fast, chaotic movements suggested she was chronically anxious. I looked her in the eye and gave her a cocky smile, ready to present my issue with a hint of drama and bordering on over confidence.

"You are looking at someone who owes more money in back child support than anyone you've ever met."

Frozen, she stared back at me and swallowed. Perhaps she thought I said the words, "armed robber," because her eyes got bigger. There was an uncomfortable silence and then a twitch manifested in her left eyelid.

She turned and typed on her keyboard, printed documents, and rattled off the filing procedure with cheetah-like speed.

As silence filled the air, she stared across the desk. "I want you to know that you're going to lose this case. You have no chance of winning," she said with a slight sadistic tone.

My feet felt cramped as my shoe tips were pressed up against the front of the desk. I pitched forward in my chair and felt my forced smile beginning to fade.

"And what do you base that belief on?" I asked as I scanned her face for nervous tics.

"The thirteenth amendment doesn't apply to child support cases." She looked away and started fiddling with her computer. "What is your argument? I mean, what is your reason for saying that?" I asked with a soft, professional tone.

"I can't get into the facts of a case. This office will only help you do the procedural work.   I'm just telling you that you're going to lose." Her comments struck me as more than pessimistic. Perhaps, like most people, she thinks child support is sacred. I pressed her for more specifics, but she dodged and blocked my questions in lawyer-like fashion before she blurted out what was on her mind. "If you won," she said, as she leaned in across the desk, "you'd destroy the entire foundation of society!"

"Yes, that's why I want to win. I want to change society— save society. I want to end child support because it's peonage." She turned away as she fiddled with papers, then swiveled back with a cold demeanor.

"This office can assist you with the procedures for filing, but nothing more. I have to stop now. Our time is up."

I met with her once again for help, but then she said her office wouldn't assist me further. Despite paperwork imperfections, the lawsuit was filed in Federal District Court against the California Department of Child Support Services.

It took over six months for the court to set a date with Federal judge, Lucy Koh. As the court date approached and the judge changed the court date from October 6th, 2011 to October 13th, I felt something historic was about to happen.

***

"Russell," I said into the phone. "It comes down to a few key ideas. Forcing someone to get a job to pay a debt is peonage, debt slavery. It's illegal and violates the thirteenth amendment to the U.S. constitution."

"The court's position," he countered, "could be that since they aren't insisting that you do one specific job for one specific employer it's not a constitutional violation."

"Right, but it's crazy. The Family Courts tell us how much money they expect a person to make and then orders a non-custodial parent to pay it. That means that you and I aren't allowed to choose the work we want to do."

"You're saying—"

"I'm saying that if a medical doctor who has the potential to make $200,000 per year wants to quit medicine and become a waiter earning $35,000 per year, the courts will say that he purposefully reduced his income to reduce his child support payments and they won't modify the amount he owes."

A moment of silence eased the intensity.

"Your point," Russell said robotically, "is that if a court orders you to make a certain amount of money it limits your career choices."

"Ahhh, yes," I said before continuing. "What if a father doesn't want to work? What if he wants to volunteer overseas for his church, or even be a bum for that matter, and live on the streets or just earn less doing a job he enjoys more? The courts say, he can't. That's involuntary servitude."

"Let me play devil's advocate," Russell countered. "A father has a duty to support his child. To support a child you have to make money one way or another."

I nodded. "That's the core issue. Do we really have to support our children? Seems bizarre, but 'support' isn't legally defined. In today's world, support means to pay money to the other parent, right?"

"Riighht," he said with a skeptical tone.

"The truth is that a parent's duty is to provide for their children—that's what the 14th amendment suggests. 'Providing' means giving children what they need to live and anything else the parents want them to have. When my child is with me, I'm providing a roof over her head, transportation, food, entertainment and anything else she needs during our time together. The mother provides nothing while the child is with me. So, time with the child forces the parent to pay for the child's needs in direct proportion to how much time they spend together."

The phone was silent for a moment before Russell countered. "What about mothers with, say, five children. The mom's not making enough money to support the kids. What then?"

"Good point. If the mother can't pay for the needs of the children, then she should give them to the father to take care of. If she won't do that, then they should split the time with the children 50–50."

"Yeah. Women will just give up their children to go along with your plan!" he said sarcastically.

"They're just as much his children as they are hers," I replied.

"But there's still going to be too many expenses for the mom, even if they split the time 50-50."

"Maybe. Which is another reason for families to stick together. From what I've read, no successful human society has ever been based on a mother—child, single family model. Only the married, two parent family has been successful."

"Ha, ha." Russell's laugh broke the intensity. "Let me get this straight. You think everyone should be married."

"No. I think if you're going to have children, then it's best if a married mother and father raise them."

"Wait, wait, wait," Russell interjected, as he held back laughter. "John, there's lots of two parent families with children that some say shouldn't have had kids at all."

"Yeah, nothing's perfect. Some people might have said that about my mother, but I'm glad she and my dad had the right to have me. I'm saying that we have an epidemic, a crisis, on our hands and it starts with how men and women relate to one another and ends with a society of fatherless children."

I paused as an uncomfortable silence lingered. "Here are some other points I'm making to the court. Child support doesn't reduce high school dropout rates, but having a father in a child's life does. Child support does not reduce drug use, but having a father in one's life does. Child support does not reduce suicide rates, but having a father in one's life does."

"You have these statistics?"

"Yes, and how 'bout this, health and behavioral problems increase without fathers in the home. Crime rates for boys and teen pregnancy for girls increase when fathers are absent. Poverty increases by five times and extreme poverty by ten times."

"I got it. Your point is that child support to the other parent doesn't solve the real problems."

"And child support creates more problems. Many fathers end up in poverty, jail or both. Let me add that one reason women are having trouble dating and marrying guys these days is because little boys didn't have male role models—fathers—in their lives."

There was a pause on the line before Russell spoke up. "When's your court date?"

"Next week," I said, as the stakes of success and failure crossed my mind.

73

Amanda chewed a chocolate bar while reading her notes. I stretched my arms overhead. She slurred her words between chocolate chunks. "The Federal Court decision was next?"

"Yeah. I got up very early in the morning, and went outside for some light exercise. It was nearly time for a landmark decision. Hours later at my computer, an email arrived from the Federal District Court. "No need to show up. The judge doesn't need to see you. You'll be mailed the decision shortly." What? I want my day in court. I want to be able to verbalize my position. This can't be good news.

One day later the judge's decision came in the mail. She ruled against me. It was the same argument a different California court had used in a similar case. If a person is not working for one boss, then involuntary servitude doesn't apply, they claim. It was a decision that lacked originality and courage. They ignored the fact that child support debt was never incurred. A parent doesn't do anything to get into this debt. Courts impose it on a person.

I sat at my small dining room table barely able to read the judge's papers. Stunned, angry and feeling hopeless, I thought about all the time and effort I'd wasted.

Later that night, Russell and I met for dinner.

We arrived at the local all-you-can-eat buffet. It was crowded and noisy, but just what we needed. We got a table in a semi-private corner. With our plates piled high we hardly had time to lift our forks before I brought up the court ruling. "The judge is wrong. She's wrong," I said, before plunging a tomato into my mouth.

"You really expected to win, didn't you?" Russell poked his fork into the leafy greens. I shook my head while eyeing my salad.

"Of course I did. I'm right."

"But the courts aren't going to let you change their system," he said.

"We need to change these laws before it gets worse," I countered.

"What happens next?"

"I'll spell it out for you. Ready? Hold on to your chair. As I've told you before, the Rockefellers are a part of the Illuminati—"

"Wait, wait," he said, nearly choking. "Let me guess! This is all manufactured by the Illuminati and because of them, you lost your court case and they want to keep child support going just to ruin families...." Russell joked, as he laughed obnoxiously.

"Well, smart guy," I said with a slight aristocratic tone, while simultaneously skimming my spoon through the lobster bisque. "You're not so far off. First of all, the Rockefellers were supporters of many eugenics programs and—"

"Hold on, John. Eugenics is what again?"

"The quest for improving the human species through mating. One means of doing that is to eliminate or kill off so called, lesser humans. That's what Hitler was into, and the Rockefellers indirectly supported him."

"Wait. You have proof of this?"

"You can find it, but let's keep going. The family courts were eugenics courts. The 1930's film, *Tomorrow's Children* is about the 1927 court case Buck v. Bell, where the Supreme Court justice famously said, 'three generations of imbeciles are enough' and then sterilized people."

"You're saying our government forcibly sterilized people?"

"It's on record, my friend. Sixty thousand that we know of, and they aren't done yet. The family courts fit into the Illuminati's plan to control the world's population."

"Wait." He grinned with spinach in his mouth. "You're trying to tell me that the Rockefellers are the Illuminati? Tell me again, who are the Illuminati?"

"The Illuminati—you'll have to look it up yourself, but the Illuminati, are those elites who believe they're enlightened and that they alone know how to run our lives better than we do. It's commonly believed that thirteen impossibly wealthy families going back many centuries, make up the Illuminati. The Rockefellers are one illuminati family."

After a quick swig of water, Russell, put his fork down to gesture. "The Illuminati wants to control the world, and to do so they want to sterilize everybody," he said, becoming more animated. "This is the craziest thing I've—"

"It's not so crazy. We can go into all the minutia of this, but what I want you to realize is one thing, the family courts are part of the plan. Their main job is to get the men out of the house, to break up families, weaken men and take control of the family."

Russell grabbed his fork, then nearly dropped it as he hurried to interject. "John," he said stone faced, as if worried about my mental health, "do you believe that the judges and lawyers and law makers are all in on this conspiracy?"

"Nooo," I said quietly. "They're not in on it consciously. They're in on it because they're part of the system. But the real powers behind this conspiracy are far removed from the courts on a day to day basis." Russell munched his salad giving me time to continue. "Look around. Men are more confused than ever about their role in society. Women are divorcing their husbands because the men aren't able to give them what they think they want. Women are in the workforce as never before doing work that used to be men's work and sometimes doing it better."

Russell bit into his mini-muffin with force, as if it were a well-done steak. "So," he mumbled, "you want to go back to the days when women were barefoot and pregnant. Is that what you're saying?"

John Farley, Jr.

"Well," I smirked, "no, although—seriously, I'm simply saying that men are becoming less manly because of a loss of male role models and mixed messages from society. Women are becoming more masculine because of societal expectations and the fact that they have to pick up where the men leave off."

"I don't see that." He grabbed his water cup.

"Open your eyes. Look around. I was talking with our friend Tina about this. She agrees with me. She's tired of being the man in her life." I pointed my fork at him. "As a forty-something divorcee, she doesn't want to compete with men anymore. This dual role women play is contributing to how they interact with men. Women can do men's work, but since they're not designed like men, it takes a toll on their femininity."

Russell sipped a spoonful of his cream of broccoli.

"Women think they want it all in life, and that pursuit stresses them. At a deep level men are wondering where they're supposed to fit in."

Russ started to get up. "I want to get some more soup. What's the next hurdle?"

"I don't know. The child support agency wants me to pay them a ton of money. Something's got to change."

74

Weeks passed. The online college I founded sold for a small sum—thank God. I needed to do something different, something successful. I'd just signed a deal to start a hypnosis clinic. December had arrived and the holiday season was in full swing.

I stood outside my condo at the mailbox and grabbed the pile of junk papers suffocating it when I saw several white envelopes. What's this? A letter from the superior court in California? What?

Once inside my condo, I dropped the bills on the table and tore open the letter. What does it say? Whaaa? An Order to Show Cause as to why I shouldn't be held in contempt for not paying $80,000 to Dee Dee. It says I have to show up at court in one week or risk jail!

Whatever else was on my mind vanished. I had to call George, my lawyer. I rushed to the phone as I flipped through my black book to find his number. George is a Harvard and Yale guy, but he's quirky. I enjoyed his upper-crust vocabulary and the sprinklings of profanity mixed with the lawyer jokes. He won me over during our first conversation.

He answered, we chatted, and I read the document.

"You have to show up," he said. "Tell them you're in court by special appearance, not general appearance. You're contesting jurisdiction only. They didn't serve you properly. That means that your due process rights have been violated."

We talked more until I understood what I had to do. For the next few days I obsessively watched every underground video on the law that I could find online. One video led to another, until...what's this ex-convict doing talking about contract law?

After I'd watched videos for twelve hours straight, I picked up the phone. "Russell, these videos online are interesting. It says the law is contract and contracts are law."

"Yeah," Russell said, not completely following or believing me.

"I remember a business law class that I took in high school. The teacher told us that if you write 'paid in full' on a check and give it to someone and they cash it, the debt is paid, even if you originally owed them more money. It has to do with contracts—offer and acceptance."

After we debated the topic awhile, I called my lawyer again to ask about it.

"I believe there's a statute against that in California," George said. "I doubt you're going to be able to pull it off."

The December court date was days away. My neck and back felt as tight as a leather glove two sizes too small. I hadn't stepped into a courtroom in over a decade. My heart pounded just at the thought. Anything can happen in a courtroom, just about anything.

75

Jasmine sat quietly as I drove her car to the San Jose courthouse. "I'm on time," I said, with my heart pounding. I felt like a Christian outside the Roman Coliseum.

"Good luck John," she said, with her soft, melodic voice, and her dark eyes. I could tell she was concerned for me. "I'll keep your things for you." She held out her hands as I emptied my pockets, except for several twenty-dollar bills.

"Thanks." I leaned over to give her a hug and a kiss.

I walked through the small parking lot carrying a thin red folder. The suit and yellow tie I wore stood out from the sea of Hispanics in jeans. The courthouse line stretched down the street and around the corner. It was filled with young and middle-aged men and a sprinkling of women. They looked poor or middle class at best. Then again, in Silicon Valley's dress down culture, for all I know they could be start up billionaires.

After a twenty minute wait, the line moved. One step. Stop. Wait. Another step. Steadily, we inched forward. After another five minutes of stop and go I was inside the building.

"Take off your belts," a deputy announced to the crowd. The young guys in front and back of me took their's off fast. I undid my buckle, but then stopped. My belt never sets off the machines at the airports.

My eyes darted to everything around me. The people. The signs. The officers. "Good morning," a female deputy said as I stood at the metal detector.

"Good morning," I replied skeptically. It must be the tie because she didn't say good morning to anyone else.

The crowd of people overflowed into the hallways. After wandering around the halls to find my courtroom, I ended up on the edge of a seat in a crowded waiting area, anxious for the battle to start.

I scanned everything as fast as possible. Who's that guy? Is that woman here to get child support? What are those officers doing over there? My mind was hyper alert. After fifteen minutes more the courtroom doors opened. The mass of people in front started to move as fast as drunk turtles.

At the entrance doors, the crowd rushed into the courtroom with the eagerness of a day after Christmas sale. An officer stood at the back near the exit and another one in the belly of the courtroom. The women only administrative staff was spread around the room.

"Excuse me." I squeezed past a plump, white, thirty-something woman on my way toward a theater style seat. I'll bet anything she's here to get child support, not pay it. A very large boardroom table stretched from the left side of the courtroom to the right. I figured it served as a barrier between the commissioner and would-be attackers.

On top of that polished table was a large flat screen television. A tall, bald man in a light suit and tie announced: "Listen up! You're going to see an important video as soon as I'm done speaking."

I'd guess he's performed this act one hundred times by the way the words rolled off his tongue. The way he spoke gave me the sense that I'm a bad guy just for being here.

"This is quasi-criminal," he said. Quasi-criminal? The law only has civil and criminal. Apparently now there's some hybrid?

"The court doesn't want to send you to jail...you've got to go on 120 job interviews in 12 weeks. If you go to only 119, then you're going to jail."

Seems the court wants to force us to get a job and extort money and if we don't pay, then they'll jail us until we do. The lights dimmed and the video came on. I sat on the edge of my seat and listened and watched. My heart raced as if I'd run five miles.

The commissioner appeared on screen. A fifty-something woman. Tall, thin, with white-gray hair and a big smile as if she were selling real estate. She mentioned our rights, including our fifth amendment right, not to be a witness against ourselves. That's only for criminal cases, not civil. So much for quasi-criminal.

After the video ended, there was a short delay as staff members took the television from the conference table. A side door near the front right corner of the courtroom opened. A deputy stood behind a man in prison garb as he came through the doorway wearing baggy, green clothes that read, Santa Clara County.

He looked to be in his forties, but sickly with his head shaved and the bony features of his face protruded as if he'd emerged from a concentration camp. His handcuffs were locked to the belt around his waist. His legs shackled at the ankles caused that all too familiar chain rattle I recalled from years ago, as he shuffled his feet.

"Sit here," the deputy directed.

The prisoner sat directly in front of us in the gallery, just on the other side of the bar. Clearly the court wanted to plant a conscious image in our minds along with a subconscious message. Then the barrel chested deputy without a neck stood in front and called out, "ALL RISE."

Everyone stood, but I didn't. The people all around sprang to their feet. A feeling of incredible social pressure engulfed me the way it does anytime you buck the crowd.

I didn't want to accidentally give the court jurisdiction over me by taking orders.

John Farley, Jr.

The commissioner came out, all smiles. "Be seated." Her demeanor reminded me of my second grade teacher. Pleasant and friendly. Until you got on her bad side. "I'll be taking roll," she said, sounding like a friendly tour guide. "When you hear your name, please announce yourself.

Name after name was read aloud. Mostly Hispanic men answered, but a couple of middle-aged white men sat in front looking sheepish.

She finally got to the bottom of the list. "O'Dell versus Farley." My heart jumped. I stood and spoke up.

"Special appearance for the respondent."

The lawyers up front cranked their heads in my direction. The commissioner raised her head from the desk and stared for what seemed a long time. After an uncomfortable pause, she continued. "What is your name?" she asked after a quick swallow.

"John."

She looked down at her papers for a full two seconds. "Your appearance is noted," she said as she gazed in my direction. After a couple more names were read, the commissioner announced, "We'll take a short recess." She stood abruptly with a blank expression and exited out the special door leading to the inner sanctum of the courtroom.

The vibes in the room seemed a little different. The two public defenders and the prosecutor converged in the front and spoke just above a whisper. Casually, the Asian public defender, in his light colored suit, walked to the back near me and after talking to several others, he turned in my direction. "John?" he asked. I met his gaze with a conscious hint of snobbishness. "What are you here for?" he asked.

"Special appearance for the respondent. I'm the administrator on the account."

"Administrator on the account," he said with a confused grin. "This isn't an account. This is a court case."

"The court case is linked to an account and I'm the administrator of the account."

"Are you—"

"Why are you asking me all these questions?" I snapped, as I leaned in with a piercing glare. He recoiled. "Well, we just want to know if you want us to defend you."

Lethal aid, I mean, legal aid. Ah, the memories.

I smirked before turning away. "I definitely don't want you defending me." Insulted perhaps or just amused, he left, and walked to the front of the courtroom.

The prosecutor was next. Mr. Phillips walked toward me, his hair and sideburns right out of the Dirty Harry days. He glared down through his glasses. "What's your name?" he demanded as if talking to a plantation serf.

"John," I said, stone faced.

"You're here for—"

"The respondent," I said.

With a split second pause, he replied, "You're the respondent. Serve him!" as he turned and strutted to the other side of the bar.

An Asian woman, hearing the cue words, approached. She held papers in both hands, close to her chest and spoke in a clear voice, "John Farley?" she said, leaning in.

Crap. Did I screw up? "No," I said, glancing at her before I turned my head in disapproval. She recoiled and hesitated before she backed up and walked away.

Moments later, the five foot six, no neck, fifty something, Hispanic court officer, with greased back hair stomped up within a few feet. "STAND UP," he shouted, as his hand moved close to his weapon. "SHOW ME IDENTIFICATION."

The other officer, commanded, "Everyone else out of the courtroom." The serfs scurried for the door. I stood and sensed that for some reason my heart rate was slowing down. I felt more relaxed, yet focused. "I don't have any," I said, with an easygoing demeanor.

"I CAN DEMAND IDENTIFICATION AND IF YOU DON'T SHOW ME I CAN SEARCH YOU." With turned up palms, raised eyebrows and a soft stare, I replied, "I don't have any." "STEP OVER HERE." He pointed behind the bar.

"Behind the bar?"

"YES! RIGHT HERE," as he gestured to one of the chairs in the belly of the courtroom.

I hesitated and swallowed, as I lifted my right foot in the air. "I'm claiming common law jurisdiction," I said, just before my foot landed on the other side of the bar.

"DON'T GIVE ME THAT COMMON LAW JURISDICTION CRAP. THE SUPREME COURT RULED COMMON LAW DOESN'T MATTER." He hovered nearby, with his gun clearly visible. The bound prisoner next to me faded out of my mind as I sat next to him.

"NOW. TELL ME YOUR NAME."

My mind raced.

"I CAN TAKE YOU AND HAVE YOU FINGERPRINTED TO FIND OUT WHO YOU ARE."

Answer only with questions, John. "Didn't that video say that I had a fifth amendment right not to be a witness against myself?"

Silence, as he walked toward his desk and back again.

"Am I under arrest?"

"NO! YOU'RE NOT UNDER ARREST," he said, as he stood in front of me, wearing a scornful scowl. "YOU'RE BEING DETAINED."

Calm and inquisitive I asked, "What's the difference?"

With that, his brow narrowed as he huffed.

I softened my facial expression fast. "I'm just asking, I don't know," I said, with as innocent a look as I could muster and my palms turned upward.

He glared at me from the corner of his eye and responded louder than necessary. "AN ARREST MEANS I'M CHARGING YOU WITH SOMETHING. DETAINED MEANS I'M

HOLDING YOU TO FIND OUT WHO YOU ARE." He started to walk back to his desk when he noticed the folder in my hand. "GIVE ME THAT."

I handed it over when I realized I almost forgot the critical question. "Am I free to go?"

"NO! YOUR'E NOT FREE TO GO," as he looked through the folder. "HE'S REDACTED IT." He strode in front of me, right in my face with pen and pad. "BIRTHDATE."

After a deep breath, I whispered, "Give me a minute," as I attempted to quiet his rage and clear my thoughts. With my birthday they can get my social security number.

He moved back to his desk again. "I don't have all day. I've got things to do." Seconds later, he was back in front of me. "BIRTHDATE."

With a sad face, I gently shook my head and glanced at him before gazing at the floor.

"THAT'S IT." He walked past me toward the exit.

The second officer motioned to him. They stood eight feet away and spoke in hushed tones. I turned my body almost 180 degrees around to watch them with a hawk eye. Amazingly, I couldn't hear them at all, but I watched. The prisoner next to me spoke in hushed tones "Go along with them. They can make—"

I raised my right hand up to silence him, while still eyeing the deputies. The prisoner stopped in mid-sentence and moments later the deputies finished their conversation.

I swallowed. Uh-oh, he's coming this way.

76

"We'll bring out the commissioner and let her handle it," he said as if nothing had happened. "Have a seat outside the bar."

I got up and made my way to the gallery. "Can I sit here?" I pointed to one of the chairs.

"Any seat you want," he said, as if suddenly he was put in charge of customer service. Why am I asking permission? I'm not detained. The other officer opened the doors for the waiting people. Within minutes, the commissioner came through the secret door. Game on. She's going to call me first. After a few moments of reading documents, she looked out at the audience. "O'Dell versus Farley."

My heart pounded again as I stood outside the bar. "Special appearance for the respondent."

"Sir, come forward," she said. I walked to the edge of the entryway then called out, "I'm claiming common law jurisdiction," as my foot landed on the other side of the bar.

"Mr. Farley..." Whatever she said next was a blur.

"My godly name is not on any of your paperwork. I don't consent to this and I waive all the benefits." The lessons I'd learned from the videos, all related to contract law.

"Mr. Farley, come closer." I took a step.

"Come closer, Mr. Farley." My knee bent and the right heel came off the ground and then I froze. She's tricking me. She's saying a name and then getting me to comply with what she just commanded. She's getting me to orally contract with her by answering to a name and doing what she says. Instantly, I stopped and placed my heel back down and straightened up.

"For the record," I said, "I don't consent to any of this. I'm here by special appearance to contest jurisdiction." The commissioner read the charges. Seventeen counts of contempt of court for not paying the money they claimed I owed. The commissioner and I verbally sparred back and forth as I told her I didn't consent to anything that was happening.

Someone must have signaled the deputy because he walked across the room toward me. I know what he's doing. He wants to serve papers on me in open court. At the last moment, I crossed my arms in front of me, palms open. I didn't want to leave myself vulnerable while also showing my defiance of their unlawful service. With a grimace, the deputy inched the papers closer to my chest.

I stood there staring past him to the bench. After a pregnant pause, he pulled the papers away and let them drop to the ground. That's all he had to do. I'd just been served. But if they'd already served me properly, they wouldn't have had to do it again, that's the point.

I put my arms down and kept eyeing the commissioner as she rattled off legal jargon. "We'll schedule the next court date for a continuation of arraignment..."

"For the record, I don't consent to being arraigned. I'm only here to contest jurisdiction."

"April 12th will continue the hearing. It will be your second general appearance..."

"No. That can't be the second general appearance because this isn't the first general appearance. This is a special appearance to contest jurisdiction." A lull happened as the prosecutor walked toward the commissioner. I bent, grabbed the papers off the floor and turned to exit. Will anyone stop me from leaving? We'll see.The commissioner asked the prosecutor,

"What amount of bail do you want?"

"Eighty thousand dollars." I walked out the door and down the hall without anyone stopping me. Once outside, I hunted for a cab.

I did it. I'm free, for now, at least. The air felt crisp under a gray sky and I was free to feel it. As I walked down the street,

I wondered if deputies were in pursuit, but I resisted the urge to look behind. I hurried around the corner, eager to get out of sight. After an expansive inhale and exhale, I noticed a police car across the street. They're not after me, relax.

The good news is I had several months to focus on my new clinic and research how to win this case. The bad news is they're closing in on me and playing hardball—and the government hates to lose.

77

Before I knew it, darkness covered the sliding glass doors off my living room. A few feet away, I sat in an uncomfortable chair staring at the computer screen. Online videos about contract law played hour after hour while I watched and forgot to eat.

Contract law? This stuff says that the judges and the cops are constantly trying to get the rest of us to contract with them orally and in writing. Even signing a driver's license is a serious contract with the government. I remembered that back in New York, my father's rights friends told me to watch out for oral contracts with cops and judges.

One video after the next drew me in. It grew late, but I decided to watch one more. If I can contract with Dee Dee to settle the debt the courts have imposed on me, then this nightmare would be over. She doesn't have to sign a contract, just sign the certified mail receipt and keep the "consideration"—that is, the payment I send.

January 10, 2012
The local post office had a lull in between the rush hours. A crowd of less than ten people waited to be served, so I joined the line.

"Next," the clerk said—I hurried to the counter.

The tall Asian man, with white hair greeted me. "Hello."

I handed over my certified letter. Normally, I don't mind chatting, but not now. The clerk processed the letter, and gave me a receipt. Next thing I know, I'm back in the car, pausing to reflect.

There. I've sent Dee Dee $20 in federal reserve notes, otherwise known as cash. The letter I sent with it spells out the agreement. If she doesn't send it back soon, she'll have agreed that the debt is paid in full. Yeah, it seems crazy, but I don't owe her. She stole my child and denied me access, so the fact that she's getting anything from me is already too much.

Later that night, I spoke with George by phone.

"I'm not sure I understand. You think there's a statute against it?" I asked.

"I believe," he hesitated, "that California has a statute that doesn't allow 'paid in full' to be valid."

"I didn't find that online," I said, with a sigh. "I'll check more and see if I find it. But doesn't a contract between she and I matter more?"

"No. Besides, it's probably against public policy to allow something like that."

"I don't see how allowing two adults to make a contract violates public policy."

"It's child support and the courts—Wait…" he said, in an upbeat tone. "Did I tell you this one? Why does the law society prohibit sex between lawyers and their clients?"

"Why?"

"To prevent clients from being billed twice for essentially the same service." We both laughed. "Keep researching and keep me posted."

The days turned into weeks.

It was February 18th. My mom passed away on this day years ago. May she rest in peace. A letter from Dee Dee, sent on Valentine's, arrived by certified mail. Valentine's Day— she does have a sense of humor.

I held the letter in the dining room, and took a deep breath before tearing it open. As I pulled out the letter inside and unfolded it as two ten-dollar bills tumbled out. She returned the money. Oh, no. I walked into the living room toward the sunlight shining through the windows and read the letter word by word.

Dear John,

I received your letter and I am returning the $20 payment you requested I accept as payment in full for the above accounts. This amount is woefully inadequate.

I'm sure you understand.

Sincerely,

Dee Dee O'Dell

My heart sank. I leaned against the living room wall. Crap. I thought she'd just ignore it. She's too smart for something so simple.

In mid-March, a letter arrived, this time from the Suffolk County family court.

"What?" I say with my eyebrows stretching as far up as they'll go. They're raising the child support fee by 15.1% for a cost of living adjustment. It's retroactive from two and one half years ago?! And to top it off, if I want to contest it, I had to have done it two and one half years ago? Are these people insane?

Before the week was up, I had a letter mailed off to the court protesting the increase, as well as the entire child support order. I have to keep researching contracts. My remedy has to be here somewhere.

April 12, 2012, downtown San Jose, CA.

Rain was falling. The court parking lot was filling up. I'd sold my beat up car when the department of child support services suspended my driver's license. It's another tactic they use to get people to pay, along with suspending passports, and raiding bank accounts.

On this day, I'd driven Russell's car to court and waited in the parking lot. God, my heart was beating way too fast. Red. I gazed down my chest. My tie is red. Power. Control. Passion.

The thud of the raindrops echoed around the car. Relax. Listen to the rain. Calm yourself. I checked my watch for the sixth time in ten minutes. This game is about to start, let's go. Fifteen minutes later, I was inside the courtroom. I sat in the gallery with many others waiting to be called by the commissioner.

A prisoner was near a deputy inside the bar. Almost for certain, he was there for child support. After all, that's what this courtroom is all about. He was a tall man with tattoos on one side of his neck and above his elbows. He wore green jail clothes while his wrists were chained to his sides.

I watched, hyper alert to everything. The way a stage is set, the back portion of the courtroom was dimly lit while the front was bright.

Then I heard it: "John Farley."

I got up and called out, "I'm here to see about that matter."

The commissioner had lots of time over the months to prepare for me. "Mr. Farley, come forward."

"I would like to do that," I said, trying to hide the shake in my voice, "conditioned upon I can step forward and engage in these proceedings with the full reservation of my unalienable rights. Do you agree?"

"I cannot accept any conditions. Step forward," she said with more force.

I swallowed and continued. "I conditionally accept your offer to step forward and engage in these proceedings conditioned upon that I can retain all of my unalienable rights."

"No, you can stay there, Mr. Farley. What's your name?" She leaned across her giant desk.

"I conditionally accept your offer to grant and convey a security interest in my property conditioned upon proof of a bona fide claim."

"This is the second general appearance..."

"This is not the second general appearance because there was no first general appearance." I gestured toward her. "This is the second special appearance." She ignored me. "I'm entering a plea of not guilty..." I opened my folder and pulled out a page with notes on it. "I want to read this into the record."

"No!" she interrupted.

The bailiff with his slicked back hair, thick neck and extra loud voice, came toward me. "Mr. Farley! The court order is to stop talking!" With his badge and uniform in my face, I froze to gauge his body language.

"I have a right to get what I want on the record," I yelled. "Let the record show that the plea is the commissioner's plea and that the commissioner has converted liability for, and accepted surety for, the defendant." All the people in the courtroom sat and ignored me as the commissioner wrote notes.

"I request that the charges be immediately revised to indicate this conversion of liability. Does anyone here, today, now, have an original charging instrument or accusatory instrument for my inspection?" I repeated myself three times before the commissioner raised her attention from her papers.

"It's in here." She tapped a folder.

"I want to see it," I said. "It will be in the clerk's office. I'm referring this case to judge Margaret Johnson. April 18th."

Apparently I was too much trouble and now she was sending me to a judge. Judges have more power than commissioners.

78

April 18th, 2012 Sunnyvale, CA

The commissioner had never mentioned a different courthouse so after traveling 25 minutes to the previous court and waiting in a long, slow line, I was told by a court officer that I had to go to the Sunnyvale Court, the one five minutes from my home.

After battling morning gridlock, I arrived back in Sunnyvale trying to stay focused.

My heart pounded as I power walked through the parking lot. I stole a glance at my wrist watch. It was nearly nine. I was cutting it close. I exhaled as I gripped the door handle. On the other side, I came face to face with the metal detector and sheriff deputies who stood behind a counter inspecting everything and everyone.

Once past the entrance, the pace slowed. The hallways were lined with people talking in small groups. The buzz of multiple conversations collided in the air around me. The signs high on the wall announced various courtrooms. Where's Department 80? There. Down the hall. Relax. I'm anxious today. There's the door. Get ready. God, I feel extra nervous.

Inside the courtroom, I found a seat in the back near a very plump man and woman, both perhaps in their late 50's. This courtroom seemed much smaller than the one in San Jose. It was more upscale and brighter. For some reason, it was more intimidating too.

Only one deputy was in here. Hispanic, not that tall. Bull-like though, and with a gun. He sat on a tall chair against the right side wall of the courtroom.

The gallery seats were theater style. It was clean. Everything seemed compact. The people filling the courtroom were mostly white and well dressed. A young, slim, pretty woman walked through the doors and stood in the aisle near me. She must be a lawyer.

Her shiny, straight blonde hair draped down past her shoulder blades in a long ponytail. The sharp creases in her stylish pants went well with her polished black shoes with two-inch heels. Her tan colored top looked professional and added a touch of femininity.

Why couldn't I find her anywhere but in a courtroom? Okay. Forget her. Focus!

"All rise!" the deputy called.

In unison and on cue, the people stood. Awkwardly, I stayed seated, hidden among the people towering around me. The legal videos I watched said standing when told means that I am under the court's jurisdiction, that is, the judge's power. It could be false, but why chance it?

As names were called I noticed a moderate tremor in my hands. The female judge emerged from behind a secret door blending almost invisibly with the wall.

"Be seated," she said, with an English accent.

I paid close attention to her every movement. A case was called. A young, clean-cut guy who looked Mexican walked past the bar and sat at the table. His pants were clean and creased and his long sleeve shirt made him look good, but average.

We learned he was a young dad who paid child support. Prior to the court date, he had to take a drug test for smoking pot.

"How are the children doing?" the judge asked him.

"Their grades in school are good..."

The judge leaned forward from her high perch. "I didn't ask you about their grades," she said in a calm, controlled, and somewhat intimidating tone. "I asked how they're doing."

He fumbled with his words and I suspected that the judge was calibrating his every syllable as they often do. Soon, that case ended and he left. That's when the inevitable happened.

"John Farley!"

In the Hotel with Amanda

Amanda and I had decided to walk around the hotel property. She held a voice recorder. We stopped at an open area high above the stylish pool and palm trees. It was so late into the evening that the pool was empty, much like the hotel hallways. The crickets chirped as we were engulfed by the crisp, fresh nighttime air.

"Your case was called?" she asked.

I leaned against the railing and caught a glimpse of her outfit. She'd brought a change of clothes for this marathon interview. Her satin beige blouse with a low cut neckline caught my attention, along with a sparkling, silver necklace that plunged out of sight. Her black pumps looked good as did the multi-colored skirt that dangled three inches above her knees, perhaps for the sole purpose of challenging my ability to stay on task.

"I stood up and announced that I was here to see about that matter. The judge told me to come forward to hear me better, but I said that I would stay right where I was and speak louder."

"What happened then?" she asked as she flipped her hair behind her.

"I repeated some contract law jargon I'd picked up online. No one seemed to know what it meant, but it certainly confused everyone."

Amanda smiled, showing off her pearly whites.

"I questioned jurisdiction. You know, the court's authority to hear the case at all. The judge acted as if she was considering the questions, then interrupted me with, "I'm the one asking the questions here, Mr. Farley." She ruled that the court had jurisdiction. I objected, and told her that my business in the court was concluded and I was leaving. Have a nice day."

415

John Farley, Jr.

"You just left?"

On The Street

I walked out of the courtroom down the hall and out the door, but my anxiety only increased. Something was wrong, I knew it. I glanced behind me. Nothing. I picked up the pace. Then—"Mr. Farley!" I pretended not to hear. "Mr. Farley!" The voices were getting closer behind me. I looked over my shoulder and that's when I knew I was in trouble. Three deputy sheriffs ran across the parking lot toward me. I stopped, and they swarmed around me. "Are you detaining me?" I asked.

The Hispanic deputy grabbed my right arm while the others grabbed my left. "You're under arrest," he said. He twisted my right arm and wrist behind me and into a martial arts joint lock.

"Ahh! I'm not resisting. I'm not resisting." They slipped handcuffs on me and walked me back to the courthouse and into an empty, unused courtroom.

"Spread your legs. Wider!" the deputy yelled. He rubbed his hands all around my legs and torso, as a younger deputy stood and watched.

"Sit in this chair."

"Okay, if I can sit in this chair?" I said. It was another oral contracting technique designed to help me avoid giving them authority over me, but I discovered it had another value. I felt more in control, and less victimized.

After what seemed like a long time, I was brought back into the original courtroom, but it was empty except for two deputies. They questioned me, put shackles around my ankles and put me into a holding cell off to the side of the courtroom. They said nothing as they shut and locked two doors to the cell.

I seriously had to pee. The toilet was right there, but I couldn't do anything with my hands cuffed behind me. I felt ready to burst.

After what seemed forever, the younger deputy opened the doors.

"I have to use the bathroom or I'm going to wet myself."

"Turn around and face the wall."

He uncuffed me, and I relieved myself.

After a long time, he came back to the cell to interrogate me. "You're going to go to the San Jose jail. Just so you know. The sheriff deputies at the jail are not going to put up with any of this stuff. Turn around."

I listened without letting him know I had some experience with this type of thing. It was time to go out the side door, and into a waiting police van. Shackles prevented my normal stride. A different young deputy escorted me to a van as I waddled along. "Walk down here," he said.

"Okay, if I can walk down here?" I replied.

The deputy driving the van opened the back doors. A middle aged man with a slight build and a pleasant demeanor greeted me. "Watch your step." The dog-like cages inside surprised me. Then I noticed him. A somewhat young, Hispanic guy dressed in a bright colored jail suit. We sat across from each other in our separate cages. After introductions were over, he told me bits of his story. "I could be locked up for 13 more years," he said casually.

I sat with my back straight, still in my suit minus the tie, watch, and cash.

"My wife gets frustrated. She takes care of our children. I told her to go, and find someone else. I understand her situation. It's really hard. She's says she's going to divorce me, but then changes her mind. It's hard. Thirteen years." He paused to take a breath. "What do they want you for?"

"Child support," I said gently. He shook his head in disbelief as his gazed at the floor.

"I heard them say that you'll come back to court Monday."

"Monday. Today's Wednesday. I—well, I hope that's not true. That's absurd." The ride seemed extra long on the hard, metal seat. The cuffs and shackles bit into my flesh. When we arrived at the prison, my new acquaintance was taken away while I waited. The cordial officer opened the back of the van and directed me to stand in front of the automatic doors.

"Okay, if I can stand over here?" I said, wanting to keep my sense of control and perhaps my rights.

A slight smile crossed his face. He was polite, perhaps humoring me. The doors opened. "Walk straight ahead."

"Okay, if I can walk straight ahead?"

"Go inside this cell."

"Okay, if I can go inside this cell?" Once inside, the cell door closed behind me. This is just a holding cell, I won't be here long.

Minutes later, the door to the cell opened. "Mr. Farley, you can come out."

"Okay, if I can come out now?"

The deputy smiled. "Stand over here." An Asian man stood behind a long counter. "What we're doing is taking your blood pressure and finding out about your health...."

Nervous energy kicked in. "I don't consent to answer any questions or medical procedures."

He reacted with surprise. "That's fine. You don't have to answer any questions," he said in a friendly manner.

Moments later, my suit jacket was taken from me and put on a chair. I was handcuffed to a row of seats like you'd see at an airport of bus station. The hard plastic wasn't designed for comfort.

A deputy no sooner cuffed me when he uncuffed me. "Walk over there."

"You!" a bulky young, hormonally arrogant deputy thirty feet away, and behind a counter, said to me.

My heart pounded. Here we go. "SIT IN THAT CHAIR," he ordered, then turned toward his photo machine. I walked toward the chair, and pointed.

"Okay, if I can sit in this chair?" A stool was against the wall eight feet in front of the photo machine.

He stopped and turned toward me with a smirk. "I'm not asking you," he said in drill sergeant style, "I'm telling you. Take off your glasses!" He flicked a switch that beamed bright light in my face.

I left my glasses on. "I'm not consenting to have my photograph taken." The bright lights went dim. The deputy glared, then turned to make an announcement.

"Hey, we got an asshole here! Until we get a photograph and prints you can't be processed. You'll spend the night right here."

"I don't consent to any of this."

"Get outta here. Go over there!" he barked, as he swept his arm through the air in anger.

I got up. "Okay, if I can go over here?" I walked toward the other prisoners, mostly black men, some Hispanics and a few whites chained to chairs. As soon as I sat, another deputy came by and cuffed my wrists, locking me into the chair.

"You're Farley, right?"

I turned and spoke in a conversational tone, "You may refer to me as Farley."

When the deputy left, a voice called to me. "Hey!" A thin, not too tall black man locked in a seat about 20 feet away was talking to me. "What's your name?" he said, with an air of indignation.

I hesitated. "John," I mouthed in a hushed tone.

"John," he repeated. "My name is Steve, Steve Garrison. I'm an attorney, not a lawyer, an attorney." Steve didn't look like either one, of course. "They have no damn right to have me here. John. Your name is John, right?"

I nodded while twisting in the chair as far as the chains would allow. I listened as Steve talked. "I'm pissed off at how they treated you. They don't have no right to treat you that way. That is *bullshit*." Steve continued while I stayed twisted to maintain eye contact. My back stiffened, as those annoying florescent lights kept flickering.

John Farley, Jr.

"Are you Farley?" a voice demanded. A deputy dressed in a green military-style uniform had come from behind.

"You may refer to me as Farley."

"What are you in here for?"

"Don't you know?"

"Are you going to answer every question with a question?"

"Aren't I allowed to?"

He shook his head as he walked away calling, "Superman over there isn't cooperating." Soon the guards started calling me Superman and Clark Kent.

Moments later, a short, tan skinned, middle aged, drunken guy, wearing a tee shirt and jeans was sat next to me. "Heeeyyyy," he slurred. "What the hell's going on? I'm an American. America is...." He trailed off, slumped over and went on mumbling.

I kept an eye on him while the deputies prowled around the room and Steve called out to me every few minutes. The drunk guy overheard Steve.

"You black piece of crap. Go back to Africa!" Steve stopped in mid sentence, while I sat awkwardly in the middle.

Steve's mouth gaped open. "Wow." He shook his head. "Wow! That's—wooow."

Being chained down like zoo animals prevented fistfights from breaking out. As the only clean cut, Caucasian wearing a button down, bright white dress shirt, and dark blue suit, I got some respect among my fellow prisoners.

The nurses brought water around to a few people. As guys needed the bathroom, deputies released their chains and sent them off to the toilet, while others were offered food. I wasn't offered anything, not even water, and I didn't ask for any either.

Many hours passed. I'd arrived at 3 p.m. and now it was 10. It wasn't worth begging for water, food, or the bathroom, unless I was ready to pass out or wet myself.

Two deputies came over. My nerves were on edge, but I did my best to appear calm. They grabbed my arms and unlocked the cuffs. "Walk there," as they pointed.

"Okay, if I can walk over there?" I sauntered back to the photo area. The young photo deputy eyed me with scorn.

"Sit down Clark Kent."

"Okay, if I can sit here?"

"What an asshole," he said while he grabbed at the machinery.

"Take off your glasses!"

"I don't consent to having my picture or fingerprints taken."

Deputies standing fifteen feet away started toward me. My heart sped up as I pulled the glasses away from my face just before they got to me. "Okay, but I don't consent to this." The short, sadistic, Asian deputy peered down at me.

"You can tell it to the judge."

As I turned toward the camera, white light flashed into my eyes. "Stand up."

"Okay, if I can stand up?"

"Walk over here."

"Okay, if I can walk over here?"

We went behind the counter to the fingerprint machine. Things had changed since the late 1990's. Ink and rollers were antiquated. In front of me was a digital machine.

The Asian deputy barked orders. "Left hand."

"I'll give it to you because I don't want to get hurt, but I don't consent to this."

As he pressed the first finger onto the glass plate, perspiration pouring out smeared the image. He lifted my finger to dab it with a cloth before he placed it back down. The perspiration returned within milliseconds. The dabbing routine continued for what seemed like twenty or thirty minutes. Each finger had to be blotted at least ten times due to the outpouring of nervous sweat.

"You know why you're here. What are you in here for?" he asked.

John Farley, Jr.

"Why don't you tell me?" I countered.

The perspiration continued to flow, but after what seemed a very long time he said, "We're done. Sit over there."

"Okay, if I can sit over there?"

The captain, an average height, stocky, middle-aged, dark skinned Hispanic guy was twenty feet away behind the chest high counter. "Farley, come here," he yelled.

I pointed to myself. "Are you referring to me?"

In a sharp tone, he slapped the counter. "I am not playing these games. Bring him over here." Two tall Asian deputies started toward me. Like a jack-in-the-box, I popped up.

"Okay, I don't want to get hurt, I'm comin' over. I don't want to get hurt."

Resisting them was a one-way ticket to the hospital and I knew it. I walked toward the deputies with hands in 'stick 'em up' posture. They grabbed, twisted and extended my arms like wings. With my wrists bent 90 degrees and palms and fingers toward the ceiling, they hauled me in front of the captain.

"THIS DOCUMENT ALLOWS YOU TO GET A COPY OF THE RULES OF THE PRISON, AND DOCUMENTS THAT WE HAVE YOUR PROPERTY SO YOU CAN GET IT BACK LATER. DO YOU UNDERSTAND?"

Understand, under stand. That's means, I stand under their authority. I looked at his dark eyes, and menacing face from my twisted position. "No. I don't understand."

"WHAT PART OF THIS DON'T YOU UNDERSTAND?"

"I really don't understand any of it."

"YOU WANT TO BE AN ASSHOLE. IF YOU WANT YOUR PROPERTY BACK, YOU SIGN THIS FORM."

"Where does my property go if I don't sign?"

"IT GOES INTO LOST AND FOUND AND ANYONE WHO FINDS IT FIRST CAN GET IT."

The deputy on my right peered at my property through the plastic bag. "That's a nice watch." The deputy on the left spoke up. "Yeah. That's a nice red tie."

I rotated my head toward him while contorted and twisted. I smiled just a little and raised an eyebrow. "That *is* a nice tie."

He cranked on my wrist for that little wisecrack as I winced with gritted teeth.

"NOW. DO YOU UNDERSTAND?" the captain repeated. I turned back to him. I know they can't force me to sign anything. Our eyes met within inches across the counter.

"No," I said, pausing for effect. "I don't."

He lashed out to grab the form as he turned from the counter in anger. "GET HIM OUTTA HERE." Fear flooded me.

"Wait. Let me read it!"

The deputies pulled me from the desk and hurried me past the chained prisoners toward a special seat in the back corner next to an old, worn out, black man. He looked weak, scattered—off in his own world and mumbling.

This time they wrapped chains across my body and locked me tightly to the chair, then cuffed my hands and shackled my legs. I sat, far off in a corner next to this mumbling man. I couldn't move more than three inches. I noticed a bad smell. This guy had pooped his pants and it smelled awful.

They're definitely angry with me now. A couple deputies and a nurse walked around to each seated prisoner. They stopped down the row from me at a big, white guy, with long, greasy black hair. From what I could tell, he was detoxifying from drugs and not handling it well. They'd put what looked like a black, bulletproof vest around him for some reason. I said a silent prayer when I saw what was happening.

79

The Hotel with Amanda

Amanda took a sip of tea and repositioned herself on the soft sofa. "This is intense. Why didn't you just go along with them this time?"

I sucked in a deep breath and arched backwards to stretch my tight muscles. "In my heart I believed that what I was doing was right. Ending debt and debtor's prison for child support and bringing back respect to fathers. That's what I'm on a mission to do. Not to mention defending freedom."

Amanda seemed lost in thought for a moment. "Ready," she said.

At the Jail

"The chained-down, bulletproof vest wearing, druggie yelled colorful language as a mob of officers in military type garb surrounded him. They blocked his feet and legs, then grabbed and twisted his arms as he struggled. That's when the nurse came over and stuck a needle in his arm as he winced and moaned.

Meanwhile, a young guy, perhaps 20, was seated a few chairs down. Hours ago, he was singing and cheerful. Now, he's a mess—slumped over, mouth stuck open in agony, as tears stained his face and dripped down alongside the drool that stretched from lip to floor. His image brought up a feeling within me. It was anguish along with deep despair, generated from a sense of helplessness from being alone and fearful. The feeling bubbled up the way a heavy meal's heartburn comes out of nowhere.

After a few more minutes, the shorter Asian officer and the thin nurse, perhaps from India, eyed me as they approached. She held a syringe, her thumb in position, cocked and ready to inject. I couldn't move because of the chains wrapped around me the way duct tape secures a cardboard box.

The nurse stood over me. "This is to protect you from communicable diseases...." The underground media and doctors have reported that these injections may have unknown viruses and other toxins in them and can end up killing a person many years down the road. Believe what you want, but I'm supposed to trust these people?

The sight of that needle made me straighten up as if I'd been poked in the rear end. "I absolutely, positively do NOT consent to any injections."

"Sir," she continued, "this is required..."

"No. I DO NOT consent to being injected with anything."

The officer glared down. "You're in prison now. You have to take this."

"I absolutely DO NOT consent. I'm feeling really threatened right now."

Instantly, the nurse gave a dismissive hand swat in the air, mumbled a few words and left with the officer close behind. It was as if I'd held up a cross, and the vampires scattered.

More time went by and they moved out the old man next to me while they left his poop-smeared seat as is. Soon, several officers brought the druggie over and shoved him into the empty chair, chained him down and left us there. He cursed and yelled, but the officers ignored him as they scattered.

He raged and I wondered if I could calm him so as not to go deaf. I spoke with a friendly, easygoing demeanor and turned to make eye contact. "It's probably best not to agitate them since they can make things more difficult."

"ARRRRGGGG," he yelled and pelted me with F-bombs as he leaned over, but the chains corralled him in. I worried he might reach me, and bite my ear off.

426

"Okay, okay," I said, "do whatever you want. Do whatever you want, never mind. Forget I said anything." I looked the other way and kept to myself. Meanwhile, the intoxicated guy was yelling at a working inmate who was strolling around with a spray bottle and rag as he wiped the windows clean.

"You're a stupid... Go back where you came from!" he spewed.

The worker's face tightened, and I could tell he wanted to body slam that wise mouth. Our inebriated friend kept taunting this very muscular, young guy who kept himself under control even though I thought I saw steam coming off his head. The young guy decided to sweep the floor. Eventually, he came my way with a frown as the broom narrowly missed my shoes.

I caught his attention with some gentle words. "That guy over there. I wouldn't let him bother you," I said with an easy smile. He turned to me looking suspicious, but then his frown softened.

"He's drunk," I said with a lighthearted chuckle, "and doesn't know what he's saying."

Instantly, his face relaxed and broke into a pleasant smile and his shoulders lowered a little. He moved with a lighter step, as if his steam valve was opened. Sure he must have known the guy was drunk, but there's something healing that happens when a person empathizes with your pain. It melts a little. I felt that I'd contributed to generating a little harmony in the place.

Another older guy who'd been brought in for disturbing the peace called over to me. He said he respected how I dealt with those officers when they were trying to get me to sign on the dotted line earlier. He too had calmed down.

It took about thirty more minutes before the druggie mellowed. Then he changed. He spoke as though we were friends. "You know, you're right. It's better not to argue with them." I grinned. His shift in attitude surprised me. By now I felt like I'd been providing therapy all day and night.

Deputies walked toward me at just past 1 in the morning. I'd arrived at this facility at 3 p.m. I hadn't had any water or bathroom and no food since breakfast the previous day.

They unchained me. "Stand up," they said. We left the waiting area toward the inner parts of the jail, out of view from the other prisoners. The captain and the tall Asian guided me into a small cell-like area. My body shook from relentless stress and anxiety.

The deputy stood by, facing the doorway, shoulder toward me, as the captain barked orders. "Take your clothes off."

"Okay, if I can take my clothes off?" I took my dress shirt off, then my suit pants and underwear as if it were no big deal. I stood naked with feet apart and hands on my hips. "Okay. What's next?" I said, as if ready to skinny dip.

The Asian looked over his shoulder with disappointment, "You have no shame."

Ahhhh—he said it and I felt the slightest of smiles flash upon my face. What was stolen in 1995 in the dungeons of Central Islip, Long Island would never be taken again, no matter what. I now felt impervious to the shame and guilt that the judges, cops and society itself had foisted upon me. It was an empowering moment.

The captain appeared with clothes. He tossed prison garb on a bench—brown pants and shirt, orange socks, underwear and tan plastic sandals. "Put these on," he ordered. "Okay, if I can put these clothes on?" I said in an effort to be consistent with the verbal contracting game we were playing. The wardrobe barely fit.

"These clothes are too small," I told the captain as he walked in.

"Don't worry about it now," the captain said.

They took me down another hallway to an open area. "Sit down here. You're gonna be interviewed."

"I'm not doing interviews. I'm not answering questions."
"SIT DOWN."

428

"Okay, if I can sit down?" I sat at a desk with at least one deputy at my back while in front was a plain clothes, tough looking white cop with a nylon cord draped around his neck and a police badge dangling at chest level.

"I'm going to ask you some questions for your safety."

"As I told the others," I said respectfully, "I'm declining to answer questions."

"How old are you?"

"Don't you already have that information?"

LISTEN. IF YOU DON'T ANSWER, YOU'RE GOING TO P.C. YOU'LL BE HOUSED WITH THE MURDERERS, THE PEDOPHILES AND THE CHICKS WITH DICKS!

Jeers erupted from officers that walked past. "What were you arrested for?"

"Why don't you tell me? What *was* I arrested for?"

"I'M NOT PLAYING THESE GAMES," he yelled inches from my face and I sensed more deputies behind me.

The Central Islip beatings flashed back. However, this time my approach was smarter. Verbal and legal, not arrogant and physical. Despite doing my best to appear calm, my insides must have been pumping out the adrenaline. "Ahh, I—I'm feeling really threatened right now," I said, with my hands close to my chest.

"THAT'S IT. GET HIM OUT OF HERE."

In seconds, I was brought down a corridor as a new guard led the way. I approached a very large, white, female officer reading at her hallway desk. Our eyes met before she gave my tight clothes a slow, expressionless once over from head to toe before her gaze gradually returned to her magazine. I sensed she was suppressing a reaction, but I wasn't sure what.

"This way," the guard said. We arrived at a dark room. "Go in here," he directed. "Get a blanket, towel and one of those bed foams lying on the floor."

I grabbed whatever looked good while my sandals slipped off with each step. The officer strode to his command desk situated in the middle of the two tiered cellblock. There, he pushed a button to unlock an upstairs cell door. With my arms loaded, I climbed about twenty five steps to the second floor while repositioning my sandals with every other step. Dim lighting was just enough to get up the stairs safely.

At the top, I pulled the unlocked cell door open, went inside the closed it. When the latch clicked, I realized I'd just locked myself into a modern dungeon. A feeling of isolation and anxiety came over me, but it wasn't unfamiliar, but rather an old feeling lying dormant. Within minutes of putting my thin, foam mattress on the hard, metal slab of the bottom bunk I heard a light tap on the door.

"Hello."

Oh no. Thank God I'm locked in here. Who's this guy? I could barely make out his dark face against the tiny door window.

"Yeah?"

With a whisper he replied, "Brother. Do you believe in our Lord and savior Jesus Christ?"

It was the perfect time for a religious conversion. "I working on it," I said sincerely.

"Do you want a copy of the New Testament bible?"

"Yes."

"I'm Marv, what's your name?"

"John."

"John, those clothes don't look right. I'll see if I can get you the right size."

It seemed as if I had someone looking out for me. It was hard to doze off that night and no sooner had I slipped into semi-sleep when the door to my cell popped open. Shadows moved past my slit of a window. Inmates poured out and down to the bottom floor. I went toward the sounds as one guy called out, "It's breakfast."

The inmates in line below resembled mannequins on a conveyor belt—nearly motionless as they waited for a plastic tray of proceeded food, and one piece of fruit. I stepped out of my cell and into the crowd. I felt as though I was the new guy on the football team showing up halfway through the season without ever having played the game.

Once breakfast was in hand, it was straight back to the cell. I opened my packet that contained a small, plastic spork: a two-in-one spoon/fork. My packet contained a toothbrush, but it was only half the regular length making brushing difficult. Worse, there's no floss allowed in jail. Not good for dental health.

Hours passed before I heard a whispering voice at my door, it was Marv. "The guy in cell four sent this." He handed me a letter. "And here's the bible."

Marv got the guard to buzz the cell door open. He slipped me a letter written in pencil. I later learned it was from an older man, a convicted murdered who was trying to prove to the court his innocence. In the letter, he said not to speak to anyone about my case, that snitches inside will rat me out in hopes of a better deal for themselves. He gave some general advice on dealing with prison life. It was a nice gesture from someone who didn't have to bother.

Hours passed. There was nothing to do in the cold, lifeless cell except read the bible, contemplate my fate, and rest in the cold air that blew through the vent. The cell door buzzed open. I went to the window to see the others walking around in the cellblock. Marv came by. "John, these clothes should fit better." He pressed a new wardrobe into my hands.

"The guard told me that they made you wear those small clothes to punish you."

Marv, I learned, received special privileges because he helped clean and do odd jobs that need doing. He'd gained the guard's trust. He and I are the same age. Marv keeps himself in good shape, and like everyone else, he wants out of jail. His goal was to have a Christian radio show to preach the bible, but for now, he preached to other inmates on Sundays.

As we stood outside my cell, Marv knocked on the door next to mine. A very tall, large and dark skinned man with more salt than pepper in his hair came out.

"John, this is Joe." Joe was missing his four front teeth, and wasn't the guy you wanted delivering pizza to your country home on a dark, cold night—or even a warm night. To my surprise the man was jovial.

"John, hmm. John—you need a better name than John to be in here," he lisped. "You need a name like Butcher Knife. Yeah, that's a good name," he said with a wide, toothless grin. "Butcher Knife. If anybody asks your name that's what you tell 'em."

I let out a nervous chuckle as my gaze shifted from Joe to Marv who laughed at the quip.

Soon, I was meeting several others and finding out their story. Some were in for violence or burglary. With California's "three strikes you're out" law, they could be here for life, or close to it, unless some small miracle happened. It's not a good law.

I discovered that any contact from the outside world, a letter, a call, a newspaper clipping sent from a friend or relative, acted as water to a dying plant. It revived the spirit and reminded each person that someone was thinking about them, that they weren't forgotten, that they're life has meaning.

Not everyone in jail should be, but everyone ought to go to jail once for a refresher on why we need to protect our personal liberties. Of course, some would never fully recover from the experience.

Twice per day, dozens of guys lined up on the ground floor as the nurses doled out medicine like Halloween candy to children. Drugs kept the masses quiet much as they do on the outside.

Days dragged on worse than a bad movie in an empty theatre and consisted of sitting, reading or doing nothing for close to 23 hours a day in a cold, lifeless, concrete cell. Usually we got an hour to talk to the other guys in the common areas or a visit to the barren gym with one basketball hoop and a pull up bar. Jail magnified the loneliness and isolation everyone feels, but faster. Fear and desperation mixed to create an anxious feeling, as if watching a slow motion accident that can't be stopped.

Chris, one of the older guys in for murder, sat and talked with Joe at a large, round metal table in the common area. I'd just finished writing a letter in pencil to the judge and rushed out of my cell before break time was over. I sailed down the stairs and took a seat at the table next to Chris and across from Joe. "Excuse, me I don't mean to interrupt, but I wanted to read this to you, if you don't mind."

The two stopped talking in mid-sentence as Chris turned to me. Joe stared from across the table. His eyes opened wide. He had "wild eyes" that reminded me of Bill Bixby's when he was about to Hulk out on the 1970's television show. It hit me that I'd just crossed a line of respect, and I gulped reflexively.

I changed course instantly. "I can come back." I said, two octaves higher. "Not a problem. I didn't mean to interrupt. I apologize. We'll do this later."

As I started to stand Joe interjected. "No, no," he said as if it was no big deal. "Read us what you wrote."

"Really? Are you sure? Okay. Dear Judge, as a hypnotist, I have clients—"

Chris interrupted. "A what?"

"A hypnotist," I said as he stared back.

"A what?" he repeated.

"A hypnotist. I'm a hypnotist."

Chris still looked confused.

"Go on," Joe said.

"And I feel awful that I'm missing my clients because of being in jail. One client, a woman in her 50's, came to me because as a young girl, she was raped by her stepbrothers. She came to me in confidence hoping I could help her. Because I'm in jail, I can't contact her or any of my clients and I feel terrible about it." I kept reading and when I was done, Joe looked placid.

"That's beautiful. Really. Just beautiful," he said. I wasn't expecting him to say that, but I was happy he did. "Thanks. I'll catch up with you guys later."

Many hours later during a short break, Chris stopped me in the hall. "John, don't send that letter. These judges have heard it all. It's not going to help you." It was too late. The letter had already been sent.

One night, a couple of us got to talking. We couldn't figure out why I was in jail. Was it for contempt? Chris said the judge could keep me in here for life whether it was legal or not, an unimaginable scenario. Each day felt like a marathon without the runner's high, only the fatigue, but not from physical exertion, but mental stress.

The hypnosis clinic occupied my thoughts. My clients, people who wanted my help, would be showing up for appointments to a locked, darkened clinic. Not good for my reputation, and I was losing money—and money was the thing the courts wanted most, besides my submission to their authority, of course.

I got along with the few guys I chatted with in prison, they—we—were a bunch of guys trying to make it through long stretches of nothingness. It was another powerful reminder that merely feeling a breeze across your face or having direct sunlight on your skin means that you have a lot of freedom to be grateful for.

Of course, human contact, talking to people, even convicts, is nourishing to the soul. So many people live isolated, unhappy lives, and yet they're physically free to change it. I realized I had more contact with my prison mates in five days than I did with most of my neighbors on the outside over five months.

After four days and nights of bible and dictionary reading, I was told that I'd be going back to court first thing in the morning. During break time, Marv and I sat in his cell and reminisced about the film *Shawshank Redemption*.

"That was a great film," I said.

Marv chuckled. "The white guy did get out first."

That night, Marv showed me an envelope and letter he was given moments before from the guards. The Department of Child Support Services was demanding child support payment or they'd suspend his driver's license, revoke his passport, put liens on his property, take his bank accounts... We shook our heads in astonishment.

"They don't even care if you have a 94-year sentence. Incredible," I said. Marv just smirked. His father pays a little money each month on his account, but the agency keeps coming after all debtors with the unrelenting persistence of a Terminator cyborg.

Unbeknownst to me, Russell had arranged for George, my lawyer, to show up in court. The next morning it would take hours for the guards and deputies to shuttle me back in front of the judge, but there I was waiting in the same cell off the courtroom. The difference being that my suit and tie were gone, replaced with prison clothes and chains, not my best look.

The deputy led me into the courtroom where George, and his female assistant sat waiting. Now, after many months of phone chats, we finally met. George had trouble walking due to overweight and diabetes, but his mind and tongue were sharp. He vacillated between serious and joking right until the judge walked in. He whispered, "The deputy told me that you don't belong in jail."

Well, that's nice to know.

The child support agency's lawyer du jour was there. A middle aged stiff with a beard that suggested he moonlighted as a Freudian psychologist and spoke as if he'd spent too much time in an upper crust graduate school. He was just another patsy who thought he was ridding the world of evil child support debtors.

After the hearing, the case was adjourned to June 26, 2012. The judge asked my lawyer to put together what's called points and authorities—a document showing court cases and the legal grounds to show that I'd been denied my due process rights

Before I was released, I had to travel back to the jail. At the prison, I was told I wouldn't get out until after midnight. That meant waiting around all day and all night. As I entered the common area, the guard directed me to my cell. No sooner had I climbed the stairs, closed my cell door, and took a bite out of the apple waiting for me since breakfast, when my cell door buzzed open. I peeked outside as the guard called, "If you want go home, grab your bedding and hurry up!"

Marv yelled to me. "John, that's the fastest we've ever seen anyone get out."

I pulled up the thin mattress and rushed down the stairs to a line on the floor where the guard told me to stand. In his military style garb he walked to a phone on the wall, picked it up, and moments later the locked door to the outer hallway opened. I stood motionless as he glanced at his clipboard and then gazed over his shoulder.

"What's your name again?"

"Farley," I said. He turned to face me with a piercing gaze and a smug smile. "*That's* what I thought it was." His remark registered in the time it takes a hard rain to penetrate a wool hat. I broke eye contact as I realized he'd tricked me into answering to a name just for the thrill of it. Touché.

Hours passed before I was released out onto the streets of San Jose with wrinkled clothes and a few dollars in my pocket. The race was on. I had to find a way to settle this case with Dee Dee once and for all. It was the end of April, and I was desperate for an escape plan.

80

The Hotel with Amanda

Amanda and I were getting our second wind. "Here's where I tell you the idea I came up with to settle this nightmare. All that time in jail doing nothing gave my subconscious an opportunity to clarify the solution."

"What was it?" she asked.

"Sally would turn 21 in a few weeks and then the weekly child support bill would end, but the back money owed, nearly $92,000, would never go away until it was paid off. At 9 percent annual interest, it was growing fast. There's no debt worse than child support. It's never really incurred, but rather imposed out of the air, which makes it the unicorn of debt—one of a kind, and unnatural."

"What about filing bankruptcy?"

"Bankruptcy doesn't end it and the government's own mafia hunts debtors all the way to other countries."

"Did you get your driver's license back?"

"At that point, I was car-less and riding my bike to my clinic each day. At night I researched contract law, specifically *offer, and acceptance*. I discovered that the non-custodial parent could, at their discretion, agree to waive outstanding child support. It would simply disappear into thin air."

"What? The mother can waive it all, just like that?"

"It happened in front of me with the court Commissioner in San Jose. A mother waived back child support and the father was off the hook, instantly."

"Is that what you did? Make a deal with Dee Dee?"

John Farley, Jr.

"I wanted to. I'd sent her emails to discuss a resolution, but she never replied. She doesn't negotiate when she doesn't have to."

"But what about for her daughter's sake? You know, get some money and just settle it."

"That's what many lawyers had suggested, but we weren't dealing with someone who wanted to settle anything."

Amanda typed quicker now. "It took a lot of digging, but I found another way. It's called *accord and satisfaction.* It's a way to settle a debt for less than what's owed. An accord is an agreement and the satisfaction refers to the legal consideration, usually money, that binds the parties to the contract. What's needed to settle the debt is getting the other party to accept the consideration."

"Wait, slow down. Consideration is money?"

"It usually is, but it can be other things too, for example, stocks and real estate. I figured that if Dee Dee and I could have a meeting of the minds, that is, we agree and she demonstrates by her actions that she's accepted my offer to settle the case, then I'd be completely released from the debt, by law."

"What did your lawyer say about that?"

"After talking with George and doing dozens of hours of legal research I found court cases going back 60 years that showed that *accord and satisfaction* is a valid defense for child support and not against public policy. George said that I was charting new legal ground with my novel approach to *accord and satisfaction.* I told him about the accord, that is, the agreement, I prepared, but he said he didn't care about that, what he cared about was *the satisfaction.*"

"You said other court cases used this method, but they failed? How are you charting new ground?"

"All the court cases I researched had failed because the debtor did something incorrect in their offer. None of them did the *accord and satisfaction* properly so the courts ruled against them, but the judges always agreed that if done right, *accord and satisfaction* is valid to settle child support debt."

"You mean you were going to do something that hadn't been done."

"Yes. The catch was that I couldn't simply pay Dee Dee less than what the government claimed I'd owed. First of all, I'd tried that with the $20, and she rejected it. Plus, with a certain type of debt, which this was, a lesser amount isn't allowed."

"So, you were stuck?"

"Until I uncovered something interesting. A debt could be paid—satisfied—if the consideration, that is, the thing being offered to the other party as payment, was in a different form or different type than what was originally owed."

Amanda stopped typing to stare at me. "You mean if you sent her a car worth $75,000 or the deed to a piece of real estate and she accepted it, then that would count?"

"The law was very clear that if she accepted something of value—and how much value doesn't matter at all to the courts—then the debt would be settled. Here's the key, acceptance can be shown by her actions, it can be implied. The court rulings said so. Not returning the consideration that's clearly sent to settle a claim implies that the offer is accepted along with the conditions spelled out in the deal. Courts had ruled that all of this was legal."

Amanda quietly typed.

"It was May 2nd, 2012 when I went to the post office to mail Dee Dee the accord and satisfaction I'd carefully prepared.

Once mailed, I drove a rental car back home and turned on the radio. The DJ announced, 'An art auction happened today in New York City at Sothebys. A pastel called *The Scream* was sold today for nearly $120 million dollars.'"

June 26, 2012 Superior Court

When the bus doors opened I stepped up and pushed the cash into the machine. The courthouse was many miles straight down the main road, but I'd be there in ten minutes. My dark pants, dress shoes, white shirt, and blue tie were ready for prime time. A woman seated just past the handicapped chairs perked up. She stared just a little too long. I took the seat one row behind and across from her when she turned and spoke to me in an admiring tone.

"You look nice." Her eyes flashed at me. "You could be a movie star," she said, as I started to feel uncomfortable. "Your eyes...they're so blue. Are you going to work?"

I must say her remarks surprised me being that it was first thing in the morning on a city bus. "Thank you," I said with an appreciative smile and a modest nod. "Ah, well, I'm going to the courthouse."

"Oh." Her gaze lingered a little longer. Then she put on her sunglasses, turned around and floated off into her own world while I floated back into mine. A movie star. That would be nice. I certainly wouldn't be on this bus, that's for sure.

In the courthouse

It was graveyard quiet. I sat in the courtroom gallery with only the deputy, a court reporter and the clerk as company. A heightened sense of awareness came over me as I reminded myself, as I always did before a court hearing, to summon my inner badass— an unnatural state for me, but required. The key I discovered to being a badass is to answer with a better response. My mentors Rhett Butler, Carey Grant and James Bond had taught me well. I was sure today would provide many opportunities to practice my renegade skills.

It was well past starting time when a woman rushed through the main door behind me,, scanned the room, then stopped in her tracks next to me. "Is your client here?"

Our eyes met and I took my time answering. "I'm the client," I said, in tough guy mode.

"Oh." She torqued her body away. Once again, mistaken for a lawyer. "Can I speak to you a moment?" she said. She plopped in a front row and motioned me to join her, which I did. Her whispers were laced with manic intensity. "We're going to trial today and the agency wants continuous jail-time, 85 days."

It's on. Even before it officially starts, this woman came out swinging. "There's no trial happening. Today is about jurisdiction only."

"No, we're having a trial today—today is scheduled for trial and we want the maximum jail time."

"No, today is about jurisdiction only, nothing else."

I could only imagine the poor slob who married this woman. It would be a living hell brought about by her demanding, nagging attitude that would surely trigger his jumping in front of a downhill bus with bad brakes. Or maybe it's just me—and my tie is a bit too tight.

Moments later, we were at the table awaiting the judge. The lawyer took a seat while I stayed upright as not to give the judge the pleasure of watching me stand up as she came in.

When the judge burst into the courtroom with the usual fanfare I stood there, unimpressed. Once we all sat, she asked for what lawyers call points and authorities. My lawyer never gave me any documentation at all and I couldn't find any court cases to back up my claim that they'd violated my due process rights and neither could the judge. She was ready, although reluctant, to rule against me when I offered a solution.

I told her that if she'd allow me about seven weeks I'd give up on the jurisdiction argument, and go to trial. She seemed surprised, but Miss Nag, didn't like it. Nonetheless, the judge agreed, and made the trial date about seven weeks out.

"And if my driver's license has been suspended I want that reinstated," I said. "Your Honor, we would require at $1,500 payment in order to do that."

"Did you hear that, Mr. Farley?"

I leaned back with raised eyebrows, and a touch of smugness as I caught the judge's eye, "I'll ride my bike." The judge stuck her nose up as she turned toward her clerk.

John Farley, Jr.

"You ride your bike then," she said with her English accented attitude. I left with a trial date set for August 7th and barely enough time for the *accord and satisfaction* to legally solidify.

August 2012 - Court

On August 7th, I came to court with all my documents, including the *accord and satisfaction*. The government lawyer made her case. During the entire trial she never attempted to prove the one thing necessary for contempt—willfulness. Meaning, that I willingly did not pay child support—that I had the money to pay it, but didn't. This was required in order for her to win, but she never bothered because she couldn't. The judge never made her prove it either.

Then it was my turn.

"Do you wish to make an opening statement?"

As I sat at the table without any notes, I leaned toward the microphone. "Yes."

I took a moment to clear my throat, and take a breath. "When I had my daughter in my life—when she was very young, three or four years old, I had to travel on the train, pick her up and travel a long distance back home—"

Miss Buzzkill broke in. "Objection your Honor. Relevance."

"I'm taking this as an opening statement and not as proof of anything, so I'll give Mr. Farley some leeway."

"...and she would always say to me, 'Tell me, tell me that story again. Tell me that story about the two little girls.'"

"About the two what?" the judge asked.

"The two little girls. I told her about the good little girl and the bad little girl. The intention of the story was to develop her self-image to be a good girl. Healthy, happy and with lots of friends and to stay away from drugs and things. She always enjoyed that story. But here's the one story I never got to tell her. It's about a knight who's always up for an adventure. Once when the knight came back from a faraway place he noticed a festival in town. He saw a woman with long hair.

"He went up to her, but she brushed him off, so he started to walk away. At that moment, she came up and handed him a note that said, 'Meet me in my land.' The knight decided to ride off to meet her and they had rendezvous' over several months. Eventually, the knight decided he had to get serious and stop these frivolous adventures and went and told the woman this. At that point, the woman left and the knight went about his life.

"Nearly a year passed when the knight returned from another adventure and saw a poster stuck to a tree. On the poster was a drawing of the woman he knew, but now she wore a queen's crown. The knight wondered, 'Who's that baby in the picture with her? Who's the father of that child?'

"Months went by until a messenger rode into town to give the knight a note from the queen requesting a meeting in her village. The knight rode out to meet her and for the first time, she invited him into her castle. There, she presented him with a baby and said, 'you're her father, but we don't need anything from you. We're fine all by ourselves.'

"The knight was shocked, stunned, and embarrassed. He went back and told the people in his town that he was the father of the baby. The queen let him see the child from time to time, but then stopped. The knight decided to visit the elders, and asked them to give him rights to his child. The elders agreed, but forced the knight to pay a tax to the queen. 'A tax?' he said. 'For what?' The elders threatened to turn the knight into a serf if he didn't pay the tax. The knight protested. 'You mean I'm not allowed to be the knight I want to be? I have to be the type of knight you want or else I become a serf?'

"Time went by and one day the knight met a pretty princess. The princess told him, 'You're no longer a knight, you're a prince now. You have to build your kingdom.' So the knight became a prince and started to build his kingdom. The queen found out and became very upset at the prince and princess and

443

sent her army to collect his gold coins, throw him in a dungeon and beat him while she watched his kingdom crumble. Finally, after many years, the frustrated princess said, 'if you're not going to give me a baby too, then I'm leaving,' and she did.

"The prince came up with an idea. He sent gold coins and a portrait to the queen as a way to settle the tax. The queen loved the portrait so much that she kept it, legally ending the tax. The prince went back to the elders and said, 'The laws of my land and the laws of her land, and even the laws of the sea agree, the prince, who would be king, is free.'"

A deafening silence fell upon the courtroom as the judge glared down with a death stare for what seemed an eternity. She swiveled to grab a folder full of documents. "Okay. Do you have anything to say about the payments that were or were not made?"

After some back and forth, I submitted my documents into evidence. "Here is the certified receipt envelope Dee Dee sent me along with her rejection letter of my January offer."

"She rejected it..." said the judge, as if that ended the issue.

"She rejected the January 10th offer. It shows that she fully understood the ramifications of accepting it. Then, on May 2nd 2012 Ms. O'Dell was sent $300 in Federal Reserve Notes, otherwise known as cash, and this handmade book of family photos and Sally's arts and crafts as satisfaction of the debt."

"I don't need to look at photos and artwork of your child. It has nothing to do with child support."

"But it does. Based on *accord and satisfaction*, there needs to be different consideration, that is, something other than what was originally called for as payment. This is it. It's different, it's new."

"I'm not disputing that you sent it. I just don't need to look at it."

"But if I had cancelled checks, and money orders that said 'paid in full' you'd want to see those."

The blue cover showed a picture of Sally and I smiling when she was five years old with my arm around her and a big, red Elmo balloon in front of us. Inside the cover were photos of baby Sally with me and many with her cousins whom she hadn't seen since she was very small. Then there were the precious cards and crafts from when she was only a few years old, comparable, if you ask me, to most of the modern art decorating city streets around the world. Inside were full color copies of a Father's Day card Sally gave me over one and one half decades ago, complete with a little girl's drawings of the yellow sun wearing dark shades, green grass and blue sky. It was signed, 'Happy Daddy Day, Love, Sally.' Other cards were there too that called me 'The best dad and great.'"

I could only imagine Dee Dee's expression when she opened the package to see *the satisfaction*, as if excavating an archaeological find of one's family. There it was, Sally with my side of the family that Dee Dee never had, along with her love cards to dad and her other art works, all in one photo book.

The judge had me read the agreement that I'd mailed.

Dear Dee Dee O'Dell,

As a release or as an accord and satisfaction, please find consideration enclosed. If you do not agree that the above referenced accounts are settled and that I am released from them, send the enclosed back within ten days. Acceptance of the items will be deemed agreement and proof that you willingly relinquish/waive any of your alleged rights on the above accounts in whatever amounts are alleged.

Photo book with photos of and from Sally O'Dell when she was a little girl.

$300 in Federal Reserve Notes.

For your celebration of Sally's 21st birthday I am providing to you these priceless items conditioned upon my release and your relinquishment of any alleged claims against me in the above matters. Written documentation showing these accounts are settled and closed is appreciated, but not required.

John Farley, Jr.

Best of luck to you, Dee Dee.
John J. Farley - Agent.

"The letter made clear that keeping the $300 cash and photo book, even without further acknowledgement, was evidence that she accepted the offer by her signature on a certified mail receipt and that I was now debt free and owed her nothing."

"I don't think $300 is enough," the judge said.

"That's why I included the photo book as consideration. That makes the offer the perfect amount, settling everything."

"I don't think Ms. O'Dell would agree to write off the balance of the child support..."

"She did. By keeping the consideration she agreed that the matter is settled, paid in full—that's the law. I have court case after court case showing that *accord and satisfaction* is a valid defense for child support. The law says she cannot accept the benefit, that is, the cash and photo book, and reject the condition, which is my release from the debt. *Accord and satisfaction* is valid. The debt is satisfied."

The judge and I debated the issue as I showed her case after case where *accord and satisfaction* was valid for child support in states scattered across the country. Then it was time for closing arguments. I started to tell her that besides the mailing of the *accord and satisfaction* to Dee Dee on May 2nd, something else happened.

"Go ahead, Mr. Farley."

"On May 2nd Sotheby's in New York held an auction."

Miss Mafia interjected. "Objection, relevance. Unless this has something to do with making child support payments..."

"Mr. Farley, is it relevant to making payments or *the satisfaction* which you believe you've accomplished?"

"It absolutely has to do with *the satisfaction*."

"Then tell me what happened in New York."

"Sotheby's held an auction and hundreds of people showed up. Five people bid and one person, in the whole world, bid

446

nearly $120 million and that piece of art was worth nearly $120 million to one person on the planet.

"Dee Dee O'Dell accepted the photo book and cash to satisfy whatever debt is alleged. She accepted the benefit therefore, she can't reject the condition."

There was a brief pause in the courtroom. My point was clear, my evidence solid and the other side didn't prove their case.

"Okay, I think Mr. Farley has made his argument," the judge said.

Some back and forth happened between the prosecutor and the judge before she leaned forward with a cold stare. "I find you guilty of contempt on 17 counts."

Guilty. The word landed like a cream pie to the face.

I sensed that not only did she enjoy saying it, but that the verdict had been decided long before I ever arrived.

"I can't believe... What are you talking about? *I* won this." I said, defiantly.

She stoically responded. "I'm the judge and I don't agree with you."

I slumped back in the chair before rebounding. Clearly, I had presented a compelling case. "I'm going to appeal this."

"You certainly have the right to appeal. You can take an appeal or a writ or whatever you want to do." I sat there angry and disappointed, but not down for the count. I have the right to an appeal, so that's what I'll do. The witch next to me wanted money put up for a bond, but the judge let me walk out the door in anticipation of a September sentencing.

Later, I spoke to Russell on the phone and relayed the story.

"Congratulations," he said.

"Congratulations? For what? I lost."

"But, the law was on your side. Neither the prosecutor nor the judge had any law to justify their position. Good job. You won, but the system will never let you beat them."

It was true. The law was on my side. The judge bent the rules every way she could to let the other side win. It was cold comfort because the day of reckoning was fast approaching.

Superior Court - September 25, 2012

The judge and the prosecutor started the sentencing hearing. "Our records indicate that Mr. Farley owes, just for the contempt period, $14,250.31 cents."

The judge paused as the number reverberated around the quiet room. The total amount the child support agency claimed I owed was closer to $92,000, that's two years pre-tax wages for the average worker in the United States.

The judge was matter-of-fact in her delivery. "Mr. Farley. $14,250.31 cents." She peered down from her perch.

I leaned forward to the microphone and gave her my best, breathy Dirty Harry impression and threw in a slight squint for effect. "I don't think I have that on me."

She continued while casually reaching for documents on her desk. "I don't have that on me either, and for good reason." After a little more banter, she hovered over her massive desk and glared. "You're not going to pay this, are you?"

It was a set up designed to fool me into committing contempt right in front of her. I shot back. "Why would I pay something that's already been paid? Why do you think I'm appealing this?"

"I'll have the deputy put the cuffs on you right now."

Panic struck. I spoke fast in a higher pitch. I sounded desperate, and then noticed her giddy reaction. She'd made me afraid, and these court vampires feed off fear, pain and misery. I caught myself and quickly went back to badass mode. "Yeah, so what do you want?"

The judge turned to the gold digger seated next to me who pulled a number out of the air. "$1,500 per month, your Honor."

The judge grinned and leaned over her desk at her. "He doesn't have that much." Then she paused and seemed to punch numbers into a calculator out of sight. "$600 per month," she said, mostly as a statement, but she seemed to be awaiting my protest.

My temper flared and I shook with anger. "Are we making a deal? Is that what this is? You want to contract with me right now?" I said with gritted teeth, wide eyes and a clenched fist. Somehow she tripped my Tyranny Alert switch. "Then let's go. Let's you and me make a deal."

"I cannot contract with you because we are not equals." Her statement shut me down for the moment.

"If I agree to this, it's only because you're coercing me. When would this amount be due?"

"On the first of each month."

"I'll agree to this because you are threatening me with jail."

"And you'll be on probation…"

"Huh? Probation! What? For what?"

"Let's take a look at the calendar…"

"You've got to be kidding me. You're going to make me come back here again? Didn't I just say that I agreed to pay? You mean you're going to waste more of my time! I don't believe it." I slumped back, and rolled my head from corner to corner.

"Yes, I'm going to waste more of your time," she said buoyantly as she thumbed through her calendar. "I want to make sure that you're complying with the order. I'll hold the 85 days in jail over your head to make sure you comply. Come back here on January 10th, 2013."

I interjected. "Let me tell you this. Unlike Dee Dee O'Dell, I've done everything I said I was going to do since day one, so if I said that I'd pay it then *it's gonna happen!*" I firmly, but lightly, rapped a pen on the table. "And if I don't pay," I said, panting in agitation, "it means *I've* decided to do the 85 days."

She glared down and didn't miss a beat. "Then you better pack your toothbrush."

I snapped back with a *Here's Johnny* grin, barely able to get the words out fast enough. "They supply them!"

"It's just an expression," she said, casually.

John Farley, Jr.

I regained my composure. "What happens if I win my appeal?"

The judge paused before answering. "If you win your appeal, then I will vacate the order."

With that I got up and glared at the judge.

Before I could turn and leave, she had one more thing to say. "$75,000 bail if he doesn't show up."

I left and all I could think about was figuring out my appeal before time ran out.

81

At the Hotel with Amanda

The two of us had dozed on the sofas and awoke at nearly the same time. Amanda ran her fingers through her hair as I rubbed the sand from my eyes.

"Gosh, what time is it?" she asked.

"Huh, just after 4 a.m.," I said, as the distant clock came into focus.

"Let me get my laptop running." As we waited I stretched and took a few deep breaths.

"Did you appeal the trial court's verdict?"

"I did. It was very difficult. Lawyers won't do appeals unless you pay them five figures, so I had to figure it out myself. When I finished the appeal, George read it."

"What did he say?"

"He said I did a very good job, and my points were legally sound. When the prosecuting attorney got around to filing a response to my appeal I was stunned. It was as if I'd studied to ace a physics exam, but showed up to a medical test."

"What do you mean? Did she cite evidence that your *accord and satisfaction* wasn't valid?"

"Not even close. She claimed I had no legal right to appeal a final judgment of contempt in the first place and cited a statute— she never bothered to address my *accord and satisfaction* argument or any of the legal mistakes the court made."

"But the trial judge said you could appeal, even encouraged you to."

"Right. That's why I couldn't believe it. But I had to file a response, and then wait many weeks for the appeal court's ruling."

"What did the court say?"

"The appeals court agreed with the lawyer that I had no legal right to appeal, and they dismissed my case. Then, to add insult to injury, they sanctioned me for the other side's court costs."

"But the judge said you could—"

"I know. Misinformation and outright lies from our government servants is par for the course. The trial was a sham, the law is a joke. Family court is a racket designed to destroy families around the world. Did you know the family law in the U.S. is on the books as 42 U.S.C. Section 666, the number of the beast? Coincidence? As Lenin, the communist leader said, 'Destroy the family, you destroy the country.'"

Amanda gave an understanding nod. "Was there anything else you could do?"

"I contacted a lawyer in New York who said I could hire him to fight the case in New York. Problem is, I was running out of cash, I mean, close to zero money, and the odds were I'd lose even if I was right. The courts had eaten up my money, time and energy. The court fights were over. On the positive side, Marv and I are still in contact through letters. I'm hoping he makes it out someday soon."

"How do I end this article? Or should I say, this book."

"Yeah, well, I didn't win the lottery. I couldn't find a rich person to become the hero, and free me from debt slavery as a humanitarian gesture. My business ventures weren't doing well. Nor could I afford to fly to New York and surprise Sally at her college before she graduated. Today, I'm picking myself up, dusting off, and putting it all behind me.

"I lost a lot and gained a lot in return. The photo book, and all the memories is one of both. What I've learned about the law and liberty is priceless. We can end the story by encouraging readers to wake up to the tyranny all around them and cherish freedom, but they can only know freedom by exercising their God given rights. Part of what I've learned is patience, and that God's ways are not our ways."

Amanda sat motionless.

"So you, Amanda, you're the final key to this story. I fought the good fight for liberty, dignity, to end debt slavery, and for my daughter. There's no Hollywood ending here, I have to let it all go, move forward, make a living, and trust that when the time is right, Sally will reach out to me. Giving one's all to a great cause is a victory for the spirit, if nothing else."

"There must be something more you can do?"

"*The accord and satisfaction* was my winning move. I know in my heart that I lawfully won, I was honorable, but the courts cheated and sometimes cheaters win. When you write this book, Amanda, and people read my story around the world, that in itself is my satisfaction. Will you promise me you'll get this story out there?"

"I promise. You remind me of Rosa Parks, the black woman who back in the 1950's wouldn't move to the back of the bus when told to give up her seat so white people could sit. One person can start a revolution."

At that moment music started to play through the hotel. "Do you hear that?" I asked.

The sound of the sitar echoed throughout. "The Beatles. It's called Norwegian Wood."

"Hmm," she said, curiously. "I first heard it when I was 12 years old while staying in Buffalo at my older brother's house for a week in the summer. For some reason I always remembered that song, but haven't heard it since."

I...once had a girl, or should I say, she once had me....

Amanda and I sat listening as I drifted into a daydream, but quickly revived myself. "What do you say we fly this coop?" I asked.

"Sure."

We fluffed the cushions we'd been resting on and started through the dining area toward the door as the music continued.

"What's this song about?" Amanda asked.

"Young men and women and their agendas."

"Ah, life and freedom are good," I said with a sigh.

We hugged at the exit. "Powerful story," she said softly, as she lingered after our embrace. Amanda's eyes looked gentler now, wiser too. "Goodbye," she said.

"My mom told me not to say goodbye. It means forever." I grinned. "She told me to say, so long."

Cold air was rolling out to the west coast. The breeze that blew through me wasn't a *January in New York* wind, but resembled instead a damp California chill that seeps through the bones the way a soggy shoe freezes the feet. I'd just come from the supermarket about one long, twisting block from my condo.

As I strolled, head down passed a line of stores with grocery bags in each hand, a young Mexican man held a sign as two toddlers circled his legs. He needed money. I switched a grocery bag from one hand to the other and reached into my pocket. A Federal Reserve Note with the profile of the man said to have ended slavery, slid out. That bill represented a lot of money to me at that moment—a lot.

The Mexican and I made eye contact for a split second. "Here you go," I said. The window shades to his soul widened. His arm stretched toward mine as his eyes stayed transfixed on me, then he clutched the cash with what seemed a combination of relief, appreciation and desperation.

A day later, I saw him again—same place. This time with his wife and children. The woman had kind eyes with a glint of the same desperation and appreciation etched on her face. As I spoke with them, I learned that they were illegal immigrants hoping to get money and permission from a court to live in Silicon Valley. It's ironic that in California illegals often drive cars without licenses, qualify for in-state or free college tuition and have even sued for the right to sit for the BAR exam and become lawyers. Child support debtors should have such value. For me, landing a job was high priority.

***

For once in my life, getting a job interview had become as difficult as it is for the average guy to land a date with a fashion model. Without work that paid good money, my life had fallen apart faster than a Hollywood marriage. Feelings of anxiety and desperation were as paralyzing to my spirit as is extra cold ice cream to the brain. At other moments, perhaps from being overwhelmed, a remarkable calm blanketed my being as if I was on a quiet mountaintop listening to the gentle sound of chirping birds.

The more I dwelled on the injustices of government the more de-motivated and rebellious I felt. Trying harder and harder to make money to buy my freedom from debt-bondage was like swimming against an unrelenting riptide. A downward spiral of negative thought, much like an ocean's undertow, led to feelings of anxiety, fear and desperation.

The thought of working to pay off a made-up "debt" to Dee Dee, like a glowing ember in a dead campfire, it still smoldered within. But my real angst was over the government's use of force against me, as if I was the lone fire hydrant in an overcrowded dog park.

Memories of the judge and the appellate court who blocked my successful win still generated a simmering scorn in my heart the way a steaming, covered pot boils over. All of this manifested into a lack of money as I'd never experienced before. Within a few months, I was broke—I mean —"where is my next meal coming from" —broke. My hypnosis center had closed and rent was overdue. It was only my sisters and brother-in-law who donated some cash to help cover the bills. Men are less likely to help other men because many believe it's disgraceful for a grown man to need help. It's men who save women and children from burning fires and floods, but strong men don't need help, the thinking goes. Make that male *white* and sympathy swirls down the circular file and gurgles back up as disdain.

Money sources were drying up. No new money was in sight. Fear was taking hold within me and the thought of being homeless was waking me in the dead of night.

It took several months to land a few job interviews accessible either by bus or a girl friend's car. Nothing positive changed in the financial arena, but my mind had relaxed a little. I was seeing hope for a brighter future. The idea that perhaps I could get a job working for a company—a concept unthinkable for more than a decade—was now willingly entertained by me as compared to sleeping on the sidewalk.

A job would instantly insert me back into the IRS and Family Court *Matrix* where money—my property—would be extracted before I ever saw it and I'd be left with practically nothing. While I wanted to live my own life, the pain of not having food or housing was too much to take. I had ambitions to pursue. Those ambitions included being in the television or movie business and also producing online self-development courses. A dating system for men based on my live seminar, *Hypnotic Seduction*.

No matter how much I watched motivational or spiritual preachers or read inspirational material, the job interviews were hard to come by. I walked into businesses and stood for hours on end filling out applications, but no luck. I posted resumes online, answered job advertisements by the dozens each week for half a year, all while directly searching for new clients on the side. The more effort I put into it, the less success I had and the more dispirited I felt. By Thanksgiving I was out of money and way behind on rent. More time passed. People I knew were away on Christmas break, traveling the world on vacation, and visiting their families.

***

Christmas Time

The day after Christmas the landlord came to the door and handed me an eviction notice. "Sorry," he gulped, while glancing at me out of courtesy. He walked into the condo to scout out its condition.

"My wife told me I should get some pictures while I'm here," he said apologetically.

"Sure," I said.

He's a smart, gray—haired engineer married to a Chinese woman. Together they have a couple of toddlers. It's a familiar scenario in Silicon Valley. Engineers marry later in life to Asian women who make them feel special, successful and appreciated. As long as the cash flows and the woman's needs and wants are met, then all is well.

The next four weeks were especially painful. Only my sisters offered to supplement the rent coming due. As if tear gas had been dropped in a crowd, my financial desperation caused some family and friends to avoid me. Homelessness was looming, but being paralyzed by fear was not an option.

While a girlfriend and I drove around in her car, we noticed white men and some women too, standing on street corners holding signs, asking for help—patiently pleading for money. It was a reminder of what Department of Child Support Services case worker—Melissa Popps— had said over the phone, "I have *clients* who pick cans out of garbage bins to pay their child support obligation."

Frankly, it's a sickening thought that the government and its insane Family Court laws degrade parents. Now, I was the one facing homelessness and no money to buy food. I was shocked and saddened by the cold rejection most friends delivered when asked for job connections or a room to rent. Even mega-millionaires, that I personally knew, turned down requests to invest in my latest business ideas for fear of loss.

The inevitable happened. I was being evicted. I had no job and no real hope of finding a place to live. Even if I did, how would I pay the rent? Fortunately, a woman who lived in the building was looking for a roommate. I'd known her from around the complex and we made a deal. The irony: she's a "man-like" lesbian and has "men issues."

I sold some furniture, stored most of my things, and crammed the rest of my belongings into one bedroom. My new room was packed like a rock concert. The shock of the move was overwhelming. Going from a spacious condo into one room in a shared space was tough. My sister had gifted me just enough money to pay rent, eat and store my things.

Before I knew it, another 60 days had passed by. After a total of eight months searching and emailing roughly 150 resumes, I'd only had four interviews which proved fruitless. With one week left before rent was due in the new place, I was down to the last $200. Once again my sister sent a final check to get me by.

***

The next day it was time to go back to court. I'd soon be face to face with a new judge and I hadn't paid a penny to the

Support Mafia since the last court date six months earlier. This lack of payment could be wrongfully interpreted as a probation violation and land me in jail. If I met with a zealous prosecutor and a unscrupulous judge, then they could have me tossed into prison all based on debt-bondage—*peonage*.

The mentality of many people is that a man, especially a white man, is somehow a disgrace if he can't find a job or is homeless. I've talked with women and men who couldn't find a job for several years. That's allowed. Society tolerates losing a corporate job and being unemployed for as long as a person can afford to be jobless. No one would call unemployment a criminal act, unless of course you owe child support. Somehow that's a crime. Government uses men's desire to provide for others as a psychological weapon against men themselves.

The late speaker Zig Ziglar said, *"You treat people the way you see them."* Those perceptions are mostly subconscious. I would add that we treat ourselves the same way, and to the same extent that we value ourselves. The challenge then, is to change the internal perception of ourselves. As we do, the people we encounter will treat of us accordingly. It works in business, in dating and even in court.

***

March 20, 2014: Poetic Justice

Another tense day at the courthouse. By now several of the deputy sheriffs knew me and said hi, chuckled or simply smiled for one reason or another as I walked through the metal detector.

The ten-minute wait for the courtroom doors to open felt more like thirty. The new male judge, a former trial attorney in his sixties sat on the bench. I found my opponent in the courtroom and we went to the hallway to talk. She was a diminutive Asian woman. We discussed the case and she was reasonable and, for what it's worth, I was treated with the dignity of a well behaved, 1850's black slave instead of a mere fat cow waiting to be shot in the head and eaten for dinner—that is to say, the usual treatment.

The Asian woman listened empathetically and then said, "Lots of people tell me stories." She grinned. "I want to have you document all the companies you apply to work for along with a list of the supervisors you interact with."

At first, her request seemed reasonable, especially when compared to a cold, lifeless prison cell. We slid back into the courtroom and waited until the case was called. After the pleasantries were handled, the judge spoke in a reflective tone. "The person in question for which support was ordered will be twenty three in May. The reason for support is long over. This sad Dickens story needs to come to an end."

A sad Dickens story. No judge ever said anything like that before. He went on to tell the prosecutor that by August the probation period would be over. This seemed to suggest that by then, no matter how much had been paid—or not paid,— California's involvement in the New York case would be over. With a calm demeanor he said that I needed to make a bonafide effort to find a job. The prosecutor demanded that I do the usual "seek work order"—that means, show up in person for ten jobs every single week; fill out applications and record all the information into a log; sign up immediately with ten temporary job agencies and mail that list to the child support office every month. A new court date was set for June 2014, just after Father's Day. The judge suggested it would be my last appearance. Leaving the courthouse, the prosecutor and I shook hands—a first in twenty years. I felt happy and relieved. Even bad options look good when compared to horrible ones.

During the bus ride home my mind recalled another bus trip along the same route less than one week earlier. I was traveling a short ride back from Mountain View, the home of many tech giants. A woman got on the bus close to my destination. There was something strange about her. The heavy coat. The pink, wool hat covered her ears. The backpack and another bag she carried seemed odd. She sat inches from me, her profile visible before she turned and smiled. I flashed a grin, but quickly looked away. Why? Why did I look away?

I felt uneasy, but I took a moment to scan her anyway. The hat, the coat, the bags—it was over 70 degrees out. Everyone was wearing t-shirts, yet she's dressed for winter. Her boots were badly worn and torn. She's homeless. A white girl in her twenties—homeless? I don't ever recall seeing an Asian person homeless. In fact, I personally know a Filipino woman who got scammed out of $170,000. A&E's Biography did a story on her. She ended up living with her parents. That's what people I knew told me to do. "Move back to the East Coast," they said. "Live with your family." Unfortunately, that's not an option for all of white America or for me.

On the streets in Silicon Valley I mostly see whites and blacks homeless on the pavement or pushing loaded shopping carts. Homelessness suggests a deeper problem happening within the families of this country. Is society spiraling out of control? Is the family being destroyed?

Reclaiming Life:

The next day after the court hearing I had a business meeting. It went well and frankly, it was as if a divine power orchestrated it with divine timing. By Monday my struggling company had received the second largest payment ever! Not that much, but enough. I was now able to get into the television production business, on my terms. It was the career I wanted to get into back in 2000 when I'd made the weight loss reality show.

Now, I'll have a chance at redemption, to live my life, my way and to do the work I want to do without bending over to satisfy the government. Win or lose. Success or failure. No one should want to succeed more than the individual himself, right? Government only demands a person find a job so it can siphon off all his or her money in order to run their anti-family racket, not to improve the individual or the family. It seemed to me a divine presence had guided my steps, although trusting a divine source was not always easy. I believe God wanted me to do certain things in this life and He opened a window after all the doors were tightly shut.

There's one preferred way to pay the government a "debt" I believe was already satisfied and wrongly applied in the first place. I'll publish and sell *The Satisfaction* and hand over the proceeds to the mafia as tribute (aka, tax). Let's have people around the world read the story for themselves. What's my new job? Selling my book and producing a television show. Of course, the judge will be asked to buy the first book.

***

The judge in my 2011 federal lawsuit against The Department of Child Support Services mentioned the rights given by the Creator and secured by government in the Declaration of Independence. "We hold these truths to be self-evident, that all men are created equal, that they are endowed by their Creator with certain unalienable Rights, that among these are Life, Liberty and the pursuit of Happiness."

Largely, that's what people want isn't it? Life—to live. Liberty—to live free, not enslaved, and the ability to pursue one's self-determined happiness without government unjustly inhibiting that pursuit. That's what I fought for; that's what the fight was all about. Thousands will oppose my viewpoints, but hopefully for the sake of freedom and family, millions will agree with it.

I'm always humbled by the sacrifices of those who have fought for freedom whether it be from a ruling nation, a tyrannical leader or a benevolent master. The founding fathers of America were men who told England "no more" we will not be your slaves any longer. Because of their innate desire to live free, America was founded for much the same reasons a person goes out and starts a company: for freedom, wealth and a chance to live their dream. Our founding father's wisdom is not antiquated, but it is still relevant today. They did not want to live bound by financial chains and working for England.

"If ye love wealth greater than liberty, the tranquility of servitude greater than the animating contest for freedom, go home from us in peace. We seek not your counsel, not your arms. Crouch down and lick the hand that feeds you. May your chains set lightly upon you; and may posterity forget that ye were our countrymen."

- Samuel Adams, Founding Father, 1776

I'd gained private funding to produce a reality television show. The stars of the show are two successful women and their colorful families. This business break was the jumpstart I needed.

By having the freedom to sell my idea and the ability to secure the funds, I'm not only able to pay myself, but also hire a film director who's the single dad of a teenage boy. He has been too proud to ask the boy's mother for child support money even when he became desperate to feed himself and his son. Now, I'd created work for him doing what he loves. Also, I was able to hire a half-dozen others to work on our project and give them jobs in their chosen careers.

Today, a Chinese woman I know, the last of ten children, will go out of her way to drive me to pick up a car I bought. She wants to help out because she likes me. It's all apropos because today is Easter Sunday, a day of resurrection. An opportunity to be re-born. From Clark Kent into a superman—or at least, a better man.

In the martial arts it's said that what matters is not how much you can dish out, but how much punishment you can take before you overcome your opponent. I've certainly been on the receiving end for a while now. A large part of life is managing fear. It's about knowing when to fight for what's right, and knowing when to go with the flow. The real test is to manage crisis with courage, style, class and dignity. In some ways, life is like a millstone. It either grinds us down or sharpens us up. The real challenge is to manage our attitude during the changes of life. It's our ability to turn "bitter" into "sweet" that determines life's quality. That's especially true when we've been wronged. Like a muscle, we have to constantly use and improve our ability to change our perceptions—make use of prayer, and then take action.

The story has been told. It has been an honor and a privilege to have you along on this journey. To paraphrase Ralph Waldo Emerson, if we are related we will meet. Perhaps we already have. To faith, family, and freedom. God bless.

Sally and friend.

A large portion of the proceeds from the sale of this book go to The Child Support Collection Unit. Order multiple copies to give as holiday gifts to those you care about. Also, visit: **CaptureYourQueen.com** for available online courses.

About the Author

John Farley, Jr. is a hypnotist and fitness professional. Currently he's in the tv/film business as a television producer. He's created several personal improvement courses.

His system for men on dating women is called *Capture Your Queen*. The skills and knowledge in the course show men of any age how to overcome the fear of rejection, attract the right women, keep the ONE, and become a stronger and more fulfilled person. Visit: **CaptureYourQueen.com and get free information now.**

Made in the USA
Middletown, DE
19 May 2023

WILLKOMMEN IN DER NEUEN ARBEITSWELT

So erwecken Sie ein Social Intranet zum Leben

Steffi Gröscho
Dr. Claudia Eichler-Liebenow
Regina Köhler

 School for
Communication and
Management

Weichselstraße 6
10247 Berlin
Tel. 030 47989789
Fax 030 47989800
www.scmonline.de

Babett-Zeichnungen: Bettina Lawrenz
Redaktion: Theresa Schulz
Lektorat: Bernd Stadelmann
Satz und Layout: Jens Guischard
Druck: Livonia Print Ltd.

Alle Rechte vorbehalten.
© SCM c/o prismus communications GmbH, Berlin 2018

2., unveränderte Auflage, September 2018
SBN 978-3-940543-43-1

NEUE ARBEITSWELT – WARUM SIE NICHT MEHR AUFZUHALTEN IST

Woran denken Sie bei „modernen Arbeitswelten"? Denken Sie an moderne Bürogebäude mit offenen Büros, Meeting-Lounges und Arbeiten im Café? Oder denken Sie an grenzenloses Arbeiten, ständige Erreichbarkeit und permanenten Stress?

Neue Arbeitswelten erzeugen viele Bilder im Kopf. Bei einigen Menschen sprechen sie die tiefsten Wünsche und Sehnsüchte an, bei anderen rufen sie eher Befremden und Unbehagen hervor. So verschieden die Bilder auch sind, es gibt eines, was alle eint: Sie drehen sich nicht um irgendwelche Software-Lösungen, sondern um eine neue Art des Arbeitens.

Das Vorhaben zur Einführung moderner Arbeitsweisen beginnt in der Regel nicht mit der Entscheidung, eine IT-Lösung einzuführen. Den eigentlichen Anstoß, über moderne vernetzte Arbeitswelten nachzudenken, liefern die Veränderungen, denen Unternehmen ausgesetzt sind und für die sie neue Arbeitsformen benötigen. Die Bereitstellung von modernen IT-Werkzeugen ist kein Selbstzweck, sondern ein Mittel, um die neuen Anforderungen besser zu erfüllen.

Doch welches sind die neuen Anforderungen, die auf Organisationen einströmen und tiefgreifend genug sind, um die Arbeitsweisen von Menschen grundlegend zu verändern? Hier eine kurze Übersicht über Herausforderungen, die uns immer wieder in Unternehmen begegnen:

ALLES IM WANDEL

Die Zeiten, da man als schwergewichtiger Tanker erfolgreich war, sind vorbei. Immer mehr Unternehmen fällt auf, dass die Erfolgsprinzipien von früher nicht mehr zuverlässig funktionieren. Hierarchien, Bürokratie, Ansagekultur – in Zeiten, da Kundenanfragen immer spezieller und komplexer werden und auch Produkte und Dienstleistungen sich immer schneller wandeln, braucht es Strukturen, in denen sich die richtigen Kompetenzträger für die Kundenanforderung schnell zusammenfinden und produktiv vernetzt arbeiten können. Agile Organisationen und Netzwerkstrukturen sind das Organisationsmodell der Zukunft. Mit der richtigen IT-Umgebung und einer passenden Unternehmenskultur gelingt der Wandel vom Tanker zum flexiblen Schnellboot.

EFFIZIENT UND TROTZDEM INNOVATIV

Effizienz- und Innovationsdruck sind zwei ganz markante Beweggründe, um sich mit vernetzten und kollaborativen Arbeitsumgebungen auseinanderzusetzen. In vielen Unternehmen herrscht noch das klassische Silodenken vor – jeder Bereich kocht sein eigenes Süppchen, keiner weiß, was der andere macht. Soziale Technologien schaffen Möglichkeiten für völlig neuartige Synergieeffekte: Sie können Prozesse verschlanken, Wissen und Ideen sichtbar machen, und sie machen das effektive bereichs- und unternehmensübergreifende Arbeiten auf einfache Weise möglich. Damit der Anspruch aufgeht, gehören jedoch einige etablierte Instrumente auf den Prüfstand: Zielvereinbarungen und Führungsstile, die Bereichsdenken fördern, sind nicht mehr zeitgemäß. Und auch das betriebliche Vorschlagswesen und Ideenmanagement bedarf häufig einer Frischzellenkur.

DIE GROSSE WEITE WELT

Immer mehr Unternehmen bewegen sich in die globalen, weltweit agierenden Märkte hinein. Internationale Vertriebsstrukturen, neue weltweite Standorte oder internationale Kooperationsnetzwerke bringen gleich mehrere neue Herausforderungen mit sich: Wie können wir trotz der Zeit- und Kulturunterschiede effektiv mit den Partnern zusammenarbeiten? Wie kann das Kundenwissen aus den verschiedenen Standorten sinnvoll gebündelt und auch anderen Standorten einfach zur Verfügung gestellt werden? Dafür braucht es Lösungen, welche die Menschen verbinden und den Austausch sowie die Zusammenarbeit praktikabel gestalten. Moderne Kollaborations- und Kommunikationslösungen schaffen dafür optimale Voraussetzungen.

ALLES DREHT SICH UM DEN MITARBEITER

Immer mehr Beschäftigte wollen selbst entscheiden, wann und wo sie arbeiten. Flexible Arbeitsmodelle stehen hoch im Kurs. Home Office, Work-Life-Balance, Mobilität – Unternehmen, die hier die richtigen Angebote entwickeln, schaffen gute Voraussetzungen, um für Leistungsträger in verschiedenen Lebensphasen ein attraktiver Arbeitgeber zu sein.

Viele Unternehmen tun sich noch schwer mit dem Gedanken, den Mitarbeitern mehr Freiräume zu gewähren und ihnen das notwendige Vertrauen zu schenken. Die Vorstellung, dass ein Mitarbeiter auch dann produktiv sein kann, wenn er nicht im Büro arbeitet, muss sich vielfach noch durchsetzen. Dabei kennen wir das alle: Konzeption und konzentriertes Arbeiten erfordern störungsfreie Arbeitsumgebungen – und das bietet ein ruhiges Büro oder Home Office eher als ein Großraumbüro. Kreatives dagegen gelingt am besten gemeinsam mit anderen in einer anregenden Umgebung. Das kann ein inspirierender Besprechungsraum ebenso sein wie eine Sonnenterrasse oder der Strand. In einer vernetzten Arbeitswelt mit der dazugehörenden Vertrauenskultur entstehen schnell inspirierende Arbeitsumgebungen.

WISSEN RETTEN VOR DER DEMOGRAFIE-FALLE

Unternehmen bekommen den demografischen Wandel immer stärker zu spüren. In den nächsten Jahren scheidet eine große Welle von Mitarbeitern altersbedingt aus den Unternehmen aus. Schon heute fällt es vielen Unternehmen immer schwerer, geeignete neue Mitarbeiter zu finden. Aber auch die Frage, wie sie das Fach- und Erfahrungswissen der ausscheidenden Mitarbeiter für die Firma erhalten und möglichst effizient an die nachfolgenden Generationen weitervermitteln können, stellt sie vor eine große Herausforderung. Schon heute stoßen klassische Schulungs- und Tandem-Konzepte im Format Face to Face an ihre Grenzen, weil sie mit hohem Aufwand verbunden sind, ohne den sich stetig weiterentwickelnden Wissensstoff tatsächlich noch vermitteln zu können. Hier sind moderne Lern-Management-Systeme gefragt, die den virtuellen Austausch von Erfahrungswissen unterstützen und dieses Wissen einfach und flexibel zur Verfügung stellen, wenn es konkret gebraucht wird. Moderne Arbeitsplattformen können das. Außerdem lassen sich mit ihrer Hilfe Abläufe verschlanken, sodass sich der oft zitierte Fachkräftemangel auch dadurch ein wenig abfangen lässt.

NEUE ARBEITSWELT – KEINE FRAGE DES OB, SONDERN DES WIE

All diese Herausforderungen zwingen immer mehr Unternehmen zu der strategischen Entscheidung, moderne soziale Plattformen einzuführen. Typischerweise werden damit folgende Erwartungen verbunden:

- Austausch fördern, damit Informationen schneller an der richtigen Stelle ankommen;
- Wissen und Experten besser auffindbar machen, um schneller gute Lösungen für komplexe Probleme zu finden;
- Zusammenarbeit und Workflows so unterstützen, dass sie wesentlich effizienter ablaufen;
- Flexible Lernumgebungen fördern, damit die Mitarbeiter das Wissen aufnehmen, wenn sie es wirklich benötigen, und ihr Erfahrungswissen wiederum der Organisation zugutekommen lassen;
- Moderne Informationskanäle bereitstellen, um alle Mitarbeiter weltweit schneller über wichtige Vorgänge auf dem Laufenden zu halten;
- Wissensweitergabe an die nachfolgenden Generationen fördern und neue Mitarbeiter schnell einarbeiten.

Eine soziale Zusammenarbeits- und Kommunikationsplattform macht nur Sinn, wenn sie lebt. Wenn sie also viele aktive Nutzer hat, die nicht nur konsumieren, sondern auch Informationen und Wissen teilen. Es ist ein Geben und Nehmen, das aber voraussetzt, dass man überhaupt bereit ist, andere am eigenen Wissen teilhaben zu lassen und eigenes Unwissen beispielsweise in Form von Fragen für andere sichtbar zu machen. Von dieser Selbstverständlichkeit sind viele Unternehmen kulturell und organisatorisch heute noch weit entfernt. Deshalb werden moderne Arbeitsweisen häufig gerade auch von Führungskräften und alt eingesessenen Mitarbeitern skeptisch betrachtet. Mühsame Aufklärungsarbeit ist erforderlich und mutige Pionierarbeit auch. Zum Glück gibt es aber auch tolle Erfolgserlebnisse mit den Mitarbeitern, die dankbar sind, dass sich ihr Unternehmen in eine moderne Arbeitswelt verwandelt und dass sie ganz vorn mitwirken können.

Dieses Buch will Ihnen Mut machen, diesen Weg zu beschreiten und ihn auch gegen Widerstände

und Begrenzungen in den Köpfen hartnäckig zu verfolgen. Es wird sich lohnen, denn die Entwicklung ist nicht mehr aufzuhalten. Die Angehörigen der nachwachsenden Generationen sind vernetztes Arbeiten und Kommunizieren bereits aus ihrem privaten Alltag gewohnt und bringen diese Gewohnheiten mit. Unternehmen, die sich davor verschließen, müssen sich darauf einstellen, dass sich die Beschäftigten ihre eigenen Wege suchen. Abstimmungen und Teamarbeiten finden dann auf nicht sicheren kostenlosen Plattformen außerhalb des Unternehmens statt. Moderne Arbeitswelten sind also keine Frage des Ob. Sie werden entstehen. Und die Vorreiter werden wahrscheinlich denen, die den Trend skeptisch beäugen, irgendwann meilenweit voraus sein – und zwar sowohl als attraktiver Arbeitgeber als auch hinsichtlich ihrer Effizienz und Innovationsstärke.

Man kann den Wandel dosiert und in verträglichen Schritten bewältigen – als Projektverantwortliche oder Entscheider haben Sie die Gestaltung des Weges in die neue Arbeitswelt ganz in der Hand. Dieses Buch will Ihnen vielfältige Anregungen geben, wie Sie das Thema angehen und erfolgreich einführen können. Es gibt nicht den einen richtigen Weg, aber es gibt Leitplanken, an denen Sie sich orientieren können. Sie helfen dabei, der einmal getroffenen Entscheidung zu vertrauen und sie selbstbewusst in Ihrer Organisation umzusetzen. Diese Leitplanken möchten wir Ihnen vorstellen.

Immer häufiger trifft man in der Praxis auf Entscheider, die den Mut haben, starke Visionen zu entwickeln und grundlegende Selbstverständlichkeiten in Frage zu stellen und die dabei ihre Organisation völlig neu erfinden. Ein mutiges Beispiel dafür ist die hhpberlin. Innerhalb weniger Jahre hat sie sich von einer hierarchisch geprägten zu einer agilen, vernetzten Organisation entwickelt und tiefgreifende Veränderungen erfahren.

Dieser Abschnitt entstand in Zusammenarbeit mit Stefan Truthän, Geschäftsführender Gesellschafter hhpberlin Ingenieure für Brandschutz GmbH

Innovative Organisationsmodelle für ein hochflexibles Projektgeschäft bei der hhpberlin Ingenieure für Brandschuz GmbH

Wir sind in den letzten zehn Jahren enorm gewachsen - von 50 auf heute 180 Mitarbeiter. Ab einem bestimmten Punkt haben wir gemerkt, dass die hierarchische Organisation für unsere Kundenstrukturen und unseren Markenanspruch nicht mehr zeitgemäß ist. Brandschutz ist ein sehr komplexes Thema, bei dem viele Faktoren zusammenwirken. Die Vielzahl der Anforderungen ist ohne umfassende Kompetenz nicht zu bewältigen. Denn in unserer modernen Gesellschaft entstehen heute Gebäude, die man in dieser Größe, Bauweise und Individualität noch vor wenigen Jahren nicht kannte. Die Folge: DAS Brandschutzkonzept, das immer anwendbar ist, gibt es nicht. Verlangt werden vielmehr sehr spezifische und individuelle Lösungen, die auf den Kunden zugeschnitten und gut durchdacht sein müssen. Wir tragen eine große Verantwortung und haben einen hohen Anspruch: Wir wollen den besten vorbeugenden Brandschutz für die Projekte unserer Kunden gestalten.

Bei uns bestimmt daher nicht die Hierarchie darüber, welcher Mitarbeiter im Projektteam eines Kunden mitwirkt, sondern das Thema. Wir haben ein Organisationsmodell geschaffen, bei dem sich wechselnde Personen mit den für den Kunden relevanten Lösungskompetenzen zu einem Team zusammenfinden können. Das Ganze ist als wandlungsfähiger Organismus angelegt – wenn sich Kundenanforderungen verändern, können ganz flexibel neue Projektstrukturen entstehen, die den Anforderungen am besten gerecht werden. Sowohl mit fachlichen Kompetenzen als auch mit dem, worauf es ebenfalls ankommt: Leute begeistern, Organisieren, Alternativen aufzeigen und Zuhören. Wir bezeichnen das als LOAZ-Organismus.

Das Organisationmodell ist darauf ausgelegt, dass Mitarbeiter ihre Stärken an der richtigen Stelle einsetzen können. Davon profitieren Kunden und Mitarbeiter gleichermaßen. Das macht unseren Spirit und unsere Begeisterung aus. Dafür benötigen wir aber auch eine IT, die diese Organisationsform „Work like a network" unterstützt. Eine IT, die themenorientiert verschiedene Akteure mit den relevanten Lösungskompetenzen zusammenbringt. Mit den Microsoft-Werkzeugen für eine agile Organisation ist uns das gelungen.

Wenn wir über neue Formen des Arbeitens nachdenken, lohnt es sich auch, scheinbare Gesetzmäßigkeiten in der räumlichen Bürogestaltung zu hinterfragen. Viel zu oft ordnen wir unsere Produktivität den räumlichen Gegebenheiten unseres Büros unter und nehmen Unterbrechungen, Ablenkungen oder andere Störfaktoren in Kauf, weil es vermeintlichnicht anders geht. Moderne Arbeitswelten verfolgen die Philosophie, die Arbeitsumgebung passend zur Arbeit bereitzustellen, damit die Mitarbeiter motiviert und leistungsfähig sind. Das Business Village Chemnitz hat einen Erlebnisraum geschaffen, der eindrucksvoll zeigt, dass sich modernes Arbeiten auch räumlich unterstützen lässt und messbare Effizienzsteigerungen bewirkt.

Business Village Chemnitz – Ein Erlebnisort für moderne Arbeitswelten

Unter dem Motto „Weil Arbeitswelten sich verändern..." wurde eine alte Fabrik zum Business Village Chemnitz ausgebaut – ein völlig neues Projekt über das Arbeiten von morgen. Geboren wurde die Idee anhand der Frage, wie man intelligent Ressourcen bündeln und einsetzen kann, damit Unternehmen sich schlank und effizient auf ihren Geschäftszweck konzentrieren können. In Zeiten des Fachkräftemangels ist dieses Thema von zunehmender Bedeutung, aber auch das Teilen statt Kaufen trifft auf einen Zeitgeist, dem sich immer mehr Unternehmen auch über die Startup-Phase hinaus öffnen.

Das Business Village Chemnitz bietet einen ganzheitlichen Ansatz zur Gestaltung einer modernen Arbeitsumgebung. Es entwirft innovative Raum- und Arbeitsplatzkonzepte ebenso wie digitalisierte Prozesse und veränderte Arbeitsmodelle. Damit können Unternehmen die gemeinschaftlich verfügbare Infrastruktur effizienter nutzen und ihren Mitarbeitern Work-Life-Modelle anbieten, die flexibel auf ihre Bedürfnisse anpassbar sind. Das schließt das Arbeiten daheim ebenso ein wie die Möglichkeit, im Büro Rückzugsorte zu finden, wenn man ungestört arbeiten oder telefonieren möchte.

Ein Mieter, der das Büro der Zukunft komplett umgesetzt hat, ist die Firma e-dox. Hier teilen sich Mitarbeiter nun weniger Schreibtische, weil festgestellt wurde, dass durch Fehltage oder Auswärtstermine nie alle Mitarbeiter gleichzeitig vor Ort sind. Benötigt man doch mehr Arbeitsfläche, reicht es, Platz im Coworking-Bereich bereitzustellen, anstatt ihn fest zu mieten. Durch Cloud Working via Office 365 und papierloses Arbeiten ist es möglich, von überall aus zu arbeiten und Zugriff auf alle Firmendaten zu haben, sofern man Internet hat. Durch diese Einsparung von Raum und Papier und die Beschleunigung von allen

Abbildung 1: Papierloses Büro und Desktop-Sharing im Business Village Chemnitz

Dieser Abschnitt erts-and in Zusammenarbeit mit Uwe Thuß, Geschäftsführer Business Village Chemnitz

internen Prozessen konnte e-dox erhebliche Kosteneinsparungen generieren. In diesem Zusammenhang mussten aber auch andere Fragen gemeinsam mit den Führungskräften und Mitarbeitern angegangen werden: „Hat der Chef ein eigenes Büro oder wird er Teil der Coworking-Community?" oder „Fühle ich mich noch wohl, wenn ich nicht mehr meinen eigenen Schreibtisch habe?".

Ein weiteres Beispiel ist die Cafeteria. Sie ist nicht nur ein Ort, um zu essen oder Kaffee zu trinken. Durch entsprechendes Mobiliar bietet sie auch die Möglichkeit, sich projektbezogen in Gruppen zusammenzufinden und dort zu arbeiten. Gleichzeitig ist sie ein kostenloser Coworking-Bereich. Jeder, der will (Freelancer, Studenten, Reisende, Selbstständige), kann in der Wohlfühlatmosphäre der Cafeteria mit kostenlosem W-LAN und Strom arbeiten. Jeder, der im Business Village arbeitet, stellt gleichzeitig auch sein „soziales Kapital" zur Verfügung. Andere sehen das Know-how der Personen und können sich über eine Webplattform vernetzen.

Abbildung 2: Flexible Büronutzung im Coworking-Space des Business Village Chemnitz

Das Business Village Chemnitz soll ein Ort für modernes Arbeiten sein und will zugleich Unternehmen inspirieren, auch in ihrem eigenen Hause moderne Arbeitsumgebungen einzuführen. Im Coworking-Bereich des Business Village Chemnitz können Teams temporär einen Arbeitsplatz bzw. einen Konferenzraum mieten, sodass sie Teil der modernen Arbeitswelt werden. Dabei erleben sie hautnah, dass es um mehr geht als nur um außergewöhnliche Möbel oder hochmoderne Technik. Den eigentlichen Nutzen moderner Arbeitsgestaltung in Form von unbürokratischen, papierlosen Prozessen und Arbeitsumgebungen, die ganz auf die berufliche Tätigkeit zugeschnitten sind, erleben Teams häufig erst, wenn sie es direkt selbst ausprobieren.

Abbildung 3: Flexibel auch als Auditorium nutzbar: Eingangsbereich des Business Village Chemnitz

Video-Tipp:
CIOs berichten –
Wie weit sind ihre
Unternehmen bei
Digitalisierung und
Transformation?
http://bit.ly/1CHNF7F

SOCIAL INTRANET – DAS HERZ DES VERNETZTEN UNTERNEHMENS

Was ist ein Social Intranet?

Dieses Buch will Unternehmen und ihre Mitarbeiter für die neue Arbeitskultur begeistern, die durch Social Intranets möglich ist. Doch worüber reden wir eigentlich, wenn wir über Social Intranet reden? Im deutschsprachigen Raum gibt es bislang keine einheitliche Bezeichnung für moderne Plattformen zur Zusammenarbeit und Kommunikation. Bezeichnungen wie „Enterprise 2.0" oder „Internes Social Media" sind ebenso geläufig wie „Kollaborationsplattform" oder „Enterprise Social Network". Diese Vielfalt an Begriffen ruft in der Praxis häufig Unklarheit und unterschiedliche Interpretationen hervor (eine Übersicht wird in Tabelle 1 gegeben).

Wir haben uns für den Begriff Social Intranet entschieden, weil er eine Klammer für die wesentlichen Aspekte moderner Plattformen bildet und Zusammenarbeit und Kommunikation einschließt: Intranets, auf die nahezu alle Mitarbeiter zugreifen können, sind in vielen Unternehmen bereits seit Jahren als Informationsplattformen etabliert. Die Möglichkeit, dass nun alle Mitarbeiter Inhalte ins Intranet einstellen und im Intranet miteinander kommunizieren, zusammenarbeiten und sich vernetzen können, wurde erst in den letzten Jahren technologisch stark vorangetrieben. Genau dies ist die neue, moderne Komponente – das „Social" in modernen Arbeitsplattformen.

Die Vorstellung einer Art „virtuellen Büros", das die Mitarbeiter morgens betreten und von dem aus sie alle anderen Arbeitsräume erreichen können, notwendige Informationen finden und sich mit Kollegen austauschen können, macht die Idee und auch die Potenziale eines Social Intranets greifbar.

Das Wort „Social" löst erfahrungsgemäß bei Entscheidern auch Skepsis und Zurückhaltung aus. Dies liegt nicht zuletzt daran, dass die aus dem privaten Umfeld bekannten sozialen Netzwerke nicht gerade mit Produktivität und inhaltlicher Qualität assoziiert werden.

Ein Social Intranet (siehe Abbildung 4) führt zum einen alle Informations- und Kommunikationsanwendungen zusammen, zum anderen ist es die Basis für die Zusammenarbeit von Teams, Abteilungen, Projektgruppen und anderen internen Communities (Social Collaboration). Hier tauschen sich die Angehörigen des Unternehmens virtuell aus. Unabhängig von ihrer Abteilungszugehörigkeit, ihrem Standort, ihrer Expertise und ihrer Position können sie Ideen, Wissen, Meinungen und Feedback einbringen. Das Social Intranet erlaubt Interaktionen und Personalisierungen, integriert oder ist der Ausgangspunkt für den Zugriff auf weitere Anwendungen. Eine unternehmensweite, systemübergreifende Suche (Enterprise Search) ist ein wesentlicher Baustein des Social Intranets.

Abbildung 4: Social Intranet integriert Social Collaboration

Abbildung 5: Social Collaboration besteht parallel zum Intranet

Reine Social-Collaboration-Plattformen (oder auch „Enterprise Social Networks" z.B. auf Basis von Confluence, Yammer oder Jive) existieren häufig parallel zum bestehenden Intranet (siehe Abbildung 5). In einigen Unternehmen gibt es nur noch die Collaboration-Plattform. Egal welche Lösung Sie für Ihr Unternehmen favorisieren – ein sorgfältig gestalteter Einführungsprozess ist immer notwendig. Im Falle einer Social-Collaboration-Plattform fällt der Projektaufwand ggf. geringer aus.

Wenn wir von Social Intranet schreiben, meinen wir also allumfassend die zentrale Hauptplattform im Unternehmen und den Einstieg in alle internen Kollaborationslösungen. Aus Sicht des Nutzers bedeutet das: Er hat das Gefühl, mit einer übergreifenden Plattform zu arbeiten, in der ggf. verschiedene Teillösungen integriert sein können.

Häufiger Sprachgebrauch „Social Intranet" in der Praxis	Häufiger Sprachgebrauch „Social Collaboration" in der Praxis
Modernes Intranet	Enterprise Social Network (ESN)
Kommunikationsportal	Unternehmensnetzwerk
Intranet 2.0	Enterprise Wiki
Intranet	Social Business Suite
Internes Unternehmensportal	Web 2.0 im Unternehmen
Enterprise Portal	Kollaborationsplattform
Enterprise 2.0	

Sprachgebrauch im Buch:

„Social Intranet" als integrierte Plattform gemäß Abbildung 4

Tabelle 1: Synonyme für Social Intranet und Social Collaboration

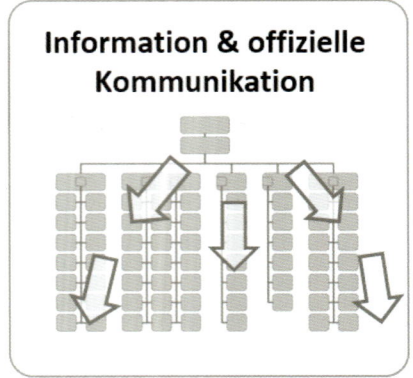

Information & offizielle Kommunikation

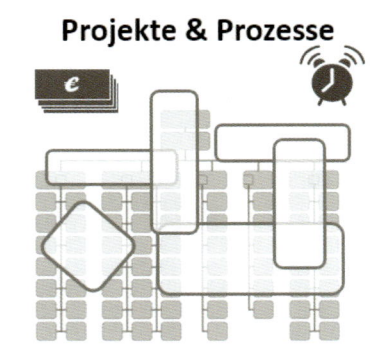

Projekte & Prozesse

Profil & persönliches Informationsmanagement

 Navigation

 Suche

 Metadaten

Vernetzung, Communities, Integration

 Activity Stream

 Dashboards

Anwendungselemente (Auswahl)

 Wiki (CMS)

 Blog (News)

 Forum

 Dokumente

 Bereiche

 Profile

 Microblog

 Umfragen

 Multimedia

 Aufgaben

 Kalender

Abbildung 6: Die vier Hauptanwendungsfälle eines Social Intranets, Quellen: T-Systems Multimedia Solutions GmbH, 2014, und detaillierte Betrachtungen in „Der Enterprise 2.0 Irrtum: Wissensmanagement im Enterprise 2.0, Teil 4" (Wolf F. , 2014)

Bei den modernen Intranet-Lösungen bilden sich folgende vier Hauptanwendungsfälle heraus:

- Information & offizielle Kommunikation,
- Projekte & Prozesse,
- Mitarbeiterprofil & persönliches Informationsmanagement,
- übergreifende Vernetzung, Communities & Integration.

In Abbildung 6 werden diese Hauptszenarien und ihre Zielgruppen dargestellt und es wird greifbarer, welche Anwendungsszenarien sich daraus konkret im Vorhaben „Social Intranet" ergeben können.

Im Zusammenhang mit modernen Arbeitswelten werden häufig auch Begriffe wie „Wissensmanagement" und „Social Business" genannt. Sie beschreiben die Chancen, welche die neue Art des Zusammenarbeitens für ein vernetztes Unternehmen bringt und werden daher in den folgenden zwei Abschnitten etwas näher erläutert.

Modernes Wissensmanagement in lebendigen Wissensnetzwerken

Schon die Pioniere des Wissensmangements, Nonaka und Takeuchi, wussten: Dokumentation, Ablage und Bewahrung von Informationen reichen für einen nachhaltigen Umgang mit Wissen und Erfahrung in Unternehmen und Organisationen nicht aus (Nonaka & Takeuchi, 1995). Als Andrew P. McAfee 2006 dann in seinem Buch „Enterprise 2.0: The Dawn of Emergent Collaboration" (McAfee, 2006) den Einsatz von Social Software in Unternehmen einläutete, atmeten viele Wissensmanagement-Enthusiasten auf.

Blickt man kritisch auf die letzten acht Jahre zurück, sieht man zwei Entwicklungen. Wissensmanagement-Ansätze folgen in der Realität noch immer dem gleichen Muster der Dokumentation, Ablage und Bewahrung. Nur die dafür verwendeten Tools sind andere. So wurden in Unternehmen keine Datenbanken, sondern die hauseigenen Wikipedias gefüllt. Die andere Entwicklung sieht man im Bereich der Zusammenarbeit von Menschen. Hier treibt der Einsatz von Web-2.0-Tools eine fortdauernde Veränderung voran, die eine stetige Intensivierung des Wissensaustausches zwischen Menschen mit sich bringt.

Es setzen sich neue Ansätze für die Verteilung von Wissen im Unternehmen durch. Unter heutigen Marktanforderungen lassen sich die Prozesse, wie Wissen vom Wissenden zum Suchenden fließt, kaum noch zentral managen. Es wird immer wichtiger, Ansätze zu realisieren, die es ermöglichen, dass Mitarbeiter eigenverantwortlich ihr Wissen untereinander teilen.

Viele Projekte zur Einführung von Social Intranets sind in den letzten Jahren gescheitert, haben ihre Ziele nicht erreicht. Es gibt aber auch die Vorzeige-Intranets und Unternehmen, die eine neue Stufe der Wettbewerbsfähigkeit erreicht haben, weil es ihnen gelungen ist, das Wissen ihrer Mitarbeiter besser zu nutzen. Die wichtigsten Aspekte, um mit einem Social Intranet zum Unternehmenserfolg beizutragen, fasst dieses Buch zusammen.

Die Einflussfaktoren für den Erfolg sind ausgesprochen vielfältig. Passen die ausgewählten 2.0-Tools zur Unternehmenskultur? Unterstützt der gewählte Ansatz die Vision des Unternehmens? Wie „social" sind die Kunden des Unternehmens? Welche Anforderungen stellen die Mitarbeiter an die Ergonomie? Wie ist das Social Intranet in die wertschöpfenden Prozesse, Arbeitsweisen und IT-Landschaften integriert?

Eine Frage hat sich jedoch als die wahrscheinlich wichtigste herausgestellt: Welche konkreten Arbeitsaufgaben werden unterstützt? Der Nutzen für das Unternehmer entsteht erst, wenn das Social Intranet für die Mitarbeiter einen direkten Nutzen schafft wenn sie also tatsächlich effektiver und effizienter arbeiten können. Die Antwort auf diese Fragestellung fällt vielen Unternehmen noch schwer. Meistens entstehen lange Wunschlisten für Features und ebenso lange Listen von Zielen die man mit dem Social-Intranet-Projekt erreichen will. Das ist noch keine ausreichende Basis, ein Projekt zu starten, aber ein deutliches Zeichen für das Potenzial, das im Unternehmen steckt. Heben Sie es!

Dieser Abschnitt entstand in Zusammenarbeit mit Stefan Ehrlich, Vorstand Knowledge Research Center Dresden e.V.

Dieser Abschnitt entstand in Zusammenarbeit mit Ulf-Jost Kossol, Leiter Social Business Technology T-Systems Multimedia Solutions GmbH

Social Business – Neue Chancen für vernetzte Unternehmen

Die Veränderungen, denen Unternehmen in ihren Märkten begegnen, haben im digitalen Zeitalter deutlich an Geschwindigkeit gewonnen. Die nahezu unbegrenzte Information und Transparenz im Internet hat das Kundenverhalten stark verändert und die Macht der Kunden wachsen lassen. Den Unternehmen verlangt das ein hohes Maß an Anpassungsfähigkeit ab, die nur entstehen kann, wenn die Mitarbeiter im permanenten Austausch mit den Kunden und Partnern, aber auch den Mitarbeitern anderer Unternehmensbereiche stehen. Klassisch werden Kunden, Mitarbeiter und Partner unabhängig voneinander betreut: Marketing, Vertrieb und Unternehmenskommunikation kümmern sich um die Geschäfts- und Privatkunden, HR und Interne Kommunikation sind für die Beschäftigten im Unternehmen zuständig, der Einkauf oder andere Mitarbeiter sind für externe Partner verantwortlich.

Ein Social-Business-Ökosystem erweitert daher die Perspektive eines Social Intranets um die Dimensionen des Extranets (externer Bereich zur Zusammenarbeit mit Partnern oder Kunden) und des Intranets, um die Wertschöpfungspotenziale von Social Media für Unternehmen darzustellen (siehe Abbildung 7). Um die Arbeitseffizienz zu erhöhen, müssen Informations-, Kommunikations- und Kollaborationspotenziale für konkrete Arbeitsprozesse über System- und Unternehmensgrenzen hinweg gehoben werden. Social Business ist ein Weg

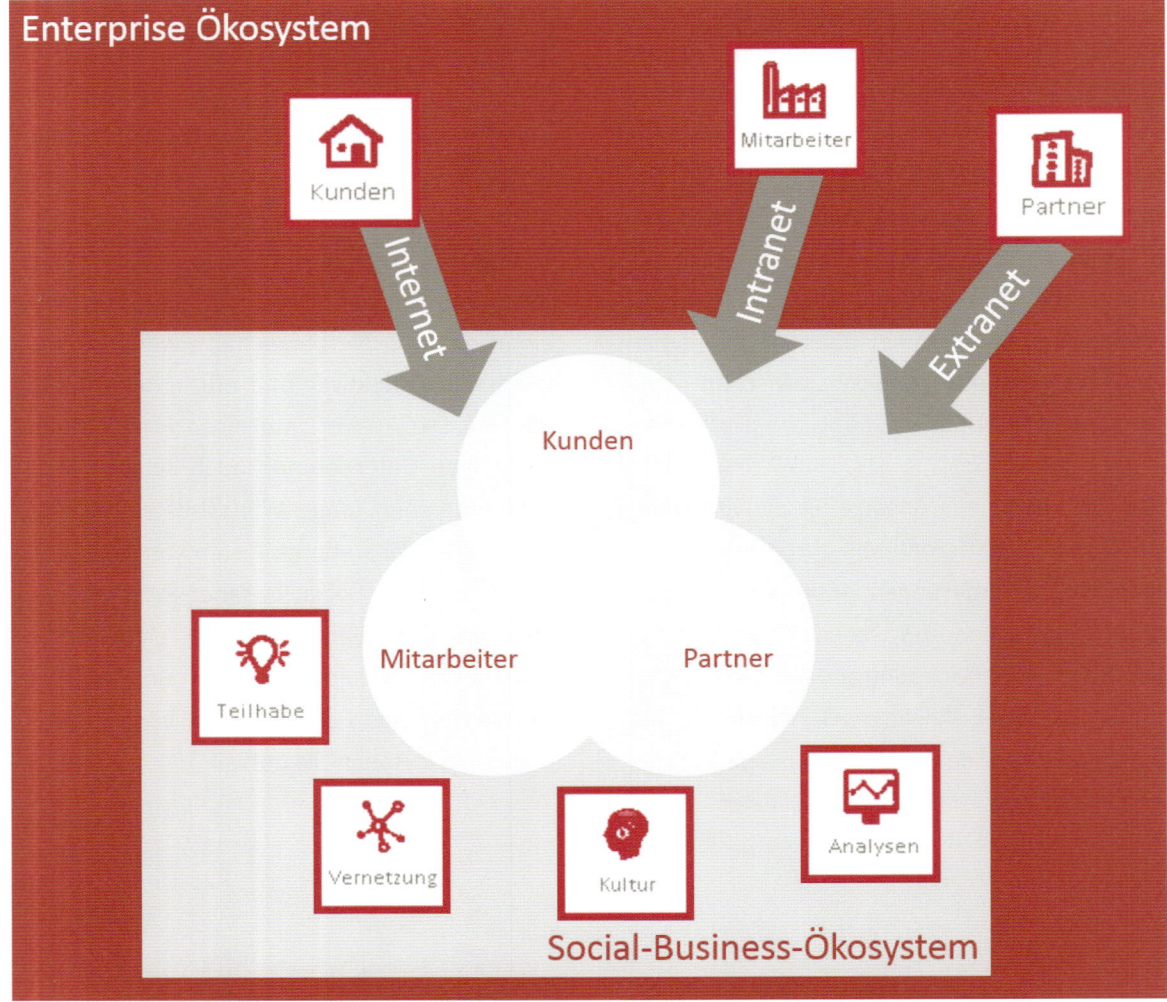

Abbildung 7: Das Social-Business-Ökosystem – Ganzheitliches Herangehen generiert mehr Wertschöpfung aus sozialer Vernetzung

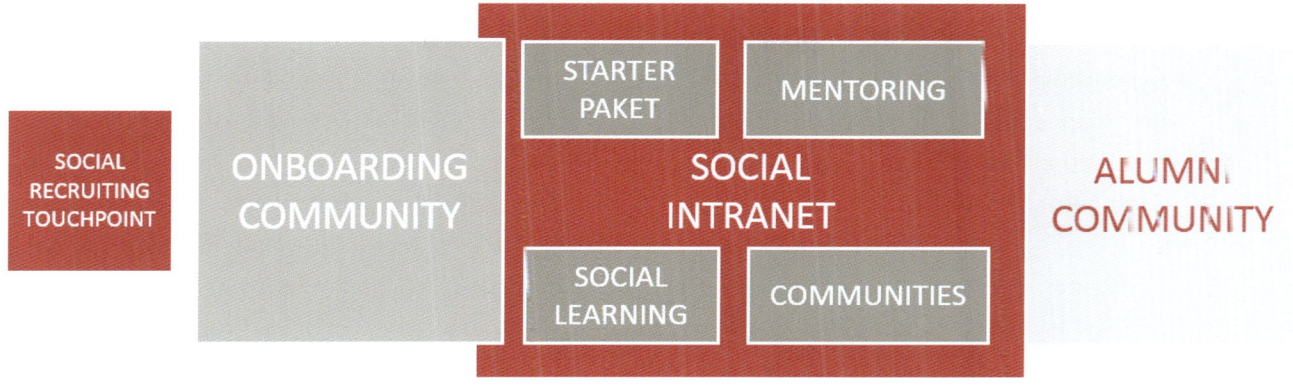

Abbildung 8: Schema eines Employer Lifecycle

zu einem anderen Geschäftsverständnis, das ökonomische Ziele und das menschliche Bedürfnis nach Kommunikation miteinander verknüpft. Ein besonderes Augenmerk liegt dabei auf der Rolle von Social Intranets (oder Social-Collaboration-Portalen), die ein wesentliches Kernelement eines Social-Business-Ökosystems darstellen.

Ein Beispiel für den gewinnbringenden Einsatz von Social-Business-Ökosystemen liefert der nachfolgend beschriebene Employer Lifecycle.

EMPLOYER LIFECYCLE

Ein Social-Business-Ökosystem wartet gerade für die Personalbeschaffer und -entwickler mit zeitgemäßen Möglichkeiten auf, um den Kampf um die besten Talente dauerhaft zu gewinnen. Es ist möglich, Mitarbeiter nicht mehr nur vom ersten bis zum letzten Arbeitstag zu verwalten, sondern sie vom ersten Kontakt über ihre Stationen im Unternehmen bis in die Zeit nach dem Austritt hinein zu begleiten. Wer ein Gesamterlebnis anbietet, wird dauerhaft als moderner und attraktiver Arbeitgeber wahrgenommen, da aktive und ehemalige Mitarbeiter die größte Nähe zum Unternehmen haben und somit die Chance besteht, sie als wirkliche Fans oder Botschafter zu gewinnen.

Wie muss man sich das nun genau vorstellen?

Der in Abbildung 8 beispielhaft dargestellte Lebenszyklus der Mitarbeiterbetreuung beginnt auf einer Karriereseite des Unternehmens im Social Web, entweder auf dem eigenen Blog oder in einem bekannten sozialen Netzwerk wie Xing oder LinkedIn. Interessierten Kandidaten werden Einblicke in die Kultur und Arbeitsweise des Unternehmens geboten, eventuell sogar über einen ersten Austausch mit „echter Mitarbeitern".

Die Zeit zwischen Vertragsunterzeichnung und erstem Arbeitstag bleibt heutzutage oftmals ungenutzt. Die Einbindung in eine Onboarding Community im externen Bereich des Social Intranets kann helfen, diese Zeit sinnvoll zu gestalten und viele Fragen, die sonst in der kostbaren Arbeitszeit gestellt werden, bereits zu beantworten. Erste Vernetzungen zwischen „den Neuen" entstehen – solche Gemeinschaften haben erfahrungsgemäß lange Bestand und geben Sicherheit.

Ab dem ersten Arbeitstag unterstützen z.B. Wikis mit einem „Mitarbeiter-Starterpaket" die ersten Schritte und machen die neuen Kollegen möglichst schnell mit ihren Aufgaben vertraut. Wenn darüber hinaus kollaboratives und informelles Lernen direkt über das Social Intranet unterstützt wird, können aufwendige Schulungen deutlich reduziert und der Wissenstransfer

beschleunigt werden. Die Vernetzung untereinander, die Begleitung durch Mentoren oder
die Mitgliedschaft in Themen-Communities
sollte durch die HR-Abteilung unterstützt und
vorangetrieben werden.

Ein Faktor, der heute noch völlig unterreprä-
sentiert ist, ist der Aufbau und die Betreuung
von Alumni-Communities. Allgemein herrscht
immer noch die Einstellung vor, dass ein Mitarbeiter nur interessant ist, solange er ange-
stellt ist. Die Potenziale einer Betreuung über
den letzten Arbeitstag hinaus werden nicht
ausgeschöpft. In unserer vernetzten und dy-
namischen Welt sollten Jobwechsel aber nicht

als unziemliche Abkehr vom Unternehmen
aufgefasst werden, sondern als etwas Normales. In einer aktiven Ehemaligen-Community
haben Unternehmen die Chance, langfristig
eine Beziehung mit einem ehemaligen Mitarbeiter aufrecht zu erhalten. Nicht nur, dass
sich dadurch Effekte für bestehende oder neue
Partnerschaften oder Aufträge ergeben können. Es wird dabei sogar die Rückkehroption
stetig aufrechterhalten.

Fazit: Für alle denkbaren Szenarien gilt:
Ein Social Intranet, das die Kommunikation
und Zusammenarbeit eines Unternehmens
vital in Fluss hält, ist heute unverzichtbar.

MIT MODERNEM CHANGE MANAGEMENT IN DIE NEUE ARBEITSWELT

Jeder stellt sich bei anstehenden Neuerungen und Veränderungen Fragen: Warum ist das Ganze notwendig? Was wird morgen für mich anders sein? Was habe ich davon? Welche Nachteile bringt mir das Neue? Wie kann ich Einfluss darauf nehmen, was mit mir geschieht?

Hinter diesen Fragen steht der Wunsch nach Sicherheit in der Unsicherheit. Vorhersagbarkeit, Kontrolle, Sinnhaftigkeit, Wertschätzung für das Bisherige – all dies sind Faktoren, die sich stark darauf auswirken, wie schnell Veränderungen akzeptiert werden. Das gilt insbesondere für Veränderungen, die den Bereich betreffen, in dem Mitarbeiter einen Großteil ihrer Lebenszeit verbringen: Die Arbeitsumgebung mitsamt den vertrauten Gewohnheiten gibt man nur ungern auf.

Social Intranets setzen da an, wo heute von den Beschäftigten immer wieder Mängel festgestellt werden, wie Mitarbeiterbefragungen zeigen: Kommunikation, Information, Zusammenarbeit und Führung. Wer mit den modernen Kommunikationsformen vertraut ist, erkennt die Chancen und Vorteile sofort. Einem Großteil der Belegschaft fehlt aber die Vorstellungskraft, was denn da genau eingeführt wird.

Dieser Vielfalt an Vorerfahrungen mit individuell angemessenen Angeboten zu begegnen, stellt Projektteams bei der Einführung von Social Intranets immer wieder vor große Herausforderungen.

Hinzu kommt: Fast jedes Unternehmen hat bereits Erfahrungen mit Veränderungsprozessen gemacht. Nicht selten ist der Begriff Change vorbelastet, weil

- große Programme initiiert wurden, die die Mitarbeiter gefühlt von der Arbeit abgehalten haben;
- alle als Ganzes durchgeschleust wurden ohne dass individuelle Gegebenheiten berücksichtigt worden wären;
- hinter verschlossenen Türen viel Papier produziert wurde, aber die Veränderungen für die Führungskräfte und Mitarbeiter nicht greifbar wurden;
- Change-Projekte top-down stattfanden und bei den Mitarbeitern das Gefühl entstand, ihnen würde etwas übergestülpt;
- die Führungskräfte zwar eine neue Strategie und Kultur predigten, aber selbst nicht vorlebten; und weil
- die Veränderungen in den Augen der Mitarbeiter mehr Schaden als Nutzen gebracht haben.

Auch wenn man große Veränderungen plant, so ist es doch in der Realität ein schleichender Prozess, der im Unternehmen durchaus in sehr verschiedenen Geschwindigkeiten ablaufen kann. Während die eine Abteilung ganz intuitiv die neuen Teamräume für sich erschließt brauchen andere Abteilungen vielleicht zusätzliche Unterstützungsangebote um zu lernen, wie man mit Communities und den modernen Kommunikations-Tools richtig arbeitet.

Veränderung ist etwas sehr Individuelles, schließlich geht es um Menschen, die sehr unterschiedliche Voraussetzungen mitbringen. Modernes Change Management legt nicht bei allen die gleichen Maßstäbe an, sondern schafft individuelle, flexible Angebote. Modernes Change Management plant nicht detailliert Monate im Voraus, sondern begleitet die Veränderungen da, wo sie gerade passieren und wo noch nachgesteuert werden muss. Modernes Change Management ist flexibel, erfolgt in kleinen Schritten und setzt auf Schneeballeffekte. Und deshalb ist es meist erfolgreicher als das klassische Vorgehen.

Modernes Change Management ist durch folgende Prinzipien gekennzeichnet:

1. Klare Ziele und eine attraktive Roadmap – Orientierung geben und Neugier wecken;

2. Anfangen, wo der Nutzen am größten ist – Die größten Schmerzpunkte erfragen und dafür attraktive Lösungen entwickeln;

3. Kleine machbare Schritte – Tun und Wirkung zeigen, anstatt sich im Analysieren zu verlieren;

4. Experimentieren und Lernen – In Pilotanwendungen lernen, bevor der große Rollout kommt;

5. Anfangen, wo es leicht ist – Mit Fans und Treibern Erfolgsstories mit Sog-Garantie produzieren, anstatt sich an den „harten Brocken" aufzureiben;

6. Storytelling und Visualisierung – Die Veränderungen verständlich machen, spielerisch und mit Humor;

7. Signale setzen – Top-Entscheider an die Spitze der Bewegung stellen.

Change Management schafft die Strukturen und Voraussetzungen, damit sich Mitarbeiter in Unternehmen permanent verändern. Damit lebt das Projekt vor, was zukünftig im Enterprise 2.0 gelebte Kultur sein wird.

Axel Springer – die richtige Projektphilosophie für eine erfolgreiche Einführung

Die Implementierung einer Kollaborationsplattform erfordert veränderte Arbeitsweisen der Mitarbeiter und hat kulturelle Einflüsse zur Folge. Auch das Pilotprojekt „CONNECT" zur Einführung von SharePoint 2013 benötigte neben den Anforderungen an die IT eine besondere Berücksichtigung dieser Aspekte. Nach circa 18 Monaten nutzen über 1.000 Anwender bei Axel Springer die neue Plattform. Eine Voraussetzung dafür bildet eine von allen Stakeholdern gelebte Projektphilosophie. Die folgenden fünf Erfolgsfaktoren spiegeln die Erfahrungen und Erkenntnisse dieser Pilotierung wider:

Dieser Abschnitt entstand in Zusammenarbeit mit Kati Sünderhauf, Referentin Change Management , Enterprise 2.0 Axel Springer SE

1. Sinn vor Funktion: Die Sinnfrage hat das Projekt von Beginn an geleitet. Wenn wir die Zusammenarbeit und Kommunikation fördern wollen, müssen wir den Mitarbeiter mit seinen Bedürfnissen in den Mittelpunkt stellen und ein Nutzererlebnis schaffen. Die Technologie und die Funktionen traten vorerst in den Hintergrund. Das Projekt wurde fortan von der Vision einer neuen vernetzten und digitalen Zusammenarbeit getragen – „CONNECT". Ideen und Themen sollen unkompliziert, abteilungsübergreifend miteinander geteilt werden und das Miteinander fördern. Jeder Mitarbeiter kann sich einbringen und sich aus seinem Wissenssilo herauslösen. Diese Vision bestimmte darüber hinaus die Herangehensweise an Einführungs- und Qualifizierungsmaßnahmen. Die Schulungen waren keine reinen IT-Schulungen. In Impulswerkstätten vergegenwärtigten sich die einzelnen Teams ihren derzeitigen Zusammenarbeitsstatus und erarbeiteten gemeinsam Ideen und Verbesserungsansätze. Auf dieser Basis haben sich die Mitarbeiter die Funktionen fallbezogen nahegebracht. Dadurch wurde der Transfer von tradierten Arbeitsprozessen in die neue Arbeitsumgebung erleichtert. Zusätzlich wurde die „CONNECT yourself"-Lernplattform etabliert. Dort bringen Kollegen ihre Anwendungstipps zu SharePoint ein, tauschen sich über aktuelle Fragestellungen aus und lernen von den Erfahrungen anderer Mitarbeiter.

2. Modern muss auch modern sein: Dieser Faktor bezieht sich vor allem auf eine ansprechende Kommunikation des Projekts. Sie bot neben dem Namen der Plattform und dem Logo wiederkehrende Farb- und Bildmotive auf Präsentationen, Handouts, Flyern und Werbemitteln. Dazu zählen auch Plakate in den Schulungsräumen und ein Erklärfilm über die neuen kulturellen Dimensionen. Mit dieser einheitlichen Bildsprache wurde IT auf einmal interessant und unterstützte das neue Arbeiten bei Axel Springer.

3. Der Weg ist bereits das Ziel: Die Pilotierung sollte nicht allein auf die Veränderungen in der Arbeitsweise vorbereiten, sondern selbst die Veränderung vorleben. Das Projektteam plante und setzte die gesamte Einführung in SharePoint 2013 um, und zwar transparent. Alle Dokumente und Informationen zum Projektfortschritt waren für alle Mitarbeiter einsehbar. Das bezog sich auch auf das „Wie" in der Einführung. Anmeldungen für Schulungen, Videos und Zusatzinformationen gab es ausschließlich auf der Plattform. Wer Hilfe brauchte, sich einbringen oder Kritik loswerden wollte, fand bei den direkten Ansprechpartnern Gehör, aber auch bei Kollegen in der Online-Community. Im Prinzip funktionierte die SharePoint-Einführung nach dem Work-in-progress-Modell. Prototypen wurden entworfen, in der Praxis direkt von den Pilotteilnehmern erprobt und weiterentwickelt. Dadurch haben die Mitarbeiter ihre zukünftige Arbeitsumgebung mitgestaltet. Damit entsteht der Wandel im Tun und wird sofort wirksam durch den viralen Effekt, mit dem die Nutzerzahl schnell stieg.

4. Die Energie des Spiels nutzen: Als gut und wirksam hat sich die Idee gezeigt, versierten Mitarbeitern eine besondere Rolle in den Einführungsteams zu geben. Diese wichtigen Akteure und Treiber für den Wandel auf Teamebene heißen bei Axel Springer Multiplikatoren. Zur Steigerung der Motivation und der Freude an der Rolle wurde ein Gamification-Ansatz gewählt. Spielen verbindet und weckt den Wettbewerbsgeist. Ein Beispiel ist das „Best Practice Battle". Hierbei konnten verschiedene Level mit unterschiedlichen „Preisen" erreicht werden. Multiplikatoren teilten ihre Anwendungsbeispiele bei regelmäßigen Stammtischen oder zeigten, wie sie ihr Team motiviert haben, Arbeitsprozesse umzustellen und dabei agiler zu werden.

5. „Offline" die Online-Idee erlebbar machen: Da SharePoint nicht einfach ein weiteres IT-Tool darstellt, sondern die Art der vernetzten Zusammenarbeit fördern sollte, musste das neue Miteinander über die Grenzen der Bereiche und Beteiligungen hinweg spürbar und erlebbar werden. Mit der Initiative „move" wurden unterschiedliche kreative Lernformate ins Leben gerufen, die die kulturellen Dimensionen wie Transparenz, das Teilen von Wissen und den Freiraum der neuen Arbeitswelt widerspiegeln. Die unkomplizierte und offene Atmosphäre während der Veranstaltungen half dabei.

INTRANET-EINFÜHRUNG
MIT METHODE

SOCIAL INTRANET ERFORDERT EINE NEUE HERANGEHENSWEISE

Um das Jahr 2011 war die Unzufriedenheit mit den klassischen Intranets und ihren Nutzerstatistiken relativ groß. Die Mitarbeiter surften, posteten und twitterten bereits im Web 2.0. Doch viele Unternehmen arbeiteten inmitten neuer Herausforderungen der Märkte noch mit traditionellen Kommunikationsformen wie E-Mail, Fax und Meeting.

Nach der Studie "Social Intranet 2012" (Dörfel & Hirsch, 2012) hatten 42% aller Intranets ein Akzeptanzproblem. Die Ursachen dafür waren vielfältig und reichten von der Fokussierung auf die reine IT über Mini-Budgets für Change und Kommunikation bis hin zu fehlender Usability der Intranets.

Ende 2012/Anfang 2013 brachten dann verschiedene Hersteller neue Versionen von Social Software auf den Markt. Diese Neuerungen präsentierten sich mit einem völlig neuen Umfang an Social Features und boten Unternehmen und Organisationen die Chance, ihre Arbeitsweisen und die interne Kommunikation grundlegend zu verändern. Allerdings machten sie auch ein verändertes Vorgehen bei der Einführung der modernen Plattformen für Kommunikation und Zusammenarbeit notwendig. Dies war die Geburtsstunde der perlrot-Einführungsmethode für Social Intranets, die auch die Grundlage für die Gliederung dieses Buches ist (vgl. Abbildung 9). Entwickelt von Steffi Gröscho, weist die Methode den Weg, wie man moderne Plattformen für Kommunikation und Zusammenarbeit erfolgreich zum Leben erweckt.

1	2	3	4	5	6
TRÄUME	ANALYSIERE	PLANE	BAUE	ERPROBE	NUTZE

Abbildung 9: Die 6 Phasen der perlrot-Methode gliedern das Buch

Die Philosophie, die hinter der Methode steckt, spiegelt sich ebenfalls im Buch wider: Sie stellt die Nutzer in den Mittelpunkt und schafft somit wichtige Voraussetzungen für die notwendige Akzeptanz. In den Projektprozess werden alle Beteiligten einbezogen: Mitarbeiter, Führungskräfte, die Fachabteilungen und Standorte, der Betriebs- und Personalrat. Die Nutzer mit ihren Anforderungen, Bedürfnissen, Ideen und Wünschen werden im Prozess und beim Bau der Lösung in ganz besonderer Weise erfasst und berücksichtigt. Change Management und Kommunikation stellen die Weichen für das Verankern der neuen Formen der Kommunikation und Zusammenarbeit im Arbeitsalltag. Natürliche Widerstände und Ängste der Nutzer werden ernst genommen.

Zu dieser Philosophie gehört auch die Überzeugung, dass die Einführung moderner Intranet-Lösungen nicht nur als technisches Projekt verstanden werden darf. Wer glaubt, dass allein mit klassischen IT-Anwenderschulungen das Wesentliche erfüllt wäre, liegt falsch. Es geht vielmehr um die Einführung neuer Arbeitsabläufe und Arbeitsweisen in der Kommunikation und Zusammenarbeit, verbunden mit allen bekannten Herausforderungen, wenn Menschen aus ihren Gewohnheiten gerissen werden und neue Routinen aufbauen müssen. Dahinter verbergen sich enorme Umstellungen. Doch damit nicht genug: Die Einführung eines Social Intranets ist auch mit gänzlich neuen organisatorischen und kulturellen Fragestellungen verbunden. Dabei geht es um virtuelle Mitarbeiterführung, Vertrauen vs. Kontrolle im Intranet, Vereinbarkeit von Beruf und Familie durch Home-Office-Angebote oder auch den Schutz der Mitarbeiter vor Informationsüberflutung und Selbstausbeutung, um nur einige Aspekte zu nennen. Genau genommen handelt es sich daher bei einem Projekt zur Einführung moderner Arbeitswelten um ein Organisationsentwicklungs-Projekt (die Gewichtung ist in Abbildung 10 veranschaulicht).

Leider begegnet man in der Praxis immer wieder der Tendenz: Sobald eine IT-Lösung eingeführt werden soll, wird das Vorhaben auf ein IT-Projekt reduziert. Allerdings ist in letzter Zeit ein gewisser Wandel zu beobachten: Aufgrund schlechter Vorerfahrungen nimmt bei Entscheidern merklich das Bewusstsein zu, dass die Einführung moderner IT-Umgebungen kein Selbstläufer ist und dass es einer sorgfältigen Einführung bedarf, damit die Investition sich auszahlt.

Die Einführung von sozialen Plattformen für Kommunikation und Zusammenarbeit erfordert eine ganzheitliche Sicht. Dabei geht es um das Zusammenspiel von Projektmanagement, Konzeption, IT, Change Management und Kommunikation. Daher haben sich für dieses Buch auch drei Expertinnen mit unterschiedlichen Schwerpunkten zusammengefunden.

Abbildung 10: „Social" werden ist mehr als ein IT-Projekt

WIE PACKT MAN ES AN?

Das vorliegende Buch befasst sich mit der Frage, wie man ein Social Intranet Schritt für Schritt erfolgreich in einem Unternehmen implementiert und etabliert. Es geht dabei weder um eine technische Einführung noch um eine weitere Theorie zu Enterprise 2.0. Das Buch will mit Ausführungen zum konzeptionellen Vorgehen den Gesamtprozess verständlich machen. Die Vermittlung eines moderaten technischen Hintergrundwissens für Projektverantwortliche ohne IT-Erfahrung kommt hinzu. Die Leser erhalten hilfreiche Grundkenntnisse, um bereits bei der Auswahl der Dienstleister gut vorbereitet zu sein und mit Schwung in ihr neues Projekt zu starten. Impulse und Tipps aus der Praxis spielen dabei eine zentrale Rolle.

AUS DER PRAXIS FÜR DIE PRAXIS

Enterprise 2.0 ist ein junges Thema und es gibt bisher keine Langzeitstudien oder ausreichend dokumentierten Erfahrungen zum Umgang mit den modernen Arbeitsweisen in Unternehmen. In Konzernen sind Social Intranets schon angekommen. Nun ermöglichen bezahlbare Cloud-Lösungen den Einzug von Social Software auch in kleinen und mittelständischen Unternehmen (KMU). Gerade diesen kleineren Unternehmen fehlen jedoch häufig die Vorbilder, von denen man lernen kann, wie man eine moderne Plattform für Kommunikation und Zusammenarbeit so einführt, dass sie auch wirklich den Nutzen bringt, den man sich davon erhofft.

Daran wollten wir drei Autorinnen etwas ändern. Das Ergebnis halten Sie in den Händen: ein Buch über praxisbewährtes und pragmatisches Vorgehen, das allen Intranet-Verantwortlichen bei der Einführung eines Social Intranets den Weg weist – aus der Praxis für die Praxis. Es soll dabei helfen, häufige Fehler zu vermeiden, die zu unzureichenden Budgetplanungen oder mangelnder Akzeptanz führen. Beispielhaft genannt seien der fehlende Bezug zur Unternehmensstrategie oder die häufig unterschätzte Komplexität eines solchen Vorhabens.

Wir danken unseren Kunden, dass wir aus unserem Arbeitsalltag berichten dürfen. 32 Beraterkollegen sowie Intranet-Verantwortliche aus Unternehmen haben ihr Praxiswissen mit uns zusammengetragen und geben in 55 Praxisboxen Einblicke in ihre Projekte. Sie leben so auch die neue Kultur des Teilens vor. Daher gilt ein großer Dank an dieser Stelle unseren Gastautoren.

Viele der Praxisbeispiele stammen von Social Intranets auf der Basis von Microsoft-Technologien. Das liegt zum einen an ihrer Marktverbreitung, zum anderen an den Projekterfahrungen der Autoren. Grundsätzlich ist das hier dargestellte Vorgehen aber technologieunabhängig.

ARBEITSPAKETE

Für jede der sechs Phasen schnüren wir im Buch Arbeitspakete, die für das Gelingen einer Intranet-Einführung wesentlich sind. Ihre Reihenfolge soll eine Orientierung geben, wie man den gesamten Projektverlauf strukturieren kann. Auf diese Weise sollen lange Anlaufphasen nach dem Prinzip „Learning by doing" vermieden werden. Stattdessen soll das Projekt schnell und zielgerichtet Fahrt aufnehmen

Das Buch ist jedoch kein fertiger Projektplan. Es versteht sich eher als Handlungsempfehlung, die bestimmte Arbeitsschritte vertieft. Die genaue Reihenfolge der Arbeitspakete in den einzelnen Phasen, aber auch die Intensität und Dauer ihrer Umsetzung sind nicht starr festgelegt. Sie können flexibel angepasst werden, so wie es die Anforderungen verlangen. Ein Beispiel: In der Regel werden Führungskräfte gleich zu Beginn, in Phase 1, mit an Bord geholt. In manchen Unternehmen kann es jedoch die bessere Strategie sein, zunächst in einem Pilotprojekt die ersten vorzeigbaren Erfolge zu

Steffi Gröscho, Geschäftsführerin perlrot, Schwerpunkte im Buch: Einführungsmethode, Kommunikation und Nutzereinbindung

Dr. Claudia Eichler-Liebenow, Social Business Consultant, T-Systems Multimedia Solutions GmbH, Schwerpunkte im Buch: Planung, Fachkonzeption und Technik

Regina Köhler, Geschäftsführerin AviloX GmbH, Schwerpunkte im Buch: Führungskräfte, Organisationsentwicklung und Change Management

Phasen:

Hauptprojekt	1. Träume	2. Analysiere	3. Plane	4. Baue	5. Erprobe	6. Nutze
Pilotgruppe HR		2	3	4	5	6
Pilotgruppe Vertrieb				4	5	6
Pilotgruppe Managementkreis					4	5	6

Abbildung 11: Pilotteams durchlaufen zeitversetzt die Phasen des Einführungsprozesses

erarbeiten, bevor die Führungskräfte eingebunden werden.

Bestimmte Anwendungsfälle mit Pilotgruppen zu erproben, bevor sie im gesamten Unternehmen ausgerollt werden, ist unbedingt empfehlenswert. Diese Pilotgruppen durchlaufen alle Phasen des Einführungsprozesses, nur zeitversetzt, verkürzt und schneller (siehe Abbildung 11). Die daraus gewonnenen Erkenntnisse im Umgang mit den zukünftigen Nutzern können dann dazu herangezogen werden, um die letzten drei Phasen im Hauptprojekt gut zu gestalten. So können beispielsweise Trainingskonzepte am Pilotteam überprüft oder erste Bausteine für den späteren Einführungs-Support entwickeltwerden.

Willkommen liebe Leserin, lieber Leser! Ich bin Babett, die virtuelle vierte Autorin dieses Buches. Ich bin eigentlich in den digitalen Welten zu Hause. Aber bei diesem Buch aus der Praxis für die Praxis lasse ich es mir nicht nehmen, Sie ausnahmsweise auch ganz direkt anzusprechen. Sie wollen also ein Social-Intranet-Projekt starten? Gratulation! Sie suchen nun nach einem Weg, der ans Ziel führt, ohne zu steil und zu steinig zu sein? Voilà – unser Buch ist ein Handlungsleitfaden dazu. Ich bin gern Ihre Wegbegleiterin.

Willkommen in der neuen Arbeitswelt! Los geht's.

TRÄUME

Wie jedes Vorhaben beginnt auch ein Social-Intranet-Projekt mit einer Vision: Welche neue Qualität wird unser Unternehmen haben, wenn unsere neue Plattform für moderne Kommunikation und Zusammenarbeit fest verankert ist? Was wird sich in der Zusammenarbeit und Kommunikation ändern und wo stehen wir durch Social Intranet in drei Jahren? Die neuesten technologischen Entwicklungen und Praxisbeispiele aus anderen Unternehmen dienen als Inspiration, um den Wert von Social Intranets zu verstehen und den angestrebten geschäftlichen Nutzen und die Ziele konkret zu formulieren.

Danach erfolgt Basisarbeit: Die Projektorganisation wird aufgestellt, Verantwortlichkeiten werden festgelegt, wichtige Befürworter aus allen Teilen des Unternehmens gewonnen und die entscheidenden Barrieren identifiziert, die den Projekterfolg gefährden könnten.

Ein sorgfältig aufgesetztes Projekt ist der beste Schutz gegen Probleme im weiteren Projektverlauf. Diese Phase benötigt daher ausreichend Aufmerksamkeit und Weitblick. Wenn das Projekt gut aufgesetzt ist, ist die erste Phase erfolgreich abgeschlossen.

INSPIRATIONEN – NEUE 1.1 MÖGLICHKEITEN FÜR KOMMUNIKATION UND ZUSAMMENARBEIT

Am Anfang eines Social-Intranet-Projekts findet man im Unternehmen immer ausgesprochen vielfältige Vorstellungen und Meinungen zu Web 2.0 vor. Wikis, Blogs, Liken und Posten – fast jeder ist schon mit ausgewählten Funktionen des Social Web in Berührung gekommen. Diese Erfahrungen stammen jedoch zum überwiegenden Teil aus dem privaten Umfeld – durch eigene Aktivitäten oder durch Schilderungen von Verwandten und Freunden.

Eine hohe Affinität und Vertrautheit im Umgang mit sozialen Tools wird häufig den sogenannten Digital Natives zugeschrieben (oder auch Generation Y und Millenials). Doch auch bei älteren Generationen von Führungskräften und Mitarbeitern findet man durchaus Offenheit und Neugier vor, die aber oft von Unklarheit begleitet werden, was diese modernen Kommunikationsformen denn konkret einem Unternehmen bringen. Auch ablehnende Vorstellungen gibt es natürlich. So begegnet man zum Beispiel häufig der Annahme, Social Features würden dazu führen, dass Mitarbeiter nur noch chatten und nicht mehr produktiv arbeiten.

Aktive Aufklärungsarbeit ist von Anfang an eine ganz wichtige Aufgabe bei der Social-Intranet-Einführung. Am besten gelingt das, indem man den Mitarbeitern und Führungskräften auf lockere und ungezwungene Weise einen Gesamtüberblick dazu verschafft, was hinter Social Intranet steckt. Praxisbeispiele aus anderen Unternehmen können helfen, den Nutzen für das eigene Unternehmen zu erkennen und Inspiration für Anwendungsszenarien zu geben. Dadurch schafft man eine ganz wesentliche Grundlage, um sachlich über die Einsatzfelder im eigenen Unternehmen zu sprechen und nicht gleich Gefahr zu laufen, aus mangelndem Verständnis heraus auf breite Ablehnung oder Desinteresse zu stoßen.

Mit solchen gezielten Vorstößen und Diskussionsansätzen zu möglichen Anwendungsszenarien im eigenen Unternehmen ist es der pfm medical ag gelungen, auf einen Schlag alle Führungskräfte dafür zu begeistern, sich mit vernetzten Arbeitswelten auseinanderzusetzen.

Dieser Abschnitt entstand in Zusammenarbeit mit Regina Wünsch, Director HR & Legal Affairs

Inspirierender Einstieg ins Thema „Enterprise 2.0" beim Führungskräftetreffen der pfm medical ag

Aufgrund des stetigen Wachstums haben sich die Führungskräfte der pfm medical ag in den letzten Jahren immer wieder die Frage gestellt, wie das Unternehmen agiler werden kann. Wie sich die Organisation angesichts der zunehmenden Komplexität besser managen lässt und wie man die Zusammenarbeit mit internationalen Standorten effektiver gestalten, Innovationen treiben und Prozessabläufe verbessern kann. Für sie war klar, man muss das Wissen der Organisation sichtbarer machen und besser nutzen.

„Einige Personen hatten sich bereits im kleinen Kreis mit dem Thema Enterprise 2.0 im Unternehmen beschäftigt. Schließlich habe ich dann in Abstimmung mit dem Vorstand den Anstoß gegeben, das Thema herauszugreifen und an prominenter Stelle zu diskutieren", berichtet Regina Wünsch, HR-Direktorin der pfm medical ag.

„Wir haben einmal im Jahr ein Führungskräftetreffen, bei dem etwa 50 Verantwortliche zwei Tage lang über aktuelle Themen sprechen. Mein Vorschlag war, in diesem Jahr das Thema „Change Management und neues Arbeiten" zu diskutieren und gemeinsam ein Konzept für pfm medical zu entwickeln. So rückte das Thema Enterprise 2.0 bei uns zum ersten Mal ins Rampenlicht.

Da ich selbst auch noch zu wenig über Enterprise 2.0 wusste, hatte ich mir externe Unterstützung von einem Experten geholt, der viel aus seinen Erfahrungen berichten konnte. Wir haben gemeinsam für den nötigen Appetit gesorgt, sodass darüber nachgedacht wurde, was möglich ist und was andere Unternehmen machen. Mit den Führungskräften haben wir dann den potenziellen Nutzen für unser Geschäft herausgearbeitet, aber auch Lücken benannt, auf die wir achten müssen. Wir haben offene Diskussionen in der sogenannten „Fishbowl" geführt zu Fragen wie: Was bewegt uns? Wo sehen wir Chancen und Risiken? Was geht uns durch den Kopf? Es war eine Mischung aus Input und konstruktiver Arbeit, die sehr gut ankam.

Dabei war eine Botschaft immer klar: Das Projekt muss zur Kultur passen. Wir können uns keine fertigen Konzepte überstülpen, sondern wir müssen das Thema gemeinsam neu gestalten. Die Ansatzpunkte dafür ergaben sich aus dem ganz konkreten Nutzen für den Einzelnen im Arbeitsablauf und in der Verbesserung der internen Unternehmenskommunikation. Das hat die Führungskräfte davon überzeugt, dass wir den Wandel zur vernetzten Arbeitswelt brauchen."

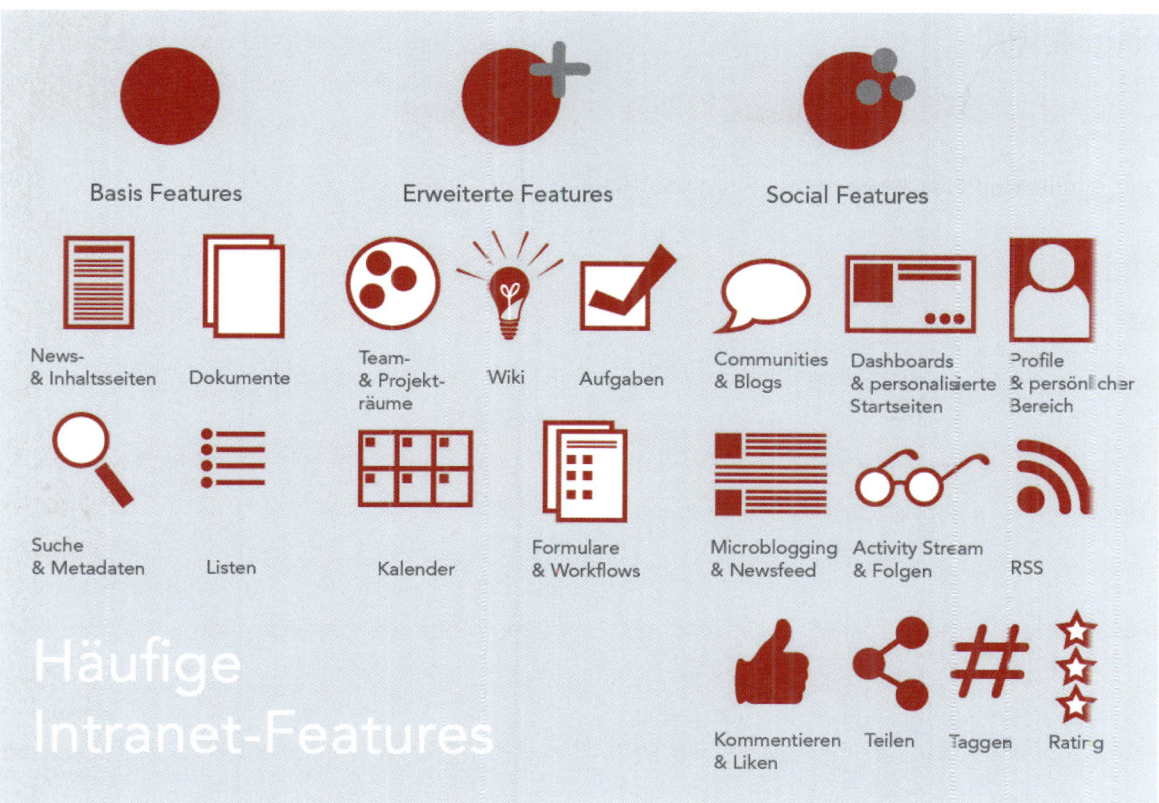

Abbildung 1.1.1: Häufige Elemente im Intranet

Im folgenden Abschnitt möchten wir Ihnen die gängigen Funktionalitäten von modernen Intranets kurz vorstellen. Dabei geht es in der Frühphase des Intranet-Projekts nicht um technische Details, sondern darum, neue Möglichkeiten und ihren Nutzen zu erkennen.

Mit der Gliederung zur Kurzbeschreibung einzelner Intranet-Funktionen in Abbildung 1.1.1 orientieren wir uns an der Historie der Intranet-Entwicklung. Viele der Basis-Features und Erweiterungen sind in bestehenden Intranets bereits abgebildet. Das soll aber nicht heißen, dass jedes Intranet über diese Elemente verfügen muss.

Basis-Intranet-Features

NEWS- & INHALTSSEITEN

Das Intranet dient vor allem dazu, intern zu informieren. Aktuelle und wichtige Nachrichten werden meist mit Überschrift und Teaser auf der Startseite angezeigt – wie bei der VHV Gruppe. Per Link gelangen die Mitarbeiter auf Nachrichten- oder Inhaltsseiten mit den kompletten Informationen. So erreichen die Unternehmens-News alle Kollegen.

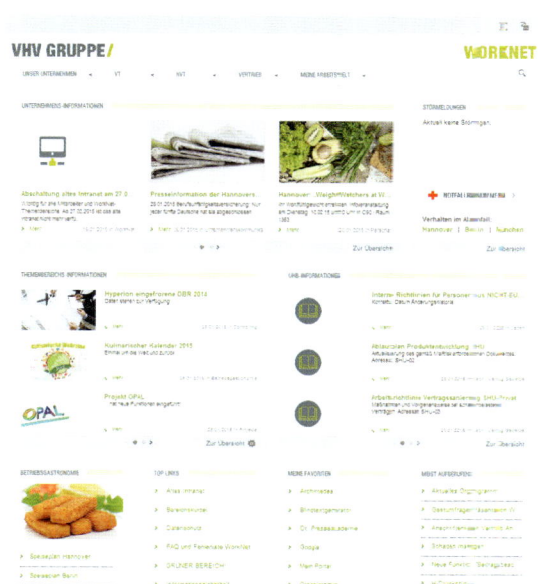

Abbildung 1.1.2: Drei Informations-Formate mit aktuellen Nachrichten – strukturiert erreichbar über die Startseite des WorkNet der VHV Gruppe (SharePoint)

DOKUMENTE

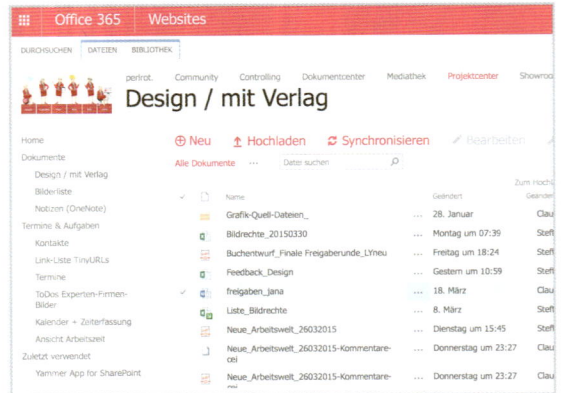

Abbildung 1.1.3: Das Dokumentencenter der Agentur perlrot (Office 365)

In modernen Intranet-Lösungen wie hier mit Office 365 bei der Agentur perlrot lassen sich Dokumente ablegen, sodass sie transparent und immer in der aktuellen Version für alle Berechtigten bereitgestellt werden. Die Mitarbeiter der Agentur können gleichzeitig gemeinsam ein Dokument bearbeiten oder bei Bedarf auf ältere Versionen zurückgreifen. Komfortabel sind Sortiermöglichkeiten und eine Dokumen-

tenvorschau. Mit Hilfe von Metadaten lassen sich Dokumente schneller auffinden. Hervorzuheben ist auch, dass Berechtigungen einfach zu vergeben und zu managen sind. Das heißt, man kann für jedes Dokument festlegen, welche User Zugriff darauf erhalten sollen und ob die Nutzer eine Lese- oder Schreibberechtigung erhalten.

LISTEN

Da das Arbeiten mit strukturierten Daten in nahezu allen Arbeitsbereichen zum Tagesgeschäft gehört, sind eine gute Darstellung und auch die leichte Bereitstellung von strukturierten Listen im Intranet gleichermaßen wünschenswert. Datenbankanwendungen für wenig komplexe Datenstrukturen oder Excel-Listen können je nach Technologie durch Listen innerhalb der Intranet-Anwendung abgelöst werden. Der Power User kann somit schnell entsprechende Listen anlegen, um gemeinsam mit anderen Mitarbeitern Daten strukturiert zu erfassen. Oft ist dann ein gleichzeitiges Arbeiten an einer Liste möglich.

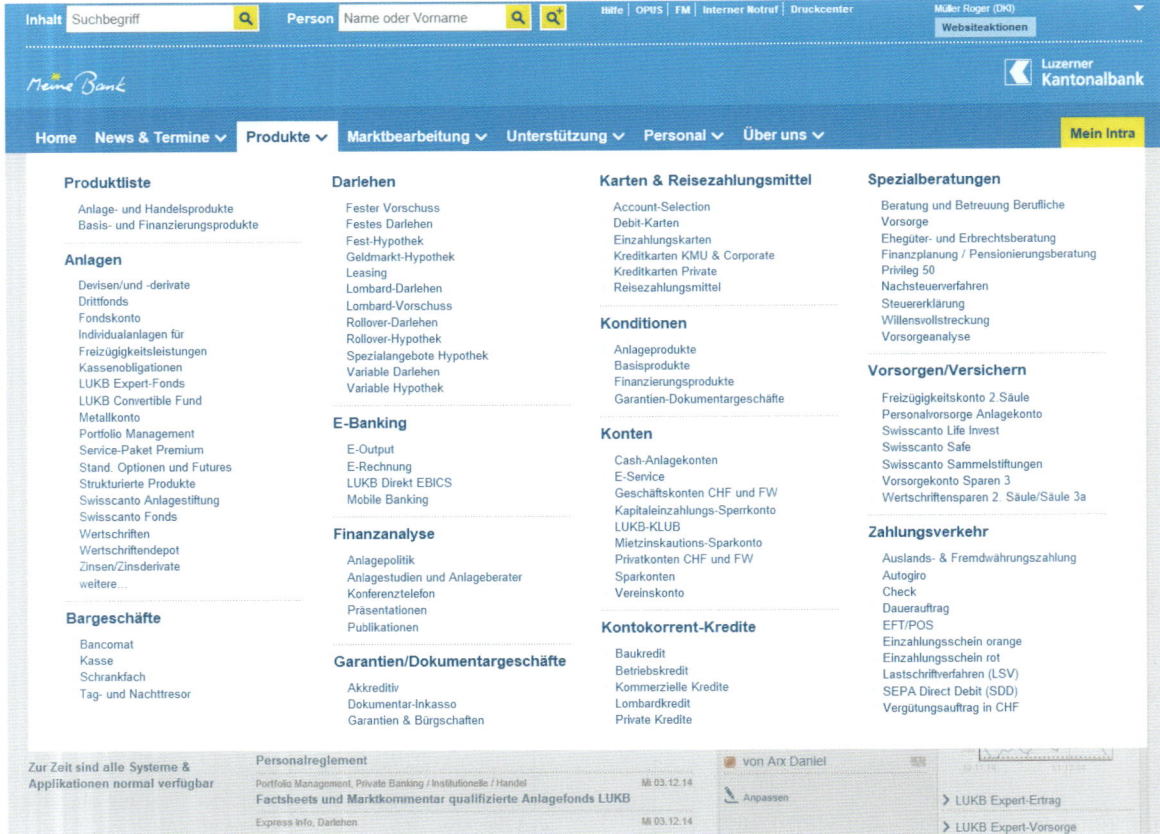

Abbildung 1.1.4: Produktübersicht für die Mitarbeiter der Luzerner Kantonalbank

Einfach und extrem hilfreich sind themenorientierte Links auf unterschiedlichen Intranet-Seiten wie bei der Luzerner Kantonalbank. Verlinkungen helfen dem Nutzer, weiterführende Informationen zu finden, Experten ausfindig zu machen sowie Zusammenhänge zu anderen Themengebieten zu erkennen. Dadurch wird das Gesamtverständnis gefördert.

SUCHE & METADATEN

Die Suche ermöglicht das schnelle und zielgenaue Auffinden von Informationen, Dokumenten oder Autoren. Indem man nach Ergebnistyp, Website, Autor, Datum und/oder Stichwort filtert, wird das Ergebnis weiter verfeinert. Es gibt nichts, was im Intranet nicht gefunden werden könnte. Wie schnell gefunden und wie gezielt gesucht wird, hängt stark von den Metadaten der jeweiligen Information ab. Metadaten werden durch Nutzer oder mit Hilfe des technischen Systems vergeben. Verfügt das Social Intranet über eine Enterprise Search wie bei der Agentur perlrot, so kann eine Enterprise Search alle indizierten internen Informationsquellen (z.B. Laufwerke, Datenbanken, Altsysteme, Mail-Ordner) umfassen. Sie liefert u.a. qualifizierte Ergebnisse bei der Expertensuche. Eine Dokumentenvorschau erleichtert das schnelle Auffinden des richtigen Dokuments zusätzlich. Für eine treffsichere Enterprise Search bedarf es einer guten Konzeption und Konfiguration.

Erweiterungen

TEAM- UND PROJEKTRÄUME

Projekt- und Teamräume gehören zu den beliebtesten Funktionen im modernen Intranet. Sie erleichtern die effiziente Zusammenarbeit über Abteilungsgrenzen hinweg. Alle Informationen rund um ein Projekt, Team oder Thema werden hier ausgetauscht. In den Community- und Projekträumen des Telekom Social Networks werden beispielsweise unabhängig von

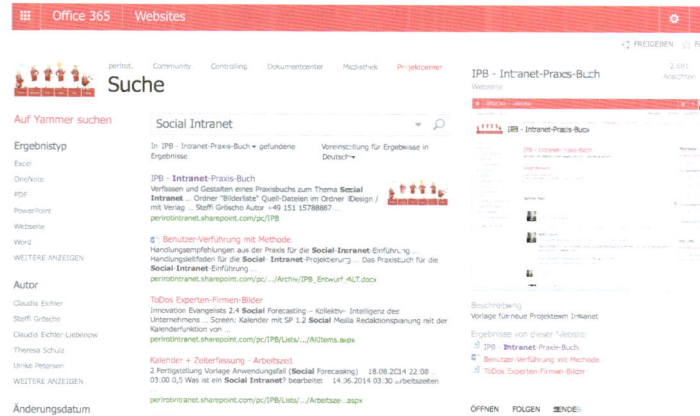

Abbildung 1.1.5: Die Enterprise Search der Agentur perlrot (Office 365)

der Organisationsstruktur diejenigen Nutzer vereint, die gemeinsam ein Projekt erfolgreich durchführen wollen. Im Raum können Dokumente gespeichert, Wikis aufgebaut sowie Aufgaben, Termine und Kontaktinformationen für alle nachvollziehbar abgelegt werden. Intranet-Räume können eigene Berechtigungen für den Zugriff haben. Im Sinne des teamübergreifenden Wissensaustausches sollten dann jedoch Statusübergänge identifiziert werden, zu denen die für eine größere Zielgruppe potenziell interessanten Informationen freigeschaltet werden.

AUFGABEN

Die Autoren und Beteiligten des vorliegenden Buches managten ihr Buchprojekt mit Office 365. Aufgaben und Fälligkeitstermine können auf diese Weise zentral gesammelt, Personen als Bearbeiter zugewiesen und der Fortschritt der einzelnen Aufgaben verfolgt und dokumentiert werden. So hat jeder einen guten Überblick über den aktuellen Arbeitsstand des Teams. Die Daten können je nach gewählter Technologie in einer Zeitleiste visualisiert und mit anderen Projektmanagement-Tools (z.B. mit Microsoft Project) und persönlicher Kalendern synchronisiert werden. Es gibt auch Technologien, mit deren Hilfe man sich die eigenen zugewiesenen Aufgaben in einem persönlichen Bereich gesammelt anzeigen lassen kann.

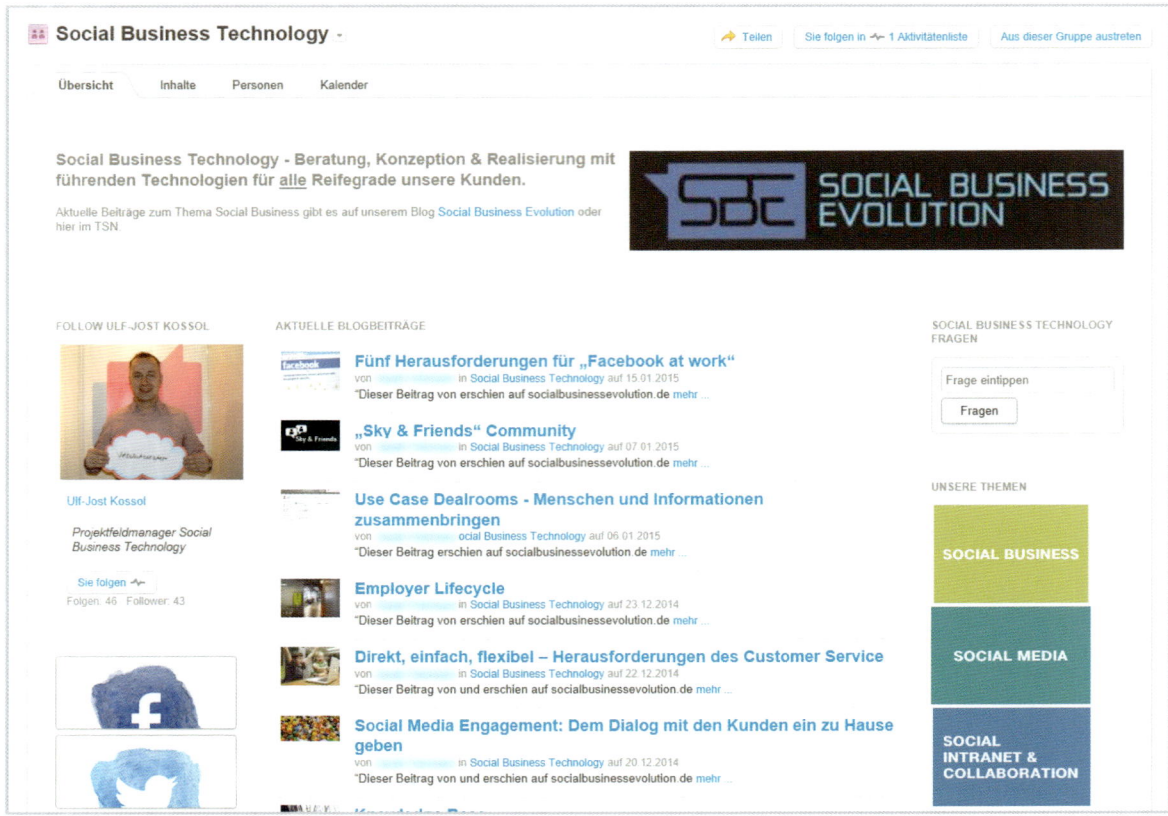

Abbildung 1.1.6: Teamraum im Telekom Social Network (Jive)

KALENDER

Eine einfachere Terminkoordination ist ein besonders häufig genanntes Bedürfnis von Mitarbeitern. Übersichten über Termine zu Veranstaltungen, einem Projekt oder Thema können manuell gepflegt oder aus den persönlichen Kalendern der Beteiligten gespeist werden. Gruppen-Kalender sind häufig mit dem E-Mail-System des Unternehmens verknüpft, sodass unkompliziert Einladungen und Änderungen zu Terminen an die richtigen Personen verschickt werden können. Bei der T-Systems Multimedia Solutions GmbH wurde durch Nutzung der Kalenderfunktion von SharePoint

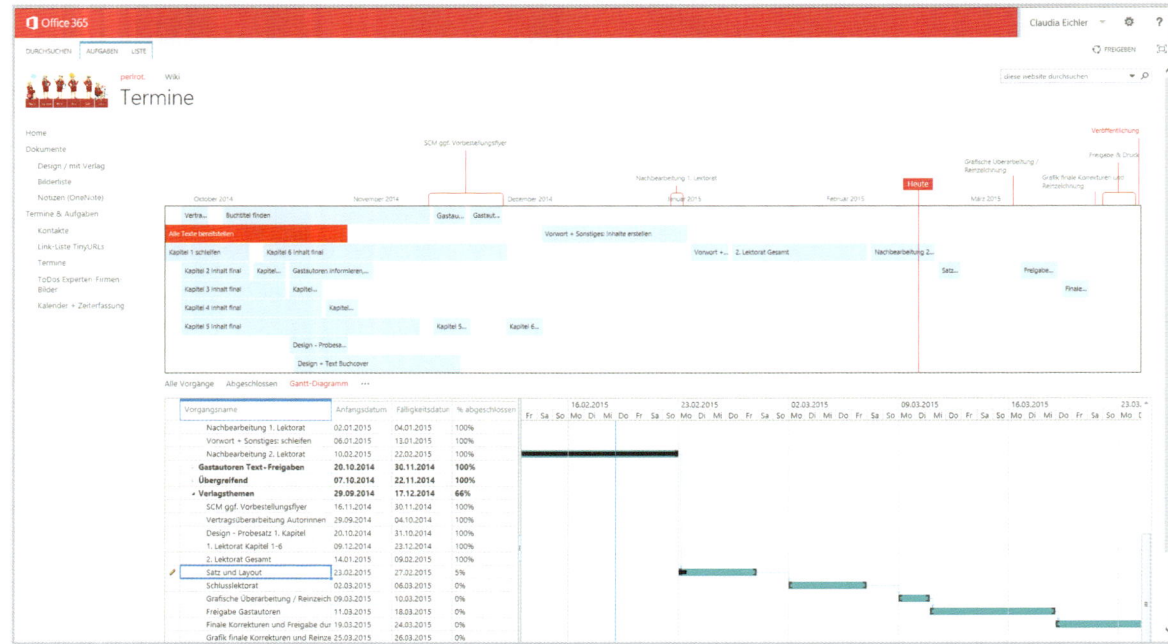

Abbildung 1.1.7: Aufgabenverwaltung bei der Bucherstellung (Office 365)

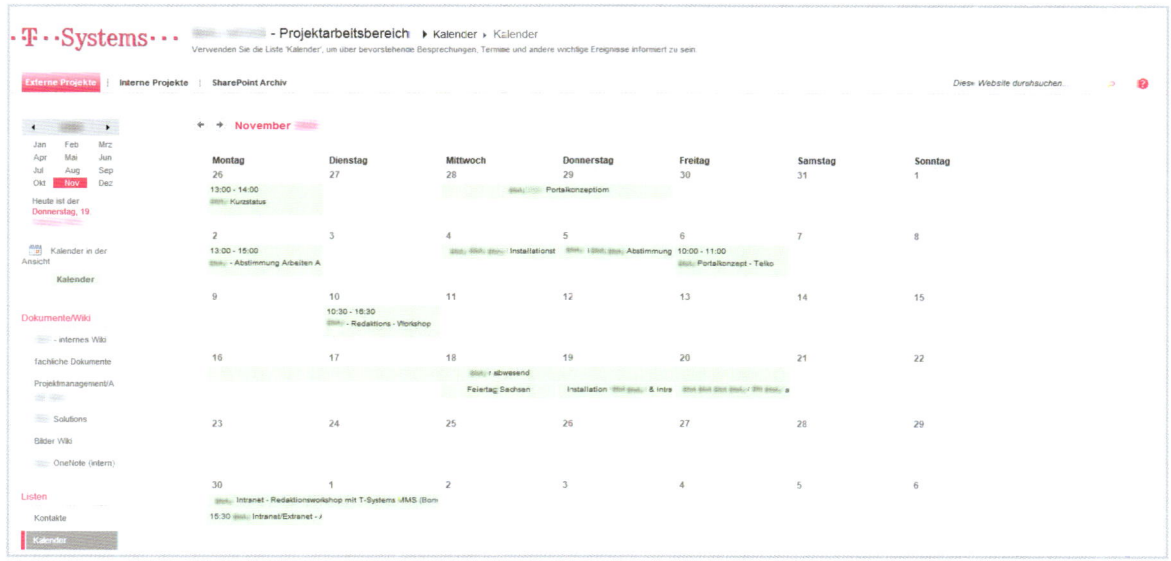

Abbildung 1.1.8: Kalendernutzung innerhalb eines Projektraums der T-Systems Multimedia Solutions GmbH (SharePoint)

für alle Projektbeteiligten die Transparenz zu Projektterminen und Abwesenheiten geschaffen. Kalenderdarstellungen für übergreifende Termine im Intranet werden auch oft gewünscht. Je nach Technologie wird dies unterschiedlich unterstützt.

WIKI

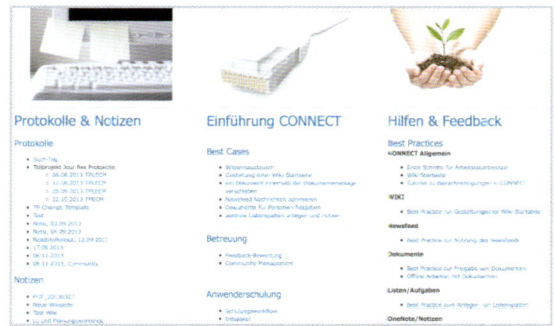

Abbildung 1.1.9: Wiki-Startseite bei Axel Springer (SharePoint)

Der IT-Abteilung von Axel Springer war es ganz wichtig, dass das Wissen, welches in der Pilotphase zur Einführung der Kollaborationsplattform „Connect" entstand, für alle sichtbar in einem Wiki erfasst und weiterentwickelt wurde.

Wenn ein Benutzer eine Seite erstellt hat, kann ein anderes Teammitglied Inhalte oder unterstützende Links hinzufügen.

FORMULARE & WORKFLOWS

Formulare erfassen Informationen zur strukturierten Weiterverarbeitung. Sie unterstützen Arbeitsabläufe und Unternehmensprozesse. In das Intranet eingebettete, webbasierte Formulare sind insbesondere aus Nutzersicht attraktiv, da keine andere Anwendung geöffnet werden muss und z.B. umständliche papiergebundene Prozesse abgelöst werden. Einige Technologien unterstützen dies direkt, in andere kann man ggf. spezielle Formularsoftware integrieren.

Die Verarbeitung von erfassten Formulardaten oder Aktionen nach Statusänderungen von Dokumenten kann über IT-gestützte Workflows gesteuert werden. Unterstützt die Intranet-Anwendung die Einbettung von Workflows, so sind dies meist Freigabeworkflows für bereitgestellte Inhalte oder auch die Umsetzung einzelner Unternehmensprozesse direkt im Intranet.

Social Features

Heute können Mitarbeiter in Organisationen immer miteinander in Kontakt treten, wenn sie es möchten – egal, wo sie sich befinden. Soziale Kommunikations- und Zusammenarbeitsplattformen vernetzen Menschen und ermöglichen den Austausch über berufliche und private Dinge. Das Unternehmen wird „social". Erfolgreiche Kommunikationstechnologien aus der Welt des Web 2.0. werden unternehmensintern genutzt.

BLOGS

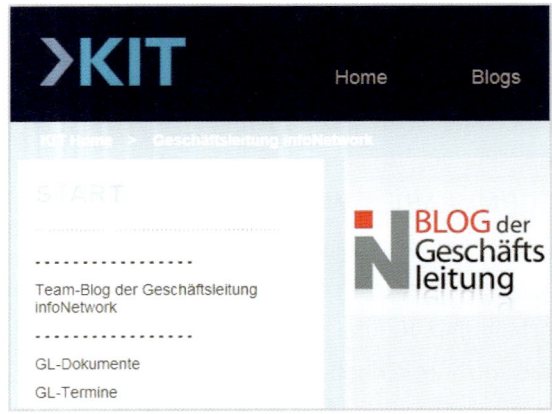

Abbildung 1.1.10: Blog der Geschäftsleitung von infoNetwork

Der Blog der Geschäftsleitung von infoNetwork informiert Mitarbeiter regelmäßig über Neuigkeiten. Blogs sind ein gutes Mittel, Wissen an andere weiterzugeben oder zur Meinungsbildung beizutragen. Außerdem regen sie Nutzer dazu an, Beiträge zu kommentieren, aktiv Ideen beizusteuern oder Fragen zu stellen.

COMMUNITIES

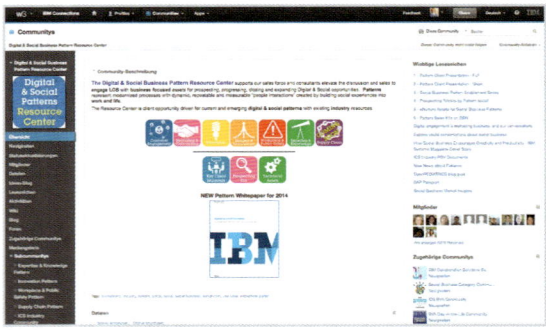

Abbildung 1.1.11: Community-Startseite eines IBM-Connections-Portals

Communities geben Raum zur Diskussion und Kommunikation. Jeder kann ausgewählten Themen folgen, mitdiskutieren, Beiträge bewerten oder auch eine eigene Community gründen. Egal, ob es um das Qualitätsmanagement geht oder um die Organisation der Laufgruppe – jeder findet sein Forum. Auch eine abteilungsübergreifende Zusammenarbeit wird ermöglicht: Mitarbeiter diskutieren z.B. Fragen rund um ein Produkt oder einen Prozess.

PERSONALISIERTE STARTSEITEN & DASHBOARDS

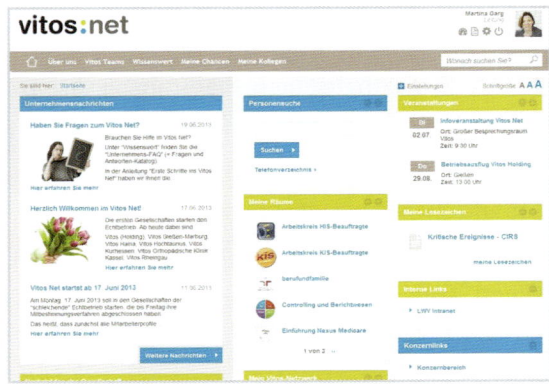

Abbildung 1.1.12: Die personalisierte Startseite von vitos (Drupal)

Die personalisierten Einstiegsseiten & Dashboards in das moderne Intranet ermöglichen den Mitarbeitern, selbst zu konfigurieren, welche Informationen sie täglich beim Öffnen des Intranets als erste benötigen bzw. zu welchen abonnierten Themen sie auf dem Laufenden gehalten werden möchten. Die Mitarbeiter von vitos sehen anhand der unterschiedlichen Überschriftfarben, welche Bereiche individualisiert werden können. Mit personalisierbaren und insbesondere beim Management beliebten Dashboards werden Daten und Informationen aus unterschiedlichsten Unternehmensanwendungen oder Informationsquellen zusammengeführt und übersichtlich dargestellt.

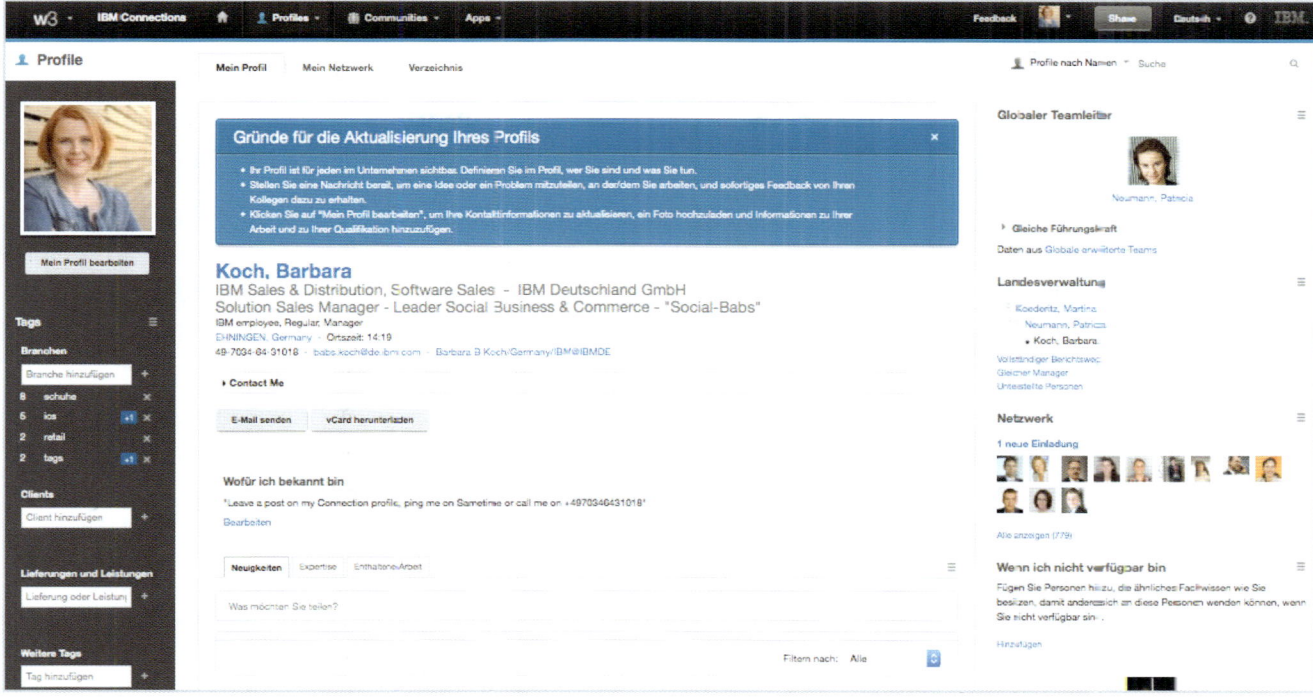

Abbildung 1.1.13: Profilseite bei IBM (IBM Connections)

PROFILSEITE UND PERSÖNLICHER ARBEITSBEREICH

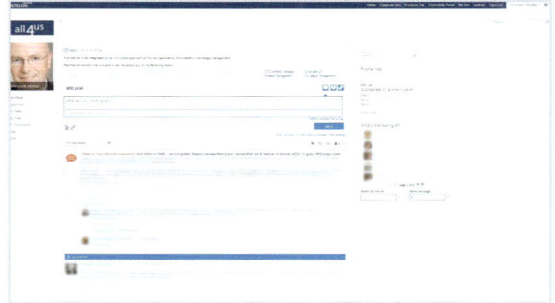

Abbildung 1.1.14: Die MySite bei der Detecon International GmbH als persönlicher Arbeitsbereich (SharePoint)

Über die Profilseite kann sich der Anwender mit Angaben zur eigenen Person im Kollegenkreis präsentieren (Foto, Position, Kontaktdaten, Expertise, Interessen etc.) So kennt jeder jeden schon einmal vom Sehen. Außerdem sind Experten leichter auffindbar. Auf der Pro-

filseite des Connections-Portals bei IBM laufen alle von der Person abonnierten Informationen zusammen. Diese Angaben sorgen für einen hilfreichen Überblick über die einzelnen Interessensgebiete. Ähnliche Möglichkeiten gibt auch der persönliche Arbeitsbereich bei der Detecon International GmbH im all4us-Intranet, welches mit Microsoft SharePoint und der Erweiterung von Sitrion umgesetzt wurde. Hier laufen persönliche Aufgaben zusammen und in der eigenen Dokumentenablage sind alle persönlichen Dokumente unabhängig vom konkreten Client-Rechner überall leicht zugänglich und gesichert. Wer mag, kann seinen Kollegen auch transparent anzeigen, welches Dokument er bearbeitet hat, welche Themen er interessant findet oder welchen Personen er folgt. Das fördert Synergien.

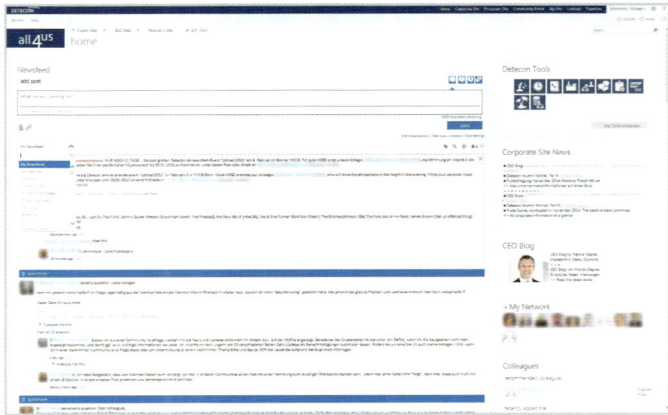

Abbildung 1.1.15: Der unternehmensweite Newsfeed der Detecon International GmbH

MICROBLOGGING ODER NEWSFEED

Wie ist der momentane Projektstand? Gibt es Ausfälle in der Produktion? Kennt sich jemand mit dem neuen Workflow aus? Im Microblog oder Newsfeed kann man kurze Nachrichten und Kommentare lesen und veröffentlichen und dabei sogar Fotos und Videos sowie nützliche Links zu Dokumenten oder Seiten im Intranet oder außerhalb einstellen.

Über den Unternehmens-Newsfeed bei der Detecon International GmbH berichten die Berater von neuen fachlichen Erkenntnissen und holen sich auch Rat und Hilfe bei anderen Kollegen.

ACTIVITY STREAM & FOLGEN

Im Activity Stream sieht der Nutzer, was im Projektraum oder im gesamten Intranet passiert. In chronologischer Reihenfolge enthält ein Activity Stream kurze Statusinformationen über neue Beiträge oder geänderte Dokumente im Intranet. Der Nutzer kann je nach Technologie steuern, was im Activity Stream erscheint oder was er angezeigt haben möchte. Das Folgen in Social Tools bedeutet, dass der Nutzer bewusst ausgewählt hat, über welche Aktivitäten und Aktualisierungen er im Newsstream informiert werden möchte. Es erlaubt die Vernetzung mit Kollegen und das Abonnieren von Neuigkeiten aus Zusammenarbeitsräumen.

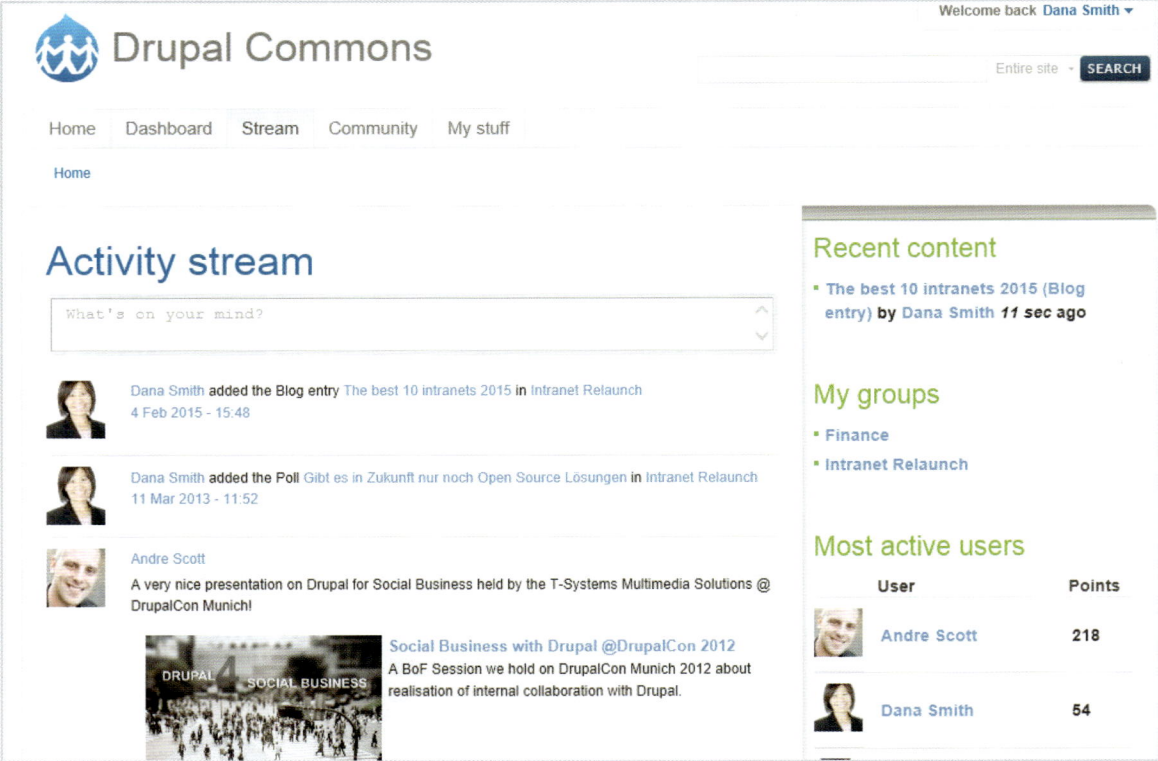

Abbildung 1.1.16: Der Activity Stream einer Drupal Community

Abbildung 1.1.17: Posten / Liken / Teilen / Taggen auf Yammer bei der AviloX GmbH

LIKEN / KOMMENTIEREN / TEILEN / TAGGEN

Wenn Mitarbeiter der AviloX GmbH Beiträge im Newsfeed oder in der Community veröffentlichen, können andere Mitglieder den Beitrag oder einzelne Antworten darauf mit „Gefällt mir" markieren. „Gefällt mir"-Bewertungen stellen eine Methode dar, öffentliche Anerkennung oder Einverständnis mit einer Nachricht zum Ausdruck zu bringen. Oft heißt ein „Like" einfach auch nur: „Ich habe die Nachricht zur Kenntnis genommen." Kommentare geben dem Autor eines Beitrags ein direktes Feedback. Durch Teilen eines Eintrags verbreitet ein Nutzer eine Information innerhalb seines Netzwerkes. Mit Hilfe des „#" können unkompliziert Schlagworte vergeben oder im Beitrag eines anderen nachträglich ergänzt werden.

RATING / BEWERTUNGEN

Für die Bewertung von Dokumenten oder Listen steht eine Fünf-Sterne-Klickfunktion bereit. Diese Bewertungsfunktion hilft den Benutzern dabei, die Inhalte selbst zu klassifizieren und damit wichtige und hochwertige Inhalte besser auffindbar zu machen.

RSS-FEED UND -AGGREGATION

Wer gern Informationen aus verschiedenen Quellen im Intranet oder Internet abonniert, kann sie sich über das RSS-Format in einer gebündelten Nachrichtenleiste anzeigen lassen. Gezielt platzierte Funktionselemente (Widgets, WebParts, Streams) aggregieren Inhalte zu einem Thema oder eines Typs aus unterschiedlichsten Bereichen des Intranets übersichtlich zusammen.

Neue Features und weitere Intranet-Trends

Die Intranet-Technik entwickelt sich rasant weiter. Anbieter setzen hier vor allem auf die Cloud, mit der es möglich ist, Kunden technische Neuerungen und Verbesserungen in kürzester Zeit zur Verfügung zu stellen. Wir gehen im Folgenden auf Trends im Intranet ein und stellen Antworten der Softwarehersteller auf die neuen Anforderungen vor. Einige Neuerungen wurden kurz vor Redaktionsschluss des Buches veröffentlicht oder von den Herstellern bereits angekündigt.

MOBILE UNTERSTÜTZUNG

Unterwegs und überall auf die Unternehmensdaten zugreifen zu können oder vom Home Office aus zu arbeiten – wer das will, benötigt zunächst die technischen Voraussetzungen für den sicheren Zugriff auf interne Unternehmensanwendungen sowie spezielle mobile Anwendungen für den Business-Alltag.

Abbildung 1.1.18: Neue Trends und Features

von Offline-Funktionen können Dateien und Ordner lokal am Rechner für die Offline-Nutzung verfügbar gehalten werden. Bei Online-Zugang werden diese Daten dann synchronisiert.

CORPORATE VIDEOS & PODCASTS

Immer mehr Unternehmen setzen auch in der Internen Kommunikation auf Bewegtbild. Office Video von Microsoft ist das Video-Portal für Office 365. Es unterstützt das Hochladen von Bewegtbild-Material. Unternehmen können Videos für den Eigenbedarf bearbeiten, kategorisieren und für mobile Endgeräte bereitstellen.

ENGE VERBINDUNGEN VON INTRANET UND INSTANT MESSAGING

Ist mein gewünschter Gesprächspartner derzeit verfügbar? Präsenzinformationen sind bei vielen Technologien zu finden. Eng damit verknüpft ist die Echtzeitkommunikation (Unified Communications & Collaborations). Viele Anbieter ermöglichen eine Chat-Funktion oder Video- und Telefon-Konferenzen aus dem Intranet heraus.

Immer mehr Intranets werden deshalb auch für Tablet-PCs und Smartphones optimiert (siehe Abschnitt 3.5 zum Thema Responsive Design).

OFFLINE-FUNKTIONEN

Die Deutsche Bahn rüstet auf, Flughäfen bieten kostenfreies W-LAN. Dennoch kann man bei Weitem noch nicht flächendeckend auf eine Internetverbindung zugreifen. Mit Hilfe

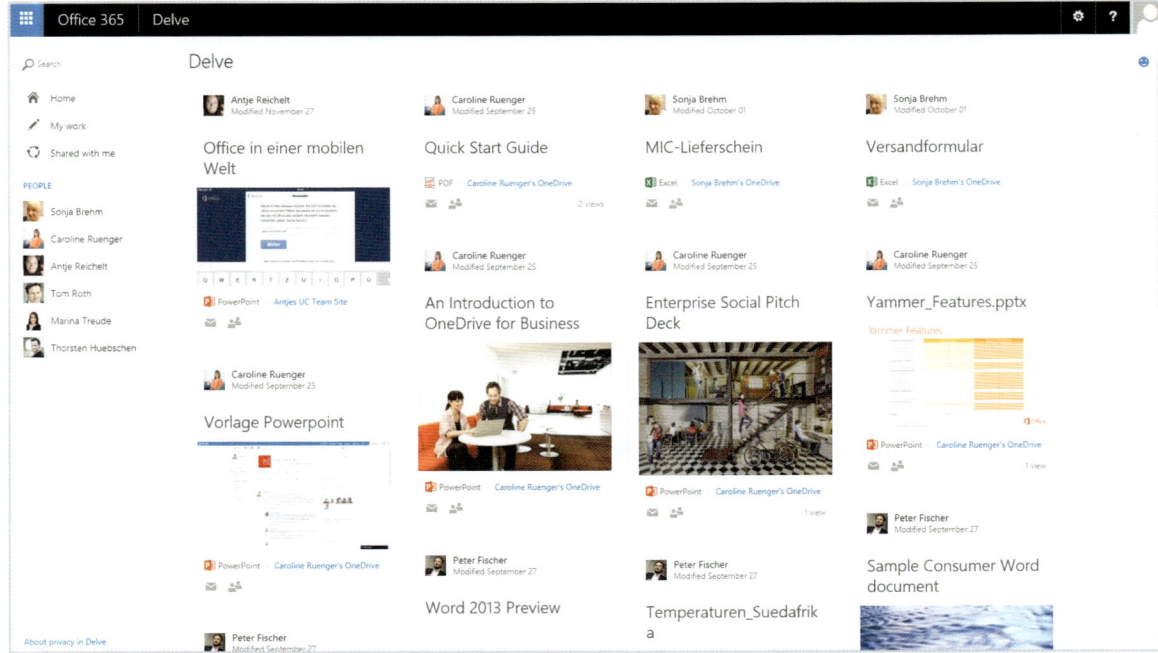

Abbildung 1.1.19: Office Delve von Microsoft (Quelle: Elmar Witte)

Abbildung 1.1.20: Auswertung von Signalen – Das Prinzip hinter dem Office Graph (Quelle: Elmar Witte)

TIEFERE VERNETZUNG UND DEREN VISUALISIERUNG

Der Trend geht im Bereich Intranet in Richtung tieferer Vernetzung und deren Visualisierung.

Diesem Trend folgt die Netzwerk-App Delve als Teil von Microsoft Office 365. Sie liefert eine individuelle Zusammenstellung von Daten aller Art im Unternehmen, ohne sie suchen zu müssen, vergleichbar mit einer „für den einzelnen Nutzer" geschriebenen Unternehmenszeitung. Delve löst damit das Problem der Informationsüberflutung und visualisiert die Informationen sehr übersichtlich und ansprechend.

Hinter der Delve-App steht der Office Graph, der über alle Office-Programme selbstlernend die wichtigsten Informationen und Dokumente zusammenstellt – wie ein persönlicher Assistent. Dabei berücksichtigt Office Graph sogenannte „Signale", die sich aus dem täglichen Arbeiten mit den Anwendungen ergeben. Ein paar Beispiele für Signale: die Teilnahme an einem Online-Meeting, welches im Kalender steht, einen entsprechenden Betreff enthält

und die Teilnehmer der Besprechung. Ein weiteres Signal ist das Verhalten des Nutzers bei Eintreffen von E-Mails. So könnte er seine Mails von seinem Vorgesetzten schneller beantworten als die Mails von seinem Kollegen. Auf diese Weise beschreibt das Verhalten detailliert, mit wem er wie zusammenarbeitet. Auch die Häufigkeit des E-Mail-Austausches ist ein Signal. Neben diesen bespielhaft aufgeführten Signalen gibt es viele weitere, die in Office Graph dazu verwendet werden, dem Nutzer zum richtigen Zeitpunkt den richtigen Inhalt sowie den dazugehörigen Experten in seinem Unternehmens-Dashboard anzuzeigen.

Office Graph stellt automatisch Beziehungen her zwischen Personen, ihren Arbeitsweisen und deren Inhalten. Je größer das Netzwerk und die zur Verfügung stehenden Workloads sind, desto besser und wertvoller arbeitet der persönliche Assistent. Die Netzwerkapplikation Delve respektiert jede Art von Rechteeinstellungen und zeigt ausschließlich solche Inhalte an, auf die der Endanwender Zugriffsrechte besitzt.

GLOBALE VERNETZUNG – SPRACH-BARRIEREN ÜBERWINDEN

Die Wirtschaft funktioniert heute global. Immer mehr Unternehmen sind international aufgestellt. Ein verbindendes, mehrsprachiges Social Intranet ist für diese Unternehmen wichtig, wenngleich die Entwicklung eines solchen grenzüberschreitenden Systems immer auch eine große technische Herausforderung ist. Im Social Intranet genügt es nicht nur, Informationsstrukturen in der jeweiligen Landessprache redaktionell bereitzustellen und technisch zu unterstützen. Vielmehr sollten Nutzer in ihrer Muttersprache Wissen teilen können, auf das die ausländischen Kollegen in Echtzeit durch integrierte automatische Übersetzungstools direkt zugreifen können. Entsprechende Technologien sind bereits entwickelt, müssen aber noch weiter verfeinert werden.

SOCIAL ANALYTICS

Um personalisierte Empfehlungen für interessante Personen, Communities und Inhalte zu erhalten, benötigt man die sogenannten Social Analytics. Ausgehend von den Profilinformationen, Tags, dem eigenen Netzwerk und eigenen Aktivitäten im Intranet werden diese Empfehlungen auf der Homepage, in Profilen und Communities zusammengestellt.

ÜBERGREIFENDE INTEGRATIONEN

Integrationen werden an Bedeutung gewinnen. Integration heißt, verschiedene Technologien so miteinander zu verbinden, dass die Nutzer gefühlt auf einer einzigen Plattform arbeiten und somit eine barrierearme Nutzungserfahrung haben. So sind Integrationsszenarien durch die Einbindung von Drittanwendungen wie CRM-, ERP-, HR-Systemen oder Prozessportalen in das Social Intranet denkbar. Sie ermöglichen es, dort direkt Daten abzurufen und zu bearbeiten, Aufgaben anzulegen und Diskussionen zu starten sowie umgekehrt Neuigkeiten aus den Drittanwendungen auch im Activity Stream angezeigt zu bekommen. Personalstammdaten liegen beispielsweise oft in einem HR-System. Verknüpft man diese Daten mit dem Intranet, können Mitarbeiter in ihrer gewohnten Intranet-Umgebung ihre Stammdaten wie Name oder Adresse ohne Aufwand selbst aktualisieren. Die Daten werden von hier wieder zurück ins HR-System gespielt.

Einfache erste Schritte sind ein einheitliches Layout, übergreifende Navigationselemente, verknüpfte Nutzerprofile (ein Profilbereich für den Nutzer im Unternehmen) und eine Enterprise Search, die alle Intranet-Quellen durchsucht.

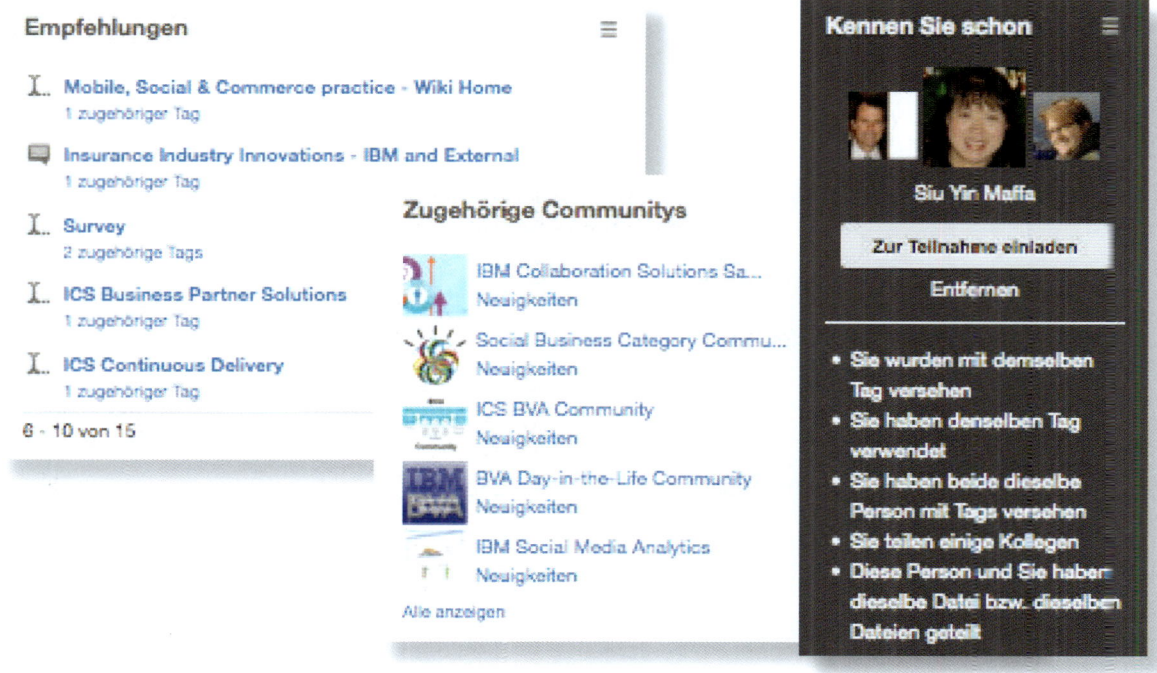

Abbildung 1.1.21: Social Analytics von IBM

1.2 DIE INTRANET-VISION ENTWICKELN

Wenn Sie Social Intranet nicht nur als Projekt sehen, sondern als eine echte Chance, Ihr Unternehmen voranzubringen und die Kommunikation und Zusammenarbeit zu modernisieren, dann brauchen Sie mehr als einen Projektplan. Sie brauchen eine Vision.

Eine Vision ist ein attraktives Bild von einer wünschenswerten Zukunft. In ihr vereinen sich die Bedürfnisse der wichtigsten Anspruchsgruppen – im Falle des Intranets sind dies vor allem die Mitarbeiter und das Management, es können aber auch die Kunden sein.

Eine Vision ist eine Vorstufe zur Entwicklung von Zielen und Strategien. Sie muss daher nicht konkret und messbar formuliert sein. Ganz im Gegenteil: Gute Visionen enthalten lediglich eine sehr kurze und emotionale Botschaft, die den Nutzen von Social Intranet auf den Punkt bringt. Diese Botschaft soll vor allem die Herzen erobern, nicht den Verstand.

Beispiele für gute Intranet-Visionen sind:
„Work like a network"
„Wir wissen, was unser Unternehmen weiß"
„Der virtuelle Schreibtisch – sämtliche Kommunikation und Information an einem Ort"
„Wissen in Chancen verwandeln – jederzeit und von jedem Ort"
„Make people more productive"
„Modernes Unternehmen – vernetzt, effizient, agil"

Die Vision der zukünftigen modernen Zusammenarbeit im Intranet sollte die Basis für jedes weitere Vorgehen sein. Je besser sie den strategischen Nutzen des Intranets auf den Punkt bringt, desto leichter wird es fallen, das Management für das Vorhaben zu gewinnen. Im besten Fall wird die Social-Intranet-Vision sogar gemeinsam mit dem Management und dem Projektteam entwickelt.

Die besten Visionen entstehen in interaktiven Strategie- und Visions-Workshops. Ein Impulsvortrag über das Thema Social Intranet ist dabei ein guter Einstieg, denn er regt die Diskussion über Erfahrungen und Wünsche für eine bessere Zusammenarbeit und Kommunikation im eigenen Unternehmen an. Durch gezielte Fragen in der Moderation und durch die Visualisierung aufgeworfener Themen und Begriffe kristallisiert sich im Laufe des Workshops ein immer klareres Bild vom strategischen Nutzen des Social Intranets für das Unternehmen heraus. Hier geht es nicht um technische Funktionen, sondern um einen Blick auf die Arbeitswelt von morgen. Der Nutzen muss anschließend nur noch in eine kurze, visionäre Botschaft gegossen zu werden, die emotionalisiert.

Folgende Fragen regen die Diskussion an:
- Welchen Herausforderungen begegnen wir als Unternehmen langfristig?
- Wie entwickeln sich die Bedürfnisse unserer wichtigsten Anspruchsgruppen?
- Welche Trends zeichnen sich insgesamt in unserem Markt ab?
- Wie können moderne Arbeitswelten uns helfen, all diesen Herausforderungen und Trends zu begegnen?

Wir empfehlen in jedem Fall, die Vision modernen Arbeitens gemeinsam mit dem Management und dem Projektteam zu entwickeln.

Dies schafft ein strategisches Gesamtverständnis bei den wichtigsten Personen im Unternehmen und sorgt für Rückenwind von ganz oben. Mit dieser positiven Aufbruchstimmung lassen sich im nächsten Schritt die Ziele und die Intranet-Strategie ableiten. Gleichzeitig wird allen Beteiligten leichter klar, dass das Vorhaben, ein modernes Intranet aufzubauen und zu etablieren, oft neue Formen der eigenen Projektorganisation erfordert.

„Integrated Social Workplace" – Die Social-Intranet-Vision der Detecon International

Die Detecon International GmbH ist seit vielen Jahren bestrebt, ihre Berater in Deutschland und den internationalen Vertretungen durch Wissensmanagement und interne Kommunikation optimal zu unterstützen. Die strategische Bedeutung von Kommunikation und Wissen für den Unternehmenserfolg ist hier längst verankert. Und doch ist alles ständig in Bewegung: Zeitgemäße Technologien werden regelmäßig evaluiert und bei Bedarf bereitgestellt. Existierende Lösungen werden in die neuen Technologien überführt und innovative Neuerungen werden eingebracht.

Im Rahmen eines Strategie- und Visions-Workshops wurden der aktuelle Stand des Arbeitsplatzes eines Detecon-Mitarbeiters rekapituliert und zukünftige Entwicklungen diskutiert. Dabei entstand die neue Detecon-Intranet-Vision des „Integrated Social Workplace", ergänzt um strategisch wichtige Funktionen und einen konkreten Umsetzungsfahrplan.

Als zukünftige zentrale Plattform wurde Microsoft SharePoint 2013 gewählt, und zwar mit der Erweiterung „Social Sites" von Sitrion, auf der bis dahin fast ausschließlich der erfolgreiche Unternehmens-Newsstream lief. Die Einführung startete mit einer Infrastruktur-Optimierung und einem einheitlichen Layout-Konzept. Communities wurden pilotiert, um daraus das Vorgehen für die Bereitstellung der Projekträume zu erarbeiten. Mit der Migration alter Intranet-Inhalte auf einen redaktionierten Bereich im neuen all4us-Intranet wurde eine weitere wichtige Komponente auf dem Weg zum Integrated Social Workplace hinzugefügt.

Dieser Abschnitt entstand in Zusammenarbeit mit Michael Schomisch, Head of Corporate ICT & Infrastructure Detecon International GmbH

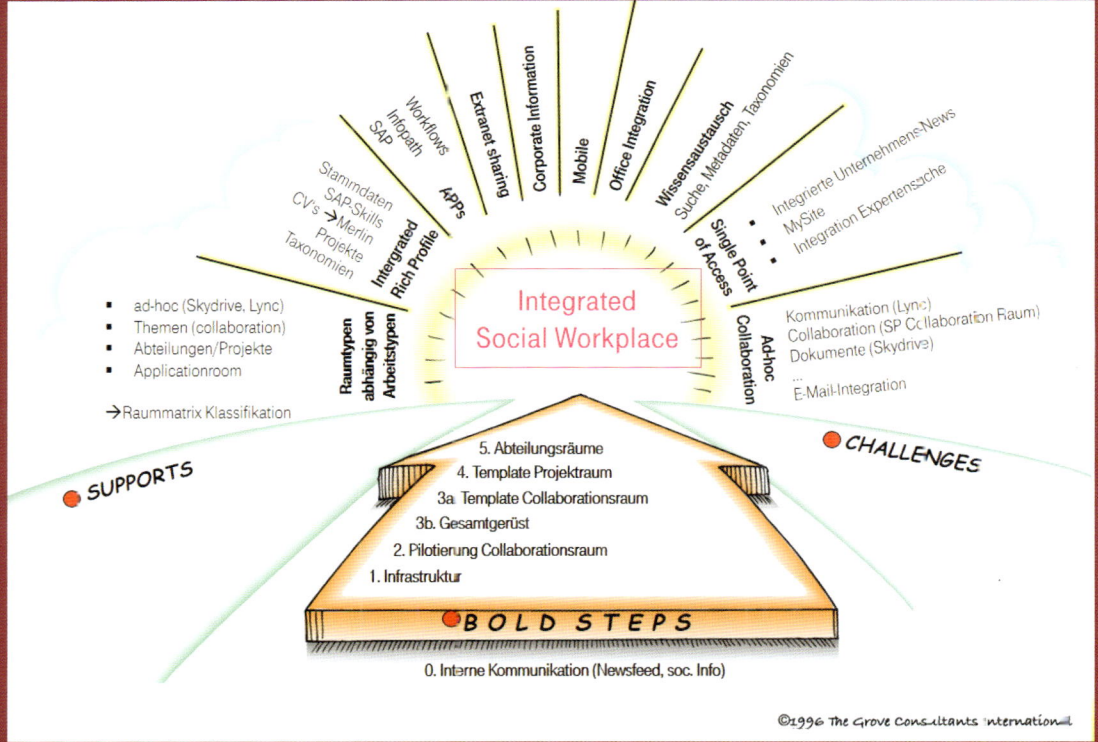

Abbildung 1.2.1: Ergebnis-Chart des Intranet-Visions-Workshops bei der Detecon International GmbH unter Verwendung der Chart-Vorlagen der Grove Consultants International (grove.com)

1.3 ZIELE, STRATEGIE, SKALIERUNG UND MESSBARKEIT

Ziele geben die Marschrichtung für ein Projekt vor. Gerade für langfristige Projekte wie die Intranet-Einführung mit einer Vielzahl an Beteiligten sind sie eine wichtige Orientierung. Strategische Ziele zeigen den langfristig angestrebten unternehmerischen Nutzen der neuen Arbeitsweisen auf, operative Intranet-Ziele wiederum sind wichtige Leitplanken, um sich bei der Einführung und Weiterentwicklung des Intranets auf das Wesentliche zu konzentrieren. Zielsetzungen in Form von Nutzerstatistiken sind ein weiteres und sehr beliebtes Mittel, um Erfolge messbar zu machen, allerdings ist deren Aussagekraft im Sinne des unternehmerischen Nutzens nur bedingt gegeben.

STRATEGISCHE INTRANET-ZIELE

Strategische Intranet-Ziele werden direkt aus der Unternehmensstrategie abgeleitet. Dies kann beispielsweise im Visions- und Strategie-Workshop passieren, der in Abschnitt 1.2 bereits erwähnt wurde. Strategische Intranet-Ziele veranschaulichen den Beitrag, den das Social Intranet zum langfristigen Erfolg des Unternehmens leistet (siehe Tabelle 1.3.1). Mit Hilfe von Kenngrößen lassen sich die strategischen Ziele messen.

Häufig werden in Projekten zur Einführung moderner Kollaborationsplattformen strategische Ziele gar nicht oder nicht ausreichend konkret formuliert. Dadurch wird wertvolle Überzeugungskraft verschenkt. Die Ableitung strategischer Ziele aus den Unternehmenszielen ist aus unserer Sicht von unverzichtbarer Bedeutung, und das aus mehreren Gründen:

- Strategische Ziele versetzen Intranet-Verantwortliche in die Lage, dem Management die Bedeutung der neuen Plattform für die Kommunikation und Zusammenarbeit im Unternehmen plausibel zu machen und entsprechend größere Budgets abzurufen.
- Durch geeignete Kenngrößen können mit Hilfe strategischer Ziele ökonomisch relevante Effekte nachgewiesen werden.

	Beispiel 1	Beispiel 2	Beispiel 3
Strategisches Unternehmensziel	Innovationsführer	Ertragsstärke	Attraktiver Arbeitgeber
Strategisches Intranet-Ziel	Effektives Wissensmanagement	Effiziente Prozesse und Workflows	Offene Unternehmenskultur
Kenngröße	Anzahl der bereichsübergreifend entwickelten Neuerungen	Bearbeitungszeiten und -kosten	Durchschnittswert in der Mitarbeiterbefragung

Tabelle 1.3.1: Beispiele strategischer Ziele

	Beispiel 1	Beispiel 2	Beispiel 3
Strategisches Intranet-Ziel	Effektives Wissens-management	Effiziente Prozesse und Workflows	Offene Unternehmens-kultur
Operative Intranet-Ziele	• kein Wissen mehr auf Laufwerken • weniger interne E-Mails • transparente Informationsflüsse im Unternehmen • weniger Suchaufwand für Informationen und Dokumente • Auffindbarkeit von Experten	• Verkürzung der Dauer des Reisekostenab-rechnungs-Workflows • Zeitersparnis bei der Terminkoordination für Schulungen • Verringerung des Ein-arbeitungsaufwands neuer Mitarbeiter • Schnelleres Finden von Dokumenten und Informationen	• höherer Informations-grad zum Gesamtkonzern • abteilungsübergreifen-der Ideenaustausch • Einbeziehung von Mit-arbeiterstimmen in Entscheidungsprozesse • sichtbare Wertschätzung durch die Führungskräfte und unter den Mitarbei-tern

Tabelle 1.3.2: Mapping strategischer und operativer Intranet-Ziele

Messbare Erfolge sind das A und O, um Führungskräfte langfristig im Boot zu halten.

- Strategische Ziele erleichtern auch den Dialog mit den Betriebs- und Personalräten, weil sie aufzeigen, dass es beim Social Intranet nicht um mehr Kontrolle, sondern um die Zukunftsfähigkeit des Unternehmens und damit auch um den Erhalt von Arbeitsplätzen geht.

Folgende Fragen helfen Ihnen, die richtigen strategischen Intranet-Ziele zu finden:

- Was motiviert uns, über Änderungen in der Intranet-Landschaft nachzudenken?
- Wie wird uns das neue Intranet verändern?
- Welche Geschäftsprozesse können effektiv durch das Intranet unterstützt oder verbessert werden?
- Wie kann uns das Intranet helfen, unsere Unternehmensziele zu erreichen?
- Woran erkennen wir, dass das Intranet einen Mehrwert bringt?

Da eine Intranet-Einführung für jedes Unternehmen ein technologisch und kulturell anspruchsvolles Vorhaben ist, sollte im nächsten Schritt eine Intranet-Strategie festgelegt werden, aus der die Prioritäten, die Reihenfolge und die grobe Zeitleiste hervorgehen. So kann beispielsweise aus Gründen der ökonomischen Dringlichkeit im ersten Schritt der Ertragsstärke ein höheres Gewicht beigemessen werden. Dies würde bedeuten, dass es im ersten Jahr vor allem auf effiziente Prozesse und Workflows ankommt und die Themen Wissensmanagement und Unternehmenskultur erst für die Folgezeit vorgesehen werden. Eine gute Intranet-Strategie gibt jeweils für die nächsten zwei bis fünf Jahre die Marschrichtung vor und zeigt anhand von klaren Kenngrößen, wie der ökonomische Nutzen über die Jahre schrittweise gesteigert werden soll.

OPERATIVE INTRANET-ZIELE

Da das Projekt für das Projektteam praktisch handhabbar sein soll, werden aus den strategischen Zielen jeweils für die nächste Realisierungsphase (meist ein Jahr) auch operative Intranet-Ziele abgeleitet. Sie erleichtern es, Prioritäten zu setzen und die vorhandenen Ressourcen richtig einzusetzen.

Intranet-Verantwortliche überspringen häufig die Formulierung der strategischen Intranet-Ziele und der Intranet-Strategie. Stattdessen starten sie ihr Projekt häufig direkt mit opera-

Dieser Abschnitt entstand in Zusammenarbeit mit Kati Sünderhauf, Referentin Change Management , Enterprise 2.0 Axel Springer SE

Ein Enterprise-Social-Network-Projekt als Teil der Gesamtstrategie bei Axel Springer

Axel Springer, der traditionsreiche Marktführer im deutschen Printgeschäft mit mehr als 13.500 Mitarbeitern und über 160 Beteiligungen, Joint Ventures und Lizenzen in 44 Ländern, geht die Digitalisierung konsequent an. Die Axel Springer SE hat sich das Ziel gesetzt, der führende digitale Verlag zu werden. Der Sprung vom tradierten Zeitungsunternehmen hin zum Anbieter mit digitalen journalistischen Angeboten ist eine große Herausforderung, die auch intern gelingen muss. Dahinter verbirgt sich ein Change-Prozess mit vielen Komponenten. Basisarbeit durch die Definition neuer strategischer Leitplanken gehört dazu, aber auch ein Kulturwandel im ganzen Haus. Eine weitere wichtige Aufgabe: Neue Talente aus der nachwachsenden Generation zu gewinnen, zu halten, zu qualifizieren und auch ältere Mitarbeiter für die digitalen Veränderungen und vernetzten Arbeitsweisen zu befähigen. Außerdem: Veränderte Anforderungen an die Arbeit verlangen nach einem modernen Arbeitsumfeld. Dafür müssen technologische Voraussetzungen geschaffen werden. So gab es mehrere Etappen auf dem Weg dorthin. Zuerst wurden mit der Initiative „Coolster Arbeitsplatz" alle Mitarbeiter bei Axel Springer mit neuen Apple Computern ausgestattet. Im nächsten Schritt startete das Pilotprojekt „CONNECT" zur Einführung von SharePoint 2013, das letztlich mit über 1.000 Anwendern in der Pilotphase erfolgreich getestet wurde. Im Jahr 2014 erlebte Axel Springer bereits eine Erfolgsstory in der Kollaborationsphase und wagt nun die nächste Ausbaustufe. Mit der Einführung von Office 365 in der Cloud soll der Kulturwandel mit mehr Mobilität und Freiraum bei der Arbeit weiter gefördert werden. Zusätzlich wird eine einfachere Zusammenarbeit mit externen Partnern ermöglicht.

Und wie hat das alles funktioniert? „Die erfolgreiche Implementierung von Kollaborationsplattformen kann nur durch das Umsetzen einer begleitenden Change-Management-Strategie gelingen. Diese Strategie rückt die Mitarbeiter ins Zentrum des Geschehens und bezieht sie von Beginn an mit ein", sagt Kati Sünderhauf, Teilprojektleiterin Einführung und Change Management von „CONNECT" und Office 365. Was genau dahinter steckt, zeigen wir an verschiedenen Beispielen in diesem Buch.

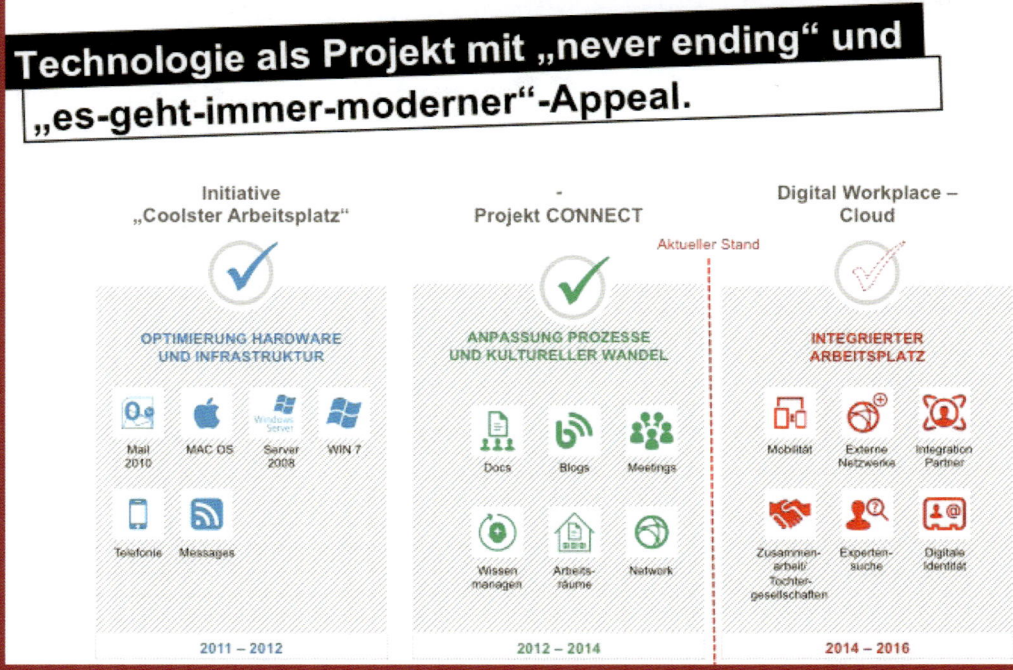

Abbildung 1.3.1: Technologieeinführung ist nie abgeschlossen – Projektphilosophie bei Axel Springer

tiven Intranet-Zielen oder gar mit Nutzungsstatistiken. Das ist zwar prinzipiell ein gangbarer Weg. Doch besteht dabei die Gefahr, dass das Social-Intranet-Projekt vom Management als zu kleinteilig wahrgenommen und daher mit wenig Aufmerksamkeit und Budget versehen wird.

Tabelle 1.3.2 zeigt, wie strategische Intranet-Ziele auf operative Ziele heruntergebrochen werden können.

Damit operative Ziele Wirkung entfalten, sind drei Grundregeln zu beachten:

1. Weniger ist mehr! Wählen Sie drei bis fünf Ziele aus, die die höchste Relevanz haben und konzentrieren Sie sich auf die Umsetzung. So behalten Sie den Überblick und den Spaß am Projekt.

2. Präzisieren Sie Ihre Ziele mit der SMART-Formel: Spezifisch – Messbar – Attraktiv – Realistisch – Terminiert.

3. Formulieren Sie Etappenziele und messen Sie anhand der Etappen die Fortschritte. So erkennen Sie Probleme frühzeitig und können rechtzeitig gegensteuern.

Viele Projektgruppen haben Schwierigkeiten mit der Messbarkeit der „weichen Auswirkungen" eines Intranets, wie z.B. Verbesserung der Mitarbeiterzufriedenheit oder der Unternehmenskultur. Doch selbst solche Ergebnisse lassen sich in der Regel mit geeigneten Instrumenten (wie z.B. Mitarbeiterbefragungen oder Stimmungsbarometern) nachweisen.

Folgendermaßen sehen SMARTe Ziele aus:

- Interner E-Mail-Verkehr: 30% weniger Datenvolumen im Vergleich zum Vorjahr;

- Befragungen: Gesamt-Durchschnittsnote 2 bei der Mitarbeiterzufriedenheit;
- Personalwesen: 10 Prozesse der Personalabteilung (z.B. Urlaubsantrag, Weiterbildungsantrag) werden bis Jahresende von allen Mitarbeitern ausschließlich über das Intranet abgewickelt.

NUTZERSTATISTIKEN

Die in der Praxis am häufigsten anzutreffende Form von Erfolgsmessgrößen sind die Nutzerstatistiken. Sie geben Auskunft über das Nutzungsverhalten. Dabei handelt es sich beispielsweise um

- angestrebte User-Zahlen,
- die Nutzungshäufigkeit einzelner Funktionen,
- die Anzahl von Communities oder Beiträgen in bestimmten Communities,
- die Anzahl von angelegten Projekträumen,
- durchschnittliche Vernetzungsgrade von Mitarbeitern.

Nutzerstatistiken schaffen einen Überblick, wie gut das Intranet angenommen wird und welche Funktionen besonders beliebt sind. Sie erleichtern es zu erkennen, wo ein Anpassungs- und Schulungsbedarf besteht. Indirekt kann man aus den Kennzahlen auch herauslesen, ob die Mitarbeiter aus dem Intranet einen Nutzen ziehen. Eine Aussage über den konkreten Wert für Unternehmen und Mitarbeiter geben sie allerdings nicht. Da Nutzerstatistiken mit der Speicherung personengebundener Daten verbunden sind, ist eine Abstimmung mit dem Betriebs- und Personalrat unabdingbar. Es ist dabei sinnvoll, sich auf einige wenige, möglichst aussagekräftige Statistiken zu konzentrieren.

Dieser Abschnitt entstand in Zusammenarbeit mit Florian Hoecherl, Manager Analytics & Tools Roland Berger Strategy Consultants Holding GmbH

Ziele als Teil der Kommunikationskampagne zum Roll-out bei Roland Berger

Die Ziele des Projekts bei Roland Berger Strategy Consultants – einer der weltweit führenden Strategieberatungen – wurden allen Mitarbeiter transparent gemacht. Zwei Wochen vor dem Go-Live der neuen Plattform wurde auf die bevorstehenden Neuerungen auf eine Art und Weise hingewiesen, die zum bewussten Lesen anregte (siehe Abbildung). Der Zusatz „Start now!" wurde dann am Go-Live-Tag mit Aufklebern realisiert.

Abbildung 1.3.2: Die Ziele des Projekts bei Roland Berger Strategy Consultants in der Kommunikation zum Launch des neuen Intranets

NUTZEN AUFZEIGEN 1.4
UND MESSEN

Am häufigsten werde ich von Intranet-Nutzern gefragt: „What's in it for me?"
Die Amerikaner haben dafür gleich wieder eine Abkürzung gefunden: WIIFM
oder auf gut deutsch: „Was bringt mir das Intranet?" Gute Projektleiter überlegen sich beim Start eines Projekts überzeugende Antworten für Manager
und Mitarbeiter. Schließlich gibt keiner von uns ohne Grund lieb gewonnene
Gewohnheiten auf und lässt sich einfach so auf Neues ein, oder?

Mehrwert für ausgewählte Abteilungen

Die Vorteile von Enterprise 2.0 kann man mittlerweile in vielen Fachbüchern nachlesen. Dabei geht es oft um den Nutzen für das Unternehmen oder für den einzelnen Mitarbeiter.
Wenn das Intranet in den Fachbereichen Nutzen
stiften soll, sollte dieser Nutzen auch mit den
Fachbereichsleitern herausgearbeitet werden.

Nachfolgend finden Intranet-Verantwortliche
erste Anregungen, die einen konstruktiven
Austausch mit den Bereichsleitern und ihren
Teams unterstützen können. Sie machen den
Führungsteams den Nutzen für ihr Verantwor-
tungsgebiet greifbarer und können durch weitere Ideen aus dem Gespräch heraus ergänzt
oder ersetzt werden. Dieser persönliche Austausch schafft zusätzliche Akzeptanz und Unterstützung für das Projekt. Ein angenehmer
Nebeneffekt: Im Gespräch erhält man wertvolle
Informationen darüber, bei welchen Anwendungsfällen das Social Intranet die Unternehmensbereiche unterstützen kann.

VORTEILE FÜR DAS MANAGEMENT

Zeit für das Führen gewinnen

Schluss mit der Fremdbestimmung durch die
Flut an E-Mails und Besprechungen! Mit einer
Social Software nutzen Führungskräfte ihre Zeit
effektiver: Information und Abstimmungen online; Strategieentwicklung, Kreation und Lernen offline.

Wissen, was das Unternehmen weiß

Social Intranet bringt das wichtigste Gut im
Unternehmen zum Vorschein: das Know-how
der Mitarbeiter. Nie war es einfacher zu über-
blicken, was im Unternehmen und am Markt
passiert. Führungskräfte entdecken frühzeitiger strategische Chancen und Risiken und die
richtigen Personen, um effektiv zu handeln.
Und Ideenmanagement 2.0 bringt neue Impulse
für's Geschäft.

Ziele erreichen

Orientierungslose Mitarbeiter? Mit Social Intranet ist das ein Thema der Vergangenheit. Mit
wenig Aufwand vermitteln Führungskräfte Ziele
an die Mitarbeiter, überprüfen die Fortschritte,
handeln, wenn etwas schief läuft, und moti-

vieren, wenn es an der Zeit ist. Durch höhere Schlagkraft im Team werden Ziele nicht nur erreicht, sondern oft auch übererfüllt.

Einfacher motivieren

Anhänger des Credos „Keine Strafe ist genug des Lobes" finden im Social Intranet einfache Tools, um über ihren eigenen Schatten zu springen. Feedback, Anerkennung und Wertschätzung erfordern weniger Aufwand denn je. Und wegen ihrer hohen Sichtbarkeit entwickeln sich im Team auch gewünschte Verhaltensweisen schneller denn je.

Unternehmenskultur entwickeln

Wer kennt sie nicht, die schlechten Resultate aus Mitarbeiterbefragungen? Information, Kommunikation, Feedback, Wertschätzung und Orientierung – die Top 5, an denen es in deutschen Unternehmen mangelt. Social Intranet eint Führungskräfte und Mitarbeiter auf einer Plattform. Es verkürzt Wege, fördert den Austausch und steigert das Gefühl dazuzugehören. Es gibt kaum bessere Tools zur Pflege der Unternehmenskultur.

VORTEILE FÜR DIE HR-ABTEILUNG

Verwaltungsaufwand senken

Endlich wieder gestalten statt verwalten! Viele Abläufe und Services lassen sich im Intranet standardisiert als Self Services einrichten: Arbeitszeugnisse anfordern, Weiterbildungen beantragen, schnelle Prüf- und Freigabeprozesse sowie aussagekräftige Performance-Reviews organisieren. Dies entlastet die HR-Mitarbeiter und setzt Ressourcen frei für die kreative Personalarbeit – ganz zum Wohle Ihrer Mitarbeiter!

Direkt im Unternehmen qualifizieren

Zwei Drittel dessen, was wir lernen, lernen wir durch direkte Kommunikation während der Arbeit. Intranets sind die optimale Unterstützung für das Lernen im Job. Diskussionen, Wikis, Präsentationen und Videos sind wahre Fundgruben für geballtes Unternehmenswissen. Und wer mehr wissen will, den führt ein Klick zum direkten Kontakt mit dem passenden internen Experten. Mitarbeiterprofile zeigen, welche Talente und Kompetenzen im Unternehmen schlummern – bereit für den Einsatz im Rahmen neuer Aufgaben und Verantwortungen.

Mitarbeiter binden

Mitarbeiter zu verlieren und zu ersetzen, wird mitunter eine teure Angelegenheit. Zufriedene und gesunde Mitarbeiter sind ein hohes Gut. Das Gefühl gebraucht zu werden, Teil einer Gemeinschaft zu sein und einen wertvollen Beitrag zu leisten, trägt wesentlich zur Zufriedenheit bei und kann sehr gut durch ein soziales Unternehmensnetzwerk gestärkt werden – und das sogar bei längerer Abwesenheit. Telekom-Mitarbeiter können sich beispielsweise während der Elternzeit mit dem Programm „Stay in Contact" auf dem Laufenden halten.

Mitarbeiter effizient einarbeiten

Wie oft werden neue Mitarbeiter am ersten Arbeitstag im Büro herumgeführt und merken sich bei all dem Neuen weder Richtlinien noch Namen? Das muss nicht sein. In einem extra dafür eingerichteten Bereich des Social Intranets können Neulinge die wichtigsten Infos selbst einholen und Bekanntschaften mit Kollegen schließen. So angeleitet, können sie die ersten Schritte in dem Tempo machen, das zu ihnen passt.

Stimmungsbilder einfangen

Mitarbeiterbefragungen sind oft sehr aufwendig und werden meist nur alle zwei bis drei Jahre durchgeführt. Mit Hilfe eines Social Intranet können jede Woche ohne großen Aufwand Umfragen stattfinden, um ein Feedback und ein Stimmungsbild aus der Organisation einzuholen. Fragen an die Mitarbeiter decken Verbesserungspotenziale auf. Fragen an das Management zeigen, welche Themen aktuell bewegen. Und warum nicht auch das Intranet nutzen, um gemeinsam mit den Mitarbeitern darüber nachzudenken, was Sie als Arbeitgeber attrak- tiv macht und wie geeignete Mitarbeiter gefunden werden können?

eLearning und optimierte Einstellungsprozesse bei United Breweries

United Breweries (UB) ist ein indischer Mischkonzern, der vor allem durch Biermarken wie Kingfisher bekannt ist und in Indien einen Marktanteil von 48% innehat. Das soziale Netzwerk Yammer wird vielfältig eingesetzt, und zwei Anwendungsfälle sollen hervorgehoben werden: eLearning und optimierte Einstellungsprozesse neuer Mitarbeiter.

Erwachsenenbildung mit Yammer setzt auf „Shared Experiences" – gemeinsame Erfahrungsräume, wo praxisnahes und relevantes Wissen auf Augenhöhe geteilt wird und durchaus auch Misslungenes zur Sprache kommt. Allen Machbarkeiten und Umsetzungsmöglichkeiten von Wissen gilt die besondere Aufmerksamkeit. Nicht nur der reine Lehrstoff wird vermittelt wie im klassischen eLearning, sondern es wird hautnah über Erfahrungen im Feld und in der Geschäftspraxis berichtet. Dabei kommen mobile Szenarien zum Einsatz, etwa wenn Mitarbeiter schnell und unkompliziert Fotos über neue Marketingkampagnen am Point of Sales der Konkurrenz posten. Auf diese Weise wird ein spürbarer Tempogewinn gegenüber den konventionellen Kommunikationsprozessen erzielt, so dass man auf Gegen- oder Alternativkampagnen rasch und agil reagieren und über die Wirkung diskutieren kann. Es ist nicht nur ein technischer Vorteil durch mobile Apps gegeben, vielmehr laden soziale Netzwerke dazu ein, dass sich Mitarbeiter über Hierarchie- und Organisationsgrenzen hinweg einbringen – auch wenn sie nicht im Marketing arbeiten, so wie in dem genannten Beispiel.

Schneller und dichter am Puls ist United Breweries auch, wenn es um interne Mitarbeiterumfragen und Stimmungsbilder geht. Dafür wird Yammer eingesetzt. Es dient dazu, schnell Maßnahmen zu generieren, wenn man Muster aus den Konversationen herausliest. Interessanterweise hat United Breweries herausgefunden, dass Lerninhalte wie Videos auf größere Beachtung und Klickraten stoßen, wenn sie mitten in eine Diskussion im sozialen Netzwerk eingestreut und so in den passenden Kontext gebracht werden. Training ist übrigens kein rein unternehmensinternes Thema. Über ein externes Yammer-Netzwerk werden auch Partner und Zulieferer geschult.

Überhaupt nutzt United Breweries intensiv diese externen Kollaborationsmöglichkeiten. Mit Studierenden wird früh Kontakt aufgenommen, wobei Yammer Bestandteil der Einstellungsprozesse ist. Wenn es zu einem Arbeitsvertrag gekommen ist, kann die Einarbeitungszeit verkürzt werden, weil die neuen Mitarbeiter sich schneller zurecht finden und mit anderen Kollegen austauschen können. Diese Netzwerke vermitteln – so United Breweries – ein Gefühl von Vertrauen, man fühlt sich in verantwortungsvollen Händen. Das sollen nicht nur die Neuen spüren. Ein externes Netzwerk für Alumnis ist in Planung. Werte und deren Vermittlung sind für United Breweries wichtig, doch ist es nicht immer einfach, sie plastisch zu kommunzieren. Storytelling auf Yammer erfüllt diesen Zweck. Stets fanden sich reichlich Beispiele von den Anwendern, um die Werte 'Pride at Workplace', 'Entrepreneural Spirit' und 'Passion for Excellence' wirken zu lassen und verständlich zu machen.

Dieser Abschnitt entstand in Zusammenarbeit mit Ragnar Heil, Customer Success Manager Office 365 Microsoft Deutschland

Yammer-Erfolgsvideo von United Ereweries http://bit.ly/1yT7Kqb

VORTEILE FÜR DIE KOMMUNIKATIONSABTEILUNG

Attraktiv kommunizieren

Gerade jüngere Mitarbeiter, denen „Posten und Teilen" in Fleisch und Blut übergegangen ist, schätzen es, wenn sie die Kommunikationsweisen aus dem privaten Umfeld auch im Job anwenden können.

Informationen leicht platzieren

Wichtige Unternehmensbotschaften und Informationen des Managements erreichen über das Intranet mit viel weniger Aufwand und viel passgenauer ihre Zielgruppe als herkömmliche Medien. Und noch besser: Aus der Einweg-Kommunikation wird eine Mehrweg-Kommunikation durch „Likes", Ratings und Kommentare der Mitarbeiter.

Redaktion entlasten

Während früher für das Intranet noch extra neue Stellen für Redakteure geschaffen werden mussten, gibt es heute viele Intranet-Redakteure, die alle relevanten Themen im Unternehmen kennen – die eigenen Mitarbeiter.

Unkompliziert auf Medien zugreifen

Die Kommunikationsabteilung muss eine riesige Menge an Informationen erstellen, erarbeiten und verteilen – und das meist unter großem Zeitdruck. Im Dokumentencenter des Intranets können Dokumente zeitgleich von mehreren Autoren bearbeitet werden. Stets steht die neueste Version eines Dokuments zur Verfügung – auch von Videos und Bildern, die übersichtlich im Mediencenter geordnet werden.

Wissen, was die Mitarbeiter bewegt

Nie war es leichter herauszufinden, was die Mitarbeiter bewegt. Bei der Datev dürfen Mitarbeiter auf der Intranet-Plattform „Nachgefragt!" ihre Fragen an das Management stellen und diskutieren. Informations- und Kommunikationslücken werden so ganz einfach aufgedeckt und geschlossen.

VORTEILE FÜR DIE PRODUKTION

Einfach dazugehören

Produktionsmitarbeiter fühlen sich oft von anderen Unternehmensteilen isoliert, weil sie meist keinen PC-Arbeitsplatz haben und viele Informationen an ihnen vorbeigehen. Bildschirme in den Pausenräumen oder Terminals an geeigneten Stellen schaffen Zugang zu Informationen und das Gefühl, dazu zu gehören.

Schichtpläne von überall abrufen

Aktuelle Schichtpläne von daheim abrufen zu können, ist ein Mehrwert, den sich viele Produktionsmitarbeiter von einem Intranet wünschen. Schichten zu organisieren, Schichten zu tauschen oder Fahrgemeinschaften zu organisieren, sind beliebte Themen von Produktionsmitarbeitern im Intranet.

Schicht ohne Informationsverlust übergeben

Ein Social Intranet vereinfacht den Austausch zwischen zwei oder drei unterschiedlichen Schichten am Tag. Wichtige Vorfälle und Übergaben werden im Intranet dokumentiert, keine Information geht mehr verloren.

Produktionsmitarbeiter in Entscheidungen einbeziehen

Führungskräfte entscheiden oft über die Köpfe der Mitarbeiter hinweg. Dabei besitzen die oft mehr Detailwissen zu den Produktionsabläufen und den technischen Anlagen. Dieses Wissen wird unkompliziert verfügbar gemacht, sodass Problemlösungen oder Entscheidungen bei Investitionen erleichtert und Qualitäts- und Produktverbesserungen befördert werden.

Aus Fehlern lernen

Wer will schon denselben Fehler anderer noch einmal machen? Beinahe-Vorfälle und Störungen können mitsamt dem Wissen um die Vermeidung und Behebung solcher Probleme im Intranet dokumentiert und leicht wiedergefunden werden. So können alle das Wissen aus Vorerfahrungen jederzeit nutzen.

VORTEILE FÜR DIE IT-ABTEILUNG

Rolle erweitern

Die IT hat eine wichtige Bedeutung, wenn Unternehmen ihre Kommunikation und Zusammenarbeit modernisieren und ihr Wissensmanagement verbessern wollen. Denn sie sorgt für ein passgenaues Social Intranet. Der IT-Verantwortliche von morgen berät seine internen Kunden, wie IT wertschöpfend in den wissens- und kommunikationsintensiven Geschäftsprozessen zum Einsatz kommt: über unternehmensweite Suchfunktionen, mobile Zugriffe und die Integration von Geschäftsanwendungen im Unternehmen.

Zeit für Kernaktivitäten gewinnen

Die Tools für Enterprise 2.0 werden in der Regel durch externe Rechenzentren (Cloud) bereitgestellt. Administrative Tätigkeiten für die Einhaltung der Datensicherheit, für die Datensicherung sowie die Verfügbarkeit fallen weitestgehend weg und geben somit der IT-Abteilung Raum für ihre Kernaktivitäten.

Anwender schneller unterstützen

Nachdem die technische Konfiguration der Dienste und die Schulung der Anwender abgeschlossen ist, werden die Communities, sozialen Netzwerke und Gruppen durch speziell geschulte Anwender (Power User, Community Manager) selbst betreut und administriert. Damit wird die interne IT-Abteilung von täglichen kleinen Anwenderfragen entlastet und Anwender erhalten schneller Hilfe.

Anerkennung spüren

Eine erfolgreiche Einführung und Nutzung von Enterprise-2.0-Funktionalitäten trägt in hohem Maße zum Ansehen der IT-Abteilung bei. Das Arbeiten mit sozialen Features ist bei den Anwendern emotional stark besetzt und macht daher den Beitrag, den die IT für mehr Spaß Effektivität und Arbeitsentlastung leistet, stärker sichtbar.

Nutzungsgrad der IT-Investitionen erhöhen

Das Social Intranet integriert im Idealfall viele IT-Anwendungen und stellt sie dem Anwender rollenbasiert zur Verfügung. Der Anwender kommt auf diese Weise mit IT-Anwendungen in Berührung, die er als sinnvoll und motivierend erlebt und die den Nutzungsgrad erhöhen. Damit lohnen sich die Investitionen in Fachanwendungen und die IT kann schneller einen Return on Investment realisieren.

VORTEILE FÜR DEN VERTRIEB

Unternehmenswissen überall mitnehmen

Vertriebsmitarbeiter sind oft unterwegs. Mit einem Social Intranet haben sie das ganze Unternehmen und die Kundenhistorie bei sich, wenn die Kundendatenbank integriert ist.

Vertriebsprozesse beschleunigen

Vertriebsprozesse, an denen mehrere Mitarbeiter beteiligt sind, werden effizienter abgewickelt, wenn jeder alle Informationen transparent über das Intranet erhält und sich die Beteiligten untereinander austauschen. Angebote werden deutlich schneller und in höherer Qualität erstellt und auch die Zusagen an den Kunden entsprechen durch interne Abstimmungen stärker den Möglichkeiten. Nie war es einfacher, sich auf den Kunden einzustellen und im Gespräch zu punkten.

Kundenerfahrungen teilen

Außendienstmitarbeiter sind das „Auge des Unternehmens". Jedes Kunden-Feedback können sie über das Intranet an alle Beschäftigten weitergeben. Die Produktion bekommt eine Rückmeldung zur Qualität, der Service kann schnell reagieren, die Entwicklungsabteilung erhält neue Impulse und das Marketing weiß, ob die letzte Kampagne angekommen ist.

Dieser Abschnitt entstand in Zusammenarbeit mit Roger Müller, Stv. Leiter Kommunikation / Mediensprecher Luzerner Kantonalbank AG

Nutzen und Nutzer im Mittelpunkt bei der Luzerner Kantonalbank

Die Luzerner Kantonalbank stellte die Nutzer der Plattform in den Mittelpunkt und schuf damit erkennbare Vorteile für alle Beteiligte: Das Intranet bietet einen echten Mehrwert im Arbeitsalltag, indem es Arbeitsprozesse optimal unterstützt. Die Informationen zu den rund 150 Produkten und Service-Paketen der Bank mussten früher aus diversen Rubriken des Intranets zusammengetragen werden. Jetzt stehen sie für die Kundenberater im Intranet übersichtlich gebündelt und gut strukturiert zum Abruf bereit. „Der Erfolg ist erkennbar", stellt Roger Müller klar. „Diese Produktseiten gehören zu den am meisten genutzten Rubriken im Intranet – neben der Personensuche und dem Speiseplan des Personalrestaurants." Damit nicht genug: Wichtige Daten wie Zinssätze und Gebühren werden automatisch an den entsprechenden Stellen eingespielt – eine echte Erleichterung für die Mitarbeiter, die diese Daten für die Beratung ihrer Kunden ständig abrufen. Oft benötigte Anwendungen sind nutzerfreundlich konzipiert, so beispielsweise das Druckcenter, bei dem Mitarbeiter Dokumente einfach wie in einem Online-Shop auswählen können. Automatisch wird per Klick daraus ein fertiges Kundendossier mit den Kontaktdaten des Beraters erstellt.

Vertriebsexpertise verfügbar machen

Die Erfahrungen, die ein Mitarbeiter im Vertrieb macht, kann er mit allen anderen teilen, vor allem mit dem Nachwuchs im Unternehmen. Das fördert das unternehmerische Denken und das Verständnis der Kundenbedürfnisse bei allen Mitarbeitern.

Experten schnell finden

Oft haben Kunden Fragen, die ein Mitarbeiter allein nicht beantworten kann. Über die Suche im Intranet kann er schnell den Kollegen mit der gewünschten Expertise finden.

VORTEILE FÜR FORSCHUNG UND ENTWICKLUNG

Kundenbedürfnisse erkennen

Social Intranet macht die von Vertrieb und Kundenbetreuung erfassten Kundenbedürfnisse leichter sichtbar. Durch den direkten Dialog mit den Kunden kann die F&E-Abteilung ihre Aktivitäten stärker auf den Markt ausrichten und die Erfolgsaussicht ihrer Innovationsprojekte deutlich erhöhen.

Viele Innovatoren gewinnen

Jeder kann im Unternehmen einen Beitrag zu Verbesserungen und Innovationen liefern. KVP, Ideenmanagement und betriebliches Vorschlagswesen erhalten im Social Intranet eine ganz neue Qualität: Ideen werden interaktiv verbessert, bevor über sie entschieden wird. Votings machen Lust auf's Engagement für Neuerungen – in der gesamten Belegschaft.

In Geschäftsmodellen denken

Die größten langfristigen Ertragschancen liegen nicht bei Produkt- und Prozessinnovationen, sondern bei innovativen Geschäftsmodellen. Warum nicht eingefahrene Denkbahnen verlassen und gängige Geschäftsmodelle mit Vertretern aus anderen Unternehmensbereichen weiterdenken?

Innovationskultur entwickeln

Social Intranet macht gute Ideen und engagierte Mitarbeiter sichtbar, ebenso aber auch Probleme und Fehler: eine Chance für die Führungskräfte, mit klaren Botschaften Mut zu machen, sich für die Umsetzung guter Ideen einzusetzen und aus Erfahrungen zu lernen.

"Working out loud" bei der Esquel Group

Esquel ist ein Kleidungsproduzent aus Hongkong mit 59.000 Mitarbeitern, der vor allem für Nike, Lacoste, Hilfiger und Ralph Lauren Shirts herstellt.

Bemerkenswert beim Einsatz von Yammer ist, dass es als Kommunikationstool genutzt wird für jede Art von Fragen. Daher das Motto: „When you doubt, Yammer it out!" Es werden also nicht wie bei anderen Unternehmen nur Spruchreifes, finale Dokumente und Hochglanzmaterial geteilt, sondern auch Halbgares. Wilkie Wong, CFO von Esquel, ergänzt dazu: „Mit Yammer backen wir den Rest fertig!" Der neue Kommunikationstrend "Working out loud" wird bereits umgesetzt und das (Top-) Management fordert die Mitarbeiter nachdrücklich dazu auf, ihre Meinungen, Ideen und Vorschläge zu äußern.

Als besonders erfolgreich hat sich eine Form des Crowdsourcing erwiesen, bei der man Entscheidungsprozesse mit einer großen Gruppe öffentlich teilt und so schneller und vor allem bessere Antworten bekommt. Vorhandenes Denken und Arbeiten in Silos soll abgebaut werden. Ideen- und Wissensmanagement wird überwiegend mit den Bordmitteln von Yammer durchgeführt. Bei sehr komplexen Themen und Projekten werden die Möglichkeiten von Office 365 und SharePoint miteinbezogen und integriert. Die mobilen Einsatzmöglichkeiten haben sehr zur Akzeptanz dieser neuen Produktivitätswerkzeuge beigetragen. Man muss nicht mehr wie früher in der Fabrik oder im VPN-Netz sein, sondern greift von überall und wann man möchte mit vielen modernen Devices auf das Wissen dieser lernenden Organisation zu, die wie ein Netzwerk arbeitet.

Dieser Abschnitt entstand in Zusammenarbeit mit Ragnar Heil, Customer Success Manager Office 365 Microsoft Deutschland GmbH

Yammer-Erfolgsvideo der Esquel Group
http://bit.ly/1ygaeu

Neue Impulse durch Open Innovation setzen

Innovation entsteht in der Regel durch die Neukombination von Bestehendem. Social Intranet führt Ideen und Know-how aus verschiedenen Teilen des Unternehmens zusammen und bringt gänzlich neue Lösungen hervor. Auch externe Innovationspartner lassen sich einfach anbinden und sorgen für zusätzliche Impulse – mit der Cloud-Technologie alles kein Problem.

VORTEILE FÜR DEN KUNDENDIENST

Exzellenten Support leisten

Nicht jeder Kundendienstmitarbeiter – sei es im Außendienst, an der Hotline oder als Korrespondenz-Sachbearbeiter – hat das gesamte Unternehmenswissen im Kopf. Im Intranet aber findet er alles. Informationen zu Produkten oder Dienstleistungen lassen sich wunderbar über Wikis abbilden. Häufig gestellte Fragen (FAQs) werden durch Experten professionell beantwortet. Bei weiterführenden Fragen reicht ein Klick und der Kontakt zum Spezialisten ist aufgebaut.

Zielgerichtet suchen

Der Support-Mitarbeiter ist darauf angewiesen, schnell und effektiv auf die jeweils relevante Information zuzugreifen. Eine klug eingerichtete und regelmäßig optimierte Suchmaschine ist für den Service-Mitarbeiter von unschätzbarem Wert und bringt dem Kunden eine spürbar höhere Beratungsqualität.

Für Kundenanfragen und Beschwerden schnell Lösungen finden

Durch die frühzeitige und transparente Bereitstellung von Kunden-Feedback an alle relevanten

Abteilungen im Unternehmen kann schneller reagiert werden. So kommen Anregungen und Hilfsangebote auch von solchen Kollegen, die sonst nicht unbedingt in die Kundenbetreuung involviert sind.

Qualitätsmängel frühzeitig beseitigen

Oft ist es schwierig, ein Feedback an das Produktmanagement weiterzuleiten. Manche Fälle erscheinen zu „unbedeutend", um extra eine Mail zu schreiben oder einen Mängelreport auszufüllen. Schneller und unbürokratischer geht es mit den Social Features.

Mit der Kunden-Community zusammenwachsen

Immer mehr Unternehmen bieten ihren Kunden Social-Media-Kanäle, um über Neuigkeiten zu informieren und den Dialog mit den Kunden zu pflegen. Moderne Unternehmen setzen noch eins drauf: Sie stellen Portale bereit, auf denen die Kunden sich bei Fragen gegenseitig unterstützen können, moderiert durch einen speziell geschulten Support-Mitarbeiter. Die dabei entstehende Kunden-Community und die schnellen, nachvollziehbaren Reaktionen aus dem Support stärken die Markenbindung und Kundenloyalität. Außerdem lassen sich wertvolle Hinweise auf aktuelle oder neu entstehende Kundenbedürfnisse entdecken.

Dieser Abschnitt entstand in Zusammenarbeit mit Jürgen Mirbach, Social Business Consultant T-Systems Multimedia Solutions GmbH

Wie misst man den Nutzen von Social Collaboration?

Die Überzeugung, dass mit Social Intranets und Social Collaboration die Arbeitsproduktivität erhöht wird, ist bereits weit verbreitet. Dennoch erregt kaum ein Thema die Gemüter stärker als die Diskussion um den Nachweis des Nutzens von Social Collaboration. In einer Diskussion in einem Intranet-Arbeitskreis wurde unlängst festgestellt, dass von ca. 25 Unternehmen in lediglich einem ein Use Case so gerechnet werden konnte, dass daraus ein

Business Case entsteht. Bei aller Schwierigkeit: Wie kann man sich dem Thema ROI (Return of Invest) und Nutzen von Social Collaboration praktisch nähern?

Das Thema ist nicht neu:
- Die Rechnung eines Business Case für Intranet-Projekte über ersparte Zeit ist bekannt und umstritten (Robertson, 2008).
- Weitere Möglichkeiten und Grenzen einer ROI-Rechnung, die einem Business Case zu Grunde liegt, sind genauso betrachtet worden, wie auch die KPIs zur Messung der Zielerreichung eines Social Intranet (Wolf, Die drei wichtigsten Ziele eines Intranet 2.0 und wie man sie messen kann, 2010).

Das Erfordernis, einen Business Case zu beschreiben, bietet die wesentliche Chance, Mehrwerte gezielt zu identifizieren und nachzuverfolgen. Ein Social Enterprise ist für sich kein Ziel – es kommt auf den spezifischen Nutzen für das Unternehmen und seine Mitarbeiter an. Die Studie „Social Collaboration in Deutschland, Frankreich und Großbritannien 2013" (Pierre Audoin Consultants, 2013) hat vier Bereiche identifiziert, die von den Fachbereichen als Handlungsfelder für Social Collaboration gesehen werden:

- Innovationsfähigkeit,
- Produktivität,
- Vernetzung und
- Management.

Diese vier Bereiche könnten eine Struktur vorgeben, in der Erfolgversprechendes gesucht und gefördert wird. Dies ist im Kern unternehmerisches Handeln, für das Controlling und Monitoring eingesetzt wird.

Vertiefende Anregungen zum Monitoring und dem damit verbundenen kontinuierlichen Verbesserungsprozess sind in Abschnitt 6.4. nachzulesen.

DAS PROJEKT RICHTIG
AUFSTELLEN

Bei den oben beschriebenen Maßnahmen ging es vor allem darum, das Bewusstsein für die strategische Notwendigkeit und für den Nutzen des neuen Intranets aus der Perspektive des Unternehmens, der Fachbereiche und der Mitarbeiter zu schärfen. Vision, Ziele und Strategie wurden umrissen, um einen Orientierungsrahmen für das Projekt zu schaffen.

Im Folgenden gehen wir darauf ein, wie man ein Social-Intranet-Projekt richtig aufsetzt. Gerade am Anfang ist es wichtig, typische Fehler zu vermeiden, um schnell ein gut organisiertes und budgetiertes Vorhaben zu entwickeln. Hier kann es besonders hilfreich sein, externe Beratungshilfen zur Unterstützung der Planungen und zur Vermeidung von Stolperfallen heranzuziehen.

Projektorganisation

Ein Social Intranet ist mehr als nur ein Technologie-Projekt. Richtig eingeführt, verändert die Social Software grundlegend die Kommunikation und Arbeitsweise im gesamten Unternehmen. Es handelt sich also um eine Neuerung, die sehr viel umfassender eine Umstellung aller Beteiligten erfordert, als dies häufig bei IT-Projekten üblich ist.

Projektteam

Ein hauptverantwortliches Projektteam sollte das gesamte Projekt steuern. Bei dessen Zusammenstellung sollte größte Sorgfalt walten. Ein zu großes Team – ideal wären etwa fünf Personen – oder eine falsche Auswahl der

Teammitglieder kann schnell dazu führen, dass sich statt einer vermeintlich schlagkräftiger Truppe tatsächlich nur eine indifferente Gruppe herausbildet.

Achten Sie bei der Auswahl der Projektteam-Mitglieder auf folgende Anforderungen:

- Leidenschaft und intuitiver Zugang zu dem Thema,
- Ressourcen, um sich langfristig im Projekt zu engagieren,
- gutes Gesamtverständnis der Organisation,
- guter Draht zu den wichtigsten Entscheidern und in die Belegschaft hinein,
- kommunikationsstark und einfühlsam,
- effektiver Arbeitsstil,
- Verantwortungsbereitschaft,
- Führungsstärke (beim Projektleiter)

Die Teammitglieder müssen keine Alleskönner sein. Die Kombination der einzelnen Stärken jedoch sollte für eine geballte Schlagkraft sorgen. Projektteam-Mitglieder kommen typischerweise aus folgenden Fachbereichen:

- Kommunikation,
- IT,
- Organisation,
- HR.

Aus der IT und der Unternehmenskommunikation sollte immer je eine Person dabei sein. Die übrigen Mitglieder sollten eher nach strategischem Schwerpunkt des Social Intranets und nach persönlicher Eignung ausgewählt werden.

Das Team braucht einen Projektleiter, der das Projekt orchestriert und gegenüber den Entscheidern vertritt. Er ist das Bindeglied zu allen Projektgremien. Projektleitung bedeutet ständige Führungsarbeit, damit das Projekt sowohl im Team als auch im Unternehmen immer genügend Fans und Unterstützer findet.

Steuerungskreis

Bei einem Intranet-Projekt gibt es eine große Bandbreite von Anspruchsgruppen, deren Erwartungen und Interessen für eine erfolgreiche Einführung zusammengebracht werden sollten.

Eine repräsentative Auswahl dieser Stakeholder, einflussreich und effektiv, bildet den Steuerungskreis (oder Lenkungsausschuss). Er gibt die Richtung vor, trifft Rahmenentscheidungen, gibt Ressourcen frei und macht seinen Einfluss bei verschiedenen Interessengruppen im Unternehmen geltend.

Steuerungskreise gehören vor allem in großen Unternehmen zu einer professionell konzipierten Projektorganisation. Bei kleinen und mittelständischen Unternehmen reicht es häufig aus, das enge Führungsteam in einer dem Steuerungskreis analogen Funktion einzusetzen. Hierbei darf jedoch nicht außer Acht gelassen werden, dass eine fortlaufende Einbindung des Betriebs- oder Personalrates elementar ist, um für das Projekt möglichst viel Rückenwind aus der Belegschaft zu erhalten.

Anhand folgender Kriterien können Sie die geeigneten Mitglieder für den Steuerungskreis bestimmen:

- einflussreicher Entscheider oder Multiplikator,
- gutes Verständnis des strategischen Wertes eines Social Intranet,

- Überzeugungs- und Entscheidungsstärke,
- kritischer Fragensteller mit Gespür für Plausibilität und Nutzen,
- Vorbildwirkung.

Je früher der Steuerungskreis bestimmt und im Boot ist, desto leichter kann das Projekt Fahrt aufnehmen.

Externe Unterstützung

Gerade für die wichtigen ersten Phasen des Projekts bringen externe Berater häufig sehr hilfreiche Erfahrungen, Methoden und technisches Fachwissen mit. Sie geben Orientierung, arbeiten mit einem Gefühl für das Gesamtunternehmen und wirken moderierend zwischen den Projektbeteiligten. Ihr Blick von außen und ihre „Draufsicht" erlauben es ihnen, Auffälligkeiten gezielter zu hinterfragen und auszusprechen als interne Beteiligte. Sie können selbst in verfahrenen Situationen oft Lösungen anbieten oder mit ihren Erfahrungen aus anderen Unternehmen völlig neue Perspektiven in ein Projekt bringen.

Jede Plattform ist anders, sie funktioniert nach den Erfordernissen des Unternehmens. Entsprechend unterschiedlich ist auch der Bedarf an externer Unterstützung. Der Dienstleister wird im Allgemeinen keine Blaupause für die Inhalte und Kosten seiner Leistungen haben. Es ist daher sinnvoll, die genauen Anforderungen im Rahmen eines Vorprojekts mit dem Dienstleister zu ermitteln, um eine realistische Budgetplanung vorzunehmen. Denken Sie dabei unbedingt daran, nicht nur einen technischen Dienstleister ins Boot zu nehmen, sondern auch einen, der die „weichen" Change-Themen bei der Einführung der neuen Arbeitsweisen beherrscht.

Technologie und Kultur gehen bei Axel Springer eine Allianz ein

Mit der Initialisierung des Projektes wurden viele Erwartungen und Anforderungen an die zukünftige Plattform für vernetzte Zusammenarbeit erkennbar. Vor allem die damit einhergehenden Auswirkungen auf Arbeitsprozesse und die kulturellen Effekte verlangten nach einer modernen Projektstruktur. Neben IT-Verantwortlichen waren Kollegen aus den Bereichen Personal, Unternehmenskommunikation und der Betriebsrat in die Konzeptions- und Umsetzungsüberlegungen eingebunden. So entstand ein interdisziplinäres Projektteam, das unterschiedlichste Blickwinkel zum Datenschutz oder zur Qualifizierung einbrachte.

Auch der Steuerungsausschuss bestand aus einer Doppelspitze aus Personal und IT. Die Projektleitung wurde zusätzlich durch einen externen Dienstleister besetzt, mit dem das Projekt nur ganzheitlich geführt wurde. Die einzelnen Teilprojekte waren gleichfalls durch eine Tandemstruktur aus einem Vertreter auf Dienstleister- und Axel Springer-Seite gekennzeichnet.

Die gesamte Einführung wurde nicht nach Art eines klassisch-linearen Projektvorgehens vollzogen. Im Projektmanagement bediente man sich agiler Methoden. Wöchentlich fand ein Sprint-Meeting statt, in dem alle Teilprojekte ihre Zwischenstände abgleichen und die nächste Woche planen konnten. Darüber hinaus gab es in der Hochphase des Projekts jeden Morgen einen 5- bis 15-minütigen Daily Stand-up via Status-Telefonat oder Webkonferenz. Durch diese enge Taktung waren alle im Team auf dem aktuellen Stand und jeder wusste, wo Unterstützung notwendig wurde. Dadurch spielte sich die Zusammenarbeit schnell ein und es entstand ein guter Zusammenhalt.

Zusätzlich wurde die Projektarbeit von Anfang an in der zukünftigen SharePoint-2013- Arbeitsumgebung umgesetzt. Es war für das gesamte Team essenziell, die Funktionen der Plattform und die Arbeitsweisen zu kennen, insbesondere die Kultur zu erleben, die bei der Implementierung ins Haus getragen wird.

Dieser Abschnitt entstand in Zusammenarbeit mit Kati Sünderhauf, Referentin Change Management , Enterprise 2.0 Axel Springer SE

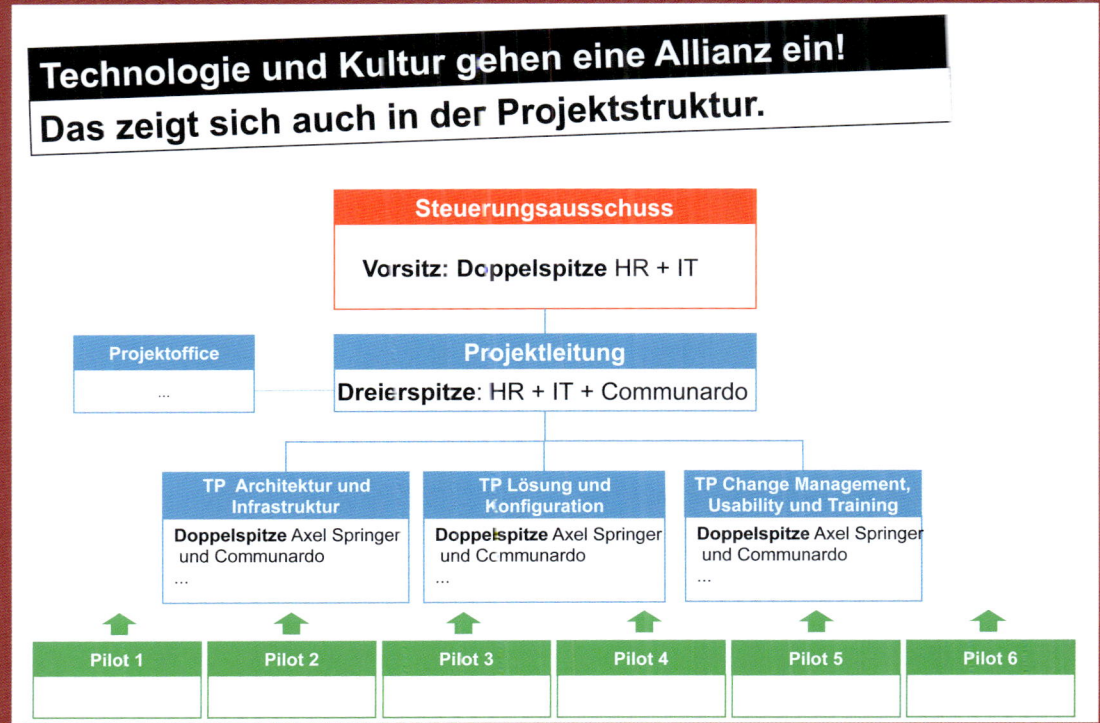

Abbildung 1.5.1: Projektstruktur, die interdisziplinäres Arbeiten fördert, bei Axel Springer

Projektinitialisierung

Die Arbeit in den Projektgremien starten

Wenn Sie Probleme und Konflikte im Projekt vermeiden wollen, sollten Sie sich am Anfang genügend Zeit nehmen, mit den einzelnen Projektgremien das Social-Intranet-Projekt sorgfältig aufzusetzen. Ein gemeinsames Verständnis der Ziele, Spielregeln, Pflichten und Aufgaben sind das A und O für einen kraftvollen Projektstart. Sie schaffen ein positives Arbeitsklima und sorgen für ein engagiertes Zusammenarbeiten aller Beteiligten.

Der Projektauftakt erfolgt am besten in Workshops, bei denen in den jeweiligen Projektgremien folgende Themen besprochen und vereinbart werden:

- Sinn und Zweck eines Social Intranets für das Unternehmen,
- Erwartungen und Zielstellungen,
- Projektgremien mit ihren klar voneinander abgegrenzten Rollen, Aufgaben und Befugnissen,
- Aufteilung der Rollen und Verantwortlichkeiten im eigenen Projektgremium,
- Chancen und Risiken im Projekt,
- Kommunikationswege im Projekt,
- Spielregeln.

Unabhängig, ob interne oder externe Dienstleister für die Umsetzung vorgesehen sind: Es wird eine klare Definition der Erwartungshaltung und der Inhalte benötigt, um spätere Konflikte zu vermeiden.

Auch wenn mit einem gemeinsamen Projektauftakt eine gute Basis gelegt wurde, sollte der Projektleiter im gesamten Projektverlauf immer ein Auge darauf haben, ob alle Beteiligten ihren Aufgaben nachkommen und ob die vereinbarten Spielregeln und Kommunikationswege eingehalten werden. Sich über solche Themen offen auszutauschen, sollte regelmäßiger Bestandteil der Gremien-Meetings sein. Im Projektverlauf wird dann auch ein strukturiertes Anforderungsmanagement zu etablieren sein (mehr hierzu in Abschnitt 3.1).

Arbeitsorganisation des Projektteams

Projektablagen, Kommunikationswege und Aufgabenverteilung müssen von Beginn an gut organisiert sein. Nur dann stimmen die Grundlagen für ein nachhaltiges Projektmanagement. Entscheiden Sie, wie Ihr Intranet-Projekt gesteuert werden soll. In Social-Intranet-Projekten eignet sich besonders ein iteratives bzw. agiles Vorgehen (mehr hierzu in Kapitel 3.1).

Ein Social-Intranet-Projektteam sollte möglichst früh auch die neue Kollaborationsumgebung für seine Arbeit nutzen. Geschieht das, so wird das Projektteam gleich als erstes an die neuen Arbeitsweisen herangeführt und entwickelt früh ein tieferes Verständnis dafür, was auf die Mitarbeiter mit dem Rollout zukommen wird. Nur in der Praxis lassen sich Erfahrungen sammeln und die Vorteile entdecken. Damit ist das Projektteam auch gleichzeitig das erste Pilotteam im Intranet-Projekt. Übrigens: Dass zu Beginn womöglich eine technische Plattform fehlt, ist kein Hindernis. Suchen Sie sich eine Pilotumgebung bei einem Dienstleister oder in der Cloud.

Projektteam als erstes Pilotteam zur Erprobung der modernen Zusammenarbeit in Office 365 bei einem Kunststoffhersteller

Beim Start des Intranet-Projekts bei einem Kunststoffproduzenten wurde auf der favorsierten Plattform Office 365 ein Projektraum eingerichtet. Die Aufgabenliste wurde grob anhand der einzelnen Projektphasen erstellt und im Projektverlauf nach und nach detailliert erweitert. Die Projektgruppe konnte alle Dokumente in einem Dokumentencenter ablegen, transparent bearbeiten und über den integrierten Yammer-Newsfeed kommunizieren. So entstanden kurze Wege in der Abstimmung innerhalb des Projektteams – sowohl innerhalb des Unternehmens als auch mit den externen Dienstleistern. Der Vorteil: Das Projektteam erprobte von Anfang an das neue Arbeiten in Office 365 und war dadurch bei der Einführung ein überzeugender und kompetenter Sparrings-Partner für alle Führungskräfte und Mitarbeiter.

1.6 STAKEHOLDER FÜR DAS PROJEKT AKTIVIEREN

Jeder, der schon einmal größere Projekte geleitet hat, weiß: Ohne die Unterstützung der wichtigsten Anspruchsgruppen kann ein strategisches Vorhaben nicht erfolgreich umgesetzt werden. Zu den wichtigsten Anspruchsgruppen zählen vor allem die Geschäftsleitung, die Führungskräfte, der Betriebsrat, Leistungsträger und einflussreiche Mitarbeiter.

Ein Social Intranet ist nicht nur ein weiteres Kommunikationsinstrument. Es bringt eine neue Art zu arbeiten mit sich und es hat das Potenzial, Arbeitsabläufe zu verschlanken und die Unternehmenskultur zu verändern. Wie bei jedem Wandel braucht auch die Einführung des Social Intranets genügend einflussreiche Unterstützer, welche die Veränderung wirklich wollen und sich dafür einsetzen. Aber auch die einflussreichen Gegner sollten im Auge behalten werden, damit die Stimmung gegenüber dem Projekt nicht plötzlich kippt.

Social-Intranet-Verantwortliche sind daher gleichzeitig auch Change Manager. Neben der Umsetzung des technisch orientierten Projektplans sollten sie sich folgende zwei Fragen stellen:

1. Wer sind die wichtigsten Einflusspersonen in meinem Unternehmen?

2. Wie kann ich diese Einflusspersonen auf die richtige Weise im Projekt einsetzen?

Stakeholder-Analyse

Eine systematische Stakeholder-Analyse ist unerlässlich für das Gelingen eines Social-Intranet-Projekts. Mit folgenden vier Schritten schaffen Sie die Grundlage für mehr Akzeptanz und Rückenwind in Ihrer Organisation:

❗Praxistipps: In vier Schritten Unterstützer gewinnen

1. Identifizieren Sie die wichtigen Einflusspersonen in der gesamten Organisation.
2. Verschaffen Sie sich anhand folgender drei Fragen ein klares Bild zu jeder einzelnen Einflussperson:
   a. Wie groß sind das Interesse und die Offenheit der Person für das Thema? Welche Interessen verfolgt sie? Auf welche Themen springt sie besonders an?
   b. Wie meinungsstark ist die Person?
   c. Wie stark ist ihr Einfluss auf andere Menschen in der Organisation?
3. Entwickeln Sie anhand dieser Erkenntnisse eine Stakeholder-Matrix nach folgendem Muster (Abbildung 1.6.1): Jeder Kreis symbolisiert eine bestimmte Person. Je größer die Kreise, umso größer ist der Einfluss der Person in der Organisation.
4. Entwickeln Sie einen Stakeholder-Plan. Dieser Plan enthält konkrete Maßnahmen, um:
   • den einflussreichsten Treibern eine

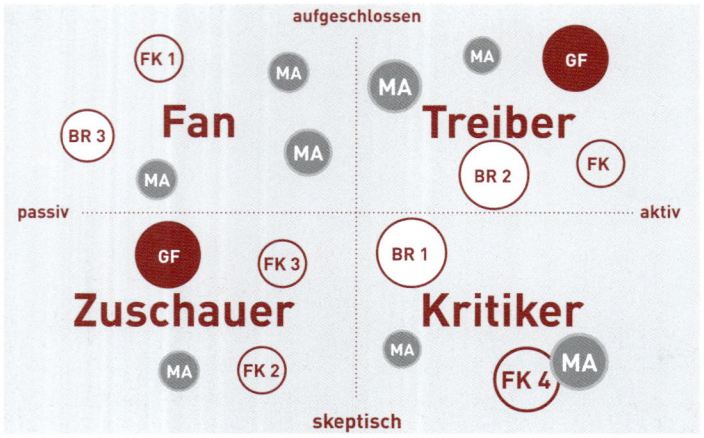

Abbildung 1.6.1: Muster für eine Stakeholder-Matrix

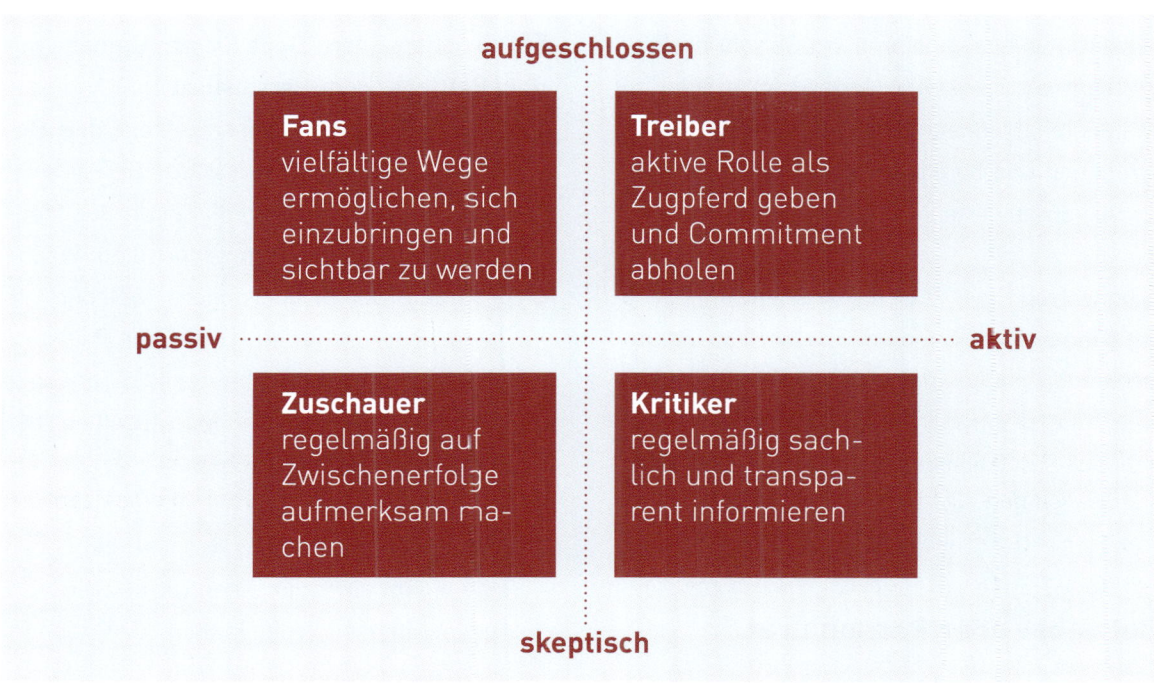

aufgeschlossen

Fans
vielfältige Wege
ermöglichen, sich
einzubringen und
sichtbar zu werden

Treiber
aktive Rolle als
Zugpferd geben
und Commitment
abholen

passiv ⋯⋯⋯⋯⋯⋯⋯⋯⋯⋯⋯⋯ **aktiv**

Zuschauer
regelmäßig auf
Zwischenerfolge
aufmerksam ma-
chen

Kritiker
regelmäßig sach-
lich und transpa-
rent informieren

skeptisch

Abbildung 1.6.2: Orientierungshilfe für das Stakeholder Management

aktive Rolle im Projekt zu geben,
- die einflussreichsten Fans zum Mitmachen zu motivieren,
- die einflussreichsten Zuschauer immer mehr vom Projekt zu begeistern und
- den einflussreichsten Kritikern den Wind aus den Segeln zu nehmen.

Es ist sehr zu empfehlen, die Tabelle gemeinsam im Projektteam auszufüllen. Die Mitglieder des Projektteams lernen auf diese Weise, wodurch ihr Projekt bedroht oder auch beflügelt wird, und

sie setzen sich leidenschaftlicher dafür ein, dass durch die richtigen Maßnahmen möglichst viel Unterstützung entsteht.

Mit Hilfe der Orientierungsregeln in Abbildung 1.6.2 lassen sich geeignete Maßnahmen entwickeln und richtig priorisieren.

Ein geschicktes Anspruchsgruppen-Management trägt maßgeblich dazu bei, die Stimmung im Unternehmen zugunsten der neuen Arbeitsformen zu verändern. Daher empfehlen wir un-

Intranet ist Chefsache, sagt meine Chefin. Und wo sie Recht hat, hat sie Recht. Wenn die Geschäftsführung nicht voll hinter dem Enterprise-2.0-Projekt steht und mitmacht, ist das Projekt zum Scheitern verurteilt.

Deshalb ist es ja so wichtig, sich für den Start des Social-Business-Portals Unterstützung auf der Führungsebene, also beim Vorstand, bei der Geschäftsführung oder wichtigen Managern zu holen.

Suchen Sie Befürworter und Meinungsmacher! Ermutigen Sie einflussreiche Führungskräfte, über das Intranet zu reden, eine Pilotgruppe zu initiieren und es natürlich selbst auch später zu nutzen, um Informationen zu verbreiten. Ob Newsfeed-Nutzung, ein Management-Kanal oder eine monatliche Videobotschaft: Es gibt viele Möglichkeiten, als Führungskraft mit gutem Beispiel voranzugehen.

bedingt, mindestens einmal im Quartal im Projektteam die relevanten Anspruchsgruppen zu analysieren, Maßnahmen zu planen sowie Beobachtungen und bereits erfolgte Entscheidungen kritisch auszuwerten.

Grundsätzlich gilt: Bleiben Sie stets im Dialog mit allen Interessierten und machen Sie Ihr Unternehmen von Anfang an auf die Zwischenerfolge im Social-Intranet-Projekt aufmerksam! So nehmen Sie Skeptikern ganz schnell den Wind aus den Segeln.

Betriebs- oder Personalrat

Das BetrVG § 87 Abs.1 sieht bei der Einführung von Intranet-Lösungen Mitbestimmungsrechte des Betriebsrates vor. Gerade bei der Einführung technischer Neuerungen, die eine Überwachung von Mitarbeitern in ihrem Verhalten und in ihren Leistungen dienen könnten, ist es wichtig, eine Genehmigung des Betriebs- oder Personalrates einzuholen. Der Arbeitgeber ist verpflichtet, sich in allen mitbestimmungspflichtigen Punkten mit dem Betriebsrat zu einigen. Üblicherweise wird dazu eine Betriebsvereinbarung abgeschlossen. Eine Betriebsvereinbarung schützt die Mitarbeiter, sorgt für Rechtssicherheit, schafft Vertrauen gegenüber neuen Technologien und sichert die Einhaltung der Vereinbarungen, auch wenn Ansprechpartner, Führungskräfte oder Mitarbeiter wechseln.

Weil Verhandlungen mit dem Betriebs- bzw. Personalrat häufig als schwierig empfunden werden, versuchen Intranet-Verantwortliche sie hinauszuschieben. Unsere Erfahrungen sagen: Gremien-Entscheidungen können dauern. Beziehen Sie die Verantwortlichen daher frühzeitig mit ein. Das spart Zeit und Geld, da Sie frühzeitig die Konfliktpunkte kennenlernen und genügend Zeit haben, sie zu lösen, ohne dass der Projektplan gefährdet wird.

! Praxistipps: Acht Tipps für den Umgang mit dem Betriebs- oder Personalrat

1. Gehen Sie positiv gestimmt auf den Betriebs- oder Personalrat zu! Er ist nicht grundsätzlich gegen die Einführung neuer Technologien. Doch gehört die kritische Prüfung von Neuerungen, welche alle Mitarbeiter betreffen, zu seinen Pflichten. Auch er hat aber ein Interesse daran, dass die Organisation ihre Marktposition behaupten oder verbessern kann.

2. Begegnen Sie ihm mit Respekt und sehen Sie in ihm nicht nur einen vom Gesetz vorgeschriebenen Handlanger: Mitarbeitervertreter sind meist sehr gut in der Organisation vernetzt. Nur wenn auch sie von den Chancen durch die Einführung von Intranet-Lösungen überzeugt sind, werden sie eine positive Multiplikatorenrolle übernehmen. Mitarbeiter stehen Änderungen offener gegenüber, wenn sie vom Betriebs- oder Personalrat unterstützt werden.

3. Der Betriebs- bzw. Personalrat ist ein gesamthaft zu betrachtendes Gremium. Hier gibt es keine Hierarchie. Alle Entscheidungen werden demokratisch getroffen und vom Vorsitzenden kommuniziert.

4. Es gibt nicht DEN Betriebs- oder Personalrat. Es ist ein Amt, das von sehr verschiedenartigen Menschen ausgeübt wird. Auch sie müssen erst die neuen technischen Möglichkeiten erkennen und verstehen, bevor sie Entscheidungen treffen. Das Amt wird übrigens mancherorts als Karrierestopper gesehen, sodass meist nicht unbedingt junge und social-affine Kollegen in dieser Funktion aktiv sind.

5. Je besser ein Betriebs- oder Personalratsmitglied die neuen Arbeitsweisen und Funktionen für sich entdeckt (und nützlich findet), desto offener wird es für Neuerun-

gen sein. Gerade die aktive Betriebs- und Personalratsarbeit ist stark kommunikativ und profitiert von den Möglichkeiten moderner Kommunikationsmedien.

6. Die Kontrolle über die Arbeit zu verlieren oder kontrolliert zu werden, ist ein großes Angstthema bei allen Nutzergruppen, auch beim Betriebsrat.

7. Zeigen Sie dem Betriebsrat die Chancen auf, doch sprechen Sie auch offen über mögliche Risiken und suchen Sie gemeinsam nach Lösungen. Führen Sie auch Anwendungsfälle für die Betriebsratsarbeit auf, um ihm zu helfen, die Vorzüge der Neuerung zu erkennen.

8. Das Bewerten von Mitarbeitern und ihrer Tätigkeit, das Kommentieren sowie die Präsenzanzeige sind wichtige Funktionalitäten in einem Social Intranet, die garantiert angesprochen werden. Bereiten Sie sich darauf vor.

Ein Schlüsselsatz, den man gegenüber dem Betriebs- oder Personalrat äußern und auch so meinen sollte, lautet: „Die neue Plattform wird nicht zur Anwesenheitskontrolle und Leistungsbewertung herangezogen." Erkennbar offenen Betriebs- bzw. Personalräten kann man sogar die Teilnahme am Pilotprogramm ermöglichen. So gehören sie zu den ersten Nutzern der modernen Technik und der Weg für eine gute Zusammenarbeit ist geebnet.

Eckpunkte der Betriebsvereinbarung eines Medienunternehmens

Mit der Einführung von SharePoint in einem Medienunternehmen wurde das Ziel verknüpft, die vorhandene Informations- und Kommunikationskultur offener zu gestalten, wobei die Persönlichkeitsrechte gewahrt werden sollen und jede technische Verhaltens- und Leistungskontrolle unterbleibt.

Wichtige Regelungspunkte für die Betriebsvereinbarung waren demnach:

* der Grundsatz, dass Mitarbeitern in den neuen Kommunikationsbereichen keine Nachteile entstehen dürfen (z.B. bei der Vertraulichkeit von Informationen und deren Kennzeichnung oder in der Veränderung der Führungskultur)
* Umgang mit personenbezogenen Daten im Allgemeinen
* Zugriffsrechte in Portalen und Arbeitsräumen, Sichtbarkeit der Teilnehmer und deren Zugriffsrechte
* Lese- und Schreibrechte im Microblogging: Wer darf kommentieren, bloggen, löschen?
* Umgang mit Mitarbeiterprofilen: Was ist ein Pflichtfeld? Was wird, wenn überhaupt, nur freiwillig eingegeben?
* Umgang mit Qualitätsbewertungen
* Ausschluss einer Delegation von Aufgaben außerhalb der disziplinarischen, fachlichen oder projektbezogenen Hierarchie
* Wikis: Umgang mit dem Teilen von Wissen, die namentliche Kennzeichnung der Autorenschaft, Zugriffsrechte beim Ändern oder Löschen, Anzeige der Änderungshistorie
* Schulungskonzept
* Regelungen, was in Konfliktfällen passiert

Bewährt haben sich Pilotierungen, um in der Pilotphase weitere Erfahrungen sammeln zu können.

Dieser Abschnitt entstand in Zusammenarbeit mit Daniel Hammer, Betriebsratsvorsitzender Niederlassung Berlin Microsoft Deutschland GmbH

Ein Vertrauensarbeitsort bei Microsoft Deutschland

Flexibles Arbeiten gehört bei Microsoft längst zum Alltag. Egal ob im Büro, beim Kunden, im Home Office oder im Café – Microsoft Deutschland legt die Entscheidung über den Arbeitsort in die Hände seiner Mitarbeiter. Diese stringente Ausrichtung basiert auf der grundsätzlichen Entscheidung, die Anwendung aktueller Technologien in den Vordergrund zu stellen und so aktiv vorzuleben.

Was bei Microsoft schon lange Praxis ist, wurde vom Betriebsrat mitentwickelt und im Rahmen einer Betriebsvereinbarung geregelt. „Mit dem Vertrauensarbeitsort schaffen wir den verbindlichen Rahmen, den wir bei Microsoft als Arbeitsplatz definieren. So liefern wir die nötige Klarheit für alle Mitarbeiter und Führungskräfte", sagt Andreas Pagel, Vorsitzender des Gesamtbetriebsrats von Microsoft Deutschland. Der „Vertrauensarbeitsort" ergänzt die bereits seit 1998 bestehende Betriebsvereinbarung „Vertrauensarbeitszeit" und bietet so den größtmöglichen Freiraum für die persönliche Arbeitsplatzgestaltung. So wird der Begriff „anwesend" während der Kernarbeitszeit durch „erreichbar" ersetzt.

Aber nicht alles kann virtuell abgewickelt werden. Damit das persönliche Miteinander nicht zu kurz kommt, gibt es klare Regeln für die Präsenzpflicht bei Teammeetings und Mitarbeitergesprächen. Coachings von Führungskräften und Mitarbeitern helfen außerdem, offene Fragen zu klären: Wie kommuniziere ich aus dem Home Office heraus mit meinen Kollegen? Was muss ich als Führungskraft beachten? Wie wird meine Leistung wahrgenommen?

Klares Ziel der Vertrauensarbeit ist eine verbesserte Vereinbarkeit von Privatleben und Beruf. Die Betriebsvereinbarung gilt auch für Mitarbeiter, die per Arbeitnehmerüberlassung bei Microsoft beschäftigt sind. Sie wurde mit dem festen Willen geschlossen, alle Mitarbeiter im größtmöglichen Maße frei entscheiden zu lassen, wann und wo die Arbeitsleistung erbracht wird. Dabei soll die Vertrauensarbeit natürlich mit den Wünschen und Bedürfnissen der Kunden und den individuellen Aufgaben in Einklang stehen. Auch die Ziele und Rollen, die Zusammenarbeit im Team sowie die gesetzlichen Erfordernisse müssen berücksichtigt werden.

Vertrauen ist gut, Zeiterfassung besser – das meinen die Gegner der Vertrauensarbeit und warnen vor Selbstausbeutung der Mitarbeiter. Befürworter loben die Zeitsouveränität, die man gewinnt. In der Vertrauensarbeit zählt allein das Ergebnis, nicht die Anwesenheit. Die Werkzeuge zur Online-Kommunikation dürfen natürlich weder zur Anwesenheitskontrolle noch zur Leistungs- und Verhaltenskontrolle durch das Management verwendet werden.

HÄUFIGE BARRIEREN BEI DER SOCIAL-INTRANET-EINFÜHRUNG

Bevor man sich auf ein Projekt einlässt, das so grundlegend in das Unternehmen eingreift, ist es gut, die „Risiken und Nebenwirkungen" im Blick zu haben. Aus den Erfahrungen vieler Workshops mit Führungskräften und Mitarbeitern haben wir jene Schwierigkeiten aufgelistet, die am häufigsten zur Sprache kommen und denen vermutlich auch Sie im Projekt immer wieder begegnen werden. Solche Barrieren sollten Intranet-Projektteams immer im Blick behalten, regelmäßig auswerten und bei Bedarf gegensteuern. Gerade die Multiplikatoren haben dabei für das Projektteam eine wertvolle seismografische Funktion.

BARRIEREN BEI DEN MITARBEITERN

Häufige Barrieren **vor** der Einführung sind:

- Mitarbeiter können sich nicht vorstellen, was Social Intranet für sie bedeutet. Sie sind verunsichert und lehnen Veränderungen erst einmal pauschal ab.
- Mitarbeiter verstehen nicht, was mit dem neuen Intranet bezweckt wird. Aus Unverständnis entstehen handfeste Befürchtungen (z.B. Personaleinsparung).
- Mitarbeiter fühlen sich nicht mitgenommen. Sie haben das Gefühl, dass ihnen das Intranet übergestülpt wird.
- Mitarbeiter setzen Transparenz mit Kontrolle gleich. Sie befürchten, für ihre Chefs „gläsern" zu werden.
- Mitarbeiter trauen dem Intranet nicht zu, die Probleme ihres Arbeitsalltags zu lösen. Sie verstehen die Vorteile nicht gegenüber dem alten System („Warum brauche ich das Intranet, wenn ich meine Dokumente auch auf dem Server ablegen kann?").

Nach der Einführung erlebt man bei Mitarbeitern häufig folgende Barrieren:

- Mitarbeiter nutzen das Intranet nicht, weil die alten Systeme noch existieren (z.B. Laufwerke, Datenbanken, Dokumentenablage, Formulare).
- Mitarbeitern fällt die Bedienung der Intranet-Werkzeuge schwer, weil sie keine Erfahrungen mit Social Media haben.
- Mitarbeiter können das Wissen aus den Schulungen nicht anwenden, weil die Neuerungen zu technisch vermittelt wurden und die Verbindung zu den alltäglichen Arbeitsvorgängen nicht verstanden ist.
- Mitarbeiter befürchten Status-Einbußen, wenn sie ihr Wissen offen weitergeben. Weil die alte Unternehmenskultur nicht zu den neuen Arbeitsweisen passt, bleiben viele wertvolle Potenziale des Intranets ungenutzt.

BARRIEREN BEI DEN INTRANET-VERANTWORTLICHEN

Typische Barrieren, die aus der **Planungsphase** resultieren, sind:

- Die Ziele der Intranet-Einführung und die Strategie der Geschäftsführung sind nicht klar. Dadurch fehlt es an Orientierung und Akzeptanz des Projekts.
- Die Kostenkalkulation endet bei der technischen Bereitstellung. Für eine sorgfältige Einführung mit Training, Kommunikationsmaßnahmen, Support und Pflege reicht das Budget nicht mehr.
- Es wird eine zu komplizierte, riesige Plattform geplant und zu viel auf einmal gewollt. Die zeitlichen Ziele werden nicht eingehalten und das Projekt wird nie fertig.

- Verantwortliche wissen nicht, wie sie im Unternehmen mit dem Intranet-Projekt starten sollen. Sie sind von der Flut an Ratschlägen überfordert und haben keine professionelle externe Unterstützung an ihrer Seite.
- Es wird zu wenig Zeit für die Einführung eingeplant. Dadurch entstehen viele Mängel und Probleme. Die Akzeptanz bei den Nutzern sinkt rapide.
- Es fehlt an einer Einführungsstrategie, die auch die Motivation der Benutzer anregt. Barrieren auf Seiten der Mitarbeiter werden nicht erkannt und behoben. Das Intranet startet als Totgeburt.

Häufige Barrieren, die mit der **Projektsteuerung** zusammenhängen, sind:

- Die Rollen und Verantwortlichkeiten für das Projekt sind nicht geklärt. Es entstehen viele Missverständnisse, ein großer Kommunikationsbedarf tut sich auf. Der Frust bei den Beteiligten steigt.
- Das Projektteam ist zu groß oder besteht aus ungeeigneten Mitgliedern. Dadurch nimmt das Projekt nur langsam Fahrt auf und sorgt nicht für genügend Aufmerksamkeit beim Management.
- Es fehlt an einer stringenten Koordination der beteiligten Personengruppen, wie beispielsweise IT-Mitarbeitern, den Angehörigen der Kommunikations- und Personalabteilung, Führungskräften, Designern und Fachabteilungen. Missverständnisse, Konflikte und Fehler entstehen und wertvolle Ressourcen werden dabei verschwendet.
- Der Betriebsrat wird nicht ausreichend informiert. Unter den Beschäftigten regt sich Widerstand gegen das Projekt.

BARRIEREN BEI DEN IT-VERANTWORT-LICHEN

Bei den IT-Verantwortlichen sind **vor** Einführung des Social Intranets folgende Barrieren regelmäßig anzutreffen:

- Das Social-Intranet-Projekt wird als reines IT-Projekt verstanden. Dadurch mangelt es an Akzeptanz bei Führungskräften und Mitarbeitern.
- Das Projekt hat keinen Bezug zu den Unternehmenszielen. Dadurch stößt es bei den Führungskräften auf wenig Interesse. Das Budget fällt entsprechend klein aus.
- Die Unternehmensprozesse sind nicht so bekannt, dass sie im Intranet abgebildet werden können.
- Die Benutzer werden nicht oder zu spät in die Konzeption der Intranet-Architektur und des Intranet-Designs eingebunden. Sehr viele Akzeptanzprobleme entstehen durch den Eindruck mangelhafter Nutzerergonomie. Wenn die Inhalte als wenig wertvoll erachtet werden, ist die Skepsis naturgemäß groß.
- Die Mitarbeiter der IT-Abteilung befürchten, dass sie mit einem modernen Intranet ihren eigenen Arbeitsplatz wegrationalisieren. Es entstehen Widerstände und Blockade-Haltungen, gerade bei Cloud-Lösungen.
- Die IT-Abteilung ist über die neuesten technischen Möglichkeiten im Bereich der Datensicherheit nur unzureichend informiert. Sie kann daher den aufkommenden Sorgen vor Sicherheitslücken im Unternehmen nicht professionell begegnen.
- Es fehlt ein gemeinsames Verständnis für die zukünftige Struktur des Portals. Dadurch werden Inhalte unsystematisch eingeordnet und die Nutzerfreundlichkeit geht zurück.

Nach Einführung des Social Intranets beobachtet man häufig folgende Barrieren auf Seiten des IT-Ressorts:

- Das Intranet überzeugt nicht als Problemlöser, weil aktuelle Probleme im Unternehmen nicht berücksichtigt wurden. Das Intranet wird daher als Zusatzaufwand gesehen und von den Mitarbeitern abgelehnt.

- Es gibt Mängel bei der Gestaltung des Mitarbeiterportals: Es ist unstrukturiert, die Navigation kompliziert und unverständlich, das Design nicht ansprechend.

- Interaktions- und Dialoginstrumente, mit denen sich die Mitarbeiter aktiv am Informationsaustausch beteiligen können, fehlen.

- Die Funktionsweise des Programms ist nicht in die Arbeitsroutine der Benutzer integriert. Alte Gewohnheiten bleiben erhalten und der Überblick bei der Arbeit wird durch das Intranet nicht vereinfacht, sondern verkompliziert.

- Es fehlt ein Support für die kleinen Probleme der Nutzer. Einfache Hilfefunktionen, um Probleme selbst zu lösen, sollte es geben. Andernfalls verlieren die Mitarbeiter das Interesse und die Aktivität im Social Intranet flaut ab.

- Die Rollenverteilung wird so angelegt, dass Intranet-Inhalte nur durch einige wenige Personen zentral eingestellt werden können. Dadurch entsteht ein künstlicher Flaschenhals mit Verzögerungen. Die mangelnde Aktualität lässt die Mitarbeiter wieder auf alte Informationskanäle zurückgreifen.

BARRIEREN BEI DEN FÜHRUNGS-KRÄFTEN

Folgende Barrieren treten bei Führungskräften oft **vor** der Einführung des Social Intranets auf:

- Die Intranet-Einführung wird als Technik-Projekt missverstanden und der Nutzen für die Fachabteilungen und die Standorte wird nicht erkannt. Das Projekt wird daher

nicht zur Chefsache erklärt, von Budgets ganz zu schweigen.

- Es gibt schlechte Vorerfahrungen mit Vorgängerversionen, so dass eine skeptische bis ablehnende Haltung vorherrscht.

- Das neue Intranet wird top-down verordnet, ohne dass den Führungskräften die organisationale Tragweite bewusst ist. Die neue Technologie wird eingeführt, ohne dass sich die Arbeitsweisen, die Organisation und Kultur verändern. Ein Investitionsgrab entsteht.

- Der Zusammenhang zur Unternehmensstrategie und zum Leitbild ist nicht klar. Damit geht dem Projekt bereits nach den ersten Einführungsschwierigkeiten die Luft aus.

- Es gibt zu wenige Befürworter unter den Führungskräften. Alte Arbeitsweisen bleiben parallel erhalten, das Neue setzt sich nicht durch.

Folgende Barrieren entwickeln sich **während** der Einführung schnell zur Gefährdung für das gesamte Social Intranet:

- Die Führungskräfte nutzen selbst nicht das Intranet und kommunizieren weiter auf die gewohnte Weise.

- Die Führungskräfte motivieren nicht zur Nutzung des Intranets.

- Die Führungskräfte äußern sich abwertend zum Intranet.

- Die Führungskräfte zeigen deutliches Missfallen, sobald ihre Mitarbeiter in ihrer Arbeitszeit den Newsfeed lesen oder in Wikis schreiben, anstatt ihre Aufgaben zu erledigen.

- Die Führungskräfte nutzen die Transparenz des Intranets, um ihre Mitarbeiter zu kontrollieren.

- Die Führungskräfte greifen nicht ein, wenn andere sich destruktiv im Intranet verhalten.

- Mitten im Projekt werden die Gelder gekürzt, zuerst meist bei allen „weichen Faktoren" wie Training, Change Management und Kommunikation.

Wenn zu viele dieser Barrieren auf Seiten der Führungskräfte auftreten und nicht beseitigt werden können, hat das Social Intranet nur geringe Chancen, das Arbeiten in Ihrer Organisation dauerhaft produktiver, ideenreicher und moderner zu machen. Die aktive Unterstützung durch die Führungskräfte ist das A und O für ein Gelingen.

Eine Chancen-Risiko-Analyse in der Form von Tabelle 1.7.1 hilft, die Barrieren und Lösungswege in Ihrem Social-Intranet-Projekt strukturiert zu erfassen und im Auge zu behalten. Sie ist ein wichtiges Arbeitsinstrument und sollte im gesamten Projektverlauf regelmäßig aktualisiert werden.

Barrieren	Lösungsansätze
Die Geschäftsleitung hat kein Interesse an Social Tools und Mehrwegkommunikation.	• detaillierte Stakeholder-Analyse durchführen • gezielt Unterstützer gewinnen • Projekt sichtbar in Einklang mit den Zielen der Geschäftsführung bringen • ökonomischen Nutzen sichtbar machen
Die interne Kommunikation ist nicht offen, es herrscht „Sonnenschein"-Kommunikation.	• Führungskräfte als Unterstützer und Vorbilder gewinnen • Diskussion über die gewünschte Kommunikationskultur im Führungskreis herbeiführen • Bewusstsein bei Nutzern schaffen: Wann sind Informationen für mich wertvoll? Wie muss ich also Inhalte erstellen, damit sie auch für andere wertvoll sind? • Schulungen für werthaltige Inhalte anbieten • Pilotprojekte durchführen mit integriertem Coaching
Erste Versuche, Wikis einzuführen, sind gescheitert.	• Interviews, um die Gründe für das Scheitern zu ermitteln • Teams finden, in denen die Wikis gut funktioniert haben, diese Teams aktivieren und Erfolgsprinzipien herausfinden • Diese Teams als Mentoren für andere Abteilungen nutzen • Erfolgsprinzipien auf alle Teams übertragen • Features finden, die einen Nutzen bringen

Tabelle 1.7.1: Erfassung von Barrieren und Lösungsansätzen bei der Social-Intranet-Einführung

Meist trage ich High Heels. Deshalb muss ich Stolpersteine in Intranet-Projekten rechtzeitig erkennen. Genauso wichtig ist es, Ausschau zu halten nach Themen, die positiv auf das Intranet-Projekt einzahlen können. Das wären z.B.:

- Wichtige Vorgänge werden über das Intranet besonders vorangebracht: Start des Intranets mit der Betriebsratswahl.
- Auf beliebte Themen der Meinungsmacher wird besonders geachtet: Business Intelligence und Mobilität.
- Besonders beliebte Mitarbeiterprogramme erhalten einen Platz: Anmeldung für geförderte Gesundheitssportgruppen.
- Workflows mit Leidensdruck werden spürbar verbessert: Reisekostenabrechnungen im Intranet noch vor dem eigentlichen Rollout.
- Wichtige Treiber werden für das Projekt gewonnen: Drei Abteilungsleiter schreiben den Blog „Die drei Fragezeichen".

1.8 AUF NEUN PUNKTE GEBRACHT

1 Ein Social-Intranet-Projekt ist mehr als ein IT-Projekt. Sie führen damit neue Formen der Zusammenarbeit und Kommunikation ein, die Ihr Unternehmen verändern und weiterbringen können. Auch wenn Sie glauben, Ihre Organisation wäre noch nicht bereit dafür – haben Sie den Mut, für die Veränderung hin zu modernen dialogorientierten Arbeitsweisen einzutreten und sich mit Ihrem Intranet-Projekt dieser Herausforderung zu stellen.

2 Es gibt viele Möglichkeiten, modern zu arbeiten. Lassen Sie sich inspirieren und nutzen Sie die Erfahrungen anderer Projektteams. Holen Sie sich auch Unterstützung von (externen) Experten, die bereits Erfahrungen mit Intranet-Projekten haben.

3 Ein Social-Intranet-Projekt bietet echte Chancen für eine Erneuerung Ihres Unternehmens. Eine Vision, die begeistert, findet immer ihre Anhänger. Denken Sie groß und mindestens drei Jahre voraus, auch wenn Sie später in kleinen Schritten voranschreiten.

4 Attraktive Ziele geben die Marschrichtung vor und sind wichtige Orientierungspunkte im Projektverlauf. Setzen Sie sich die Ziele realistisch und langfristig, vergessen Sie dabei nicht den angestrebten Nutzen für das Unternehmen und planen Sie ausreichend Zeit für die Einführung des Intranets ein.

5 Niemand ändert gern lieb gewordene Gewohnheiten. Arbeiten Sie deshalb den Mehrwert der neuen Plattform für das Unternehmen und die Mitarbeiter gezielt heraus.

6 Entscheiden Sie mit Sorgfalt, wenn es um das Projektteam, die Ziele, die Ressourcen und die Suche nach Unterstützern geht. Mit dem Projekt kommen Sie dann sehr viel leichter voran. Investieren Sie jetzt in ein sorgfältig aufgesetztes Projekt und entwickeln Sie es mit der modernen Technologie weiter.

7 Die Einführung einer modernen Arbeitsplattform ist Chefsache. Holen Sie Führungskräfte an Bord, die später die neuen Arbeitsweisen vorleben und auch mal klare Ansagen machen können. Sprechen Sie in dieser Phase vor allem mit Treibern, Fans sowie wichtigen Meinungsmachern und vergessen Sie den Betriebs- oder Personalrat nicht.

8 Es ist wichtig, die „Risiken und Nebenwirkungen" zu kennen. Erfassen Sie systematisch und kontinuierlich die Barrieren in Ihrem Social-Intranet-Projekt und treffen Sie geeignete Gegenmaßnahmen.

9 Erfolge motivieren und wecken Aufmerksamkeit. Machen Sie sich Ihre Fortschritte regelmäßig bewusst und kommunizieren Sie von Anfang an Zwischenerfolge.

1 TRÄUME   2 ANALYSIERE   3 PLANE   4 BAUE   5 ERPROBE   6 NUTZE

ANALYSIERE

Nachdem in der ersten Phase das Projekt aufgesetzt wurde, geht es nun in die Analysephase. Welchen Bedarf haben Unternehmen und Nutzer? Was konkret möchten Anwender in ihrem neuen Intranet vorfinden? Welche Workflows und Prozesse sollen im Intranet abgebildet werden? Die Mitarbeiter als zukünftige Nutzer werden spätestens in der Analysephase ins Boot geholt und mit ihren Ansprüchen an das Intranet erfasst. Erste Lösungsansätze werden aufgezeigt.

Wenn durch den Analyseprozess ein Überblick über zukünftige Anforderungen an die Arbeit im Social Intranet geschaffen wurde und alle bis zu diesem Zeitpunkt ermittelten Anwendungsszenarien systematisiert vorliegen, ist die zweite Phase beendet. Die Ergebnisse dieser Phase bilden die Basis für eine fundierte Entscheidung zur finalen Technologie und zur Art des zukünftigen Betriebs der Plattform in Phase 3.

ANALYSE DER
AUSGANGSSITUATION

Egal, ob Unternehmen Intranet-Neulinge sind oder bereits über eine Intranet-Landschaft verfügen: Eine sorgfältige Bestandsaufnahme zu bisher eingesetzten Instrumenten und den damit verbundenen Erfahrungen und Gewohnheiten bildet eine wichtige Grundlage, um den Prozess zur erfolgreichen Einführung von Social Intranets richtig zu gestalten. Eine erste Bestandsaufnahme sorgt für ein klares Bild zur Ausgangssituation des Projekts. Dabei wird in viele Richtungen geschaut:

1. Vorhandene IT-Landschaft

Die meisten Unternehmen verfügen über eine gewachsene IT-Landschaft prozessunterstützender Anwendungen. Das Feedback von Nutzern deutet jedoch darauf hin, dass die unterschiedlichen Unternehmensanwendungen häufig nicht integriert sind und die Nutzung sehr unbefriedigend ist. Ein Intranet-Projekt kann dann entweder Ergebnis oder Anlass für das Aufstellen einer IT-Roadmap für die nächsten drei Jahre sein. Dabei werden Business-Anforderungen und die neuen Möglichkeiten der IT in Übereinstimmung gebracht. Welche Software-Lösungen werden übernommen, welche bestehenden Systeme werden in die neue Plattform eingebunden oder welche Parallelsysteme können abgeschaltet werden? So trägt ein Intranet-Projekt zu einer Konsolidierung der IT-Landschaft bei.

2. Bestehendes Intranet

Intranets sind vor allem in größeren Unternehmen bereits verbreitet. Die Nutzung erster Social Features ist jedoch verschieden ausge-

prägt. Bereitgestellte Tools wie Wikis, Blogs und Teamräume sind mehr oder weniger erfolgreich in einzelnen Unternehmensbereichen etabliert, in anderen dagegen haben sie noch gar keinen Einzug gehalten.

Statistiken geben einen Überblick über die Nutzung einzelner Intranet-Bereiche, vor allem jene, die mangels Aufrufen grundlegend erneuert oder abgeschaltet werden sollten. Ein kritischer Blick auf die Inhalte zeigt, was wirklich übernommen wird und welcher Ballast neuen frischen Inhalten weichen sollte.

3. Analyse der Unternehmenskultur

Ausgeprägte Hierarchien, Mängel in der Kommunikation und eine nachteilige Feedbackkultur behindern die Einführung moderner Social-Plattformen. Ein besonderes Augenmerk sollte deshalb der Analyse der Unternehmenskultur gelten. Mehr dazu im Abschnitt 2.2.

4. Stand der Kommunikation

Wie ist der momentane der Stand der Kommunikation, welche Kommunikationswege werden bisher genutzt und wo können die Mitarbeiter der Kommunikationsflut nicht mehr Herr werden? Das entstandene Bild zeigt schnell, wo neue Tools erforderlich sind und welche Medien (wie z.B. der einmal monatlich erscheinende Mitarbeiter-Newsletter) besser auf der neuen Plattform verortet werden sollten.

5. Erfahrungen mit bisherigen Projekten

Auch die Rekapitulation bisheriger Einführungsprojekte mitsamt der darin vorgesehenen

Ziele und Vorgehensschritte liefert hilfreiche Informationen. Im Rückblick ist zu verstehen, welche der Schritte wertvoll waren und nachahmenswert sind. Welche Dinge wurden versäumt oder nicht gut genug umgesetzt und haben damit den Projekterfolg gemindert?

6. Identifizieren von Bedürfnissen und Schmerzpunkten der Nutzer

Wie arbeiten die Mitarbeiter heute? Welche Anforderungen an die Arbeitsunterstützung haben die Intranet-Nutzer? Welche Workflows gilt es zu verbessern, was kann mit Hilfe des Intranets effizienter bearbeitet werden? Welche neuen Features wünschen sich die Nutzer? Bei der Zusammenarbeit werden oft Datensilos und Abteilungsdenken als Hemmnisse genannt und

bedürfen neuer Lösungen. Wir stellen Nutzer in das Zentrum eines Intranet-Prozesses und widmen ihnen deshalb den separaten Abschnitt 2.3. Im Ergebnis dieser Bestandsaufnahme gewinnen Sie einen guten Überblick über bestehende Anwendungen und deren Nutzung, ebenso wie über die konkreten Bedürfnisse und Befürchtungen der Nutzer. Das bildet vor allem die Basis für

- eine sorgfältige Planung und Beschreibung der Anwendungsszenarien (siehe 2.4),
- eine strategisch durchdachte Technologieentscheidung (siehe 2.5),
- die Migrationsplanung (siehe 3.9),
- die zu planende Kommunikations- und Einführungsbegleitung (3.11) sowie
- eine erste Roadmap.

ANALYSE DER 2.2
UNTERNEHMENSKULTUR
UND KOMPETENZEN

Die gelebte Unternehmenskultur ist ein entscheidender Dreh- und Angelpunkt, um festzustellen, ob ein Unternehmen wirklich die Chance hat, „social" zu werden. Ein Enterprise 2.0 verändert den Firmenalltag, es führt in vielerlei Hinsicht zu Wandlungsprozessen in traditionell geführten Unternehmen.

Es muss nicht schon bei Einführung eines Social Intranets eine ausgereifte 2.0-Kultur vorhanden sein, aber es sollte eine Perspektive da sein, dass diese Kultur entwickelt werden kann. Der „Regler" in Abbildung 2.2.1 sollte also in den einzelnen Dimensionen nicht ausschließlich auf Enterprise 1.0 stehen, sondern es sollte Teams und Führungskräfte im Unternehmen geben, bei denen schon Ansätze der Kultur 2.0 erkennbar sind. Sonst entstehen später in der Einführung unangenehme Überraschungen. Alles steht und fällt hierbei natürlich mit der Geschäftsleitung, die in der Zukunft das neue Arbeiten und die neue Kultur nicht nur einfordern, sondern auch vorleben sollte.

Eine Kulturanalyse kann sehr hilfreich sein, um genau zu ermitteln, wo sich die Abteilungen zwischen den oben dargestellten Dimensionen verorten lassen. Hierfür können Sie sowohl schriftliche Befragungen als auch Interviews

Abbildung 2.2.1: Unterschiede in Bezug auf Arbeiten und Führung zwischen einem traditionellen Unternehmen und einem Enterprise 2.0

oder Team-Workshops nutzen (Tabelle 2.2.1). Wenn in Ihrem Unternehmen bereits regelmäßig Mitarbeiterbefragungen stattfinden, liefern auch sie hilfreiche Hinweise für die Kulturanalyse.

Vorteile schriftlicher Befragungen	Vorteile persönlicher Interviews oder Workshops
• Geringerer Umsetzungs- und Auswertungsaufwand • Höhere Abdeckung des Unternehmens bei überschaubarem Aufwand • Guter allgemeiner Überblick • Leichtere Messbarkeit und Möglichkeit, die Messergebnisse für das Management aufzuarbeiten	• Höherer Informationsgehalt „zwischen den Zeilen" • Mehr Beispiele, die man gegenüber dem Management zitieren kann • Möglichkeit, die Teilnehmer persönlich dafür zu sensibilisieren, dass sich auf dem Weg zum Social Business auch die Kultur verändern muss

Tabelle 2.2.1: Vorzüge schriftlicher und persönlicher Befragungen zur Kulturanalyse

Die persönliche Ansprache durch Interviews oder Workshops ist zwar wesentlich zeitaufwendiger, liefert aber einen unvergleichlich höheren Informationsgehalt, sodass Sie darauf nicht verzichten sollten. Wenn es sich anbietet, können Sie auch beide Ansätze kombinieren, indem Sie sich über eine schriftliche Befragung einen guten Gesamtüberblick verschaffen und dann durch persönliche Interviews bestimmte Ergebnisse vertiefend analysieren.

Wenn Sie die Chance haben, persönlich mit Mitarbeitern zu sprechen, dann nutzen Sie sie, um den entscheidenden Aspekten wirklich auf den Grund zu gehen. Dafür kann Ihnen die Critical-Incidents-Technik helfen. Die Grundidee besteht darin, genau herauszufinden, welche Verhaltensweisen für eine effektive Kommunikation und Zusammenarbeit besonders wichtig sind. Erfragen Sie bei Ihren Interviewpartnern konkrete Ereignisse aus der Vergangenheit, aus denen sich „Erfolgsfaktoren" ableiten lassen. Sammeln Sie in den für den Unternehmenserfolg wichtigsten Bereichen Erfahrungen mit besonders kritischen Momenten, die ein Projekt zum Scheitern brachten. Mit dieser Art der Kulturanalyse finden Sie genau heraus, wo Sie ansetzen müssen, um eine Kulturveränderung anzustoßen. Die Social-Intranet-Anwendungsfälle entwickeln Sie auf diese Weise genau an den kritischen Stellen der Zusammenarbeit, also an Reibungspunkten und Störstellen, deren

Behebung sich positiv auf das weitere Vorgehen auswirken wird. Scheiterten beispielsweise frühere Versuche der bereichsübergreifenden Zusammenarbeit daran, dass kein transparenter Informationsfluss vorhanden war und dadurch auch kein Vertrauen entstand, so sollte dieses Thema später bei der Einführung des Social Intranets besondere Berücksichtigung finden.

Im Ergebnis der Kulturanalyse sollten zu folgenden Fragen verlässliche Aussagen stehen:

☑ **Checkliste: Sechs Fragen für den Einstieg in eine Kulturanalyse**

1. Welcher Art ist die aktuelle Kultur? Wo lässt sie sich im Kontinuum zwischen Enterprise 1.0 und Enterprise 2.0 einordnen? (Siehe Abbildung 2.2.1)

2. Welche Elemente einer 2.0-Kultur sind im Unternehmen (bei den Führungskräften / in den Teams / bei den Mitarbeitern) bereits gut ausgeprägt? Wo besteht der größte Nachholbedarf?

3. Wie wird das Management / die Führung von den Mitarbeitern wahrgenommen?

4. Wie werden die Mitarbeiter vom Management wahrgenommen?

5. Wie sind die Web-2.0-Medienkompetenzen im Unternehmen ausgeprägt (u.a. Informationen finden, Informationen managen, effektiv kommunizieren, Inhalte erstellen, Inhalte und Personen vernetzen)?

6. Welche Teams haben kulturell bereits einen Vorsprung, sodass sie sich als Pilotteam besonders eignen?

Die Ergebnisse der Analyse sollten nun dem Management vorgestellt und ausführlich diskutiert werden. Dabei ist wichtig, die Diskrepanz zwischen Ist und Soll genau aufzuzeigen und mit Beispielen zu belegen, damit die Führungskräfte eine bessere Vorstellung vom Veränderungsbedarf in ihrem Unternehmen und in ihrer Führungskultur bekommen. Denn wenn Mitarbeiter sich frei im Intranet bewegen sollen, dann brauchen sie die Führungskräfte als Vorbilder. Ohne Bewegung in den Köpfen und im Verhalten wird im Unternehmen kein Wandel zum Enterprise 2.0 erfolgen. Oder anders ausgedrückt: Leitbilder sollten zukünftig nicht nur offline, sondern auch online authentisch gelebt werden.

Ja, liebe Führungskräfte, ich wette: Wörter wie "Kulturwandel" oder „Change Management" stehen auf Ihrer Schwarzen Liste ganz, ganz weit oben. Ich kann Sie verstehen. Sie haben das schon öfter erlebt oder anders gesagt: Schon so „manche Sau wurde durch´s Dorf getrieben". Viel Trara – leider oft für nichts.

Nun, ich bin keine Change Managerin, sondern Umsetzungsbegleiterin. Jetzt, wo wir so ein schickes Intranet einführen, will ich Sie keinesfalls vergraulen, rufe kein neues Change-Projekt aus und hänge die Sache auch gar nicht erst an die große Glocke. Ich gehe lieber subtil vor und lasse die Themen ganz von selbst in Workshops aufkommen. Zugegeben, ein paar richtig gute Fragen stelle ich auch, und sicher rütteln wir dann auch ein wenig an bestehenden Kulturproblemen und sprechen notwendige Veränderungsmaßnahmen an. Aber keine Sorge: Wir packen die Themen zusammen in kleine, machbare Maßnahmenpakete und ich lasse Sie damit nicht allein.

Kommen die neuen Kommunikationstools erst einmal zum Einsatz, stehe ich Ihnen gern weiter zur Seite. Führungskräfte bekommen bei mir immer ein eigenes Pilotprojekt, in dem sie im „geschützten Raum" die Tools ausprobieren und ein paar Tricks kennenlernen. Auch zu wichtigen kulturellen Aspekten im Zusammenhang mit der Führung vernetzter Teams. Dann sprechen wir beispielsweise darüber, wie es sich anfühlt, wenn ich eine Frage stelle und niemand antwortet. Oder wie motivierend es ist, wenn ich ein „Like" für mein Arbeitsergebnis oder eine Nachfrage bekomme.

2.3 NUTZER IN DIE ANFORDERUNGSANALYSE EINBEZIEHEN

Wenn man Nutzer schon frühzeitig in das Intranet-Projekt einbindet, hat das zwei entscheidende Vorteile. Zum einen kann man die Anforderungen an eine neue Plattform viel genauer erfassen und damit den Erwartungen der Anspruchsgruppen treffsicherer begegnen. Zum anderen sind Mitarbeiter und Führungskräfte, die frühzeitig mitgestalten können, offener, die späteren Veränderungen auch im eigenen Arbeitsumfeld umzusetzen. Dabei werden die Anforderungen und Szenarien mit Blick auf die Zukunft erhoben, denn die Technologieentscheidung fällt mindestens für die nächsten drei Jahre.

Für alle Zielgruppen bei der Anforderungsanalyse gilt: Der Weg ist das Ziel. Nur wer verstanden hat, welche modernen Formen der Kommunikation und Zusammenarbeit es gibt, und wer richtig einschätzen kann, welchen Nutzen sie schaffen, ist in der Lage, neue Lösungen zu erarbeiten. Dafür eignen sich Impulsvorträge, inspirierende Beispiele aus anderen Unternehmen oder erstes Ausprobieren für besonders Engagierte.

Verantwortliche befürchten oft, dass das Einbeziehen der künftigen Nutzer in den Intranet-Entwicklungsprozess den Zeitplan aus dem Ruder bringt und unnötige Abstimmungen und Gegenwehr erzeugt. Wir haben damit jedoch beste Erfahrungen gesammelt. Es braucht Zeit, das Neue am Arbeiten 2.0 zu verstehen und sich nach und nach darauf einzulassen. Deshalb sind Inspiration und das Einbeziehen der Nutzer kein Umweg, sondern sinnvolle Prozesse während der notwendigen Reifezeit. Den Mehrwert von „Social" kann man versuchen zu erklären, viel wirkungsvoller ist es jedoch, wenn das neue Arbeiten 2.0 erlebt wird. Dafür eignen sich Probierwerkstätten und andere kreative Formate, die mit Gamification-Elementen Lust darauf machen, sich noch stärker mit dem Thema auseinanderzusetzen. Erfahrungen zeigen, dass die größten Gegner von Social diejenigen sind, die auch privat noch nie soziale Plattformen wie XING, Facebook, What's App oder Dropbox getestet haben.

Da meist auch für das Projektteam die modernsten Formen der Kommunikation und Zusammenarbeit neu sind, ist das Einschalten von externen Beratern zu empfehlen. Gerade wenn es um Überzeugungsarbeit bei Führungskräften oder dem Betriebs- oder Personalrat geht, haben sie erprobte Beispiele, Argumente und Methoden parat.

Die Beteiligung der Nutzer bei der Anforderungsanalyse sollte möglichst direkt und persönlich erfolgen. Workshops, World-Cafés und Interviews machen das Thema begreifbarer und zeigen dem Projektteam sehr gut, wo das Unternehmen aktuell steht und welche Gestaltungsfelder zu bewältigen sind. Online-Befragungen und Umfragen müssen schon wirklich qualitativ sehr hochwertig und motivierend sein, damit die Nutzer daran teilnehmen und zufriedenstellende Ergebnisse liefern. Meistens erfordern sie einen großen Aufwand für das Projektteam, ohne dass sie wirklich neue Ideen mit sich bringen, da die Teilnehmer zu wenig Einblick in die neuen Möglichkeiten haben und bei ihren Vorschlägen vom alten System ausgehen.

Nutzerfeedback einholen

Aus Befragungen und Interviews lassen sich häufig wesentlich mehr Erkenntnisse über die alltäglichen Herausforderungen der Mitarbeiter ziehen, als man gemeinhin vermutet. Ein etabliertes Verfahren zur systematischen Datenanalyse ist beispielsweise der Grounded-Theory-Ansatz. Nach den Worten seiner Begründer handelt es sich dabei um „keine Theorie, sondern eine Praktik, um die in den Daten schlummernde Theorie zu entdecken [...] [und] analytisch über soziale Phänomene nachzudenken" (Legewie & Schervier-Legewie, 1995).

Zunächst analysiert der Anwender dabei die vorliegenden Daten durch theoretisches Kodieren. Sodann werden aus den erfragten Daten sinnhafte Kategorien gebildet. Damit wird sichergestellt, dass

1. die analysierten Daten strukturiert werden (z.B. nach „Schmerzpunkten von Mitarbeitern im Rahmen der Informationsgewinnung" und „Schnittstellen einer Job-Rolle zu anderen Rollen");

2. die gefundenen Kategorien zueinander in Beziehung gebracht werden (z.B. „Schmerzpunkte treten häufig rollenübergreifend auf") sowie

3. die zentrale Kategorie ermittelt wird, siehe z.B. „Vermittlung des Nutzens von Enterprise Social Networks für Mitarbeiter" (Aycin, 2012).

Ein weiterer wesentlicher Bestandteil der Grounded Theory ist das theoretische Sampling. Die Daten werden unmittelbar nach der Datenerhebung ausgewertet und für weitere Befragungen berücksichtigt. Sobald durch eine zusätzliche Datenerhebung keine neuen Erkenntnisse mehr zu vermuten sind (die sog. theoretische Sättigung), wird die Befragung abgeschlossen.

Bei der Microsoft Deutschland GmbH wurde die Grounded Theory angewendet, um Anwendungsfälle für Yammer im Großkundenvertrieb für Banken und Versicherungen zu ermitteln.

Dieser Abschnitt entstand in Zusammenarbeit mit Sebastian Klenk, Technical Evangelist Microsoft Deutschland GmbH

Dieser Abschnitt entstand in Zusammenarbeit mit Alexander Strahled, Geschäftsbereichsleiter Banken und Versicherungen Microsoft Deutschland GmbH

Qualitative Befragung zur Beschreibung von Anwendungsfällen für die Einführung von Yammer im Großkundenvertrieb für Banken und Versicherungen bei Microsoft Deutschland

In einem verteilten Vertriebsteam der Microsoft Deutschland GmbH wurde die Nutzung des Business-Netzwerkes Yammer im Vertriebsalltag untersucht. Die Analyse sollte dabei helfen, Anwendungsfälle herauszuarbeiten und deren Verbreitung im Unternehmen gezielt zu unterstützen.

Die erforderlichen Informationen wurden durch eine zweistufige qualitative Befragung erhoben. In einem ersten Arbeitsgang lieferten Interviews mit dem Vertriebsteam – also den unmittelbaren Benutzern des sozialen Unternehmensnetzwerkes – hilfreiche Erkenntnisse über Schmerzpunkte der Kollegen im Rahmen ihrer Vertriebstätigkeiten. Dabei wurden insbesondere die rollenspezifischen Herausforderungen und die individuellen Erfahrungen mit sozialen Netzwerken im privaten und beruflichen Umfeld ermittelt. In der zweiten Stufe fanden Experten-Interviews statt, um die Erkenntnisse aus den Mitarbeiter-Interviews besser einschätzen zu können. Dabei konnte gezielt die Meinung erfahrener Experten zur Einführung und Nutzung von Enterprise Social Networks im Unternehmen eingeholt werden.

Für beide Zielgruppen wurde ein separater Leitfaden für ein einstündiges Interview ausgearbeitet. Die Auswahl der Interview-Partner bei den Experten erfolgte über Empfehlungen aus dem Kollegenkreis, über eigens geknüpfte Kontakte zu internen und externen Fachleuten, über Partner aus dem Microsoft-Partnernetzwerk sowie über Kunden. Auf diese Weise konnten unterschiedlichste Erfahrungen und Sichtweisen in die Datenerhebung einfließen.

Auf Grund der dezentralen Aufstellung des Vertriebsteams wurden die meisten Interviews als Videokonferenz mit Microsoft Lync durchgeführt. Die Interview-Leitfäden wurden während des Gesprächs mit handschriftlichen Notizen und Querverweisen versehen (u.a. mit digitaler Handschrifteingabe unter Verwendung von Microsoft OneNote). Die Analyse der Daten aus den Befragungen erfolgte mittels Grounded Theory.

Aus den gewonnenen Erkenntnissen wurden in Workshops mit ausgewählten Vertriebsmitarbeitern Anwendungsfälle (engl. Use Cases) entwickelt, die anschließend in einer teaminternen Umfrage priorisiert wurden. Beispielsweise wird Yammer im Großkundenvertriebsteam für Banken und Versicherungen bei Microsoft Deutschland dazu eingesetzt, Best Practices innerhalb des Vertriebsteams zu teilen. Die Beschäftigten werden dadurch auf besonders erfolgreiche Aktivitäten von Kollegen aufmerksam gemacht und können sie innerhalb des Yammer-Netzwerkes diskutieren und für ihre eigene Rolle adaptieren. Die Diskussionen stehen darüber hinaus auch teamübergreifend allen weiteren Microsoft-Mitarbeitern innerhalb des weltweiten Yammer-Netzwerkes zur Verfügung. Ein weiterer Anwendungsfall ist das Teilen und die anschließende Diskussion aktueller Nachrichten zu Kunden aus der Banken- und Versicherungsbranche.

Für die ausgewählten Use Cases wurden schließlich Pilotprojekte gestartet. Dort erhielt jeder Mitarbeiter ein Gefühl für Yammer in der Praxis, sodass er unmittelbar die Vorteile für sich kennenlernen konnte. Beispiele dafür sind etwa die erleichterte Expertensuche oder das Finden und Verstehen von Diskussionen aus der Vergangenheit. Hiervon profitierten vor allem neue Mitarbeiter, die keinen Einblick in zurückliegende E-Mail-Verläufe der Kollegen hatten. Eines der Pilotprojekte zur praktischen Anwendung von Yammer im Vertriebsalltag war die Bildung virtueller Projektgruppen, um zwischen den Vertriebsmitarbeitern die Accounts abzustimmen. Darüber hinaus wurde Yammer direkt genutzt, um im Vertriebsteam und unter Beteiligung des Managements die Vision und Leitlinien für die zukünftige Kommunikation und Zusammenarbeit auszuarbeiten.

Welche Zielgruppen mit besonderen Anforderungen sind nun in einem Social-Intranet-Projekt zu berücksichtigen, um daraus die wichtigsten Anwendungsszenarien abzuleiten? Die nächsten Seiten geben Ihnen hierzu Aufschluss.

Mitarbeiter beteiligen

In der Vergangenheit wurde das Intranet hauptsächlich von der IT-Abteilung entwickelt und den Mitarbeitern als fertige Lösung vorgesetzt. Entsprechend niedrig war der Nutzungsgrad. Oftmals wurde schon froh verkündet, dass 60% der Mitarbeiter das Intranet wenigstens einmal wöchentlich besuchen. Wir hingegen sind erst mit 100% täglicher Nutzung zufrieden.

Mitarbeiter wissen oft am besten über ineffiziente Abläufe und Probleme in der Zusammenarbeit mit anderen Abteilungen Bescheid. Sie sind schließlich diejenigen, die täglich die Arbeitsvorgänge ausführen. Dadurch sind gerade sie es, die schnell Lösungsansätze finden. Die Intelligenz und Erfahrung vieler sorgt für attraktive Intranet-Inhalte.

Wenn Mitarbeiter die Inhalte mitgestalten dürfen, zeigen sie erfahrungsgemäß eine höhere Akzeptanz für die Plattform und nutzen das Intranet später aktiver. Das erspart Ressourcen für Motivationsmaßnahmen. Power User können durch eine Projektbeteiligung von Anfang an, beispielsweise in einer Testplattform oder in Pilotprojekten, an die neuen Funktionalitäten herangeführt werden. Das senkt den Trainingsaufwand und liefert zudem früh vorzeigbare Ergebnisse, die für die Projektkommunikation entscheidend sind.

An welchen Stellen lohnt es sich also, Mitarbeiter in das Intranet-Projekt einzubeziehen?

Wir erzielen den größten Erfolg

- beim Auflisten von Schwachstellen in der Kommunikation und Zusammenarbeit;
- beim Erfassen gewünschter Inhalte;
- beim Dokumentieren von Prozessabläufen, die im Intranet abgebildet werden sollen;
- bei der Auswahl des Inhalts, der aus dem bestehenden Intranet in das neue überführt werden soll;
- beim Testen der Navigation und Usability sowie
- beim Trainieren von Kollegen.

Als **Formate** eignen sich Mitarbeiter-Befragungen, Umfragen, World-Cafés, Workshops, Interviews, Pilot- und Testgruppen.

Folgende Wünsche stehen bei Mitarbeitern meist ganz oben in der Prioritätenliste:
- schnelles Finden von Informationen oder Dokumenten;
- Übersicht über möglichst alle Projekte, auch die anderer Abteilungen;
- zeitnahe Informationen vom Management;
- offenere Kommunikation mit dem Management;
- Arbeit von Zuhause aus;
- Anbindung externer Partner;
- moderne eLearning-Angebote im Intranet;
- Schnelleinstiege zu wichtigen oder häufig besuchten Seiten wie Projektseiten, Wikis, dem Kantinen-Speiseplan oder dem Schwarzen Brett;
- verbesserte Workflows bei der Beantragung von Urlaub, Reisen oder Weiterbildungen sowie
- Spaß haben.

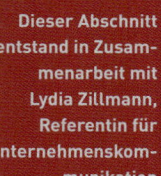

Dieser Abschnitt entstand in Zusammenarbeit mit Lydia Zillmann, Referentin für Unternehmenskommunikation CONTAS KG

Die Wende zur Offenheit – Social Software und Unternehmenskultur http://bit.ly/1yHAAJM

Geschäftsprozesse mit den Mitarbeitern verbessern: Der Einstieg in das Wissensmanagement-Projekt bei der CONTAS KG

Ein guter Veränderungsprozess beginnt damit, bei allen Beteiligten eine gemeinsame Wahrnehmung der Ausgangssituation zu schaffen. Also startete die CONTAS KG, eine Leipziger Beratungsgesellschaft für integrierten Strategie- und Kulturwandel, das Social-Collaboration-Einführungsprojekt mit einer Analyse der Geschäftsprozesse. Dabei wurden die Mitarbeiter von Anfang an mit einbezogen. Stärken und Schwächen der Arbeitsabläufe wurden gemeinsam analysiert und anschließend mit allen Beschäftigten in einem Dialog-Workshop erörtert. Alle Geschäftsprozesse wurden dabei „auseinandergenommen" und leicht verständlich skizziert. Anschließend wurden konkrete Verbesserungsmöglichkeiten mit Blick auf die strategischen Unternehmensziele erarbeitet. Dabei hatten die Mitarbeiter die Möglichkeit, ihre Wünsche zu äußern, wobei sie praktisch von selbst auf die Idee kamen, dass Social Features bestimmte Arbeitsabläufe entscheidend verbessern können. Auf diese Weise konnte beispielsweise für den Vertriebsprozess ermittelt werden, wie die Phase der Angebotserstellung durch den Einsatz von Blogs und einer gemeinsamen Dokumentenplattform spürbar beschleunigt und verbessert werden kann. Um bei der Umsetzung von Beratungsprojekten besser das Wissen aus früheren Projekten zu nutzen, wurde der Einsatz von Wikis und Such-Schlagworten als besonders wichtig angenommen.

„Durch die Möglichkeit, bei der Anforderungsanalyse mitzuwirken, haben sich alle Mitarbeiter intensiv mit den neuen Social Features auseinandergesetzt. Was einigen vorher nur vom Hörensagen bekannt war, wurde für die Mitarbeiter plötzlich fassbar, weil sie anhand ihrer eigenen Arbeitsabläufe überprüft haben, wie ihnen die neuen Features helfen können. Auf diese Weise konnten wir bei den Mitarbeitern ein starkes Interesse an diesen Tools wecken. Der Nutzen wurde direkt klar", erinnert sich Lydia Zillmann, welche die Einführung von IBM Connections in dem Beratungsunternehmen mitverantwortete.

Mitarbeiter ohne Bildschirmarbeitsplatz – eine besondere Zielgruppe

Wenn Mitarbeiter keinen Bildschirmarbeitsplatz haben – wie z.B. Produktionsarbeiter, Straßenbahnfahrer oder Anlagentechniker – ist es nicht einfach, sie in das Intranet einzubeziehen. Folgende Fragen brauchen Antworten:

- Warum ist es wichtig, dass auch diese Zielgruppe das Intranet nutzen kann?
- Was leistet das Intranet? Was müssen Mitarbeiter ohne Bildschirmarbeitsplatz erfahren? Wo ist ihre Mitarbeit wichtig?
- Wo könnten die Bildschirme stehen – in den Pausenräumen oder im Kantinenbereich?
- Nutzt man Flatscreens, Smartphones, Tablets oder stattet man Infopoints mit Terminals aus?

- Bekommen die Mitarbeiter nur Lese- oder auch Schreibrechte?
- Stimmt der Betriebsrat zu? Dürfen die Mitarbeiter das Intranet nur in den Pausen oder auch während der Arbeitszeit nutzen oder gar mobil von daheim aus zugreifen?
- Wie und wann werden die Mitarbeiter geschult? Kann man die Intranet-Bereiche so gestalten, dass kein Training notwendig ist und Videounterweisungen ausreichen?
- Wie sichert man den Support in der Startphase, wenn Fragen gehäuft und sogar in den Pausenzeiten auftreten?
- Was kann man den Mitarbeitern bieten, damit sie regelmäßig im Intranet vorbeischauen?
- Wie viel Budget muss investiert werden, um die notwendigen Geräte zur Verfügung zu stellen?

Ein Kunststoffhersteller bindet die Produktion an das Social Intranet an

Wie führt man ein Social Intranet ein, wenn von der tausendköpfigen Belegschaft 700 Mitarbeiter keinen Bildschirmarbeitsplatz haben und in Schichten arbeiten? Dieser Herausforderung stellte sich ein Kunststoffhersteller, der von Anfang an die Produktionsmitarbeiter in die Anforderungsanalyse mit einbezogen hat. Schnell wurde dabei klar, dass eine „Zwei-Klassen-Gesellschaft" am Standort hinderlich ist und jeder einen Zugang zum neuen Intranet erhalten sollte.

In einem Interview zeigte der Produktionsleiter auf, wo die vielversprechendsten Anwendungsfälle in der Produktion liegen:

- Informationen über Schichtpläne und Schichtplanänderungen werden im Intranet veröffentlicht, sodass Anrufe bei Änderungen wegfallen.
- Inhalte der meist überladenen Schwarzen Bretter werden digital aufbereitet, damit alle Informationen übersichtlich zu lesen sind.
- Alle betrieblichen Informationen werden künftig zwischen den vier Schichten über das Intranet weitergegeben, damit das Wissen dokumentiert vorliegt.
- Der Austausch zwischen den Mitarbeitern, auch über die Arbeitsthemen hinaus, wird unkomplizierter, um das Wir-Gefühl zu stärken.
- Die Schichtleiter können die Social Features nutzen, damit sich die neue Anerkennungskultur leichter etablieren kann.

Diese Anwendungsfälle wurden in einem Workshop mit Produktionsmitarbeitern noch weiter ergänzt.

Zunächst wurde festgelegt, dass in der Produktion selbst kein Intranet-Zugang eingerichtet wird, nur in den Pausenräumen. Inzwischen testet jedoch eine Pilotgruppe, in welchen Bereichen sich Intranet und die Einhaltung strenger Arbeitsschutzauflagen und Qualitätsrichtlinien nicht ausschließen.

Dass die Produktionsmitarbeiter bereits in einer frühen Phase des Intranet-Projekts einbezogen wurden und dass ihre Wünsche mit hoher Priorität berücksichtigt wurden, nahm übrigens bei der Einführung den Gegnern allen Wind aus den Segeln. Dem Hauptargument „Das braucht doch keiner!" konnte so entschlossen begegnet werden.

Führungskräften die Arbeit erleichtern

Es ist wichtig, dass die Führungskräfte das Intranet als Teil der Unternehmensstrategie begreifen. Formulieren Sie deshalb die Business-Anforderungen für das Intranet so, dass die Strategie bestmöglich umgesetzt werden kann. Genauso wichtig ist es, bei der Gestaltung der Intranet-Anwendungen immer auch die Führungskräfte und ihre Arbeitsanforderungen besonders im Blick zu haben, denn deren Tätigkeiten unterscheiden sich in der Regel erheblich von denen der Mitarbeiter. Wenn Sie bei der Präsentation Beispiele für Arbeitserleichterungen, Zeitersparnis oder Prozessvereinfachungen aufzeigen, sorgen Sie für Aha-Erlebnisse und gewinnen Verbündete.

Spezielle Lösungen für Führungskräfte können sein:

- ein Kanal (auf der Startseite), auf dem Neuigkeiten aus dem Management schnell kommuniziert werden können;
- geschlossene Projekträume, in denen sich Führungskräfte austauschen, vertrauliche Dokumente ablegen und gemeinsam bearbeiten können;
- virtuelle Meeting-Räume, durch die Dienstreisen eingespart werden können;
- mobile Lösungen, die Zugriffe auf Unternehmensdaten von unterwegs aus gewährleisten;
- Newsfeed, Videobotschaften und Blogs für die schnelle und direkte Mitarbeiterkommunikation;

- aufbereitete Reports und Kennzahlen;
- Management Self Services.

Gleichzeitig kann abgefragt werden, welche aktuellen Projekte es momentan gibt. Davon eignet sich vielleicht eines als Pilotprojekt, das unter besonderer Anleitung eines externen Beraters mit Hilfe der neuen Tools zum Erfolg geführt wird.

Nutzen Führungskräfte das Intranet selbst und gehen mit gutem Beispiel voran, hat das eine positive Signalwirkung auf die Mitarbeiter. Haben sie den Nutzen für das eigene Arbeiten erkannt (siehe auch Punkt 1.2), können auch weitere Anwendungsfälle für Mitarbeiter herausgearbeitet werden.

Ein Kunststoffhersteller mobilisiert seine Führungskräfte

Was tun, wenn frühere Erfahrungen mit dem Intranet dazu führen, dass Führungskräfte einem SharePoint-Einführungsprojekt eher skeptisch gegenüber stehen? Das Projektteam eines Kunststoffherstellers wählte eine Vorwärtsstrategie und lud die Führungskräfte zu einem Workshop ein, bei dem ihnen die Chancen der neuen Arbeitswelt demonstriert werden sollten. Mit einem Geschäftsführer, der vorher ins Boot geholt wurde und sich viel von dem Projekt versprach, war klar, dass die Veranstaltung für alle einen hohen Stellenwert hatte. Entsprechend hoch war die Teilnehmerzahl.

Als Einstieg in den Workshop wurden den Führungskräften das Projekt und die Möglichkeiten modernen Arbeitens erläutert. Beispiele aus anderen Unternehmen, aber auch ein bereits erfolgreich im eigenen Hause absolviertes Leuchtturmprojekt machten den Teilnehmern die Veränderungen durch „Social Business" vorstellbar. Damit es nicht bei der Inspiration blieb, sammelten die Führungskräfte in Gruppen anhand von Störfaktoren im Führungsalltag die wichtigsten Anwendungsfälle für das neue Intranet. Typische Themen waren Meeting-Organisation, Schichtübergaben und Führungskommunikation. Zu jedem dieser Themen wurden in einer gemeinsamen Diskussion erste Anregungen dazu gegeben, wie die Cloud-Lösung Office 365 hierbei konkret entlasten und unterstützen kann. In der sehr offenen Gesprächsatmosphäre äußerten die Führungskräfte auch ihre Bedenken und Zweifel, sodass diesen Einwänden unmittelbar begegnet werden konnte. Eine Sorge war beispielsweise, dass ältere Mitarbeiter möglicherweise mit den neuen Medien nicht mehr Schritt halten könnten oder dass der persönliche Kontakt zu den Mitarbeitern durch das Social Intranet leiden könnte.

Unter dem Strich haben drei Stunden intensiver Workshop-Arbeit dazu geführt, dass das Projekt bei den Führungskräften eine deutlich höhere Akzeptanz erfuhr und einige Teilnehmer gegenüber dem Projektteam im Nachhinein sogar spezielle Angebote für Pilotprojekte machten.

Fachabteilungen einbeziehen

Wenn das oberste Management und die Führungskräfte ein Bild davon haben, wie das Intranet die internen Abläufe unterstützen kann, muss ein weiterer wichtiger Schritt getan werden: Die Abteilungen selbst müssen sich im Intranet wiederfinden. Das Social Intranet ist keine reine Informationsplattform mehr, sondern auch eine Zusammenarbeitsplattform, in der wichtige Vorgänge aller Abteilungen abgebildet werden.

Nicht selten aber sind die Beziehungen zwischen der IT und den Fachabteilungen belastet, frühere Software-Projekte haben Spuren hinterlassen. Zudem gibt es unterschiedliche Vorstellungen: Während die IT-Experten versuchen, das Projekt vom Aufwand her in einem überschaubaren Rahmen zu halten, haben die Fachabteilungen meist spezielle Anforderungen und fühlen sich – wenn ihre Wünsche nicht erfüllt werden – unverstanden. Streitigkeiten um Budgets und Ressourcen tun ihr Übriges.

Es ist also kein Wunder, dass sich Projektteams oftmals scheuen, bei der Planung groß zu denken und auf die Abteilungen zuzugehen. Halten Sie jedoch Kurs.

Folgende Vorteile sprechen klar für die Einbindung der Fachabteilungen:

- Die Aufgaben bei der Entwicklung des Intranets werden auf mehrere Schultern verteilt.
- Die IT kann genau das liefern, was die Fachabteilungen wirklich benötigen.
- Einige Fachabteilungen sind bereit, als Sponsoren für das Projekt zu fungieren.
- Es können Abteilungen gefunden werden, die sich in einem frühen Stadium zu Pilotprojekten bereit erklären und so für vorzeigbare Erfolgserlebnisse sorgen.
- Den Fachabteilungen wird nichts übergestülpt, sondern sie können den Prozess aktiv mitgestalten und das Intranet später bestmöglich nutzen.

Um ein gutes Projektklima zu schaffen, kann es sehr nützlich sein, externe Berater in den Prozess einzuschalten, die sich mit den Arbeitsabläufen in verschiedenen Unternehmensbereichen auskennen. Sie müssen die Anforderungen des jeweiligen Bereichs in die „Plattform-Sprache" übersetzen. Gleichzeitig sollten sie über Methoden verfügen, um die Kommunikation und Zusammenarbeit zwischen IT und Fachabteilungen zu fördern und bei Konflikten zu moderieren.

Bei der Aufnahme von Anforderungen haben wir sehr gute Erfahrungen mit Impuls-Workshops gemacht. Auch Interviews mit den Abteilungsleitern sind sehr hilfreich.

IT-ABTEILUNG

Die IT-Abteilung ist für die technische Verankerung der Intranet-Lösung im Unternehmen zuständig. Nicht immer kann vorausgesetzt werden, dass die Mitarbeiter dieser Abteilung die neue Software gleich beherrschen. Durch die Affinität zu Software-Lösungen generell ist aber davon auszugehen, dass sie ohne große Schwierigkeiten ein Pilotprojekt meistern können. Die neuen Formen der Zusammenarbeit müssen auch hier erst erprobt werden.

Oft gewünschte Features der IT-Abteilung sind

- ein Hilfebereich mit wichtigen Dokumenten, Videos und FAQ zur Software, um beim Rollout nicht mit Nutzeranfragen überhäuft zu werden;
- ein Support-Newsfeed, damit die Power-User Fragen zur Funktionsweise selbst beantworten können;
- eine Anzeige des IT-Systemstatus oder die Möglichkeit, Wartungsarbeiten auf der Startseite anzukündigen;
- eine Übersicht zu Verantwortlichkeiten und Supportzeiten der einzelnen IT-Abteilungsmitarbeiter;
- ein Projektraum zur Steuerung der IT-Projekte.

KOMMUNIKATIONSABTEILUNG

Den Mitarbeitern der Kommunikationsabteilung kommt bei der Anforderungsermittlung eine Doppelrolle zu. Neben der Bedarfserhebung für den eigenen Fachbereich wissen sie am besten, welche Kommunikationsmittel und -wege im gesamten Unternehmen bestehen bleiben sollten und welche durch neue Features ersetzt werden müssen.

Zwei Beispiele: Statt des wenig gelesenen monatlichen Newsletters gibt es jetzt aktuelle News, die regelmäßig auf der Startseite des Intranets erscheinen. Die Mitarbeiterzeitung wird weiterhin gedruckt, weil sie oft mit nach Hause genommen wird, sodass auch Familienangehörige darin lesen können. Ausgewählte Texte erscheinen parallel im Intranet.

Oft gewünschte Features der Kommunikationsabteilung sind:

- Newsbereich auf der Startseite;
- Bereich für Presseinformationen;
- Bilder- und Videobereich (Mediathek);
- Newsfeed, Communities und Blogs, damit sich die Mitarbeiter selbst mit Informationen versorgen können;
- Feedback-Möglichkeiten;
- Umfragen;
- Redaktions-Workflows, in die mehrere Redakteure eingebunden sind.

PERSONALABTEILUNG

Wer wissen will, was das Intranet können soll, kommt um intensive Gespräche mit der Personalabteilung nicht herum. Diese Bedarfserhebung ist vielschichtig:

1. Personalverantwortliche können dem Intranet mit ihrem Wissen eine besondere Richtung geben. Sollte beispielsweise dem Wissensmanagement eine stärkere Bedeutung beigemessen werden, weil viele ältere Arbeitnehmer in den nächsten Jahren ausscheiden? Gibt es Nachwuchsprobleme und sollte man über attraktive Features für junge Mitarbeiter nachdenken? Gegebenenfalls sind die Personalfluktuation oder der Krankenstand so hoch, dass man das Intranet-Projekt als Chance nutzen kann, hier Verbesserungen zu erzielen.

2. Das HR-Team hat bestimmte Anforderungen an die Gestaltung eines Abteilungsarbeitsraums. Vorhandene Personalinformationssysteme müssen ggf. mit dem Intranet verkoppelt werden.

3. Die Personalabteilung stellt für Mitarbeiter viele Services bereit. Mit Hilfe des Intranets und eines entsprechenden HR-Bereichs können diese Dienste stark vereinfacht werden.

4. Mit Hilfe moderner, in das Intranet integrierter eLearning-Angebote können die Beschäftigten für die Arbeitswelt 2.0 effizient geschult werden.

5. Das Entstehen einer Organisation 2.0 ist immer ein längerfristiger Change-Prozess, der von der Personalabteilung begleitet werden muss. Gerade als direkter Ansprechpartner für den Betriebs- oder Personalrat leistet die Personalabteilung wertvolle Unterstützung.

Oft gewünschte Features der Personalabteilung sind:

- ein eigener HR-Bereich mit Self Services für Mitarbeiter;
- ein Weiterbildungsbereich mit Informationen zu Angeboten, Anmeldemöglichkeiten und Nachverfolgung der Teilnahme;
- Workflows, beispielsweise für Urlaubsanträge und deren Genehmigung;
- Anbindung an bestehende Personalverwaltungssysteme wie z.B. in SAP;
- Integration von Social Talent Management Suites;
- Cockpit mit Reports und Kennzahlen;
- eLearning- und Social-Learning-Features, um mehr Möglichkeiten für eigenverantwortliches Lernen-on-demand zu schaffen;

- eine eigene Rubrik auf der Startseite, um über Personal-News schnell zu informieren;
- Umfragetools;
- ein Onboarding-Prozess für neue Mitarbeiter, um sie reibungslos in das Unternehmen einzuführen.

Internationale Standorte im globalen Intranet

Ein Hauptgrund für das Scheitern von standortübergreifenden Intranets war in der Vergangenheit auch die Bereitstellung der Inhalte. Wenn nur die Zentrale dafür verantwortlich ist, werden Inhalte oft nicht bedarfs- und zeitgerecht aktualisiert, sodass das Intranet seine Attraktivität verliert. Hinzu kommt, dass sich die einzelnen Standorte nicht ausreichend im Intranet präsentiert fühlen. Schließlich möchten die Mitarbeiter wissen, welche Neuigkeiten es vor Ort und anderswo gibt, und das am liebsten in ihrer Landessprache.

Mit dem Intranet-Projekt werden nicht selten Kulturprobleme zwischen Mutter- und Tochtergesellschaften aufgedeckt, die sich sogar darin widerspiegeln, dass es neben dem zentralen Intranet noch hier und da ein Standort-Intranet gibt. So kommen globale Nachrichten nicht mehr bei jedem an und die Nutzerstatistiken sind schlecht.

In Zeiten der Globalisierung steht somit die Frage im Raum: Wie können wir unser Intranet zu einer global attraktiven Plattform entwickeln und wie beziehen wir einzelne internationale Standorte dafür besser ein?

! **Praxistipps:** Sechs Tipps für die Anbindung von internationalen Standorten

1. Alle Organisationseinheiten werden in die Analysephase einbezogen. Erfahrungen zeigen, dass es oft zielführender ist, wenn das Intranet-Team persönlich vor Ort Gespräche führt und die Anforderungen aufnimmt oder Verantwortliche an den Standorten dazu befähigt. Der Aufwand dafür zahlt sich aus, wenn das Intranet-Projekt auch als eine Chance verstanden wird, dass die Standorte näher zusammenrücken.

2. Die Startseite des Intranets enthält neben den News aus der Zentrale auch Neuigkeiten des jeweiligen Standorts. Dafür wird ein Redaktionssystem bereitgestellt, sodass Inhalte dezentral ohne spezielle IT-Kenntnisse und von unterschiedlichen Organisationseinheiten aus gepflegt werden können. Dezentrale Redakteure werden gefördert, aber zentral betreut.

3. Intranet-Inhalte werden mehrsprachig angeboten. Standort-News erscheinen in jedem Fall auch in der Sprache des Standorts.

4. Die Mitarbeiter erhalten personalisierbare Startseitenbereiche, auf denen sie selbst bestimmen können, wie viele globale Inhalte sie abonnieren. Zielgenaue, individuelle Informationen verringern die Informationsbelastung der Nutzer.

5. Für die organisationsweite Kommunikation und Zusammenarbeit werden Tools wie Projekträume, Communities, Newsfeed usw. zur Verfügung gestellt. Sie bieten die Möglichkeit, sich auszutauschen und Gruppen zu bilden – egal, wo sich der Arbeitsplatz befindet.

6. Ggf. werden automatische Übersetzungstools integriert, sodass auch die Aktivitäten von Mitarbeitern anderer Länder bei Interesse verfolgt werden können.

Intranet-Relaunch bei der Reedereigruppe Hamburg Süd – Nicht ohne globale Standorte!

Die Reedereigruppe Hamburg Süd ist mit rund 4.500 Mitarbeitern in über 300 Büros rund um den Globus vertreten. Jede Region hatte bis zum Launch ihr eigenes Intranet, sodass sechs regional unabhängige Portale zu einem integriert werden mussten. Informationsstände, Redaktionen, Nutzungsgrade und Anforderungen waren zu bündeln und zusammenzuführen.

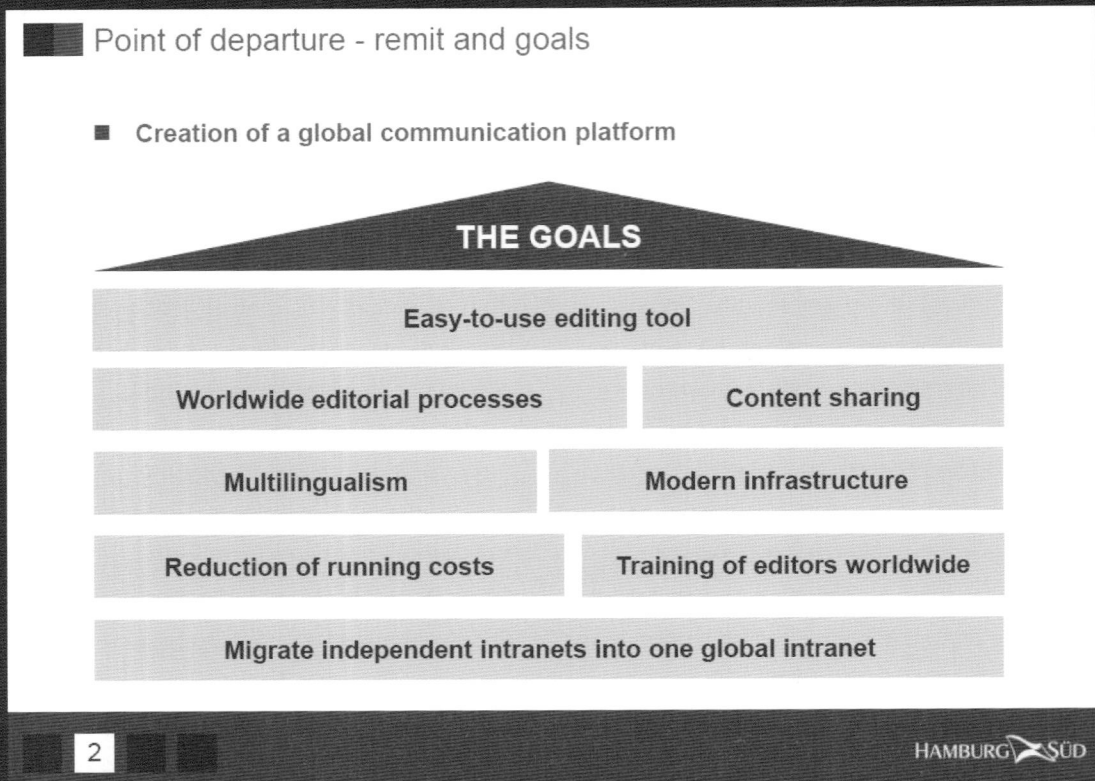

Abbildung 2.3.1: Ziele des Intranet-Relaunchs bei Hamburg Süd

Bei der Hamburg Süd starteten die mit dem Projekt betrauten Mitarbeiter der Hauptabteilung Corporate Communications mit einer Anforderungsanalyse. Um die Bedürfnisse und Wünsche der Mitarbeiter weltweit kennenzulernen, wurde zusätzlich eine Befragung durchgeführt – ein Online-Umfrage-Tool ging an alle Regionalleiter. Die wiederum bildeten kleinere Spezialteams, um eine möglichst große Bandbreite an Antworten zu erhalten – sowohl von den Fachbereichen als auch von den Regionen.

Die einzelnen Ergebnisse gingen zur Auswertung zurück ins Headquarters, wo anhand der Antworten ein Konzept erarbeitet und das weitere Vorgehen geplant wurde. Ein Hamburg Süd-Projektteam war rund eine Woche in jedem der fünf regionalen Head-Offices weltweit unterwegs, um den Rollout genau abzustimmen und die Dauer der Migration der Inhalte abzuschätzen. Gemeinsam mit den Redakteuren wurden Vorgaben erarbeitet, zum Beispiel wie lange es dauern soll, bis die Inhalte eingestellt sind. Hierbei zeigte sich, dass eine Face-to-Face-Kommunikation mit den Projektbeteiligten vor Ort deutlich effektiver ist als eine anonyme Online-Kommunikation. Etappenweise wurde das Intranet dann in den einzelnen Regionen gelauncht.

Betriebs- und Personalrat einbinden

Die Arbeitnehmervertretung ist eine wichtige Zielgruppe im Social Intranet. Schon so mancher Projekt-Verantwortliche stöhnte über schwierige und aufreibende Abstimmungen mit dem „widerspenstigen Verhinderer Betriebsrat". Aus unserer Sicht aber kommt ihm – wie in Abschnitt 1.6 beschrieben – eine tragende Rolle bei der Einführung neuer Technologien zu, auf Basis seiner Mitbestimmungspflicht auch zu Recht: Er ist dem Schutz der Mitarbeiter verpflichtet, deckt Risiken im Datenschutz auf und achtet auf kritische Aspekte im Arbeitsrecht oder in Fragen kultureller Natur. Damit ist er genau der Richtige, um die Social-Intranet-Einführung ganzheitlich im Blick zu behalten. Denn letztlich haben wir ein gemeinsames Ziel: Die Arbeitsumgebung und die Bedingungen für Mitarbeiter zu verbessern.

Social-Intranet-Lösungen sind übrigens auch hervorragend dazu geeignet, die Betriebsratsarbeit zu optimieren.

Oft gewünschte Features des Betriebs- und Personalrats sind:

- Vorstellung der Betriebsräte mit ihren Arbeitsschwerpunkten;
- Betriebsratsneuigkeiten, Hinweise und Termine;
- Einrichten eines öffentlichen Betriebsrats-Bereichs mit allen wichtigen Dokumenten (z.B. Betriebsvereinbarungen);
- Einrichten eines geschützten Betriebsratsbereichs, z.B. in Form von Projekträumen für die Betriebsratsarbeit 2.0.

Datenschutz- und IT-Sicherheitsbeauftragte

Der Sicherheit persönlicher Daten und der Unternehmensdaten ist die höchste Priorität einzuräumen. Vor der Anschaffung neuer Software-Lösungen, mit denen personenbezogene Daten verarbeitet werden, ist in Deutschland eine Vorabkontrolle durch den Datenschutzbeauftragten gemäß Bundesdatenschutzgesetz (BDSG) durchzuführen. Somit prüft der Datenschutzbeauftragte bei der Einführung einer Intranet-Lösung insbesondere, wie Informationen über Mitarbeiter oder Kunden vor einem unbefugten Zugriff zu schützen sind.

Dies schließt die Prüfung IT-sicherheitsrelevanter Aspekte und Maßnahmen gegen Angriffe von außen ein, sodass alle erforderlichen Vorkehrungen zur Einhaltung der Datensicherheit getroffen sind. Der IT-Sicherheitsbeauftragte wird insbesondere bei Einsatz einer Cloud-Lösung oder einer mobilen Lösung für das Intranet neue Prüfprozesse etablieren müssen, denn die Sicherheitsstandards und Sicherungsmöglichkeiten haben sich in den letzten Jahren enorm gewandelt. Es kann in jedem Fall sehr hilfreich sein, einen externen Experten zu Rate zu ziehen, um alle notwendigen Maßnahmen zur Sicherung zu konzipieren und deren Umsetzung zu prüfen.

2.4 ANWENDUNGSSZENARIEN – DEN ANFORDERUNGEN STRUKTUR GEBEN

Wenn Sie die Ausgangssituation umfassend beleuchtet und die Anforderungen an das moderne Intranet erfasst haben, können Sie sich nun in wichtige Anwendungsfälle vertiefen.

Welche Szenarien stoßen bei Management und Mitarbeitern in besonderer Weise auf Zustimmung?

Nützliche Anwendungsszenarien tragen dazu bei, die Akzeptanz für Intranet-Portale zu erhöhen. Denn nur wenn das Intranet-Portal Nutzertools bietet, die Mitarbeitern helfen, ihren Job besser zu erledigen, werden sie immer wieder darauf zurückgreifen. Selbst einfache Basis-Tools wie Mitarbeiterprofile oder einfache Redaktions-Workflows können ein Schlüssel zur Nutzerzufriedenheit sein. Spezielle Schlüsselanwendungen für Führungskräfte und das Management, wie z.B. die Einbindung

von Business Intelligence oder der Einbau eines Managementblogs, können genau diese Zielgruppe motivieren, die für den Portalerfolg so wichtig ist.

Ob Digitaler Vertriebskoffer, Wissenscenter oder Innovationslabor – holen Sie sich für erste Lösungsansätze Inspiration von anderen Projekten. Nicht vergessen: Beginnen Sie nicht mit der Frage, was die jeweilige Technik kann, sondern prüfen Sie zunächst Ihre Zielstellung. Prüfen Sie dann in einer ersten Grobanalyse, welche Intranet-Features besonders passend erscheinen. Damit lässt sich bereits viel besser einschätzen, welche Technik geeignet ist und welche Anforderungen Sie in der Planungsphase berücksichtigen sollten. Verwenden Sie viel Sorgfalt darauf, solche businessrelevanten Anwendungsfälle zu identifizieren und genauer auszugestalten.

Analysen

Vorhandene IT-Landschaft

Bestehendes Intranet

Stand der Kommunikation und Zusammenarbeit

Erfahrungen bisheriger Projekte

Identifizieren neuer Bedürfnisse und Schmerzpunkten bei den Nutzern

Analyse der Unternehmenskultur

Grobkonzeption

Identifizierung von Anwendungsszenarien und übergreifenden Anforderungen

Steckbriefe Anwendungsszenarien:
- Herausforderung
- Lösungsansatz
- Mögliche Hürden
- ggf. ausführlichere Beschreibung

Technische Plattform

Vorauswahl

Entscheidungsmatrix

Proof of Concept

Entscheidungsvorlage

Entscheidung

Technologieorientierte Fachkonzeption

UseCases und UserStories zu den Anwendungsszenarien formulieren

Ausarbeitung Details zu funktionalen und nichtfunktionalen Anforderungen

Informationsarchitektur und Design

Basis für technische Implementierung

Basis für Releaseplanung

Abbildung 2.4.1: Anforderungsaufnahme und -verarbeitung in der Übersicht: von der Analyse zur Fachkonzeption

Erstellen Sie einen Steckbrief. Mit Steckbriefen wird das Intranet-Vorhaben in all seinen Verästelungen für Sie greifbar und Sie können die skizzierten Möglichkeiten zur Umsetzung weiterreichen. Abbildung 2.4.1 veranschaulicht die Zusammenhänge einer gezielten Anforderungsbeschreibung für eine Social-Intranet-Planung.

? Fragenliste: Verfassen eines Steckbriefs für Anwendungsszenarien

Herausforderung

- Welches Problem soll gelöst werden?
- Welchen Mehrwert würde dies für Ihr Unternehmen schaffen?
- Welche Zielgruppen werden angesprochen?

Lösungsansatz

- Wie könnte grob eine Lösung dafür aussehen?
- Wie könnte sie technisch umgesetzt werden?
- Welche Intranet-Features werden benötigt?
- Gibt es Beispiele, an denen man sich orientieren kann?
- Mit welcher Komplexität ist in etwa zu rechnen?

Mögliche Hürden

- Welche sowohl technischen als auch kulturellen Schwierigkeiten könnten bei der Umsetzung auftreten?
- Welche Stolpersteine sind aus anderen Erfahrungen bekannt?
- Welche Abhängigkeiten sind zu berücksichtigen?

Mit Anwendungsfällen zu arbeiten bringt mehr Genauigkeit in gesammelte Anforderungen. Von Mitarbeitern wird beispielsweise vielfach der Wunsch geäußert, Blogs einzuführen. Hier ist nun genauer zu definieren, worüber gebloggt werden soll. Aus dieser Analyse kann sich zum Beispiel folgende Kurzbeschreibung des Anwendungsszenarios „Wochenbericht zu den Projekten" ergeben:

Beispiel: Blog zu den Projekt-Wochenberichten
Herausforderung: Jedes Projektteam soll zum Projektstatus eine wöchentliche Zusammenfassung bereitstellen, die unternehmensweit nachlesbar ist.

Lösungsansatz: Je nach Konzeption erfolgt entweder eine Blog-Statusmeldung oder es sind vordefinierte Dokumente bereitzustellen. Zur Umsetzung des Szenarios „Projekt-Statusmeldung" sind somit die Intranet-Features Blog und Dokumentenvorlagen-Unterstützung notwendig.

Mögliche Hürden: Ist der Zugang zum Ort, wo diese Statusmeldung abzugeben ist, nicht intuitiv auffindbar oder ist der Umgang mit den Tools kompliziert, so wird der Anwender sie sehr ungern oder gar nicht verwenden.

Spätere Technikentscheidung

Erst in einem nächsten Schritt prüfen Sie, welche Software Ihnen am besten bei der Umsetzung der Anforderungen helfen kann. Gegebenenfalls gibt es am Markt schon passende Spezialtools, wie z.B. eine CRM-Lösung für den Vertrieb oder eine einfache App, um Meetings zu organisieren. Solche Tools können Sie einfach anbinden oder integrieren und so Entwicklungskosten sparen. Bei der ins Auge gefassten Software-Lösung gibt es bestimmt Standard- oder Social-Funktionalitäten, die auf Anhieb viele Probleme lösen.

Personalisierbar, rollenbasiert, mehrsprachig – Weitere übergreifende Anforderungen

Neben den Anwendungsszenarien wird es auch weitere übergreifende Anforderungen geben, die Auswirkungen auf die Auswahl der technischen Plattform, auf die Konzeption und Umsetzung haben. Themen wie Mehrsprachigkeit, Design & Layout, Barrierefreiheit oder Barrierearmut, Browsertypen, mobiler Zugriff, Performance & Stabilität der Plattform, Servicelevel, Sicherheitszertifikate und Lifecycle-Manage-

Blog-Beitrag von H als Überblick zu de Herausforderunge der Mehrsprachigk im Intranet
http://bit.ly/1CynX

Blog-Beitrag auf besser2.0 zum Umgang mit Barrierefreiheit in Social Tools
http://bit.ly/1uNGh

ment bilden eigene Anforderungsblöcke. Häufig wird deren Umsetzung von mehreren Anwendungsszenarien benötigt. Im Rahmen eines Grobkonzepts sollten daher auch hierzu so früh wie möglich erste Betrachtungen zu den benötigen Rahmenbedingungen erfolgen

Für ausgewählte Anwendungsszenarien haben wir gemeinsam mit zahlreichen Gastautoren folgende Steckbriefe erstellt. Lassen Sie sich davon zum Weiterdenken und Umsetzen inspirieren:

Dieser Abschnitt entstand in Zusammenarbeit mit Vincent U. Aydin, Head of Business Development innosabi GmbH

Ideen- und Innovationsmanagement – Die Intelligenz der Vielen nutzen

HERAUSFORDERUNG

Aus unserer Erfahrung lassen sich die typischen Herausforderungen von Unternehmen im Innovationsmanagement gut in drei Bereiche aufteilen: Erstens soll Innovationsmanagement wieder Spaß machen. Zweitens geht es um mehr Effizienz in Innovationsprozessen, d.h. die hohe Flut an Informationen soll effektiv durch passende Algorithmen kanalisiert werden, um die Qualität der Lösungsfindung zu erhöhen. Und drittens haben viele Unternehmen verstanden, dass die Öffnung nach innen und außen entscheidend ist für die Qualität der entstehenden Innovationen.

LÖSUNGSANSATZ

Modernes softwaregestütztes Ideen- und Innovationsmanagement setzt genau an die oben genannten Herausforderungen an. Es macht sich die Prinzipien des Crowdsourcings zunutze, um dem Innovationsgeschehen im Unternehmen wieder Schwung und Qualität zu verleihen.

Wer ein herkömmliches betriebliches Vorschlagswesen ablösen oder verbessern will, braucht Systeme, mit denen es Spaß macht,

Ideen zu teilen. Viele Unternehmen haben bereits Systeme für den Austausch von Ideen eingeführt, aber mit wenig Erfolg. Ganz oft scheitern sie daran, dass Mitarbeiter das Gefühl haben, sie müssten zusätzliche Aufgaben erledigen und auf Krampf Ideen produzieren. Das ist natürlich nicht Sinn der Sache. Eine Software, die das Sammeln und Generieren von Ideen unterstützt, sollte ähnlich viel Lust machen wie der tägliche Besuch auf Facebook. Die Sache ist vergleichbar mit einer Kaffeeküche, in der man sich trifft und mit den Kollegen plaudert – nur digital: Da schaut man immer mal rein, unterhält sich oder schreibt einfach Ideen nieder. Und manchmal liest man auch gern einfach mal so mit und kommt auf ganz neue Gedanken.

Es ist nämlich der Grundgedanke modernen Ideen- und Innovationsmanagements, die gesamte Organisation und gegebenenfalls auch externe Personen auf einer Plattform zusammenzuführen, sodass sie gemeinsam an Ideen arbeiten. Es geht nicht mehr wie bisher darum, DIE EINE exzellente Idee herauszufiltern und einen Wettbewerb zu schaffen, sondern die Community soll gemeinschaftlich attraktive Ideen ausarbeiten und weiterentwickeln. Innovationen sind damit explizit eine Leistung von mehreren Personen. Das ist ein völlig anderes Verständnis, als es vielerorts praktiziert wird.

Bei internem Crowdsourcing greift man auf den im Unternehmen vorhandenen Wissens- und Ideenschatz zurück. Bei externem Crowdsourcing bezieht man auch Kunden, Lieferanten oder andere Personengruppen in einen Innovationsprozess mit ein, um ihn mit neuen Perspektiven und Ideen zu bereichern. Das kann man sich so vorstellen:

Am Anfang steht eine konkrete Fragestellung, die man lösen möchte. Eine solche übergeordnete Fragestellung wird heruntergebrochen in Teilfragestellungen, weil diese leichter bear-

beitet werden können. Wenn Sie beispielsweise ein neues Duschgel entwickeln wollen, können Sie Ihre Frage direkt an einen Kunden weitergeben. Die Antworten können hierbei jedoch auch in sehr verschiedene Richtungen gehen. Wenn Sie den Mitentwickler animieren, sich über den Duft, das Aussehen und den Namen Gedanken zu machen, dann erhalten Sie mehr Informationen. Die Teilnehmer geben Ideen ein, diskutieren sie und bewerten am Ende auch alle Ideen. Schritt für Schritt lässt sich so mit Tausenden von Teilnehmern etwas entwickeln, das die Ideen der gesamten Community widerspiegelt.

MÖGLICHE HÜRDEN

Bei der Einführung eines modernen Ideen- und Innovationsmanagements schlägt einem zunächst häufig Ablehnung entgegen, auch von Personen, die man eigentlich als Fürsprecher gewinnen möchte. Ein nicht selten gehörtes Argument lautet: Das Neue sei nicht Teil der Aufgabenbeschreibung. Die Teilnahme am Ideenmanagement wird oft als lästige Extra-Arbeit aufgefasst.

Diese Ablehnung hängt auch mit dem „Not-invented-here-Syndrom" zusammen. Für den Mitarbeiter fühlt es sich so an, als gäbe es künftig irgendeine externe Plattform, in die er seine Ideen hineinkippen muss. Das verursacht automatisch Vorbehalte. Wenn Sie Widerständler haben, die keine Lust oder keine Zeit haben, ist es sehr schwierig, intern Begeisterung auszulösen.

Eine weitere wichtige Hürde ist die Unternehmenskultur. Hier unterscheiden sich die Branchen sehr stark. Vielerorts gibt es enorme Vorbehalte, wenn es um das Preisgeben und Teilen von Wissen und Ideen geht. In einer solchen sehr traditionellen Kultur mit festen hierarchischen und statusorientierten Strukturen muss man natürlich ganz anders vorgehen als bei Unternehmen, die schon sehr offen und vernetzt agieren.

Community entwickelt bei Kärcher Innovation mit Hochdruck

Kärcher nutzte Crowdsourcing, um einen Hochdruckreiniger für den japanischen Markt zu entwickeln. Dabei war es dem Unternehmen von Anfang an wichtig, dass dieses Produkt über einen Homeshopping-Partner vertrieben werden sollte. Also wurden neben bestehenden Kärcher-Kunden auch Homeshopping-Kunden in die Produktentwicklung mit einbezogen.

Das aus dem Crowdsourcing entstandene Produktkonzept erfüllt die extrem spezifischen Bedürfnisse der dortigen Konsumenten. Ein Anwendungsfall waren beispielsweise Hochdruckreiniger für das Bad. Die Community hat so spezifische Hinweise an die Produktentwickler gegeben, mit welchen Features ein solcher Reiniger ausgestattet sein sollte, dass es nicht schwer war, daraus Prototypen zu skizzieren, die wiederum der Community zum Bewerten zurückgespielt wurden.

Dieser Abschnitt entstand in Zusammenarbeit mit Markus Raatz, Vorstandsvorsitzender Ceteris AG

Business Intelligence (BI) – Aktuelle Informationen für alle Mitarbeiter

HERAUSFORDERUNG

Im Intranet sollen wichtige Kennzahlen für breite Anwendergruppen effizient bereitgestellt werden.

- Derzeit sind aktuelle Zahlen in vielen Organisationen „Herrschaftswissen": Im Controlling sind Auswertungen vorhanden, die Geschäftsleitung kann sie dort erhalten, aber alle anderen Mitarbeiter wie Teamleiter, Schichtleiter oder Projektleiter, die auch auf der Grundlage neuartiger Daten bessere Entscheidungen treffen könnten, gehen leer aus.

- Es werden standardisierte Berichte über produzierte Stückzahlen, Fehlerraten oder Unfälle aufwendig manuell ausgedruckt und ans „Schwarze Brett" gehängt ohne die Möglichkeit, mit wenigen Klicks mehr über die Details zu erfahren.

- Der Mangel an aktuellen, aufbereiteten Unternehmenszahlen führt oft dazu, dass an vielen Stellen die gleiche Arbeit doppelt getan wird: Die wenigen Zahlen, die es gibt, werden noch per Excel-Tabelle mühevoll aufbereitet. Es entsteht eine „Schatten-BI", die sehr wichtige Auswertungen oft manuell per E-Mail verteilt. Die darin enthaltene Datenmenge ist dann eine Herausforderung für schwach ausgestattete Computer.

LÖSUNGSANSATZ

Nicht jede Organisation hat das Geld oder das Know-how für ein von der IT maßgeschneidertes Intranet-Berichtsportal, in dem man qualitätsgeprüfte Daten erhält, die stets aktuell sind. Moderne Intranet-Projekte stellen mehr und mehr Self-Service-Funktionalitäten in diesem Umfeld zur Verfügung, bei denen die Power User, die schon bisher manuelle Excel-Aus-wertungen improvisiert haben, ihre Berichte für alle im Portal publizieren können. Die Daten hinter diesen Berichten aktualisieren sich dabei automatisch über Nacht.

Nicht zufällig werden offizielle BI-Dashboards vielfach weniger genutzt als solche Berichte und Auswertungen, die direkt aus den Fachabteilungen kommen. Sie sind einfach immer 100% praxisrelevant, antworten gezielt auf die Herausforderungen des Alltags und enthalten viel Business-Wissen, oft sogar kombiniert mit Spezialdaten, die nur in den Fachabteilungen bekannt sind.

Als Werkzeug zur Erstellung dieser Lösungen durch den Anwender ist Excel sehr gut geeignet, vor allem wegen seiner Visualisierungsmöglichkeiten. Lädt ein Power User die fertigen Sheets nun in den SharePoint-Server hoch und nutzt die Funktionalität der Excel Services, brauchen die Betrachter keine Daten lokal herunterzuladen oder eine Software installieren, sondern betrachten alles über ihren Webbrowser. Selbstverständlich ist diese Ansicht auch im Intranet interaktiv, über Filter oder Datenschnitte (Slicer).

MÖGLICHE HÜRDEN

- Diejenigen Power User, die ein gutes Datenverständnis und gute Excel-Kenntnisse haben, sodass sie solche Auswertungen bauen können, sind im täglichen Geschäft ohnehin beliebte Mitarbeiter. Es ist also gut möglich, dass sie für ihre Hauptaufgaben intensiv gebraucht werden und wenig Zeit haben, sich noch um Berichte für andere Abteilungen zu kümmern.

- Die automatische Aktualisierung solcher Auswertungen kann derzeit, um die Quellsysteme nicht zu beeinträchtigen, maximal einmal am Tag geplant werden. Bei manueller Ausführung geht es natürlich auch häufiger.

Abbildung 2.4.2: Power-View-Dashboard mit Kartenanbindung: Die Karte kommt aus dem Internet, die Daten aus PowerPivot

- In der Begeisterung darüber, ihre persönlichen Leistungen im Unternehmen breit präsentieren zu können, veröffentlicher manche Power User eine Unzahl von Berichten, was die Anwender eher verwirrt als informiert. Eine gute Intranet-Suche kann hier helfen, aber natürlich ist es sinnvoll, den Power User noch vor der Veröffentlichung um eine Kategorisierung und Kurzbeschreibung der Berichte mit ihren Datenquellen zu bitten.

- Zu viele publizierte Berichte, teilweise mit vielen Daten dahinter, die sich täglich aktualisieren, verschlingen Ressourcen des Intranet-Servers und der Quellsysteme. Hier hilft ein Management Dashboard, das anzeigt, welche Abfragen wie lange dauern, welche Berichtsmappen wie groß geworden sind und wie viele Nutzer diese aufgerufen haben. Selten genutzte, aufgeblähte Auswertungen können dann ausgelagert oder gelöscht werden.

AUSFÜHRLICHERES ZUM ANWENDUNGS-FALL BI

Das radikal Neue bei der Self-Service-BI ist, dass breite Anwenderschichten Zugang zu Auswertungen bekommen, und zwar gerade deshalb, weil die Mitarbeiter selbst solche Auswertungen erstellen. Daneben sollte man aber nicht vergessen, dass der klassische Kunde für Business Intelligence meistens in der Führungsebene der Organisation zu finden ist. Es ist sinnvoll, für die dort beliebten Dashboards, KPIs und Scorecards dieselbe Technologie und Datenbasis zu verwenden, wie sie der Allgemeinheit zugänglich gemacht werden.

Weil Fachanwender über Self-Service-Funktionalitäten einen größeren Beitrag zur Business Intelligence in der Organisation leisten können, ist eine BI-Initiative bei der IT noch lange nicht überflüssig. Die Integration von mehreren Datenquellen mit unterschiedlichen, komplexen Strukturen und abweichenden Stammdaten bleibt meist eine Aufgabe für Spezialisten, die

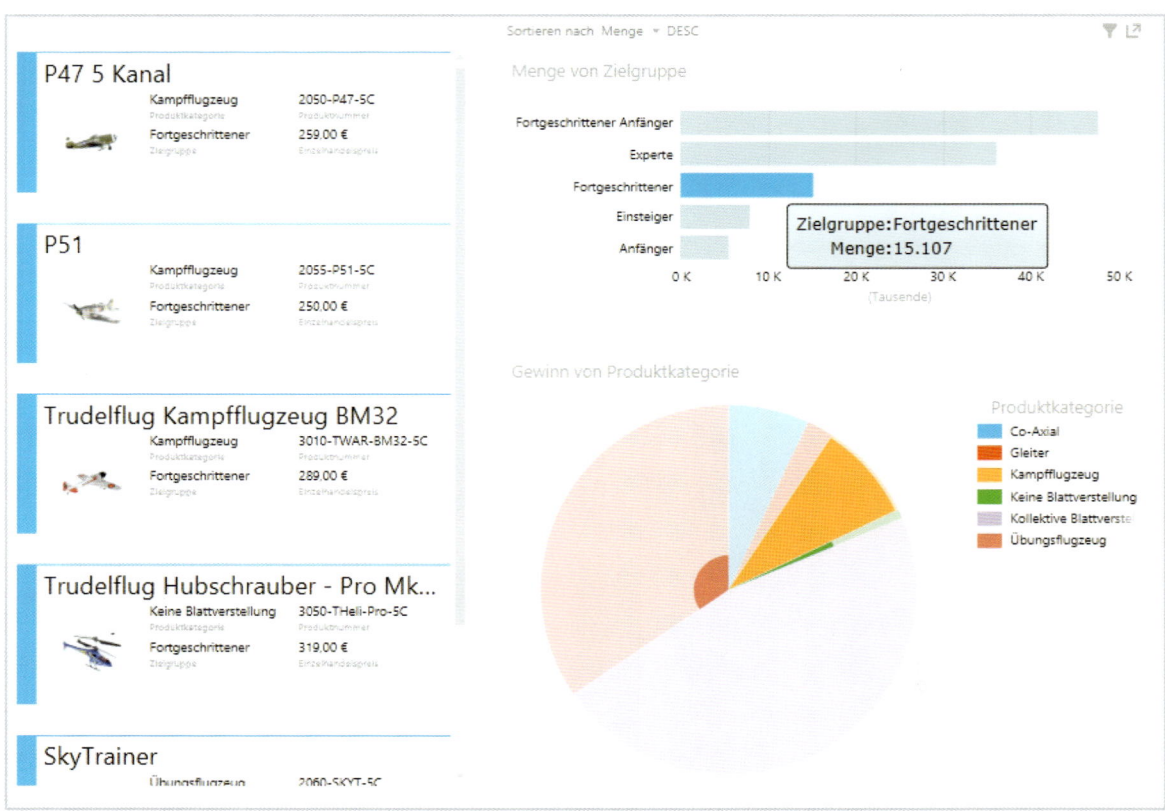

Abbildung 2.4.3: Interaktive Power-View-Ansicht: Jeder Klick auf ein Berichtselement filtert automatisch den gesamten Bericht. Hier der Blick auf eine Zielgruppe.

die Ergebnisse in einer leicht verständlichen Struktur und mit viel Business-Logik den Fachanwendern zur Verfügung stellen. Eine solche Datenbank, die nur Auswertungszwecken dient und oft als Data Warehouse oder Datamart bezeichnet wird, ist die ideale Grundlage für die Berichte der Fachanwender.

An mehreren Stellen kann dabei eine externe Unterstützung der Fachanwender oder der internen IT sinnvoll sein, um das Projekt in die richtigen Bahnen zu lenken und eine Überforderung der Beschäftigten im Unternehmen zu vermeiden:

- Externe Dienstleister können bei der Bereinigung und Vereinheitlichung unterschiedlicher Datenquellen in einer Analysedatenbank helfen, weil sie dafür erprobte Verfahren kennen;
- Externe können einen Standard-Satz von Berichten und Auswertungen der Geschäftsleitung ebenso wie den Anwendern zur Verfügung stellen, wenn Power User damit zeitlich zu stark gefordert wären.

Außerdem können sie auch ihr Know-how zur leicht verständlichen Visualisierung von Berichten in ein solches Projekt einbringen, damit die Grafiken gleichartig und damit einfach interpretierbar werden.

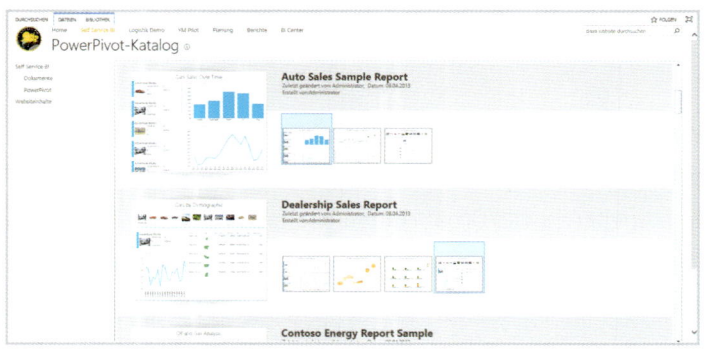

Abbildung 2.4.4: Ein PowerPivot-Katalog im SharePoint zeigt im Webbrowser Momentaufnahmen der hochgeladenen Berichte an, ohne dass sie extra geöffnet werden müssen.

Gleich gestaltete Berichte werden gelesen und verstanden!

Berichte brauchen eine einheitliche visuelle Sprache. Das bedeutet: gleiche Darstellung von Sachverhalten in jeder Auswertung, übersichtliche Visualisierungen, keine unnötigen Details.

Es empfiehlt sich ein Blick auf die Website vor Prof. Rolf Hichert, www.hichert.com, insbesondere in den „Schreckenskeller". Wer dort nicht lachen muss, weil er eigene „Berichts-Sünden" wiedererkennt, hat noch nicht genug Reports gebaut!

Self Service Business Intelligence bei StarBack

StarBack, ein internationaler Hersteller und Großhändler von Tiefkühlbackwaren, hat vor kurzem sein ERP-System von Dynamics NAV auf SAP umgestellt. Dabei ist aus Kostengründen weitgehend auf Customizing verzichtet worden, wie es bei dem Vorsystem noch üblich war, und nun fehlte eine Reihe von Zusatzinformationen für das Reporting. Das betraf vor allem Kategorisierungen, Plandaten und länderspezifische Strukturen, die die Fachanwender in Excel-Sheets und Access-Datenbanken nachgebildet hatten.

Der erste Schritt zur Business Intelligence war nun die Einführung von PowerPivot in Excel. Ein Power User aus dem Einkauf erhielt Lesezugriff auf eine SQL-Server-Analysedatenbank, in die die relevanten SAP-Daten nächtens hineinkopiert werden. Unter der Anleitung externer Berater entstand ein erstes gemeinsames Datenmodell. Die im SAP fehlenden Zusatzdaten wurden dabei durch Import aus Access und Excel ins Modell eingebunden und verknüpft, und dann erste PivotChart-Grafiken darauf erstellt. Diese fertigen Berichte wurden anfangs vom Power User manuell verteilt und gewannen schnell an Beliebtheit. Erst geschah dies als PDF, da viele Anwender noch mit Office 2010 und ohne PowerPivot-AddIn arbeiteten, aber dann wurde der Wunsch nach täglicher Aktualisierung laut.

Um die Verteilung zu vereinfachen, ermöglichte man es dem Power User, seine Sheets in einen PowerPivot-Katalog im SharePoint hochzuladen. Die anderen Benutzer betrachteten sie jetzt einfach im Browser über Excel Services, ohne selbst PowerPivot installiert zu haben, und genossen dennoch die Interaktivität der Abfragen über Pivot-Filter und Datenschnitte. Ein grafisch begabter Kollege erstellte auf dem bestehenden Modell sogar animierte Power-View-Analysen im selben Katalog. Über eine automatische serverbasierte Datenaktualisierung waren die Zahlen jeden Morgen wieder aktuell.

Bei den Anwendern konnte man einen Generationsunterschied feststellen: Viele, gerade ältere Kollegen, konsumierten die Berichte nur und stellten maximal einen Filter auf eine andere Kostenstelle o.ä. um. Jüngere Anwender waren oft mutiger; sie pivotierten die Zahlen und bauten neue Auswertungen, aber kaum einer außer dem Power User öffnete die PowerPivot-Verwaltung und modellierte selbst. Die Herausforderung war nun, aus anderen Abteilungen weitere „Datenkonsumenten" zu selbstständigen „Datengestaltern" zu machen. Dies versuchten die Power User selbst – nach der Devise „Gib einem Hungrigen einen Fisch und er wird einen Tag satt sein. Lehre ihn zu fischen, und er wird nie wieder Hunger haben".

Zwar wurde StarBack gerade von einem internationalen Konzern übernommen, dessen Intranet-Strategie keinen SharePoint-Server zulässt. Die Fachanwender haben aber bereits über einen Ausweg nachgedacht: Wenn der lokale SharePoint abgeschaltet werden muss, wird man in die Cloud umziehen und SharePoint Online im Office 365 verwenden. Die dort angebotenen Power-BI-Funktionalitäten bieten sogar noch mehr als das lokale SharePoint, so etwa die Möglichkeit, die Lieblingsberichte auf mobile Geräte zu synchronisieren und Abfragen auf die Daten in natürlicher Sprache zu formulieren.

Dieser Abschnitt entstand in Zusammenarbeit mit Joerg Jasper, Technology Sales Professional Microsoft Dynamics CRM Microsoft Deutschland GmbH

Collaborative Customer Relationship Management – Mehr Vertriebs-PS auf die Straße bekommen

HERAUSFORDERUNG

Die meisten Unternehmen setzen heute klassische CRM-Systeme wie Salesforce, Dynamics CRM, Update oder CAS ein. Oftmals sind sie bereits mit den bestehenden ERP-Systemen wie SAP oder Dynamics AX integriert, um einen 360°-Blick auf die Kunden zu erhalten. Was diese Systeme in den meisten Fällen heute noch nicht berücksichtigen, sind die in den letzten Jahren in Unternehmen gewachsenen Kollaborations- und Kommunikationsplattformen.

Vielfach werden Kundenmanagement-Systeme heute noch sehr starr als Arbeitswerkzeug für den einzelnen Vertriebsmitarbeiter und Kundenbetreuer sowie als Reporting-Werkzeug für die Führungskräfte verstanden. Besonders im Zusammenhang mit den gewachsenen Ansprüchen der Endkunden an eine exzellente Kundenerfahrung wirken viele CRM-Systeme wie aus einer anderen Zeit.

Die Vertriebsmannschaft eines Unternehmens ist vor allem dies: ein Team. Keiner steht alleine. Häufig muss im Rahmen eines Kundenvorgangs weit ins Unternehmen hinein kommuniziert werden, müssen Wissen und Information abgefragt und ausgetauscht werden, muss an Dokumenten, Angeboten, Präsentationen kollaboriert werden. Dies ist in vielen heutigen CRM-Systemen unzureichend oder überhaupt nicht abgebildet, sodass neben dem Kundenmanagement-System von den Mitarbeitern oder einzelnen Teams individuelle Randlösungen und Wissensinseln verwendet werden. Fazit: Der Aufwand ist höher, Kenntnisse gehen verloren und schlussendlich leidet die „Kundenerfahrung" darunter.

Moderne CRM-Lösungen sind daher:

1. moderne Kollaborationsplattformen, die eine direkte, flexible Zusammenarbeit mit unstrukturierten Daten und Informationen erlauben und dies mit den streng relationalen Daten des CRM-Systems verbinden; oder sie sind

2. mit bestehenden Enterprise Social Networks verknüpft, um den unternehmensweiten Austausch über Kunden, Projekte und Verkaufschancen zu fördern.

LÖSUNGSANSATZ

Zu 1) CRM als moderne Kollaborationsplattform

Jedes CRM System unterstützt heute die Möglichkeit, an einen Datensatz – egal ob zu Kunde, Verkaufschance oder Projekt – ein Dokument

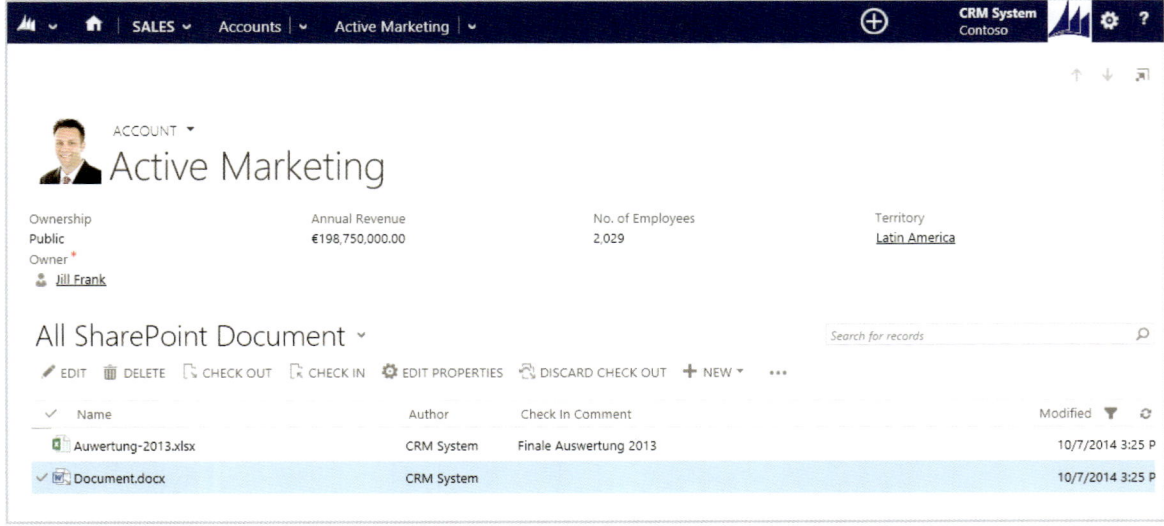

Abbildung 2.4.5: Beispiel Dokumentenablage in SharePoint aus der Sicht des CRM

als Anhang hochzuladen. Das Problem dabei ist, dass damit bis auf weiteres jede Zusammenarbeit an diesem Dokument unterbunden ist.

Die Aufgabe lautet daher, wie oben beschrieben, zu jedem Zeitpunkt ein Dokument an einen Datensatz hängen zu können, das aber in einer Kollaborationsplattform verortet ist und jederzeit aus dem CRM heraus direkt angesteuert werden kann. Gelingt dies, können alle Vorteile einer modernen Kollaborationsplattform genutzt werden; nämlich:

- die Workflow-Unterstützung bei der Bearbeitung und Freigabe von Dokumenten;
- die Versionierung oder
- die Funktion, das Dokument ad hoc im Browser zu betrachten oder schnell einige Informationen online zu editieren, ohne das Dokument zuvor herunterladen zu müssen.

Möglich ist aber auch, dass Mitarbeiter des Vertriebsteams durch Kollegen aus anderen Bereichen aktiv bei der Erstellung und Bearbeitung der Dokumente (Verträge, Angebote, Präsentationen, Marketingmaterialien) unterstützt werden können. So kann beispielsweise die Revision eines Vertrages durch die Rechtsabteilung losgelöst vom CRM vonstattengehen. Der „Freigabeworkflow" der Dokumentenmanagement-Funktion auf der Kollaborationsplattform spiegelt die finale Freigabe des Vertrags im CRM wider, sodass der Verkaufsprozess automatisiert in den nachfolgenden Arbeitsschritt gehen und das Vertriebsteam entsprechend informieren kann.

Eine Dokumentenablage in SharePoint aus der Sicht des CRM ist in einem Beispiel in Abbildung 2.4.5 zu sehen: Innerhalb von Dynamics CRM ist dies in der Integration mit Microsoft SharePoint in einer einfachen ersten Form bereits realisiert. Seit der Version CRM 2013 und SharePoint 2013 (oder den jeweiligen Online-Varianten) ist auch eine Server-Synchro-

nisation verfügbar, um nach der Konfiguration für Firmen, Kontakte oder weitere Entitäten in SharePoint Dokumentenbibliotheken anzulegen. Wenn Sie daraufhin ein Dokument zu einem Kunden ablegen wollen, wird für den Kunden in SharePoint ein Ordner angezeigt und das Dokument dort abgelegt. Dies alles geschieht vollkommen transparent aus dem CRM heraus.

Eine solche Integration ist ein erster Schritt in die richtige Richtung, da sie die Anforderung an eine gemeinsame Arbeit an Dokumenten im Team aus dem CRM heraus unterstützt und somit die Fülle an bekannten Funktionen zur Kollaboration auch für das CRM nutzbar macht.

Es gibt jedoch auch Anwendungsszenarien, in denen weiterführende Lösungsansätze gefragt sind:

- Die Beteiligung an Ausschreibungsverfahren ist ein hochgradig kollaboratives Anwendungsszenario. Hier geht es nicht mehr nur darum, einzelne Dokumente zu bearbeiten und effizient zu verwalten, sondern am besten einen vollständigen Projektarbeitsbereich für die Bearbeitung der Ausschreibungsunterlagen und die Zusammenarbeit mit den Kollegen aus anderen beteiligten Bereichen einzurichten. Dieser Projektarbeitsbereich wäre von einer Kollaborationsplattform bereitzustellen und eng mit dem Vorgang „Verkaufschance Ausschreibung" im CRM zu verknüpfen. Alle wichtigen Informationen aus dem CRM (Stakeholder beim Kunden, Mailverkehr, Vertriebsteam) würden direkt im Projektarbeitsbereich sichtbar werden. Der Einstieg in den Projektbereich liefe über das CRM. Gegebenenfalls könnte auch die Einstiegsseite des Projektes, welche z.B. die wichtige Projektskizze zeigt, direkt im CRM angezeigt werden.

- Ein weiteres vielversprechendes Anwendungsfeld sind gemeinsam gepflegte Sammlungen von unstrukturierten Notizen, Gedanken, Fotos, Audiohinweisen und Brainstormings zu Kunden, Verkaufschancen oder Projekten. Damit ließe sich dem beliebten Trend, dass jeder Vertriebsmitarbeiter eigene Notizbücher, Excellisten o.ä. irgendwo und irgendwie pflegt, effektiv begegnen, ohne den Komfort dieser individuellen Lösungen zu schmälern. Hervorragend ließe sich ein solches Szenario z.B. mit Microsoft Office OneNote und SharePoint lösen, wenn für den Datensatz (z.B. Verkaufschance) direkt aus Dynamics CRM heraus ein solches Notizbuch angelegt und anschließend das Vertriebsteam dazu eingeladen wird.

Verschiedene Microsoft-Partner bieten genau für diese Szenarien bereits abgestimmte Lösungen an, um CRM und SharePoint sowie OneNote für eine effiziente Teamzusammenarbeit und Dokumentenkollaboration zu verbinden.

Zu 2) CRM als integraler Teil des Enterprise Social Networks

Für Unternehmen, die bereits Enterprise Social Networks (ESN) und damit neue, schnelle und vereinfachte Formen der internen Kommunikation etabliert haben, bieten sich mit Social CRM noch weitere interessante Perspektiven.

Wenn das CRM ein integraler Teil des Social Intranets ist, dann können Fragen oder Anliegen der Kunden, aber auch Hilfegesuche für problematische Verkaufsgespräche im CRM eingestellt und automatisch über das Social Intranet für andere Mitarbeiter in der Organisation sichtbar gemacht werden, um deren Antworten zu erhalten. Wichtig hierbei ist jedoch, dass die gesammelten Ideen wiederum ihren Weg auch ins CRM finden, damit die Informationen für den Kunden- oder Vorgangs-Datensatz nicht verloren gehen.

Die beiden großen CRM-Anbieter Microsoft und Salesforce haben dies bereits erkannt und ihre Enterprise Social Networks eng mit ihren CRM-Lösungen verbunden, um genau dies zu ermöglichen: eine freie, schnelle und direkte Kommunikation über die CRM-Grenze hinweg mit dem gesamten sozialen Netzwerk des Unternehmens, um das verborgene Wissen der Mitarbeiter in die Kommunikation mit dem Kunden zu bringen.

MÖGLICHE HÜRDEN

Beide Lösungsansätze – der zweite sogar noch mehr als der erste – leben von einer offenen Unternehmenskultur, die das Teilen schätzt und fördert.

Plattformen, auf denen man Dokumente teilen und gemeinsam bearbeiten kann, sind heute vor allem im privaten Bereich weit verbreitet. Umso stärker werden Mitarbeiter es zukünftig als Mangel empfinden, wenn im Vertriebsprozess Informationen verloren gehen oder eine gemeinsame Dokumentenbearbeitung nicht möglich ist. Enterprise Social Networks sind noch nicht so häufig in Unternehmen anzutreffen. Wenn sie aber erfolgreich eingeführt wurden, wird der Wunsch, sie auch im Zusammenhang von CRM zu nutzen, schnell zunehmen.

Das Ingenieurbüro hhpberlin verzahnt Kundenmanagement-Software und Kollaborationsplattform

Das Ingenieurbüro hhpberlin verwaltet im Dynamics CRM strukturiert alle relevanten Daten rund um Kunden und Projekte. Hier sind alle Ansprechpartner, die Kommunikationshistorie, Anfragen und Projektaufträge angelegt, wie auch die entsprechenden Aufwendungen im Projekt und die jeweiligen Rechnungen. Auf der anderen Seite ist jedes Projekt mit einer SharePoint Site verbunden. Sobald ein neues Projekt im CRM erfasst wird, legt ein Prozess im Hintergrund nach den angegebenen Kriterien eine Projektwebsite an, auf der die Projektbeteiligten zusammenarbeiten können. Gerade durch diesen zentralen Kollaborationsort und ein hinterlegtes OneNote-Notizbuch in jeder Projektsite gehen auch kurze Notizen und Merkhinweise nicht verloren. Die Verbindung mit Dynamics CRM erlaubt es den Mitarbeitern, relevante E-Mails durch zwei einfache Klicks über Outlook im CRM zu verfolgen und einem konkreten Vorgang / Projekt zuzuordnen. Damit wird die gesamte Kommunikationshistorie erfasst und durch eine von hhpberlin realisierte Integration auch im SharePoint-Projekt sichtbar gemacht. Zudem werden allen Projektbeteiligten die Kennzahlen zum Budgetverbrauch angezeigt. Allein diese Kennzahlen haben dazu beigetragen, dass Stunden schneller erfasst werden und dem Kunden dadurch zeitnaher in Rechnung gestellt werden können, was den Cashflow positiv beeinflusste.

Ein wichtiger und sicher ein entscheidender Vorteil der Kombination aus Dynamics CRM und den SharePoint-Projektsites ist der Umstand, dass sich hier bei hhpberlin ein Zentralbereich für alle relevanten Informationen rund um einen Kunden und ein Projekt etabliert hat. Für solche Erfolgsbeispiele braucht es Visionäre wie Stefan Truthän, der unablässig seine Mitarbeiter befragt hat, was sie zusätzlich brauchen könnten, um effizienter zu arbeiten, und der parallel all seine Ideen eines produktiven Arbeitens festgehalten hat.

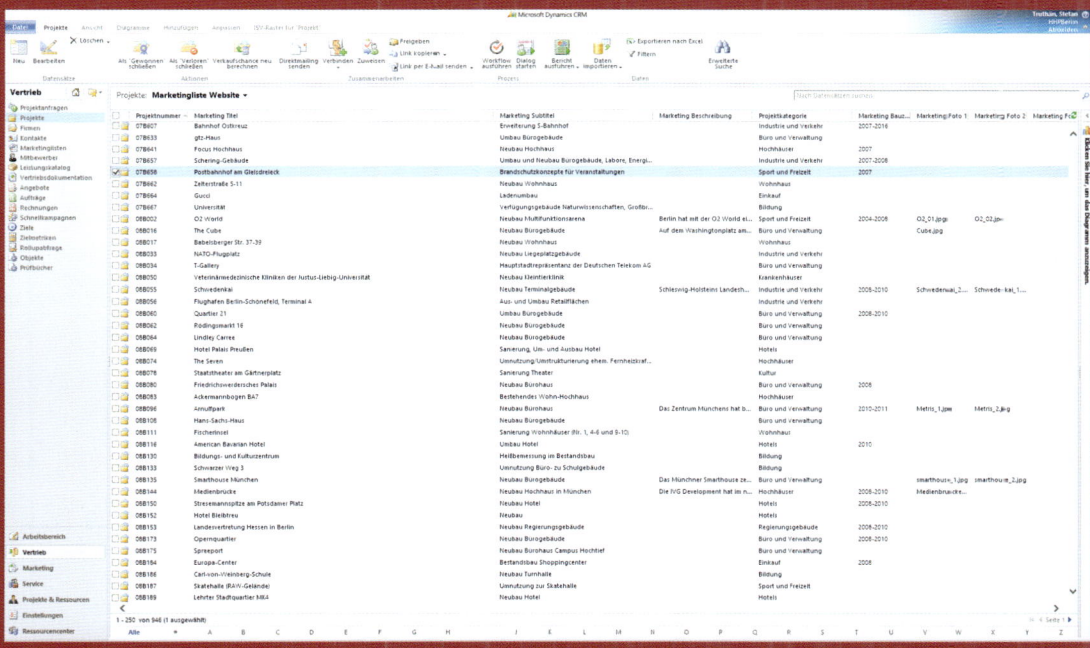

Abbildung 2.4.6: Liste der Projekte im CRM

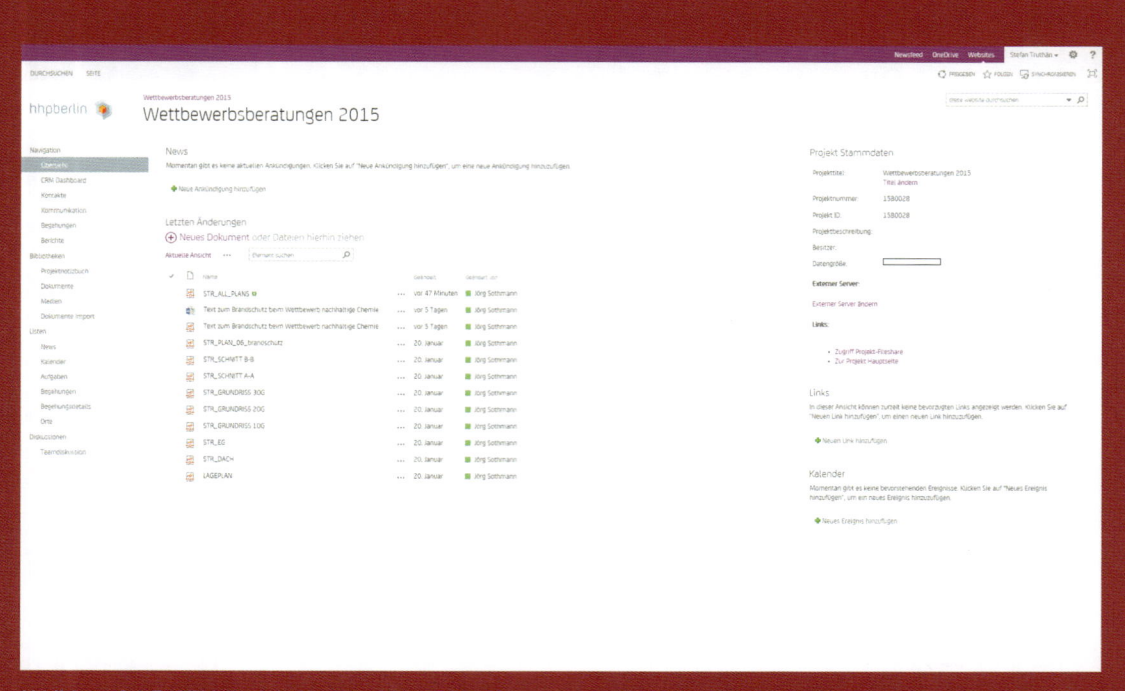

Abbildung 2.4.7: CRM-Projekt in einer SharePoint Site

Social Forecasting – Kollektive Intelligenz des Unternehmens nutzen

HERAUSFORDERUNG

Unternehmen, die sich in Branchen mit aggressivem Wettbewerb bewegen, müssen Innovationen schnell generieren und an den Markt bringen, um sich immer wieder Marktanteile zu sichern.

Dabei steht das Management stets vor der Herausforderung, möglichst zuverlässige Produkt- und Absatzprognosen zu treffen, obwohl die Entscheidungsparameter sehr unsicher sind. Um Entscheidungen zu fundieren, greifen Manager häufig auf die klassische Marktforschung in Form von Zielgruppenbefragungen zurück. Sie aber sind meist kostspielig und zeitaufwendig – das Potenzial der internen kollektiven Intelligenz bleibt ungenutzt.

LÖSUNGSANSATZ

Langzeituntersuchungen zeigen, dass Prognosen mittels Social Forecasting:

- nachweislich genauere Prognosen liefern. Social Forecasting ist in 76% aller Fälle genauer als die klassische Marktforschung.
- schneller als die Marktforschung sind. Innerhalb einer Woche sind fundierte Ergebnisse für eine Managemententscheidung möglich.
- zweimal geringere Kosten verursachen als Befragungen, Experten und Konzepttests.

Social Forecasting liefert eine kostengünstige und schnelle Methode, um im Rahmen von Entscheidungsprozessen systematisch die kollektive Intelligenz im Unternehmen zu erfassen und präzisere Vorhersagen treffen zu können. Es braucht dafür ein durch soziale Technologien vernetztes Unternehmen und eine in das Intranet eingebettete Prognosebörse.

Eine Prognosebörse funktioniert im Prinzip wie ein Aktienmarkt und enthält hohe Anteile von Gamification. Fachbereiche können dort Fragen einstellen, zu denen sie sich schnell die Meinung und Beurteilung vieler Menschen einholen wollen. Aus der Erfahrung eignen sich primär Fragen, die man an externe Marktforschungsagenturen abgeben würde, z.B. zu Absatzprognosen, Produktbeurteilungen, Innovationsbewertungen, R&D-Steuerung, Fragen zu Pricing, Beurteilung von Geschäftsmodellen oder ganz konkrete Fragen zur Positionierung gegenüber Wettbewerbern.

Jeder Mitarbeiter hat Zugang zu der Plattform und kann sein virtuelles Kapital einsetzen, um die Fragen zu beurteilen. Zahlreiche Gamification-Elemente sorgen dafür, dass Mitarbeiter Spaß daran haben, ihr Wissen dem Unternehmen zur Verfügung zu stellen.

Ein Prognosemarkt ist eine Plattform, die Folgendes umfasst:

- Profile von Experten zu den verschiedensten Themengebieten;
- die Eingabe von Prognosefragen mit Raum für Informationen, Bilder, Videos oder Grafiken;
- Ranglisten der guten Prognostiker;
- eine Übersicht des „Spielgeldes" der Mitarbeiter;
- Voting Tools für verschiedene Fragearten;
- Top-Prognosen und Fragen, die im Activity Stream sichtbar sind;
- die Möglichkeit, offene und geschlossene Prognosemärkte durchzuführen;
- die Möglichkeit, Teilnehmer einzuladen sowie

Datenquellen folgender Art:

- Stammdaten z.B. aus Nutzerverwaltungssystemen oder HR-Systemen;
- Nutzerprofile (durch Nutzer eingegeben);
- Umfangreiche Informationen zu den Fragen (durch den Fachbereich eingegeben);
- Teilnehmerdaten (aus Nutzersystemen oder via Schnittstelle zu Datenbanken, Excel o.ä.).

Dieser Abschnitt entstand in Zusammenarbeit mit Stephan Grabmeier Geschäftsführer Innovation Evangelist

MÖGLICHE HÜRDEN

- Es ist ein intelligentes Gesamtkonzept vonnöten, um die Prognosebörse für die Mitarbeiter auch auf lange Sicht attraktiv zu gestalten. Das Konzept sollte deshalb anhand der Erfahrungen immer weiter verbessert werden.
- Eine frühzeitige Einbindung und Überzeugung des Betriebsrates ist unabdingbar.
- Wissenschaftliche Studien zeigen, dass man mehr als 30 Personen benötigt, damit eine Prognose valide wird.
- Dem Culture-Change-Aspekt ist weit mehr Bedeutung zu widmen als der technischen Infrastruktur. Erst wenn das Management diese Arbeitsform als neue Chance erkennt und Wissen nicht mehr als Machtinstrument betrachtet, ist die Voraussetzung für einen wirkungsvollen Einsatz gegeben.

Prognosemärkte bei der Deutschen Telekom AG

Bei der Telekom erhielt jeder Mitarbeiter ein Startkapital von 5.000 „Telekom Dollar", die er wie bei einem Aktienmarkt in Ideen und Fragen investieren konnte.

Wir haben einen Prozessablauf entwickelt, der es dem Management ermöglicht, binnen fünf Arbeitstagen quantifzierte Ergebnisse der Telekom Crowd zu erhalten. Jeweils bis Montagnachmittag konnte eine Frage mit Hintergrundinformationen eingestellt werden, die einen Handelszeitraum von drei Tagen bis Donnerstagabend hatte. Der Freitag diente zur Auswertung der Ergebnisse. Am Montag darauf lag der Report des Prognosemarktes für das Management vor.

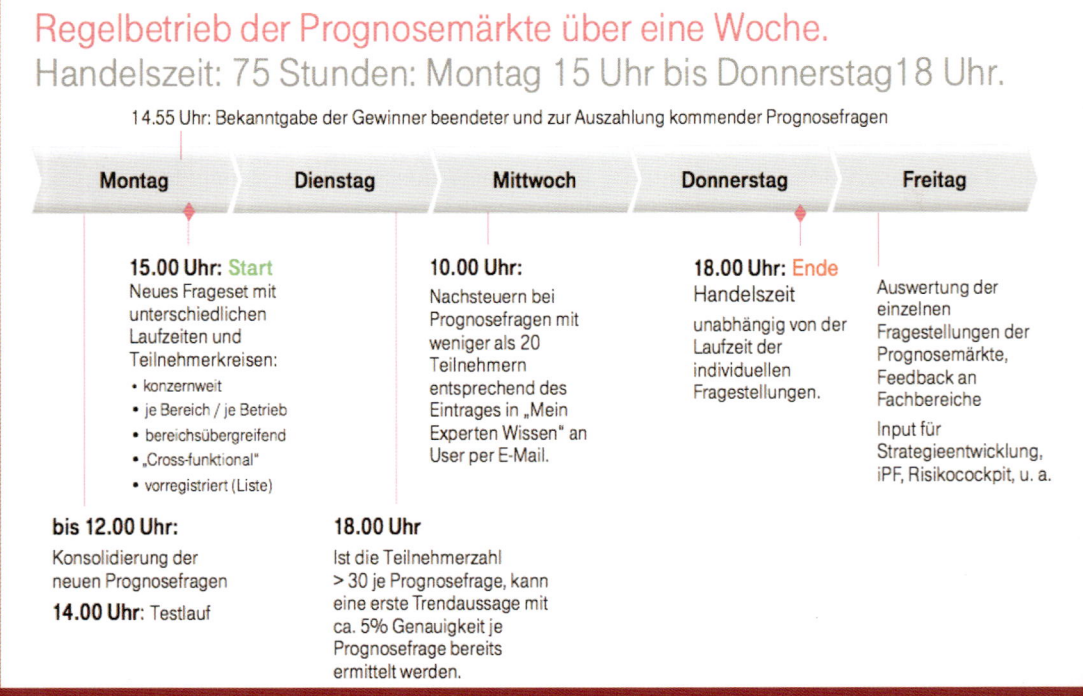

Abbildung 2.4.9: Handelszeit Prognosemärkte

Jährlich werden viele hundert Fragen online gestellt und durch die Cowd bewertet. Unsere wissenschaftlichen Untersuchungen zeigen, dass bereits 30 Beschäftigte ausreichen, um valide Ergebnisse von der Crowd zu erhalten.

Die folgende Übersicht zeigt Informationen aus dem Jahr 2013. Besonders hervorheben lässt sich der Wert von 83% Genauigkeit der Prognosen der Telekom Crowd. Industrieübergreifende Benchmarks weisen i.d.R. einen Wert < 70% auf.

Die Telekom Prognosemärkte in 2013:
das Jahr in Zahlen.

Mehr als
3.000
Registrierte Nutzer sind bei den Telekom Prognosemärkten dabei - Experten aus allen Fachbereichen.

Über
150.000
Prognosen wurden 2013 abgegeben, mehr als bei allen Wahlumfragen zur Sonntagsfrage des stern/RTL-Wahltrends im gesamten Jahr 2013.

73
Fragen aus 20 Fachbereichen wurden gestellt.

 Präzise: **94% Genauigkeit**
Pulsbefragung Nov.2013

 Wegweisend:
Geschäftsfahrrad

Mehr als
6.500
Kommentare haben alle Teilnehmer geschrieben. Würde man alle in einem Buch zusammenfassen, hätte es **350 Seiten** und wäre so dick, wie der erste Harry Potter Band.

6 Mio.
Telekom-Dollar haben alle Nutzer bei allen Fragen umgesetzt. Im Durchschnitt hat jeder Nutzer **271 T$ pro Frage** umgesetzt.

83%
Genauigkeit wurden durchschnittlich bei allen Fragen mit tatsächlichem Endergebnis erzielt. Bei mehr als der Hälfte der Fragen lag die Genauigkeit sogar bei über 90%.

 Smart:
Smart Home

 Lebensnah:
Digitales Testament

 Verspielt:
Arenafever

Was ist wichtig? Was wird heiß diskutiert? Trends, Prognosen, Hintergründe. Bleiben Sie auch 2014 am Ball!

 ERLEBEN, WAS VERBINDET.

 prognosemaerkte.telekom.de

Abbildung 2.4.10: Telekom Prognosemärkte – das Jahr in Zahlen

Mit Hilfe des Social Forecasting ist die Deutsche Telekom in der Lage, die Marktforschungsbudgets um über 70% zu reduzieren und gleichzeitig eine sicherere und schnellere Entscheidungsbasis für das Management zu schaffen. Für die Mitarbeiter entstand eine hohe Wertschätzung und ein motivierender Spaßfaktor beim Einsetzen des eigenen Wissens.

Zwei Beispiele zur konkreten Umsetzung der Telekom Prognosemärkte:

Entwicklung der Produkt-Roadmap im Bereich Product & Innovation

Eine Business Unit im Marktbereich Product & Innovation entwickelte mit den Telekom Prognosemärkten ihre Produkt-Roadmap für 2013/2014. In drei Wellen von je einer Woche wurden in einem geschlossenen Prognosemarkt mit knapp 200 Teilnehmern 47 Produkt- und Service-Ideen gehandelt und beurteilt. Im letzten Durchgang ließ das Management ein Ranking der Top-15-Produkte durchführen. Das Management nutzte die Ergebnisse der Crowd und setzte die zehn am besten bewerteten Produkte auf die Roadmap. Noch nie zuvor hatte ein Bereich mit dieser Methode in der Deutschen Telekom seine Planungsentscheidung auf die Basis kollektiver Intelligenz gestellt.

Pricing neuer Produkte bei T-Systems

Im Bereich New Business Development der T-Systems sollte das Pricing für Web Services in Deutschen Fußballstadien festgelegt werden. Das Expertenteam aus diesem Geschäftsbereich prognostizierte Einnahmen von rund einem Euro pro User. Der Vorstand stoppte die Entwicklung dieses Produktes, da es mit dieser Erlös-

Video „So funktioniert Social Forecasting am Beispiel der Telekom Prognosemärkte" http://bit.ly/1wwErE8

prognose nicht wirtschaftlich umsetzbar gewesen wäre. In dieser Phase stellte das Web Services Projektteam diese Herausforderung als Frage in die Telekom Prognosemärkte und ließ den Preis durch die Crowd ermitteln. Der Crowd-Erlös lag bei 3,89 EUR pro User. Eine erste Validierung mittels externer Marktforschung ergab exakt den gleichen Betrag.

Auf Basis der Prognosen wurde das Pricing angepasst und in den Vertragsverhandlungen damit argumentiert. Der Vorstand gab die Investitionen frei für die Produktentwicklung. Im April 2013 wurde das erste Produkt im Stadion von Bayer Leverkusen vorgestellt. Die zweite Validierungsstufe, die Nutzung durch die Fans und Kunden im Stadion, untermauerte die richtige Pricing-Prognose. Mit Hilfe der Telekom Prognosemärkte konnten somit siebenstellige Zusatzeinnahmen pro Stadion erzielt werden.

Das Feedback der Mitarbeiter für die neuen Formen der crowdbasierten Innovation mittels der Telekom Prognosemärkte war überwältigend gut. Die Bestätigung der offenen Dialogformen zeigte uns, wie sehr der Bedarf an Formaten mit Enterprise 2.0 vorhanden ist.

Projektmanagement – Herzstück für die Teamarbeit

HERAUSFORDERUNG

Schaut man in die Unternehmen, so sind dort neben den Regel- oder Prozessaufgaben stets auch zeitlich befristete Vorhaben oder Aufträge umzusetzen. Nicht jeder nennt es so, aber es sind Projekte. Ob klein oder groß, in vielen Projekten sind aktuelle Informationen im Team auszutauschen, Dokumente zu bearbeiten, Aufgaben zu erfassen und zu steuern, Anforderungslisten zu pflegen, Listen mit Verantwortlichkeiten und Ansprechpartnern zu verwalten.

In vielen Unternehmen wird Projektmanagement mit Excel-Dokumenten, E-Mails und einer Dokumenten-Ablage auf Laufwerken betrieben. Nicht verwunderlich sind daher die am häufigsten genannten Verbesserungswünsche von Projektmitarbeitern:

- Informationen schneller finden;
- Dateien gemeinsam bearbeiten;
- besserer Überblick über den Projektstatus.

Teure Projektmanagement-Tools sind häufig zu komplex und unflexibel für Projekte kleiner oder mittlerer Größe und daher entsprechend unbeliebt. Eine echte Alternative bieten moderne Kollaborationsplattformen, auf denen Projektteams an einem Ort alle Informationen finden, die sie für die effiziente Projektumsetzung benötigen.

LÖSUNGSANSATZ

Kollaborationsfunktionen sind das Herzstück der meisten Social-Software-Lösungen. Unternehmen, die bereits ein Social Intranet haben, können den Projektteams mit geringem Aufwand die technischen Features zur Verfügung stellen, die sie für eine effiziente Teamarbeit benötigen. Dies erfolgt durch die Bereitstellung eines Team-Raums bzw. einer Team-Community, die in der Regel standardmäßig Aufgabenlisten, Blogs und Newsfeeds, Wikis, Kalender und Dokumentenablage enthalten.

Obwohl die technische Bereitstellung mit ein paar Mausklicks erledigt ist, lehrt die Erfahrung, dass Teamräume insbesondere zu Beginn oft nur zögerlich oder gar nicht genutzt werden. Manchmal ist auch das Gegenteil der Fall und es entsteht schnell ein Wildwuchs an Teamräumen, bei dem man als Anwender den Überblick verliert.

Um dies zu vermeiden, empfiehlt es sich, vor der unternehmensweiten Einführung von

Teamräumen zunächst ausgewählte Pilotprojekte durchzuführen. Dabei verwenden bestehende Projektteams die neuen Features und versuchen durch kontinuierliche Verbesserungsmaßnahmen, einen immer höheren Effizienzgewinn durch die neue Technologie zu erzielen. Außerdem helfen die Pilotprojekte dabei zu erkennen, welche anderen Unternehmensanwendungen mit dem Projektraum verknüpft werden sollten. Das kann beispielsweise die automatische Vorbefüllung schon beim Anlegen eines Projekts sein, wenn in SAP oder CRM bereits Projektstammdaten vorhanden sind, oder – um ein anderes Beispiel zu nennen – die Integration von Projektmanagement-Tools wie Microsoft Project.

Sobald genügend Erfahrungen und Erfolge gesammelt sind und notwendige Verknüpfungen fehlerfrei funktionieren, lässt sich der Einführungsprozess im gesamten Unternehmen viel leichter gestalten.

MÖGLICHE HÜRDEN

Gerade die Projektarbeit bedarf einer effektiven Vorgehensweise und gemeinsamer Überzeugungen angesichts eines gemeinsamen Ziels. Damit sind - in der Art zu arbeiten – Umstellungen verbunden, was eine der größten Hürden bei der Einführung von Projektmanagement 2.0 darstellt.

Die Motivation, der Wille, das System haben zu wollen, ist die Grundlage für alles Weitere. Das steht, wie schon erläutert, am Anfang. Wird die Plattform dann angenommen und genutzt, besteht als nächstes die Gefahr eines Wildwuchses von Projektablagen. Klare Nutzungs-Guidelines sind deshalb nötig und gut gestaltete Einführungsprozesse, damit die verschiedenen Teamräume homogen bespielt werden und der Verwaltungsaufwand für die Intranet-Verantwortlichen überschaubar bleibt. Ein Community Manager (siehe auch 3.10) hat sich in vielen Unternehmen bewährt, um Qualität, Nutzer-

akzeptanz und Effizienzverbesserungen in der Projektarbeit zu erzielen.

Eine weitere Hürde stellt die zunehmend gewünschte Anbindung externer Nutzer, vor allem Partner oder Kunden, dar. Hier betreten wir das Anwendungsszenario Extranet, welches später beschrieben wird.

Relevant für die Umsetzung dieses Anwendungsszenarios ist die in Abschnitt 3.4 beschriebene Raumkonzeption.

Social HCM – Human Capital Management als echten Service begreifen

Dieser Abschnitt entstand in Zusammenarbeit mit Andrej Doms, Associate Partner – Portals & Social Con\ista Consulting.

HERAUSFORDERUNG

Neue Arbeitszeit- und Arbeitsplatzmodelle sorgen dafür, dass Mitarbeiter moderner Unternehmen immer weniger ortsgebunden sind und zu den üblichen Bürozeiten vielfach nicht arbeiten müssen. Diese Flexibilisierung bedeutet auch, dass diese Menschen nicht mehr an den zumeist papier- und ortsgebundenen Prozessen im Personalbereich teilnehmen können. Dokumente werden per Post versandt, Medienbrüche geschaffen und Prozesslaufzeiten verlängern sich. Im klassischen Ansatz werden die Prozesse in einem Content-getriebenen Intranet beschrieben, aber völlig losgelöst davon per Post, E-Mail oder Telefon umgesetzt. Dabei sind Information, prozessbezogene Daten und Kommunikation verteilt über verschiedenste Systeme.

Diese Komplexität erleben nicht nur Ihre Mitarbeiter, sondern auch Personalsachbearbeiter und Führungskräfte. Das Management steht vor der neuen Herausforderung, solche Prozesse an die Realitäten im Arbeitsalltag der Mitarbeiter anzupassen und als flexible Services bereitzustellen, die von den Mitarbeitern unabhängig von Zeit, Ort oder Gerät abgerufen werden können.

LÖSUNGSANSATZ

Wenn Sie HCM-Prozesse als Service für Ihre Mitarbeiter betrachten, dann müssen Aufbereitung und Präsentation der Services völlig neu gestaltet werden. In einem einheitlichen Service Portal sollten alle Informationen, Kommunikation und Services zusammenlaufen und den Menschen eine gesamtheitliche Sicht auf HCM-Prozesse bieten. Ihre Mitarbeiter sind bereits im Web 2.0 angekommen. Einen Service Ihres Personalbereiches zu nutzen, muss genauso einfach sein, wie eine Buchbestellung bei Amazon oder ein Schuhkauf bei Zalando.

An folgende Bestandteile sollten Sie für Ihr Portal denken:

Personalisierte Service-Center-Startseite

Eine personalisierte Startseite ermöglicht dem Mitarbeiter einen leichten Zugang zu seinen Daten und Prozessen und bietet bereits die wichtigsten Punkte auf einen Blick. Ein einfacher Zugang zu komplexen Szenarien ist das wichtigste Ziel für HCM-Prozesse.

Präsentation der Services und Ansprechpartner

Dies verschafft Ihren Mitarbeitern eine Übersicht über die Prozesse und bringt über die Vorstellung der Ansprechpartner eine wichtige persönliche Note in ein sehr sensibles Thema. Aus „der Personalabteilung" wird „mein Personalsachbearbeiter", mein persönlicher Dienstleister, ganz so wie bei einem Finanzdienstleister oder in der Kfz-Werkstatt meines Vertrauens. Durch diesen emotionalen Wandel im Qualitätsempfinden der Mitarbeiter bereiten Sie den Weg für die Umstellung der internen Personaldienstleistungen auf Self-Service-Szenarien.

Informationen zu den Prozessen

Die klassische Präsentation der HR-Informationen in Dokumenten und langen Websites wird durch wenige einfach und klar strukturierte Webseiten ersetzt, die die Sachverhalte vereinfachen und mit den wichtigsten Informationen darstellen. Tiefgreifende und umfängliche Dokumentationen werden optional angeboten. Denken Sie an eine gut aufgebaute Webseite einer Krankenversicherung, die komplexe Sachverhalte so vereinfacht, dass jedermann sie nachvollziehen kann. Aus diesen Informationsseiten können jederzeit die zugehörigen Services gestartet werden.

Self-Service-Online-Dienste

Self-Service-Dienste in einem HCM-Portal bieten Ihren Mitarbeitern Zugang zu jeder Zeit und an jedem Ort. Formulare werden online ausgefüllt, Genehmigungen im Portal ausgelöst und Belege eingescannt, Bescheinigungen automatisiert erstellt und vom Mitarbeiter ausgedruckt. Lange Wartezeiten entfallen. Ihre HR-Mitarbeiter können sich auf die wesentlichen Aufgaben im Personalmanagement und der Personalentwicklung konzentrieren und sind von zeitraubenden Standardvorgängen befreit. Die Services bedienen sich dabei direkt aus ihren vorhandenen HCM-Stammdaten und Prozessen, die Sie z.B. bereits in SAP HCM realisiert haben.

Ein zentrales Aufgaben-Center rund um HCM-Prozesse

Das zentrale Aufgaben-Center ist Teil des personalisierten Portals. Wiedervorlagen, Fristen und Freigaben werden hier genauso für Mitarbeiter wie für Führungskräfte geführt. Per E-Mail werden die Mitarbeiter regelmäßig über fällige Aufgaben informiert. Stellvertreter-Regelungen bei Urlaub oder Krankheit werden transparent. Auch komplexe Prozesse wie z.B. das Onboarding neuer Mitarbeiter werden hier plötzlich transparent und können effizienter durchgeführt werden. Auf einen Blick kann jeder Prozessbeteiligte erkennen, welche Aufgaben noch offen sind und an welchem Punkt der Prozess momentan steht.

Moderne Kommunikationsmöglichkeiten über soziale Features

Newsfeeds, die in die Self Services eingebunden sind, erlauben eine einfache prozessgebundene Kommunikation mit den Personalsachbearbeitern. Befreit von den Limitierungen einer E-Mail, stehen die Antworten auf die wichtigsten Mitarbeiterfragen allen Beteiligten zur Verfügung. Vorgesetzte können direkt in diese Kommunikation eingebunden werden.

Mobiler Zugang zu allen Services

Mobiler Zugang zu wichtigen Services ist kein Luxus mehr, sondern ein essenzieller Bestandteil einer modernen Prozesslandschaft. Man ist befreit von der Notwendigkeit, am Schreibtisch oder über das Notebook permanent „angebunden" zu sein, weil auch unterwegs am Smartphone oder zwischen zwei Terminen Kontakte mit dem Unternehmen (z.B. Genehmigungen) erfolgen können, ohne lange zu warten oder den Tagesfluss zu durchbrechen. Mit der Kamera des Smartphones oder Tablets können Belege einfach abfotografiert und korrigiert werden, über die eingebauten Druckfunktionen auch außerhalb des Büros z.B. im Hotel Bescheinigungen ausgedruckt werden. Sogar die Gehaltsabrechnung sollten Sie nicht mehr mit der Post verschicken müssen.

Ein attraktives und gut gestaltetes HR-Portal ist ein wichtiger Anziehungspunkt für Mitarbeiter und häufig einer der meistbesuchten Bereiche von Intranets. Evaluationen nach der Einführung von Social HCM zeigen in der Regel die stärksten Effekte in folgender Hinsicht:

- nachweislich deutlich höhere Zufriedenheit mit den HR-Services bei den Mitarbeitern;
- deutliche Steigerung der Effizienz der HCM- Prozesse;
- Entlastung des Personalbereichs von administrativen Tätigkeiten und dadurch mehr Ressourcen für strategische Personalarbeit.

MÖGLICHE HÜRDEN

- Nötig ist ein intelligentes Gesamtkonzept, um ein HCM-Portal und Self Services für die Mitarbeiter attraktiv zu gestalten. Dieses Konzept sollte entsprechend der alltäglichen Erfahrungen im Betrieb kontinuierlich verbessert werden.
- Eine frühzeitige Einbindung und Überzeugung des Betriebsrates ist auch hier unabdingbar.
- Dem Cultural-Change-Aspekt ist besondere Aufmerksamkeit zu widmen. Der Service und der Self-Service-Gedanke müssen erst an die Menschen herangetragen werden.
- Die Akzeptanz der Mitarbeiter für diese Lösungen hängt sehr stark von der Qualität der Präsentation und der intuitiven Bedienung ab. Interface-Designer sind in der Lage, gefällige und einfache Lösungen zu schaffen.
- Besonders beim Schutz persönlicher Daten haben die Beteiligten – je nach Position und Rolle – häufig sehr unterschiedliche Standpunkte. Sorgen Sie für eine einheitliche Sichtweise, damit Missverständnisse nicht zu Show-Stoppern werden.

HCM-Self-Service bei einem Anlagenbauer

Bei einem Anlagenbauer mit 4.000 Mitarbeitern weltweit werden aus Deutschland heraus alle HCM-Prozesse gemanagt. Es gibt in den regionalen Niederlassungen keine HR-Abteilungen, lediglich einzelne Fachkräfte.

Um den Mitarbeitern in aller Welt einen hochwertigen mehrsprachigen HR-Service anbieten zu können und dabei die zentrale HRM-Abteilung weiter in die Lage zu versetzen, strategische Personalmanagement-Aufgaben wahrzunehmen, wurde beschlossen, ein zentrales HCM-Self-Service-Center zu schaffen. Dieses Service-Center sollte ein zentraler Anlaufpunkt in einem neuen Intranet werden.

Das HCM-Self-Service-Center wurde als erster Baustein eines Social-Intranet-Projekts konzipiert und umgesetzt. Dabei wurde insbesondere Wert auf einen einfachen Zugang und eine unkomplizierte Integration in die SAP-basierten HCM-Prozesse gelegt. Die Prozesse und Stammdaten verblieben im SAP. Das User Interface für Employee- und Manager-Self-Services jedoch sollte im Intranet und auf den mobilen Devices verfügbar sein. Insbesondere für die Führungskräfte war der mobile Zugriff besonders wichtig, da auch die Teams international aufgestellt sind und erhebliche Reisetätigkeiten anfallen.

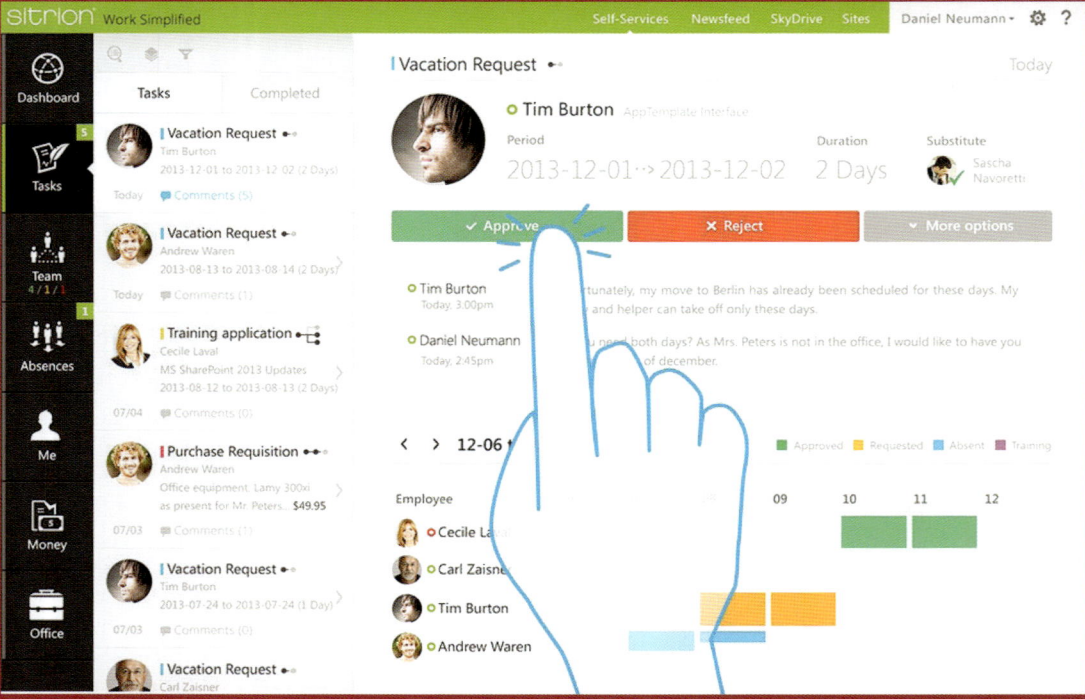

Abbildung 2.4.11: Mit diesem HR-Self-Service-Portal erreicht man alle wichtigen Personalprozesse mit der Fingerspitze.

In den letzten acht Jahren hat sich die Mitarbeiterzahl auf 4.000 Mitarbeiter verdoppelt. Der Arbeitsanfall im HCM-Team hat sich in der gleichen Zeit durch die Internationalisierung, hohe Fluktuation und durch Restrukturierungen mehr als vervierfacht. Mit Hilfe der Harmonisierung und der Automatisierung manueller Prozesse sowie der Verlagerung in Self Services konnten diese Steigerungsraten ohne eine personelle Anpassung bewältigt werden.

Für die Mitarbeiter bedeutet dieser Service eine höhere Flexibilität und eine deutliche Vereinfachung der HCM-Prozesse, da die Services auch mobil abgerufen werden können und die Komplexität hinter leicht zu bedienenden Oberflächen versteckt wurde.

Das HCM-Self-Service-Portal gehört in dem genannten Unternehmen zu den drei meistbesuchten Seiten und erhält durchweg positives Feedback. Insbesondere die mehrsprachige Umsetzung und die einfache Vernetzung mit den HR-Fachkräften über den Einsatz von Newsfeeds werden ausgesprochen positiv bewertet.

Hier noch zwei konkrete Beispiele für Prozesse, die im Self-Service-Portal umgesetzt wurden:

Anlegen einer neuen Stelle im SAP

Das Anlegen einer neuen Stelle im SAP ist ein sehr komplexer Prozess, der viele Transaktionen und teilweise auch eine manuelle Datenübernahme in die unterschiedlichen Teilprozesse erfordert. Bisher wurden diese Prozesse durch komplexe papiergebundene Formulare von der Führungskraft initiiert, manuell in das SAP HCM-System übertragen und dann in verschiedensten Transaktionen verarbeitet. Der Prozess verläuft rein iterativ und hat sehr lange Laufzeiten.

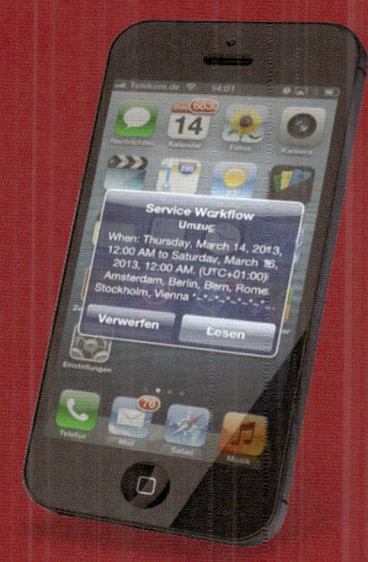

Abbildung 2.4.12: Freigabe von Prozessen über das Smartphone

Im neuen Self-Service-Portal wird für das Anlegen einer neuen Stelle ein einfaches elektronisches Formular angeboten, das mit einer Vorgabe bzw. vorgeschlagenen Werten aus dem SAP vorbelegt ist. Dabei werden bereits beim Ausfüllen des Formulars wichtige Validierungen durchgeführt und die Führungskraft auf eventuelle Stolpersteine hingewiesen. Die Transaktionen im SAP werden nach einer Prüfung durch die HR-Fachkräfte automatisch durchgeführt und der Fortschritt im Self-Service-Center dokumentiert. Die Laufzeiten für das Anlegen einer neuen Stelle konnten um ca. 70% reduziert werden. Papiergebundene Formulare werden überhaupt nicht mehr benötigt. Dieser Prozess konnte in leicht reduzierter Form auch für Stellenänderungen etabliert werden.

Mitarbeiter-Self-Service bei Stammdatenänderungen

Stammdatenänderungen und Gehaltsnachweise sind klassische papiergebundene Prozesse. Für Veränderungen an den Stammdaten sind Unterlagen einzureichen, die z.B. beim Einwohnermeldeamt oder bei Krankenkassen ausgestellt werden. Im Unternehmen sind ebenfalls papiergebundene Formulare auszufüllen und bei der HR-Abteilung einzureichen.

Neben den notwendigen Postwegen innerhalb und außerhalb des Unternehmens sorgen papiergebundene Genehmigungsprozesse sowie die Kommunikation bei Rückfragen für lange Laufzeiten. Die Dokumentation der Prozesse erfolgt im Rahmen dicker papiergebundener Personalakten. Im Self-Service-Portal können die Mitarbeiter die Prozesse direkt durch ein elektronisches Formular initiieren und werden durch Formularassistenten durch den gesamten Vorgang geführt. Dabei werden Eingaben validiert, unnötige Eingaben ausgeblendet und die Auswirkungen z.B. einer veränderten Steuerklasse direkt erklärt. Der Prozessverlauf wird transparent gemacht und dokumentiert. Anlagen reichen die Mitarbeiter z.B als Handyfoto ein. Der gesamte Vorgang wird nicht nur im SAP prozessiert, sondern auch in einer digitalen Personalakte archiviert. Die Mitarbeiter im HR-Bereich überprüfen die Vorgänge und geben die Transaktionen in einem elektronischen Prozess frei.

Dieser Abschnitt entstand in Zusammenarbeit mit Andreas Rohr, Freiberuflicher Software-Architekt/ Senior-Berater conaro

Integrationen – Nutzerfreundliches Arbeiten ohne Grenzen

HERAUSFORDERUNG

Ein Intranet sollte keine Insel sein. Weder inhaltlich noch technologisch. Um einen Mehrwert für die Benutzer eines Intranets zu schaffen, ist es meist notwendig, Daten aus anderen Unternehmensanwendungen zu beziehen oder sogar sich an deren Prozesse anzuknüpfen.

LÖSUNGSANSATZ

Um das Integrationsszenario geeignet auszugestalten, sollten die Stärken und Schwächen des zu integrierenden Systems sowie die Vorteile der Intranet-Nutzer bei einer Integration ausführlich analysiert werden. Darauf aufbauend sind drei Stufen der Integration in Betracht zu ziehen:

- **Stufe 1:** Reine Datenintegration,
- **Stufe 2:** Alternatives User Interface,
- **Stufe 3:** Vollständige Prozessintegration.

Für die technische Umsetzung von Integrationsszenarien gibt es je nach Intranet-Technologie bereits zahlreiche unterstützende Schnittstellen und Frameworks, die jedoch stets einen unternehmensindividuellen Konfigurations- oder Entwicklungsbedarf erfordern.

MÖGLICHE HÜRDEN

Die größte Hürde bei Integrationsszenarien ist nicht die initiale Umsetzung, sondern die Sicherstellung, dass die Integration langfristig stabil und kompatibel läuft. Kritische Punkte sind hier beispielsweise Updates und Upgrades eines der Systeme oder der zielgerichtete Umgang mit Störungsanalysen.

AUSFÜHRLICHERES ZUM ANWENDUNGSFALL

Vor einigen Jahren war es schon ein Fortschritt, wenn im sogenannten Self-Service-Bereich die üblichen Unternehmensformulare im PDF-Format zum Download angeboten wurden.

Doch wieviel Attraktivität würde ein Intranet gewinnen, wenn es nicht nur das Formular, sondern den gesamten Prozess bzw. Workflow anbieten könnte? Wenn also der Benutzer durch eine z.T. vorausgefüllte Erfassungsmaske empfangen und bei den nächsten Schritten begleitet würde. Dabei würden dann die benötigten Daten aus den entsprechenden Quellsystemen herangezogen.

Ein Klassiker dafür ist der Urlaubsantrag. Diesen Antrag könnte der Benutzer im Intranet eingeben. Er würde dabei sehen, wie hoch sein verbleibender Urlaubsanspruch ist und u.U. auch, ob es bereits von Kollegen Anträge für denselben Zeitraum gibt. Die Informationen könnten dabei aus dem SAP HR-System stammen. Und auch die nächsten Schritte erfolgen zumeist im SAP HR-System. Bei einer entsprechenden Integration würde das Intranet dem Benutzer die HR-Daten aus SAP anzeigen, die erfassten Antragsdaten an das SAP-System weiterreichen und den Status des entsprechenden SAP-Workflows an den Intranet-Benutzer kommunizieren.

Ein ähnlicher Klassiker ist der Prozess der internen Bestellung bzw. Bedarfsanforderung. Hier erwartet der Benutzer, dass er einen hübsch anzuschauenden Warenkatalog durchstöbern kann, so wie er es im privaten Bereich dank Amazon & Co. gewöhnt ist. Muss er seine Bestellung jedoch mittels SAPGUI absetzen, wird er eines Besseren belehrt. Und auch sein Vorgesetzter, der die Bestellung beispielsweise prüfen und gegebenenfalls genehmigen soll, wird keinen Komfort im zuständigen System antreffen. Dementsprechend sind solche Tätigkeiten auch eher unpopulär. Gerade bei solchen Prozessen, bei denen sich sogenannte Gelegenheitsnutzer mit den Quellsystemen (wie hier im Beispiel SAP) schwertun, bietet es sich an, ein alternatives vereinfachtes User Interface zu schaffen – etwa direkt im modernen Intranet.

Diese Beispiele zeigen, dass man bei der Integration eines Intranets von mehreren Stufen sprechen kann:

Stufe 1 – Reine Datenintegration

Das Intranet konsumiert Daten aus anderen Quellsystemen und zeigt diese Daten in Listen oder als Auswahlmöglichkeiten innerhalb des Intranets an. Eine Sonderform dieser Stufe ist die Integration über die Suchfunktion. Dabei sind die Daten oder zumindest Teilbereiche der Daten und der Quellsysteme für das Intranet lesbar und können als Suchergebnisse innerhalb der User Interfaces des Intranets angezeigt werden.

Stufe 2 – Alternative User Interfaces

Das Intranet dient dabei quasi als Erfassungswerkzeug und stellt sein User Interface zur Verfügung. Die erfassten Daten werden dann in einer Einbahnstraße an das entsprechende zuständige System weitergereicht.

Stufe 3 – Vollständige Prozessintegration

Dies ist gewissermaßen eine Ausbaustufe der zuvor genannten Stufe. Hierbei werden die vollständigen Prozesse eingebunden. Die Daten werden nicht nur über ein alternatives Frontend erfasst und übergeben, sondern die Prozessschritte werden überwacht. Es kann sogar sein, dass einige Prozessschritte im Intranet erfolgen. Das setzt u.a. eine Workflow-Engine beim Intranet voraus, hört sich aber komplexer und aufwendiger an, als es tatsächlich ist.

Oft wird man je nach Bedarf Mischformen dieser Integrationsstufen antreffen.

Aber neben diesen eher klassischen Integrationsformen, die zumeist strukturierte Daten und Prozesse betreffen, werden derzeit dank Social Business und Generation Y auch neue Formen der Integration intensiv diskutiert:

Wie kann man beispielsweise Daten aus anderen Unternehmensanwendungen in Newsfeeds einbinden? Soll man Daten für diese Unternehmensanwendungen quasi intern „twittern" können? Wann macht so etwas Sinn? Oder sollte man Daten und Objekte des Quellsystems besser „liken", so wie wir es schon im privaten Bereich bei Facebook tun? Wie kann ich die Strukturen der klassischen Datenwelt mit der eher adhoc-gesteuerten „neuen" Arbeitswelt zusammenführen?

Ansätze und Prototypen gibt es bereits. Spannend wird es, ob und wie sie sich durchsetzen und unsere Arbeitswelt bereichern werden.

Zusammenfassend kann man festhalten, dass eine wie auch immer geartete Integration des Intranets IMMER einen Mehrwert generiert. Man sollte den entsprechenden Aufwand natürlich im Auge behalten, aber die meisten Leser werden staunen, was mittlerweile technisch mit überschaubaren Mitteln möglich ist. Es ist definitiv keine Zauberei.

Experten finden – Erfahrungen und Know-how im Unternehmen besser nutzen

HERAUSFORDERUNG

Im Intranet sollen die richtigen Ansprechpartner für spezielle Problemstellungen und Themen zielgerichtet gefunden werden. Hierbei sollen auch die Experten auffindbar sein, die Kenntnisse in bestimmten Bereichen unabhängig von ihrem aktuellen Tätigkeitsprofil haben.

LÖSUNGSANSATZ

Experten werden gefunden auf Basis folgender Informationen:

- Entsprechend der Abteilungen, die für gewisse Themen verantwortlich sind;
- gemäß offizieller Stellenbeschreibungen;
- gemäß den vom Nutzer selbst im Profil angegebenen Schwerpunkten und Interessen;
- gemäß bisheriger durchgeführter Projekte, Tätigkeiten und den Skills aus dem Lebenslauf;
- gemäß Aktivitäten im Intranet zu bestimmten Themen (Dokumente, Blogbeiträge, Kommentare);

Datenquellen:

- Stammdaten aus Nutzerverwaltungssystem und HR-Systemen;
- Nutzerprofile (durch Nutzer angereichert mit eigenen Informationen);
- Aktivitätenstrom;
- Profile in unterschiedlichen Ausprägungen, etwa als
  - statische Profilseiten, generiert aus Mitarbeiterstammdaten,
  - durch Mitarbeiter gepflegte Profile (z.B. MySite von Microsoft),
- ggf. sind Projektdatenbanken gekoppelt mit den Nutzerprofilen, so dass bei jedem Mitarbeiter automatisch die Information zugeordnet wird, in welchen Projekten er bereits gearbeitet hat.

Zur Umsetzung dieses Szenarios sollten mindestens die Intranet-Features „Profilseite" und „Suche" sowie die Verschlagwortungsmöglichkeit bereitgestellt werden.

MÖGLICHE HÜRDEN

- Mit dem Betriebsrat und dem Datenschutzbeauftragten muss im Rahmen des Intranet-Projektes die Verfügbarkeit der personenbezogenen Daten im Intranet abgestimmt sein. Hierzu gehört die Diskussion über Gründe von personenbezogenen Suchanfragen sowie die Auswertbarkeit der Daten. Solche Themen bergen meist strittiges Potenzial, doch müssen sie nicht zwangsläufig durch technische Restriktionen gelöst werden. In jedem Fall aber ist der Umgang mit den Daten als Bestandteil von Betriebsvereinbarungen zu verankern.
- Führungskräfte wollen nicht, dass die eigenen Leute gefunden werden – das Potenzial für Effizienzverbesserung und Synergiefindung wird deshalb in der Firma nicht hinreichend wahrgenommen.
- Die Qualität der Expertensuche wird sich erst mit entsprechender Zeit und mit gut angereicherten Profildaten und Intranet-Inhalten entwickeln, ggf. ist die Erwartungshaltung am Anfang zu hoch.
- Vielleicht sind die Informationen noch gar nicht vollständig erfasst und müssen zunächst harmonisiert werden. Auch gibt es den Fall, dass Mitarbeiter nicht gefunden werden wollen. Hier schließen sich wieder Mitarbeiteraktivierungsthemen an.

AUSFÜHRLICHERES ZUM ANWENDUNGSFALL

Die Umsetzung solch einer Expertensuche kann je nach Technologie, Ausbaustufe des Intranets und Tagesgeschäft des eigenen Unternehmens sehr unterschiedlich sein. Beginnen Sie daher mit der Bestandsaufnahme von bereits vorhandenen Informationen und planen Sie die gezielte Verbindung mit den Mitarbeiterprofilen und die Integration in die Suche. Besonderes Augenmerk kann dann darauf gelegt werden, welche Suchmöglichkeiten in unterschiedlichen Medien angeboten bzw. wo diese integriert werden. Expertensuchen können neben einer klassischen Suchmaske auf der Intranet-Seite u.a. auch in die Instant Messaging Software integriert werden (z.B. in Microsoft Lync).

Social Learning – Moderne Personalentwicklung für eine lernende Organisation

HERAUSFORDERUNG

In vielen Unternehmen werden vor allem die Mitarbeiterentwicklung und das tägliche Geschäft getrennt voneinander betrachtet. Lernen geschieht entweder im Klassenraum oder als eLearning-Einheit. Nicht selten erleben Personalentwickler eine Art Schulungsmüdigkeit, da die Angebote nicht mehr dem entsprechen, was Mitarbeiter sich wünschen.

Die Trends in diesem Bereich zeigen, dass Mitarbeiter nicht mehr bereit sind, zu einer bestimmten Zeit an einem bestimmten Ort zu lernen. Auch von anonymen eLearning-Angeboten nehmen Arbeitnehmer zunehmend Abstand. Es besteht der Wunsch nach Interaktion mit „realen" Personen (Video Chat statt Einzel-eLearning-Kurs) und nach zeit- und ortsunabhängigen, auch mobilen Lernangeboten, die sich nahtlos in den Arbeitsalltag integrieren lassen (Pappas, 2014).

In einer immer stärker globalisierten Geschäftswelt beschäftigen sich immer mehr Unternehmen damit, wie Social Learning als zeitgemäße Form der flexiblen bedarfsgerechten Personalentwicklung in die interne Lern- und Wissensstrategie integriert werden kann. Was Social Learning ausmacht, ist nicht nur die Anwendung von Web-2.0-Funktionalitäten wie Blogs, Wikis und Kommentaren in der Geschäftswelt, sondern die Integration dieser Funktionalitäten in mitarbeiterbezogene und arbeitsnahe Anwendungsfälle.

LÖSUNGSANSATZ

Heutzutage ist es wichtig zu verstehen, dass Lernen nichts ist, was losgelöst passieren sollte. Das Lernsystem ist eng an die täglichen Arbeitsprozesse und die konkreten Situationen, in denen Lernbedarf entsteht, anzuknüpfen. Moderne Learning-Management-Systeme (LMS) sind heutzutage sehr gut mit Web-2.0-Technologien wie Communities, Blogs Wikis etc. ausgestattet, jedoch werden sie meist außerhalb der traditionellen Social-Business-Anwendungen gesehen. Das Lernen wird dadurch für Mitarbeiter zu etwas, was sie zusätzlich machen müssen.

Für Unternehmen sollte deshalb wichtig sein, dass moderne Social-Learning-Anwendungsfälle in die täglichen Arbeitsabläufe des Mitarbeiters integriert werden. Im besten Fall merkt der Lernende gar nicht, dass er gerade dabei ist, etwas zu lernen. Diese Entwicklung erfordert von jedem Unternehmen eine Begleitung:

- Die Mitarbeiter müssen darin gefördert werden, selbstständig Lerninhalte zu suchen und sich weiterzuentwickeln. Kresse spricht in diesem Zusammenhang von einer „Mitmach-Personalentwicklung" (Kresse, 2011). Hier bedarf es vielerorts einer neuen Qualität von Vertrauenskultur dem Lernenden gegenüber, aber auch einer gezielten Förderung der Such- und Selbstlernkompetenz von Mitarbeitern.
- Auch werden sich die Rollen in der Lernkultur eines Unternehmens stark verändern. Führungskräfte und Personalentwickler geben weniger vor, sondern agieren in der Rolle des Enablers, der die Voraussetzungen für erfolgreiches eigenverantwortliches Lernen schafft. Trainer dagegen werden in Zukunft weniger losgelöste Angebote schaffen, sondern den Lernenden kontinuierlich begleiten in der Rolle eines Community Managers (Robes, 2011).

MÖGLICHE HÜRDEN

- Social Learning wird zu technisch betrachtet (Nutzung von Web-2.0-Funktionen).
- Die Anwendungsfälle des Social Learning müssen in ein ganzheitliches Lernkonzept integriert werden (Strategische Planung).

Dieser Abschnitt entstand in Zusammenarbeit mit Sandra Brückner, Social Business Consultant Pokeshot///SMZ

- Für die Verankerung des Social Learning ist ein aktives und vorausschauendes Change Management zwingend notwendig.

Wie genau aber können die neuen Formen des Lernens aussehen? Welche Anwendungsfälle gibt es bereits und welche Erfahrungen lassen sich daraus ableiten? Im Folgenden finden Sie ein konkretes Beispiel eines sehr beliebten Anwendungsfalls für Social Learning: den Onboarding-Prozess.

Onboarding bei einer großen Versicherung

Das Onboarding von Mitarbeitern ist die erste Chance eines Unternehmens, einer Abteilung oder eines Projektteams, neue Kollegen an Prozesse zu gewöhnen und grundlegendes Wissen zu vermitteln. Aber auch andersherum bringen neue Kollegen oft Wissen mit, das für das Unternehmen interessant ist.

Mit dem Ziel, neue Mitarbeiter schnell zu integrieren und schnell deren Vertrauen für eine langfristige Bindung aufzubauen, führte ein großer Versicherungsdienstleister eine Onboarding Community ein. Diese basierte auf dem Social-Learning-Produkt „SmarterPath", dessen Social-Learning-Elemente gezielt an die Bedürfnisse des Unternehmens angepasst wurden. Als Besonderheit wurde beispielsweise ein Onboarding Path entwickelt.

Mit modernen Social Learning Tools wie z.B. SmarterPath ist es möglich, jedem Mitarbeiter einen individuell zugeschnittenen Einarbeitunsplan (Enablement Path) zuzuordnenden. Dabei können dem personalisierten Plan nicht nur eLearning-Kurse, sondern auch interaktive Community-Elemente (Verbindung zu Personen, Gruppen, etc.) zugeordnet werden. Der Lernende erhält durch SmarterPath einen genauen Überblick, welche Elemente er bereits durchgeführt hat und welche nicht. Individuelle Pläne lassen sich in SmarterPath speichern und können jederzeit neuen Mitarbeitern zugeordnet werden.

Weiterführend entwickelte das Umsetzungsteam eine Gamification-Strategie, um durch motivierende Aspekte wie z.B. Badges oder Punkte das Onboarding zusätzlich zu unterstützen.

Eine Evaluation durch das Umsetzungsteam ergab folgenden konkreten Nutzen:
- Alle Informationen befinden sich an einem Platz in der Community (integriertes Lernen).
- Alle Angebote werden über eine Plattform („SmarterPath") zur Verfügung gestellt. Bei Pflichtschulungen ist es nicht mehr notwendig, in ein separates Lernsystem zu wechseln.
- Ein individueller Plan erleichtert den Einstieg des Mitarbeiters in das Unternehmen, er vernetzt sich automatisch und erhält weitere wichtige Informationen.
- Die Gamification-Elemente schaffen einen motivierenden Spaßfaktor.

Aufbauend auf diesem Anwendungsfall hat das Versicherungsunternehmen immer mehr Anwendungsfälle für Social Learning über SmarterPath realisiert. Beispielhaft zu nennen sind ein integriertes Sales Enablement (Qualifizierung, Zertifizierung) oder Talent Management (Talente identifizieren, Talente fördern, Talente halten).

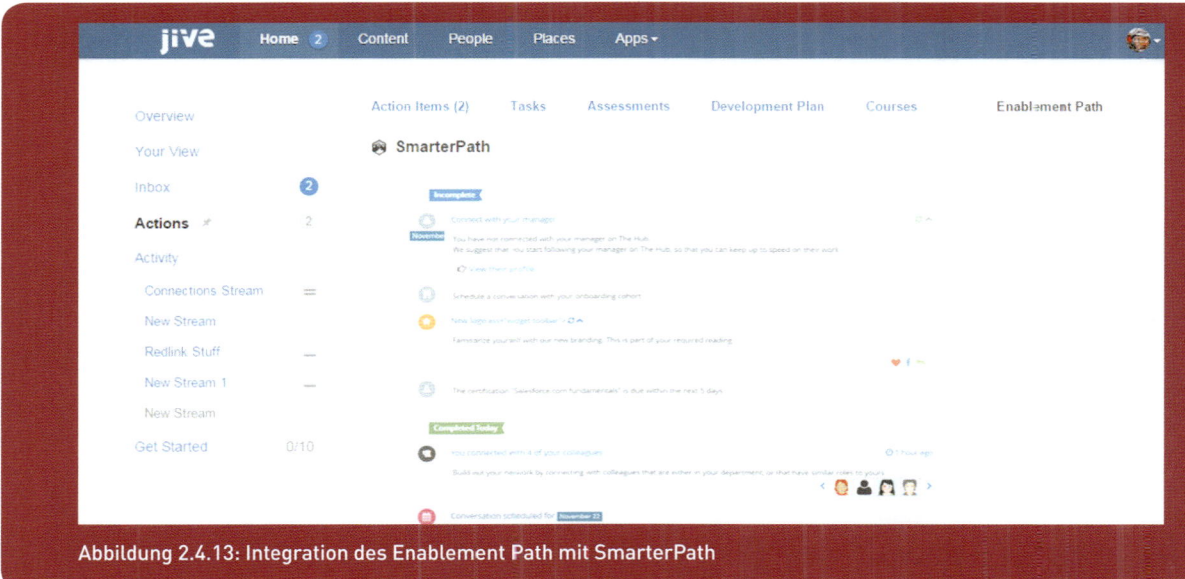

Abbildung 2.4.13: Integration des Enablement Path mit SmarterPath

Support-Communities – Ausgezeichneter Service für die Nutzer

HERAUSFORDERUNG

Führt ein Unternehmen eine neue interne Plattform mit Social-Media-Elementen ein, funktioniert dies meist nicht ohne intensive Betreuung und Einführung.

Mitarbeiter beginnen die Plattform zu nutzen, zu erforschen und in ihren Arbeitsalltag einzugliedern. Dabei stoßen sie auf Fragen, welche sich meist auf die Art und Weise der Plattformnutzung oder auch um die verschiedenen „neuen" Funktionalitäten, deren Bedienung und eventuelles Fehlverhalten beziehen.

Die einfachste Möglichkeit ist ein Support über die im Unternehmen gewohnten Kanäle, wie z.B. ein Helpdesk mit Formular oder ein Telefon mit angebundenem Ticketingsystem. Diese Abwicklung über den Servicedesk hat meist eine, in erster Linie nicht nachhaltige 1:1-Kommunikation zur Folge und führt zu einem gewohnt hohen Aufwand. Demnach wird jede Anfrage individuell beantwortet und kein Nutzer hat Zugang zu bereits beantworteten Fragen oder den Lösungen, die andere Nutzer ohne den Support anzufragen, selbst gefunden haben.

LÖSUNGSANSATZ

An dieser Stelle hilft ein Blick auf die im externen Umfeld bestehenden Support-Communities. Mit dem Ansatz der Support-Communities wird versucht, die viel zitierte „Weisheit der Massen" zu nutzen und für den eigenen Service und Support einzusetzen. Ziel ist es, sogenannten Super-Usern eine Plattform zu geben, ihr Wissen mit anderen Nutzern zu teilen und diesen Nutzern zu helfen. Ziel einer solchen Support-Community ist es, mit Hilfe der Nutzer die eigenen Supportkosten zu reduzieren. Beispiele in Deutschland sind hierfür neben der wohl bekanntesten Support-Community, der „Telekom Hilft Community", das „Vodafone Kundenforum", die „Sky & Friends Community" oder auch die „Datev Newsgroup". In Anlehrung an deren Erfolg liegt es praktisch auf der Hand, diesen Use-Case auch auf der internen Plattform zu initiieren.

Kommunikative Social Features bieten die Grundlage zur Abbildung einer internen Support-Community. In einem Forum können Fragen gestellt und in Wikis oder Blogs bestimmte Themen zu FAQs bzw. Anleitungen zusammengefasst werden. Eine Suchfunktion ermöglicht das Suchen in schon bestehenden bzw. gelösten Servicefragen.

Dieser Abschnitt entstand in Zusammenarbeit mit Erik Frömder, Social Business Consultant T-Systems Multimedia Solutions GmbH

Durch das einfache Erstellen von Inhalten werden Barrieren zur Teilnahme an der Community abgebaut und jeder Nutzer kann faktisch zum Supportmitarbeiter werden.

Konkrete Vorteile dieses Anwendungsszenarios:

- einfach zu verstehen;
- direkt auf der neuen Plattform – kein Medienbruch;
- Entlastung des Services durch Nutzer-helfen-Nutzern-Konzept;
- Motivation der Nutzer durch Möglichkeit zur Positionierung und Reputation beim Beantworten von Nutzerfragen;
- Adaptierung für weitere Services rund um bestehende Applikationen und Programme.

MÖGLICHE HÜRDEN

Das im externen Umfeld erwünschte Nutzer-helfen-Nutzern-Konzept kann im internen Umfeld zu Spannungen führen. In externen Communities bildet die Positionierung über Gamification und hohe Teilnahme bzw. Beantwortung von Serviceanfragen die Grundlage für den Erfolg des Use-Cases. Im Gegensatz dazu kann die zu hohe Beteiligung von Nutzern in einer internen Service-Community zu der Frage führen, wie dieses Engagement im Zusammenhang zu den regulären Aufgaben des helfenden Mitarbeiters steht.

Sinnvoll ist es hier, ausgewählten Mitarbeitern ein Mandat zu übertragen, die interne Service-Community zu managen. Natürlich ist es weiterhin gewollt, dass Fragen auch von „normalen" Nutzern in der Community beantwortet werden.

Sie sollten aber, ähnlich wie in externen Support-Communities, nicht nur sich selbst überlassen sein. Mitarbeiter als Community Manager und Moderatoren einzusetzen, lohnt sich. Zu den Aufgaben dieser Mitarbeiter gehören neben dem Beantworten der Fragen auch die Zusammenfassung und das Erstellen von Hilfedokumenten. Darüber hinaus leiten sie nachgelagerte Serviceeinheiten weiter und sind ganz generell für die gesamte Kommunikationsbetreuung da.

Neben diesen „klassischen" Servicefällen sind die Moderatoren und Community Manager als aktive Repräsentanten der Plattform auch für die Aufnahme von Wünschen, Anregungen und neuen Anforderungen an das allgemeine System zuständig. Die allgemeine Sorge für „gute Stimmung" in der Community gehört somit auch zum Aufgabenfeld des Community Managers.

In die Releaseplanung sollten Service-Community-Mitarbeiter gezielt einbezogen werden, da sie durch ihre Kenntnisse über das zu Grunde liegende Konzept befähigt sind, zwischen Fehlverhalten in der Plattform und konzeptionell bedingten Einschränkungen zu unterscheiden.

Externe Communities nutzen motivierende Gamification-Elemente, um ihren Nutzern noch mehr Anreize zu bieten und Fragen zu beantworten. Die Motivation durch Gamification verlangt im internen Umfeld gesonderte Aufmerksamkeit. Insbesondere hinsichtlich der Leistungskontrollen und Ranglisten sollte eine Einbeziehung des Sozialpartners stattfinden.

Trotz der angesprochenen Hürden bietet die Support-Community einerseits eine Entlastung des 1st-Level-Supports und führt andererseits zu einer verbesserten Akzeptanz der Plattform.

Die Support-Communitiy des Telekom Social Networks

Innerhalb des Telekom Social Networks (TSN) gibt es aktuell über 90.000 angemeldete Nutzer (davon über 70.000 in Deutschland) in über 9.000 Gruppen. Neben den bekannten Supportkanälen über den Service-Desk wird für das TSN ein Community-Support angeboten. Die Gliederung des TSN (Telekom Social Network) erfolgt über Gruppen, also jeweils eigene Communities. Auch der TSN-Community-Support (Abbildung 2.4.14) wird mit solch einer Gruppe abgedeckt. Aktuell wird das Community Management in der Supportgruppe von zwei Personen durchgeführt.

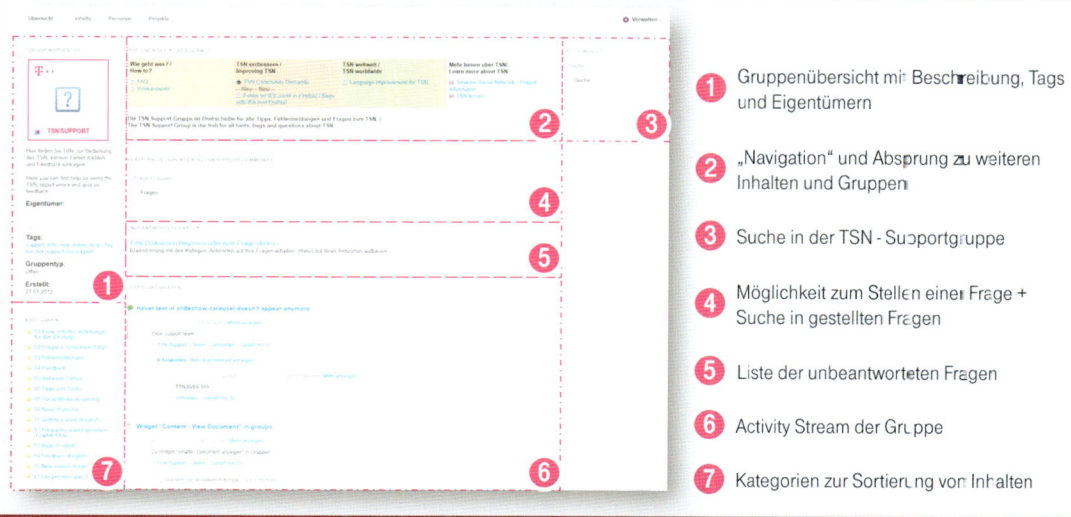

1. Gruppenübersicht mit Beschreibung, Tags und Eigentümern
2. „Navigation" und Absprung zu weiteren Inhalten und Gruppen
3. Suche in der TSN - Supportgruppe
4. Möglichkeit zum Stellen einer Frage + Suche in gestellten Fragen
5. Liste der unbeantworteten Fragen
6. Activity Stream der Gruppe
7. Kategorien zur Sortierung von Inhalten

Abbildung 2.4.14: Support-Community des Telekom Social Network

Die Gruppenstartseite dient als Eingangstor zur Support-Gruppe und setzt sich aus folgenden Widgets zusammen

No.	Name	Beschreibung
1	Gruppenübersicht mit Beschreibung, Tags und Eigentümern	TSN Standard Gruppenübersicht auf der der Nutzer schnell eine Beschreibung, zugehörige Tags sowie die Eigentümer der Gruppe als Ansprechpartner vorfindet
2	„Navigation" und Absprung zu weiteren Inhalten und Gruppen	Verweis auf relevante Supportinhalte zum einen in der Support-Gruppe direkt, zum anderen auch in weiteren interessanten Gruppen
3	Suche in der TSN-Supportgruppe	Allgemeine Suche in den Gruppeninhalten
4	Möglichkeit zum Stellen einer Frage plus Suche in gestellten Fragen	Hier können Supportfragen gestellt werden. Das Widget sucht automatisch beim Eingeben der Frage in bestehenden Inhalten, um Dopplungen zu vermeiden.
5	Liste der unbeantworteten Fragen	Die Liste der unbeantworteten Fragen zeigt zum einen dem Community Support alle neuen, unbeantworteten Fragen. Gleichzeitig wird hier anderen Nutzern die Möglichkeit gegeben, auf unbeantwortete Fragen selbst zu reagieren.
6	Activity Stream der Gruppe	Im Activity Stream werden dynamisch alle letzten Aktivitäten innerhalb der Gruppe angezeigt.
7	Kategorien zur Sortierung von Inhalten	Für ein besseres Auffinden der Inhalte, die in der Support-Gruppe erstellt werden, werden diese verschiedenen Kategorien zugeordnet.

Tabelle 2.4.1: Beschreibung der Widgets der TSN Support-Community

Dieser Abschnitt entstand in Zusammenarbeit mit Gernot Kühn, Technologieberater Office 365 Microsoft Deutschland GmbH

Dokumentenablage – ein pragmatischer neuer Nutzeransatz

HERAUSFORDERUNG

Das Thema „Struktur der Ablage von Dokumenten" nimmt in der Diskussion rund um die Gestaltung einer neuen Zusammenarbeitsplattform oft einen sehr großen Raum ein. Dabei dominiert es teilweise vollständig alle anderen Gesichtspunkte des Intranets. Warum das so ist? In den Augen vieler Entscheider sind Dokumente nach wie vor die wesentliche Quelle der Unternehmensinformation. Ergo: Wenn ich die Dokumentenablage sehr gut organisiert habe, habe ich auch mein Unternehmenswissen optimal organisiert. Aber wie stellt sich das in der Praxis derzeit dar? Eine sehr (oder zu) strukturierte, kategorisierte und komplexe Ablageform führt in der Regel nicht zu einer erhöhten Nutzung durch die Anwender. Aber genau das wollen wir ja erreichen!

Der klassische Ansatz, ein Dokumentenmanagement zu realisieren, ist häufig weit entfernt von dem, was die Anwender wirklich brauchen:

1. Man erstellt ein Fachkonzept (Pflichtenheft) für das Dokumentenmanagement-System (DMS).

2. Die entsprechenden Arbeitsprozesse und Arbeitsanweisungen werden aufgezeichnet bzw. modifiziert.

3. Man definiert Zugriffsmodelle und organisiert die Rechtevergabe.

4. Es wird eine Strategie für die Migration der bestehenden Daten ins neue System festgelegt.

5. Schnittstellen zu weiteren Systemen werden definiert.

6. Eine Dokumentenklassifikation (Kategorisierung, Verschlagwortung) wird erarbeitet.

Im Ergebnis entstehen oft Ablagestrukturen, die wiederum für den Nutzer zu bürokratisch und damit unattraktiv sind.

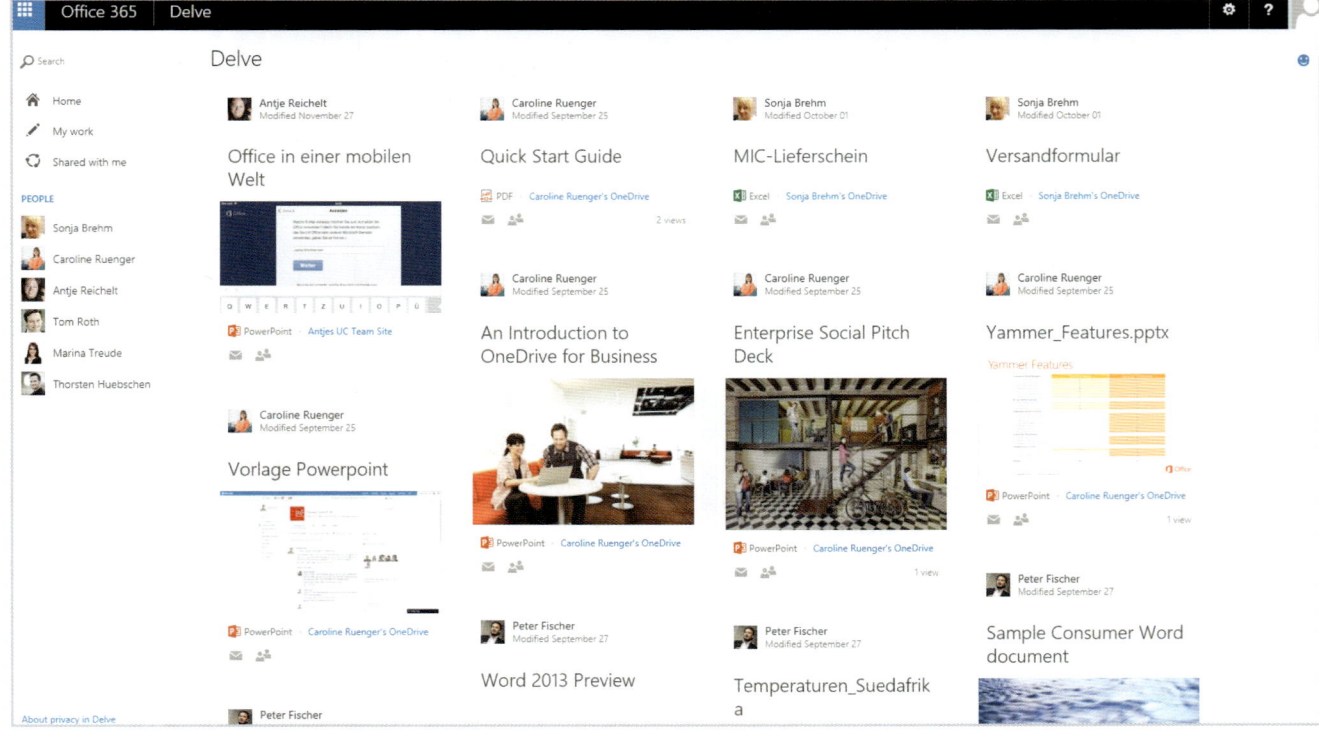

Abbildung 2.4.15: Beispiel zu Microsoft Delve (Quelle: Elmar Witte)

Unternehmens-Anforderungen	Sicht der Anwender	Lösungsmöglichkeiten
TYP AD HOC: Schnelles und intuitives gemeinsames Arbeiten an aktuellen Dokumenten im Unternehmen und mit externen Personen	**Meine Dokumente** Intuitives Freigeben von Dokumenten, gemeinsames Online-Arbeiten, Oberfläche wie Dateiablage (eigene Dateien), Kommentierung von Dokumenten	OneDrive for Business auf der Basis von Office 365, Dokumente und Notizen in Yammer, Präsentation der Dokumente in Delve
TYP STRUKTUR: Geordnetes Arbeiten an Dokumenten, evtl. auf der Basis von Vorlagen und integrierten Arbeitsabläufen (Workflows)	**Unsere Dokumente im Team** SharePoint Räume für Teamaufgaben (direkte Zuordnung zu bestimmten Personen), Prozesse sind vorbereitet (Projektabwicklung u.ä.)	SharePoint-Seiten, Vorlagen für Projekte, vorbereitete WebParts und SharePoint Apps
TYP SYSTEM: klassifiziertes Ablagesystem	**Alle Dokumente im Unternehmen** Klare Struktur mit vorgeschriebener Kategorisierung der Dokumente, Zugriff über ein ausgearbeitetes Berechtigungskonzept	SharePoint-Dokumenten-Center ggf. kombiniert einer Unternehmens-Taxonomie ergänzt mit einem Archivierungssystem

Tabelle 2.4.2: Typen von Dokumentenablagen und Lösungsmöglichkeiten am Beispiel von Microsoft-Produkten

LÖSUNGSANSATZ

Einen Lösungsansatz wollen wir nun auf Basis von Microsoft SharePoint aufzeigen, das Konzept und Vorgehen lässt sich jedoch auch auf andere Technologien übertragen. Während sich bisher alles um den Aufbau komplexer Strukturen und die bereichsspezifische Organisation von Daten drehte, liegt der Fokus zukünftig auf der Nutzung der Dokumente so nah wie möglich an der Stelle, wo der Anwender sich zur Zeit der Bearbeitung „aufhält". Am besten lässt sich das am Beispiel der kontextbezogenen Suche erklären, wie sie derzeit von Microsoft Delve realisiert wird (siehe Abbildung 2.4.15).

Delve stellt Informationen über die Themen zusammen, an denen man arbeitet, und zeigt die Aktivitäten von Personen im eigenen Netzwerk auf der Grundlage von gemeinsam angegebenen Interessen auf.

Neben der unternehmensweiten Suche nach Dokumenten kann man auch organisatorische Strukturen in der Dokumentenablage so anlegen, dass der Weg der Dokumente zum Anwender möglichst kurz ist.

Mit Hilfe des in Tabelle 2.4.2 beschriebenen Ansatzes – hier am Beispiel der Microsoft-Technologien aufgezeigt – können Sie die Anforderungen in Ihre Organisation aufnehmen.

Mit zunehmender Komplexität steigt auch der Grad der Gestaltung durch den System-Administrator. Während dieser im AD-HOC-Modus noch überschaubar ist, wird beim Typ SYSTEM ein hoher Gestaltungsaufwand erforderlich.

Das klassische DMS (Typ SYSTEM) ist bereits weiter oben kurz beschrieben und in der

Dokumente speichert man in OneDrive für Unternehmen, wenn...	Dokumente hinterlegt man in Bibliotheken von Teamseiten in SharePoint, wenn...
... man nicht beabsichtigt, sie mit jemanden zu teilen. Die Voreinstellung ist auf „privat" gesetzt, außer man legt sie in den Ordner „shared with everyone".	... man den Mitgliedern im Team relevante Dokumente präsentieren will, z.B. für ein bestehendes Projekt.
... man plant, mit jemanden zu teilen, aber das Dokument nur für kurze Zeit aktuell ist. Ein Beispiel ist das Einstellen eines Entwurfs, um vor der Veröffentlichung Feedbacks von Kollegen zu bekommen. Eine Freigabe auf das Dokument ist schnell erstellt und die Kollegen bekommen einen Link und die Berechtigung zur Bearbeitung zugeschickt.	... man Berechtigungen und Kontrolle für eine Reihe von Dokumenten an eine breite Gruppe von Mitarbeitern einräumen möchte. So können weitere Personen einfach die Steuerung übernehmen und sehen, wie sich die Dokumente weiter entwickeln.
... man noch keine Teamseite zu einem Thema findet und trotzdem schon erste Dokumente zu einem Thema sammeln möchte, auch schon in Zusammenarbeit mit einzelnen Kollegen.	... man Berechtigungen auf der Basis von ganzen SharePoint-Seiten vergeben will, statt nur auf der Dokumentenebene. Haben also die Anwender berechtigten Zugang zur Seite, dann auch auf alle dort abgelegten Dokumente. Das ist einfach und bedeutet einen geringeren Aufwand.
	... man schon in einem Projekt auf SharePoint-Basis arbeitet. In diesem Fall macht es natürlich Sinn, auch die dazugehörenden Dokumente dort abzulegen.
	... man Arbeitsabfolgen (Workflows) für das Einchecken und Weiterbearbeiten von Dokumenten benötigt.

Tabelle 2.4.3: Guideline Dokumentenablage – persönlicher Bereich vs. gemeinsame Ablagen (abgeleitet aus: Microsoft, 2014)

Nutzung vielen Anwendern vertraut. Unklar ist vielen Nutzern jedoch häufig, wann man SharePoint-Seiten nutzt (Typ STRUKTUR) und wann „OneDrive für Unternehmen" (Typ ADHOC). Die Tabelle 2.4.3 liefert Aufschluss dazu.

MÖGLICHE HÜRDEN

Die Dokumentenablage ist immer ein hochgradig emotionales Thema, geht es doch auch um Organisation, Struktur und Zugriffsberechtigungen von unterschiedlichen Abteilungen mit oft eigenen Sichtweisen. Bewährtes Arbeiten wird dabei in Frage gestellt. Der „Besitz" von Dokumenten gibt Mitarbeitern Sicherheit, und die Kenntnis von Ablagestrukturen bedeutet auch immer etwas Herrschaftswissen. Neue offene Strukturen werden von Mitarbeitern daher auch häufig als eine Gefahr empfunden, so dass nicht unbedingt von einer überschwänglichen Freude und Bereitschaft auszugehen ist.

Unternehmen versprechen sich häufig mit einer ausschließlich zentralen Dokumentenablage eine sichere Datenquelle für die Zukunft. Man erhofft sich eine optimale Auffindbarkeit der Dokumente, indem man sie kategorisiert. Dies ist leider ein Trugschluss, der über viele Jahre in Fachberichten und Lehranstalten propagiert wurde und ein wesentlicher Grund dafür ist, warum heute häufig ein unternehmensweites DMS eingeführt wird, ohne dass die konkreten Nutzeranforderungen detailliert erhoben worden wären.

Organisation der Dokumentenablage bei einer Stiftung

Ende 2014 wurde mit einer international tätigen Stiftung mit Hauptsitz in Berlin, eine Neustrukturierung der Dokumentenablage umgesetzt. Das Hauptanliegen der Verantwortlichen war es, die Unmengen an Dokumenten, die sich im Laufe der Zeit auf Dateiservern und vielen Ordnern angesammelt hatten, zentral in ein Dokumentenmanagement von SharePoint zu füllen. „SharePoint kann das doch, oder?", so die Frage gleich am Anfang. Grundsätzlich klar, SharePoint kann das natürlich. Nur werden dabei auch die eigentlichen aktuellen Themen der Anwender in der Stiftung berücksichtigt?

Begonnen wurde also mit einer detaillierten Aufnahme der Vorgänge, bei denen Dokumente derzeit in der Stiftung verarbeitet werden. Dort wurden Themen (und damit auch die begleitenden Dokumente) für den Typus ADHOC und STRUKTUR identifiziert. Dokumente sollten dort nah am Anwender bleiben und seine aktuelle Arbeit unterstützen. Vorgänge der aktiven Zusammenarbeit wurden in Projekt-Seiten auf der Basis von SharePoint abgebildet. Hinzu kam eine Reihe von Anwendungsfällen, die nun in Yammer stattfinden, z.B. die eigentliche Erstellung von zentralen Dokumenten in einer übergreifenden Diskussion.

Die Zusammenarbeit zwischen den Sachbearbeitern in der Stiftung konnte somit auf der Basis von SharePoint-Team-Seiten gelöst werden. Die Zusammenarbeit an Dokumenten mit den vielen externen Ressourcen wird zukünftig mit Hilfe von OneDrive für Unternehmen unterstützt. Die dann verbliebenen Dokumente, von denen sich viele als reine Archivdokumente herausstellten, konnten mit weniger Aufwand als geplant, d.h. ohne eine Vielzahl an Kategorisierungsfeldern, in einer Zentral-Ablage organisiert werden.

Was wurde erreicht? Die Sachbearbeiter finden ihre Arbeitsdokumente schnell in den SharePoint-Seiten und müssen dafür nicht immer in die Zentralablage. Die Adhoc-Zusammenarbeit an Dokumenten (Erstellung, Freigabe, Bereitstellung) wurde individuell mit den Sachbearbeitern in der Stiftung anhand ihrer Wünsche besprochen und umgesetzt. Aus dem software-getriebenen Ansatz (SharePoint hilft uns beim Dokumentenmanagement) wurde eine szenarien-getriebene Umsetzung anhand konkreter Anwendungsfälle, bei denen Dokumente eine bestimmende Rolle spielen.

Im Ergebnis waren die Sachbearbeiter zufrieden mit der neuen Lösung, weil sie bei ihrer Erarbeitung mitwirken konnten. Daraus ergab sich eine hohe Akzeptanz. Es haben sich neue Möglichkeiten mit Yammer als internes und externes soziales Netzwerk ergeben, die vorher nicht in Betracht gezogen wurden. Gerade die neuen Möglichkeiten wie das gemeinsame webbasierte Arbeiten an Dokumenten und das Teilen der Dokumente mit Externen hat den größten Nutzen für die Stiftung.

Dieser Abschnitt entstand in Zusammenarbeit mit Frank Wolf, Mitgründer von Eyo Mitarbeiterapp

Mobiles Intranet – kein Feature, sondern Quantensprung

„Nur der informierte Mitarbeiter identifiziert sich mit seinem Unternehmen und setzt sich für dessen Ziele ein." Prof. Dieter Georg Herbst

HERAUSFORDERUNG

Aus drei Gründen findet die Mobilisierung von Intranets immer mehr Interesse:

1. Das Intranet hat vielerorts die Mitarbeiterzeitung als Leitmedium der Internen Unternehmenskommunikation abgelöst. Moderne Intranets stehen für personalisierbare, stets aktuelle Informationen sowie die Möglichkeit der aktiven Beteiligung über Kommentare und Bewertungen. Um in den Genuss dieser Vorteile zu kommen, brauchen Mitarbeiter jedoch einfache Zugriffe auf das Intranet. Viele Mitarbeiter haben jedoch keinen festen Arbeitsplatz. „Alibilösungen" wie die oft installierten Terminals werden kaum genutzt und sind weit davon entfernt, ein verlässlicher Informationskanal zu sein.

2. Auch Mitarbeiter mit bestehendem Intranet-Zugriff am Arbeitsplatz wünschen sich ein mobiles Angebot. Unternehmensneuigkeiten, Marktinformationen, neue Ideen oder aktuelle Fragen in der Organisation sind in kompakter Form verfügbar und daher ideal für den mobilen Zugriff geeignet. Die Informationen können schnell nebenbei aufgenommen werden, sodass die eigentliche Arbeit nicht darunter leidet. Das stärkt deutlich die Reichweite und Verlässlichkeit des Intranet-Kanals im Unternehmen.

3. Sicherer Zugriff auf Basisinformationen von unterwegs. Basisinformationen wie beispielsweise Telefonbuch, Vertriebsinformationen, Ansprechpartner, Arbeitsanweisungen und Informationen über Standorte benötigen häufig einen sicheren Zugriff von unterwegs und sollten nach Möglichkeit auch offline verfügbar sein.

Auf den ersten Blick ist die Mobilisierung eines Intranets eine einfache Aufgabe. Die bislang eher wenigen Beispiele zeigen jedoch, dass es einige Herausforderungen gibt:

- Zu großer Funktionsumfang: Moderne Intranets enthalten Funktionen zur Unterstützung von Wissensarbeit, Vernetzung und Projekten. Beispiele hierfür sind virtuelle Arbeitsräume, erweiterte Profile oder Dokumentenbibliotheken. Das macht diese Systeme für mobile Gelegenheitsnutzer schnell sehr kompliziert und unübersichtlich.

- Fehlende Funktionen: Klassische Unternehmenssoftware setzt die Existenz aller Nutzer in bereits vorhandenen Verzeichnissystemen voraus. Die administrative Interaktion mit dem Nutzer erfolgt über eine Firmen-E-Mail-Adresse. Viele gewerbliche Mitarbeiter verfügen allerdings nicht über eine eigene E-Mail-Adresse. Für sie müssen einfache alternative Zugriffsmethoden gefunden werden.

- Hohe Kosten für Standardsoftware: Die Lizenz für eine geeignete Intranet-Software verursacht Kosten, die für viele Unternehmen im Kontext von gewerblichen Arbeitsplätzen zu hoch sind. Oft sind diese Arbeitsplätze stark strukturiert und knapp kalkuliert, so dass wenig Spielraum für zusätzliche Kosten besteht.

- Hohe Kosten für individuelle Lösungen: Eine Eigenentwicklung ist teuer in der Anschaffung und insbesondere bei mobilen Apps mit ihren häufigen Updates sehr aufwendig im Unterhalt. Dazu müssen oft noch verschiedene Apps für zumindest zwei Umgebungen (iOS und Android) gepflegt werden.

- Vertraulichkeit: Insbesondere dann, wenn Inhalte auch auf privaten mobilen Geräten verfügbar sein sollen, wird eine bewusste Trennung des mobilen Inhalts von den unternehmenskritischen Inhalten erforderlich.

LÖSUNGSANSATZ

Der wichtigste Schritt zur Lösung dieser Herausforderungen ist eine Einsicht: Die mobile Verfügbarkeit eines Intranets ist kein einfaches Feature unter vielen anderen, sondern eine zentrale und kritische Anforderung. Um diese Anforderung umzusetzen, muss die Intranet-Lösung von Anfang an inhaltlich und technisch mobil gedacht werden. Dabei gibt es unter anderem zwei wesentliche Kernfragen:

- Wer stellt die Endgeräte zur Verfügung?
- Welche Anwendungsfälle sollen mobil unterstützt werden?

Wer stellt die Endgeräte zur Verfügung?

Die Ausstattung aller Nicht-Büro-Arbeitsplätze mit mobiler Hardware und Internetzugriff war bislang aufgrund der Kosten für die meisten Unternehmen keine Option. Mit der Verbreitung von privaten Smartphones und der zunehmenden Nutzung von privaten Geräten für Unternehmens-Apps steht plötzlich ein neuer Distributionskanal zu den Mitarbeitern zur Verfügung. Über 80% der Mitarbeiter mit eigenen Smartphones nutzen diesen Kanal bereits für ihre Arbeit (Griffith, 2014).

Es gibt demgegenüber auch aktuelle Beispiele wie Berlin Transport. Das Unternehmen hat seinen 1.800 angestellten Busfahrern zentral Smartphones und eine Intranet-App zur Verfügung gestellt. Der Vorteil dieses Verfahrens ist die garantierte Abdeckung aller Mitarbeiter. Dadurch können auch verbindliche Informationen und zeitkritische Anweisungen kommuniziert werden.

Welche Anwendungsfälle sollen mobil unterstützt werden?

Kommunikation

Der Anwendungsfall Kommunikation hat eine hohe Relevanz für die mobile Verfügbarkeit. Das Intranet rangiert in der Relevanz bzgl. Informationen zum Unternehmen und Arbeitsumfeld heute oft noch hinter Mitarbeiterveranstaltungen, Printmedien und E-Mail-Newslettern (Hirsch, 2014). Wer die vollen Potenziale eines Intranets heben möchte, muss insbesondere den Kommunikationskanal besser, einfacher und überall verfügbar machen.

Zielgruppe: alle Mitarbeiter; Komplexität: gering; Sicherheitsbedarf: gering.

Information

Ein gemischtes Bild zeigt sich bei statischen Informationen wie Arbeitsanweisungen, Kontaktdaten oder Standortbeschreibungen. Hier sollte nicht das komplette Intranet verfügbar sein, denn dort existieren in großen Unternehmen oft Tausende an Inhaltsseiten, die mobil keinen Mehrwert bieten. Die Leitfrage sollte daher lauten: Welche Informationen sind für möglichst

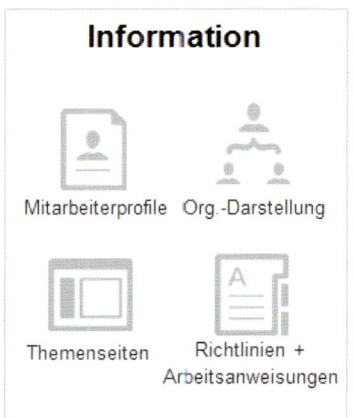

Abbildung 2.4.16: Die wichtigsten Anwendungsfälle für einen digitalen Arbeitsplatz. Was davon sollte mobil verfügbar sein?

viele Mitarbeiter wichtig und nicht sicherheits-kritisch. Hinzu kommt die Anforderung, möglichst einfach auf sie zugreifen zu können.

Zielgruppe: alle Mitarbeiter; Komplexität: mittel; Sicherheitsbedarf: gering

Zusammenarbeit

Bei Inhalten aus Zusammenarbeit und Projekten sprechen insbesondere zwei Gründe gegen eine volle mobile Priorität. Zum einen die Informationssicherheit, denn in diesem Anwendungsfall werden unternehmenskritische Informationen und Dokumente bewegt. Eine – wenn auch passwortgeschützte – Verfügbarkeit auf privaten Geräten kommt für viele Unternehmen deshalb nicht in Frage. Zum anderen geht es in vielen Projekten um Wissensarbeit, um das Kreieren statt Konsumieren. Hier stoßen mobile Geräte deutlich an ihre Grenzen. Wer von uns nutzt ein Smartphone oder Tablet, wenn er einen längeren Text schreiben muss? Eine Ausnahme bildet die reine Team-Kommunikation in Projekten. Microblogging-Dienste wie Yammer sind mobil verfügbar und werden von vielen Teams erfolgreich zur Kommunikation genutzt.

Zielgruppe: Informationsarbeiter; Komplexität: mittel bis hoch; Sicherheitsbedarf: mittel bis hoch.

Prozesse

Die Mobilisierung von Unterstützungsprozessen für Rechnungsfreigaben oder Urlaubsanträge hängt stark von den Merkmalen des einzelnen Vorgangs ab. Die Leitfrage lautet: Welche Prozesse sind für möglichst viele Mitarbeiter wichtig, nicht sicherheitskritisch (personenbezogene Daten), aber zeitkritisch? Sicherheitskritische Kernprozesse können ebenfalls mobil abgewickelt werden. Der hohe Aufwand für eine solche Lösung muss dann durch den tatsächlich realisierten Prozessnutzen abdeckbar sein.

Zielgruppe: Prozessarbeiter; Komplexität: mittel bis hoch; Sicherheitsbedarf: mittel bis hoch.

MÖGLICHE HÜRDEN

- Die variablen Ausspielkanäle verursachen technische Komplexität und erzeugen einen hohen kontinuierlichen Pflegeaufwand einer mobilen Lösung. Der mobile Kanal wird deshalb eine massive Standardisierung der Intranet-Lösungen befördern. Schon heute erfolgen die meist gut funktionierenden mobilen Szenarien über Standardtools im Bereich Teamkommunikation.

- Sicherheitskritische Inhalte werden auch zukünftig einen hohen Aufwand bei der Mobilisierung erfordern und haben nichts auf privaten Mobiltelefonen verloren. Die Entscheidung, welche Anwendungsfälle mit welchen technischen Lösungen realisiert werden, wird damit zukünftig stark von Sicherheitsüberlegungen beeinflusst.

Abbildung 2.4.17: Die drei wichtigsten mobilen Szenarien für einen digitalen Arbeitsplatz

- Unternehmens-Apps auf privaten Geräten führen zu einer zusätzlichen Fragmentierung der Nutzer. Viele Mitarbeiter, die bislang keinen Zugriff hatten, kommen zwar dadurch besser an aktuelle Informationen. Wer jedoch kein privates Smartphone besitzt, hat weiterhin keinen Zugriff.

DIE ZUKUNFT: DAS INTRANET „VERAPPT"

Die Zukunft des digitalen Arbeitsplatzes liegt nicht in einer großen übergreifenden Plattform, die alle beschriebenen Anwendungsfälle abbilden kann. Das hieße, den Fehler der großen Mitarbeiterportale zu wiederholen, als viel Geld und Zeit in „Integrationspaläste" geflossen ist, die am Ende kein Beschäftigter mehr benutzen konnte und wollte.

Den Weg in die Zukunft zeigen die mobilen Geräte selbst, die mit einer einfachen Logik verschiedenste Anwendungen (Apps) auf einer leicht zu navigierenden Oberfläche zusammenführen. Der Nutzer kann cann bestimmte Anwendungsfälle mit der jeweils besten passenden App bearbeiten. Der moderne digitale Arbeitsplatz wird aus einzelnen, standardisierten, aber hochfunktionalen Anwendungen bestehen, die alle über Basisdienste (z.B. Nutzer, Suche, Startseite, Navigation) miteinander verbunden sind. Die noch immer viel zu langen Planungs- und Konzeptionsphasen von Intranets werden einer kontinuierlichen Aktualisierung oder Neuorientierung der einzelnen Anwendungen weichen. Einige Anwendungen werden überall verfügbar und mobil leicht zugänglich sein, andere nur im Unternehmensnetzwerk.

Der digitale Arbeitsplatz wird technisch und funktional näher am Puls der Zeit sein können und damit auch endlich im Unternehmen eine dem privaten Gebrauch ebenbürtige Nutzererfahrung bieten.

Beispiel: Mobiles Intranet für ein Logistikunternehmen

Mehr als 50% der Mitarbeiter eines norddeutschen Logistikdienstleisters hatten zum Projektstart keinen Zugriff auf das bestehende Intranet. Mitarbeiterkommunikation fand über Führungskräfte, das schwarze Brett und eine quartalsweise erscheinende Mitarbeiterzeitung statt. Daraufhin wurde das Ziel ausgegeben, die Mitarbeiter schneller und aktueller zu informieren. Die Mitarbeiter sollten mit ihren privaten Geräten, mit den Laptops oder Smartphones, auf den neuen Kommunikationskanal zugreifen können. Der mobile Kanal sollte aus nativen Apps für iOS und Android bestehen und sehr einfach und ohne Schulung handhabbar sein. Aus Sicherheitsgründen sollte das bestehende Intranet nicht mit mobilen Eigenschaften hochgerüstet werden.

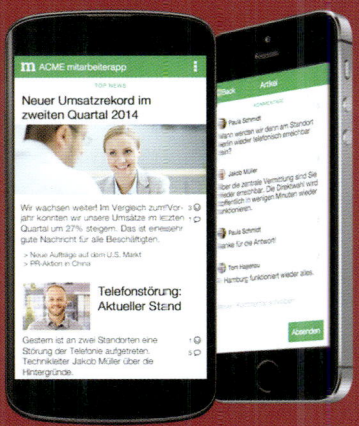

Abbildung 2.4.18: Mobile Ansicht einer Intranet-App

Die Lösung war die Mitarbeiter-App, eine Standardlösung für eine mobile Unternehmenskommunikation, die aus einem eigenen Content-Management-System und verschiedenen Ausspielkanälen wie nativen Apps, Web-Apps und dem Web besteht. Redakteure können entweder Inhalte in der Mitarbeiter-App selbst anlegen oder aus beliebigen Quellen (z.B. Intranet, Website, Social Media) importieren. Ein wichtiges Kriterium für die Auswahl der Lösung war auch die Möglichkeit, Mitarbeiter ohne firmeneigene E-Mail-Adresse einfach einzubinden und später auch administrieren zu können.

Redaktionelle Inhalte – verbindliche Informationsdarstellung bleibt

HERAUSFORDERUNG

Das klassische Intranet-Szenario, bei dem Informationen redaktionell erstellt werden, hat auch in modernen Intranet-Lösungen seine Daseinsberechtigung. Dies betrifft insbesondere solche Informationen, die einen verbindlichen Charakter haben, besonders wichtig sind und deshalb korrekt sein müssen. Die Intranet-Plattform soll Funktionalitäten und Berechtigungsstrukturen unterstützen, die wegen solcher Inhalte nur von zugelassenen Personen oder Personengruppen verändert werden können. Layout-Templates und Freigabe-Workflows sind optional zu unterstützen. Zusätzlich sollte ein modernes Intranet aber auch Interaktionsmöglichkeiten aufweisen, sodass direkt und einfach auf die redaktionellen Inhalte reagiert werden kann und, je nach Inhalt, interessenbezogene Benachrichtigungen möglich sind.

LÖSUNGSANSATZ

Im Konzept für die Informationsarchitektur und im Rollen- und Rechtekonzept wird identifiziert, in welchen Bereichen des Intranets redaktionelle Inhalte in welcher Form bereitgestellt und durch wen sie formuliert und freigegeben werden sollen. Im Rahmen des Design-Konzeptes können Elemente definiert werden, die solche Inhalte gesondert kennzeichnen, z.B. durch die prominente Benennung der verantwortlichen Abteilung oder des Autors.

Dem Redakteur wird durch intuitive Bedienoberflächen die Arbeit erleichtert. Besonderes Augenmerk sollte hierbei auf die Schlagworterstellung („Tagging") gelegt werden. Denn damit unterstützt die Redaktion

diejenigen Nutzer, die sich für bestimmte Themen interessieren und diese nachverfolgen wollen. Auch die redaktionell gepflegten Inhalte werden somit Bestandteil von Inhalten in Dashboards und Activity Streams (siehe Design).

Nicht zwingend erforderlich, jedoch empfehlenswert ist für dieses Anwendungsszenario eine technische Plattform, die Content-Management-Funktionen unterstützt. Folgende Intranet-Features werden für dieses Szenario benötigt: Inhalts- und Newsbereitstellung, Dokumente, sowohl Listen als auch RSS, Folgen und Interaktionsfunktionen wie Likes, Kommentare, Teilen, Taggen, Rating sowie gegebenenfalls Dashboards und persönliche Startseiten.

MÖGLICHE HÜRDEN

Wenn Interaktionsfunktionen wie Likes oder Kommentare direkt an den redaktionell bereitgestellten Inhalten zugelassen werden, ist es erforderlich, die Nutzer im qualifizierten Umgang mit der Kommentarfunktion zu schulen, ebenso wie die Redakteure im konstruktiven Umgang mit den Reaktionen der Mitarbeiter.

AUSFÜHRLICHERES ZUM ANWENDUNGSFALL

Es ist wichtig, das hier grob beschriebene Anwendungsszenario bereits in der Analysephase zu identifizieren, um die entsprechenden technischen Voraussetzungen von Beginn an einzuplanen und ins Berechtigungskonzept einfließen zu lassen. Die eigentlichen Herausforderungen für die Redaktion der Inhalte selbst sind dann fachlicher und organisatorischer Art. Hierauf wird in der Phase „Erprobe" im Abschnitt 5.4 eingegangen.

Verbindliches Informationspaket – der Kompass im Informationsdschungel

HERAUSFORDERUNG

In einem gut etablierten Mitmach-Intranet entsteht täglich eine Fülle an neuen Informationen, die zumeist auch allen Mitarbeitern zugänglich sind. Dies ist die Basis für einen offenen Wissensaustausch. Bei dieser Informationsfülle muss sichergestellt werden, dass alle Mitarbeiter wissen, welche Informationen sie verbindlich und regelmäßig abzurufen haben. Diese verbindlichen Inhalte können sich in unterschiedlichsten Bereichen des Intranets befinden.

LÖSUNGSANSATZ

Verbindliche Informationen werden redaktionell im wöchentlichen oder monatlichen Rhythmus zusammengestellt. Hierbei sind zwei Varianten denkbar:

- Über speziell zu vergebende Metadaten und eine automatische Aggregation der Verweise auf die Beiträge sind die verbindlichen Informationen an einer markanten Stelle in der Intranet-Navigation abrufbar.
- Über eine manuell zusammengestellte Inhaltsseite mit Verweisen auf die jeweiligen Inhalte im Intranet können die Informationen abgerufen werden.

Hilfreich für den Nutzer ist eine Markierung, sodass er erkennen kann, welche der verbindlichen Inhaltsseiten er bereits besucht hat.

MÖGLICHE HÜRDEN

- Organisatorisch zu klären ist, wer im Unternehmen entscheidet, was in die verbindlichen Informationspakete aufgenommen werden darf.
- Eine unklare Rollen- und Rechtevergabe für die Erstellung und Freigabe darf es nicht geben.
- Zuweilen besteht in Unternehmen der Wunsch, bei verbindlicher Informationen die Kommentar- und Bewertungsfunktion abzuschalten. Diese Aspekte sollten vorausschauend im Projekt diskutiert und entschieden werden.

Verbindliches Informationspaket der T-Systems Multimedia Solutions GmbH

Seit 2008 entstehen im Social Intranet der T-Systems MMS kontinuierlich neue Informationen durch die Mitarbeiter. Anfängliche Akzeptanzhürden beim Mitmachweb sind überwunden, sie gibt es nicht mehr. Die Bewältigung und Strukturierung der Informationsflut aber blieb lange eine Aufgabe für alle. Ende 2011 wurde entschieden, dass monatlich ein Informationspaket aus neuen Meldungen unterschiedlichster Themen zusammengestellt und redaktionell aufbereitet wird. Ein Kriterienkatalog gab vor, welche Meldungen weitergegeben werden sollten. Die Informationen sollten betreffen:

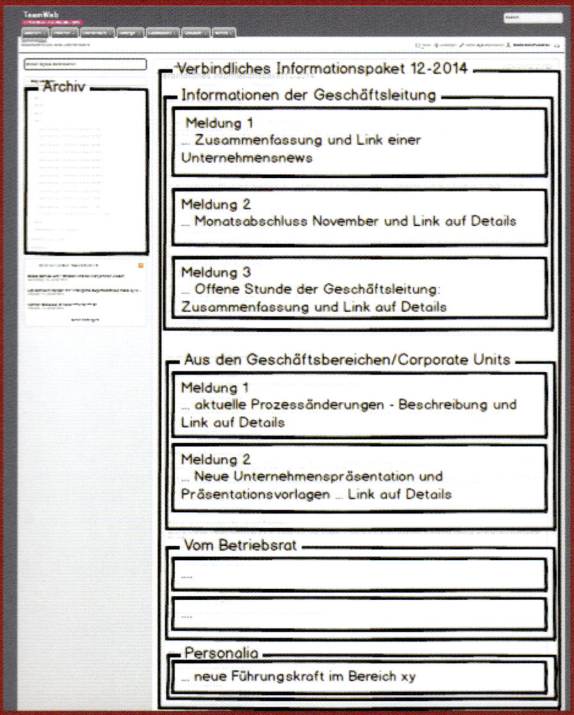

Abbildung 2.4.19: Aufbau des verbindlichen Informationspakets der T-Systems Multimedia Solutions GmbH

- Rechtliche Vorgaben und Richtlinien;
- Vorgaben der MMS und des Konzerns (Betriebsvereinbarungen, Hausordnung, Prozesse, Arbeitsanweisungen);
- Strategische und operative Entscheidungen der Geschäftsleitung und des Führungskreises, die direkte Auswirkungen auf die Mitarbeiter haben bzw. von den Mitarbeitern umgesetzt/eingehalten werden müssen und/oder die bei Nichteinhaltung zu einem Schaden für das Unternehmen bzw. den Mitarbeiter führen können;
- Informationen zu einer veränderten wirtschaftlichen und finanziellen Situation des Unternehmens.

Für den Leser werden diese Informationen geclustert nach Informationen der Geschäftsleitung, der Geschäftsbereiche und Corporate Units, des Betriebsrats und der Personalia. Jede Meldung wird kurz zusammengefasst, relevante Links auf weiterführende Details aus verschiedensten Bereichen im Social Intranet zum Thema zusammengestellt und die Ansprechpartner und Verantwortlichen genannt. Das Archiv ermöglicht auch die spätere Nachvollziehbarkeit (Struktur der Darstellung siehe Abbildung 2.4.19).

Extranet – mit externen Partnern und Kunden unkompliziert zusammenarbeiten

HERAUSFORDERUNG

Immer mehr Unternehmen haben das Bedürfnis, mit Kunden, Partnern und Dienstleistern genauso schnell, sicher, transparent und effektiv Informationen und Dokumente auszutauschen, wie sie das intern gewohnt sind. Solche zugriffsbeschränkten Plattformen, deren Inhalte nur ausgewählten externen Personenkreisen zugänglich sind, werden Extranet genannt.

Die wichtigste Herausforderung besteht darin, hier Möglichkeiten anzubieten, die konform zu den eigenen Sicherheits- und Datenschutzrichtlinien, gleichzeitig aber auch attraktiv in der Handhabung und Nutzung sind. Die fachlichen und inhaltlichen Anforderungen an solche

Zusammenarbeits- und Informationsbereiche decken sich mit vielen Intranet-Anwendungs-szenarien und haben dennoch andere Anforderungen an Rollen- und Berechtigungskonzepte sowie an die Nutzerauthentifizierungen. Als Extranets können bezeichnet werden:

- Projektzusammenarbeitsbereiche für verteilte Projektteams,
- Externe Netzwerke/Gruppen in Enterprise Social Networks wie Jive, Yammer, Tibbr,
- Kunden-Communities,
- Open-Innovation-Netzwerke,
- Informations- und Supportportale für Kunden und Partner.

Die Bereitstellung eines Extranets stellt im Grunde eine Erweiterung der Intranet-Landschaft dar. Daher sollte insbesondere für die Benutzer im eigenen Unternehmen der Zugriff einfach sein und keine große Hürde im Umgang darstellen.

LÖSUNGSANSATZ

Für die Bereitstellung eines Extranets bietet sich oft die Verwendung derselben Technologie an, die auch für das Intranet verwendet wird. Intranet-Bausteine wie Layout oder Kollaborations-Tools können oft direkt übertragen werden. Hat man noch im Intranet Bedenken, überhaupt über das Thema Cloud nachzudenken, ist man bei der Technologieauswahl für das Extranet sehr viel schneller bei der Entscheidung hin zu einem Cloud-Service (siehe auch 2.6). Die Vorteile:

- schnelle Verfügbarkeit – für Hosting und Betrieb ist gesorgt;
- einfache Skalierbarkeit;
- sehr gute Unterstützung mobiler Endgeräte;
- für den sicheren Zugriff auf die Daten wurde bereits durch den Cloud-Anbieter gesorgt.

Einige Nachteile einer vom Unternehmensnetzwerk losgelösten Umgebung lassen sich durch Integrationsszenarien und die Anbindung von eigenen Nutzer-Verwaltungssystemer lösen.

MÖGLICHE HÜRDEN

Sobald Informationen die geschlossene IT-Landschaft des Unternehmens verlassen, entstehen besondere Sorgen um die Sicherheit der eigenen Daten. Es gibt ausreichend geeignete und geprüfte Konzepte und Strategien, mit denen sich IT-Abteilungen und Entscheider sorgfältig auseinandersetzen sollten. Je umsichtiger diese Entscheidung getroffen wird, desto leichter wird es im gesamten Umsetzungsverlauf, Kritikern den Wind aus den Segeln zu nehmen. Bei dieser Gelegenheit sei gesagt: Unternehmen, die sich gänzlich diesem Szenario verschließen, riskieren häufig, dass die Mitarbeiter ihren Bedarf an Austausch und Kollaboration mit unternehmensfremden Lösungen stillen. In diesem Fall sind mögliche Sicherheitslücken für die IT-Abteilung kaum zu steuern.

Gerade aufgrund der hohen Sicherheitsbedenken und der häufig noch ungewohnten Fähigkeiten, über Extranets Wissen mit Außenstehenden zu teilen, sollten die Nutzer schon vor der Einführung intensiv einbezogen und bei der Arbeitsaufnahme begleitet werden. Konzeptionell ist einiges an Vorarbeit zu leisten, um klar zu definieren, welche Informationen auf welche Weise im Extranet abgelegt werden dürfen und wie das dazugehörige Rollen- und Rechtekonzept aussieht. Sorgfältige Schulungen sind unerlässlich, ebenso wie gute Supportangebote.

Eine weitere Hürde besteht in der Aktivierung der externen Nutzer, vor allem, wenn sie noch keine Erfahrungen mit Kollaborationsplattformen gesammelt haben und sich dennoch auf der Plattform mit eigenem Wissen einbringen sollen. Auch das ist eng zu begleiten und idealerweise über ausgewählte Pilotgruppen vorab zu testen.

Weitere Anwendungsszenarien

Weitere Ideen, welche Szenarien Sie bei der Planung berücksichtigen könnten, haben wir in Abbildung 2.4.20 aus verschiedensten Intranet-Projekten aufgelistet. Gleiche Szenarien haben oft auch unterschiedliche Bezeichnungen in den Unternehmen. Wählen Sie daher unbedingt eine Bezeichnung, die zu Ihrer Firma passt und von den Mitarbeitern verstanden wird. Anwendungsszenarien müssen übrigens überhaupt nicht technisch komplex sein. Es geht immer um die Frage: „Was will ich mit dem Intranet tun?". Das kann die Spannbreite von „Senioren & Jubiläen" bis hin zum „Digitalen Vertriebskoffer" haben und damit sehr komplex sein.

Einarbeitungs-prozess	Vernetzung mit Kollegen	Organigramme	Geschäfts-verteilungsplan	Unternehmens-handbuch
Nachschlagwerke	Glossar	Vorstellung neuer Mitarbeiter	Jubilare	Wissensspeicher
How-To's / FAQs / Ratgeber	Management-Kanal	Kolumne	Online-Support	Schwarzes Brett
Software- oder Prozesstutorials	Produktportal	Event Promotion	Echtzeit-kommunikation und Desktop Sharing	Video und Web-conferencing
Kunden-Communities	Medien-, Bild oder Literatur-datenbanken	Speiseplan	Stellenaus-schreibungen	Formular- und Vorlagencenter
Ablösung papierbasierter Formulare und Vorgänge	Freigabe von Urlaubsanträgen	Interne Stellenaus-schreibungen	Buchung von Ressourcen und Räumen	Digitaler Vertriebskoffer
Mitarbeiter-Self-Service	Umfrage	Informelles Lernen	Hilfe und Unterstützung für technische Probleme	...

Abbildung 2.4.20: Weitere Anwendungsszenarien

Nun nimmt das Ganze Gestalt an. Die Anwendungsszenarien liegen vor – fein durchdacht in einem Steckbrief. Sie umzusetzen, darum geht es jetzt. Natürlich starten wir mit den Anwendungsfällen, die für die Chefs, Führungskräfte und Mitarbeiter besonders dringend sind. Dank Zielgruppenanalyse sind alle bestens im Bilde und wissen, was gebraucht wird. Dann kann uns später keiner damit kommen, wir würden hier Geld zum Fenster rauswerfen.

TECHNISCHE 2.5
PLATTFORM

Nachdem in den vorangegangenen Phasen der strategische Business-Nutzen und die wichtigsten Anwendungsszenarien herausgearbeitet wurden, ist es nun an der Zeit, die richtige Technologie für das Social Intranet auszuwählen. Die Entscheidung sollte bewusst erst zu diesem Zeitpunkt getroffen werden, weil dafür erst jetzt alle wichtigen strategisch relevanten Informationen vorliegen.

Sie treffen in diesem Projekt die Entscheidung für ein System, das die Arbeitswelt Ihrer Mitarbeiter nachhaltig verändern wird. Dafür werden Sie entsprechende Budgets, Mitarbeiter und auch Zeit zur Verfügung stellen müssen. Diese Entscheidung sollte also unbedingt fundiert und mit Weitblick getroffen werden. Die Auswahl des erstbesten Systems auf Basis einer einfachen Liste mit wünschenswerten Features kann langfristig gravierende Folgen haben, denn ein solches System auf eine geeignetere

Plattform zu migrieren, ist mit hohen Kosten und mit Daten- und Wissensverlusten verbunden. Dokumente und Dateien sind noch recht einfach zu migrieren, Newsfeeds und Blogs nur sehr schwierig oder gar nicht.

Von fachlicher Seite sind insbesondere die strategischen Anwendungsszenarien zu berücksichtigen. Von IT-Seite werden Themen wie die Integration in die bestehende Systemlandschaft, der Wartungsaufwand und die Verfügbarkeit von Fachwissen bei der Auswahl der Plattform ins Gewicht fallen.

Dieser Abschnitt entstand in Zusammenarbeit mit Andrej Doms, Associate Partner – Portals & Social ComVista Consulting

Technologieauswahl – ein strukturierter Prozess in sechs Schritten

Um eine fundierte Entscheidung über die geeignete Technologie zu treffen, sollten Sie sich an folgenden Schritten orientieren:

Abbildung 2.5.1: Phasen bei der Technologieauswahl

Anwendungsszenario	News- & Inhaltsseiten	Dokumente	Listen	Suche & Metadaten	Team- und Projekträume	Aufgaben	Kalender	Wikis	Formulare & Workflows	Blogs	Communites	Dashboards & personalisierte Startseiten	Profile & persönlicher Bereich	Microblogging & Newsfeed	Activity Stream	RSS	Folgen	Interaktionsfunktionen (Like, Kommentare, Teilen, Taggen, Rating)	Information & Kommunikation
Bereitstellung redaktioneller Inhalte	X	X	X										X			X	X	X	Information & Kommunikation
Projektarbeit gemeinsam managen		X	X	X	X	X	X	X							X				Projekte & Prozesse
Experten finden				X						X			X		X				Persönliches Informationsmanagement
Social HCM																			Projekte & Prozesse
Ideen- und Innovationsmananagement																			Communities & Vernetzung
Social Forecasting																			Communities & Vernetzung
Social Learning																			Communities & Vernetzung
Business Intelligence																			Projekte & Prozesse
SAP Integration																			Projekte & Prozesse
A more Social & Collaborative CRM																			Projekte & Prozesse

Abbildung 2.5.2: Beispiel reduzierte Featureliste: Übersicht benötigter Intranet-Features je Anwendungsszenario

ERSTER SCHRITT: REDUZIERTE FEATURE-LISTE

Die identifizierten Anwendungsszenarien erlauben eine sehr gute Einschätzung, welche Intranet-Features benötigt werden und durch die künftige Technologie unterstützt werden müssen. Anhand der Tabelle in Abbildung 2.5.2 können Sie sich einen Überblick verschaffen, wie eine reduzierte Feature-Liste aussehen kann.

Je häufiger ein Feature benötigt wird, desto höher sollte diese Anforderung bei der Softwareauswahl priorisiert werden.

ZWEITER SCHRITT: VORAUSWAHL

Ein guter Startpunkt für die Vorauswahl ist der Blick in die IT-Strategie und die bestehende Systemlandschaft. Viele Unternehmen setzen bei ihren wichtigsten Anwendungen auf Produkte großer Hersteller, z.B. Microsoft und SAP oder IBM und Oracle. Ein erster Blick sollte also den Angeboten dieser Hersteller gelten, die im Allgemeinen auch entsprechende Social-Intranet-Lösungen anbieten. Der Vorteil liegt auf der Hand. Diese Systeme integrieren sich zumeist gut in die bestehende Landschaft, und die Einarbeitung für die Mitarbeiter ist relativ leicht, da sie bereits mit Systemen dieser Hersteller arbeiten. Ein weiterer Pluspunkt ist, dass diese großen Hersteller schon sehr lange im Markt sind und ihre Roadmaps regelmäßig veröffentlichen. Informationen rund um die weitere Entwicklung einer Plattform sind hier zumeist verfügbar, mit Überraschungen muss kaum gerechnet werden. Das erleichtert eine langfristige Planung und stellt sicher, dass Sie auch in den nächsten Jahren noch Support für Ihre Plattform bekommen. Kleinere Anbieter werden gerne mal von anderen geschluckt oder ändern ihre Strategie radikal, was für Ihre Ziele nachteilig sein kann. Andererseits sind aber gerade die kleineren Hersteller sehr agil und passen sich schnell neuen Markttrends an. Hier werden neue Entwicklungen oft in Wochen marktreif, wofür die großen Anbieter gern mal zwei Jahre brauchen.

Eine Konsolidierung der Systemlandschaft ist in vielen Unternehmen ein wichtiges Thema. Über die Jahre wurden viele unterschiedliche Technologien und Lösungen angeschafft, die allein durch ihre große Anzahl Probleme machen, den Betrieb und die Wartung erschweren und somit Kosten verursachen. Hier müssen Sie entscheiden, ob Sie mit vielen Speziallösungen arbeiten wollen, die eine Aufgabe besonders gut bewältigen, oder ob Sie lieber mit wenigen übergreifenden Technologien umgehen wollen, die zwar „Out-of-the-Box" nur 80% Lösungen anbieten, aber gut anpassbar, integrierbar und erweiterbar sind.

Denken Sie auch an Ihre Anwender, die mit vielen verschiedenen Systemen und Benutzeroberflächen überfordert sein könnten. Die Spezialisten bieten oft sehr tolle, aber leider auch sehr unterschiedliche Bedienkonzepte, während Generalisten meist ein durchgängiges Bedienkonzept über alle Anwendungen liefern. Einige Speziallösungen, besonders die Cloud-basierten Angebote, sind gerne auch mal radikal, wenn es um die Features und Funktionen ihrer Angebote geht. So passiert es zuweilen, dass Funktionen über Nacht verschwinden oder sich komplett ändern, ohne dass die T oder die zuständigen Fachadministratoren darüber informiert worden sind. Die Verwirrung bei den Anwendern ist danach meist komplett, auch die Zahl der Supportanfragen steigt rasant.

Einige Anwendungen sind auch nur aus der Cloud zu beziehen, d.h. diese Anwendungen können Sie gar nicht im eigenen Rechenzentrum betreiben. Neben den rechtlichen Fragen, die mit der Auslagerung von IT-Technologie und Daten verbunden sind, stellt eine Cloud-basierte Lösung auch ganz andere Anforderungen an Ihre IT-Administratoren und Ihre IT-Sicherheitskonzepte. Mehr zum Thema Cloud können Sie in Kapitel 2.6. nachlesen.

Ein guter Startpunkt für Ihre Überlegungen ist auch der Gartner-Quadrant „Magic Quadrant for Social Software in the Workplace" (Drakos, Mann, & Gotta, 2013). Hier wird eine Auswahl aus den am Markt erfolgreichsten Plattformen nach verschiedensten Aspekten eingestuft und bewertet. Eine einfache Visualisierung in einem Koordinatensystem gibt eine erste Übersicht über die Marktführerschaft, die Visionäre und die Verfolger. Dazu gehört immer ein recht umfangreiches Dokument, welches die Bewertungen dokumentiert und erläutert und wichtige Hinweise für Einsatzszenarien, Stärken und Schwächen der Plattformen liefert. Der vollständige Report ist zwar kostenpflichtig, die Investition macht sich aber schnell bezahlt.

Allerdings kann der Gartner-Quadrant nur einen ersten Anhaltspunkt liefern. Es gibt weit mehr als 20 Produkte am Markt und über die Eignung der Technologie für Ihr konkretes Projekt kann hier natürlich keine Aussage getroffen werden. Publikationen wie z.B. vom Institut für Medien- und Kommunikationsmanagement der Universität St. Gallen bieten oft einen deutlich größeren Überblick, allerdings nicht so komprimiert. Eine weitere gute Informationsquelle sind Konferenzen und regionale oder überregionale User Groups, die sich mit dem Thema befassen.

Erweitern kann man diese Auswahl bereits jetzt um eine Einschätzung der IT, in welchem Umfang diese Technologien in die bestehende Systemlandschaft integriert und der T-Betrieb der Lösung sichergestellt werden kann. Das muss nicht in der Tiefe erfolgen, sondern zunächst ganz grob.

Auch das Thema externer und mobiler Zugriff kann hier schon grob behandelt werden. Prüfen Sie, ob eine App für Smartphones oder zumindest mobile, responsive Weboberflächen zur Verfügung stehen und ob die Anwendung sicher für den externen Zugriff über eine Internetverbindung veröffentlicht werden kann. Gleichen Sie diese Informationen mit der IT-Strategie für Mobile Devices und externen Zugriff ab.

Für diese erste Auswahl sollten sie nicht mehr als acht Produkte vergleichen, da es sonst sehr schnell sehr unübersichtlich werden kann. Produkte, die auf den ersten Blick nicht passen, gehören hier nicht rein, sondern werden sofort ausgelassen. Vergleichen Sie nur „echte Kandidaten", die sich nach oberflächlicher Betrachtung eignen könnten.

Um die IT von Anfang an mit einzubinden, sollten Sie auch Vorschläge aus dem IT-Bereich hinzuziehen, da die Mitarbeiter dort möglicherweise

Universität St. Gallen – regelmäßig aktuelle Studien und Publikationen rund um Medien und Kommunikation
http://bit.ly/1ALJoK

Gartner – Magic Quadrant for Social Software in the Workplace: Überblick zur Technologie und deren Bewertung
http://gtnr.it/1yihve

James Dellow vergleicht in seiner Blogpost die Empfehlung der Jahre 2007-2013. Von den 70 dargestellten Unternehmen waren nur 7 in allen Jahren dabei: Microsoft (nun inklusive Yammer), IBM, Jive Software, Atlassian, OpenText blueKiwi and Telligent (Zimbra)
http://bit.ly/1AavqB

bereits Erfahrungen mit einem oder mehreren der in Frage kommenden Systeme haben.

Die besonders geeigneten vier Technologien, die aus diesem Prozess hervorgehen, qualifizieren sich für die detailliertere Analyse im Rahmen einer Entscheidungsmatrix.

Denken Sie auch an die Einbeziehung eines Dienstleisters, der sie kompetent bei der Software-Evaluierung begleiten kann und sich bei den von Ihnen präferierten Lösungen auskennt, der Testzugänge zu den Technologien beschaffen kann und überhaupt vergleichbare Erfahrungen mitbringt.

DRITTER SCHRITT:
VERGLEICH ANHAND EINER ENTSCHEIDUNGSMATRIX

Um nun einen tieferen Blick auf die möglichen technischen Plattformen zu bekommen, ist auch eine detaillierte Auseinandersetzung mit den Anforderungen nötig. Hier reicht nicht die reine Auflistung benötigter Features, sondern - wie von uns bereits getan, der Blick auf die konkreten Anwendungsszenarien und die dort formulierten Lösungsansätze, die mit Blick auf die Technologien nun vertieft werden sollten.

Ein gutes Beispiel dafür ist das Feature „Formulare & Workflows". Das Feature an sich stellt noch keine Anforderung dar. Hier ein paar Hinweise:

Was für Formulare wollen Sie umsetzen?
- Einfache Word-Formulare, vorgefertigte Webseiten zur Inhaltspräsentation oder Business-Formulare, die Teil eines wichtigen Business-Prozesses sind?

Welche Workflows benötigen Sie?
- Viele technologische Plattformen schreiben auf dem Datenblatt, dass sie Workflows beherrschen, aber welche genau?
- Reichen Ihnen einfache Freigabe- oder Statusprozesse oder muss der Workflow komplexe Business-Prozesse leisten, Daten umformen, Dokumente verschieben?
- Muss die Workflow-Engine erweiterbar sein oder eine API besitzen, damit Sie sie mit einer Programmierung erweitern können?
- Können diese Funktionen über eine zusätzliche Software abgebildet werden?

Es genügt also nicht, Formulare und Workflows als Feature in die Anforderungen zu schreiben. Stattdessen verfeinern Sie nun die Betrachtungen zu den Szenarien, die Workflows enthalten wie z.B. Urlaubsfreigabe, Dokumentenarchivierung, Webseiten-Veröffentlichung und so weiter. Auch die Ausbaufähigkeit kann man recht gut bewerten.

Für eine Entscheidungsmatrix bietet sich Excel als einfach zu bedienendes Tool an. Sie erstellen eine entsprechende Tabelle, in der die Technologien nach dem Schulnotenprinzip bewertet werden können.

Teilen Sie die Anforderungen in funktionale und nicht-funktionale Anforderungen auf, skizzieren Sie Risiken und lassen Sie auch Kosten für Software, Hardware und die benötigte Dienstleistung in Ihre Betrachtung einfließen. Ein vereinfachtes Beispiel für eine solche Tabelle bietet das folgende Bild.

Hersteller		A	B	C	D
Produkt		Modernes Intranet	Social Collaboration	Dokumenter-center	Prozesse & Workflows
Kriterium	Gewichtung	Bewertung	Bewertung	Bewertung	Bewertung
A. Nicht-Funktionale Anforderungen	30%	1,9	1,8	1,3	1,9
B. Funktionale Anforderungen	35%	2,1	1,9	1,4	2,2
C. Risiko	15%	1,8	1,6	1,0	2,0
D. Kosten	20%	2,5	2,5	1,5	2,0
Angepasste Zwischenbewertung	Gewichtung 2/3	2,1	1,9	1,3	2,0
Administration und Wartung	25%	2	3	1	3
Ausbildung / Schulung	25%	2	4	1	3
Verfügbarkeit von Fachkräften	25%	3	4	2	2
Gesamteindruck	25%	1	3	1	1
Bewertung POC	Gewichtung 1/3	2,0	3,5	1,3	2,3
Gesamtbewertung		2,0	2,5	1,3	2,1

Tabelle 2.5.1: Beispiel Evaluierungsauswertung für die Technologieauswahl

Selbstverständlich gibt es unterhalb der Themenbereiche noch eine Reihe von Anforderungen, die aber das Format eines Buches sprengen würden.

Ein weiteres Auswahlkriterium sind häufig die Lizenzkosten. Leider haben die Hersteller sehr unterschiedliche Modelle: Kaufen, Mieten, Software-Assurance, jährliche Gebühren etc.

Gewichten Sie Themenbereiche entsprechend Ihren Bedürfnissen, d.h. nachdem Sie zu allen Anforderungen eines Themenbereichs einen Durchschnittswert gebildet haben, legen Sie fest, zu wieviel Prozent er für die Endnote relevant ist. Auf diese Weise können Sie sehr gut steuern, zu wieviel Prozent ein Themenkomplex in die Endwertung einfließt. Individualisieren das Ergebnis genau auf Ihre Anforderungen. Nach der detaillierten Einstufung in diese Matrix kann optional noch ein weiterer Schritt hinzukommen, der allerdings Kosten verursachen kann: Ein Proof of Concept.

VIERTER SCHRITT: PROOF OF CONCEPT

In einem Proof of Concept (PoC) wird ein vereinfachter Anwendungsfall beispielhaft mit den oben ausgewählten Plattformen realisiert. Bei einem PoC kann man direkt mit der Umsetzung auf den Plattformen Erfahrungen sammeln, einen ersten Eindruck gewinnen und Risiken besser abschätzen. In einem PoC kann man z.B. über folgende Faktoren eine grobe Einschätzung erhalten:

Machbarkeit

- Kann der vereinfachte Prozess abgebildet werden?
- Kommen bereits hier erste Grenzen zum Vorschein?
- Was geht „Out-of-the-Box", was muss durch aufwendiges Customizing realisiert werden?

Zu erwartende Aufwände

- Kann innerhalb einer vorgegebenen Zeit ein Ergebnis realisiert werden?
- Wieviel Fachwissen ist in der IT bereits vorhanden?
- Wie stark ist die Einbindung der Fachabteilungen?

Zeithorizont

- Wie lang sind Entwicklungszeiten?
- Wie schnell sind Fachkräfte am Markt verfügbar?

Wartung und Pflegeaufwand

- Ließ sich das System einfach und schnell aufsetzen?
- Wie hoch war der administrative Aufwand während des PoC?
- Wie lange dauern Deployments und Patches?

Gesamteindruck

- Wirkt die erarbeitete Lösung schlüssig und rund?
- Ist das Benutzungskonzept durchgängig oder gibt es viele Brüche?
- Wie werden Ihre Anwender diese Lösung akzeptieren?
- War die Umsetzung problemlos oder gab es Hindernisse?

Ausbildung/Schulung

- Wie einfach kommen Mitarbeiter und IT-Personal mit dem System zurecht?
- Wie lange müssen Fachanwender geschult werden?
- Wieviel Ausbildung brauchen IT-Mitarbeiter, um das System betreiben zu können?
- Sind entsprechende Schulungen überhaupt verfügbar?

Positionierung am Markt

- Sind Fachkräfte am Markt verfügbar, die extern unterstützen können?
- Was kosten diese Fachkräfte?
- Sind Fachkräfte zur Festanstellung verfügbar?

Wie sieht die Strategie des Anbieters für die nächsten 2-3 Jahre aus?

- Wird die Plattform vom Hersteller als strategisch erachtet und entsprechend lange angeboten?
- Wie steht es um die Versorgung mit Patches und Updates?
- Gibt es eine Roadmap, die Ihnen Planungssicherheit verschafft?

Es gibt sicher noch deutlich mehr Fragen, die Sie sich stellen können. Diese kleine Auflistung soll Ihnen einen ersten Startpunkt für Ihre eigenen Überlegungen bieten.

FÜNFTER SCHRITT: ENTSCHEIDUNGSVORLAGE

Aus der Entscheidungsmatrix erarbeiten Sie nun eine Entscheidungsvorlage für das Entscheidergremium. Hier werden die Ergebnisse der Matrix kommentiert und unterfüttert. Es gibt immer Argumente und Themen, die aus der Matrix nicht unbedingt hervorgehen, für die Entscheidungsfindung aber wichtig sind. In diesem Dokument können Sie auch wirtschaftliche Betrachtungen (TCO = total cost of ownership bzw. ROI = return of invest) erläutern und bereits eine Roadmap für die nächsten Schritte definieren.

Übersicht der gängigsten Plattformen

Inzwischen gibt es eine Vielzahl von Social-Software-Anbietern auf dem Markt. Vergleicht man die einzelnen Software-Lösungen, so findet man grundlegende Funktionalitäten, die meist jedes dieser Tools unterstützt und jedes Social Intranet haben sollte. Auch die Anbieter reiner Content-Management-Systeme, mit denen bisher Intranets gebaut wurden, reichern ihre Software inzwischen um Social Features an oder bieten Schnittstellen zu Social Network Frameworks.

Hier ein kurzer Überblick über einige der gängigsten Plattformen.

SHAREPOINT

SharePoint hat sich in den letzten Jahren als die erfolgreichste Plattform für Social Intranets und Collaboration in Unternehmen entwickelt. Keine andere Plattform ist am Markt so erfolgreich und wird in so vielen Unternehmen eingesetzt. SharePoint kann fast alle o.g. Anforderungen erfüllen und ist leicht anzupassen und zu erweitern. Der wichtigste Vorteil ist aber die perfekte Integration in die anderen Microsoft Produkte wie Office, Dynamics CRM oder den SQL Server. Wenn Sie bereits viele Microsoft Produkte einsetzen, können Sie durch diese Integrationsszenarien das Maximum aus der Plattform schöpfen und Ihre Produktivität deutlich verbessern.

IBM CONNECTIONS

Connections ist IBMs Social-Networking-Plattform, welche die Vernetzung, Zusammenarbeit und Wissensarbeit der Mitarbeiter optimiert. Sie bietet gängige Funktionen wie Profile, Communities, Blogs, Wikis und Dateiablage. Auch eine mobile App ist vorhanden. Die intensive Integration in andere IBM-Produkte wie Lotus Notes, WebSphere oder FileNet machen Connections zu einer interessanten Lösung für alle Unternehmen, die eine starke IBM-Strategie verfolgen. Für Unternehmen ohne eigenes IBM-Know-how kann der Einstieg in die Technologie unter Umständen schwierig werden, da die technologische Basis auf IBM-Produkte setzt. IBM Connections kann on premise oder Cloud-basiert betrieben werden.

JIVE

Jive verbindet Collaboration-Szenarien mit Social-Community-Funktionen und hat sehr früh auf Social Networking als zentralen Bestandteil in allen Funktionen der Plattform gesetzt. Der Collaboration-Ansatz von Jive kann als „Real-Time" bezeichnet werden. Es integriert sich sehr gut in andere Plattformer wie z.B. SharePoint, CRM oder Office. In den Bereichen Social Analytics und Gamification gehört Jive sogar zu den Technologieführern. Jive kann nicht nur als Cloud Service bezogen werden, sondern auch von Jive betrieben in Ihrem eigenen Rechenzentrum gehostet werden, so dass Ihre Daten niemals Ihr Unternehmen verlassen. Diesen Service bietet momentan kein anderer Anbieter. Auch Jive bietet hervorragende Apps für alle wichtigen mobilen Plattformen.

SITRION SOCIAL WORKPLACE

Vielen noch unter dem Namen Newsgator Social Sites bekannt, hat Newsgator 2013 die Firma Sitrion Software gekauft und unter dem Sitrion Label die Produkte vereint. Sitrion Social Workplace ersetzt den Social Stack von SharePoint on premise und erweitert somit die Plattform um moderne Social Features. Es bietet eine nahtlose Integration mit den eigenen Produkten zur SAP-Integration und ermöglicht es so, auch Self-Service-Szenarien z.B. aus dem HR-Bereich abzubilden, die mit den anderen Technologien nur sehr aufwendig zu realisieren wären. Hervorzuheben sind die Apps, die den mobilen Zugriff auf die Social Funktionen und SAP-basierte Inhalte sehr einfach machen.

Social Software Tools im Vergleich findet man inklusive Screencast-Serie in den Themenwochen im Blog „Social Business Evolution" http://bit.ly/1CqDOm

DRUPAL

Das Open-Source-System Drupal hält als Content-Management-System für nahezu jeden Anwendungsfall in Bezug auf Collaboration und Social Features durch die sehr große Entwicklergemeinde bereits viele fertige Module und Erweiterungen parat. Der Einsatz dieser Frameworks für interne Kommunikation und Collaboration, aber auch für Internetplattformen und externe Communities gewinnt an Attraktivität aufgrund der lizenzkostenfreien Verfügbarkeit. Abgerundet für den Enterprise Einsatz wird diese Attraktivität dadurch, dass Dienstleiter die Lücke zwischen Open Source und Business-Tauglichkeit schließen, entsprechende Lösungskonzepte für Social Intranets auf Basis Drupal anbieten und umfassend supporten.

OFFICE 365 / YAMMER

Office 365 bietet die Standardplattformen SharePoint, Exchange und Lync als Cloud-basierte Plattformen an. Der Umfang ist noch weitestgehend identisch zu den On-Premise-Varianten. In den nächsten Jahren werden aber alle neue Features, zunächst „Cloud First", immer erst in Office 365 verfügbar sein, bevor sie in die On-Premise-Werkzeuge integriert werden. Einige Features werden auch nur in der Cloud verfügbar sein. Office 365 kann noch um Business-Intelligence-Funktionen, CRM Online und Yammer erweitert werden.

Yammer ist eine reine Social-Network-Lösung, die entweder Stand-Alone betrieben werden kann oder die Social-Funktionen von SharePoint im Office 365 ersetzt. Yammers große Stärken sind die intuitive Bedienung, die Anwendern den Einstieg leicht macht, und die auf allen wichtigen mobilen Plattformen verfügbaren Apps. Da Yammer eher auf Kommunikation und Ad-hoc-Zusammenarbeit setzt, ergänzt es sich sehr gut mit SharePoint. Allein genutzt stoßen manche Unternehmen sehr schnell an Grenzen.

CHATTER

Chatter ist das Social-Networking-Produkt von Salesforce und besticht durch die hervorragende Integration in Salesforce. Ähnlich wie z.B. Yammer konzentriert sich die Plattform auf Kommunikation und Vernetzung. Chatter ist ein reiner Cloud-Service.

ATLASSIAN CONFLUENCE

Atlassian Confluence wurde zunächst als Enterprise Wiki für Unternehmen konzipiert. Inzwischen ist Confluence zu einer sehr modernen Social-Collaboration-Plattform gewachsen, die sich hervorragend für Wissensmanagement und übergreifende Zusammenarbeitsszenarien z.B. in Projekten eignet. Es kann als On-Premise-Lösung oder Cloud-basiert betrieben werden

INTERACT INTRANET

Interact Intranet positioniert sich als Intranet-zentrierte Alternative zu SharePoint. Während SharePoint sich mehr um Enterprise Content Management positioniert und Intranet als einen Anwendungsfall bietet, präsentiert sich Interact Intranet als Plattform, die möglichst alle Szenarien ohne zusätzlichen Erweiterungsaufwand abbilden kann. Interessant für Umsteiger ist das Versprechen, dass Interact allen SharePoint Content kostenlos in eine neue Interact- basierte Plattform migriert. Neben den üblichen Social-Intranet-Funktionen ist der sehr schnelle Einstieg in die Plattform ein wichtiges Argument. Interact kann als On-Premise-Lösung oder Cloud-basiert betrieben werden.

WEITERE ALTERNATIVEN

Diese Auflistung ist sicherlich nicht repräsentativ, zeigt aber, wie viele unterschiedliche Lösungen am Markt verfügbar sind. Nur kurz erwähnen möchten wir noch Just, Coyo oder IntreXX, die ebenfalls Lösungen für Social Intranets bieten und einen Blick wert sind.

Alles neu oder Vorhandenes zusammenführen?

Eine einheitliche Technologie für alle gewünschten Komponenten der Social-Intranet-Landschaft ist nicht für jedes Unternehmen realisierbar oder gewünscht. Es gibt häufig mehrere technische Lösungen zur Unterstützung aller relevanten Anwendungsfälle. Basierend auf der Erkenntnis, dass die Orientierung und somit die Akzeptanz des Intranet-Nutzers schnell verloren gehen kann, werden immer häufiger übergreifende Integrationsszenarien betrachtet und umgesetzt. So wird beispielsweise die Verknüpfung des bestehenden redaktionellen Intranets mit einer Zusammenarbeitsplattform und/oder einer Community-Software vorgenommen oder es werden vorhandene Dokumentenmanagement-Systeme angebunden.

Einfache erste Schritte sind ein einheitliches Layout, übergreifende Navigationselemente, verknüpfte Nutzerprofile (ein Profilbereich für den Nutzer im Unternehmen) und eine Enterprise Search, die alle Intranet-Quellen durchsucht.

Ein weiteres wichtiges Integrationsszenario ist die Einbindung von Drittanwendungen wie CRM-, ERR-, HR-Systemen oder Prozessportalen in das Social Intranet, um dort direkt Diskussionen starten zu können und umgekehrt Updates aus den Drittanwendungen auch im Activity-Stream angezeigt zu bekommen.

Allen Aktivitäten gemein sollte der Blick auf die durchgängig stimmigen Anwendungsszenarien aus Nutzersicht sein. Brüche beim Übergang von einem System in das andere sind zu vermeiden.

2.6 CLOUD ODER NICHT CLOUD

Dieser Abschnitt entstand in Zusammenarbeit mit Martina Grom, MVP Office 365 atwork GmbH

In unserer modernen vernetzten Welt liegen viele Chancen, etwa für Unternehmen, die durch die neuen Möglichkeiten zur Kommunikation und Zusammenarbeit mit wenig Aufwand weltweit operieren können. Gleichzeitig sind viele neue Herausforderungen hinzugekommen. Die Frage nach Sicherheit und Datenhoheit rückt immer mehr in den Fokus von IT-Beauftragten und Datenschützern. Das Internet hat unsere Welt verändert, im Business-Umfeld genauso wie im Privaten. Als Anwender sind wir es gewohnt, unsere Daten in der Cloud zu speichern und Dienste aus der Cloud zu verwenden. Über Apps (für Applikationen, sprich Software) nutzen wir Dienste am Computer genauso wie am Smartphone und kommunizieren im Unternehmen und privat mit der ganzen Welt.

CLOUD – WAS IST DAS EIGENTLICH?

Der Begriff „Cloud" (Wolke) wird oft anstelle von „Cloud Computing" (Rechnen in der Wolke) verwendet und ist ein Sinnbild der Informationstechnologie für Rechnernetze, die meist entfernt stehen und deren Inneres unbekannt ist. „Cloud" steht somit sinngemäß als Standort von bereitgestellten Diensten für mehrere Computer, die über das lokale Netzwerk im Unternehmen (LAN, Local Area Network) oder über das Internet (WAN, Wide Area Network) verbunden sind.

Die Anzahl der Server in der Cloud ist meist riesig, oft stehen in den Rechenzentren (Hundert-)tausende Rechner. Allein die Dimension und der sichere Betrieb von Rechenzentren sind beeindruckend.

Blicke in das Microsoft Datenzentrum http://bit.ly/18hfokb

Über sog. „Load-Balancer" (Lastenverteiler) wird die Arbeitslast, die von außen kommt, gleichmäßig auf einzelne Rechner verteilt. Als Anwender ist man über eine App sprichwörtlich mit der Cloud – tatsächlich jedoch nur mit einem bestimmten zugewiesenen Rechner – über ein Service verbunden. Über diesen Informationskanal können Daten (Texte, Bilder, Sprache und Videos) mit den Internetprotokollen HTTP und HTTPS gesendet und empfangen werden. Die Daten werden in einem zentralen Speicher gesichert und können nach erfolgreicher Authentifizierung von allen Rechnern in der Cloud verwendet werden. Alle Daten sind immer redundant, das bedeutet mehrfach, an verschiedenen Orten gespeichert. Es spielt somit keine Rolle, auf welchem Rechner man „landet", als Anwender kann man immer auf seine Daten zugreifen. Auch wenn viele Rechner im Netzwerk ausfallen würden, übernehmen die restlichen die Arbeitslast und die Anwender bemerken den Ausfall nicht. Die Cloud ist also skalierbar und hochverfügbar.

PRIVATE UND PUBLIC CLOUD

Private Cloud

Im Grunde kann jedes Unternehmen sein eigenes Rechenzentrum, seine eigene Cloud betreiben. Vor allem große Unternehmen wie Banken, Versicherungen, Finanzmärkte, Händler, Forschung und Industrie besitzen oft eigene Datenzentren. Man spricht dabei von einer Private Cloud. Auch staatliche Institutionen wie Militär und Verwaltungsstellen besitzen und betreiben eigene Rechenzentren. Somit geben die Eigentümer selbst die Regeln vor und kontrollieren den Zugriff auf die gespeicherten Daten durch

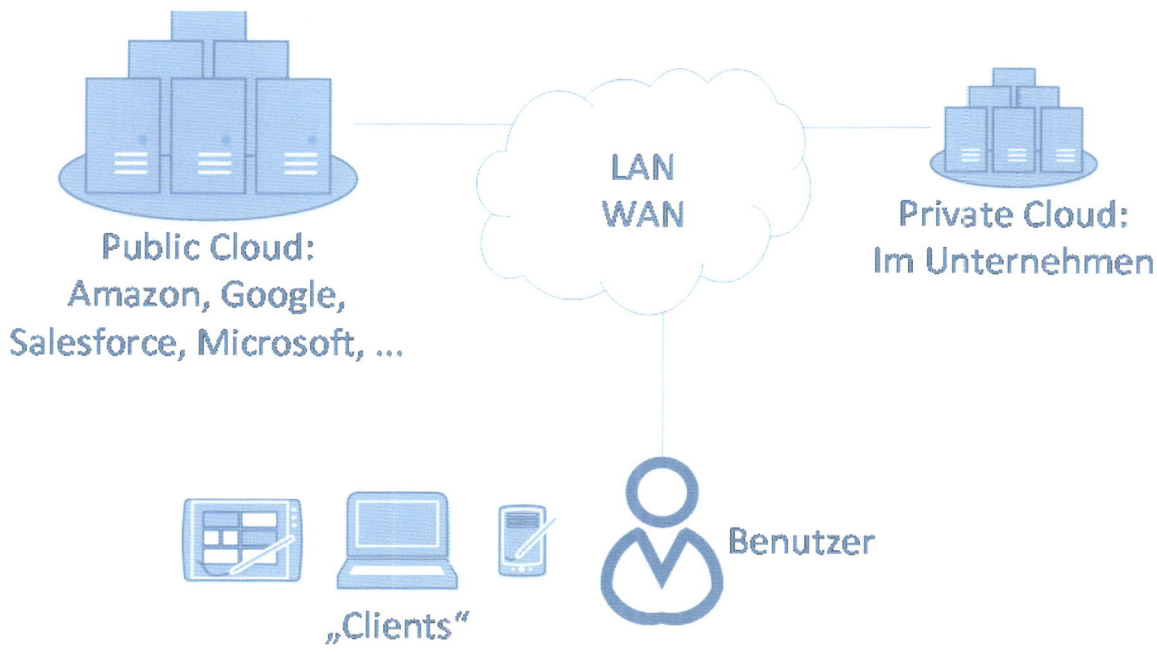

Abbildung 2.6.1: Schaubild Public Cloud und Private Cloud

(bestimmte) Anwender in der eigenen Organisation. Der eigene Rechner in der Besenkammer oder im Serverraum macht dabei jedoch noch keine Private Cloud aus, es muss schon ein Rechenzentrum mit allgemein gültigen Sicherheitsstandards sein.

Public Cloud

Im Gegensatz hierzu steht die Public Cloud, die von beliebigen Personen und Unternehmen genutzt werden kann. Die bekanntesten Anbieter sind Amazon, Google, Salesforce und Microsoft. Hier wird vor allem das Modell „Software as a Service" (SaaS) genutzt, privat wie im Unternehmensumfeld. Anwender sind selbst dafür verantwortlich, welche Daten sie in die Public Cloud stellen.

CLOUD-DIENSTE

Die Cloud wurde maßgeblich von den weltweit operierenden Internetfirmen geprägt. Sie alle verwenden Cloud Computing für die Bereitstellung ihrer eigenen Dienste und bieten sie für Unternehmen und Endanwender an. Technisch gesehen gibt es mehrere Dienstarten, die über Cloud Computing bereitgestellt werden.

IaaS (Infrastructure as a Service)

Mit IaaS können eigene virtuelle Rechner in der Cloud verwendet werden. Dabei verhält sich eine virtuelle Maschine genauso wie ein eigener Computer: Er kann ein- und ausgeschaltet werden, man kann beliebige Software darauf installieren und man ist selbst für die Wartung verantwortlich. Der Zugriff auf die virtuellen Maschinen erfolgt über Webinterfaces oder über Remote-Desktop-Verbindungen (Fernzugriff). IaaS ist oft für IT-Abteilungen sinnvoll die sich nicht um die Hardware-Anschaffung und deren physischen Betrieb mit allen erforderlichen Themen wie Strom, Kühlung, Security, Performance, Festplatten-Tausch, Backup usw. kümmern wollen. Ein weiterer verbreiteter Einsatzzweck sind Test- oder Demo-Umgebungen, die schnell erzeugt werden wollen und auch nach Bedarf ein- und ausgeschalten werden.

PaaS (Platform as a Service)

PaaS ist ein von einer Hardware völlig abstrahierter Dienst. Dabei wird eigene Software für das jeweilige PaaS-System – wie beispielsweise Microsoft Azure – geschrieben und vom Entwicklungsrechner meist direkt in die Wolke installiert. Die Software, etwa eine Webseite, ein

Webdienst oder eine Applikation, läuft nur in der Cloud und ist speziell dafür angepasst. Die Cloud stellt die Plattform, das Betriebssystem, ein Datenbanksystem und weitere Dienste wie Authentifizierung, Mobile Dienste, verteilte Datenbanken etc. bereit, je nach Cloud-Anbieter. Entwickler sind dabei selbst für die Aktualisierung ihrer eigenen Software verantwortlich. Die Cloud-Betreiber kümmern sich um alle Wartungen, auch dass die Lösung hoch verfügbar bereitsteht.

SaaS (Software as a Service)

Als SaaS-Lösung (Software as a Service) werden Dienste bezeichnet, die Standard-Software und Anwendungsprogramme für Benutzer bieten. Darunter fallen etwa E-Mail (Outlook & Co), Instant Messaging (Skype, WhatsApp, etc.), Telefonie- und Videokonferenz-Systeme (Skype, Lync & Co), Webshops (Amazon & Co), Intranet Portale (SharePoint Online, etc.), CRM und ERP-Systeme (Salesforce, Microsoft CRM, Microsoft Dynamics, etc.), Applikationen (YouTube, GoogleDocs, Microsoft Office 365, etc.), private Online-Speicher (iCloud, Dropbox, OneDrive, etc.) und vieles mehr. Als Benutzer hat man keinen Zugang auf das dahinter liegende System, sondern nutzt diese Standard-Dienste direkt aus der Cloud. SaaS bezeichnet die Möglichkeit, sämtliche Software-Leistungen nicht mehr zu kaufen bzw. zu lizenzieren, sondern lediglich die Nutzung der Software zur Verfügung zu stellen. Bezahlt wird nach dem „Per use"-Modell, d.h. bezahlt wird tatsächlich, was man verwendet. Microsoft Office 365 gehört in diese Kategorie.

Es gibt einige Hersteller, die sich auf Cloud Services konzentrieren. Die wichtigsten sind:

- Microsoft (deckt mit Azure und Office 365 den gesamten Bereich ab: IaaS, PaaS und SaaS),
- Google (SaaS, IaaS),
- Amazon (IaaS).

VORTEILE DER CLOUD

Jedes System hat Vor- und Nachteile. Die Cloud stellt eine logische Weiterentwicklung von einzelnen Server-Systemen zur Bereitstellung von übergreifenden Diensten über zentrale Server-Farmen in der Informationstechnologie dar. Hier finden Sie einige positive Eigenschaften von Cloud Computing.

Der Weg in die Cloud sollte wie jede andere Entscheidung auch gut durchdacht sein, indem die Vor- und Nachteile abgewogen werden. Für Unternehmen entstehen immense Vorteile durch die Social Software als Cloud-Lösung: Endlich mit einer professionellen Lösung arbeiten zu können, keine Angst mehr davor haben, dass der Server im Homeoffice oder im Büro ausfällt oder die Internetverbindung mal nicht funktioniert. Keine unnötigen Hardwarekosten haben, schnell agieren und sich auf das Wesentliche konzentrieren können. Seien wir ehrlich: Welches kleine oder mittlere Unternehmen (KMU) leistet sich heute ein geo-redundantes Rechenzentrum?

Elastizität

Durch Abstraktion und Virtualisierung ermöglichen die Cloud-Systeme Leistungs- und Kostenvorteile gegenüber konventionellen Computer-Systemen. Software und Hardware müssen nicht selbst angeschafft werden und können ganz nach eigenem Bedarf genutzt werden. So macht etwa der Online-Händler Amazon im Weihnachtsgeschäft mehr als die Hälfte seines Jahresumsatzes und benötigt nur in den letzten drei Monaten des Jahres ein Vielfaches an Rechenleistung für den Shop und die Abwicklung der Bestellungen. Dann wird kurzfristig die Rechenleistung erhöht, die danach wieder reduziert wird. Die Nutzung je nach Bedarf wird als „Elastizität" bezeichnet.

Kostenvorteil

In der Cloud werden im Regelfall nur jene Leistungen bezahlt, die genutzt werden, das Prinzip lautet „Pay per use". Beim SaaS gibt es eine monatliche Pauschale, je nach bestelltem Paket. So kostet etwa ein E-Mail-Zugang wenige Euro pro Monat bis hin zum vollen Funktionsumfang. Firmen können so einfach kalkulieren, es gibt keine versteckten oder unvorhersehbaren Kosten, keine eventuell erforderliche Neuanschaffungen für die Infrastruktur, keine eigene Wiederherstellung von Systemen und Backups, keine zusätzlichen Personalkosten usw.

Verfügbarkeit

In der Cloud werden alle Daten redundant gehalten. Das bedeutet, es liegen (üblicherweise) mehrere Kopien der Daten an verschiedenen Speicherorten vor. Der Lieferant des Services kümmert sich um den Betrieb, die Verfügbarkeit und die Backups. Ein Service Level Agreement (SLA) garantiert für Business-Services, z.B. eine Verfügbarkeit von 99.9%. Damit ist ganz klar, was der Kunde an Leistungen und Kosten von seinem Cloud-Dienst erwarten darf.

Standardisierung

Ein weiterer Vorteil von Cloud-Diensten ist die Standarisierung. Kunden verwenden ein vorgegebenes System. Dieses wird automatisch gewartet, aktualisiert und stellt definierte Schnittstellen zur Verfügung. Kein Wildwuchs, keine proprietäre Software, keine unbekannten Kosten. Das Gleiche gilt auch für Prozesse und Abläufe innerhalb der Rechenzentren. Es gibt keinen unbefugten Zugriff und alle (Wartungs-) Arbeiten sind genau definiert.

Zentrale Daten

Gerade in Unternehmen ist die Zusammenarbeit extrem wichtig. Alle gemeinsam genutzten Daten liegen an einer einzigen, zentralen Stelle – in der Cloud, wo die Daten mehrfach gespeichert sind. Alle berechtigten Benutzer können somit überall damit arbeiten.

Effizienz

Die Standardisierung führt auch dazu, dass kleine oder private Clouds selten so effizient betrieben werden können wie große Rechenzentren. Die Maßnahmen beginnen bei der Anschaffung der optimierten Server und reichen über Strom- und Umweltschutzmaßnahmen wie Kühlung und Internetzugang bis hin zu Security-Standards.

NACHTEILE DER CLOUD

Eigentlich gibt es nur wenige Nachteile der Cloud. Hier eine Liste von Themen, die man beachten sollte, wenn man im Unternehmen oder privat Daten in die Cloud speichert.

Konnektivität

Es erscheint offensichtlich, ist jedoch oft ein Ausschlussgrund: Man benötigt eine (gute) Internetverbindung. In einer Region, wo es vielleicht nur einen ADSL-Anschluss mit geringer Bandbreite gibt, ist es wahrscheinlich keine gute Idee, alle eigenen Daten ausschließlich in die Cloud zu legen. Wenn keine Internetverbindung vorhanden ist, gelangt man mitunter nicht mehr zu seinen Daten. Abhilfe schafft eine Synchronisation, wie sie etwa OneDrive oder SharePoint Online mit OneDrive for Business liefert. Dabei sind die Daten lokal am eigenen Rechner gespeichert und können offline verwendet werden. Sobald wieder eine Internetverbindung vorhanden ist, kümmert sich eine App im Hintergrund darum, dass die geänderten Daten wieder in die Cloud synchronisiert werden.

Anpassungen

Durch die Standardisierung in SaaS ist es nicht möglich, größere kundenspezifische Anpassungen vorzunehmen. Der Lieferant gibt die Software für ALLE Benutzer vor. Für Kunden, die das Aussehen von Lösungen oder Prozesse ändern wollen, gibt es meist keine Möglichkeit, diese Änderungen entsprechend den eigenen Bedürfnissen anzupassen (Customization). Kunden, die darauf bestehen, müssen diese (oder eine andere) Lösung kaufen, anpassen und in ihrem eigenen Rechenzentrum installieren und betreiben oder ein sogenanntes dediziertes System anmieten. In manchen Fällen bieten Software-Hersteller ihre Lösungen für die eigene Installation (On-Premise) und für die Cloud an. Von diesem Thema sind auch Kunden betroffen, die beispielsweise die Kontrolle über die installierten Updates haben wollen. In einer SaaS-Lösung kümmert sich der Hoster um Updates, aber für alle.

Rechtliches

Die Daten in der Cloud gehören dem Ersteller, also Ihnen! Zur Herausgabe von eigenen Daten ist – genauso wie bei einer realen Durchsuchung – ein Gerichtsbeschluss nötig. Dieser Gerichtsbeschluss muss dem Inhaber der Daten – also Ihnen – vorgelegt werden. Sie sind dann für die Herausgabe der Daten verantwortlich. Die Benachrichtigung erfolgt nur dann nicht, wenn es sich um den schweren, dringenden Verdacht einer Behörde handelt, etwa bei Terrorverdacht (Stichwort: Gefahr im Verzug). Für die Herausgabe von Daten gibt es beim Dienstleister meist ganz klare Richtlinien. Microsoft etwa veröffentlicht regelmäßig Statistiken über solche Anfragen. Sie können auf der Website zum sogenannten „Transparency Report" (Microsoft, Low Enforcement Report, 2014) angesehen werden. Rechtlich funktioniert die Datenherausgabe also genauso wie bei Daten, die im Unternehmen gespeichert sind. Es gilt das lokale Datenschutzgesetz oder innerhalb der EU das entsprechende EU-Recht.

Security

Wichtige Unternehmensdaten bedürfen immer eines Sicherheitskonzepts und einer Klassifizierung. Je nach Schutzwürdigkeit wird ein Dokument dann entweder verschlüsselt oder mit Rechtemanagement versehen abgelegt. Dies gilt natürlich auch für E-Mails. Bei Forschungsunternehmen oder in der Industrie sind die Sicherheitsaspekte ganz anders als bei einem Händler, Dienstleister oder Einzelunternehmen. Die Rechenzentren selbst sind mehrfach gesichert und verfügen über eigene Sicherheitsstandards. Dort gelangt kein Unbefugter zu den Computern und Datenspeichern, alle Vorgänge werden überwacht und ausgewertet. Die Sicherheitsstandards in der Cloud sind jenen von normalen Unternehmen oft haushoch überlegen. Der physische Standort des Rechenzentrums entscheidet nicht über die Schutzwürdigkeit der Daten – das entscheidet der Dateninhaber selbst!

Was die Cloud betrifft, ist mein Wetterbericht optimistisch: zunehmende Bewölkung. Doch komme ich mit Managern ins Gespräch, reichen die Gegenargumente von der Datenspionage hinter den Unternehmenstüren bis hin zur NSA nach Amerika. Wie gehe ich damit um? Unverdrossen und guten Mutes!
Nicht nur Ihre Mitbewerber haben sich bereits für die Cloud entschieden, auch Ihre Mitarbeiter sind mit Dropbox oder WhatsApp schon fleißig dabei, oder? Datensicherheit ist auch keine Frage des Social Intranets. Es lohnt sich also, über die Chancen und Risiken nachzudenken. Vielleicht ist ja eine Hybridlösung genau das Richtige für Sie. Ich komme jedenfalls gern ins Haus und bringe mit: mein mobiles Intranet und den Cloud-Berater von nebenan.

EINSATZ DER CLOUD

Für Dienste und Lösungen in der Cloud ist ein riesiges Potenzial vorhanden. Aus gewisser Sicht stellt sich für Unternehmen nicht die Frage, ob die Cloud genutzt wird, sondern wann die Cloud genutzt wird. Im privaten Umfeld sind wir die Nutzung von Cloud-Lösungen vom Smartphone oder Tablet bereits gewöhnt.

Bevor jedoch SaaS Public-Cloud-Services eingesetzt werden, sollte sich Ihr Unternehmen über folgende Themen im Klaren sein:

- Wie oben erwähnt, sind die SaaS Cloud-Dienste nicht individuell bestimmbar.
- Die Services unterliegen den Regeln des Cloud-Anbieters.
- Ein Cloud-Betreiber behält sich aus Datenschutzgründen oft vor, Kundendaten in ein anderes Rechenzentrum zu verschieben (etwa bei Ausfall eines ganzen Rechenzentrums). Das geschieht aus Gründen der garantierten Serviceverfügbarkeit.
- Kunden haben keinen eigenen Zugang zu den Daten, etwa für Audits. Sie müssen bei Bedarf mit dem Cloud-Arbieter extra vereinbart werden oder man greift auf bereitgestellte Audit Reports zurück.
- Bei Ausfall eines Cloud-Dienstes gibt es bei Business Services oft eine Geld-Zurück-Garantie. Das gilt jedoch nur für die Kosten des Dienstes. Nicht erhalten sind etwaige Forderungen nach entgangenen Gewinnen oder ähnliche geschäftliche Aspekte oder Forderungen.
- Sie können nicht bestimmen, wann eine neue Version eines Cloud Services ausgerollt wird.
- Der Cloud-Anbieter unterstützt nur eine bestimmte Anzahl an Vorversionen, Sie sollten mit Ihrer Software also auf dem aktuellen Stand bleiben.

Für den erfolgreichen Einsatz von Cloud-Lösungen sind die obigen Punkte individuell für Ihr Unternehmen zu beantworten. Wenn das getan ist, kann eine technische Umstellung von IT-Diensten in die Cloud erfolgen.

Office 365 im Überblick

Office 365 enthält jene Tools, die uns bei unserer täglichen Arbeit unterstützen und die mittlerweile zentraler Bestandteil jeder Office-Umgebung sind: Microsoft Exchange, SharePoint Online, Lync Online, Office Online und Office Professional Plus.

Office 365 enthält für uns gewohnte Applikationen: Microsoft Exchange für den Versand und den Empfang von E-Mails, SharePoint Online für die Zusammenarbeit, die Dokumentenablage, Gruppenfunktionen wie Kalender und Adressbücher, Lync Online für die Onlinekommunikation via Chat, Videokonferenz und -telefonie und Office Professional Plus als vertraute Bürosoftware im Alltag.

Dabei wählen Sie selbst das derzeit für Sie passende Endgerät aus, sei es ein PC, Notebook, Mac, ein Tablet, ein Windows Phone, BlackBerry, Android oder iPhone.

Mit Microsoft Office 365 Pro Plus, welches nach wie vor auf dem Client zu installieren ist, gibt es eine gute Integration mit den oben genannten Produkten. Die Abbildung 2.6.2 zeigt die einzelnen Komponenten, die je nach erworbenem Office-365-Paket, den sogenannten Plänen, verfügbar sind.

Lestetipp:
Cloud-Fachwissen ganz einfach: „Microsoft Office 36 für kleine Unternehmen". (Grom, 2012)

Abbildung 2.6.2: Elemente von Office 365

Beispiele der Nutzung von Office 365

Das Schöne an Office 365 ist, dass diese Cloud-Lösung genauso für Einzelpersonen wie für weltweit operie-
rende Unternehmen eingesetzt werden kann. Hier einige Beispiele von Firmen, die mit Office 365 arbeiten:

- Eine kleine Druckerei in Wien hatte Probleme mit einem alten, nicht mehr gewarteten E-Mail-Server. Da
  funktionierende E-Mails für den Geschäftsbetrieb absolut erforderlich sind, war es wichtig, das eigene
  System möglichst rasch zu ersetzen und eine Lösung zu finden, die stabil und kostengünstig funktioniert,
  ohne dass wieder ein eigener Server angeschafft und betrieben werden musste. Mit Office 365, Exchange
  Online und Outlook konnte die Umstellung aller Mitarbeiter innerhalb eines Tages erfolgen. Seitdem gibt
  es keine Probleme mehr und alle Mitarbeiter können E-Mails jederzeit über Smartphones, Tablets, PCs
  und Mac-Systeme abrufen und bearbeiten.

- Ein Studenten-Verein in Deutschland verwendete eine alte, nicht mehr angepasste Mitgliederverwal-
  tung. Alle Mitglieder sollten eine E-Mail-Adresse vom Verein und gemeinsame Plattformen für die
  Kommunikation von News, Veranstaltungen und Leistungen rund um den Verein erhalten. Es wurde ein
  Office-365-Mandant angelegt. Somit erhalten alle Mitglieder Outlook Online und eine vollwertige Exch-
  ange-Mailbox mit Kalender und Kontakten aller anderen Mitglieder. SharePoint Online stellt ein gemeinsames Portal und einzelne Portale für die Geschäftsstellen, Alumni und Projekte bereit. Für die zentrale
  Verwaltung wurde ein Webportal in Microsoft Azure erstellt, welches die Benutzer aus Office 365 mit ihren Mitgliederinformationen verknüpft und alle wichtigen Operationen bereitstellt.

- Ein weltweit operierender Baukonzern bekam den Auftrag, eine neue Metro im Persischen Golf zu bauen.
  Zur Abwicklung der Baustellen war es erforderlich, ein gemeinsames System einzuführen, um eine mul-
  tinationale Arbeitsgemeinschaft gut zu organisieren und eine flexible und standardisierte IT zu verwenden. Dabei musste die Umsetzung rasch und kostengünstig erfolgen. Mit Office 365 war die Lösung sofort
  ohne eigene, aufwendige Server-Installationen einsetzbar. Nun können die Teilnehmer auf ihre E-Mails
  zugreifen und gemeinsame Dokumente bearbeiten und Videokonferenzen über Lync Online durchführen.
  Nach Beendigung des Projekts wird der Office-365-Mandant einfach archiviert und stillgelegt. Das ganze
  System kann auf die Projektdauer begrenzt zu budgetierbaren, fixen Kosten verwendet werden und stellt
  eine optimale Lösung dar.

Chancen der digitalen Zukunft

Die Welt ist im Wandel – und das in einem Ausmaß, wie es die Wirtschaft bisher selten erlebt hat. Unsere Welt entwickelt sich immer mehr zu einer digitalen Welt, zu einer digitalen Realität. Daraus ergeben sich viele Möglichkeiten, die nur darauf warten, in den Unternehmen umgesetzt zu werden. Für die Wirtschaft gilt es, jetzt anzufangen, jetzt loszulegen, jetzt die Chancen zu nutzen, bevor es alle anderen tun. Es müssen die Voraussetzungen innerhalb der Unternehmen geschaffen werden, um die digitale Welt zu meistern. Dabei kann beispielsweise die Cloud-Lösung Office 365 sehr gut helfen.

Edgar K. Geffroy
Keynote Speaker |
Consultant | Autor |
Geschäftsführer
Geffroy GmbH

Daten synchronisieren und sicher teilen

Wir nutzen Office 365 bereits seit einigen Jahren und als Geffroy Consulting haben wir einige Microsoft-Projekte begleitet. Was mich persönlich am meisten begeistert hat: Office 365 ist eine passgenaue und individuelle IT-Komplettlösung, die maximale Flexibilität, eine optimale IT-Infrastruktur sowie Datensicherheit gewährleistet und gleichzeitig die Kosten gering hält. Daten können laufend mit Ihren lokalen Rechnern synchronisiert werden und sind jederzeit mobil auf Smartphone und Co. verfügbar. Die Anschaffung einer solchen IT-Lösung verändert das Unternehmen erst einmal grundlegend – bietet aber auch große Vorteile.

Edgar K. Geffroy im
Video über Office 365
http://bit.ly/1tdVsYy

Machen Sie aus Change eine Chance!

Wir leben in einer Zeit, in der Wandlungsfähigkeit überlebenswichtig und die Grundlage für zukünftige Erfolge ist. Einfach gesagt, aber schwer umzusetzen. 84% der Menschen haben Angst vor Veränderungen und 98% der Unternehmen nutzen ihre digitalen Chancen nicht. Doch wir werden die nächsten Jahrzehnte in einem Zeitalter des permanenten Wandels leben. Deshalb müssen Unternehmer ihren Fach- und Führungskräften die Angst nehmen und sie dafür begeistern, dass die Zukunft eine Chance darstellt.

Praxisbericht im
Video zur erfolgreichen Umstellung auf
Office 365
http://bit.ly/1CqEIP...

Wir brauchen Provokateure, die neue Wege gehen wollen. Wir brauchen Pioniere und Herausforderer.

2.7 AUF NEUN PUNKTE GEBRACHT

1 Wer mitgestalten durfte, der nimmt das neue Intranet auch schneller an. Beziehen Sie alle zukünftigen Nutzergruppen von Anfang an mit ein und erfragen Sie die Abläufe, die momentan den meisten „Schmerz" verursachen. Trauen Sie den Mitarbeitern zu, Lösungsansätze für ihre Aufgaben am Arbeitsplatz selbst zu finden.

2 Schnittstellengespräche mit den Fachabteilungen sorgen dafür, dass Sie Ihre Lösung bedarfsgerecht bauen und Synergieeffekte mit anderen Projekten sichtbar werden. Binden Sie die Fachabteilungen also in die Planung ein und informieren Sie die zukünftigen Nutzer kontinuierlich über Projektfortschritte.

3 Ob einzelne Standorte zukünftig das zentrale neue Intranet nutzen oder auf eigene Lösungen setzen, das liegt in Ihrer Hand. Gehen Sie auf die Wünsche an den Standorten ein und räumen Sie für die dortigen Mitarbeiter auch auf der Startseite regional betreute Informationsplätze ein.

4 Ihre Strategie und die Nutzerbefragungen zeigen klar, wo im Unternehmen Handlungsbedarf besteht. Bestimmte Probleme lassen sich schnell mit der neuen Software-Lösung beheben. Definieren Sie die Anwendungsfälle und bringen Sie sie in eine für das Unternehmen wertvolle Reihenfolge.

5 Der Wandel zur Unternehmenskultur 2.0 geschieht nicht von heute auf morgen. Wenn es eines Kulturwandels bedarf, dann stellen Sie sich auf einen langfristigen Weg ein. Rufen Sie in einer wandelmüden Organisation aber nicht das nächste Change-Projekt aus, sondern lassen Sie den Wandel einfach als „Zusatzprodukt" Ihres Intranet-Projekts entstehen.

6 Vollständige IT-Konzepte, losgelöst von der Zieltechnologie, machen wenig Sinn – ihre Umsetzung verursacht entweder hohe Kosten oder Kompromisse, die das Konzept wieder in Frage stellen. Schauen Sie sich deshalb frühzeitig nach einer geeigneten Basistechnologie um und lassen Sie sie von Software-Experten auf den neuesten Stand bringen.

7 Cloud ist keine Frage des Ob, sondern lediglich des Wann. Stellen Sie alte Bedenken auf den Prüfstand, denn sowohl die Technik als auch die Rahmenbedingungen und Gesetze befinden sich ständig in Änderung.

8 Ein Intranet-Projekt ist selten als einzelne Ausschreibung planbar und durchführbar. Planen Sie interne Ressourcen und Budgets für mehrere Phasen.

9 Kein Projektteam möchte alte Fehler wiederholen. Machen Sie sich die Erfahrungen aus vorangegangenen Projekten bewusst und lernen Sie daraus.

1 TRÄUME   2 ANALYSIERE   3 PLANE   4 BAUE   5 ERPROBE   6 NUTZE

PLANE

In der dritten Phase erfolgt die fachliche und technische Spezifizierung der Lösung. Wichtige Funktionalitäten und Features werden geprüft. Hier entscheidet sich endgültig, welche Software für das Intranet eingesetzt wird. Danach können die Pläne für die Entwicklung und Einführung aufgestellt werden – von den technischen Plänen über den Personalent-wicklungsplan bis hin zum Mitarbeiteraktivie-rungsplan. Jetzt sind die Kosten auch genauer kalkulierbar.

Wenn der weitere Projektablauf bis einige Wochen nach dem Launch des neuen Intra-nets grob geplant ist, ist die dritte Phase erfolgreich absolviert.

VON ANFORDERUNGEN UND AGILITÄT IM MANAGEMENT VON INTRANET-PROJEKTEN

Bei der Einführung des modernen Intranets sind viele Aspekte zu berücksichtigen. Für das Projektmanagement gibt es in vielen Unternehmen bereits etablierte Richtlinien und Prozessvorgaben. So ist eine übergreifende Koordination erforderlich, auch ein detailliertes Anforderungsmanagement sollte es geben, und der Entwicklungsleiter muss die angemessene Vorgehensweise für die technische Implementierung auswählen. Für was man sich letztlich entscheidet, hängt von vielen Umständen ab. Die Wahlmöglichkeiten reichen vom phasenorientierten „klassischen" bis zum agilen Management (z.B. Scrum in der Software-Entwicklung), wobei insbesondere die Vielzahl der Anforderungen an ein Social Intranet oft für ein agiles Vorgehen spricht.

Erfolgsrezept Anforderungsmanagement

Ob komplexe Anforderungen zu steuern sind oder für die Intranet-Planung auf viele Standards gesetzt wird – gleich zu Projektbeginn sollte das Entwicklerteam festlegen, wie die Anforderungsdokumentation erfolgt und auf welche Weise Änderungen an den Anforderungen nachvollziehbar erfasst und freigegeben werden. Anders als beim klassischen Vorgehen befindet sich beim agilen Vorgehen das Intranet in einem kontinuierlichen Veränderungsprozess. Um diesen Prozess überschaubar zu halten, sollten die vorgenommenen technischen Änderungen für jeden nachvollziehbar sein. Die Rolle des Anforderungsmanagers ist daher erfolgs-

entscheidend für die pünktliche und bedarfsgerechte Intranet-Bereitstellung.

Modernes tool-gestütztes Anforderungsmanagement schafft Transparenz, die insbesondere für das Testen und in der Weiterentwicklung der Intranet-Lösung wichtig ist. Es hilft, Auswirkungen von Änderungsanforderungen richtig zu bewerten und Akzeptanzkriterien zielgerichteter zu identifizieren.

Ein agiles Vorgehen bei der technischen Umsetzung und die damit einhergehende strukturierte Aufbereitung der Anforderungen über User Stories im Produkt-Backlog bieten eine sehr gute Chance, das Anforderungsmanagement nachvollziehbar zu etablieren. Ob „Anforderungskatalog" oder „Produkt-Backlog" – eine nachvollziehbare Struktur inklusive Nummerierung ist für das spätere Referenzieren auf die ursprüngliche Anforderung hilfreich.

Klassisches oder agiles Projektmanagement – eine Entscheidungshilfe

Um Projektteams eine Entscheidungshilfe an die Hand zu geben, welches Vorgehensmodell für ihr Intranet-Projekt das geeignete ist, werden in Tabelle 3.1.1 (gemäß Schneegans, 2012 und Hagen, 2014) die beiden verbreitetsten Formen – das klassische und das agile Projektmanagement – gegenübergestellt und in den nachfolgenden Abschnitten noch genauer beschrieben.

Dieser Abschnitt entstand in Zusammenarbeit mit Christian Glessner SharePoint MVP Experts Inside

Weitere Betrachtungen und Vergleiche sind zu finden unter:
ttp://bit.ly/18l3eqp

Aspekt	Klassischer Ansatz geeigneter	Agiler Ansatz geeigneter
Art des Projekts	• Investitionsprojekte • Organisationsprojekte	• (Software-) Entwicklungsprojekte
Umfeld	• stabil • fachlich komplizierte Probleme	• dynamisch • systemisch-komplexe Probleme
Projektziele	• gleichbleibend • klar, spezifisch, messbar, abgrenzbar (Qualität, Kosten, Zeit)	• unscharf • veränderlich (MoSCoW: must, should, could, won't)
Auftraggeber	• gleichbleibend • „klassischer Typ" • ziel- und kennzahlenorientiert	• eventuell wechselnd oder mit schwankenden Zielstellungen • „agiler dynamischer Typ"
Team	• räumlich verteilt, virtuell • eher groß • Projekt ist eines von mehreren Projekten/Aufgaben • braucht klare Führung	• eher lokal • eher klein • frei von weiteren Aufgaben und Projekten • eigenständig, selbstorganisiert
Externe Dienstleister	• viele Dienstleister • viele Abhängigkeiten untereinander • benötigen klare Aufgaben- und Terminvorgaben	• wenige • geringe Abhängigkeiten • vom „Mindset" geeignet für agiles Arbeiten • agiles Vorgehen lässt sich vertraglich abbilden
Stakeholder	• viele Stakeholder, die Anforderungen festlegen • hoher Abstimmungsbedarf und Zeitaufwand • Termine müssen eingehalten werden, weil Aktivitäten von Stakeholdern vom Termin abhängen • Termine wichtiger als Leistungsumfang	• wenige Stakeholder • Qualität wichtiger als Termin • Aktivitäten der Stakeholder weitgehend unbeeinflusst vom Projekt
Dokumentation	• Rechtliche Anforderungen erfordern hohe Dokumentationsqualität • Zukünftige Weiterentwicklung und Pflege haben großen Stellenwert	• Keine externen Zwänge und Normen • Für zukünftige Zwecke geringe Relevanz

Tabelle 3.1.1: Klassisches oder agiles Vorgehensmodell? – Eine Entscheidungshilfe

Beide Varianten des Projektmanagements müssen nicht als Entweder-oder betrachtet werden. Je nach Unternehmenskontext kann auch eine Mischform Sinn machen, welche die passendsten Elemente beider Ansätze miteinander verbindet.

KLASSISCHES VORGEHENSMODELL BEI INTRANET-PROJEKTEN

Das bekannteste Vorgehensmodell im klassischen Projektmanagement von Software-Entwicklungsprojekten ist das Wasserfallmodell. Ähnlich wie das Wasser den Wasserfall Stufe für Stufe hinunterläuft und dann im Tal weiterfließt, werden im Wasserfallmodell die einzelnen Phasen wie Planung, Entwicklung und Testen sequenziell durchlaufen, ohne dass es zwingend einen Rückfluss gibt.

Im Wasserfallmodell ist jede Phase klar definiert durch einen Start- und einen Endpunkt in Form eines Meilensteins und konkreter damit verbundener Zielstellungen.

Das klassische Projektmanagement eignet sich besonders für Projekte, die gut vorhersehbar und planbar sind. Wenn sich die Anforderungen in der Planungsphase relativ präzise beschreiben lassen und im Zeitverlauf nur geringfügig ändern, spricht dies für ein klassisches Vorgehen. Typische Beispiele sind klar definierbare, in sich geschlossene Anwendungen, bei denen dem Anforderer von Beginn an klar ist, was er braucht und die Entwicklung klar abzuschätzen ist.

Klassisches Projektmanagement, häufig visualisiert über Gantt-Charts, hat den Vorteil, dass es häufig einfach und verständlich ist und die Aktivitäten in einer klaren Reihenfolge abgearbeitet werden können.

Im Allgemeinen ist das klassische Vorgehen problemlos erfolgreich, wenn überschaubare Vorhaben umzusetzen sind, also z.B. bei der Verwendung fertiger Frameworks und Dienste, der Umsetzung einzelner Anwendungen. Mehr hierzu auch im übernächsten Abschnitt.

AGILES VORGEHENSMODELL IN DER SOFTWARE-ENTWICKLUNG NACH SCRUM

Ein agiles Projektmanagement zeichnet sich durch ein schrittweises, auf Wiederholungen setzendes Vorgehen aus. Es ist werteorientiert, seine ideelle Grundlage ist das agile Manifest, welches u.a. folgende Prinzipien postuliert (agilemanifesto.org, 2001):

Die 12 Prinzipien der agilen Manifests http://bit.ly/1Enpb9

Lesetipp: Boris Gloger: „Scrum: Produkte zuverlässig und schnell entwickeln (Gloger, 2013).

- Individuen und Interaktionen sind wichtiger als Prozesse und Werkzeuge.
- Funktionierende Software ist wichtiger als umfassende Dokumentation
- Zusammenarbeit mit dem Kunden ist wichtiger als Vertragsverhandlung.
- Reagieren auf Veränderung ist wichtiger als das Befolgen eines Plans.

Das mittlerweile bekannteste agile Vorgehensmodell für Software-Entwicklung heißt Scrum. Die Umsetzung der agilen Prinzipien möchten wir in diesem Abschnitt anhand von Scrum etwas detaillierter vorstellen. Über Scrum gibt es mittlerweile sehr viele Bücher, die dieses Kapitel selbstverständlich nicht ersetzen kann. Doch soll an dieser Stelle ein Grundverständnis für ein agiles Vorgehen vermittelt werden, da es sich doch deutlich von den üblichen Projektmanagement-Ansätzen unterscheidet.

Die zentralen Elemente von Scrum sind

- das Produkt-Backlog (anstelle des klassischen Lastenhefts),
- verschiedene Rollen (Product Owner Scrum Master, Scrum Team) sowie
- verschiedene Elemente der Arbeitsorganisation (Scrum Sprint, Sprint Planning, Daily Scrum Meeting, Review Meeting, Retrospective Meeting).

Wer?	Was?	Warum?
Als Mitarbeiter	möchte ich auf der Startseite einen Newsbereich	um über das Unternehmen aktuell informiert zu sein.
Als Mitarbeiter aus dem Vertrieb	benötige ich alle Produktinformationen aktuell in einer Übersicht	damit ich Kunden immer die aktuellen Daten zur Verfügung stellen kann.
Als Herr Müller aus dem Management	möchte ich die neuesten Unternehmenskennzahlen zentral einsehen können	um nicht bei jeder Nachfrage auf andere Abteilungen angewiesen zu sein.

Tabelle 3.1.2: Beispiele für User Stories

EIN AUF HÖCHSTEN NUTZEN AUSGERICHTETES, ANPASSUNGSFÄHIGES „LASTENHEFT" – DAS PRODUKT-BACKLOG

Das sogenannte Produkt-Backlog ersetzt das Lastenheft des klassischen Projektmanagement. Er wird mit allen umzusetzenden Anforderungen befüllt. Diese Anforderungen werden in Form von sogenannten User Stories formuliert. Dabei handelt es sich um kurze Sätze, die nach der folgenden Formel erstellt werden:

„Als <Rolle> möchte ich <Ziel/Wunsch>, um <Nutzen>"

Es wird beschrieben, wer was warum möchte. Es wird nicht beschrieben, wie dies umgesetzt werden soll. Die Auswahl der geeignetsten Tools und Features liegt später in der Verantwortung des Scrum Teams.

Die User Stories im Produkt-Backlog sind entsprechend ihres Geschäftswerts absteigend sortiert. Es können jederzeit User Stories hinzugefügt oder entfernt werden. Auch die Priorisierung kann sich im Laufe des Projekts noch ändern, solange die Umsetzung noch nicht in eine Sprintplanung aufgenommen wurde. Die User Stories werden zunächst grob erfasst (siehe Beispiel in Tabelle 3.1.2), für die Priorisierung und Auswahl zur Umsetzung verfeinert und erst während des Sprints zur Umsetzung detaillierter ausgearbeitet.

KLARE VERANTWORTLICHKEITEN – DIE ROLLEN IM SCRUM

Der Product Owner ist dafür verantwortlich, dass das Social Intranet den maximalen Geschäftsnutzen entfaltet. Er ist für das Produkt-Backlog verantwortlich und gibt beim Scrum Team jeweils die werthaltigsten User Stories in Auftrag. Seine Aufgabe ist es, die Anforderungen detailliert zu beschreiben und bezüglich der Priorisierung Entscheidungen zu treffen.

Der Scrum Master ist der „Hüter" des gesamten Entwicklungsprozesses. Er moderiert die Scrum Meetings, überwacht den Gesamtprozess und muss Störfaktoren wie z.B. eine langsame Entwicklungsumgebung so schnell wie möglich beseitigen. Für diese Rolle braucht es ganz besonders gute Soft Skills und ein gutes Standing gegenüber dem Management.

Das Scrum Team ist für die eigentliche Umsetzung verantwortlich. Es besteht in der Regel aus zwei bis acht Personen mit gemischten Expertisen wie z.B. Entwickler, Berater und Tester. Es arbeitet eigenverantwortlich, bestimmt seine Geschwindigkeit selbst und entscheidet, wie viele User Stories in einem Sprint umgesetzt werden.

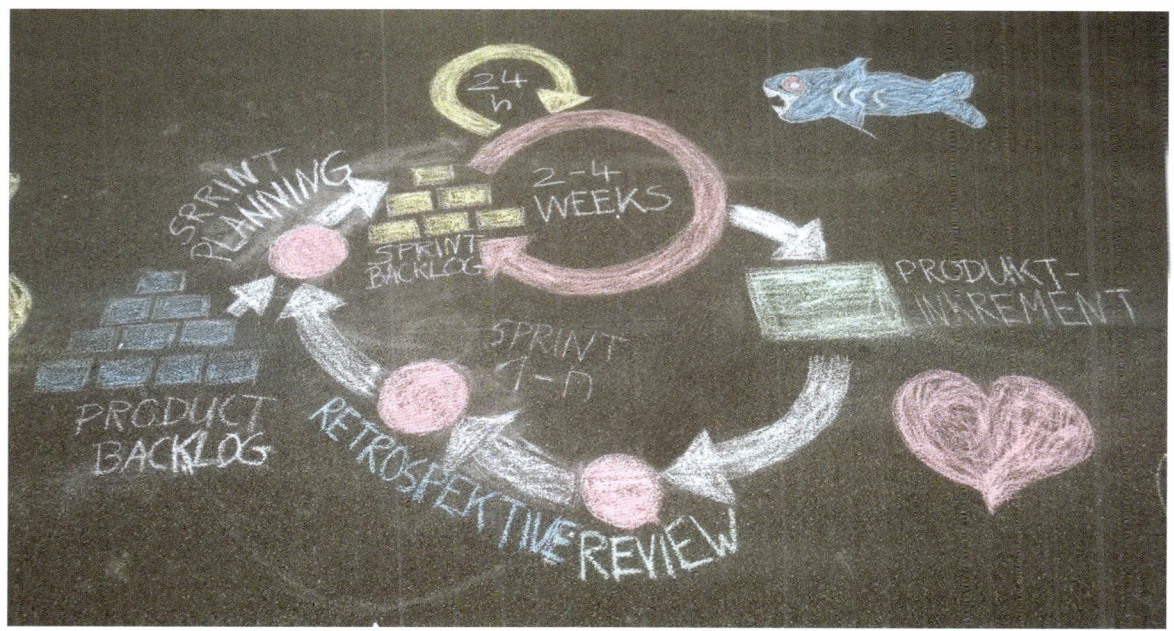

Abbildung 3.1.1: Scrum-Ablauf – auf die Straße gebracht von Christian und Lilly May Glessner

HOHER KUNDENNUTZEN UND KURZE LERNSCHLEIFEN – ARBEITSORGANISATION BEI SCRUM

Scrum funktioniert in kurzen Iterationsschleifen – den sog. Sprints – mit einer typischen Dauer von zwei bis vier Wochen. Der Ablauf eines Sprints ist in Abbildung 3.1.1 dargestellt.

Ein Sprint beginnt mit dem sogenannten Sprint Planning Meeting. Hierbei setzen sich Scrum Master, Product Owner und das Scrum Team zusammen, um den nächsten Sprint zu planen. Zu Beginn des Meetings stellt der Product Owner dem Team die Vision für den nächsten Sprint vor sowie die User Stories, die aus seiner Sicht im nächsten Sprint umzusetzen wären. Das Scrum Team stellt jetzt so lange Fragen an den Product Owner, bis es sich in der Lage fühlt, den Aufwand der User Stories zu schätzen. Es ist auch sinnvoll, mit dem Product Owner Abnahmekriterien (Definition of Done) für die einzelnen Stories zu definieren, zum Beispiel dass die Funktionalität mehrsprachig sein muss.

Die Aufwandsschätzung erfolgt meist mit Hilfe des sogenannten Planning Poker. Jedes Mitglied des Scrum Teams bekommt einen Satz Karten mit ansteigender Zahlenfolge und

schätzt den Aufwand der User Story. Wird der Aufwand durchgehend als sehr hoch eingeschätzt, wird die User Story in kleinere Stories zerlegt und erneut geschätzt Die Aufwandsschätzung erfolgt in mehreren Schleifen, bis das Scrum Team weitgehend einen Konsens entwickelt hat. Dieser Ablauf wird so lange wiederholt, bis das Scrum Team entscheidet, keine weiteren User Stories mehr in den Sprint aufzunehmen. Damit ist der sogenannte Sprint Backlog befüllt und kann in korkrete Aufgaben heruntergebrochen werden.

Nun kann der eigentliche Sprint beginnen. Jeden Morgen trifft sich das Scrum Team zum Daily Scrum Meeting. Dabei informieren sich alle Teammitglieder gegenseitig in kurzer und knapper Form über erledigte und anstehende Aufgaben sowie Probleme. Auf diese Weise behält das Team einen sehr guten Überblick über die Fortschritte, und Hürden können frühzeitig erkannt und beseitigt werden.

Ein Sprint wird beendet durch ein Review Meeting. Darin stellt das Scrum Team dem Product Owner das Ergebnis des letzten Sprints vor. Am Ende eines jeden Sprints muss ein potenziell releasefähiges Produktinkrement stehen, welches einen echten Wert für den Kunden darstellt. Auf Basis dieser Zwischenerfolge kann der Product Owner den Produkt-Backlog weiterentwickeln und hat gleichzeitig ein gutes Gefühl, dass das Projekt vorangeht.

Agile Softwareentwicklung misst dem Nutzen, aber auch dem Lernen einen hohen Stellenwert zu. Dafür dient u.a. das Retrospective Meeting, welches nach einem Review Meeting stattfindet und bei dem das Scrum Team den Ablauf des vorigen Sprints reflektiert und gegebenenfalls optimiert.

Projektmanagement bei der Social-Intranet-Einführung

Insbesondere Intranet-Projekte sind lebendige Projekte und sollten sich mit der Firma und Firmenkultur parallel weiterentwickeln. Gerade in der heutigen Zeit ist es wichtig, schnell auf Veränderungen reagieren zu können. Agile Vorgehensmodelle eignen sich hierfür besser als klassisches Projektmanagement. Agiles Vorgehen wirkt sich positiv auf die Motivation der Projektteams aus, weil es dem eigenverantwortlichen Arbeiten einen großen Stellenwert einräumt und das entwickelte Endprodukt auch vom Kunden gut akzeptiert wird. Häufig bestehen Bedenken, dies wäre risikobehaftet, aber das Gegenteil ist der Fall. Durch die ständigen Produktinkremente, die getestet werden bzw. sogar live gehen könnten, entstehen ständig Werte, und das Feedback der Tester und Mitarbeiter kann in den nächsten Sprint einfließen. Das Risiko eines fachlichen Fehlschlags ist somit sehr gering. Nicht verschweigen wollen wir, dass Scrum zugunsten der Qualität auch höhere Kosten verursachen kann durch die notwendige kontinuierliche Bereithaltung des Teams und die intensiven Abstimmungstreffen (insbesondere für die ersten Phasen bis sich das Team eingearbeitet hat). Risiken im agilen Vorgehen verlagern sich eher auf Punkte wie unklare Rollenverständnisse und Ausfälle im Team. Da kann es passieren, dass die Anforderungen noch nicht feinabgestimmt sind und der Entwickler frei hat.

Ein weiteres Hindernis in der Praxis ist die Angebotsgestaltung. Agiles Vorgehen eignet sich schlecht für Festpreis-Projekte, dafür aber am besten für Angebote nach Aufwand – der Albtraum eines jeden Einkaufs. In der Praxis haben wir gute Erfahrungen mit Projekten auf der Basis von Budgets gemacht. Hierdurch hat der Einkauf ein Kostendach, allerdings ist der Funktionsumfang variabel. Diese Art von Angebot setzt großes Vertrauen in den Partner voraus, insbesondere bei einem initialen Projekt. In unserem Einführungsmodell durchlaufen wir verschiedene Phasen, in denen der Rückfluss von Feedback und Erkenntnissen in die Intranet-Umsetzung und Einführungsbegleitung ein entscheidender Erfolgsfaktor ist. Eine Adaption des agilen Vorgehens nach Scrum, bezogen auf die Intranet-Einführungsmethodik, bedeutet, detaillierte Planungen möglichst nur für kurze Zyklen und überschaubare Lieferinhalte vorzunehmen. Für Lieferleistungen sind auch Vertragsgestaltungen „nach Aufwand" möglich. Dabei wird berücksichtigt, dass die Projektbeteiligten meist erst im Projektverlauf durch neue Erkenntnisse und das Fortschreiten einzelner Entwicklungsstufen die Anforderungen viel zielgenauer formulieren können. Das Realisierungsteam setzt dann genau das um, was auch gebraucht wird.

Die hier im Buch vorgestellte Methode gibt eine Gesamtschau auf notwendige, sinnvoll aufeinanderfolgende Projektschritte – von der Vision bis zur Nutzung der neuen Plattform im Arbeitsalltag. Sie bietet jedoch keine festgezurrte Planung an, sondern empfiehlt Flexibilität je nach den Rahmenbedingungen des Projekts. Das Phasenmodell kann sich dabei sowohl auf das klassische als auch auf das agile Vorgehen der IT einstellen. Das Team erarbeitet Schritt für Schritt, welche Arbeiten im nächsten, überschaubaren Zeitraum anstehen und schätzt den benötigten Zeitaufwand. Es definiert so Maßnahmen und Dauer der einzelnen Projektphasen – natürlich unter Beachtung der zur Verfügung stehenden Ressourcen.

Liebe Freunde des Pflichtenheftes, wir alle lieben Kontrolle. Doch in Zeiten des schnellen Wandels birgt diese vermeintliche Sicherheit ein Risiko! Das Verfassen des Pflichtenheftes für das Gesamtvorhaben wird schnell zur Last und dauert länger, als technische Neuerungen in Cloud-Versionen gelauncht werden. Wir können nicht schnell genug auf Markt- und User-Anforderungen reagieren.

Je öfter die neuesten technischen Features angewandt werden, desto genauer können Bedarfe vom Nutzer beschrieben werden. Agiles Vorgehen berücksichtigt diesen Lerneffekt. Seien Sie mutig, nutzen Sie ein agiles oder iteratives und flexibles Projektmanagement. Zerlegen Sie das Bauen des neuen Intranets in einzelne Launch-Phasen, die jeweils ein Bündel neuer Anwendungsszenarien für Ihre Nutzer bereithält.

3.2 ROADMAP – KATEGORISIEREN UND PRIORISIEREN

Die Analysen und Ergebnisse aus den Befragungen und Workshops aus Phase 2 liegen nun vor. Die gewünschten Anwendungsfälle und Feature müssen in der Folge sortiert und priorisiert werden.

Betrachten Sie dabei:

1. **die Priorität für das Unternehmen**, um die strategischen Ziele zu erreichen. Starten Sie mit den am schnellsten benötigten Dingen (Schmerzpunkte) und denen, die eine sichtbare Verbesserung schaffen. Schauen Sie aber auch nach einfach zu erreichenden Zielen („low hanging fruits" oder „quick wins").

2. **die Attraktivität für die Mitarbeiter**, damit sie die neue Plattform später nutzen. Die Tauschbörse steht auf Ihrer Agenda nicht sehr weit oben? Wenn Sie für Ihre Mitarbeiter wichtig ist, schenken Sie ihnen einfach so etwas zum Start und freuen Sie sich, dass damit die neuen Social-Funktionen perfekt erlernt werden.

3. **den Organisationsaufwand** bei der Umstellung von alt zu neu. Beginnen Sie mit Dingen ohne großen Aufwand, um schnelle Erfolge sichtbar zu machen.

4. **den Umsetzungsaufwand der IT**, denn er bestimmt maßgeblich das Machbare an Ressourcen und Budget.

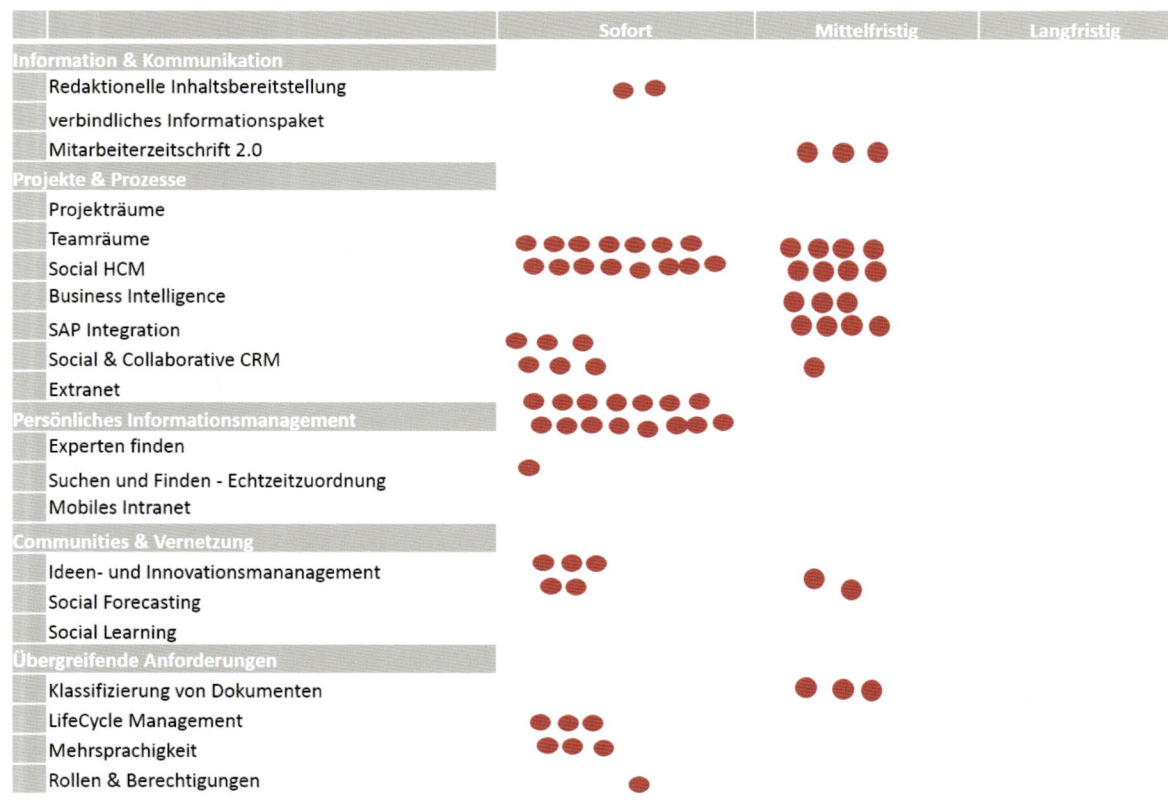

Abbildung 3.2.1: Beispiel Workshop-Ergebnis zur Priorisierung

Nutzen Sie dafür Klebepunkte, Scrum-Karten zur Aufwandschätzung oder Excel-Tabellen mit Schulnoten (siehe Beispiel in Abbildung 3.2.1).

Anhand dieser vorgenommenen Sortierung und Priorisierung ergibt sich ein erstes Bild für mögliche Inhalte der einzelnen Releases und deren Abhängigkeiten mit den benötigten Basisfunktionalitäten der technischen Plattform. Die Inhalte der Roadmap sind häufig durch das begrenzte Budget bestimmt. Daher benötigen wir erste Aufwandschätzungen für die Umsetzung der Szenarien. Dabei wird bewertet, welche Anforderungen mit den Standardfeatures der ausgewählten Basisplattform abgedeckt werden und welche Anforderungen einer weiteren Entwicklungs- und Konfigurationsleistung bedürfen. Der Aufwand für organisatorische Maßnahmen und der eigene Ressourcenaufwand muss gleichfalls analysiert werden.

Die grobe Vorstellung, was in welchem Zeitrahmen erreicht werden soll, erfassen Sie in einer Intranet-Roadmap, die visualisiert werden sollte. Die Roadmap betrachtet die Vorgehensweise über einen längeren Zeitraum hinweg – in der Regel mehr als ein Jahr –, ist jedoch kein detaillierter Projektplan. Die Grobplanung der Roadmap hilft aber, das langfristige Vorhaben eines umfassenden und gut genutzten modernen Intranets in einzelne Phasen aufzuteilen.

In vielen Einführungsprojekten für moderne Intranets findet man Rollout-Pläne vor, in denen schrittweise neue Anwendungsszenarien freigeschaltet wurden. Es gibt Vor- und Nachteile der unterschiedlichen Einführungsstrategien (siehe hierzu Abschnitt 6.1) Die dort beschriebenen Strategien helfen, eine eigene Roadmap zu entwickeln

3.3 ERFOLGSFAKTOR USABILITY

Eine gute Nutzerfreundlichkeit und ein positives Nutzererleben sind die Erfolgsgeheimnisse für hohe Akzeptanz von Intranets. Leider sind Intranets oft über Jahre hinweg erweiterte Systeme mit entsprechend unübersichtlichen Informationsstrukturen, welche schnell alle positiven Effekte hemmen können.

Intranet-Usability beschreibt, wie gut ein Intranet den Mitarbeitern im Arbeitsalltag hilft, bestimmte Ziele schnell, einfach und zufriedenstellend zu erreichen. Die Benutzerfreundlichkeit berücksichtigt darüber hinaus auch die emotionalen Aspekte des gesamten Nutzererlebnisses (User Experience). Die ideale User Experience erfüllt alle Nutzeranforderungen, ermöglicht eine einfache Bedienung und erzeugt Freude bei der Nutzung.

Häufige Mängel bei der Gestaltung des Intranets sind eine wenig ergonomische Struktur, ein unattraktives Design, schwer auffindbare Inhalte sowie eine komplizierte und unverständliche Navigation. Darin liegen meist auch die Hauptgründe für eine geringe Nutzung des Intranets.

Mit einfachen Schritten können solche Mängel relativ schnell behoben werden. Viele Faktoren beeinflussen die Usability einer Intranet-Seite. Nutzerfreundliche Seiten begeistern, sie führen die Nutzer elegant durch die Inhalte und machen die Nutzung so intuitiv wie möglich. Eine wichtige Voraussetzung dafür ist eine gute Balance aus Logik und Design. Logisch strukturierte, aber optisch fade Seiten schrecken Nutzer ebenso ab wie brillant designte Seiten, deren Struktur sich dem Nutzer jedoch nicht erschließt.

Um eine gute Usability zu gewährleisten, sollten Sie von Anfang an den zukünftigen Nutzer in den Mittelpunkt des Entwicklungsprozesses stellen. Ein solcher, am User zentrierter Designprozess berücksichtigt in einem ständigen Kreislauf alles, was gebraucht wird: Nutzerbedürfnisse, geeignete Angebote und deren permanente Bewertung durch die Nutzer so lange, bis das Ergebnis stimmt.

! Praxistipps: Zehn Tipps zur Nutzerfreundlichkeit im Intranet

1. Untersuchen Sie möglichst frühzeitig, womit die Zielgruppen Ihres Intranets bisher unzufrieden sind. Decken Sie durch Befragungen vorhandene Schwachstellen und Nutzungsprobleme auf und ermitteln sie den vorhandenen „Frustrationsgrad".

2. Platzieren Sie wichtige Informationen zentral auf Ihrer Startseite. Dann können Ihre Mitarbeiter im Arbeitsalltag schnell und einfach darauf zugreifen. Sie werden schnell merken, wie der gefühlte Mehrwert bei den Mitarbeitern steigt. Achten Sie dabei unbedingt auf die Aktualität der Inhalte!

3. Sorgen Sie dafür, dass Anwendungen und Systeme, die für den Arbeitsalltag benötigt werden, in jedem Fall miteinander und mit dem Intranet kompatibel sind. Verringern Sie die sogenannte „Tool-Time", d.h. die Zeit, die Ihre Mitarbeiter durch inkompatible Systeme verlieren. Manuelles Übertragen von Daten oder Speicherfehler sind No-Gos für nutzerfreundliche Intranets

4. Berücksichtigen Sie bei der Entwicklung des Intranets die verschiedenen Aufgabenbereiche und Rollen in Ihrem Unternehmen. Eine personalisierte Ansicht und ein rollenbasierter Aufbau der Funktionen sind von großem Vorteil, da die Mitarbeiter je nach Funktionsbereich verschiedene Features und Inhalte benötigen.

5. Auch für den Aufbau der Intranet-Seiten gilt: Die Form sollte der Funktion folgen. Erarbeiten Sie daher zuerst den Nutzungszweck einer Seite, bevor Sie sich dem Layout und anderen Feinheiten zuwenden.

6. Beschränken Sie sich bei der Gestaltung der Elemente und Informationen auf das Wesentliche nach dem bewährten Grundsatz: So wenig wie möglich, so viel wie nötig. Sorgen Sie auf Textseiten für optische Auflockerung durch geeignete Grafiken oder Videos.

7. Achten Sie auch auf allgemeine Konventionen, mit denen Nutzer bereits aus dem Internet vertraut sind. Für Intranet-Seiten wäre beispielsweise das horizontale Scrollen unerwartet und im Arbeitsalltag hinderlich. Ein einheitlicher Aufbau aller Unterseiten ist zudem empfehlenswert.

8. Intranet-Räume mit bestimmten Funktionen wie z.B. Projekträume sollten gestalterisch angepasst und von anderen Seiten unterscheidbar sein, damit User verschiedene Umgebungen innerhalb des Intranets schnell erfassen und sich intuitiv zurechtfinden können

9. Unterstützen Sie die Nutzerführung durch aussagekräftige Überschriften und Bezeichnungen. Auch Icons eignen sich hervorragend zur einfachen Navigation. Beachten Sie dabei, dass Elemente mit ähnlichen Funktionen auch als solche zu erkennen sind.

10. Ist Barrierefreiheit in Ihrer Organisation ein wichtiges Thema? Dann sorgen Sie für die Möglichkeit, die Schrift zu vergrößern, sowie für eine Vorlesefunktion.

Wie werden Intranet und Social Network barrierefrei?
http://bit.ly/1wy4q

Planen Sie in jedem Fall mehrere Testläufe und Korrekturschleifen für die Benutzerführung und die Benutzeroberfläche ein, bevor Sie das neue Intranet freigeben. Beziehen Sie auch dabei die späteren Nutzergruppen ebenso ein wie völlig unabhängige Testpersonen.

Die Erkenntnisse dieser Usability-Betrachtungen bieten die Grundlage für die Informationsarchitektur und das Design, auf die wir nun eingehen werden.

3.4 INFORMATIONS-ARCHITEKTUR

Überblick

"The art and science of structuring, organizing and labelling information to help people find and manage it."
Louis Rosenfeld
(Rosenfeld, 2011)

Im Intranet geht es vorrangig darum, die tägliche Arbeit zu unterstützen, indem Inhalte bereitgestellt werden und abrufbar sind, sodass die Kommunikation untereinander erleichtert wird. Dafür braucht es eine schnelle Orientierung und eine leichte und intuitive Bedienbarkeit für die unterschiedlichen Nutzergruppen mit ihrem jeweils sehr individuellen Suchverhalten. Aus Unternehmenssicht wiederum ist es von hohem Interesse, dass die Informationen verwaltet werden können, ohne dass technische und budgetäre Schranken überschritten werden. Den Spagat aus diesen beiden Zielrichtungen zu meistern, ist Aufgabe der Informationsarchitektur des Intranets.

Diese Ziele vor Augen, gilt es zunächst, Inhalte zu klassifizieren und zu strukturieren. Zur Methodik der Konzeption von Informationsarchitekturen gibt es spezielle Literaturangebote. Im Buch „Social Intranet - Kommunikation fördern - Wissen teilen - Effizient zusammenarbeiten" (Wolf, 2011) gehen Jan Jursa und Ulf Sthamer auf die Besonderheiten der Informationsarchitektur von Social Intranets ein. Dabei ist von Bedeutung, dass eine externe Unterstützung fast immer hilfreich für die Methodik des Projekts ist, zumal der Blick von außen einer vielfach waltenden Betriebsblindheit der Insider entgegenwirkt. Bei näherer Betrachtung des Schwerpunktes "Organisieren" von Inhalten verdeutlich Abbildung 3.4.1 die zur Verfügung stehenden Elemente der Planung.

Abbildung 3.4.1: Wichtige Themen bei der Konzeption einer Informationsarchitektur

Eine besondere Herausforderung ist dabei die große Zahl unterschiedlicher Autoren in einem Social Intranet. Ohne adäquate Unterstützung der Nutzer kann dies zu

- inkonsistentem Umgang mit Daten,
- unterschiedlichen Benennungen,
- einer abweichenden Gestaltung der Seiten
- und der ungleichen Strukturierung von Inhalten

führen. Die Wiederauffindbarkeit von Inhalten wäre damit erschwert. Eine Informationsarchitektur versucht, solche Probleme schon in der Konzeptphase aufzugreifen, um ihnen vorzubeugen.

Die wesentlichen Themenbereiche, die bei der Konzeption einer Informationsarchitektur zu berücksichtigen sind, haben wir hier zusammengefasst:

GESTALTUNG UND NAVIGATIONS-ELEMENTE

Die bereits erfolgten Betrachtungen zur Usability werden in diesem Baustein der Informationsarchitektur berücksichtigt und später mit der Designentwicklung umgesetzt. Für intuitives Bedienen spielt die Optik eine herausragende Rolle.

Verschiedene Navigationselemente sorgen für eine gezielte Benutzerführung und versetzen den Nutzer in die Lage, Informationen, die er benötigt, auf unterschiedlichen Wegen zu finden.

- **Navigationsbaum:** Der normale planmäßige Weg wird durch den Navigationsbaum beschrieben. Nutzer klicken sich durch eine horizontale und vertikale Navigation und erreichen dadurch ihr Ziel.

- **Abkürzungen:** Sie beschreiben einen direkten Weg. So kann durch eine Verlinkung auf der Startseite eine Inhaltsseite schneller erreicht werden

- **Verwandte Themen:** Es gibt immer auch „ungeplante" Strecken. Damit sind Navigations-Elemente gemeint wie 'Verwandte Themen" oder "Siehe auch"

- **Bottom-Up-Navigation:** Sie macht es möglich, dass der Nutzer den Weg von einer einzelnen Seite wieder zurück in die übergeordneten Inhaltsseiten findet.

- **Gestalterische Elemente:** Sie sorgen für die Lesbarkeit und eine schnelle Wiedererkennbarkeit von Funktionen und Inhalten. Wichtige Informationen müssen hervorgehoben werden und weniger relevante in den Hintergrund treten. Dafür sind Standards für die Übersichts- und Inhaltsseiten zu definieren.

- **Editoren:** Im Social Intranet sind die Nutzer meist weder geübt noch geschult, wie Inhalte darzustellen sind. Daher kann eine Beschränkung der Eingabe auf kurze Textbeiträge und eine Bildvorschau sinnvoll sein. An den Stellen, wo mehr gebraucht wird, helfen gute Editoren mit Hervorhebungen in Kombination mit Formatvorlagen (z.B. Überschriften, Links, Tabellen) und Seitentemplates.

- **Personalisierung und Individualisierung:** Im Umgang mit der Informationsflut helfen Personalisierungen auf der Basis der Nutzerinformationen (Standort, Abteilung etc.) und Individualisierungen durch die Nutzer. Nutzer können selbst bestimmen/konfigurieren, was ihnen wichtig ist und angezeigt wird (konfigurierbarer Newsfeed, Dashboards, meine Links, meine Dokumente, RSS-Feed). Aber Achtung: Auch hier gilt: Weniger ist mehr! Zu viele Einstellmöglichkeiten führen schnell zu Verwirrung und Frustration bei den Nutzern.

BENENNUNGEN, TAXONOMIEN UND METADATEN

Einheitliche Benennungen, prägnant und spezifisch, helfen dem Nutzer, schneller zu erkennen, um welchen Typ von Inhalt es sich handelt. Zugleich hilft dies der Suchmaschine, die Relevanz von Treffern genauer zuzuordnen. Gezielte Vorschläge bei der Eingabe (Autocomplete-Funktionen) unterstützen den Ersteller einer Information und helfen, Wildwuchs zu vermeiden. Moderne Technologien unterstützen auch eine Rechtschreibhilfe in den Metadaten oder stellen einfach auswählbare, unternehmensweit einheitliche Schlagworte bereit. Dabei ist es wichtig, eine gesunde Balance zu finden zwischen freier Handhabung und Pflichtfeldern/Vorgaben.

Die Entwicklung von unternehmensweiten Schlagwort-Katalogen (sog. Taxonomien) gehört ebenfalls in die Konzeption der Informationsarchitektur. Hierbei ist auch festzulegen, wie und wann diese Taxonomien als Metadaten mit den Informationselementen verbunden werden sollen. Da sie sich im Lauf der Zeit ändern können, sollte ihre Weiterentwicklung und Pflege als feste Aufgabe und Verantwortlichkeit in der Organisation verortet werden.

STRUKTURIERUNG UND NAVIGATION

Informationsstrukturen sind auf ganz unterschiedlichen Ebenen und Elementen vorhanden und zu definieren. Die hierarchische Anordnung in Form einer Navigation spielt ohne Frage die wichtigste Rolle. Jedoch auch

- die Unterstützung von Informations-Netzen (dargestellt z.B. durch Tag Clouds oder semantische Graphen),

- die Informationsablage in und Informationsflüsse aus Intranet-Räumen (z.B. durch Activity Streams oder Workflows),
- die Darstellung und Erreichbarkeit der Informationselemente innerhalb einer Hierarchieebene sowie
- der inhaltliche Aufbau in den Seiten selbst

geben den Informationen im Intranet weitere Strukturen. Der Blick auf Themen, Aufgaben, Zielgruppen, geografische Attribute, Beliebtheit und Aktualität oder alphabetische Ordnung sind die Kriterien, nach denen z.B. kategorisiert und angeordnet werden kann.

SUCHE

Eine Suche funktioniert nicht allein dadurch gut, dass sie installiert wurde und die Startseite des Intranets als zu durchsuchende Datenquelle konfiguriert wurde. Wenn dies der Fall wäre, dann würde niemand seine Unzufriedenheit über die Intranet-Suche äußern. Die Konzeption der Suche als Bestandteil der Informationsarchitektur beschäftigt sich damit, wie die Inhalte in der Suche aufgefunden werden, nach welchen Prinzipien indexiert und die Suchergebnisse dargestellt werden sollten. Aufgrund der herausragenden Bedeutung der Suchfunktion werden diese Aspekte an späterer Stelle in diesem Kapitel weiter vertieft.

Die Ergebnisse aus der Konzeption der Informationsarchitektur werden in Form von SiteMaps, Wireframes und Übersichten der Planung zukünftiger Inhalte dokumentiert und fließen inhaltlich in die Governance-Richtlinien ein. In den folgenden Abschnitten werden die Themen Navigation, Raumkonzeption und Suche für die interessierten Leser weiter vertieft.

Wie man eine gute Navigation entwickelt

STRUKTUR UND NAVIGATIONSELEMENTE

Natürlich ist es unabdingbar, dass Sie zum Start des neuen Intranets eine grundlegende Struktur für die redaktionell vorgegebenen Bereiche haben. In aller Regel sind bereits vorhandene Strukturen dafür eine gute Basis. Es gibt eine Startseite und darunter gruppieren sich dann Standorte oder Abteilungen. Es gibt Navigationspunkte zu fachlichen Themen wie Personalangelegenheiten oder Projekte. Diese Top-Level-Punkte zu identifizieren, geht vermeintlich recht schnell. Sobald es dann daran geht, die Details der Unternavigation zu planen, merkt man allerdings ebenso schnell, dass das Thema leider nicht so einfach ist, wie es vielleicht anfangs schien.

„Organisieren wir nur nach Standorten oder auch nach Abteilungen? Was ist jedoch, wenn es Abteilungen an mehreren, aber nicht an allen Standorten gibt?" Dies ist nur eine von vielen typischen Fragestellungen, die auftauchen, wenn man sich näher mit der Navigationsstruktur beschäftigt. Hier gibt es kein allgemeingültiges Rezept, wohl aber ein paar Ansatzpunkte, um zu einem guten Ergebnis zu kommen.

Empfehlenswert ist es, von Anfang an auf eine Technologie zu setzen, die es erlaubt, die Navigation flexibel zu handhaben. Bewährt hat sich z.B. eine sogenannte „Metadatenbasierte Navigation". Dabei wird jede neue Seite und jeder neue Bereich durch Zuweisen einer Metainformation in der Navigation verortet. Eine neue Seite über ein Projekt in England kann so beispielsweise unter Standorte > England > News platziert werden. Mit diesem flexiblen Ansatz kann man auf unkomplizierte Weise auf Veränderungen über die Lebenszeit der Internetplattform hinweg reagieren. Die Zusammenlegung von Abteilungen, das Hinzukommen neuer Standorte – das verursacht alles keine Probleme mehr.

Beispiele für weitere Navigations-Elemente sind:

- Haupt-Navigation (Top-Navigation und Themen/Bereichs-Navigation);
- Breadcrumb-Navigation (Pfad von der Hauptseite zur aktuellen Unterseite);
- "Schaufenster-Navigation" (Quick Links);
- Kontextabhängige Navigation (z.B. "Siehe auch");
- Service-Navigation (Links zu Hilfen, Einstellungen oder persönlichen Bereichen);
- Personalisierte Navigationselemente.

Die Abbildung 3.4.2 zeigt exemplarisch eine Bereichs-Startseite der Abteilung Human Resources. Das "Schaufenster" ist hierbei eine Art Quick-Link-Sammlung und enthält die wichtigsten Links zu Inhalten in diesem Bereich.

Es ist auch eine Überlegung wert, Benutzern die Möglichkeit zu geben, sich einen Teil der Navigation selbst zu gestalten. Techniken, die wir vom Webbrowser kennen, z.B. das Setzen von Favoriten, können ohne großen Aufwand in die Navigation eines Social Intranets integriert werden. Indem der Benutzer Seiten abonnieren kann, schafft er sich seine ganz eigene Navigationsstruktur, die er nach seinen Bedürfnissen immer wieder anpassen kann.

VOM CARD SORTING ZUR TOP-NAVIGATION

Ein zentrales Element der Navigation ist die Haupt-Navigation. Sie besteht im Regelfall aus zwei Elementen, der „Top-Navigation" und der „Themen- und Bereichs-Navigation". Beide zu entwickeln, ist kein Projekt sondern ein Prozess – d.h. die Navigationsstruktur sollte in regelmäßigen Abständen neu getestet werden. Oft erleben wir, dass das Thema Hauptnavigation lediglich als ein Randthema in einem Intranet-Projekt gesehen wird. Unserer Meinung nach ist die Entwicklung einer aufgaben- und themenorientierter Top-Navigation ein wichtiger Erfolgsfaktor in einem Intranet-Projekt.

Dieser Abschnitt entstand in Zusammenarbeit mit Sven Lindenhahn, Social Business Consultant T-Systems Multimedia Solutions GmbH

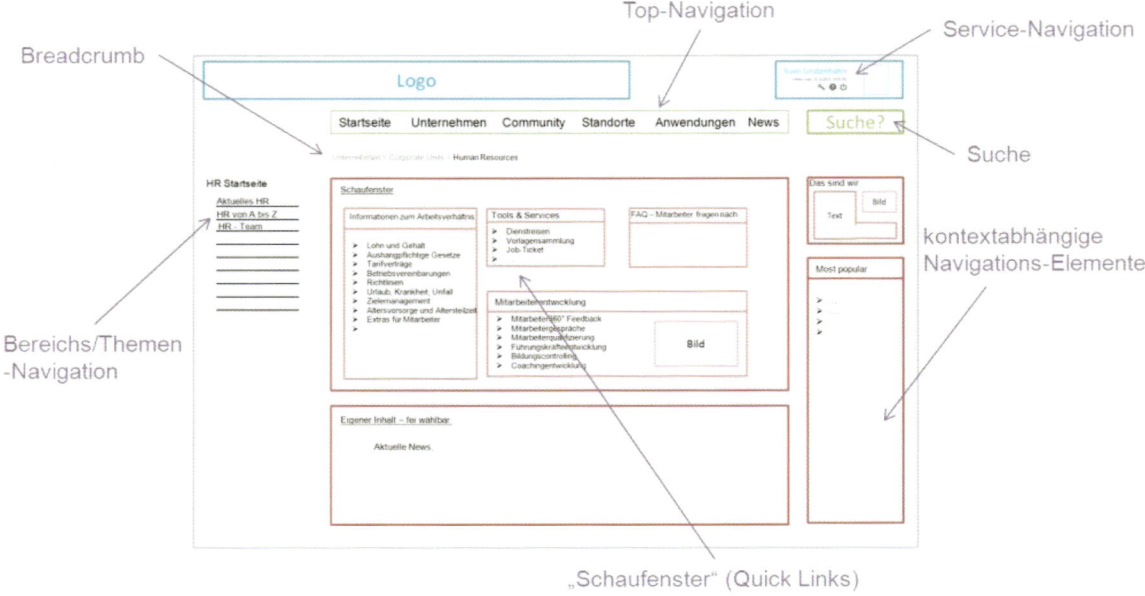

Abbildung 3.4.2: Navigationselemente einer Bereichs-Startseite

Mit Hilfe der Card-Sorting-Methode kann man die Top-Navigation in Zusammenarbeit mit den zukünftigen Nutzern entwickeln und sie auf diese Weise elegant in den Entwicklungsprozess integrieren. Es ist immer wieder schön zu sehen, mit welcher Begeisterung der Großteil der Teilnehmer am Card Sorting teilnimmt und welche Ergebnisse in der Zusammenarbeit dabei entwickelt werden. Zudem wird über die-

sen Weg auch den Teilnehmern bewusst, welch komplexe Herausforderung es ist, eine für die Mehrheit der Nutzer verständliche, robuste themenorientierte Navigation zu ermitteln. Oberbegriffe sind dabei eindeutig, verständlich und überschneidungsfrei zu formulieren und das, obwohl jeder Mitarbeiter eine eigene Sicht auf das Unternehmen hat. Die Entwicklung einer für alle Nutzer idealen Hauptnavigation ist ein nicht zu erreichendes Ziel. Aber ein guter Kompromiss für alle sollte gefunden werden.

Card Sorting bedeutet vereinfacht: Teilnehmer müssen Karten, auf denen Begriffe stehen, thematisch sortieren. Dies kann online oder in Workshops stattfinden, wobei wir ein mehrstufiges Vorgehen empfehlen (siehe Abbildung 3.4.3). Für den Einstieg empfiehlt sich ein Workshop in einem kleineren Teilnehmerkreis. Dabei erhält jeder Teilnehmer Karten mit vorgegebenen Begriffen und die Aufgabe, diese Karten zu sortieren und jeweils Oberbegriffen zuzuordnen. Es sollte vorab entschieden werden, ob die Oberbegriffe vorgegeben werden (geschlossenes Card Sorting) oder selbst zu entwickeln sind (offenes Card Sorting). Die Einzelergebnisse werden dann der Gruppe vorgestellt und kommentiert: Warum habe ich mich für diese

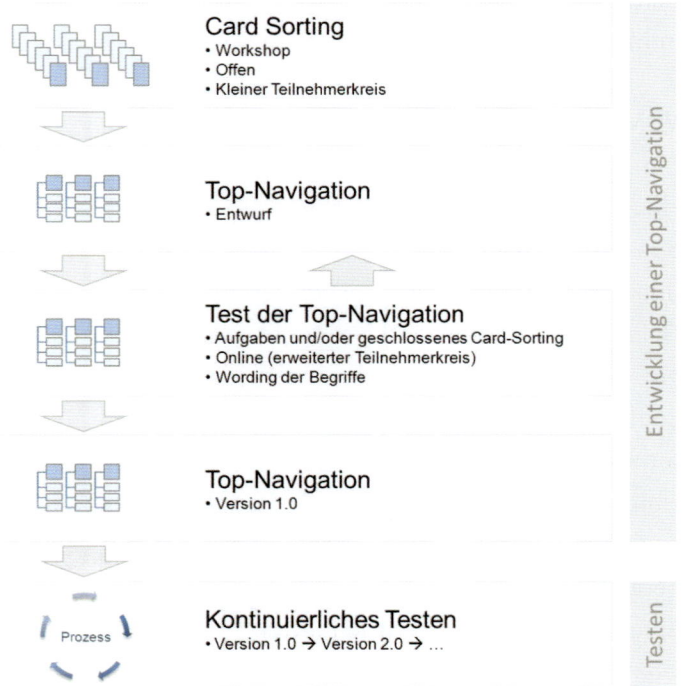

Abbildung 3.4.3: Der Weg vom Card Sorting zur Top-Navigation

Lösung entschieden? Wobei hatte ich Schwierigkeiten? Welche Begriffe waren unklar und fehlen womöglich? Gibt es noch wichtige Themen? Anschließend werden die Oberbegriffe im gemeinsamen Dialog zu einer Top-Navigation konsolidiert.

Folgende Best-Practice-Regeln für offene Card Sortings resultieren aus unseren praktischen Erfahrungen:

- Begriffe in max. acht Gruppen einsortieren;
- Untergruppen können erstellt werden (max. eine weitere Ebene);
- Oberbegriffe (Name der Gruppen) können auch Begriffe sein;
- Leere Karten für die Teilnehmer, um fehlende Begriffe zu ergänzen;
- Unklare Begriffe nicht zuordnen und zur Seite legen;
- Zeit: ca. 30 Minuten – kein Problem, wenn es länger dauert;
- Jeder sollte möglichst für sich arbeiten.

Der im Workshop gewonnene Entwurf wird im Anschluss nochmals überprüft und kann dann über ein Online Card Sorting einer großen Teilnehmerzahl zur Abstimmung vorgelegt werden. Die Mitarbeiter erlangen so das Gefühl, am Intranet-Projekt aktiv mitwirken zu können. Zudem ist es ein gutes Kommunikationsmittel, um die Beschäftigten über den aktuellen Stand des Intranet-Projekts zu informieren. Die folgende Abbildung 3.4.4 zeigt beispielhaft ein geschlossenes Online Card Sorting, welches nach denselben Regeln erfolgt wie die Workshop-Variante.

Bestenfalls kristallisiert sich schnell eine Navigationsstruktur heraus, die auf breite Zustimmung trifft. Falls nicht, sollte ein solcher Konsens durch weitere Iterationsschleifen angestrebt werden.

Eine empfehlenswerte, englische Internetseite zu Details des Card Sortings stellt die Firma steptwo bereit: http://bit.ly/1A8Jd2

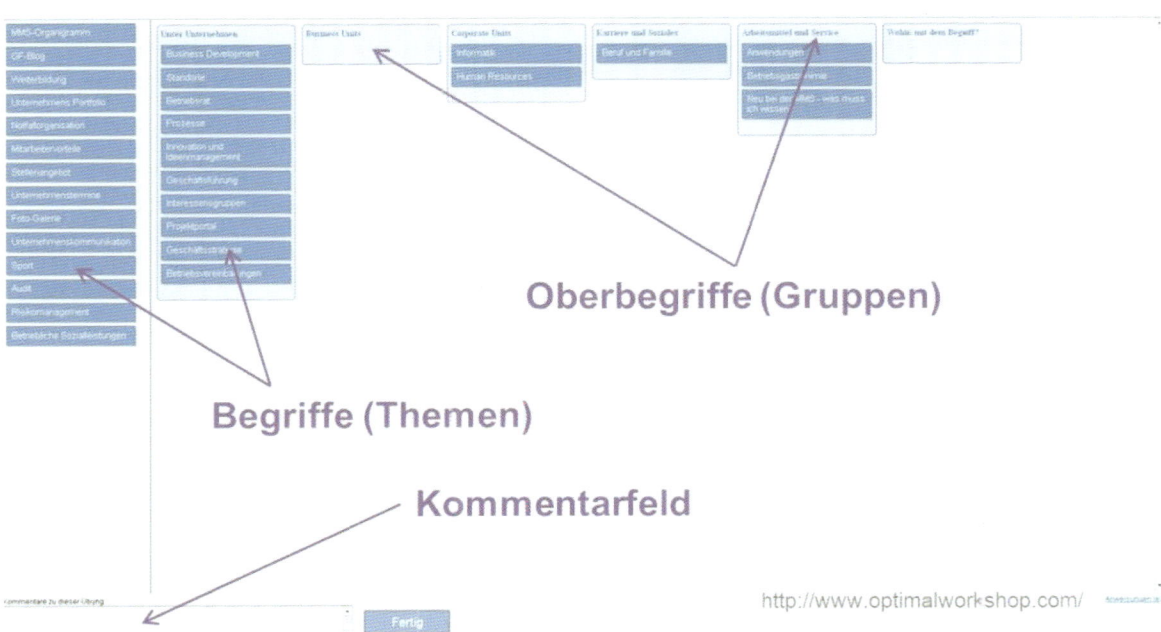

Abbildung 3.4.4: Beispiel für geschlossenes Card Sorting - Online mit www.optimalworkshop.com

TEST DER HAUPTNAVIGATION

Es besteht die Möglichkeit, eine Top-Navigation gezielt durch Aufgaben zu testen. Dafür müssen die Testpersonen definierte Aufgaben erhalten, die sie zu lösen haben. Wie beim Card Sorting kann dieser Test sowohl als Workshop als auch online durchgeführt werden. Die folgende Abbildung zeigt beispielhaft die Online-Variante mit der Aufgabe: Sie sind neu bei der T-Systems und möchten sich über Ihren Standort informieren. Wo finden Sie Informationen zum Standort Dresden?

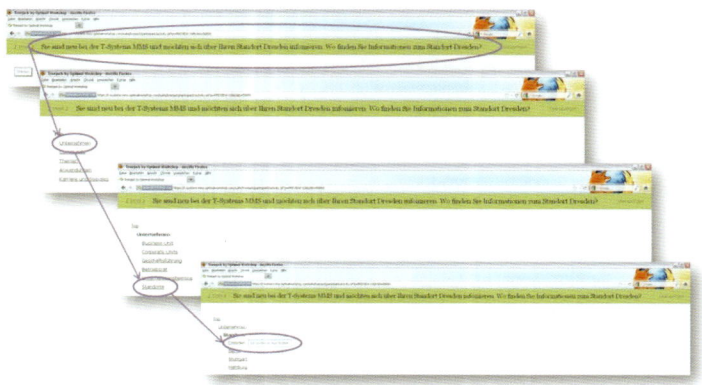

Abbildung 3.4.5: Beispiel zum Test der Navigation „Wo finden Sie Informationen zum Standort Dresden?"

Mit Hilfe von drei Kennzahlen erfolgt schließlich die Bewertung der getesteten Top-Navigation:

1. Zielerreichung, d.h. haben die Testpersonen den richtigen Weg gefunden?
2. Abweichung vom direkten Weg;
3. Zeitaufwand.

Die ersten beiden Kennzahlen sind hier von besonderer Bedeutung bei der Bewertung. Sie zeigen auf, inwieweit der Nutzer auf den ersten Blick den richtigen Weg findet.

Raumkonzepte

Für jedes Social Intranet sind auch Zusammenarbeitsräume wichtig. Ob für Teams, Projekte oder Communities – es besteht der Bedarf an einem definierten Arbeits- und Inhaltsraum für den fokussierten und effektiven Informationsaustausch. Jedem Beteiligten ist klar, wo er welche Inhalte bereitstellen und finden kann. Im Sinne des unternehmensweiten Informations- und Kommunikationsflusses sind diese Räume offen für alle oder nur für gewisse Zielgruppen.

In vielen Unternehmen findet die Zusammenarbeit aktuell über ein gemeinsames Netzlaufwerk und/oder über E-Mail-Postfächer statt. Zuweilen werden diese bereits ergänzt durch ein Wiki oder durch spezielle Seiten im bestehenden Intranet. Die Übersichtlichkeit ist nicht immer zufriedenstellend.

Mit der Bereitstellung von Zusammenarbeitsräumen sollen die Arbeitsabläufe der jeweiligen Zielgruppe unterstützt und in die Unternehmenslandschaft eingebettet werden. Die Raumkonzeption bereitet dies durch spezielle Betrachtungen je Raumtyp vor. Unterschiedliche Raumtypen sind bei der Nutzungsaufnahme ggf. auch unterschiedlich zu begleiten.

Dabei ist es nicht immer ganz leicht, den Sinn für die richtige Technologie zu entwickeln. Erfahrene Berater, die das Team bei der Konzeption begleiten, sollten deshalb unbedingt hinzugezogen werden. Oft stecken auch einige Stolpersteine in der Software, die bei technologieabhängigen Fachkonzepten frühzeitiger umgangen werden, wodurch Kosten bei der Umsetzung gespart werden können.

Die benötigten Raumtypen orientieren sich an den vier Hauptanwendungsfällen in Social Intranets (siehe Einführung, S. 10):

1. Information und offizielle Kommunikation,
2. Projekte und Prozesse,
3. Profil und persönliches Informationsmanagement,
4. Vernetzung, Communities, Integration.

Bei diesem Ansatz stellten wir fest, dass sich das gesamte Intranet in verschiedene Raumtypen clustern lässt. Die Abbildung 3.4.6 enthält eine Übersicht von typischen Räumen, aber auch Produkt- oder Partnerräume sind denkbar.

Die aufgeführten möglichen Raumtypen können wie folgt beschrieben werden:

- **Informationsraum**: Strukturierte, übergreifende, verbindliche Informationen und gut konzipierte Navigationsstrukturen; im modernen Intranet werden sie mit Social Features konzipiert. Daten aus und über die anderen Räume werden hier gleichfalls angezeigt und integriert. Der Informationsraum löst das Intranet 1.0 als Push-Kommunikation ab.
- **Team- oder Organisationsräume**: Moderne Zusammenarbeitsbereiche für die Teams im Unternehmen, Räume mit abgestimmten, auf den Arbeitsprozess des jeweiligen Teams angepassten Inhalten und Funktionalitäten.
- **Prozess- und Anwendungsräume** Für spezielle Prozesse kann es spezielle Anwendungsräume geben, in denen die Unternehmensanwendung entweder direkt auf Basis der neuen Technologie umgesetzt wird oder in denen alle Informationen und Verbesserungsimpulse rund um eine Unternehmensanwendung (oder einen Geschäftsprozess) gebündelt werden. Eine Ausprägung kann auch ein „Produktraum" sein, der alle Informationen und Aktivitäten rund um ein Produkt wiedergibt.
- **Projekträume**: Unterstützung der Bearbeitung von Vorhaben mit zeitlich begrenzter Laufzeit;
- **Profilraum**: Darstellung des Mitarbeiters, angereichert um Informationen dieses Mitarbeiters, z.B. zu den eigenen Skills und Erfahrungen oder auch ein eigener Blog. Über diesen Raum erfolgt zumeist die di-

Abbildung 3.4.6: Mögliche Raumtypen

gitale Vernetzung der Mitarbeiter untereinander.
- **Communities**: Unternehmensübergreifende Arbeitsgruppen oder Themenräume, die meist für alle offen sind
- **Suchraum**: Die Heimat für die Informationssuche.

Wenn Sie die benötigten Raumtypen identifiziert haben, dann erarbeiten Sie für sie konzeptionell folgende Fragestellungen:

? Fragenliste: Raumtypen konzipieren

- **Zielgruppen**: Wird der Raum öffentlich oder nur für einen geschlossenen Nutzerkreis zugänglich sein? Oder gibt es Teile im Raum, die nur ausgewählten Nutzern zur Verfügung stehen?
- **Raumbereitstellung**: Wie werden neue Räume angelegt? Soll dies über einen Self Service von interessierten Mitarbeitern erfolgen oder sind spezielle Beantragungsprozesse zu etablieren?
- **Vorlagen und Templates**: Sind Templates und Vorlagen für die Raumgestaltung vorhanden? Wie werden sie weiterentwickelt und aktualisiert?
- **Lebensdauer**: Welche Lebensdauer hat ein Raum? Besteht er zeitlich unbegrenzt

oder kann er – wie zum Beispiel ein Projekt-traum – nach einer gewissen Laufzeit oder nach gewisser Zeit ohne Zugriff archiviert oder gelöscht werden? Was geschieht mit Informationen und Dokumenten, die als Wissensbasis für das Unternehmen oder einzelne Personen interessant sind? Wie wird der Nutzer darin unterstützt, keine Schattenkopien anzulegen?

- **Navigation**: Welche Navigationsmöglich-keiten sind innerhalb des Raumes anzubie-ten, die die Arbeit im Raum selbst ergän-zen? Welche Balance von Eigenständigkeit des Raumes in Darstellung und Navigation und der Einbettung ins gesamte Intranet muss geschaffen werden?
- **Elemente**: Welche Medien und Elemente sollen im Raum unterstützt werden (Doku-mentenvorlagen, Bildergalerien, Filmarchi-ve, Kontaktlisten, …)?
- **Rechte**: Welche besonderen Rollen und Rechte sind im Raumkontext notwendig? (Siehe hierzu auch 3.6)

Das Intranet in Raumtypen einzuteilen, dient dem besseren Verständnis von unterschiedli-chen Funktionsumfängen der verschiedenen Intranet-Bereiche. Das erleichtert die Erstel-lung von Teilkonzepten je Raumtyp.

Konzeption der Suche

In vielen Intranets steigt mit zunehmender Zahl an Informationen auch die Unzufriedenheit mit den Suchergebnissen. Eine erfolgreiche Enter-prise Search braucht ein Konzept zur Konfigu-ration der Suche. Suche und Datenstrukturen stehen dabei in engem Zusammenhang. Struk-turen in den Informationen werden für eine er-folgreiche klassische Suche über Suchbegriffe benötigt. Umgekehrt können über die Suche Strukturen in den Informationen an die Ober-fläche gebracht werden. In dem Fall spricht man auch von Search Driven Content Publica-tion, also dem Publizieren von Inhalten, die im Suchindex vorhanden sind und in Inhaltsseiten im Intranet analog dem redaktionellen Inhalt zur Anzeige gebracht werden.

Allgemeingültige Richtlinien für die Einführung einer Enterprise Search gibt es nicht. Ein paar Punkte sollten dabei jedoch grundsätzlich be-achtet werden:

DATENQUELLEN

Am Anfang der Planung einer unternehmens-weiten Enterprise Search steht immer die Herausforderung, die unterschiedlichen Da-tenquellen innerhalb der Unternehmensland-schaft zu identifizieren. Generell unterscheidet man hier zwischen zwei Arten von Datenquel-len. Einerseits gibt es die strukturierten Daten, die aus Datenbanken, LOB Anwendungen (LOB = Lines of Business Integration) oder struktu-rierten Fileablagen kommen. Andererseits sind viele Informationen in unstrukturierten Daten wie Wiki-Seiten, Informationsportalen oder the-menbezogenen Fileablagen mit gewachsenen Ablagestrukturen zu finden. Alle diese Quellen können gut mit Enterprise-Suchlösungen indi-ziert werden. Der Zugriff und die genauen Be-reiche, die indiziert werden sollen, müssen aber klar abgesteckt und geplant sein.

METADATEN

Zusammen mit den Fachbereichen sollte defi-niert werden, welche Metadaten in der Suche als Filter zur Verfügung stehen sollen und wel-che Themenbereiche redaktionell vorgegeben werden sollen.

SUCHERGEBNIS-ANZEIGE

Moderne Enterprise-Search-Lösungen bieten komplexe Sucheingabemasken und Ergeb-nisseiten. Themenbereiche und vorkonfigurier-te Suchfelder beziehen sich meist auf kontextu-elle Aspekte wie z.B. „nach Personen suchen", „nach Produkten suchen", oder „nur Daten aus einer speziellen Niederlassung anzeigen". Die

Anforderungen an bereitzustellende Facetten (Einschränkungen nach Kategorien) und föderiertes Suchen (Einbindung externer Datenquellen) sollten gut konzipiert werden. Suchergebnisse können für ausgewählte Themen auch anders dargestellt werden als übrige nhalte, beispielsweise lässt es sich konfigurieren, dass Personen immer mit Bild angezeigt werden. Beliebt sind auch Previewer für Suchergebnisse und die Anzeige von Informationen im Kontext des Suchbegriffes.

SECURITY

Ziel des wichtigen Punktes Security ist es, Anwendern Daten anzubieten, von denen sie möglicherweise gar nicht wussten, dass sie im Unternehmen vorhanden sind. Wenn Berechtigungen auf die Inhaltsquellen, die von der Suche indiziert werden, nicht korrekt gesetzt sind, kann das zu unerwünschten Ergebnissen führen. Es ist vermutlich richtig, dass z.B. der verantwortliche Projektmanager Zugriff auf die Bilanzzahlen seiner Projekte hat, ob er aber auf der Search Driven Site, die ihm die Bilanzen seiner Projekte aggregiert, auch die Unternehmensbilanz sehen soll, ist fraglich. Daher ist es immer ratsam, beim Einführen einer unternehmensweiten Suche die Berechtigungen sauber zu prüfen. Es empfiehlt sich, bevor eine Suchlösung für die Anwender freigegeben wird, mit Testbenutzern aus verschiedenen Bereichen zu evaluieren, ob die Berechtigungen richtig und vollständig greifen. In Umgebungen mit komplexen Strukturen kann das natürlich sehr schnell recht umfangreich werden. In solchen Fällen empfiehlt es sich zum Beispiel, mit Skripten eine automatisierte Validierung der Berechtigungen durchzuführen.

STATISTIKEN

Ein weiterer Aspekt sind die Statistiken der Suche. Einige Funktionen von Enterprise-Suchlösungen basieren auf Statistiken. Darunter fallen zum Beispiel das Relevanz Ranking, die Option

„Meinten Sie..." oder auch Features wie ‚andere Benutzer haben gesucht". Diese Statistiken werden durch die Suchlösung erstellt. Dazu müssen Daten über die Nutzung der Suche und das Benutzerverhalten gesammelt werden. Dieser Aspekt muss klar kommuniziert werden und mit dem Betriebs- bzw. Personalrat abgestimmt sein.

SEARCH DRIVEN FEATURES

Es ist ratsam, am Anfang sparsam mit den Search Driven Features umzugehen. Die Idee hinter Enterprise Search ist es, dem Anwender Informationen, Daten und Wissen leichter zugänglich zu machen. Wenn Mitarbeiter, Partner oder Kunden damit überfrachtet werden, sinkt die Akzeptanz für solche Lösungen sehr schnell.

SUCHBASIERTES DATENMANAGEMENT

Enterprise-Suchlösungen bieten in der Regel Funktionen an, um Suchergebisse redaktionell zu beeinflussen, Inhalte im Ranking hoch oder herunter zu stufen oder bei bestimmten Suchworten ganz explizite Ergebnisse hervorzuheben. Dies ist ein sehr mächtiges Feature im Bereich des unternehmensweiten Datenmanagements, muss aber, damit es funktioniert, gut geplant sein, die Zuständigkeiten müssen klar geregelt sein und die Daten aktuell gepflegt werden.

Die Möglichkeiten einer Enterprise Search im Unternehmen sind sehr umfangreich. Planen Sie zum Start mehr als nur die Installation der Suche, konzipieren Sie die Dinge gut, die Ihre Nutzer an der bisherigen Suche am meisten vermisst haben. Der Erfolg des neuer Intranets wird auch daran gemessen, und zwar in nicht unerheblichem Maße. Mit wachsendem Inhalt und steigender Nutzung werden Sie noch genügend Gelegenheit zum Feintuning der Suche haben, sofern Sie die Ressourcen dafür auch einplanen.

3.5 DESIGN

Intranets haben zwar nicht die Aufgabe der Außenvermarktung eines Unternehmens, dennoch sollten sie professionell und ansprechend gestaltet sein. Ein gutes Design entscheidet maßgeblich über die Nutzerakzeptanz.

Braucht das Intranet ein spezielles Design? Diese Frage kann ganz klar mit „Ja" beantwortet werden, da Intranet-Seiten (Arbeiten, Austauschen) im Vergleich zu Internet-Seiten (Verkaufen, Unterhalten) andere Funktionen haben. Dementsprechend müssen sie auch andere Anforderungen erfüllen. Das heißt: Intranet-Seiten müssen im Gegensatz zu gewöhnlichen Webseiten für den Einsatz im 8-Stunden-Arbeitsalltag eingerichtet sein. Das erfordert oft eine leichte Anpassung des Corporate Designs.

Es ist dringend davon abzuraten, das Screen Design der Unternehmens-Homepage eins zu eins auf das Intranet zu übertragen. Die Nutzer sollen auf den ersten Blick das eine Medium vom anderen unterscheiden können und genau wissen, wann sie sich in einem geschützten internen Bereich bewegen und wann in einem öffentlich zugänglichen.

Die besondere Stellung der Startseite

Eine besondere Aufmerksamkeit im Design und auch bei der Usability kommt der Startseite des Intranets zu. Warum?

Der erste Eindruck, den die Nutzer von der neuen Plattform haben, entsteht beim Öffnen der Startseite. Der erste Klick, das Öffnen des Browsers entscheidet oft über Gefallen oder Nichtgefallen und damit auch über die Akzeptanz.

Die Startseite ist der zentrale Eingang zum virtuellen Unternehmen und zu weiteren Seiten im Intranet. Hier präsentiert sich das Unternehmen, hier verkörpern die Inhalte die Unternehmenskultur, in deren Umfeld die Mitarbeiter eine „virtuelle Heimat" finden oder nicht finden. Die Intranet-Homepage erfordert deshalb meist besondere Redaktionsvorgaben und sollte unbedingt mehrmals wöchentlich neue Inhalte bieten.

Auch für das laufende Intranet-Projekt hat die Startseite eine wesentliche Bedeutung: In vorhergehenden Projektphasen wird viel über das Intranet gesprochen, aber erst die gestaltete Startseite gibt dem Intranet ein unverwechselbares Gesicht, mit dessen Aussehen langsam alle Beteiligten gemeinsam ein erstes tatsächliches Bild vom Vorhaben entwickeln können. Möchte man andere Zielgruppen vom Projekt überzeugen oder über Projektfortschritte berichten, kann die Startseite als ein erster Erfolg bestens präsentiert werden.

Es lohnt sich also, in das Design der Startseite in hohem Maße zu investieren.

INHALTE DER STARTSEITE

Vergleicht man verschiedene Intranet-Portale miteinander, so fällt auf: Jede Homepage sieht anders aus. Bei näherer Betrachtung lassen sich jedoch einige Gemeinsamkeiten bei den Inhalten erkennen. In unseren Projekten empfehlen wir sehr oft folgende Elemente:

Intranet-Startseite des Goethe-Instituts

Durch die stetige Entwicklung des Internets und moderne Sehgewohnheiten wachsen die Ansprüche der Nutzer an das Design. Auch wenn Intranets nicht jeder Mode des Webs folgen müssen, entwickeln sie sich doch parallel zum Internet mit. Das Intranet sollte zumindest der Unternehmenswebsite in Modernität nicht nachstehen, vor allem auf der Startseite.

Im folgenden Beispiel sind der Wandel und die Entwicklung der Startseite des Goethe-Instituts von 1995 bis 2013 zu sehen.

Abbildung 3.5.1: Intranet-Startseite des Goethe-Instituts: 1995, 2005, 2009, 2013

NEWS

Auf der Startseite sehen die Nutzerneuigkeiten aus dem Unternehmen, aus den Abteilungen oder von den Mitarbeitern. Sie werden meist nur angeteasert und bieten mehr Informationen über einen Link auf Unterseiten. Erstreckt sich das Intranet über viele Standorte, sollte überlegt werden, ob die Startseite einen e genen Standortbereich für ihre News enthält.

GESICHTER

Die Nutzer in den Mittelpunkt zu stellen heißt auch, sie auf der Startseite zu präsentieren. Ihre Vorbildfunktion im Intranet können die Führungskräfte über einen Manage-

ment-Blog auf der Startseite wahrnehmen. Wichtige Zahlen aus dem Management können auf der Startseite Platz finden. Über die Vorstellung neuer Mitarbeiter, die Würdigung des „INTRANETters der Woche" oder Jubiläen zeigen Mitarbeiter Gesicht. Umstritten ist der Newsfeed auf der Startseite. Gerade bei Unternehmen, die mit „Social' erst starten, dürfte das Geschriebene auf der Homepage eher ein Hemmnis sein, sich an Unterhaltungen zu beteiligen.

MITARBEITERAKTIVIERUNG

Es gibt zahlreiche Elemente um Mitarbeiter zu aktivieren und in Interaktion zu bringen: Eine

Umfrage, Gewinnspiele, die Zahl der Woche oder das Bild des Tages sind einige Möglichkeiten für eine attraktive Gestaltung.

SCHNELLEINSTIEGE

Ob Mitarbeiterverzeichnis, Speiseplan oder Wiki – auf die am häufigsten genutzten Elemente sollten die Nutzer einen Schnellzugriff über Verlinkungen erhalten. Attraktiv ist ein Link über Icons. Viele Projektteams bieten den Nutzern einen personalisierten Bereich auf der Startseite an, in dem sie sich selbst Links zu wichtigen Unterseiten einstellen können.

NAVIGATION

Eine übersichtliche Navigation führt Nutzer zielgerichtet weiter. Zurzeit geht der Trend zu modernen Megamenüs.

SUCHE

Selbstverständlich sollte es ein Suchfeld auf jeder Intranet-Seite geben.

BILDER ODER VIDEO

Eine Homepage darf und soll emotional ansprechen. Dafür sorgen attraktive Bilder. Verstärkt werden auch Videos auf der Intranet-Startseite eingebunden.

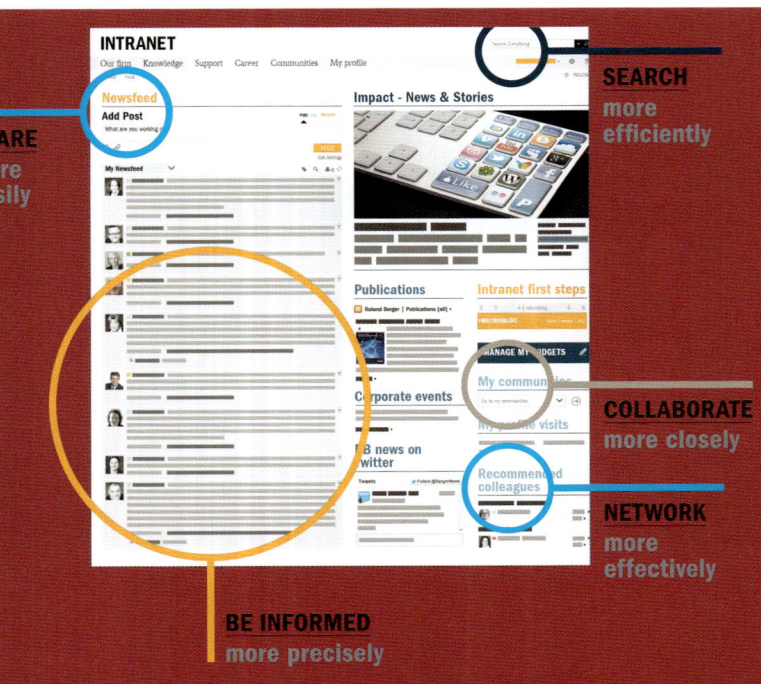

SEARCH more efficiently

COLLABORATE more closely

NETWORK more effectively

BE INFORMED more precisely

SHARE more easily

Abbildung 3.5.2: Startseite des Intranets

Startseite von Roland Berger Strategy Consultants

Bei Organisationen, die überwiegend Social-Starter in der Belegschaft haben, kann das Posten auf einem Newsfeed, wenn es sichtbar auf der Einstiegsseite zum Intranet geschieht, zuweilen eine Hemmschwelle sein.

Nicht so bei den Beratern von Roland Berger. Dort waren der zentrale Austausch und das Vernetzen Hauptziele der Einführung eines Sozialen Intranets. Technisch wurde es auf Basis von SharePoint 2013 und Sitrion implementiert. Schon auf der Startseite kann man die enorme Bedeutung, die Social Collaboration zukommt, erkennen.

Dieser Abschnitt entstand in Zusammenarbeit mit Florian Hoecherl, Manager Analytics & Tools Roland Berger Strategy Consultants Holding GmbH

Die gesamte linke Hälfte der Startseite wird vom Newsfeed dominiert. Auf der rechten Seite sind Unternehmens-News mit moderner Slider-Funktion platziert. Die Mitarbeiter können mit der zusätzlichen Funktion „Manage My Widgets" ihre Startseite individuell in einem vorgegebenem Rahmen anpassen. Die Mitarbeiter navigieren das Intranet mit Hilfe eines Megamenüs, das auf jeder Seite verfügbar ist.

Alle wichtigen Informationen sind so mit einem Klick erreichbar, ohne dabei durch zugrunde liegende Share-Point-Strukturen begrenzt zu sein.

Beim Design stehen verschiedene Farben für unterschiedliche Bereiche des Intranets. So hebt Orange beispielsweise persönliche Inhalte hervor.

Entwicklungsprozess Design

Der typische Ablauf des Intranet-Design prozesses gestaltet sich meist so:

1. **Anforderungen aufnehmen**: Zuerst werden die Anforderungen und Wünsche der Nutzer erfasst. Welche Elemente sind auf der Startseite erforderlich? Ist das Portal eher informations- oder prozessgetrieben? Bei prozessorientierten Seiten greift man oft auf das Standarddesign zurück oder geht zumindest behutsam bei der Anpassung vor. Informationsseiten werden häufig grafisch anspruchsvoller gestaltet.

2. **Wireframes**: Mit Hilfe von Wireframes entstehen sehr früh konzeptionelle Entwürfe von Webseiten. Die Gestaltung spielt noch keine Rolle, es geht um die Anordnung der Elemente, um Benutzerführung und Navigation.

   Es gibt zwei Arten eines Wireframes: Statische Wireframes zeigen eine schematische Darstellung einer einzelnen Seite, bei der die grundlegenden Elemente der Seite festgehalten werden. Dynamische Wireframes bestehen aus mehreren Seiten, die als funktioneller Prototyp interaktiv miteinander verknüpft sind. So ist eine Navigation von einer Seite zur anderen Seiten möglich.

   Auf dieser Grundlage kann man in die Diskussion und zu ersten Korrekturen gehen. Erkenntnisse aus vorangegangenen Usability-Untersuchungen und Mitarbeiterbefragungen spielen an diesem Punkt eine ausschlaggebende Rolle und müssen in die Entwürfe eingebunden werden.

   Aus technischer Sicht muss man überlegen, für welche Browser und für welche mobilen Endgeräte das Intranet eingerichtet werden soll (siehe Abschnitt Responsive Design).

3. **Designentwürfe**: Nun kann das eigentliche Screendesign beginnen: Bilder, Farben Icons usw. Mit diesem Arbeitsschritt erfahren alle Beteiligten noch vor der technischen Umsetzung, wie das Intranet künftig aussehen wird. In einem Klickdummy ist schon ersichtlich, was beim Klicken auf einzelne Navigationselemente oder bei „Mouse over" passiert. Dabei müssen dann auf jeden Fall die Gegebenheiten der ausgewählten Intranet-Software berücksichtigt werden. Der Designer sollte sich also mit der Web- und Intranet-Technologie gut auskennen und außerdem ein geschultes Auge für die Usability mitbringen.

4. **Technische Umsetzung**: Danach können die Entwürfe technisch umgesetzt werden. Hierbei setzen die Entwickler die Designs in HTML, CSS und JavaScript um. Es werden Page Layouts für unterschiedliche Seitentypen erstellt – z.B. Newsseite, Themenseite, Produktseite usw. Es ist sinnvoll sich vorher mit dem Designer auf ein bestimmtes Layout Raster bzw. Gridsystem zu einigen. Das Gridsystem bestimmt die Positionierung, Ausrichtung und Abstände der Elemente. In der Praxis wird meistens das Bootstrap Grid als Grundlage verwendet. Bootstrap bringt von Haus aus schon Unterstützung für Responsive Designs. HTML Frameworks wie Bootstrap erleichtern die Arbeit und senken den Aufwand.

5. **Portal lebendig halten!** Der Umgang mit dem Design ist ein Prozess, der nie statisch ist. Eine Auffrischung zum Firmenjubiläum oder etwas mehr Frühlingsfarben zur Osterzeit sind nicht sehr aufwendig und bringen Leben ins Portal.

Usability und
responsive design:
p://bit.ly/1EUZC97

Responsive Design

Responsive Design ist die dynamische Veränderung des Erscheinungsbildes einer Website in Abhängigkeit von Ausrichtung und Bildschirmgröße des Ausgabegerätes. Responsive Design bietet einen Lösungsansatz für die Designproblematik der Webgestaltung vor dem Hintergrund einer wachsenden Zahl von Endgeräten.

Auch im Bereich des Intranet-Designs gibt es diese Problematik, denn mittlerweile ist der reine Desktop-Arbeitsplatz in vielen Unternehmen Vergangenheit. Das bedeutet: Die Inhalte des Intranets sollten auch mit mobilen Endgeräten wie Smartphones und Tablet-PC`s optimal nutzbar und zugänglich sein, so z.B. die Anpassung von Navigation, Texten, Bildern und Spalten.

Folgende Eigenschaften werden beim Responsive Design vorrangig als Planungskriterien herangezogen:

- Größe des Gerätes und seine Bildschirmauflösung,
- Orientierung (Hoch- oder Querformat),
- Eingabemöglichkeiten (Tastatur, Fingergeste [Touch], Spracheingabe),
- Navigation (sollte groß und feststehend sein, damit sie auch mit Touch bedienbar ist),
- Priorisierung von Inhalten und Funktionalitäten.

❗ Praxistipps: Fünf Tipps zum Responsive Design

1. Stellen Sie den Nutzen des mobilen Intranet-Zugriffs dar und bringen Sie in Erfahrung, wie Ihre Mitarbeiter am besten davon profitieren, z.B. welche Funktionalitäten mobil gebraucht werden.

2. Fragen Sie Ihre Mitarbeiter, welche Funktionen am wichtigsten sind und am häu-

figsten genutzt werden. So können sie ihre Funktionen leichter ordnen.

3. Die Intranet-Startseite sollte auch in der mobilen Version eine hohe Priorität haben und die Kultur und Ziele Ihres Unternehmens darstellen.

4. Wesentliche Informationen und Funktionen müssen schnell erreichbar und auffindbar sein, deshalb sollten sie zentral platziert werden.

5. Die User Experience muss nicht zwingend auf allen Geräten identisch sein. Einheitlichkeit ist zwar wichtig, es sollte jedoch die Benutzerfreundlichkeit im Vordergrund stehen.

VORTEILE VON RESPONSIVE DESIGN

Responsive Design für Intranets anzuwenden bietet viele Vorteile, da Nutzer jederzeit, an jedem Ort mobil auf das Internet zugreifen und standortunabhängig arbeiten können. Mitarbeiter können so auch mit ihren persönlichen Geräten auf das Intranet zugreifen und sie für die Arbeit nutzen. Responsive Design macht das Erstellen, die redaktionelle Pflege und technische Wartung mehrerer Spezialversionen einer Intranet-Seite überflüssig. Das bringt erhebliche Budgeteinsparungen mit sich. Das Intranet behält seine Flexibilität, denn Größe und Art der Endgeräte ändern sich schnell. Responsive Design bietet auf beliebigen Endgeräten immer das beste Nutzererlebnis, das Design ist autonom und reagiert auf den Nutzer und dessen Anforderungen.

WIE FUNKTIONIERT RESPONSIVE DESIGN?

Um auf die Bedürfnisse der mobilen Nutzung einzugehen, ist das Verständnis der grundlegenden Funktionalität ausschlaggebend. Die drei Hauptelemente, die ein Responsive Design möglich machen, sind folgende:

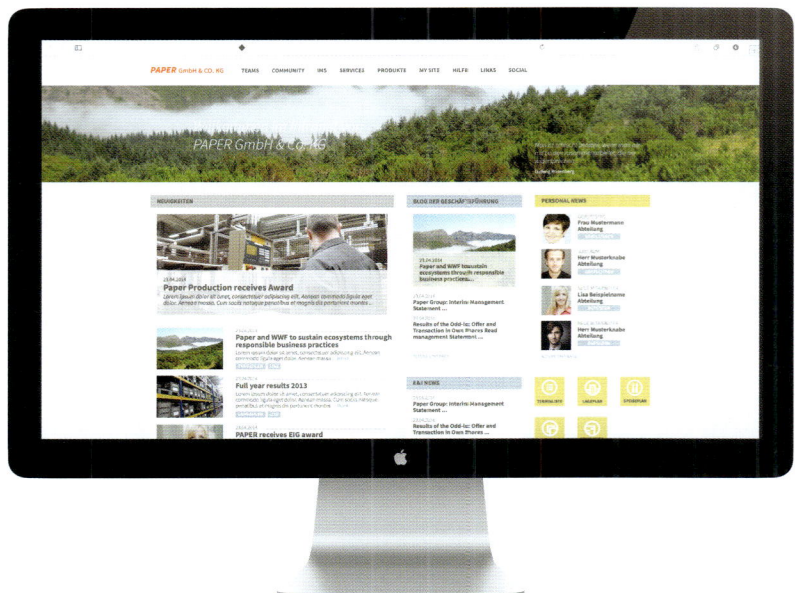
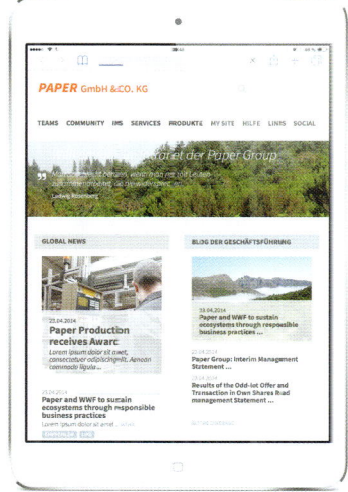

Abbildung 3.5.3: Flexible Grids (Quelle: Oliver Jungmann)

MEDIA QUERIES

Mit dieser CSS-Technik wird die Layoutanpassung für verschiedene Bildschirmgrößen ermöglicht. Spezielle Funktionen der jeweiligen Endgeräte können genutzt werden, um das Layout optimal zu gestalten. Zu diesem Zweck können Elemente beispielsweise neu angeordnet, verborgen oder durch andere ersetzt werden (z.B. eine ganze Navigationsleiste durch ein Icon in der mobilen Version).

FLEXIBLE GRIDS

Im Gegensatz zu normalen Layoutmasken oder -mustern, deren Positionen feststehend sind, platziert sich das flexible Grid bei einem Responsive Design je nach verfügbarem Platz um.

Elemente werden nach bestimmten Vorgaben, je nach Bildschirmgröße oder Größe des Anzeigefensters neu positioniert

RESPONSIVE IMAGES

Ladegeschwindigkeiten von Web- und Intranet-Seiten sind wichtig. Es ist notwendig, dass Inhalte so datenfreundlich wie möglich angeboten werden, da Art und Weise der mobilen Verbindungen qualitativ schwanker.

Mit Responsive Images ist die Möglichkeit gemeint, Abbildungen maßgeschreidert anzubieten indem mehrere Varianten derselben Abbildung auf verschiedenen Endgeräten angezeigt werden.

Mehr zu Design, Usability, Card-Sorting, Wireframes und der modernen Startseite des Goethe-Institus der Babetteria 37:
http://bit.ly/1dhzQ22

3.6 RECHTE, ROLLEN, GRUPPEN

In diesem Abschnitt beschäftigen wir uns mit der Planung, wie die Nutzer des Intranets je nach ihrer Rolle gruppiert und mit Berechtigungen ausgestattet werden können. In Abschnitt 1.6 hatten wir uns einerseits mit den Stakeholdern des Intranets beschäftigt und in Abschnitt 2.3 mit unseren Nutzern und ihren Bedürfnissen. Hierauf bauen wir nun auf. Die folgende Grafik stellt vereinfacht dar, dass in der Hierarchie der unterschiedlichen Intranet-Bereiche Nutzer und Nutzergruppen gewisse Rollen als Menge von Einzelrechten erhalten.

Zunächst hierzu einige Begriffserklärungen:

Rechte
Sie betreffen in einem IT-System Einstellungen, die einem Benutzer gewisse Handlungen auszuüben erlauben (z.B. „Elemente bearbeiten", „Elemente löschen", „Berechtigungen verwalten", „Seiten hinzufügen", ...). Diese granularen Rechte oder Teilrechte liegen fest, denn sie sollen ja nicht jedes Mal einzelnen Personen zugewiesen werden.

(Technische) Rollen
Rechte bündelt man zu Rollen (z.B. „Leser", „Redakteur", „Teilnehmer", „Verwalter", ...). Während die Liste der möglichen Rechte in einem IT-System im Allgemeinen fest definiert ist, sind Rollen oft dynamisch konfigurierbar.

Berechtigungsstufen
Die Berechtigungsstufen (z.B. „Lesen", „Mitwirken", „Bearbeiten", „Entwerfen", „Vollzugriff", ...) sind bei einigen Herstellern als Zwischenebenen zu finden. Das heißt: Auch sie bündeln einige Rechte, sodass eine oder mehrere dieser Berechtigungsstufen einer bestimmten Rolle zugewiesen werden kann.

Nutzer oder Nutzergruppen
Ihnen werden eine oder mehrere Rollen zugewiesen, die je nach Intranet-Bereich auch völlig unterschiedlich sein können.

Fachliche Rollen
Die Bindeglieder zwischen der Technik und unseren vorherigen Analysen und Planungen sind die sogenannten fachlichen Rollen (Beispiel Abbildung 3.6.2) sowie die Anwendungsszenarien.

Im Verlauf unserer Planung muss also geprüft und entschieden werden, welche fachlichen Rollen wir auf Basis der Analysen und Anwendungsszenarien benötigen. Diesen fachlichen Rollen werden dann technische Rollen zugeordnet. Die gewählte Technologie unterstützt Standard-Rollen und Rechte, für die es laut Hersteller typische Einsatzszenarien für Unternehmen gibt.

Abbildung 3.6.1: Zusammenhang Rechte, Rollen, Gruppen und Nutzer

Abbildung 3.6.2: Beispiel – fachliche Rollen im Intranet

Orientieren Sie sich bei der Planung an diesen Hinweisen. Setzen Sie jedoch nicht starr die eingeschliffenen Rollenvorgaben um. Prüfen Sie vielmehr, was sich davon auf das eigene Unternehmen übertragen lässt. Notwendige eigene Rollen und Rechte sind je nach Technologie jederzeit definierbar – wenn auch ihre Umsetzung im System meist mit einem gewissen Mehraufwand verbunden ist. Darüber hinaus wird ein Nutzer in unterschiedlichen Bereichen des Intranets unterschiedliche Rollen und somit unterschiedliche Rechte haben. Ein Bezug zur definierten Informationsarchitektur muss also hergestellt werden.

Ein weiterer Punkt für die Berechtigungsplanung ist der Umstand, dass Nutzeraccounts und -informationen oft zentral in einem von der gewählten Intranet-Technologie unabhängigen System verwaltet werden. Sinnvoll ist die Anbindung des Systems, um ein Single-Sign-On (also eine Anmeldung, die für verschiede Systeme gültig ist) zu ermöglichen. Klären Sie daher, in welchem System Nutzergruppen zu verwalten sind.

Bevor Sie Berechtigungen im Intranet genauer planen können, gilt es einen genaueren Blick auf die Anwendungsszenarien zu werfen. Die unterschiedlichen Personengruppen und fachlichen Rollen der Intranet-Akteure müssen identifiziert werden. Beispiele relevanter Personengruppen im Unternehmen sind:

- Vorstand,
- Executives & Managementgroup,
- Abteilungsleiter,
- Office-Arbeiter,
- Produktionsmitarbeiter ohne PC-Arbeitsplatz,
- Standortmitarbeiter,
- Redakteure,
- HR Mitarbeiter,
- Mitarbeiter Unternehmenskommunikation,
- Mitarbeiter je Organisationseinheit.

Diese Personengruppen oder Personen nehmen im Intranet fachliche Rollen wahr, die wir gemäß Tabelle 3.6.1 für unser Unternehmen nun näher beschreiben.

Fachliche Rolle	Sprechender Name?
Beschreibung	Ausführliche Beschreibung zu den Aufgaben, die diese Rolle im Intranet ausführen soll. Für welche Ergebnisse ist sie verantwortlich?
Anwendungsszenarien	In welchen Anwendungsszenarien wird diese Rolle benötigt?
Intranet-Bereich	In welchem Bereich des Intranetportals wirkt diese Rolle?
Personengruppe	Welche Personengruppen im Unternehmen nehmen diese Rolle typischerweise oder konkret wahr?
Befähigung	Welche fachlichen Fähigkeiten und Kompetenzen werden zur Wahrnehmung der Rolle vorausgesetzt? Welche Voraussetzungen werden benötigt?
Berechtigung und Besetzung fachlich/organisatorisch	Welche organisatorischen, fachlichen Rechte benötigt der Rolleninhaber innerhalb der Organisation? Wie wird die Rolle praktisch besetzt?
Technische Rolle	Welche technische Rolle wird benötigt, um die Aufgaben erfüllen zu können?

Tabelle 3.6.1: Beschreibungsvorschlag fachlicher Rollen

Diese Einteilung bedeutet nicht, dass wir deshalb sehr viele unterschiedliche technische Rollen im System definieren müssen. In dem Beispiel aus der Abbildung 3.6.2 unterscheiden sich die technischen Rollen für den Bereichs- und Abteilungsredakteur nicht – sie werden z.B. einer Rolle „Redakteur" zugeordnet. Die fachliche Unterscheidung wird hier gewählt, um in der Kommunikation zur unterschiedlichen inhaltlichen Verantwortung eines Bereichs- oder eines Abteilungsredakteurs oder bei der Schulung speziell vorgehen zu können. Ein weiteres Beispiel sind Projektraum-Owner und Community Manager – sie werden voraussichtlich eine technische Rolle „Besitzer" im jeweiligen Projektraum oder der Community erhalten. Jedoch wird ein Projektraum-Owner vor dem Hintergrund geschult und begleitet, welche prozessbegleitenden Möglichkeiten in Projektraum bestehen und wie diese bestmöglich eingesetzt und genutzt werden können. Der Community Manager hingehen wird sensibilisiert, wie er die Community aktiv unterstützt und begleitet.

Die Namensgebung für die technischen Rollen werden je nach Unternehmen, die Basistechnologie und Standardsprache variieren. Einige Beispiele für die Beschreibung häufiger technischer Rollen:

Besucher (oder Leser)
Besucher haben den Zugriff „Lesen" für Seiten und Inhalte. Um sie trotz dieser eingeschränkten Zugriffsrechte aktiv einzubinden, können für sie gesondert berechtigte Kommentar- und Bewertungsfunktionen (z. B. soziale Tags, Likes) eingerichtet werden.

Mitglieder (oder Teilnehmer oder Beteiligte)
Mitglieder haben in der Regel den gleichen Zugriff wie die „Besucher". Das heißt: Diese Nutzer brauchen die gleiche Einführung wie Besucher, müssen aber zusätzlich verstehen, wie man Inhalte, Metadaten und Beiträge hinzufügt.

Besitzer (oder Verwalter, Owner oder Manager)
Besitzer haben in der Regel neben den Zu-

griffsrechten „Lesen" und „Beitragen" noch das Recht „Design". Das bedeutet, dass sie Strukturen, Listen und Ablageordner modifizieren sowie Inhalts-und Metadaten hinzufügen können. Als Gestalter brauchen sie eine Einführung und Ausbildung, die auch Intranet-Grundsätze und -Richtlinien umfasst. Darüber hinaus müssen sie grundlegende Informationen zur Architektur und Website Usability besitzen.

Da die praktische Umsetzung je nach Technologie sehr variiert, hier noch einige allgemeine Hinweise zur Vorgehensweise.

! Tipps: Neun Tipps für mehr Übersichtlichkeit und Verständlichkeit der Berechtigungen im Intranet

1. In einigen Systemen werden Nutzergruppen und Rollen gleichgesetzt oder gleichbenannt. Das verwirrt etwas. Merken Sie sich einfach, dass Gruppen der praktischen Verwaltung von Nutzern dienen und Rollen die Theorie abbilden.

2. Nutzergruppen können in unterschiedlichen Portalbereichen auch verschiedene Rollen innehaben. Die Pflege der Mitglieder einer Gruppe, die meist einer höheren Dynamik unterliegt, ist somit unabhängig von der Berechtigungspflege im Intranet, die seltener verändert wird. Einprägendes Beispiel sind Gruppen, die die Organisationsstruktur abbilden: Ein neuer Mitarbeiter wird der Gruppe hinzugefügt und schon hat er seine notwendigen Rechte im Intranet – auch an unterschiedlichen Stellen.

3. Die Vergabe von Rollen an einzelne Nutzer ist für umfangreiche Inhaltsbereiche nicht zu empfehlen, da die spätere Nachvollziehbarkeit nicht gegeben ist. Diese Möglichkeit („Share", „Teilen") sollte daher möglichst nur in thematisch abgeschlossen Bereichen für Adhoc-Zusammenarbeiten wie in Teamräumen oder Communities ermöglich werden.

4. Technische Rollen sollten aufeinander aufbauen, d.h. eine Rolle mit mehr Rechten sollte auch die Rechte der Rolle mit weniger Rechten enthalten.

5. Innerhalb der Portalstruktur sollten sich Berechtigungen hierarchisch vererben und erst da verändert („gebrochen") werden, wo es nötig ist.

6. Klären Sie, wer Rollen vergeben und entziehen darf. Ebenso ist „Löschen" nicht immer die Lösung zur Reduzierung der Informationsflut. Nichts ist unbefriedigender, als die Tatsache, dass abgelegte oder gefundene Informationen – also Elemente des eigenen Wissensspeichers – zu einem späteren Zeitpunkt nicht mehr zugänglich sind oder gelöscht wurden, weil andere Personen der Meinung waren, dass sie nicht mehr relevant sind, weil die fragliche Person inzwischen an einem anderen Projekt arbeitet.

7. Scripte und Vergabe-Workflows sowie spezielle Tools (vom Hersteller der Intranet-Technologie selbst oder von Drittanbietern) unterstützen beim Verwalten.

8. Prüfen Sie, wie sich Gruppenstrukturen ihrer vorhandenen Nutzerverwaltung für die im Intranet benötigten Gruppen nachnutzen lassen und welche ggf. neu angelegt werden müssen.

9. Ein Namensgebungskonzept für Gruppen in den einzelnen Intranet-Bereichen erleichtert die Übersichtlichkeit.

Die in dieser Planungsphase erarbeiteten Berechtigungsstrukturen sind auch später anpassbar. Daher gilt: Bauen Sie sich im Rahmen der Intranet-Organisation eine Struktur auf, die Änderungen auch später nachvollziehbar dokumentiert. Die Umsetzung der Berechtigungen muss in die Tests einbezogen werden, um Überraschungen und die ungewollte Freigabe von schützenswerten Informationen zu vermeiden.

3.7 GOVERNANCE FÜR DAS SOCIAL-INTRANET-PROJEKT

Blogbeitrag zum Thema Governance mit Infografik
tp://bit.ly/1Ewb6Te

nfografik zu Governance in SharePoint
tp://bit.ly/1EVOJnF

atenschutzwiki des Bundes
tp://bit.ly/1uM4eZc

„Web-Governance versucht Personen, Richtlinien, Technologien und Prozesse zu nutzen, um kurz- und langfristige Ziele zu erreichen und Konflikte innerhalb des Unternehmens, die im Zusammenhang mit dem IT-System stehen, auszuräumen." (Ganser & Müller, 2012)

Das Thema Intranet-Governance wird in Unternehmen sehr unterschiedlich gehandhabt. Eins aber wollen alle: Das Intranet soll administrierbar sein und mit wenig Aufwand übersichtlich und aktuell gehalten werden. Gleichzeitig sollten aber die angestrebten Intranet-Business-Ziele, die Offenheit, Flexibilität und Attraktivität nach Möglichkeit nicht eingeschränkt werden.

In den vorangegangenen Phasen haben Sie einen detaillierten Einblick darüber gewonnen, welche Vision und welche Business-Ziele hinter dem Social-Intranet-Projekt stehen, welche Anforderungen auf Seiten der Stakeholder bestehen und wie sich die Ausgangssituation in Ihrem Unternehmen darstellt. Aus diesen Informationen lassen sich nun die Intranet-Richtlinien entwickeln, die mit der Strategie und Governance Ihres Unternehmens in Einklang stehen.

NOTWENDIGKEIT VON GOVERNANCE

Wenn weit umspannende Technologien wie ein Social Intranet eingeführt werden, sind klare Rahmenbedingungen und Regeln erforderlich, um

- Verantwortlichkeiten zu regeln;
- gesetzliche Vorschriften einzuhalten;

- ein gemeinsames Verständnis für angestrebte Zustände und Vorgehensweisen zu entwickeln;
- technische Rahmenbedingungen abzustecken;
- Voraussetzungen für einen langfristig Nutzen zu schaffen;
- eine hervorragende Usability zu gewährleisten;
- Wildwuchs bei den Strukturen in Portalen und Webseiten zu vermeiden;
- einen gewissen Standard zu halten und die Qualität der Inhalte zu sichern;
- die Benutzer zu befähigen, mit dem Portal und den neuen Möglichkeiten und Freiheitsgraden im modernen Intranet verantwortungsbewusst umzugehen;
- blockierende Streitigkeiten zu vermeiden;
- die zielgerichtete Weiterentwicklung zu gewährleisten – selbst wenn Verantwortliche wechseln.

INHALTE DER GOVERNANCE

Die Intranet-Governance sollte somit alle organisatorischen, inhaltlichen und technischen Rahmenbedingungen und Aktivitäten zusammenführen, welche die Steuerung des neuen Intranets beeinflussen. Sie fungiert als eine Art Kompass für Richtlinien, Regelwerke und Steuerungselemente im Intranet. Dafür gibt es zwar Governance-Vorlagen, an denen Sie sich orientieren können. Beachten Sie dabei aber, dass eine Intranet-Governance immer sehr unternehmensspezifisch entwickelt werden sollte, damit der strategische Kontext ausreichend berücksichtigt wird.

Es empfiehlt sich, kein allumfassendes Governance-Werk zu verfassen (das keiner lesen möchte), sondern die einzelnen Themen in leicht handhabbare Pakete zu verpacken und die Umsetzung der eigenen Intranet-Governance direkt in die Intranet-Planung einfließen zu lassen.

GOVERNANCE-PAKETE

1. Kommunikation über

- Strategie, Vision und Ziele des Intranets,
- Erwartungen der Shareholder und Stakeholder bezüglich des Nutzens der Plattform.

2. Etablierung einer Intranet-Organisation, in der

- Sponsoren, Verantwortlichkeiter und Entscheidungskompetenzen definiert sind;
- die Interessen aller Stakeholder im Intranet-Kontext berücksichtigt und abgestimmt werden;
- die Unterstützung der Nutzer effizient geregelt ist und Spezialfälle zeitnah behandelt werden.

3. Richtlinien

- Design-Richtlinien (CI/CD, Farben, Formen, Schriften) zur Förderung von Standards und mit dem Ziel der Wiedererkennung und Vereinheitlichung;
- Redaktions-Richtlinien (Qualitätskriterien für Inhalte und Redaktionsprozesse);
- Guidelines und Netiquette für die Nutzer beim Umgang mit dem neuen Portal;
- Richtlinien für Compliance-, Datenschutz- und Sicherheitsvorgaben;

- Technologie-Richtlinien (technische Anforderungen und Rahmenbedingungen wie Betriebssysteme, Bildschirmauflösungen, mobile Geräte);
- Richtlinien zur Integration von Systemen und Applikationen.

4. Verwaltung und Optimierung des Intranets durch

- Einhaltung der definierten Richtlinien;
- Bereitstellung von Diensten und Lösungen, die das Kerngeschäft fördern und die Arbeit des Einzelnen und der Teams effizient unterstützen;
- Ablösung schwer zu wartender Altsysteme bzw. Abbau redundanter Technologien.

Eine klare Governance hilft Konflikte zu vermeiden oder schneller zu lösen und die Qualität und Attraktivität sowie den Wertschöpfungsbeitrag des Social Intranets innerhalb der gesamten IT-Landschaft langfristig sicherzustellen. Aus diesem Grunde sollte mit der Entwicklung der Governance-Richtlinien bereits in dieser frühen Phase begonnen werden. Sie kann später in der Phase „Baue" weiter ausdifferenziert werden (siehe dazu Abschnitt 4.3).

Gleichwohl sollte die Governance ein lebendiges Regelwerk sein. Sie sollte sich an verändernde Rahmenbedingungen und die konkreten Erfahrungen aus dem Betrieb des Intranets anpassen, jedenfalls soweit das notwendig ist.

Die Grundlagen für eine gute Governance werden durch die Konzeptionsschritte der Planungsphase geschaffen. Usability-Betrachtungen, Informationsarchitektur, Design sowie Berechtigungskonzept sind wesentliche Elemente für die Governance.

Ich gebe zu, das Thema Governance ist nicht gerade sexy. Wenn Sie mich aber trotzdem nach meinen Beobachtungen fragen, sage ich Ihnen Folgendes:
1. Weniger Ärger im Projekt macht den Aufwand wett!
2. Rom wurde nicht an einem Tag erbaut und so muss sich Governance auch nach und nach entwickeln.
3. Während früher das Intranet 1.0 meist zentral verwaltet wurde, wird die Governance eines Social Intranets hier und da eher dezentral verwaltet.
4. Die Welt ist im Wandel und das gefühlt jeden Tag ein bisschen schneller. Deshalb sollte auch das Thema Governance flexibel und wandlungsfähig angegangen werden, damit die Weiterentwicklung nicht irgendwann stockt.
5. Nicht die Kontrolle, sondern das Erreichen gemeinsamer Ziele ist Zweck der Governance. Die Akzeptanz ist umso höher, je weniger einengend sie formuliert ist.

! Praxistipps: Intranet-Verwaltung leicht gemacht

Das Bundesamt für Sicherheit in der Informationstechnik und die Hersteller selbst stellen häufig Governance-Konzepte und Vorlagen auf ihren Portalen bereit. Sie sind aber sehr allgemein und umfänglich gehalten und bedürfen daher einer kritischen Prüfung. So gehen Sie dabei vor:

1. Laden Sie sich ein Template herunter, welches zu Ihrem Projekt passt. Im Falle eines SharePoint-Intranet-Projekts ist das z.B. das SharePoint-Governance-Template von Microsoft.

2. Prüfen Sie kritisch, welche Bereiche dieses fast 100 Seiten umfassenden Dokuments auf Ihr Projekt und Ihre Umgebung zutreffen. Die übrigen streichen Sie.

3. Beziehen Sie nun die einzelnen Fachbereiche ein und definieren Sie für die einzelnen Kapitel Ihre unternehmensspezifischen Vorgaben.

Intranet-Governance wird schnell zu einem bürokratischen Monster, wenn sie nicht auf ein sinnvolles Maß hin entwickelt wird. Es geht um Handhabbarkeit und Effizienz. Keiner liest gerne Hundert-Seiter und kein Mitarbeiter sieht sich gern in der Rolle, Woche für Woche die gleiche Checkliste abzuarbeiten und z.B. zu kontrollieren, ob auf dem Server XY noch genügend freier Festplattenspeicher verfügbar ist.

Automatisieren Sie Ihre Governance, wo immer das möglich ist. Mit Tools wie z.B. SCOM können gerade wiederkehrende Aufgaben und Überwachungsfunktionen gut automatisiert werden. Die Automatisierung lässt sich auch problemlos auf Themen wie die Dokumentation der Umgebung ausdehnen. Für alle gängigen großen Intranet-Systeme gibt es entweder eingebaute Funktionen, um die Systemlandschaft zu dokumentieren oder 3rd-Party-Lösungen, die das für Sie erledigen. Der Umfang reicht dabei vom grundlegenden Aufbau, über das Konfigurieren und Einstellen bis hin zur Dokumentation der Berechtigungsstrukturen und Ressourcenverteilung. Ändert sich also etwas an Ihrem Intranet-System, kommt z.B. ein neuer Server dazu oder wird ein weiterer Standort einbezogen, müssen Sie nicht mehr manuell Ihr Governance-Konzept nachziehen. Das erledigt mit wenigen Klicks Ihre Governance-Software-Lösung.

PROTOTYPING UND TECHNOLOGIEORIENTIERTE KONZEPTE

Dieser Abschnitt entstand in Zusammenarbeit mit Alexander Döhling, SharePoint Architekt T-Systems Multimedia Solutions GmbH

Zur Planungsphase gehört auch die technische Konzeption. Das umfasst alle strukturierten Betrachtungen dazu, was aus Entwicklungs- und Betriebssicht notwendig ist, um die fachlichen Anforderungen und formulierten Anwendungsszenarien auf der gewählten technischen Plattform abzubilden. Welche Besonderheiten oder Herausforderungen bergen Social-Intranet-Plattformen? An dieser Frage orientieren wir uns in diesem Abschnitt, tiefere Details zur technischen Konzeption überlassen wir den im Projekt benannten Architekten, Entwicklern und Technikern.

Was macht ein Social Intranet zu einem besonderen Projekt aus Sicht der IT?

Die IT muss einen sicheren und effektiven Betrieb einer Plattform sicherstellen, jedoch sind die Nutzungsintensität, die Datenvolumina und zukünftige Anforderungen oft noch gar nicht exakt bestimmbar. Folglich muss die Infrastruktur und Systemarchitektur mit einem Blick in die Zukunft geplant werden, sodass die Plattform skalierbar ist: bei höherem Nutzungs- und Datenaufkommen muss sie leicht erweiterbar sein. Dies ist auch ein Grund, warum Unternehmen auf Cloud-Dienste setzen. Ein Social-Intranet-Projekt kann somit zu einem wichtigen Baustein in der IT-Strategie des Unternehmens werden.

Die Anwendungsarchitektur des Social Intranets ausbaubar zu konzipieren, ist eine größere Herausforderung als die Planung einer einzelnen IT-Anwendung. Auch wenn wir mit ersten Anwendungsszenarien auf der Plattform starten, dürfen Entscheidungen über die Entwicklungs- oder Anwendungsframeworks spätere Erweiterungswünsche nicht unmöglich machen oder dann überproportionalen Mehraufwand bedeuten.

Ein besonderer Aspekt kann auch sein, dass durch den Einsatz einer Standardsoftware aus IT-Sicht „nur" noch die Konfiguration und Administration der Plattform konzipiert werden muss. Auch dann gehört ein umfassendes Verständnis aller Rahmenbedingungen und System-Schnittstellen sowie die Bewertung der Auswirkungen auf existierende Richtlinien und Sicherheitsvorgaben dazu. Bei der Verwendung einer Cloud-Lösung stehen IT-Abteilungen häufig das erste Mal vor der Herausforderung, unternehmensinterne IT-Systeme wie z.B. das federführende Nutzerverwaltungssystem an eine externe Anwendung sicher anzubinden und zu integrieren.

Überblick verschaffen

Der Übergang von der Analyse der Anforderungen und fachlichen Planung zur technischen Umsetzung ist für das Projektteam einfacher, wenn es gelingt, das Zielbild und die Gründe für Entscheidungen allen Beteiligten klar zu vermitteln. Bereiten Sie deshalb möglichst gemeinsam mit dem Architekten ein Kickoff für die Entwicklung vor, in dem Sie dann auch auf die Historie zum bisherigen Projektverlauf und zur Anforderungsaufnahme eingehen. Nur unter dieser Voraussetzung wird das Projekt vom „Mitdenken" und Wissen aller Teammitglieder profitieren.

Visualisierungen helfen den Anforderungsmanagern und Architekten dabei, sich in die Denkmuster der wichtigsten Stakeholder hineinzufühlen. Je nach Zielgruppe und bereits vorhandenem Vorwissen zu dem Projekt ist eine unterschiedliche Detaillierung in den Visualisierungen hilfreich und zu empfehlen.

Für den Einstieg in das Projekt und zur Vermittlung des Projekt-Scopes und der Vision hilft ein sogenanntes „Big Picture"-Schaubild (siehe Abbildung 3.8.1). In diesem Bild werden auf abstrakter Ebene die „Building Blocks" (Hauptbestandteile) der zukünftigen Lösung vorgestellt. Auch eine Abgrenzung zu benachbarten Systemen kann sehr hilfreich sein, da hier bereits erste wesentliche Informationen zu Schnittstellen und möglichen Engpässen enthalten sein können.

Ausgehend hiervon wird in vielen Projekten das relativ grobe Big Picture in mehrere Architekturschaubilder verfeinert, deren Anzahl und Tiefe sich an den Bedürfnissen der Projektbeteiligten ausrichten sollten. Grundsätzlich gilt für die Dokumentation: So viel wie nötig und so wenig wie möglich.

Den Vorgang, die Lösungsarchitektur vom Groben zum Feinen zu beschreiben, nennt man das „Top-Down-Prinzip". Daneben gibt es weitere Herangehensweisen (wie z.B. Bottom-Up, Outside-In, Inside-Out), die andere Aspekte der Lösung ggf. besser visualisieren können.

Neben den bereits genannten Schaubildern sind weitere technische Konzepte für die Beschreibung der geplanten Lösung notwendig bzw. zu empfehlen.

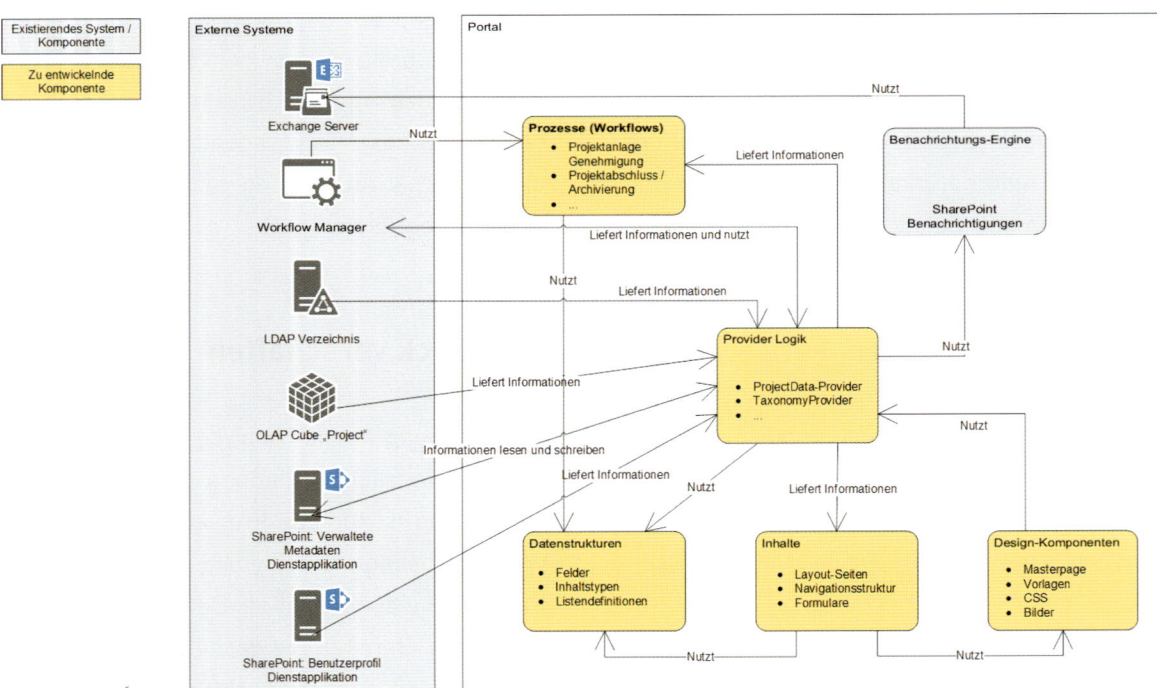

Abbildung 3.8.1: Beispiel eines Big Pictures einer Social-Intranet-Landschaft

Langsam, langsam! Bevor Sie nun gleich ein Konzept erstellen, erarbeiten Sie die notwendige Struktur der Konzepte erst einmal in einem Projekt-Wiki oder einer anderen, in Ihrem Unternehmen eingesetzten Software für Mind-Mapping oder für digitale Notizbücher (z.B. MindManager, Apple Evernote, Microsoft OneNote). Übrigens: Das Konzept selbst kann dann ebenso ganz transparent in einem Wiki geschrieben werden.

Dazu gehören:

1. ein technologieorientiertes Fachkonzept,

2. eine technische Feinkonzeption inklusive

- Informationsarchitektur (die Struktur, Mengen und Typen von Inhalten),
- Laufzeitsicht der Lösung und damit das Zusammenspiel der einzelnen Module und Komponenten,
- Verteilungssicht der Module/Komponenten,
- Integrations- und Schnittstellenkonzepte,
- Rollout- und Update-Strategie,
- Berechtigungskonzept,

3. die Infrastruktur- und Betriebskonzeption,

4. Styleguide für die visuelle Gestaltung des Intranets,

5. Sicherheitskonzepte,

6. eine Testkonzeption.

Auch hier gilt wieder das Prinzip der Verhältnismäßigkeit. Für jedes Konzept sollte der Nutzen und der dafür notwendige Aufwand für die Erstellung und die Pflege berücksichtigt werden.

Technologieorientierte Fach- und Feinkonzeption

Die ausformulierten Grundlagen für die Entwicklung und Umsetzung einer Lösung bilden das technologieorientierte Fachkonzept und die technische Feinkonzeption. Wichtigste Konzeptionsgrundlage sind die Anforderungen aus den Anwendungsszenarien und deren Verfeinerungen im Anforderungskatalog bzw. Produkt-Backlog.

Ein Social Intranet wird heutzutage meist auf Basis eines vorhandenen Frameworks oder eines Social-Software-Produkts aufgebaut. Deshalb sollten Konzepte nicht losgelöst von der ausgewählten Technologie erstellt werden. Standardfunktionen und Lösungskomponenten des Herstellers und von Drittanbietern sind zur Umsetzung der Anforderungen einzuplanen und nur begründet durch Eigenentwicklung zu ersetzen oder zu erweitern. Es muss entschieden werden, welche Komponenten „nur" konfiguriert und welche entwickelt werden müssen. An dieser Stelle kommen aus dieser technischen Bewertung heraus auch Rückfragen und Empfehlungen, Anforderungen ggf. auch zu verändern, um Dinge zu vereinfachen oder kostengünstiger umzusetzen. Seien Sie hier offen, auch auf diese Vorschläge einzugehen.

TECHNOLGIEORIENTIERTES FACHKONZEPT

Im technologieorientierten Fachkonzept wird jedes Anwendungsszenario mit den übergreifenden Anforderungen ausformuliert. Erste Konzeptbausteine wie die fachlichen Betrachtungen zur Informationsarchitektur, dem Design und den Berechtigungen fließen hierbei ein. Wireframes und Klickdummies sind wichtig zur Festigung des gemeinsamen Verständnisses der Anforderung einerseits und der technologischen Machbarkeit andererseits. Klickdummies sind zwar aufwendiger, jedoch auch sehr sinnvoll, da sich dort bereits Klickpfade nachvollziehen und die ersten Usability-Aspekte prüfen lassen.

Die Inhalte der technologieorientierten Fachkonzeption müssen vom Projektteam verstanden und bestätigt (also abgenommen) werden, bevor die Umsetzungsplanung beginnen kann. Wenn Sie dies zu diesem Zeitpunkt noch mit Interpretationsspielraum formulieren, so akzeptieren Sie hinterher auch das, was auf dieser Basis umgesetzt wurde. Dieses Fachkonzept muss kein einzelnes Dokument sein, die detaillierten Beschreibungen je Szenario und Use Case können auch in einem Tool zum Anforderungsmanagement (Requirements Engineering), auf das alle Projektmitglieder Zugriff haben, erfasst werden. Eine Nachverfolgung von Diskussionen, Abstimmungen und Entscheidungen ist hier oftmals sogar viel besser möglich. Aus der nun folgenden technischen Feinkonzeption können sich auch nochmals Änderungsempfehlungen an einzelnen Fachanforderungen ergeben, die erneut zu bewerten sind.

TECHNISCHE FEINKONZEPTION

In der technischen Feinkonzeption (auch DV-Konzeption oder technische Spezifikation) beschreiben die Architekten und Entwickler die technischen Einzelheiten, mit denen die abgenommenen Anwendungsszenarien re-alisiert werden können. Wichtige Entscheidungen zur Umsetzung der Datenstrukturen und -typen, der (nicht-flüchtigen) Speicherung der Daten, den Schnittstellen zu anderen Systemen sowie der Oberfläche werden hier getroffen. Der Architekt plant während dieser Konzeptionsphase auch die Aufteilung der Anforderungen in einzelne und bestenfalls parallel bearbeitbare Arbeitspakete für die Steuerung der Entwickler.

PROTOTYPEN UND PROOF OF CONCEPTS

Eine bewährte Methode zur Konzeption der geeigneten Umsetzungsvarianten und zur Prüfung der technischen Machbarkeit sind sogenannte Proof of Concepts (PoC) und die Entwicklung von Prototypen.

Für ein Social-Intranet-Projekt spielt das Thema Nutzerprofile eine wichtige Rolle, da Profilinformationen von Nutzern oft erstmalig personalisiert in internen Systemen für andere Anwender angezeigt werden. Demzufolge kann es empfehlenswert sein, diese Funktion in einem Proof of Concept zu validieren. Ein mögliches Ergebnis für den PoC könnte sein, dass der Import der Informationen für die Nutzerprofile aus verschiedenen Drittsystemen wie einem LDAP (Lightweight Directory Access Protocol)-Verzeichnis (z.B. Active Directory) und einer HR-Datenbank erfolgreich durchgeführt werden kann. Ein weiteres Ziel könnte lauten, dass Nutzer über die Unternehmenssuche die öffentlichen Informationen der Profile durchsuchen können, aber gleichzeitig sichergestellt ist, dass nicht-öffentliche Informationen nicht gefunden werden. Auf die Konzeption der Suche sind wir bereits unter 3.4 eingegangen. Die Ergebnisse des PoC fließen anschließend in die Feinkonzeption und in die aufgenommen Anwendungsszenarien ein.

Ein Prototyp ist bereits ein fertiges Stück Software, welches dem Anforderer präsentiert wird, um direkt mit ihm in die Diskussion treten zu können. Anhand einer lauffähigen Software lassen sich die umgesetzten Funktionen einfacher besprechen und es lässt sich feststellen, ob die Entwicklung in die richtige Richtung geht. Der Aufwand hierfür zahlt sich durch bessere Qualität und durch frühzeitige Identifizierung von Problemen oder nur sehr aufwendig umsetzbaren Anforderungen aus. Oftmals sind Ergebnisse aus den PoC und den Prototypen später nachnutzbar.

ENTWICKLUNGSVORGEHEN

Die Planung des Entwicklungsvorgehens findet gleichfalls zu diesem Zeitpunkt statt. Die für das Projekt gültigen Entwicklungsrichtlinien und die Nachvollziehbarkeit der entwickelten Komponenten wird geregelt durch den Einsatz von Quellcodeverwaltungstools wie z.B. TFVC (Team Foundation Version Control), Git und Subversion. Im Entwicklungsteam werden gemeinsam mit den sog. Build- und Release-Managern die Strategien bei der Veröffentlichung einer Version der Software sowie der Umgang mit unterschiedlichen Quellcodezweigen für die Weiterentwicklung der Software und ihrer Fehlerbehebung besprochen und festgelegt. Im Allgemeinen werden solche Strategien innerhalb eines Unternehmens (hoffentlich) bereits existieren, so dass diese Überlegungen nicht immer von Neuem durchgeführt werden müssen. Allerdings kann es dennoch zu kundenspezifischen Anpassungen kommen, die dann allerdings einen erheblichen Mehraufwand bedeuten.

Gängige Software-Entwicklungssuiten wie Visual Studio und Eclipse sowie viele der dafür kostenfrei verfügbaren Erweiterungen vereinfachen und beschleunigen die Entwicklung. Natürlich werden auch gerne andere Tools wie spezielle Text-Editoren eingesetzt. Sie können für einzelne Entwickler die besseren Programmierumgebungen sein als eine komplette Software-Entwicklungssuite. Innerhalb eines Teams jedoch sollte auf eine möglichst hohe Homogenität geachtet werden.

Tools wie TFS (Team Foundation Server), Jira und Redmine helfen bei der Steuerung von Anforderungen, Entwicklungsaufgaben, Statusnachverfolgung, Dokumentation und Fehlernachverfolgung als auch bei der Sprintplanung in der agilen Software-Entwicklung.

DEPLOYMENT- UND TESTKONZEPTION

Bewährt haben sich auch Prozesse zur automatischen Bereitstellung (Deployments) auf Test- und Produktiv-Umgebungen. Durch sie kann regelmäßig, bei verringerter Fehlerquote und ohne das Entwicklerteam zu benötigen, ein Deployment auf eine Testumgebung ausgeführt werden, auf der dann entweder manuell oder ggf. auch automatisiert die Software getestet werden kann. Umfang und Art der Qualitätssicherung werden in der Testkonzeption geplant. Beginnt die Testkonzeption schon in dieser Planungsphase, so können ausgearbeitete Testfälle bereits in den Entwicklertests berücksichtigt werden.

Infrastrukturplanung, Entwicklungs-, Test- und Demo-Umgebungen

INFRASTRUKTURKONZEPTION

Mit der Infrastrukturkonzeption wird ermittelt, wie die Intranet-Serverlandschaft aufzubauen ist, um die ersten Anforderungen zu realisieren und gleichzeitig eine sogenannte skalierbare Plattform zu haben, die auch für die strategischen Ziele ausbaubar ist. Die Infrastrukturplanung beinhaltet:

- eine Analyse der Anforderungen an die Technik, basierend auf den fachlichen Anforderungen der erwarteten Datenmengen und des wahrscheinlichen Nutzerverhaltens. Dazu muss das Mengengerüst ermittelt werden, inklusive der Art und Größe der Daten (z.B. Videos, große PDF-Dateien oder nur Wordfiles im Bereich 500kbyte) sowie die voraussehbare Zahl der Zugriffe von unterschiedlichen Unternehmensstandorten.
- Infrastrukturschaubilder und Spezifikation benötigter Hardware: Server (bzgl. Typ, Leistung, Arbeitsspeicher, Speicherplatzbedarf) Router, Firewall, Switch, Storage, Backup- und Monitoringsysteme etc.;
- Ermittlung benötigter Software und Lizenzen;
- Beschreibung des Vorgehens zur Erweiterung der Plattform bei steigender Anforderung;
- Planung der Authentifizierung und Autorisierung;
- Prüfung der Belastbarkeit der vorhandenen Netzinfrastruktur (Netzwerk LAN und WAN Bandbreiten), ggf. Ausbau oder Tuning planen;
- ggf. Konzeption der Realisierung zur Bereitstellung von Zugriffen durch externe Nutzer;
- Beschreibung von Konfigurationen der Systeme inklusive des sicherheitsrelevanten Härtens (Hardening) der Server;
- Konzeption zur Umsetzung von Ausfallsicherheit und Optimierungsmaßnahmen zur Last- und Performancesicherung;
- Ermittlung von organisatorischen Maßnahmen zur Beantragung von Zertifikaten, Freischaltungen und die Anlage von System-Accounts etc.;
- Anbindung weiterer notwendiger Systeme wie z.B. eines E-Mail-Servers zum Versenden von Benachrichtigungen;
- Sicherheitskonzept;
- Definition von Backup- und Recovery-Strategien.

Auch bei der Nutzung von Cloud-basierten Plattformen (siehe auch 2.6) entfällt die Infrastrukturkonzeption nicht – zumeist genügt dann ein geringerer Umfang, da viele Punkte durch den Cloudservice-Provider bereits geregelt und vorgegeben sind.

Bei der Planung der Infrastruktur sind existierende Best Practices und Whitepaper zu beachten. Sie enthalten Hinweise auf mögliche bekannte Stolpersteine und darauf, welche Komponenten am besten harmonieren. Gerade in Bezug auf die Netzinfrastruktur oder speziell anzubindender Systeme gibt es immer wieder schwer zu identifizierende Probleme.

TEST-, ABNAHME-, ENTWICKLUNGS- UND DEMOSYSTEME

Anhand der Parameter für die Zielplattform müssen weitere Umgebungen geplant werden. Dazu gehören Test- und Abnahmeumgebungen und Entwicklungs- und Demosysteme, die in der Konfiguration im Wesentlichen dem Zielsystem entsprechen sollten. Was die Datenkapazität und Performance anbelangt, können sie aber auch einfacher ausgestattet sein. Entwicklungs- und Demo-Umgebungen sind häufig virtuelle oder Cloud-basierte Umgebungen.

Papier ist geduldig, die Treiber des neuen Intranets vermutlich nicht. Hiermit meinen wir nicht die Termine, sondern die Ungeduld, endlich ein besseres Gefühl dafür zu bekommen, wie die einzelnen Anforderungen nun tatsächlich im neuen Intranet umgesetzt werden und funktionieren. Sinnvoller Weise entscheidet man sich für eine existierende Basisplattform, die auf die Bedürfnisse Ihres Unternehmens angepasst werden kann. Eine Demonstrations- und Test-Umgebung ist daher im Allgemeinen mit wenig Aufwand einzurichten. Das Projektteam sollte zeitig eine Basisschulung im Umgang mit dem System erhalten – das erhöht das gemeinsame Verständnis während der

Diskussion um Anforderungen und deren Ausprägungen ungemein. Später können ggf. auch erste Entwicklungen auf dieser Demo-Umgebung eingespielt werden. Mögliche Gebühren für diese Nutzung sind ein sinnvoller Invest mit folgenden Vorteilen:

- Die Plattform wird kennengelernt.
- Sie kann frühzeitig getestet werden; Feedback ist zeitiger vorhanden und kann somit noch berücksichtigt werden.
- Sie können selbst auch anderen Personen aus dem Unternehmen etwas zeigen.
- Auf dieser Umgebung sind Sie vielleicht selbst der Administrator, natürlich auch mit allen Rechten und Pflichten.
- Diese Umgebung kann der Entwicklung von Hilfetexten, Einführungsvideos oder Schulungshandbüchern dienen und ist früher vorhanden, als das künftige Produktionssystem verfügbar ist. Etwaige Testdaten lassen sich leicht wieder entfernen.

Wichtig ist dabei, dass die Erwartungshaltung an die Demo-Umgebung nicht zu hoch sein darf. Haben Sie Vertrauen in das Umsetzungsteam. Meist werden die eigentlichen Anforderungen später viel genauer umgesetzt als im Demo.

Betriebskonzept und Weiterentwicklung der technischen Lösung

Ein Betriebskonzept definiert die Bedingungen, unter denen die zukünftige Plattform in der täglichen Nutzung laufen soll. Es beschreibt alle Prozesse und Rollen, die Schnittstellen und Tätigkeiten, die notwendig sind, um das Intranet nutzen zu können. Es regelt die Beseitigung von Störungen und sorgt für einen reibungslosen Betrieb der Plattform. Das Betriebskonzept wird in dieser Phase begonnen und mit Fortschreiten des Umsetzungsprojektes verfeinert und ausgearbeitet. Das zukünftige Serviceteam sollte früh in die Infrastrukturplanung und die Testdurchführung einbezogen werden. Das erleichtert den Übergang von der Entwicklung zur Betreuung der Anwendung im Betrieb.

Von Anfang an muss sich das Betriebsteam auf die kontinuierliche Weiterentwicklung der Plattform und viele Anfragen einstellen. In der zukünftigen Intranet-Organisation müssen diese Aufgaben (siehe Abschnitt 3.10) verankert werden.

3.9 MIGRATIONSPLANUNG

Die Migration stellt alle Beteiligten vor ganz eigene, oftmals ungeahnte Herausforderungen. Oft wird das Migrationsthema aus der IT heraus getrieben, weil beispielsweise für alte Systeme der Support ausläuft oder im Rahmen der IT-Strategie eine Harmonisierung der IT-Landschaft angestrebt wird. Die Migration von Intranet-Plattformen ist dabei aber nicht mit der Migration von gewöhnlichen IT-Backendsystemen wie Datenbankservern oder Fileservern zu vergleichen. Zusätzlich ergeben sich durch das neu konzipierte Intranet in der Regel ganz andere Datenstrukturierungen und Funktionen, in die die bisherigen Informationen und Funktionalitäten überführt werden müssen, sofern sie noch relevant sind. Somit untergliedert sich ein Migrationsvorhaben in die Aspekte Inhalte, Nutzerdaten und technische Komponenten.

Aspekte einer Intranet-Migration

Um das Migrationsprojekt zu einem Erfolg werden zu lassen, ist es wichtig sich ein paar entscheidende Fakten bewusst zu machen:

! **Praxistipps: Acht wichtige Fakten für eine erfolgreiche Migration**

1. **Klare Ziele:** Es ist ganz entscheidend, dass Sie von Anfang an aufzeigen, welche Ziele Sie mit der Migration verfolgen. Dabei können die Gründe ganz unterschiedlich sein. Wenn beispielsweise migriert wird, weil die aktuelle Version Ihrer Software aus dem Support des Herstellers ausläuft, muss das klar kommuniziert werden. Sonst erwarten die Fachbereiche, dass auch neue

Funktionen oder Anforderungen umgesetzt werden. Wenn es darum geht, Systeme zu konsolidieren, um Ressourcen oder Lizenzen einzusparen, dann machen Sie auch das gegenüber Ihren Mitarbeitern ganz deutlich. Also z.B. „Wir kaufen die neue Version zu einem Preis von Summe X, dafür sparen wir aber diese und jene Lizenz ein, was uns Summe Y als Ersparnis bringt."

2. **Neue Möglichkeiten ausschöpfen:** Manchmal ist ein technischer Grund der Auslöser für die Migration. Es wäre dennoch verschenktes Potenzial, wenn Sie nicht die Möglichkeiten der neuen Softwareversion nutzten. Planen Sie diesen Umstand ein, setzen Sie sich mit den neuen Funktionalitäten auseinander und eruieren Sie ihre Einsatzmöglichkeiten.

3. **Nicht einfach nur migrieren:** Es ist nicht damit getan, die alte Plattform 1:1 in das neue System zu migrieren. Mit der Einführung von Enterprise-2.0-Software ändern sich die Arbeitsweisen im Unternehmen grundlegend und viele alte Dinge werden von den Nutzern nicht mehr benötigt bzw. durch neue Funktionen anders gelöst. Überlegen Sie daher, was wirklich migriert wird.

4. **Falsche Erwartungen:** Oft werden in die neue Softwareversion hohe Erwartungen gesetzt. Mit der neuen Version wird aber nicht automatisch alles besser. Sicher bringen neue Versionen oft auch Verbesserungen und neue Funktionen mit sich. Um einen produktiven Mehrwert zu erzielen, ist aber eine durchdachte Ein-

führungsstrategie erforderlich, wie wir sie in unserem Buch dargestellt haben.

5. **Ungeplantes Deployment/Upgrade:** Für den Anwender gibt es nichts Schlimmeres als morgens an den Arbeitsplatz zu kommen und nicht mehr die gewohnte Umgebung vorzufinden – selbst wenn es nur Änderungen im Design sind. Sorgen Sie dafür, dass die Anwender wissen, dass Systeme migriert werden und welche Änderungen dabei auf sie zukommen.

6. **Tools zur Unterstützung:** Selten lässt sich eine Migration einfach nur durch die Installation einer neuen Version der alten Software abbilden. Gerade wenn Sie die Gelegenheit nutzen möchten, um aufzuräumen, Altlasten loszuwerden oder Bereiche zu konsolidieren, ist oftmals der Einsatz von 3rd-Party-Produkten notwendig.

7. **Testmigration mit realen Daten und Benutzern:** Es ist essenziell, dass Migrationstests anhand von realen Bedingungen durchgeführt werden. Testen Sie mit repräsentativen Inhalten und Benutzern. Das bedeutet nicht, dass die Tests mit Ihren produktiven Daten erfolgen sollen. Wenn Sie aber 500 MB große Dateien in Ihrem System haben, dann erhalten Sie aus Migrationstests mit 150kB keine brauchbaren Ergebnisse. Genauso verhält es sich mit den Benutzern. Wenn auf das aktuelle System Benutzer aus verschiedenen Standorten oder sogar externe Nutzer Zugriff haben, dann muss auch das in Ihren Tests berücksichtigt werden.

8. **Altlasten und Designfehler loswerden:** Unternehmen verändern sich mit der Zeit, Abteilungen werden zusammengelegt, neue kommen dazu oder weitere Standorte entstehen. Nutzen Sie die Gelegenheit einer Migration, das Intranet stets den aktuellen Gegebenheiten anzupassen.

Vorgehensplanung

Sie dürfen das Thema Migration nicht unterschätzen, sich aber auch davor nicht scheuen. Viele der oben genannten Punkte gelten auch bei der Intranet-Einführung und sind hier im Buch bereits beschrieben worden. Wir wollen nun am Ende der Analysephase überprüfen, ob wirklich an alles gedacht wurde.

⚠ Praxistipps: Drei Optionen für das Migrations-Vorgehen:

1. **Nichts migrieren:** Dafür erstellen Sie zwar einen Index mit alten Inhalten. Neue Inhalte werden jedoch nur im neuen System abgelegt.
2. **Alles aufräumen und migrieren:** Dann herrscht zwar Ordnung, aber das Vorgehen ist sehr zeitaufwendig, was das Projekt ggf. unnötig verzögert.
3. **Nur den letzten Inhalt aufräumen und migrieren:** Dadurch können Benutzer schnell die Vorteile der neuen System-Features wie Suche, Tagging, soziale und Feedback-Funktionen auf vorhandene Daten anwenden.

Auch eine inhaltsabhängige Mischung dieser drei Optionen ist möglich.

Eine Übersicht, welche Altanwendungen und Funktionen entfallen und welche in den Anwendungsszenarien und übergreifenden Anforderungen enthalten sind, muss beim Aufstellen des Migrationskonzeptes erfolgen.

Haben Sie sich für das Aufsetzen einer vollständig neuen technischer Intranet-Landschaft entschieden, wird dieser Plattformaufbau wie ein neues Projekt geplant. Schwerpunkte hierbei ist die Migration von Daten sowie der bestehenden Nutzerprofil-Informationen in das neue System.

Wenn Sie den Intranet-Relaunch mit einem Versions-Upgrade des Herstellers auf der bestehenden Intranet-Plattform verbinden, dann können Sie darauf bauen, dass die bereitgestellten Whitepapers des Herstellers zum Upgrade-Vorgehen die richtige Grundlage sind. Doch müssen auch immer wieder Sonderfälle beachtet werden. Erfahrungsgemäß erfolgt das Auslesen der vorhandenen Installation und der Datenstrukturen durch individuell angepasste Skripte.

Proof of Concepts für die weitere Lauffähigkeit von Teilkomponenten sind ebenso notwendig wie eine Einführungsbegleitung für die Nutzer. Welche Änderungen der neuen Version dabei besonders erläutert werden müssen, sollte vorher überdacht werden.

Da gerade Migrationen eine gute Gelegenheit sind, Systeme und Portale an aktuelle Entwicklungen im Unternehmen anzupassen, sollte man sie nicht ungenutzt verstreichen lassen. So könnte endlich mal in der Nutzerverwaltung aufgeräumt werden, mit Hilfe von Tools ließe sich ein Mapping der Benutzerkonten durch-

führen. Der Anwender findet in jedem Fall nach der Migration seine vertrauten Berechtigungen und Zugriffsmöglichkeiten wieder, auch wenn sich im Hintergrund wesentliche Strukturen geändert haben. Das Neustrukturieren von Portalen oder aber das Zusammenlegen vormals getrennter Strukturen geschieht in aller Regel auch durch den Einsatz von Migrationstools. Regelbasiert kann hier vieles automatisiert werden. Beispielsweise könnte man sich vorstellen, dass erst mal kein Dokument, das seit einem Jahr nicht mehr geändert wurde, mitmigriert. Im Ergebnis wären danach nur die aktuellsten Daten im neuen System. Losgelöst davon können die Fachbereiche entscheiden, was von den alten Daten zusätzlich noch benötigt wird. Ähnlich verhält es sich mit der Automatisierung von Qualitätskontrollen. Regelbasiert könnten z.B. nur die Inhalte migriert werden, die einen eindeutigen Status wie z.B. „Freigegeben" oder „Draft" haben. Über alle anderen Inhalte muss der Fachbereich neu entscheiden. Sie sehen schon an diesen wenigen Beispielen, wie mächtig 3rd-Party-Tools und Erweiterungen im Rahmen einer Migration sein können.

PLAN FÜR DIE ORGANISATIONS- UND PERSONALENTWICKLUNG

Soziale Technologien lösen Grenzen auf, Grenzen zwischen Bereichen und Abteilungen und Grenzen vom Unternehmen zu seiner Umwelt. Nie war es leichter, Informationen zugänglich zu machen, und Menschen, die sich sonst nie begegnet wären, miteinander zu vernetzen.

Diese Möglichkeiten werden die Art und Weise, wie Organisationen funktionieren, sehr stark verändern. Hierarchien werden immer stärker vernetzten Organisationsmodellen weichen. Formale Kontrolle wird zunehmend von informellen Informationsflüssen und selbstorganisierten Arbeitsweisen abgelöst.

Die Tragweite dieser Veränderungen ist den Intranet-Verantwortlichen und den Entscheidern häufig nicht bewusst. Es fehlt oft das Vorstellungsvermögen, weil es an Erfahrungswerten aus ähnlichen Projekten mangelt. Kulturelle und organisatorische Stolpersteine werden daher häufig erst in der Umsetzung erkannt

Was Ihnen auf dem Weg in die moderne Arbeitswelt alles passieren kann

Egal wie gut man vorbereitet ist auf die Einführung von Social Business – der Weg zum modernen Arbeiten ist mit Hürden versehen, die sich oft erst in der Umsetzung zeigen. Schließlich geht es hier um Menschen, und jeder Mitarbeiter geht sehr unterschiedlich mit dem neuen Intranet um.

Praxiserfahrungen zeigen, dass Folgendes bei der Einführung passieren kann:

- Führungskräfte zeigen ein deutliches Missfallen, sobald ihre Mitarbeiter in ihrer Arbeitszeit anderen Abteilungen Wissen zur Verfügung stellen, statt an der Erreichung der eigenen Abteilungsziele zu arbeiten.
- Führungskräfte misstrauen Mitarbeitern, die im Home Office arbeiten, weil sie sich nicht mehr persönlich davon überzeugen können, dass die Mitarbeiter wirklich arbeiten.
- Ideen und Anregungen aus anderen Abteilungen werden nicht genutzt
- Führungskräfte und Mitarbeiter trauen sich nicht, Fragen im Intranet einzustellen, weil sie dann als Unwissende dastehen.
- Mitarbeiter lesen nur, aber schreiben nichts ins Intranet aus Sorge, öffentlich kritisiert zu werden.
- Führungskräfte und Mitarbeiter weigern sich, ihr Wissen anderen zur Verfügung zu stellen; sie lassen sich von der Vorstellung leiten, andernfalls bald ersetzbar zu sein.
- Alle Projekträume werden als geschlossene Communities angelegt, weil sich die Teams davor scheuen, transparent zu machen, wie sie arbeiten.
- Führungskräfte sind beleidigt, wenn ihre Mitarbeiter sich bei der Lösung von Problemen Unterstützung im Unternehmen suchen, ohne sie zu fragen.

Wer nicht nur eine Technologie einführen, sondern ein leistungsfähiges Enterprise 2.0 entwickeln möchte, kommt um eine systematische Organisationsentwicklung nicht herum. Hier ist ein ganzheitliches Vorgehen erforderlich, bei dem Personal- und Organisationsentwickler ebenso wie das Management gefragt sind.

Leider sind Personalleiter dem Wandel zum modernen vernetzten Unternehmen häufig nicht gleich zugetan. Sei es, weil sie der alten Schule (und Kultur) angehören, sei es weil sie die Befürchtung umtreibt, bei diesen modernen Themen abgehängt zu werden – sie gehören eher zu den Zögerlichen und nicht zu den Gestaltern, den Zupackenden. Mit Umsicht und durchdachtem Handeln lassen sich solche anfänglichen Ängste aber reduzieren. In jedem Fall müssen genügend Treiber im Management zu finden sein, die das Social-Intranet-Vorhaben unterstützen und dabei über einen langen Atem verfügen.

Organisationsentwicklung – Gestaltungsaufgabe für Management und Betriebsrat

Organisation und Kultur sind immer eng miteinander verzahnt. Ein Enterprise 2.0 funktioniert weder mit traditionellen hierarchischen Strukturen noch inmitten einer althergebrachten statusorientierten Unternehmenskultur. Folgende Gestaltungsaufgaben sollten daher unbedingt von der Personalabteilung und der Unternehmensführung angegangen werden:

1. Mit dem vernetzten Arbeiten werden sich die Strukturen im Unternehmen verändern. Nötig ist eine eindeutige Abgrenzung zwischen Aufbau-, Ablauf-, Projekt- und Netzwerk-Organisation mit klaren Zielen, Rollen, Befugnissen und Ressourcen. Den Mitarbeitern sollte danach klar sein, welche Teile ihrer Arbeitszeit sie für welche Art von Aufgaben investieren können, und auch den Führungskräften sollte dies klar sein. Geschaffen werden muss der Verantwortungsbereich eines Community Managers, auch neue Gremien wie das Social Intranet Governance Board müssen eingerichtet werden, um sicherzustellen, dass das neue Intranet mit hoher Qualität genutzt wird und für eine spürbare Wertschöpfung sorgt. Alte Rollen wie die des Intranet-Redakteurs werden sich stark verändern. Auch neue Fähigkeiten sind in der neuen Arbeitswelt gefragt: Während früher Fachwissen und soziale Kompetenzen karrieretauglich waren, werden jetzt Medienkompetenz, Networking-Kompetenz, informelle Führungskompetenz sowie Change-Kompetenz immer wichtiger. Die Unternehmen sollten entsprechende Karriereoptionen bereitstellen. So müssen etwa für die neu entstehende Rolle des Community Managers Laufbahnwege entwickelt werden, sodass Talente motiviert und schnell ausgebildet werden.

LOAZ-Organismus – Der Bauplan für eine agile Organisation bei hhpberlin

Die hhpberlin Ingenieure für Brandschutz GmbH hat im Zuge ihres Wachstums ihr Organisationsmodell grundlegend reformiert. Klassische Hierarchien wurden aufgelöst und agile Teamstrukturen geschaffen. Der sogenannte „LOAZ Organismus" orientiert sich an den Grundprinzipien der Anpassungsfähigkeit biologischer Strukturen und wurde als Bauplan für agile Organisationen adaptiert:

1. Es wird angenommen, dass nicht jede Person in einem Team über alle Charaktereigenschaften im gleichen Maße verfügen kann, um alle notwendigen Themen abzudecken, die für eine Weiterentwicklung jedes Teams notwendig sind. Es gibt vier Charaktere: L – Leute begeistern, O – Organisieren können, A – Alternativen aufzeigen und Z – Zuhören können. In einer LOAZ-Zelle sind diese Eigenschaften auf verschiedene Talente verteilt.
2. Wenn Zellen im biologischen Sinn größer werden oder sich verändern, dann teilen sie sich. So entstehen auch bei LOAZ neue Zellen.
3. Führungskräfte werden Freie Radikale genannt: Sie docken sich dynamisch an die Zellen an und unterstützen die Themen überall dort, wo sie gebraucht werden.
4. Es gilt: Das Thema führt! Arbeitsweisen werden also nicht hierarchisch, sondern themenbezogen gestaltet. Die Themen werden in Form von Layern organisiert und zur Verfügung gestellt. Es gibt Layer vom Typ Projekte, Lösungskompetenzen, Standorte, Forschungsvorhaben, Saisonale Themen und Operatives Geschäft.
5. Jeder kann sich in den verschiedenen Layern engagieren, je nach Interesse und Stärken. Dadurch kommt es zu einer Vielfalt. Menschen brauchen Anerkennung und Perspektiven, am besten eine individuelle Karriereperspektive. Ob Fach- oder Projektkarriere, Führungskompetenz oder Sozialkompetenzen: Es geht um das Wollen und Können, weniger um das Sollen und Müssen.
6. hhpberlin hat keine flache und schon gar keine klassische Hierarchie. Vielmehr ist es eine extrem komplexe themenorientierte Struktur. Diese benötigt eine IT als Betriebsmittel, um überhaupt die Vielfalt in Potenzial umzuwandeln.
7. In der hhpberlin-Organisation werden die Geschäftsführer Dynamos genannt. Sie treiben den Organismus an.
8. Durch die Kreisform des Modells vergrößert sich der Organismus – die Menschen bleiben dabei aber im Mittelpunkt. Sie sind das wichtigste Gut einer wissensgetriebenen Gesellschaft.

Dieser Abschnitt entstand in Zusammenarbeit mit Stefan Truthän, Geschäftsführender Gesellschafter hhpberlin Ingenieure für Brandschutz GmbH

Mehr zum Bauplan für eine agile Organisation unter QR-Code:
http://bit.ly/197D9I

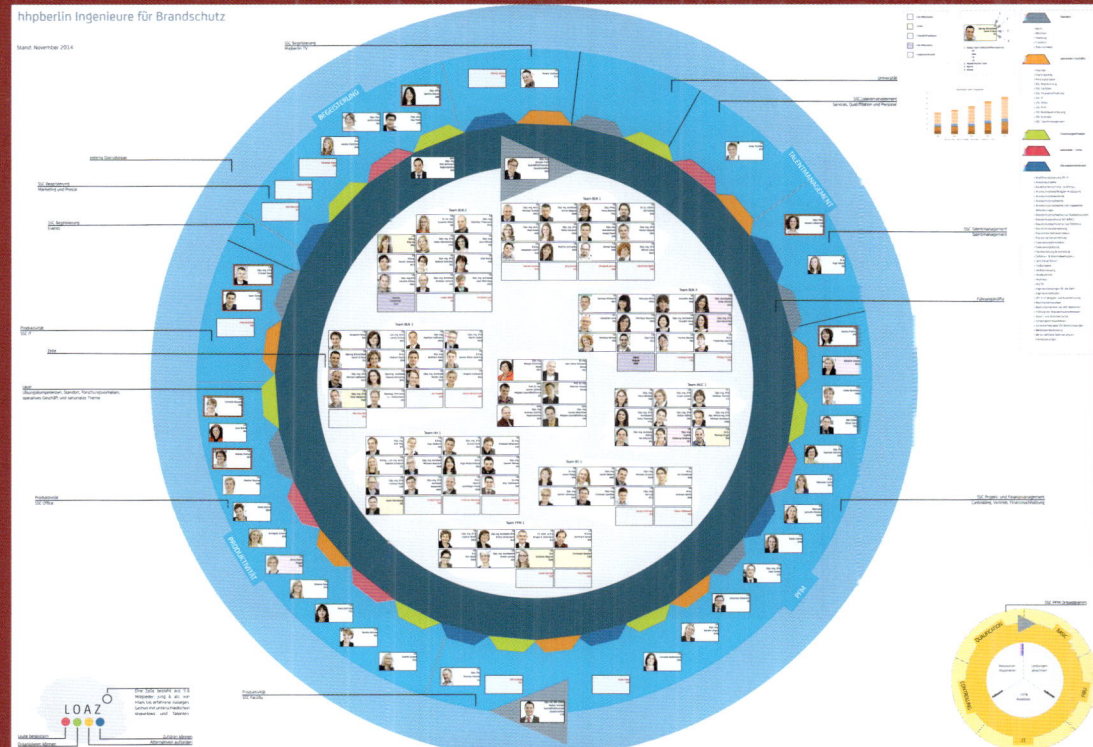

Abbildung 3.10.1: LOAZ-Organismus

2. Während Unternehmen mit voller Kraft moderne Formen der Zusammenarbeit und Kommunikation ansteuern, stammen ihre Unternehmensleitbilder häufig noch aus einer längst vergangenen Zeit. Werte-Leitbilder bedürfen bei der Einführung sozialer Technologien unbedingt einer Überprüfung und bei Bedarf auch einer Anpassung. Vorangehen sollte ein intensiver Diskurs unter den Führungskräften und bei den Mitarbeitern des ganzen Unternehmens darüber, welches Verhalten und welche Einstellungen in Zukunft im Unternehmen belohnt werden sollen. Das Teilen von Wissen und Erfahrungen müsste beispielsweise nicht mehr nur geduldet, sondern als wünschenswertes Verhalten in die Verhaltensgrundsätze, Stellenprofile, Zielvereinbarungen, Beurteilungs- und Entlohnungssysteme integriert werden. Zudem sind Entwicklungsangebote nötig, um die Führungskräfte und Mitarbeiter beim Erwerb der neuen Kompetenzen zu unterstützen (z.B. Leadership 2.0, Medienschulungen, etc.).

Dieser Abschnitt entstand in Zusammenarbeit mit Lydia Zillmann, Referentin Unternehmenskommunikation CONTAS KG

Social-Collaboration-Ziele finden ihren Einzug in Mitarbeitergespräche bei CONTAS

Bei der CONTAS KG wurden nach der Einführung von IBM Connections die Mitarbeitergespräche um Ziele im Zusammenhang mit dem vernetzten Arbeiten ergänzt. Das war für die Mitarbeiter ein ganz klares Signal, dass die Nutzung der Social-Collaboration-Plattform eine hohe strategische Relevanz besitzt, die vom Management explizit gewünscht ist. Gleichzeitig wurden die Erwartungen an sie auch fassbar, da sie über die Mitarbeitergespräche klären konnten, welche Rolle sie künftig in der Community übernehmen, welche (strategischen) Themen sie darin verantworten und woran ihr Beitrag gemessen wird. Aufgaben und Ziele sahen beispielsweise so aus:

- Bereitstellen von Informationen, Wissen und Erfahrungen aus den eigenen Projekten und Kundengesprächen, welche neben dem fachlichen und methodischen Know-how auch solche Erfahrungen enthalten, aus denen andere lernen können, auch wenn sie selbst nicht mit vor Ort waren;
- Proaktives Einbringen von Ideen und Unterstützen der anderen Teams;
- Fördern von Reflexions- und Lernprozessen in den eigenen Kernschwerpunkten mit Hilfe der Social Software (etwa durch Einladungen zu Diskussionsforen), aber auch außerhalb davon;
- „interne Vermarktung" von eigenen Projekten, Ideen oder Informationen, die von allgemeinem Interesse im Unternehmen sind und dem Erreichen der strategischen Ziele dienen. Vor allem die interne Zusammenarbeit soll so unterstützt und etwa durch Einladungen zur gemeinsamen Weiterarbeit an Projekten vorangetrieben werden.

Im Zuge dieser Entwicklungen wurden die Stellenprofile um die damit verbundenen Rollen im Social Intranet erweitert. Die Funktion des Projektmanagers umfasste beispielsweise auch das Community Management für die von ihm verantworteten Projekte. Der Projektmanager trägt in diesem Sinne persönlich dafür Verantwortung, dass die Erfahrungen aus seinem Projekt auch anderen Teams zugutekommen und die relevanten Projektinformationen fortlaufend sichtbar gemacht werden.

3. Werden im Rahmen des Social-Intranet-Projekts auch flexible Arbeitsmodelle eingeführt, welche ein mobiles, zeit- und ortsunabhängiges Arbeiten unterstützen, so ergeben sich noch weiterführende Fragestellungen: Wie gestalten wir unsere Regelungen zum Arbeitsort und zur Arbeitszeit? Wie gewährleisten wir den optimalen Versicherungsschutz für unsere Mitarbeiter? Wie gehen wir mit dem Thema Datensicherheit um, wenn unsere Mitarbeiter von jedem Ort auf unsere Daten zugreifen können? Wie regeln wir die Nutzung privater Endgeräte für die Arbeit oder die private Nutzung beruflicher Endgeräte? Wie fördern wir die Gesundheit der Mitarbeiter in flexiblen Arbeitsmodellen, welche viele Gefahren der Selbstausbeutung mit sich bringen? Wie gestalten wir unser Bürokonzept um – wie viele feste Arbeitsplätze braucht das Unternehmen noch, wie sollten diese Arbeitsplätze gestaltet sein und wie nutzen wir den zusätzlich gewonnenen Raum am besten? Viele dieser Themen sind für die Unternehmen nicht neu, bedürfen aber in diesem Zusammenhang einer neuerlichen Überprüfung auf Aktualität, Vollständigkeit und Praktikabilität.

Flexibles Arbeiten – richtig geregelt und räumlich gestaltet bei Microsoft Deutschland

Bei Microsoft Deutschland entscheidet jeder Mitarbeiter selbst, wo er arbeitet: Im Microsoft Büro, beim Kunden, von zu Haus oder anderswo. In diesem Zusammenhang wird auch ein neues Bürokonzept eingeführt, das kurze Informationswege und einen intensiven Informationsaustausch unterstützt. Nicht mehr jeder Mitarbeiter benötigt einen eigenen Arbeitsplatz. Daher werden feste Arbeitsplätze reduziert zugunsten des Ausbaus von Meeting- und Rückzugsräumen. Bei der Einführung des neuen Bürokonzepts wurden feste Regeln angewandt, um die richtige Anzahl der vorzuhaltenden Arbeitsplätze zu ermitteln. Aktuell wird zwischen vier verschiedenen Arbeitsstilen unterschieden, für die es jeweils verschiedene Anforderungen gibt. Mitarbeiter im Außendienst unterliegen anderen Anforderungen als die Kollegen im Innendienst, Verwaltungstätigkeiten benötigen andere Regularien als Entwicklungsbereiche.

Jedem Mitarbeiter steht es frei, unabhängig von seiner Rolle mindestens einen Tag pro Woche außerhalb des Microsoft Büros zu arbeiten. Für alle Arbeitnehmer gelten Arbeitsschutzvorschriften-Verordnung und Aufgaben für Sicherheit und Gesundheit, unabhängig vom gewählten Arbeitsort. Außerhalb des Büroarbeitsplatzes gilt selbstverständlich auch der Daten- und Informationsschutz im Rahmen der gesetzlichen und betrieblichen Regelungen (z.B. BDSG, GBV zur beschränkten privaten Nutzung von IT Systemen).

Der im Betrieb gewährte Versicherungsschutz gilt mit wenigen Einschränkungen überall: Die vom Mitarbeiter eingesetzten Arbeitsmittel sind versichert, soweit sie von Microsoft zur Verfügung gestellt sind. Die Beweislast für das Auftreten eines versicherungsrelevanten Ereignisses während der Arbeit außerhalb des Büros trägt der Mitarbeiter, wobei die hierfür geltenden versicherungsrechtlichen Bestimmungen wichtig sind. Die Anerkennung eines Unfalls als Arbeitsunfall wird durch die verantwortliche Berufsgenossenschaft immer im Einzelfall geprüft, gleichgültig, wo es passiert ist. Grundsätzlich gilt aber: Ein Arbeitsunfall ist dann gegeben, wenn der Beschäftigte im Rahmen seiner versicherungspflichtigen Tätigkeit einen Unfall erleidet.

Arbeitsregelungen auf Vertrauensgrundlage können dann problematisch werden, wenn Mitarbeitern das eigene Zeit-Management fehlt. Die Gefahr, dass sie zu lange arbeiten, ist hoch. Und wenn Zeit nicht erfasst wird, gibt es keinen Beleg für einen Ausgleich. Ob nun Zeiterfassung oder Vertrauensarbeitszeit: Arbeitsschutzgesetze gelten für alle Arbeitnehmer. „Mehr als zehn Stunden pro Tag darf nicht gearbeitet werden und Zeiten über acht Stunden müssen dokumentiert sein", sagt Frank Brenscheidt, Arbeitszeitexperte in der Bundesanstalt für Arbeitsschutz und Arbeitsmedizin in Dortmund.

Dieser Abschnitt entstand in Zusammenarbeit mit Daniel Hammer, Betriebsratsvorsitzender Niederlassung Berlin Microsoft Deutschland GmbH

4. Auf dem Weg zum sozial vernetzten Unternehmen ergeben sich zahlreiche Fragestellungen, die mitbestimmungspflichtig sind. Der Betriebs- bzw. Personalrat ist möglichst frühzeitig einzubinden, um rechtzeitig vor dem Rollout die erforderlichen Betriebsvereinbarungen abgeschlossen zu haben. Mehr zu diesem Thema können Sie im Abschnitt 1.6 nachlesen.

Die vier genannten Gestaltungsaufgaben übersteigen die Kompetenzen und den Zielrahmen des Intranet-Projektteams. Und doch wird das neue Arbeiten nur so gut funktionieren wie auch diese Rahmenbedingungen durchdacht und angepasst sind. Achten Sie bereits in den ersten beiden Phasen Ihres Intranet-Projekts darauf, genügend Unterstützer im Management zu finden, die sich dieser Themen annehmen. Idealerweise sind das der Personalleiter selbst sowie die Geschäftsführung.

Die Personal- und Organisationsentwicklungs-Aufgaben, die in jedem Fall zum Scope Ihres Projekts dazugehören, finden Sie im nun folgenden Abschnitt.

Heute schon an die Rollen von morgen denken

Das neue Intranet steht noch nicht – trotzdem sollten Sie sich bereits in der Planungsphase Gedanken machen, wer nach dem Launch die neue Kommunikations- und Zusammenarbeitsplattform betreut und langfristig für die Einhaltung der Governance verantwortlich zeichnet. So kann es nicht zu Ressourcenengpässen kommen.

Über welche Aufgaben und Rollen sprechen wir? Letztlich geht es um die technische Pflege, um die inhaltliche Betreuung und die strategische Weiterentwicklung der Plattform.

In der Planungsphase sollten Sie gemeinsam mit der Personalabteilung die in Abbildung 3.10.2 beschriebenen Aufgaben in der Organisation verankern. Gehen Sie dabei folgendermaßen vor:

Technische Betreuung
· Technischer Betrieb und Systempflege
· Anforderungsmanagement
· Portalverbesserung
· Umsetzung Weiterentwicklung

Inhaltliche Betreuung
· Inhaltspflege
· Community Management
· Qualitätssicherung
· Richtlinienkontrolle

AUFGABEN
&
ROLLEN

Strategische Weiterentwicklung
· Business Value Monitoring
· Sicherstellung und Anpassung Governance
· Planung neuer Anwendungen
· Change Management

Abbildung 3.10.2: Aufgaben und Rollen für die zukünftige Entwicklung und Betreuung des Social Intranet

❗ Praxistipps: Vier Schritte zur Personalplanung der langfristigen Intranet-Organisation

1. Veraltete und neue Aufgaben ermitteln
- Aufgaben aus Abbildung 3.10.2 konkret beschreiben;
- Überblick verschaffen, welche Aufgaben nicht mehr gefragt sein werden.

2. Rollen- und Stellenprofile entwickeln
- Für jede Aufgabe entscheiden, ob sie über Funktionen und Stellen oder über Rollen und Gremien realisiert werden soll;
- Profile für die Funktionen/Stellen sowie die Rollen/Gremien entwickeln (Aufgaben, Zielsetzungen, Erwartungen, Befugnisse und Kompetenzanforderungen).

3. Organisationsplan entwerfen
- neue Aufgaben im Organigramm verorten;
- überprüfen, wer in der Organisation von veralteten Rollen und Aufgaben betroffen ist;

- überprüfen, wer in der Organisation für die neuen Anforderungen grundlegend geeignet ist und ob ggf. neues Personal benötigt wird;
- Übergang von bisherigen Aufgaben/Rollen zu zukünftigen Aufgaben/Rollen planen (Personalplanung, Personalentwicklungs-Maßnahmen, Budgets);
- Organisationsplan freigeben lassen.

4. Umsetzung Organisationsplan
- geeignete Personen ansprechen;
- externe Stellenbesetzung planen.

Neue Rollen können entweder durch frühzeitige Stellenausschreibungen besetzt werden oder es wird bei bestehenden Mitarbeitern das entsprechende Know-how aufgebaut. Egal ob intern oder extern – die künftig Verantwortlichen sollten so schnell wie möglich die Chance bekommen, im Projekt mitzuwirken.

Karrierelaufbahn Interner Community Manager bei der Robert Bosch GmbH

Bei der Robert Bosch GmbH entsteht für den Internen Community Manager bereits heute ein eigenes Stellenprofil mit eigener Karrierelaufbahn und eigenem Vergütungsmodell. Das neue Berufsbild gilt dabei als „Triebkraft und Transformator im hochvernetzten Unternehmen". Der Community Manager ist als formaler Leiter einer oder mehrerer unternehmensinterner oder -externer Communities angedacht, zu dessen Aufgabenfeld alle Maßnahmen für die Planung, den Aufbau, Betrieb, das Wachstum und den Erfolg von Communities gehören. Sein vorrangiges Ziel besteht darin, Wertschöpfung durch Co-Kreation und Kollaboration zu schaffen. Den Karrierepfad gestaltet Bosch dabei in drei Stufen: yellow, green und black belt. Während der Junior Community Manager (yellow) noch fast rein operativ unterwegs ist, übernimmt der Senior Community Manager (green) auch Consulting-Aufgaben wie beispielsweise die strategische Use-Case-Beratung oder die Prozessoptimierung. Der Advanced Community Manager schließlich soll wie ein Unternehmer im Unternehmen agieren können, der neue Ideen für Communities, Anwendungen etc. generiert und eigenverantwortlich für das Set-up, die Pflege und Entwicklung von strategisch relevanten und komplexen Communities verantwortlich ist.

Für die Kompetenzentwicklung des Community Managers hat Bosch eigene Qualifizierungskonzepte für die jeweiligen Karrierelevels entwickelt, die von Webinaren über mehrtägige Seminare bis zu 10-wöchigen Online-Kursen reichen.

Quelle: (Göhring & Perschke, 2014)

Die Geburt eines neuen Berufsbildes: der Community Manager

Ein Community Manager ist der soziale Kopf einer Community. Seine Aufgaben sind vergleichbar mit denen eines Klassensprechers in der Schule oder denen eines Gärtners: Die Plattform muss gehegt und gepflegt werden wie ein Garten und manchmal muss dem Wildwuchs Einhalt geboten werden. Der Community Manager ist Teil der Community. Er zeigt Präsenz, agiert authentisch und ist Vorbild für andere. Community Manager sehen am besten dreimal täglich nach dem Rechten.

Der Community Manager ist der erste Ansprechpartner der Gruppe und unterstützt sie in einer moderierenden aktivierenden Rolle. Es gehört nicht zu seinen Aufgaben, alle Fragen in der Community selbst zu beantworten oder die Community mit Inhalten zu bereichern. Vielmehr motiviert er die Mitglieder, sich aktiv in der Community zu engagieren. Er gibt Tipps, damit die Community allen Teilnehmern etwas nützt. Und er sorgt vor allem durch Wertschätzung und Mediation für ein positives Klima, in dem sich alle Mitglieder wohlfühlen.

Community Manager setzen Themen, regen Diskussionen an, posten interessante Inhalte, laden Experten ein, schaffen Kommunikationsanlässe, planen Aktionen wie z.B. Umfragen und geben Nutzer-Tipps. Bei entstehenden Diskussionen moderieren sie. Sie wissen: Communities haben meist eine eigene Intelligenz und durchaus die Fähigkeit, sich in den meisten Fällen selbst zu regulieren. Kommt es dennoch zu einem Streit, ist es die Aufgabe des Community Managers, rechtzeitig und vermittelnd einzugreifen und auf die Einhaltung der Netiquette zu achten.

Neben diesen Aufgaben ist der Community Manager aber auch eine wichtige Anlaufstelle für Community-Mitglieder und die Personen, die für die Qualität und strategische Weiterentwicklung der sozialen Plattform verantwortlich sind. So trägt er die Bedürfnisse der Nutzer nach Weiterentwicklung und Schulungen weiter, kommuniziert aber auch Neuerungen in die Communities hinein.

Yammer-Community-Management bei Microsoft

In der Microsoft Deutschland GmbH hat sich über die Jahre die Yammer-Gruppe „Windows Phone" als die Aktivste herauskristallisiert. Woran kann man den Erfolg festmachen?

1. Kleine, einfache Portionen für kurze Aufmerksamkeitsfenster

Die Community ermöglicht aller Teilnehmern einen leichten Zugang zu Themen, vor allem den Mitgliedern, die sich nicht hauptberuflich mit Smartphones beschäftigen. Im Vordergrund stehen nicht die technischen Details, sondern Konsumententhemen (Kaufempfehlungen, aktuelle Angebote, neue Apps, neue Features). Sehr geschätzt wird vor allem die schnelle, unmittelbare Hilfe.

2. Sehr breites Thema, das viele Leute mit hoher Reichweite und persönlicher Relevanz anspricht

Jeder Microsoft Mitarbeiter besitzt ein Windows Phone, was im Wesentlichen den Erfolg dieser Gruppe ausmacht. Das Thema ist über Abteilungs- und Organisationsgrenzen hinweg von großem Interesse.

3. Proaktive Community Manager

Der Community Manager ist ein aktives und engagiertes Mitglied mit sehr hoher Fachkompetenz. Er besitzt einen Informationsvorsprung, den er in vielen Fällen an die Gruppe weitergibt. Er weist auf Fehler in Beiträgen hin und kann Feedback an die Produktgruppe senden. Er ist dafür autorisiert.

4. Beginnen mit einer Mission und dem Ende im Kopf

Die Gruppe hat sich ein Mission Statement gesetzt mit klaren Zielen, die zum Unternehmensziel passen: Microsoft-Mitarbeiter sollen sich noch besser mit (ihren) Windows Phones auskennen und sie überzeugend in ihrem Umfeld präsentieren können. Außerdem gibt es klare Rollen und Verantwortlichkeiten in der Gruppe.

5. Vernetzung auch in der Kohlenstoffwelt (Vernetzung im wirklichen Leben)

Die Stimmung in der Gruppe wird mitbestimmt durch die Tatsache, dass sich die Mitglieder auch außerhalb von Yammer treffen, sich unterstützen und helfen, also aktiv Beziehungen pflegen. Diese zwischenmenschlichen Aspekte, der soziale Kitt, sind sehr wichtig für den Erfolg. Hin und wieder werden Mitglieder auch auf Yammer gelobt (dafür gibt es eine spezielle Funktion), wenn sie Wesentliches beigetragen haben oder Erfolge verzeichnet werden konnten. Die Yammer-Gruppe hatte eine Vorgängerin, die komplett abgeschafft worden ist: die E-Mail-Verteilerliste!

6. Einfache Benutzeroberfläche und leichter mobiler Einsatz

Die Technologie des sozialen Netzwerks darf die eigentlichen inhaltlich-fachlichen Dialoge nicht übertrumpfen, sondern tritt idealerweise in den Hintergrund. Es funktioniert einfach und baut somit Hindernisse ab. Von überall aus kann man Nachrichten schreiben und lesen. Schnell mal die App öffnen und Neues erfahren, während man auf die Bahn wartet.

7. Win-Win oder „Was ist für mich drin?"

Rewards, Gamification und ein ausdifferenziertes Erfolgssystem können die Motivation kurzfristig ankurbeln. Gutscheine werden in anderen Gruppen für besonders gehaltvolle Beiträge vergeben, sind aber in der Windows Phone Gruppe nicht von Bedeutung. Die Teilnehmer sind grundsätzlich motiviert, Wissen zu teilen und eine Reputation als Experte zu erlangen. Sie freuen sich, neue Devices über Vorteilsangebote zu kaufen, die auf Yammer angekündigt werden. Es ist sinnvoll, das Teilen von Wissen auch an persönliche Zielvereinbarungen zu koppeln, sodass ein Engagement in der Community auch im Mitarbeitergespräch durch den Manager honoriert wird – in welcher Form auch immer.

Dieser Abschnitt entstand in Zusammenarbeit mit Ragnar Heil, Customer Success Manager Office 365 Microsoft Deutschland GmbH

10 Tipps für das Community Management im Enterprise 2.0
http://bit.ly/1nH0h

Bundesverband Community Management e.V.
http://bit.ly/Se8Cn

3.11 GROBPLÄNE FÜR DAS USER-ONBOARDING

Wenn mit der IT abgestimmt worden ist, welche Features zu welchem Zeitpunkt in der neuen Plattform umgesetzt werden und die strategische Personal- und Organisationsentwicklung aufgestellt sind, kann das User-Onboarding nach und nach projektiert werden. Wie führen wir unsere künftigen Nutzer an die Plattform heran?

Wir empfehlen Pläne aufzustellen für

- das Training und den Support,
- die Einführungsdramaturgie und die Kommunikation,
- die Mitarbeiteraktivierung und Incentivierung.

Warum es notwendig ist, bereits in Phase 3 an diesen Plänen zu arbeiten, wird beim Trainings- und Support-Plan am deutlichsten: Für Training und Support richten viele Projektteams bereits Bereiche im Intranet ein.

Egal, ob eine Liste aller Multiplikatoren, ein Trainingsbereich mit Trainingsvideos oder die wichtigsten Fragen und Antworten (FAQ) zur neuen Plattform: Alles muss die IT für die technische Umsetzung in Phase 4 einplanen. Außerdem haben alle Pläne Auswirkungen auf die Budgetierung und die Ressourcen. Die Pläne für das User-Onboarding werden Schritt für Schritt im weiteren Projektverlauf verfeinert.

Trainings- und Support-Plan

Im Trainings- und Support-Plan wird festgehalten, wie die Nutzer des Intranets an die Technik herangeführt werden, neue Arbeitsweisen erlernen und wie sie nach dem Start unterstützt werden.

? **Fragenliste: Wichtige Fragen zur Erarbeitung eines Trainings- und Support-Plans**

1. Wie sind die Mitarbeiter auszubilden, damit sie das Intranet gut nutzen können?

2. Welche neuen Arbeitsweisen und Fähigkeiten müssen in den Teams neu entwickelt werden?

3. Wann sollte das Training angeboten werden?

4. Wo können die Trainings stattfinden?

5. Wer kann die Trainings durchführen?

6. Welche Trainingsarten eignen sich am besten für welche Zielgruppe?

7. Welche Ausbildungsinhalte sind angemessen für die einzelnen Zielgruppen?

8. Welche Lernmodule und Schulungsmaterialien müssen bereitgestellt werden?

9. Wie sieht der Trainings- und Supportbereich im Intranet aus?

10. Wo kann sich der Nutzer vor allem in den ersten vier Wochen nach dem Start Unterstützung holen?

11. Welche Support-Angebote gibt es?

12. Welche Mitarbeiter sind für Unterstützungsangebote zuständig?

13. Wie können die Nutzer selbst in den Trainings- und Support-Prozess einbezogen werden?

14. Wie können die Pilotgruppen zum Trainingserfolg der gesamten Organisation beitragen?

15. Welches Budget benötigen wir dafür?

Weiteres zum Thema Training und Trainingsmaterialien in Abschnitt 4.4.

Einführungsdramaturgie und Kommunikationskonzept

Der Kommunikationsabteilung kommt bei der Bekanntmachung und beim Start des neuen Intranet eine herausragende Rolle zu. Daher sollte sie unbedingt in die Planung einbezogen werden.

Die meistdiskutierte Frage beim Launch: Soll der Rollout als großer Aufschlag, als „Big Bang" erfolgen oder in mehreren Wellen? Unsere Erfahrungen zeigen, dass ein Big Bang große Risiken in sich birgt. Technische Probleme oder nicht durchgehend getroffene User-Erwartungen vermiesen dann leicht die Stimmung in der gesamten Organisation, und Korrekturen müssen aufwendig kommuniziert werden. Schaltet man die neue Plattform hingegen zu kleinteilig frei, beispielsweise nur die Startseite, kann der Nutzer womöglich den Mehrwert des Ganzen gar nicht richtig spüren und wechselt zwischen gewohnten und neuen Arbeitsweisen hin und her. (Weitere Einführungsstrategien beschreiben wir in Abschnitt 6.1)

Wir favorisieren – auch zur Entspannung des Projektteams – eine Freischaltung des neuen Intranets in mehreren sinnvoll aufeinander abgestimmten Etappen. Dies könnte beispielsweise so aussehen:

1. Pilotgruppen: Einzelne neue Teile wie die künftigen Projekträume (Aufgaben, Newsfeed, Dokumentenablage) werden für einzelne Pilotgruppen oder Abteilungen zur ersten Nutzung freigeschaltet – vor dem eigentlichen Launch.

2. Einzelne Abteilungsseiten gehen vorab in den Testbetrieb, z.B. die Personalseite

3. Offizieller Launch: Informationsseiten wie die Startseite, die Betriebsratsseite oder der Überblick über die Gesundheitskurse werden unternehmensweit im ersten Rollout zur Verfügung gestellt. Der Zugriff auf die Projekträume steht nun allen Nutzern frei. Social-Funktionen können genutzt werden. Abteilungsseiten gehen online. Es darf gefeiert werden, weil die wichtigste Etappe geschafft ist.

4. Weitere nützliche Workflows und Prozesse werden ausgerollt.

? **Fragenliste:** Wichtige Fragen für einen Einführungs- und Kommunikationsplan

1. Mit welcher Strategie starten wir – Big Bang oder Welle? (siehe Einführungsstrategien im Abschnitt 6.1)

2. Wann wird was an wen kommuniziert?

3. Gibt es eine spannende Dramaturgie?

4. Welche Kommunikationsmaterialien benötigen wir? (Poster, Give aways, …)

5. Welche möglichen Stolpersteine sollten wir in der Kommunikation beachten?

6. Wie erfolgt der Launch? (Große Party, pures Online-Event, …)

7. Planen wir eine Party? Wenn ja, was benötigen wir dafür? (Catering, Raum, …)

8. Wie binden wir die Mitarbeiter und verschiedenen Standorte in den Launch ein?

9. Welche wichtigen Stakeholder binden wir ein?

10. Welche technische Ausstattung benötigen wir für den Start (z.B. extra bereitgestellte Monitore, um erste Erfolge zu zeigen)?

11. Welche Pilotgruppen können Leuchtturmprojekte sein, deren Erfolge wir beim Start feiern?

12. Welches Budget benötigen wir?

13. Wer ist für Teilbereiche verantwortlich, wer steuert?

Mehr Informationen zum Thema Kommunikation finden Sie in den Abschnitten 4.2 und 6.1.

Pläne für Mitarbeiteraktivierung und Incentives

Wie in Phase 1 beschrieben, wird das Intranet nur genutzt, wenn die Mitarbeiter den Mehrwert im Arbeitsalltag wirklich erfahren haben – nicht vorher. Doch lässt sich der konkrete Nutzen nur erleben, wenn man im Intranet arbeitet. Es gibt also ein Huhn-Ei-Problem. Deshalb ist es aus unserer Sicht ein guter Weg, das Intranet als Produkt zu betrachten, das man den Mitarbeitern „schmackhaft" macht und vor allem im ersten Monat nach dem Start gezielt „bewirbt". Zahlreiche Anreize sollen zum Blick in die vielfältigen Intranet-Bereiche motivieren. Auch hier gilt: Kommunikation kann aus einem schlechten Produkt kein gutes machen!

? **Fragenliste:** Wichtige Fragen für einen Mitarbeiteraktivierungs- und Incentive-Plan

1. Welche Tools und Features sind besonders attraktiv für Mitarbeiter oder die Organisation und sollen beworben werden?

2. Welche Features gelten als schwierig und benötigen unsere besondere Aufmerksamkeit (z.B. Nutzer wollen kein Bild von sich in die Profilseite einstellen)?

3. Wie können Mitarbeiter für die gezielte Nutzung bestimmter Funktionen aktiviert werden?

4. Welche gewünschten Verhaltensweisen sollen mit Anerkennung versehen werden?

5. In welcher Form wird gewünschtes Verhalten belohnt?

6. Wie wird welcher Schritt im Intranet belohnt?

7. Wo kann Incentivierung einen nachhaltigen Erfolg sichern helfen? (Beispiel:Smartpho- nes werden verlost, weil die neue Plattform vor allem über mobile Geräte genutzt wer- den soll.)

8. Welches Budget benötigen wir?

Mehr Informationen zum Thema Mitarbeiterak- tivierung finden Sie im Abschnitt 6.2.

3.12 AUF NEUN PUNKTE GEBRACHT

1 Intranet-Projekte sind lebendige Projekte. Haben Sie Mut, sich vom klassischen Festpreis-projekt zu entfernen und mit agilem oder iterativem Vorgehen flexibler auf die sich verän-dernden Anforderungen einzugehen.

2 Eine strukturierte Aufarbeitung der gesammelten Anforderungen, Wünsche und Anwen-dungsszenarien hilft bei der weiteren Planung des Intranet-Projektes. Priorisieren Sie nach Wichtigkeit für das Unternehmen, Attraktivität für die Mitarbeiter, Organisationsauf-wand und Umsetzungsaufwand der IT.

3 Eine hohe Usability, eine gute Informationsstruktur und viele interaktive Tools sind eine Grundvoraussetzung für rege Aktivitäten des Social Intranets. Überprüfen Sie mit einfa-chen Methoden wie dem Card Sorting, ob sich die Nutzer gut zurecht finden werden.

4 Das Intranet braucht ein ansprechendes Outfit, schließlich möchte jeder von uns auch in einer einladenden Umgebung arbeiten. Ihre individuellen Design-Vorgaben sollten das be-rücksichtigen, ebenso eine mobile Verfügbarkeit. Investieren Sie vor allem in eine attraktive Startseite!

5 Eine vertrauensvolle, enge Zusammenarbeit mit der IT ist Gold wert. Gehen Sie auf die IT-Umsetzer zu, denn die kümmern sich in Phase 3 um die Informationsarchitektur, um Rechte und Rollen, Governance und die Migrationsplanung.

6 Es lohnt sich, heute schon darüber nachzudenken, was sich mit der Einführung des neuen Intranets verändern wird und wie Sie diese Veränderungen gestalten wollen. Erarbeiten Sie aufeinander abgestimmte Pläne für die Einführung, Kommunikation, das Training und den Support sowie die Mitarbeiteraktivierung. Sammeln Sie erste Ideen zum Vorgehen und erweitern Sie diese Überlegungen im Laufe des Projektes.

7 Ein Intranet-Projekt ist mehr als ein IT-Projekt. Ein lebendiges Intranet verändert Ihre Organisation und die Art und Weise, wie bei Ihnen gearbeitet wird. Schenken Sie der Organisations- und Kulturentwicklung ausreichend Aufmerksamkeit und gestalten Sie den Weg zu einem modernen vernetzten Unternehmen mit viel Rückenwind von oben!

8 Bei der Roadmap und der langfristigen Grobplanung sollte man stets das Budget im Auge behalten. So vermeiden Sie, auf halber Strecke „liegen zu bleiben". Kalkulieren Sie neben den IT-Ausgaben auch Kosten für die Kommunikation, das Training, die Einführung sowie die Pflege des Intranets nach dem Launch.

9 Eine starke Motivation des Teams ist ein erheblicher Erfolgsfaktor für das Intranet-Projekt. Unterschätzen Sie nie die menschliche Komponente während der Projektplanung und im Projektverlauf!

1	2	3	4	5	6
TRÄUME	ANALYSIERE	PLANE	BAUE	ERPROBE	NUTZE

BAUE

In der vierten Phase werden Navigations-, In-
formations- und Rechtestruktur angelegt. Die
Infrastruktur wird bereitgestellt, erste Prototypen werden gebaut und die Lösung wird
entwickelt. Während der Lösungsentwicklung
ist ausreichend Zeit für die Anfertigung von
Kommunikations- und Trainingsmaterialien,
die ab Phase 5 benötigt werden.
Wenn die Lösung installiert ist, ist die 4. Phase
beendet.

TECHNISCHE UMSETZUNG
UND RELEASE-STEUERUNG

Die umfangreiche Planung aus der vorange-gangenen Phase gilt es nun abzuarbeiten. Es werden die notwendigen Konfigurationen durchgeführt und Software-Komponenten ent-wickelt. Der Umfang dieser Arbeitspakete dürf-te in den verschiedenen Projekten, die denkbar sind, sehr stark variieren. Jedoch sollte allge-mein beachtet werden, dass die Größe solcher Arbeitspakete nicht zu voluminös angesetzt wird, da dann kein effektives Controlling mehr möglich ist. Der Grund dafür ist, dass der Fer-tigstellungsgrad eines so großen Arbeitspakets mit einer Dauer über etliche Tage sehr viel schwerer abzuschätzen ist als bei einer kürze-ren Dauer von, sagen wir, nur einem Tag.

Die vorgestellten, nicht technikbezogenen Vor-gehensweisen und Methoden im Buch eignen sich sowohl für den Einsatz von fertigen Lösun-gen und Frameworks, als auch für individuali-sierte, komplexe Intranet- oder Zusammen-arbeitslandschaften. Somit haben wir diesen Abschnitt kurz gehalten und gehen nur auf allgemeine Aspekte und Erfahrungswerte ein, mit dem Ziel, von den Nichttechnikern besser verstanden zu werden.

Bei der Vorstellung technologieorientierter Konzepte wurde bereits definiert, wie die Ent-wicklung abläuft und welche Guidelines gelten (siehe Abschnitt 3.7). Danach werden Arbeiten auf verschiedene Personen verteilt, und zwar so, dass unabhängig voneinander entwickelt wer-den kann und die entwickelten Lösungskompo-nenten dann auch korrekt zusammenspielen. Die benötigten unterschiedlichen Kenntnisse

und Fähigkeiten sind in der Zusammenset-zung des Entwicklungsteams abzubilden. Pro-jektmanagement und enge Abstimmungen im Entwicklungsteam etwa durch tägliche „Stand-up"-Meetings sind ganz wichtige Erfolgsfakto-ren. Nur so kann die Planung in eine gewisse Balance gebracht werden, denn zu klären sind:

- die erledigten Aufgaben, über die systema-tisch berichtet werden muss;
- die Fragen und Probleme sowie Abhängig-keiten zwischen einzelner Aufgaben;
- die bevorstehenden Aufgaben;
- die Testszenarien für die nächsten Aufga-ben;
- die zeitliche Verfügbarkeit der Personen, sobald sie benötigt werden;
- die Risikobewertung: Risiken diskutieren, aktualisieren und ggf. neue diskutieren und aufnehmen;
- über Themen informieren, die andere Sta-keholder bearbeiten und diskutieren.

In Abschnitt 3.1 sind wir auf den agilen bzw. iterativen Software-Entwicklungsprozess und die Sprintplanungen eingegangen. Diese Vor-gehensweise wird nun angewendet. Der agile Ansatz oder ein iteratives Vorgehen haben sich bewährt: Einzelne Funktionalitäten sind je Ent-wicklungszyklus fertigzustellen und zu testen. Ändern sich innerhalb eines Sprints die Anfor-derungen oder werden Fehler gefunden, wer-den die Anpassungen und die Fehlerbehebung nicht sofort im aktuellen Zyklus umgesetzt, sondern erst im darauf folgenden berücksich-tigt. Damit stellen wir sicher, dass am Ende

Dieser Abschnitt entstand in Zusam-menarbeit mit Alexander Döhling, SharePoint Architek[...]-Systems Multime[...] Solutions GmbH

eines jeden Zyklus eine potenziell ausrollbare Software, ein sog. Sprint-Release, bereitgestellt werden kann, welcher im folgenden Zyklus von den Testern auf Fehler geprüft werden kann.

Wichtig ist, dass klar geregelt ist, wie erkannte Fehler (Bugs) zu erfassen und zu handhaben sind, insbesondere wenn der Anforderer auch gleichzeitig Tester ist (z.B. die Fachabteilung des Auftraggebers). In der Bewertung eines vermeintlichen Fehlers ist zwischen „Fehler in der Umsetzung" oder „neue Anforderung" zu unterscheiden. Dies ist eine häufig unterschätzte und bei komplexen Vorhaben eine zeitlich aufwendige Rolle, die z.B. durch den Anforderungsmanager oder den Architekten wahrzunehmen ist. Sie haben den besten Überblick über bisherige Anforderungen an das System. Wenn die Bewertung „neue Anforderung" erfolgt, ist zumeist mit einer technischen Änderung und mit Änderungen an den Konzepten und der Dokumentation zu rechnen, was ziemlich arbeitsintensiv ist. Auch vermeintlich kleine Änderungen wie das Hinzufügen neuer Felder zu einer Datenstruktur können ab einem bestimmten Fertigstellungsgrad zu einem hohen Mehraufwand führen. Gleichzeitig sorgen immer wieder neue Anforderungen oder ihre Änderung für einen Stillstand im Projektfortschritt, da der Architekt mit der Bewertung der Änderung und mit der Konzeption für ihre Umsetzung beschäftigt ist, sodass er die Rolle als Controller im Entwicklungsteam nicht mehr wahrnehmen kann.

Releases werden im besten Fall automatisch, d.h. vollständig über Skripte, auf eine Referenz- oder Testumgebung eingespielt (deployed). So wird sichergestellt, dass beim Einspielen keine Fehler gemacht werden, die dann fälschlicher Weise als Umsetzungsfehler dem Release zugerechnet werden. Vorausgesetzt werden muss jedoch, dass die Skripte korrekt funktionieren und über die Projektlaufzeit regelmäßig auf den aktuellen Stand gebracht werden. Darum testen Sie auch den Release-Prozess, indem Sie regelmäßig und oft ein Deployment auf einer Ihrer Testumgebungen durchführen. Dadurch finden Sie Fehler im Deployment-Prozess schon Tage oder Wochen, bevor der Live-Gang einsetzt.

Ein Release muss nicht zwingend neu entwickelte Features enthalten, es können auch Anpassungen am Backend oder am Quellcode zur Fehlerbehebung oder zur Restrukturierung (Refactoring) umgesetzt worden sein. Daneben ist es möglich, dass auch redaktionelle und administrative Tätigkeiten durchgeführt werden. In der Praxis werden durch ein Release meist mehrere und unterschiedliche Arten von Änderungen eingespielt. Zu einem Release gehört neben der Software auch immer die Änderungshistorie (Release Notes) zum vorherigen Release. Und falls manuelle Schritte zur Installation notwendig sind, gehört dazu auch eine Dokumentation dieser Schritte.

Lassen Sie sich jetzt nicht von Ihrem Plan abbringen und schützen Sie Ihr Social-Intranet-Projekt vor den vielen gutgemeinten Änderungen der Anforderungen während der Umsetzungsphase. Die sind nämlich oft der beste Weg, Ihr Projekt scheitern zu lassen. Konzentrieren Sie sich auf das Wesentliche und beschwichtigen Sie die Drängler. In der Ruhe liegt die Kraft!

Nachdem das Release auf der Test- oder Referenzumgebung eingespielt wurde, führen die Tester oder die fachlichen Anforderer die Testszenarien aus der Testkonzeption entweder manuell oder teilweise automatisiert durch. Erst wenn der Test erfolgt und die betreffende Version abgenommen ist, stellt man sie auf der Produktionsumgebung bereit.

Migrationen und Konsolidierung von mittleren und großen Umgebungen sind von Ihrer Komplexität und vom Aufwand her, je nach der Anzahl und Art der Anpassungen, gleichzusetzen mit Entwicklungsprojekten. Nutzen Sie in Ihrer alten Umgebung ausschließlich Standardfunktionen des von Ihnen gewählten Produktes. Helfen können bei der Migration oft Tools von Drittanbietern, um die Anpassungen und Umbauten im Unterbau von Systemen und Portalen in die neue Umgebung zu überführen. Dabei bleiben die Datenstrukturen, der Aufbau, die Architektur, die Berechtigungen, die Navigation und weitere Basiskomponenten in der Regel unverändert. Wurden jedoch tiefergehende Anpassungen oder selbstentwickelte oder eingekaufte Lösungen in Ihrer Umgebung bereitgestellt, steigt die Komplexität stark an. Oft müssen dann Tools für die Migration neu entwickelt oder fehlende Funktionalitäten nachprogrammiert werden.

❗Praxistipps: Wichtige Botschaften von Architekten und Entwicklern an die Intranet-Planer

1. Geben Sie dem Projekt-Setup ausreichend Zeit, bevor Sie konkrete Ergebnisse erwarten. Das Einspielen des Entwicklungsteams, die Basiskomponenten und die Etablierung von Deployment-Szenarien sind wie das Fundament eines Hauses – es muss solide sein für all die Dinge, die später noch geplant sind.

2. Schützen Sie Ihr Projekt vor zu vielen Änderungswünschen und lassen Sie sich die Änderungen von einem Grem um bestätigen.

3. Seien Sie vorsichtig mit zu frühen Terminzusagen und mit verbindlichen Aussagen zur Fertigstellung.

4. Planen Sie für die Zukunft und nutzen Sie Standardfunktionalitäten, wo immer es geht. Jede Anpassung kostet Geld für die Konzeption, die Entwicklung und den Test. Gleichzeitig erschweren tiefgreifende Anpassungen ein zukünftiges Upgrade und machen es wiederum teurer.

5. Bei Änderungswünschen (Change Requests, CRs) machen Sie sich immer die Motive, ihre tatsächliche Notwendigkeit und Dringlichkeit bewusst. Erwarten Sie nicht, dass Änderungen sofort im geplanten Entwicklungszyklus eingearbeitet werden. Das stört. Dringende CRs können ggf. in die Planung für den nachfolgenden Zyklus aufgenommen werden.

6. Verbreiten Sie keine Hektik im Team. Die Erfahrung lehrt: Je verständnisvoller der Umgang, desto zeitiger werden Sie auch über eventuelle Probleme informiert. Andernfalls versucht das Team bis zur letzten Minute das Problem zu lösen und erst kurz vor der Einspielung gesteht es Verzögerungen ein.

4.2 KOMMUNIKATION
VOR DEM START

Wir erörtern die Kommunikation des Intra-net-Projekts hier in Phase 4. Je nach Projekt-situation und Rahmenbedingungen sollte damit jedoch schon in früheren Projekt-Phasen be-gonnen werden. Wir starten bei ausgewählten Zielgruppen meist schon in Phase 2. Auch noch einige Wochen nach dem Launch (siehe 6.1) sollte man erklären und erläutern.

Im Wesentlichen folgt die Kommunikation zum Intranet-Projekt gängigen Regeln und Maß-nahmen der Internen Kommunikation. Gibt es dennoch Besonderheiten, die zu beachten sind? Die Antwortet lautet: Ja, besonders wenn man bedenkt, dass die Nutzer in kurzer Zeit für völ-lig neue Arbeitsweisen begeistert werden müs-sen und so Kommunikation immer auch Chan-ge-Kommunikation ist.

Während das Intranet 1.0 noch stark vermarktet werden musste, können Sie bei der Einführung des Social Intranets darauf bauen, dass Ar-beitsprozesse darin so verankert werden, dass Ihre Mitarbeiter sich zwangsläufig früher oder später mit dem neuen System auseinanderset-zen müssen, wenn sie auf dem Laufenden blei-ben wollen. In der Regel entscheidet das Gefühl des persönlichen Nutzens und des Sinns dar-über, wie schnell und intensiv die Mitarbeiter die neue Plattform nutzen und ihr Wissen tei-len. Spätestens dann wird schnell klar: Ein gu-tes Kommunikationskonzept ist Gold wert und spart Ihrem Unternehmen Zeit und Geld.

Das Social-Intranet-Projekt als Marke mit Zugkraft

Mit der Kommunikation Ihres Intranet-Projekts beginnen Sie am besten in Phase 2, wenn Sie Ihr Vorhaben den Führungskräften, dem Be-triebsrat oder Anwendern präsentieren. Schon früh sind Sie vor die Wahl gestellt: Wollen Sie ein „normales" unauffälliges Projekt oder wol-len Sie ein interessantes Projekt, das Aufmerk-samkeit und Neugier weckt.

Wir alle kennen die Kraft von Marken. Sie ver-führen uns, Produkte zu kaufen, weil wir von der Qualität oder dem Wertversprechen überzeugt sind. Auch das Social-Intranet-Projekt kann eine Marke mit Zugkraft werden, allerdings gibt es dabei einiges zu beachten:

1. Entwickeln Sie mit allen bereits erarbeiteten Erkenntnissen aus den Phasen „Träume" und „Analysiere" ein gemeinsames Ver-ständnis zu folgenden Fragen: Wozu gibt es das Projekt? Was ist die langfristige Vision? Welchen Nutzen soll das Social Intranet stif-ten? Was hat der Mitarbeiter davon, was das Unternehmen? Welchen Bedürfnissen wird damit begegnet? Fassen Sie Ihre Erkennt-nisse in klaren, griffigen Aussagen zusam-men. Die sprechen die Ebene des Verstan-des an und liefern Ihnen in allen wichtigen Situationen geeignete Argumente.

2. Entwickeln Sie daraus eine passende Pro-jekt-Story für die verschiedenen Zielgrup-pen. Jeder Mensch liebt Geschichten. Vor allem solche, die einen bei den eigenen Be-dürfnissen und Sehnsüchten packen. Das kann die Sehnsucht nach Vertrautheit, Nähe und Verbundenheit sein, ebenso wie die

Sehnsucht nach Austausch und Anschluss. Geschichten sprechen nicht die Verstandesebene, sondern die emotionale Ebene an. Deshalb haben sie eine viel stärkere Wirkung als jede Power-Point-Präsentation. Wer zeitgemäßes Marketing machen will (egal wofür), kommt um Storytelling nicht herum.

3. Entwickeln Sie eine spannende Kommunikations-Dramaturgie. Sie müssen nicht alles auf einmal preisgeben. Definieren Sie einen Regieplan, welche Inhalte und Werkzeuge zu welchem Zeitpunkt und in welchem Rahmen bekannt gemacht werden. Damit helfen Sie den Nutzern, eine positiv besetzte „innere Bilder- und Gedankenwelt" zu erschaffen, die den Wunsch nach und die Neugier auf die neuen Arbeitsformen erhöht – das berühmte „Kopfkino". Bauen Sie einen Spannungsbogen auf, indem Sie zu Beginn eine eher vage emotional ansprechende Story kommunizieren und im späteren Verlauf anhand der Erfolgsgeschichten aus den Pilotprojekten in der Phase 5 immer klarer aufzeigen, was das neue Arbeiten alles bewirken kann. Nutzen Sie in Pre-Launch-Szenarien eine geheimnisvolle, vielleicht sogar magische und mystische Sprache. Bleiben Sie aber auf dem Boden der Tatsachen und rufen Sie keine Revolution aus, damit bis zum Launch-Tag die Energie und Neugier der Mitarbeiter erhalten bleibt.

Ist Ihr Projekt spannend inszeniert mit ansprechenden Botschaften, dann sind Interesse und spätere Nutzerbereitschaft (fast) vorprogrammiert. Aus folgenden Kommunikationselementen sollten Sie ein stimmiges Gesamtkonzept gestalten:

- ein zugkräftiger Name und Claim für das Intranet/das Projekt,
- eine ansprechende Wort- bzw. Wort-Bild-Marke,
- stimmige Botschaften sowie
- eine überzeugende und spannend erzählte Projektstory.

Doch wie entwickelt man Kommunikationselemente, die wirklich ankommen?

!Praxistipps: Acht Tipps zum methodischen Vorgehen bei der Entwicklung vor Kommunikationselementen

1. Entwickeln Sie die Kommunikationselemente nicht allein im Projektteam, sondern lassen Sie kreative Kollegen mit möglichst vielfältigen Erfahrungshintergründen mitwirken.

2. Verwenden Sie projektive Methoden wie Bilder und assoziative Verfahren, um den Kopf von Sachargumenten frei zu machen und die eigentlichen Bedürfnisse der zukünftigen Nutzergruppen herauszufinden.

3. Lassen Sie sich und den Teilnehmern genügend Zeit zum Sammeln von Ideen und passenden Bildern. Gehen Sie nicht zu früh in eine Wertung und Vorentscheidung über, denn die besten Stories entstehen, wenn man verschiedene Bilder und Ideen miteinander verknüpft.

4. Entwickeln Sie mit den Teilnehmern einen roten Faden für eine Story indem verschiedene Bilder miteinander verknüpft werden.

5. Achten Sie auf eine interessante Dramaturgie, die einen Spannungsbogen erkennen lässt und neugierig macht.

6. Finden Sie möglichst „Personas", welche die Hauptrollen der Geschichte verkörpern und finden Sie eine geeignete Visualisierung (z.B. als Comic).

7. Sammeln Sie nach dieser kreativen Vorarbeit Ideen für den Namen. Tragen Sie dafür die wichtigsten Themenfelder zusammen und verwenden Sie Kreativitätsmethoden, um daraus den passenden Namen und Claim zu generieren.

8. Formulieren Sie abschließend aus den bereits entwickelten Sachargumenten stimmige emotionale Botschaften.

Entwicklung einer Markenstory für die Einführung eines Wissensnetzwerks in der ifm-Unternehmensgruppe

Der Start des Projekts „Wissensnetzwerk" fand bei ifm in einem kleinen Team statt. Schnell wurde dem Team klar, wie umfangreich das Projekt werden würde und dass dies eine gänzlich neue Arbeitsplattform und Arbeitsweise für alle ifm-Mitarbeiter mit sich bringen würde.

Daher war es dem Projektteam wichtig, rechtzeitig die Führungskräfte und die Mitarbeiter aller 43 internationalen Standorte für das Wissensnetzwerk zu begeistern, und das auf eine möglichst ansprechende, international verständliche Weise.

Deshalb dachten ein paar kreative Köpfe aus verschiedenen Unternehmensbereichen über eine geeignete Projektstory nach. Aus einer Vielzahl von bereit gestellten Bildern konnte jeder Beteiligte diejenigen auswählen, die seiner Meinung nach die Motive für das neue Wissensnetzwerk besonders gut darstellten. Das Erstaunliche dabei war: Die Geschichten, welche sich um die persönlichen Bilder rankten, waren sich sehr ähnlich, so dass es nicht schwer war, gemeinsam einen roten Faden für eine Geschichte zu spinnen.

Ausgangspunkt der Projektstory waren die zwei Unternehmensgründer, die vor 45 Jahren mit einer Idee den Grundstein für das Familienunternehmen gelegt hatten, das mittlerweile auf weltweit 5.200 Mitarbeiter angewachsen ist. Natürlich, Erfolg und Wachstum über die Landesgrenzen hinweg hatten es im Laufe der Jahrzehnte immer schwieriger gemacht, ein Gefühl der Verbundenheit und das „Familiäre" quer durch alle Unternehmensteile weiter zu pflegen. Das neue Wissensnetzwerk wurde deshalb als Chance gesehen, ebendies unter den Mitarbeitern weltweit zu tun. Die Geschichten wurden mit Hilfe einer Präsentation verdichtet und es entstanden erste grafische Entwürfe für die Bildsprache, die sich nun durch alle Medien des Projekts ziehen sollte: Angefangen von der ersten Hingucker-Präsentation über die Trainingsmaterialien bis hin zum Startfilm des Wissensnetzwerkes.

Die Namensfindung für die Plattform fand zunächst im kleinen Kreis statt. Der Name sollte möglichst in der Unternehmenssprache Englisch sein und einen positiven Klang haben. Er sollte aussagen, welcher Wert darin steckt und eine Assoziation zum Wissensnetzwerk darstellen. Und er sollte im täglichen Gebrauch sprechbar sein. Schließlich müssen ihn die Nutzer leicht in Sätze einbauen können wie „Leg es im NAME ab." oder „Das findest du auf NAME." Für die finale Auswahl des Namens wird nun ein größerer Nutzerkreis einbezogen.

Abbildung 4.2.1: Erste Entwürfe für die Projektstory der ifm-Unternehmensgruppe (Quelle: Lydia Zillmann)

Abbildung 4.2.2: Kommunikationsmaßnahmen flachen Täler ab (nach Elisabeth Kübler-Ross)

Zum richtigen Zeitpunkt emotionale Täler ausfüllen

Da die Intranet-Einführung eine Änderung der gewohnten Arbeitsweisen bedeutet, sehen Ihre Mitarbeiter diesem Prozess oft mit gemischten Gefühlen entgegen. Gehen Sie davon aus, dass die Emotionen während des Einführungsprozesses einem wiederkehrenden Muster von Höhen und Tiefen unterliegen, die Ihre Mitarbeiter bewältigen müssen. Es ist ein richtiger Change-Prozess, der wie alle anderen Change-Prozesse auch mit Frustrationen, Ängsten und Widerständen verbunden sein wird (siehe Abbildung 4.2.2). Das emotional Schwierigste dabei ist die Umstellung von alten auf neue Gewohnheiten, denn sie verlangt vom Mitarbeiter, Sicherheiten und Routinen aufzugeben und sich darauf einzulassen, Neues zu lernen und eventuell dabei auch Fehler zu machen.

Mit einer einfühlsamen Begleitung, den richtigen Angeboten in diesem Veränderungsprozess und entsprechender Kommunikation lässt sich die Abwärtskurve ins „Tal der Tränen" abfedern, sodass die Mitarbeiter mit den neuen Tools schneller die Vorteile höherer Produktivität erleben. Dies ist gerade in der Phase kurz vor und nach dem Start von besonderer Bedeutung.

Halten Sie besonders für diese Zeit entsprechende Maßnahmen bereit.

Die Faktoren, die ein schnelleres Aufnehmen der neuen Arbeitsweisen begünstigen, sind:

- eine klare Ziel- und Nutzenformulierung;
- eine Projekt-Marke, welche die zukünftigen Nutzer emotional anspricht und ihre Bedürfnisse adressiert;
- die transparente Vermittlung von Art und Umfang der geplanten Veränderung;
- eine plausible Erklärung der notwendigen Veränderung alter Arbeitsweisen;
- kontinuierliche Updates zum aktuellen Projektstand und zu den nächsten Schritten;
- ein Aufzeigen, mit welchen Maßnahmen die zukünftigen User befähigt und unterstützt werden sollen;
- ein glaubwürdiges Statement, dass für jeden Nutzer – egal ob Mitarbeiter oder Führungskraft – das neue Arbeiten eine Umstellung und einen Lernprozess erfordert und dass Ausprobieren und Lernen erlaubt sind;
- Berührungspunkte mit dem neuen System schaffen, um die Veränderungen vorstellbarer zu machen;
- der ausdrückliche Wille der Geschäftsleitung zum Wandel inkl. des Vorlebens.

Hah, es gibt bestimmt Leser unter Ihnen, die Kurven und Modelle lieben. In der Theorie sind sie ja auch sehr hilfreich und erklären einiges, wie z. B. die Phasen, die Nutzer bei der Einführung des Social Intranets durchlaufen. Aber Vorsicht: In der Praxis sieht es meist ganz anders aus. Da lässt sich nicht schon vorher sagen, wann User die Täler erreichen. Jeder tickt anders! Deshalb mein Tipp: Stellen Sie sich vorbeugend auf das Tal der Tränen ein, finden Sie passende Argumente für Kritiker und kommunizieren Sie proaktiv, wie Sie die Nutzer unterstützen werden. Und dann hören Sie sich einfach in Ihrem Unternehmen um und stellen sich jede Woche neu auf die Geschehnisse ein.

Kommunikationsthemen in der Phase vor dem Start

Die Kommunikation baut sich langsam auf und ist in der Phase vor dem Start am dichtesten. Welche Themen können aufgegriffen werden?

- Vision und Ziele;
- Nutzen-Botschaften (Welche Schwachstellen sollen mit der neuen Plattform behoben werden?);
- Markenstory des Projekts inklusive Name für das Intranet;
- Was kommen wird;
- Projektstatus;
- Führungskräfte-Statements zum Projekt, inklusive Notwendigkeit und Chancen;
- Was sich ändern wird;
- Neue Inhalte im Intranet;
- Erste Projektfortschritte;
- Ergebnisse aus den Nutzer-Workshops und gewünschte Features;
- Erste Erfolgsgeschichten aus den Pilotteams;
- Dinge, von denen man sich verabschieden wird;
- Vorstellung des Projektteams und der ersten Testnutzer;
- Startseite und besonders tolle Seiten oder Funktionen;
- Vorweggenommene Befürchtungen und deren Entkräftung;
- Wie machen es andere und was kann man von ihnen lernen?

Spannungsbogen aufbauen

Ein wichtiger Faktor in der Launch-Kommunikation ist der Aufbau eines Spannungsbogens, der Neugier und Lust auf das neue Intranet weckt.

❗ **Praxistipps:** Zehnmal Inspiration für die spannungsvolle Ankündigung des Starts

1. **Wir-Gefühl aufbauen:** Einer der großen Triebfedern beim Spannungsaufbau ist das "WIR"-Gefühl. Sie sind der Trainer einer tollen Mannschaft. Sprechen Sie nicht darüber, welche Vorteile die Nutzer haben, sondern lieber darüber, was WIR gemeinsam erreichen. Geben Sie den Nutzern eine Steilvorlage und lassen Sie die anderen die Tore schießen.

2. **Persönlichkeiten nach vorn schicken:** Binden Sie Führungskräfte ein – ohne dass sie zuviel vorwegnehmen. Führungskräfte sind von Natur aus Motor, Innovator, Querdenker und Sprachrohr. Jemand, der stets voranschreitet und dabei die Kontrolle bewahrt, ist für Menschen magisch und anziehend. Charisma gewinnt! Seien auch Sie eher unbequem, eckig und kantig als stromlinienförmig und langweilig.

3. **Zeigarnik-Effekt nutzen:** Dieser, aus der Psychologie bekannte Effekt besagt, dass man sich an unterbrochene, unerledigte

Aufgaben besser erinnert als an abgeschlossene Aufgaben, weil die Spannung erhalten bleibt. Beschreiben Sie das neue Intranet vor dem Start niemals voll und ganz, sondern nutzen Sie den Effekt. Je geheimnisvoller und zurückhaltender Sie kommunizieren, desto mehr Spannung und Aufmerksamkeit erregen Sie. Zeigen Sie, was kommt, ohne jedoch alles haarklein zu beschreiben. Sagen Sie, dass eine neue Plattform kommen wird, bleiben Sie aber beim Termin vage.

4. **Das Neue herausstellen:** Das Unbekannte hat einen unglaublichen Reiz, wir sind von Natur aus neugierig. Alles was neu ist, erfährt automatisch ein gesteigertes Interesse. Beschreiben Sie daher in der Pre-Launch-Phase, was neu ist und was an Neuem zu erwarten ist. Aber niemals vollständig.

5. **Überraschend sein:** Nichts fesselt unsere Aufmerksamkeit so sehr wie Überraschungen. Sie lösen tiefenwirksam positive Emotionen aus. Spielen Sie, legen Sie eine Spur aus Lockelementen aus, der die Mitarbeiter folgen können. Lassen Sie vielversprechende Nebenbemerkungen fallen, verteilen Sie Geschenke. Machen Sie etwas, was es in Ihrer Organisation bisher noch nie gab.

6. **Charme versprühen:** Seien Sie in Ihrer Launch-Kommunikation charmant. Flirten Sie in gewisser Weise mit den neuen Nutzern. Freundlich, einladend, herzlich, authentisch und liebevoll ist besser als laut, aggressiv und dominant. Drücken Sie Ihren Mitarbeitern nicht die eigene Meinung auf und lassen Sie sie zu Wort kommen.

7. **Zur Aktion aufrufen:** Sagen Sie konkret, was der Nutzer wann und wo tun soll. Spannen Sie die potenziellen Nutzer möglichst intensiv mit in den Pre-Launch ein, sodass sie mit zunehmender Launch-Dauer immer mehr "Teil des Projektes" werden. Call to Action, jetzt geht es ums Mitmachen!

8. **Mit Verknappung arbeiten:** Nein, nicht alle dürfen sofort einen Blick auf die neue Plattform werfen. Den verdient man sich, z.B. durch das Ausfüllen einer Umfrage oder die Beteiligung an einer Fotoaktion. Sagen Sie nicht sofort ja, wenn weitere Abteilungen die neue Plattform nutzen wollen oder sich Leute für Pilotprojekte bewerben. Begrenzen Sie kommunikativ die Zahl von Workshop-Plätzen (aber für den größten Raum). Dies wird auf dramatische Art und Weise das Begehren rund um die neue Plattform verstärken. Spannung entsteht durch Zurückhaltung einer Sache, einer Person oder Information. Verknappung hat die Macht, geradezu Begehren hervorzurufen. Sagen Sie nein und erzählen Sie im gleichen Atemzug immer wieder von Ihrem modernen neuen System und welchen Nutzen es stiften wird.

9. **Zunehmend Gas geben:** Erhöhen Sie bis zum Start nach und nach die Geschwindigkeit der Kommunikation. Die stärkste Frequenz und Präsenz sollte zum Launch-Tag erreicht werden und ca. 2 Wochen auf hohem Niveau gehalten werden. Verzichten Sie auf einen gleichmäßigen Veröffentlichungsrhythmus. Kommunizieren Sie lieber in unterschiedlicher Intensität und Emotionalität.

10. **Countdown starten:** Ein Countdown zeigt an, wann das Warten ein Ende hat. Noch 10 Tage, noch 9 Tage … 3, 2, 1 – Start!

Quelle: in Anlehnung an (Kroof, 2011)

Die Kommunikationsmaßnahmen in Vorbereitung des Launches hängen natürlich stark von der gelebten Unternehmenskultur ab: Ob eher eine spielerische Ankündigung oder ein schleichender Prozess mit stetigen Hinweisen passend ist, sollte wohlüberlegt getroffen werden. Eines sollte in der Ankündigungskommunikation auf keinen Fall fehlen: Motivieren und Neugierde wecken.

Wer auf der Suche nach kreativen Maßnahmen für die Einführung ist, findet viel Inspiration im externen Marketing. Schließlich geht es auch hier um Vermarktung, nur dass die Kunden die eigenen Mitarbeiter sind. Mit ein bisschen Fantasie lassen sich auch schnell Analogien z.B. zur Autowerbung finden: Plakate, Werbespots, Spielzeug-Autos als Geschenk, Einladungen zu Testfahrten, Gewinnspiele und so weiter. Doch Achtung! Nicht das Produkt Social Intranet („Auto") sollte im Fokus der Kommunikation stehen, sondern der Nutzen und der Mehrwert („Fahrspaß, Geschwindigkeit, Sicherheit, Komfort, ...").

! **Praxistipps: Dreizehn Anregungen, auf das Intranet einzustimmen:**

1. **Werbemittel:** Für die Verbreitung des Intranet-Namens haben Sie ein ganzes Maßnahmenpaket parat. Bedruckte Büroutensilien wie Mousepads, Notizzettelblöcke und Tassen mit dem Intranet-Namen, Logo und URL verbreiten die frohe Kunde schnell. Erwägen Sie aber auch Außergewöhnliches: z.B. schrullige Bekleidung wie Flip-Flops oder Regencapes – alles was Mitarbeiter dazu bringt, darüber zu reden.

2. **Druckerzeugnisse**: Poster, Flyer, Karten, alles funktioniert! Ob eine digitale Plattform mit traditionellen Kommunikationsmethoden zu bewerben ist, wird oft in Frage gestellt. Aber mal ehrlich: Ein Ding zum Anfassen ist bei so viel Digitalisierung ein wichtiger Kontrapunkt.

3. **Kommunikationskanäle:** Natürlich nutzen Sie alle bisherigen Kommunikationskanäle, um das Neue anzukündigen. Vergessen Sie dabei nicht die Medien, die durch das Intranet eventuell ersetzt werden wie das Schwarze Brett, den Newsletter oder das Mitarbeitermagazin. Verfassen Sie eine würdige "Verabschiedungsgeschichte" für „alte" Medien, die nicht mehr benötigt werden.

4. **Digitales:** Bildschirmschoner, Signatur, Unternehmens-TV, Videos, Mailings mit Hinweis zum neuen Intranet – bestücken Sie alles. Vergessen Sie bei der Auswahl der passenden Materialien jedoch nicht, auch Mitarbeiter einzubeziehen, die über keinen Computerarbeitsplatz verfügen.

5. **Im Bilde:** Veranstalten Sie eine Fotosession für die Profilseite. Egal ob Sie einen Profifotografen engagieren oder eine Kamera mit Selbstauslöser aufstellen. Hauptsache es macht Spaß und die Mitarbeiter kommen ins Gespräch. Schenken Sie jedem Teilnehmer an der Fotosession etwas, z.B. ein Vorab-Bild von einer Intranet-Seite.

6. **Wettbewerbe:** Veranstalten Sie Wettbewerbe oder kleine Gewinnspiele rund um das Intranet schon bei der Namensfindung. Veranstalten Sie aber auch Wettbewerbe „Alt" gegen „Neu". Messen Sie die Zeit, die ein Protagonist braucht, um die Antwort auf eine Frage bei 10 Mitarbeitern einzuholen und die Ergebnisse auf einen Blick darzustellen. Und zwar per Telefon, Mail und per Newsfeed. (Der Newsfeed gewinnt immer!)

7. **Werkstätten:** Alles was hilft, sich mit dem Neuen schon im Vorfeld auseinanderzusetzen, zahlt auf den Start ein. Diskutieren Sie, probieren Sie, testen Sie mit einer ausgewählten Nutzerschar.

8. **Probefahren:** Laden Sie interessierte Nutzer zu einer Testrunde ein oder veranstalten Sie Intranet-Verkostungen. Hauptsache, der Nutzer kann schon bestimmte Bereiche ausprobieren in einem würdig inszenierten Rahmen.

9. **Riesenpuzzle:** Verteilen Sie Riesenpuzzleteile, mit deren Hilfe sich Kollegen im Unternehmen zu einem Netzwerk zusammenfinden können. Alle Teile zusammen ergeben ein großes Bild – z.B. die Abbildung des neuen Teamraums oder der Community.

10. **Information:** Eines der bewährtesten Mittel gegen Kritik und Unsicherheit ist Aufklärung. Geben Sie den Nutzern Möglichkeiten, sich detaillierter zu informieren (Webinare, Broschüren), konkreter nachzufragen (Intranet Hotline) oder sich zu beteiligen (FAQs, Verbesserungsvorschläge).

11. **Mobile Universität:** Die Mitarbeiter entdecken die mobilen Varianten des Intranets. Sie sind überrascht, dass das Lernen rund ums neue Intranet auch auf iPad/iPhone abrufbar ist. Das ist natürlich davon abhängig, ob das Unternehmen auch entsprechende Endgeräte wie iPhones oder iPads bereitstellt.

12. **Best-Practice-Raum:** Von anschaulichen Beispielen lässt sich gut lernen. Ein spezieller Projektraum des Intranets dient vor dem Starttermin als Schaufenster für erfolgreiche Anwendungsbeispiele. Die Beispiele werden gesammelt und auch über die Launch-Phase hinaus fortgeführt, um Lösungsmöglichkeiten für aktuelle Fragen aus dem Intranet-Arbeitsalltag zu zeigen.

13. **SMS-Kampagne:** Eine begleitende und kostengünstige Kommunikationsunterstützung durch ein etabliertes Instrument wie SMS hilft, auf neue Praxisbeispiele, Anwendungen und Werkzeuge hinzuweisen. Doch Vorsicht: In der alltäglichen Informationsflut kann eine SMS auch schnell untergehen.

Likes und Likies für die Mitarbeiter eines Kunststoffherstellers

Für einen Kunststoffhersteller war der neu einzuführende Gefällt-mir- bzw. Like-Button das zentrale Element bei der Kommunikation. Er tauchte überall auf – und zwar in Keksform:

- Auf allen Trainings- und Kommunikationsmaterialien waren die Likie-Kekse dekoratives Element.
- Am Werkstor erhielten Produktionsmitarbeiter am Launch-Tag eine Mini-Kekstüte mit Likies. Bei allen Schulungen wurden solche Tüten an die Teilnehmer verteilt.
- In kurzen Ankündigungsfilmen erklärten die Multiplikatoren, was ihnen im Intranet besonders gut gefällt. So wurden einzelne Bereiche des Intranets besonders beworben und der Nutzen erklärt. Die Kekstüte mit den Likies war in jedem Film mit im Bild – sogar auf dem Schreibtisch des Geschäftsführers war sie zu sehen, und im Archiv auch. Am Ende des Films kam ein übergroßer Likie-Keks ins Bild. Der Intranet-Name wurde mit den Keksen nachgebildet und mit Aufforderungen versehen wie „Erfahre mehr im Intranet!" oder „Vernetze dich im Intranet!"

Abbildung 4.2.3: Auch der Intranet-Name lässt sich aus Likies legen.

Mmmmh, diese Momente zum Schwachwerden! Like-Pralinen und Likie-Kekse verteile ich zu gern in meinen Workshops und Kampagnen. Falls Sie Ihren Intranet-Nutzern den Plattform-Start versüßen möchten:

Goethe Schokoladentaler Manufaktur Leipzig,
www.goethe-schokoladentaler.de/index.php/leipzig.html
Verdener Keks- und Waffelfabrik, Hans Freitag GmbH,
www.hans-freitag.de

Abbildung 4.2.4:
Gefällt-mir-Button
in Keksform

Videos für das Intranet

VIDEOS ALS KOMMUNIKATIONSMEDIUM

Inzwischen ist vielen Verantwortlichen die Bedeutung von Videos für Unternehmen und Organisationen klar geworden: Das Management und vor allem die Mitarbeiter akzeptieren Videos als nützliches Tool und erwarten sogar den Einsatz von Videos in der Internen Kommunikation. So ist es nicht verwunderlich, dass in dem Maße, wie die externe Nutzung der bekannten Internet-Video-Plattformen (YouTube u.ä.) stetig weiter steigt, auch die Erwartungshaltung der Anwender an ihre interne Arbeitswelt steigt. Sie bringen ihre Freizeiterfahrungen mit an den Arbeitsplatz.

Der Report „Magic Quadrant for Enterprise Video Content Management" (Andrews, 2013) bestätigt diesen Trend. Aktuell werden in großen Unternehmen im Schnitt 10,8 Stunden Videofilm pro Anwender und Monat konsumiert, bis 2016 sollen es 16 Stunden sein, prognostiziert Gartner die positive Entwicklung.

Was könnten also die Geschäftsgründe sein, weshalb Unternehmen sich im Rahmen des Intranets näher mit Video beschäftigen? In erster Linie geht es darum, Aufmerksamkeit für die Informationen im Intranet zu gewinnen und die Ziele eines Intranets erfolgreich zu erreichen.

Vier Probleme der Internen Kommunikation könnten mit Hilfe von Videos behoben werden:

1. **Mangel an Interesse:** Videos sind eindeutig interessanter als eine lange Mail oder ein Dokument. Comscore fand heraus, dass Besucher einer Webseite 2 Minuten länger verweilen, wenn die Seite Videos bietet (Three Motion, 2013).

2. **Mangel an Klarheit und Verständnis:** Videos verbinden auf emotionale Weise Visuelles mit Ton und Text. Sie können ein Produkt und Personen in Aktion präsentieren. Somit sind Videos der beste Weg, etwas klar zu ZEIGEN – und nicht nur darüber zu sprechen oder zu schreiben.

3. **Mangel an Vertrauen:** Der Zuschauer kann im Video den Sprecher sehen und hören, er erkennt auch die Zwischentöne und wird emotional angesprochen. Diese emotionale Nähe, auch über Organisationsgrenzen hinweg, schafft Glaubwürdigkeit und Vertrauen.

4. **Mangel an Engagement:** Kommunikation sollte das Wissen erweitern, Verhalten und Einstellungen ändern und Aktivitäten ankurbeln. Das Video ist dafür das geeignete Medium – inspirierende Videos motivieren zu konkreten Handlungen. So hat ReelSEO herausgefunden, dass 4 von 10 Besuchern nach dem Ansehen eines Videos ein Geschäft aufgesucht haben (online oder persönlich) (Three Motion, 2013).

Dieser Abschnitt entstand in Zusammenarbeit mit Gernot Kühn, Technologieberater Office 365 Microsoft Deutschla GmbH

VIDEO-FORMATE FÜR DAS INTRANET:

Für das Intranet eignet sich eine Vielzahl von Formaten:

- **Interview:** Experten werden befragt und geben unabhängig und glaubwürdig Auskunft.

- **Tagebuch:** Als kurze Videos geben Tagebücher einen persönlichen und authentischen Einblick in Geschehnisse und Gedanken.

- **Erklärung:** Erklärvideos sind überall geeignet, wo komplexe Sachverhalte kurz und prägnant dargestellt werden sollen – nicht nur bei Schulungen, sondern auch bei Produkt- und Dienstleistungsvorstellungen.

- **Screencast:** Für die Vorstellung einer Software oder den Umgang mit ihr werden Bildschirmaufzeichnungen verwendet.

- **Rundgang:** Rundgänge geben einen kurzen Einblick in die Arbeitsweise von Abteilungen und Teams, stellen Arbeitsplätze, Messen und Projekte vor.

- **Case Study:** Reale Fallbeispiele in Form von Interviews, ggf. auch in Kombination mit Screencast und Rundgang, geben beispielhaft Anregungen und Motivation.

Sammlung von Launch Videos von Ellen van Aken http://bit.ly/1vkigHt

- **Support/Training:** Die Kombination aus Erklärung und Screencast vermittelt anschaulich Trainingsinhalte.

- **Webcast:** Eine Präsentation (PowerPoint) wird aufgezeichnet, ggf. mit Sichtbarkeit des Sprechers oder in Kombination mit einem Screencast.

VIDEOS BEGLEITEN DEN INTRANET-START

Es gibt eine Vielzahl von Möglichkeiten, den Start bzw. Relaunch eines Intranets mit Videos zu begleiten. So können Schulungen für Power User aufgezeichnet und als Video-Schulungen in einem speziellen Trainingsbereich abgelegt werden. Auch die IT kann kleine Screencasts in einem Hilfe-Bereich ablegen, um die ersten Anwenderfragen im Umgang mit der neuen Intranet-Software ohne Personalaufwand zu beantworten. Die Kommunikationsabteilung stellt das neue Intranet mitsamt seinen einzelnen Bereichen vor. Der Geschäftsführer weiht das neue Intranet vor laufender Kamera ein. Er wendet sich mit einer Videobotschaft an seine Mitarbeiter und ruft zur aktiven Nutzung des neuen Portals auf.

Video-Einsatz bei der ANWR GROUP

Die ANWR GROUP realisierte beim Start von „MY ANWR" gleich mehrere Videos.

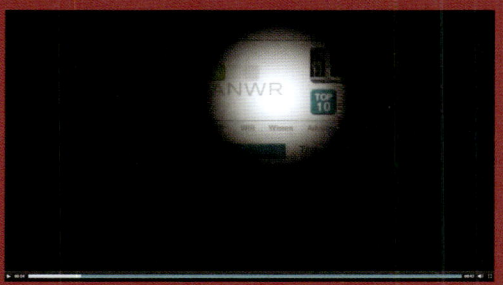

Abbildung 4.2.5: Beispiel ANWR GROUP – Blick auf kleine Portalausschnitte

„Großes Kino", das neugierig macht: Kurz vor dem Portal-Start wird in einer persönlichen Mail ein Teaser-Film an alle Mitarbeiter versendet. Er ist geheimnisvoll in Szene gesetzt, dem Zuschauer wird nur ein Blick auf kleine Portalausschnitte gewährt.

Ohne die oberste Instanz läuft nichts: Vorstandsvorsitzender Günter Althaus schwört die neue, 600 Mitarbeiter starke Community in einer Videobotschaft auf das neue ANWR GROUP-Portal ein, bedankt sich beim Projektteam für die geleistete Arbeit und zerschneidet feierlich ein rotes Band als Symbol der offiziellen Eröffnung von MY ANWR.

Abbildung 4.2.6: Beispiel ANWR GROUP – Bilder aus der Videobotschaft

Abbildung 4.2.7: Beispiel ANWR GROUP – Leitfigur Michelle

Das Intranet zeigt Gesicht: Die Leitfigur Michelle führt durch das Intranet. In einem aufwendigen Einführungsvideo erklärt sie auf unterhaltsame Weise die Funktionalitäten und Vorteile von MY ANWR. Sie zeigt, dass es so einfach wie bei Facebook ist, mit dem Intranet Kontakte zu Kollegen zu finden und zu pflegen. Zum besseren Kennenlernen gibt es die Option, sich über private Interessen auszutauschen - auch das wie bei Facebook, nur besser, denn keiner liest heimlich mit. Dokumente müssen nicht mehr lange gesucht werden, sondern sind klar strukturiert und immer aktuell abgelegt. Über die News ist man über alles top informiert: Staugefahr? Cabrio-Wetter? Lieblingsessen in der Kantine? Mit MY ANWR weiß man schneller Bescheid.

Dieser Abschnitt entstand in Zusammenarbeit mit Nadine Pachali, Unternehmenskommunikation ANWR GROUP

Videofilme der ANW anschauen: http://bit.ly/1yj7sVv

Dieser Abschnitt entstand in Zusammenarbeit mit Gernot Kühn, Technologieberater Office 365 crosoft Deutschland GmbH

AUSBLICK: WIE WIRD DIE INTERNE NUTZUNG VON VIDEOS KÜNFTIG AUSSEHEN?

Videos im Unternehmensalltag werden sich zur Normalität entwickeln. Die Bereitstellung (hochladen und abrufen) wird technisch und in der Handhabung einfacher werden. Neue Nutzungsszenarien für Online/Offline auf mobilen Geräten werden zu einer weiteren Verbreitung beitragen. Videos kann man mit Hilfe von Social-Komponenten anreichern und damit dokumentieren, welchen Zuspruch das Video von den Kollegen erhalten hat. Klassische eLearning-Systeme werden durch Eigenproduktionen von internen Experten ergänzt, vielleicht sogar ersetzt. Damit überholt sich das textbasierte Lernen in Lektionen und entwickelt sich zu einer projektbezogen interaktiven Wissensweitergabe von Kollege zu Kollege.

Das Microsoft Academy Portal

Das unternehmensinterne Portal „Microsoft Academy Mobile" stellt durch Anwender angefertigte Videos bereit, um den Wissensaustausch und das Lernen innerhalb des Unternehmens zu verbessern. Es basiert auf SharePoint-Technologien und bietet Social-Elemente wie Rating und Like. Die Anzahl der Views und Downloads sind transparent und werden für Ansichten im Portal wie „Am besten bewertete Videos" oder „Meist geladene Videos" genutzt. Heute gibt es eine mobile Zugriffsmöglichkeit per Windows und Windows Phone App.

Das Portal wurde 2008 ins Leben gerufen und hat sich seitdem enorm entwickelt. Es bietet viele Arten von Trainings, virtuellen Konferenzen, Live-Events, On-Demand-Podcasts und individuellen Screencasts.

Das Academy-Portal hat viele Microsoft-Manager, Produktgruppen und einzelne Experten aktiviert und ermutigt dazu, einen Peer-to-Peer-Austausch von Wissen mittels Video-Informationen in Gang zu setzen. Zu Beginn des Community-Projekts wurden Anwender nachhaltig aktiviert. Als Gegenleistung für ihr Engagement wurden den Community-Mitgliedern per „Podcast-in-a-Box" Leihgeräte bereitgestellt: eine Flip-Videokamera, Demo-Recording-Software und ein Audio-Recorder. Die Kollegen verpflichteten sich im Gegenzug, regelmäßig Inhalte zu produzieren – drei Videos im Quartal. Mit dem Anerkennungsprogramm konnten die Video-Podcaster je nach der Anzahl von Downloads, Bewertungen und Kommentaren Punkte sammeln und attraktive Preise (z.B. Fotoapparate, Rollkoffer) in einem Bereich von Academy einlösen.

Die Nutzung des Academy-Portals hat zu einem Rückgang der Vor-Ort-Schulungen beigetragen und zu einer intensiveren Verwendung der bestehenden Trainings geführt. In den ersten drei Jahren hat Microsoft damit nachweislich einen signifikanten Return on Investment (Kada, 2010) generiert. Academy erreichte nach drei Jahren immerhin 50 Prozent der Microsoft-Mitarbeiter und im Geschäftsjahr 2010 gab es mehr als 9.000 Academy-Podcast-Uploads und fast 1 Million Downloads.

	2008	2009	2010
Adoption Metrics (annual, not cumulative)			
Media uploads (videos and webcasts)	2,344	6,241	9,123
Downloads	95,900	272,563	940,412
Number of unique users (% of Microsoft headcount)	10,203 (11%)	27,465 (30%)	47,300 (53%)
Social Media Metrics			
Number of ratings	696	1,773	7,541
Number of comments	111	748	980

Tabelle 4.2.1: Key Growth Metrics for the Microsoft Academy Portal (Kada, 2010)

The Academy Porta
Microsoft's corpora
YouTube channel
http://bit.ly/1BHSCI

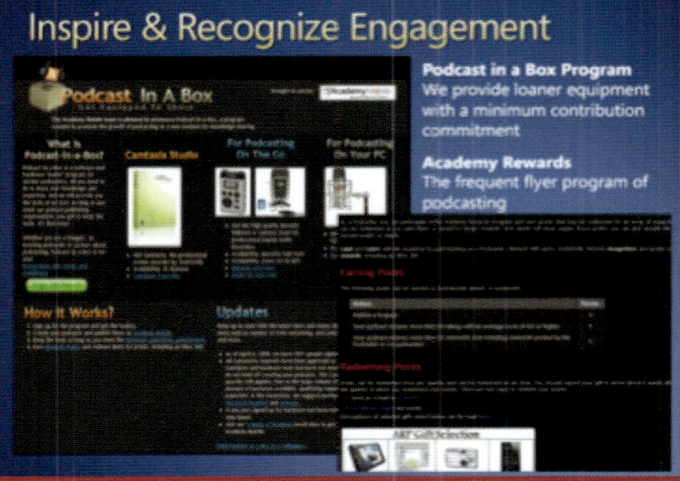

Abbildung 4.2.8: Screen Microsoft Academy Mobile

4.3 GUIDELINES UND NETIQUETTE

Erinnern wir uns daran, wie es war, als wir zum ersten Mal Plattformen wie XING, twitter & Co betraten: Alles war ungewohnt und wir wussten nicht genau, was üblich ist, was man tun darf und lassen sollte. Genauso geht es den Nutzern, wenn sie sich erstmals in der neuen Kommunikations- und Zusammenarbeitsplattform bewegen. Intranet-Guidelines können hier als „Leitplanken" dienen und dem Nutzer helfen, sich über den rechtlichen Rahmen, neue Möglichkeiten aber auch über eventuelle Risiken zu informieren.

In der Praxis findet man häufig folgende Arten von nutzerorientierten Richtlinien:

- Netiquette: Regeln für das Verhalten in der Community mit gewünschten zwischenmenschlichen Verhaltensweisen;
- Guidelines für Community Manager: Empfehlungen für das Aktivieren und Moderieren einer Community;
- Redaktions-Guidelines: Hinweise zu Inhalten und zum Verfassen von Beiträgen, zu Qualitätskriterien sowie zu redaktionellen Abläufen und Freigaben;
- Intranet-Guidelines: Nutzungsrichtlinien, auch mit Informationen zu gesetzlichen Rahmenbedingungen und eventuellen Risiken für den Nutzer.

Die Richtlinien sollten eher einen einladenden, aktivierenden und motivierenden Charakter haben. Das Verfassen der Guidelines ist stets eine Frage der Balance: Wie viel muss gesteuert werden und wie viel kann man einfach frei laufen lassen? Alles hängt stark von der Unternehmenskultur, der Größe eines Unterneh-

mens und dem Reifegrad sowie den Vorerfahrungen der Nutzer in sozialen Netzen ab. Meist führt die Angst davor, dass Mitarbeiter nur noch „daddeln" oder ein Shitstorm durch das Portal gehen könnte, zur Überregulierung. Solche Befürchtungen sind meist unbegründet, denn jeder Mitarbeiter ist als Absender von Beiträgen erkennbar und hat auf seinen guten Ruf zu achten, nicht nur in der Firma – auch online. Gehen Sie zudem davon aus, dass sich durch das Bewerten von Beiträgen (Like, Rating, Kommentare) ein Selbstregulierungs-Mechanismus in Gang setzt. Denken Sie daran: Auf jeden Fall müssen die Richtlinien nicht nur mit den Führungskräften abgestimmt sein, sondern auch mit dem Betriebs- bzw. Personalrat. Beide haben ein Mitbestimmungsrecht.

! Praxistipps: Wichtige Inhalte für Intranet-Guidelines

- **Beschreibung der neuen Plattform:** Name der Plattform, Ziele, Nutzen, Verantwortlichkeiten

- **Rechtliche Rahmenbedingungen:** Distanzierung von rassistischen oder menschenverachtenden Äußerungen; geltendes Recht für verlinkte Beiträge oder Verlinkungen darauf; Verwendung von Bildern, Videos, Tonaufnahmen; Recht am eigenen Bild

- **Sicherheit:** Datenschutzerklärung, Sicherheit der Software, Speicherung welcher Daten (z.B. auch Geburtsdatum, E-Mail, Personalnummer, Bild auf Freiwilligenbasis), Einhaltung des Datenschutzrechts, Umgang mit dem Passwort, Schutz vor Einblicken Dritter, Geheimhaltung, Wahrung von Betriebsgeheimnissen, Beachtung von Passagen des Arbeitsvertrags

- **Respektvoller Umgang:** gewünschte Umgangsformen, Recht auf Meinungsäußerung, Vermeidung unsachlicher Diskussionen, Klärung von Problemen in persönlichen Gesprächen oder Nachrichten – und nicht öffentlich auf der Plattform

- **Neue Möglichkeiten der Kommunikation und Zusammenarbeit:** Hinweise auf neue Möglichkeiten wie Communities, Blogs usw., gewünschte neue Verhaltensweisen wie Wissensaustausch und teamübergreifende Zusammenarbeit

- **Regeln für digitale Zusammenarbeit:** Dokumentenablage, Taggen von Beiträgen, Umgang mit Metadaten, Verlinkungen, Hinweise zur Aktualisierung, zum Löschen und Archivieren

- **Verantwortung für Inhalte:** Eigenverantwortung der Nutzer für Veröffentlichungen; Langlebigkeit der Inhalte im Portal; Umgang mit Fehlern

- **Empfehlungen zum Stil:** Wegfall von Mimik und Gestik in der schriftlichen Kommunikation; mögliche Missverständnisse bei der Verwendung von Ironie, Sarkasmus und anderen Formen des Humors; Verwendung der Ich-Form; Vermeidung von Abkürzungen, von Texten ausschließlich in Großbuchstaben, von SMS-Stil sowie von Schimpfwörtern; Hinweis auf Unterstützungs- und Hilfeangebote: Link zum Support-Bereich im Portal

- **Konsequenzen:** Folgen bei Verstößen gegen die Richtlinien

Nachfolgend finden Sie ein Beispiel, wie die Allianz ihre Guidelines für ihre Plattform ASN formuliert hat. So erhalten Mitarbeiter eine wertvolle Handlungsorientierung und Sicherheit im Umgang mit dem neuen Medium.

Beispiel: Guidelines für die Kommunikationsplattform ASN der Allianz

- ASN ist eine offizielle Kommunikationsplattform der Allianz; die Nutzung ist freiwillig.
- ASN bietet vielfältige Möglichkeiten, sich mit Kollegen in der Allianz zu vernetzen und miteinander zu kommunizieren und erleichtert so die Zusammenarbeit.
- Sie suchen Informationen? Nutzen Sie ASN, um die Gemeinschaft zu fragen!
- Sie haben Informationen, die wertvoll für andere sind? Teilen Sie diese mit anderen im ASN!
- Wer Gedanken und Ideen teilt, macht sie fruchtbar und nützlich für viele Menschen und stärkt damit das ganze Unternehmen.
- Jeder Eintrag ist willkommen und auch konstruktiv-kreatives Querdenken ist ausdrücklich erwünscht.
- Wenn Sie Hilfe auf der Plattform bekommen haben, bestätigen Sie diejenigen, die Ihnen geholfen haben. Positive Rückmeldung motiviert!
- Wenn Sie einen neuen Weg finden, ASN effektiv zu nutzen, berichten Sie darüber.

Ein paar einfache Regeln erleichtern die Kommunikation im ASN:

- Verwenden Sie die Ich-Form: Das Feedback beschreibt das, was Sie wahrgenommen haben.
- Vermeiden Sie Verallgemeinerungen (im positiven wie negativen Fall): Das Aufzeigen eines Problems bedeutet nicht, dass ein Gesamtsystem nicht funktioniert.
- Denken Sie daran, dass bei der schriftlichen Kommunikation nonverbale Faktoren (Mimik, Gestik, Sprache) wegfallen!
- Humor, Ironie o. ä. können unterschiedlich aufgefasst werden.
- ASN ist ein zusätzlicher Kommunikationskanal, ersetzt aber nicht das persönliche Gespräch. Insbesondere Konflikte sollten Sie nicht im ASN lösen.
- Bedenken Sie mögliche Folgen, bevor Sie etwas schreiben und handeln Sie so, dass Sie es mit gutem Gewissen vertreten können.
- Die Daten des ASN befinden sich auf internen Servern der Allianz. Dennoch sollte der Austausch von sensiblen Informationen ausschließlich in privaten Gruppen geschehen.
- Veröffentlichen Sie auch in privaten Gruppen grundsätzlich keine persönlichen oder privaten Daten sowie Bilder von Kollegen ohne deren Zustimmung.
- Verraten Sie keine Betriebsgeheimnisse und halten Sie sich an die entsprechenden Passagen Ihres Arbeitsvertrages.
- Beleidigungen, sexistische oder rassistische Äußerungen sind verboten, ebenso wie das kommerzielle oder private Anbieten von Waren und Dienstleistungen.

Quelle: direkt zitiert aus: (Wegscheider, 2012)

TRAININGS UND
TRAININGSMATERIALIEN

DIE USER FIT MACHEN

Wer seine Mitarbeiter richtig vorbereiten will, entscheidet sich für Intranet-Trainings. Damit die Trainings Lust auf das neue Intranet machen, müssen sie passgenau auf Anforderungen an die Mitarbeiter und ihre Nutzungsgewohnheiten zugeschnitten sein. Die Trainings funktionieren dabei wie das Intranet selbst. Sie vernetzen Mitarbeiter untereinander. Sie bieten Abwechslung in den Workshop-Formaten und Darstellungsformen und setzen auf vielfältigen Medieneinsatz abseits von der klassischen PowerPoint-Präsentation. Den Mitarbeitern bietet sich ein spannender Raum für Entdeckungen rund um das Intranet, für Fragen und Diskussionen. Sie erhalten wertvolle Tipps im richtigen Umgang mit dem neuen Medium und lernen es live im Austausch mit anderen kennen. Das steigert das „Wir-Gefühl" im Team und in den Abteilungen, leistet aber auch wertvolle Hilfe für abteilungsübergreifendes Arbeiten, das künftig sicher eine noch wichtigere Rolle spielen soll. Welche Gestaltungsmöglichkeiten der Trainingsbereich bietet, zeigt unsere virtuelle Trainerin Babett.

1. Kreative Trainingsformate

Für die erfolgreiche Intranet-Einführung kommt es maßgeblich auf die richtige Art des Trainings an.

Nicht nur Rücken- und Armmuskeln sind zu trainieren, sondern auch das Herz!

Wer sagt also, dass Trainings nur frontal im Fitnessstudio – äääh – Schulungsraum stattfinden müssen? Sicher, die üblichen Face-to-Face-Schulungen haben den größten Trainingseffekt. Aber probieren Sie doch auch mal etwas Neues, z.B. Intranet-Werkstätten, Brown-Bag-Sessions oder erklären Sie Newsfeed und Community-Blogs beim Kaffeeküchen-Klatsch.

2. Medienvielfalt

Setzen Sie auf unterschiedliche Medien. Gerade dann, wenn viele Mitarbeiter zur gleichen Zeit startklar gemacht werden müssen oder die Ressourcen begrenzt sind. Außerdem werden Sie so auch unterschiedlichen Lernstilen gerecht. Richten Sie im Intranet eine Trainingsecke ein für Lernvideos, Screencasts, Schulungskarten, Webcasts und Webinare.

3. Unterschiedliche Formate für verschiedene Nutzer

Kein Intranet-User will ins kalte Wasser geworfen werden. Jeder soll das für seine Business-Rollen notwendige Training erhalten.

Die Besucher mit „Lese-Zugriff" müssen die verschiedenen Bereiche des Intranets kennen. Außerdem sollten Sie wissen, wie sie Beiträge liken oder bewerten können. Dürfen Sie auch Beiträge z.B. an der virtuellen Pinnwand posten, dann sollte das WIE vermittelt werden.

Mitglieder mit Lese- und Schreibrechten müssen verstehen, wie man Inhalte, Metadaten und Beiträge hinzufügt. Sie müssen lernen, wie sie die neuen Formen der Zusammenarbeit in der Praxis umsetzen können. Wie bearbeiten wir Dokumente gemeinsam und tauschen Wissen aus?

Betreiber können Strukturen, Listen und Bibliotheken modifizieren. Diese Anwender benötigen eine umfassende „how to"-Ausbildung sowie ein vollständiges Verständnis aller Internet-Grundsätze und -Richtlinien. Darüber hinaus müssen sie grundlegende Dinge zur Architektur und Website Usability verstehen. Nicht zu vergessen sind spezielle Trainings für Redakteure und Migrationslotsen.

4. Unternehmenspotenzial nutzen

Als erstes und am intensivsten werden die Multiplikatoren geschult. Sie geben ihr Wissen an Power User und Kollegen weiter. Bringen Sie in Trainingsgruppen auch Schnellstarter mit den Social-Entdeckern zusammen, die Generation Facebook mit den älteren Kollegen. Die „Digital Natives" sind es gewohnt, Inhalte nicht nur zu konsumieren, sondern sich aktiv an der Entwicklung von Inhalten zu beteiligen. Machen Sie sich das beim Erstellen des Trainingsbereichs im Intranet zunutze!
Auch Anerkennung ist wichtig. Veröffentlichen Sie z.B. eine „Galerie der zertifizierten Multiplikatoren und Social Power User" im Trainingsbereich.

5. Abteilungsspezifisch schulen

Auch die einzelnen Abteilungen müssen sich in der neuen Plattform durchboxen. Wenn sie einen spürbaren Trainings-Effekt für ihr Business erzielen sollen, schulen Sie nah am Arbeitsalltag und geben Sie einzelnen Abteilungen ein spezielles Teamsite-Training gerade für abteilungsspezifische Prozesse und Workflows. Hier ist es auch von Vorteil, wenn die Abteilungsleiter Unterstützung beim Überführen der Arbeitsabläufe und Inhalte in die neue Plattform erhalten.

6. Führungskräfte trainieren

Auch Führungskräfte müssen auf die Trainerbank. Dem Management bietet ein Social Intranet ganz neue Möglichkeiten, Mitarbeiter zu führen. Wie Führen 2.0 funktionieren kann, zeigen FührungskräfteWerkstätten. Doch auch die Tools der Social-Plattform gilt es zu beherrschen. Wie kommuniziere ich mit den Mitarbeitern? Welche Tools kann ich nutzen, um Leistungen anzuerkennen und Feedback zu geben?

7. Perfektes Timing

Trainings sind ideal unmittelbar vor dem Start Ihrer neuen Lösung. Während das Power-Training für Power User vor der Testphase beginnt, trainiert man die Mehrheit der Nutzer zeitnah vor der Einführung und die Nutzer mit nur Lesezugriffen genau zum Start der Lösung. Danach plant man Trainings als kontinuierliche Basis, wenn Anwender neue und erweiterte Fähigkeiten benötigen.

8. Richtige Trainingslänge

Auch bei der Trainingslänge ist Individualität das Stichwort. Mehrtägige Trainings können sinnvoll und angemessen sein für einige Ihrer Power User und Administratoren. Aber für die Mehrheit der Benutzer sind häufige Mini-Schulungen besser, die es Usern erlauben, dann zu konsumieren, wenn sie es brauchen. Schließlich soll es keinen Muskelkater geben! Na dann: Auf die Plätze! Fertig! Los!

TRAININGSMATERIALIEN

Die meistdiskutierte Frage beim Thema Trainingsmaterialien lautet: Brauchen wir ein gedrucktes Schulungshandbuch? Die Erfahrung zeigt: Keiner liest gern lange Bedienungsanleitungen. Deshalb kann die Diskussion um Schulungshandbücher nur in eine Richtung gehen: Sie sind nicht unbedingt notwendig! Gedruckte Inhalte machen viel Arbeit und veralten sehr schnell. Oftmals treten bei den Nutzern Fragen auf, die bei Ihren Vorüberlegungen und Planungen nicht hinreichend berücksichtigt wurden, und ausgerechnet diese Fragen stehen dann nicht im Handbuch.

Aktuell und zeitgemäß ist ein spezieller Trainings-, Support- und Hilfebereich im Intranet, in dem die Nutzer alles finden, was sie benötigen – gern auch das stets aktuelle Online-Benutzerhandbuch. Welche Hilfsangebote können sie Ihren Mitarbeitern machen, damit Sie sich besser orientieren können?

☑ **Checkliste:** Der Support- und Hilfebereich im Intranet kann folgende Dinge enthalten

- eine Liste des Projektteams und der Multiplikatoren, die wichtige Ansprechpartner zeigt und die Vorreiter würdigt;
- ein Support-Newsfeed oder -Blog in dem die Nutzer sofort Antworten erhalten;
- FAQs zum Intranet, die stets aktuell gehalten werden können;
- Hilfedokumente oder das Online-Benutzerhandbuch, die in Wort und vor allem im Bild ausgewählte Handlungsschritte veranschaulichen;
- Hilfevideos (Screencasts), die zeigen, wie es funktioniert;
- die Anmeldung zu Trainings oder Listen mit Trainingsterminen, um sich für die Schulungen komfortabel einzutragen;
- Feedback zu den Trainings, damit alle Übungen laufend optimiert werden können;

Abbildung 4.4.1: Eine Broschüre erklärt den Nutzern des MAN Diesel & Turbo Intranets die Vorteile und Möglichkeiten des gemeinsamen Arbeitsbereichs

- einen Hilfebereich für Führungskräfte oder Multiplikatoren, die in einem geschützten Bereich spezielle Unterstützungsangebote erhalten, z.B. zu Leadership 2.0 oder den Umgang mit Ängsten;
- Feedback zum Intranet, damit das Projektteam schnell reagieren kann.

Wird ein Intranet relaunched, kann den Nutzern auch eine visualisierte Darstellung helfen. So zeigt man ihnen eine Art Landkarte, wo die alten Inhalte des Intranets im neuen verortet sind. Die Mitarbeiter ersparen sich dadurch Frust beim Suchen nach bewährten Inhalten, verlieren keine Zeit und sind schneller wieder handlungsfähig.

Das ändert sich

Abteilungsgrenzen

Abteilungsübergreifende und direkte Kommunikation auf Augenhöhe

Mühevolle Suche

Zentrales Auffinden von Dokumenten, Ansprechpartnern und Informationen

Abbildung 4.4.2: Trainingskarten eines Kunststoffherstellers vergleichen alte und gewünschte neue Arbeitsweisen

Bei den Trainingsmaterialien sollte beachtet werden, dass Darstellungen von bisherigen Arbeitsroutinen den neuen gewünschten Arbeitsweisen gegenüber gestellt werden. Die Mitarbeiter erhalten dabei in möglichst verständlicher Sprache nützliche Informationen für den Arbeitsalltag: Was ändert sich? Welche Vorteile ergeben sich für die Zukunft?

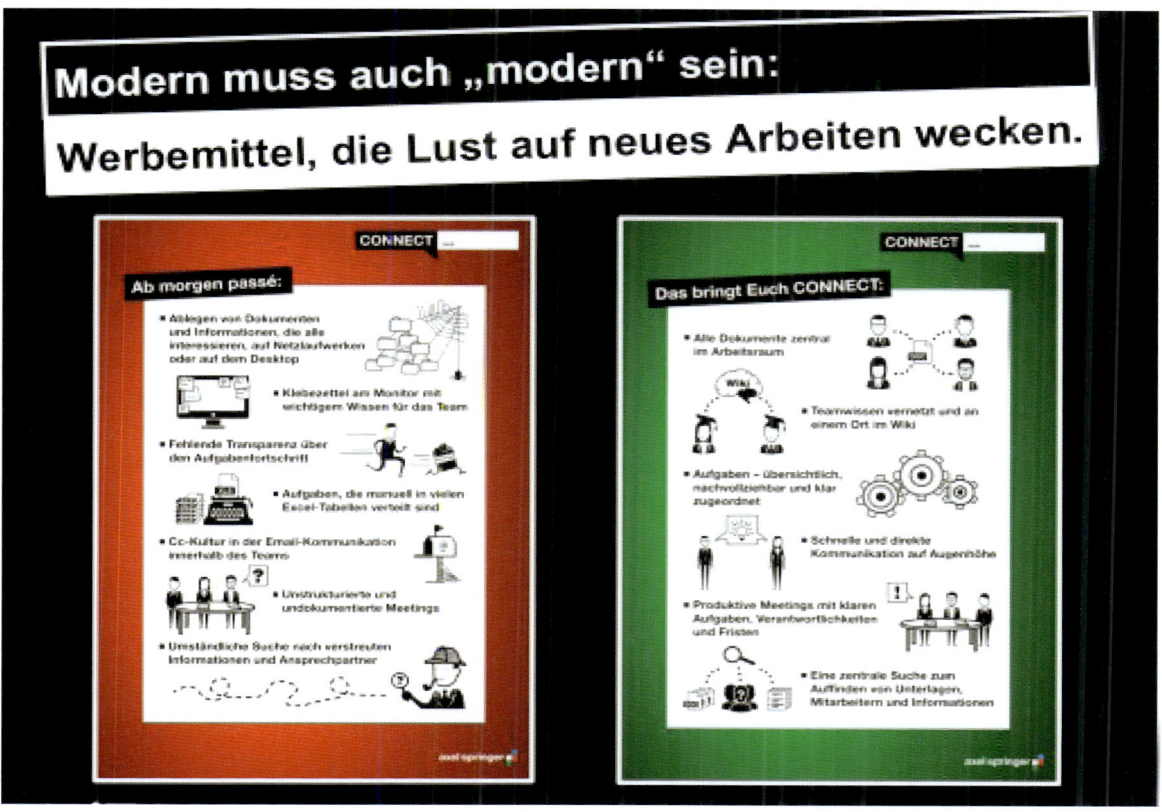

Abbildung 4.4.3: Trainingskarten für die neue Plattform CONNECT bei Axel Springer

Abbildung 4.4.4: Aus dem Erklärfilm zur Einführung von CONNECT – Einfache Bildsprache, klare Botschaften

4.5 AUF NEUN PUNKTE GEBRACHT

1 Die technische Umsetzung der Nutzeranforderungen wird die IT in Phase 4 zum Schwitzen bringen. Halten Sie Nervennahrung bereit!

2 Es bringt nichts, mit dem Fuß auf dem Gaspedal zu stehen. Haben Sie Geduld! Besonders in dieser Phase können zwei Schritte zurück manchmal langfristig mehr Erfolg bringen, als stetig mit hoher Geschwindigkeit voranzupreschen.

3 Emotionen während des Change-Prozesses unterliegen einem wiederkehrenden Muster von Höhen und Tälern. Stellen Sie sich darauf mit geeigneten Maßnahmen ein, welche die Veränderungen für die Mitarbeiter positiv erlebbar machen.

4 Hervorragende Kommunikationsideen gab es schon vor Einführung des Intranets. Machen Sie die besten ausfindig, peppen Sie sie auf und bereiten Sie etwas vor, was es in Ihrem Unternehmen bisher noch nie gab.

5 Intranet-Guidelines können als „Leitplanken" dienen und dem Nutzer helfen, sich über den rechtlichen Rahmen, neue Möglichkeiten und eventuelle Risiken zu informieren. Legen Sie Ihre Guidelines und Richtlinien fest und berücksichtigen Sie dabei Ihre Unternehmenskultur. Achten Sie auf einen ausgewogenen Umfang, anstatt Nutzer mit unnötigen Vorschriften zu erschlagen!

6 Für Anfänger ist es nicht so einfach, mit der neuen Plattform umzugehen. Bereiten Sie eine unterstützende und motivierende Netiquette vor.

7 Beginnen Sie mit der Anfertigung von Trainings- und Kommunikationsmaterialien. Denken Sie dabei zeitgemäß und richten Sie für diesen Zweck einen Trainings-, Support- und Hilfebereich in Ihrem Intranet ein.

8 Ein Training ist oft der erste Kontakt der Nutzer mit dem neuen Medium. Gestalten Sie das Training attraktiv und machen Sie neben den technischen Fragen auch die neuen Arbeitsweisen zum Thema.

9 Die Bedeutung von Videos ist enorm gewachsen. Nutzen Sie die Vorteile dieses Mediums und bieten Sie Filme für Trainings und für Ihre Markenstory an!

1 TRÄUME **2** ANALYSIERE **3** PLANE **4** BAUE **5** ERPROBE **6** NUTZE

ERPROBE

Noch vor dem Start folgen funktionale und technische Tests. Erste Pilotgruppen können die Lösung in ausgewählten Bereichen testen und die neuen Arbeitsweisen erproben. Maßnahmen zur Personalentwicklung sowie Trainings- und Kommunikationsmaßnahmen gehen in ihre intensivste Phase. In dieser Phase erfolgt auch die erste Inhaltsredaktion und ggf. die Durchführung von Migrationen.

Wenn das ganze Unternehmen für den Rollout vorbereitet ist und Fehler in der Software beseitigt sind, ist die fünfte Phase erfolgreich abgeschlossen.

TESTEN, TESTEN,
TESTEN

Neue Systeme, egal welcher Art, müssen getestet werden. Das gilt auch für unser neues Intranet. In diesem Abschnitt wollen wir dem Leser einen Überblick über verschiedene Testarten geben. Getestet wird auch schon in den früheren Phasen. Ohne geplantes und koordiniertes Testen werden Fehler nicht zeitig genug erkannt und Nutzer beim Start unnötig enttäuscht. Ihre intensive Einführungskommunikation könnte verpuffen.

Die Tests starten in der Planungsphase und stützen sich dabei auf unsere Konzepte für die verschiedenen Anwendungsszenarien.

FACHLICHE TESTS

Fachliche Tests erproben nicht die funktionale Umsetzung, sondern konzeptionelle Bausteine wie Navigationsstrukturen, die Verständlichkeit von Oberflächen und Namensgebungen. Sie zeigen, ob die zur Verfügung stehenden Funktionen den Arbeitsablauf und die Informationssuche auch wirklich unterstützen. Man redet somit von Usability Tests, die möglichst zeitnah auf Basis von Prototypen oder durch Pilotgruppen durchgeführt werden sollten. Bei den Korrekturen und Verbesserungen geht es aber nicht um sofortige Änderungen an der Spezifikation, sondern zunächst um die Identifizierung von Hürden, die bei der praktischen Nutzung auftreten können. Notwendige Umbenennungen, andere Strukturen, bessere Hilfen etc. werden erfasst und auf redaktionelle Umsetzbarkeit geprüft. Sind technische Änderungen notwendig, so muss bewertet werden, wie schnell und mit welchem Aufwand sie umgesetzt werden kön-

nen. Solche Schwachstellen sollten offen kommuniziert werden. Der Nutzer muss damit umgehen können und er soll auch erfahren, wann er mit einer Optimierung rechnen kann.

TECHNISCHE TESTS

Technische Tests der funktionaler Anforderungen und der technischen Plattform können sein:

Entwicklertests

Diese sogenannten Modultests führt die Entwicklung direkt durch – jeder Entwickler ist dafür verantwortlich, vorzuprüfen, ob der von ihm bereitgestellte Code die an ihn gestellten Anforderungen erfüllt. Fehler in der Anwendung resultieren äußerst selten aus Fehlern der Programmierung selbst, sondern aus Fehlern in der Interpretation der formulierten Anforderungen, aus Lücken in Konzepten oder dem Zusammenspiel von Komponenten.

Funktionstests und Testautomatisierung

In diesen meist toolunterstützten Tests werden die zuvor konzipierten Testfälle für das jeweilige Release strukturiert durchgeführt. Diese Fälle umfassen im allgemeinen Tests mit Nutzern in den verschiedenen Rollen, mit Zugriff über verschiedene Browser, Betriebssysteme und Endgeräte. Gerade bei iterativen Entwicklungen und absehbar häufigeren Releases lohnt es sich, über Testautomatisierungen für einzelne Anwendungsbereiche nachzudenken.

Integrationstests

Die Ergebnisse dieser Tests sind die am meisten gefürchteten in den Projektteams. Hier wird das

Zusammenspiel der zukünftigen Plattform mit anderen Systemen geprüft. Dies sind im Allgemeinen gemeinsam genutzte Systeme wie z.B. die Nutzerverwaltung und -autorisierung oder die E-Mail-Plattform. Die Integrationstests sind auf der Referenz- und der Produktiv-Plattform durchzuführen. Auch hier gilt, wer Zeit einplant, die Schnittstellen sauber definiert und frühzeitig antestet, kann eventuelle Probleme noch vor der ersten Release-Einspielung erkennen.

Last- und Performance-Tests

Durch die Simulation eines gleichzeitigen Zugriffs vieler Nutzer von unterschiedlichen Standorten aus wird die Netz- und Serverinfrastruktur getestet. Auch die Anwendungsarchitektur wird erprobt. Es muss sichergestellt sein, dass das System für die Zahl der Mitarbeiter im Unternehmen und für das wahrscheinliche Zugriffsverhalten richtig ausgelegt ist. Getestet wird am besten das Produktivsystem, bevor erste echte Nutzerdaten enthalten sind. Wichtig ist hier auch ein modulares Testen, um mögliche Schwachstellen schneller einkreisen zu können. Nichts ist nervenaufreibender als gegenseitige Schuldzuweisungen zwischen Entwicklungs- und Betriebsteam. Übrigens können auch die Testskripte aus der Testautomatisierung ggf. herangezogen werden, um ein unterschiedliches Verhalten in der Systemnutzung zu simulieren.

Sicherheits- und Penetrationstests

Die Tester dieses Fachgebietes verstehen sich auf interaktive Plattformen und ihre Schwachstellen bei möglichen Attacken auf das System. Auch die Identifizierung von Fehlern in Serverkonfigurationen und Rechtevergaben muss beherrscht werden, sodass keine Informationen an Unbefugte ausgegeben werden.

Migrationstests

Wenn es sich beim neuen Intranet nicht um eine Neu-Implementierung handelt und auch Daten aus bestehenden Systemen migriert

werden, so muss das in der Testphase berücksichtigt werden. In den Kapiteln „Migrationsplanung" und „Technische Umsetzung" wurde schon einiges zum Thema Migration gesagt. Es ist von entscheidender Bedeutung, dass Tests mit realen Daten, Datenmengen und Szenarien auch für zu migrierende Daten und Strukturen durchgeführt werden. Die Testphase ist eine gute Gelegenheit, Erkenntnisse, Laufzeiten von Migrationen und kritische Aspekte in einer Migrationscheckliste zu erfassen. Diese Checkliste dient dann bei der Durchführung als Drehbuch und stellt sicher, dass kein Aspekt vergessen wird.

Besondere Aspekte beim Test der Enterprise Search

Auch die Sucheigenschaften müssen getestet werden. Die Suche sollte so konfiguriert sein, dass alle relevanten Inhalte in den Index aufgenommen sind. Da z.B. die Führungskräfte sehr wohl auch mal nach Stichworten wie „Auslastungszahlen" etc. suchen, finden sich auch dazu Inhalte im Index. Nicht gewollt ist natürlich, dass Unbefugte über die Suche Zugriff auf sensible Daten erhalten. Gerade in gewachsenen Strukturen sind Berechtigungen nicht immer konsequent abgegrenzt, weil etwa die Vererbung von Rechten irgendwann nicht unterbrochen wurde, um nur ein Beispiel zu nennen. So kommt es immer wieder vor, dass Anwender Zugriffsrechte auf Daten haben, von denen sie gar nichts wissen.

In der unendlichen Menge an Daten geht dieser Aspekt im Alltag meist unter. Überhaupt sollte geprüft werden, ob die Schlagwortsuche auf die Frage nach sensiblen Daten zielgerichtet reagiert und was geschieht, wenn nach abseitigen Begriffen wie „Weihnachtsfeierfotos" gefahndet wird. Es gehört zu den obersten Geboten bei der Einführung einer unternehmensweiten Enterprise-Suchlösung, vor dem Start solche realitätsnahen Szenarien durchzuspielen. Moderne Suchlösungen umfassen auch sogenannte

Black-Listen, also Listen mit Suchbegriffen, zu denen grundsätzlich keine Treffer zurückgegeben werden. Zusammen mit richtig gesetzten Berechtigungen können Sie damit vermeiden, dass ungewollte Inhalte zutage gefördert werden.

In Firmen mit mehrsprachiger Umgebung muss bei den Tests darauf geachtet werden, dass die Suchlösung sprachliche Besonderheiten wie Umlaute oder unterschiedliche Datumsformate richtig behandelt und die Treffermenge dem zu erwartenden Ergebnis entspricht. Je nach verwendeter Technologie werden auch nicht alle Dateiformate automatisch volltextindiziert. Es gibt Grenzen, was die Größe der zu indizierenden Dateien angeht. Solche technischen Rahmenparameter müssen im Vorfeld geklärt sein und im Rahmen der Tests evaluiert werden.

❗ Praxistipps: Vier Tipps zur Durchführung von Tests

1. Die Tests sollten unbedingt durch Teams erfolgen, die mit dem Prüfen von IT-Anwendungen vertraut sind und die Erfahrungen mit der Basissoftware des jeweiligen Intranetsystems haben.

2. Vermeiden Sie zum Zeitpunkt des Testens fachliche Diskussionen über Mockups, Screenentwürfe und ausführliche Use-Case-Beschreibungen aus früheren Projektphasen. Jede Änderung, die auf nicht korrekten oder missverstandenen fachlichen Anforderungen beruht, ist zeit- und kostenintensiv.

3. Berücksichtigen Sie, dass auch bei der Installation einer Standardsoftware als Basis und der Einrichtung spezieller Anwendungsszenarien Fehler auftreten können. Dies hat meist wenig mit mangelnder Sorgfalt der Entwickler zu tun, sondern ist in der Regel auf das hochkomplexe Zusammenspiel vieler verschiedener Faktoren zurückzuführen.

4. Wichtig: Die Pilotnutzer sollten die Plattform erst auf die Eignung der Raumfunktionalitäten testen, wenn die technischen Tests abgeschlossen sind. Eine instabile Plattform würde die Akzeptanz des neuen Intranets gefährden.

5.2 PILOTIERUNG UND LEUCHTTURMPROJEKTE

Dieser Abschnitt entstand in Zusammenarbeit mit Katharina Simon, Senior Social Business Consultant/ Spezialist Social Enabling Systems Multimedia Solutions GmbH

Damit der Rollout von Anfang an unter einem guten Vorzeichen steht, ist es mittlerweile bewährte Praxis, im Vorfeld Pilotprojekte zu starten, sodass einzelne Teams die neue Plattform direkt am Arbeitsplatz nutzen können. Das hat den Vorteil, dass hier Erfolgsgeschichten entstehen, die Ihnen helfen, immer mehr Fans für das neue Arbeiten zu gewinnen. Außerdem lernen Sie aus den Pilotprojekten, was möglicherweise noch verbessert werden muss, um den Rollout vorzubereiten.

Damit aus Pilotprojekten wirkliche Leuchtturmprojekte werden, sollten Sie ein paar Hinweise beachten.

❗ Praxistipps: Sieben Tipps, um Pilotprojekte zum Leuchten zu bringen

1. **Sorgfältige Auswahl des Pilotprojekts:** Am besten eignen sich Geschäftsbereiche oder Projekte, die für das Unternehmen von hoher Bedeutung sind und vom Management sorgfältig beobachtet werden. So stellen Sie sicher, dass regelmäßig im Kreis der Entscheider über das neue System gesprochen wird. Vermeiden Sie jedoch zeitkritische Unternehmensfelder. Das Einführen neuer Arbeitsweisen beansprucht Zeit.

2. **Entwicklung von Zielen und KPIs:** Gleich zu Beginn des Pilotprojekts sollten Sie mit dem Projektteam analysieren, welche konkreten Businessziele das neue Social Intranet unterstützen soll. Geht es um Effizienzsteigerung – wenn ja, was sollte effizienter werden? Geht es um Qualitäts-

steigerung – wenn ja, wo konkret soll eine höhere Qualität erzielt werden? Geht es um Mitarbeiterzufriedenheit – wenn ja, wo genau gibt es Unzufriedenheit? Legen Sie die Ziele mit dem Pilotteam messbar fest, entscheiden Sie auch, wie oft sie überprüft werden. Im Laufe des Pilotprojektes ist es wichtig, die gewählten KPIs auf den Prüfstand zu stellen.

3. **Sorgfältige Auswahl der Pilotteilnehmer:** Das Management der Abteilung oder aber der Projektleiter des Pilotprojektes sollten der neuartigen Arbeitsweise gegenüber von vornherein aufgeschlossen sein. Sie sollten zudem motiviert sein, das Projekt zum Erfolg zu führen und die Erfahrungen, Erfolge und Learnings im Unternehmen weiter zu verbreiten.

4. **Train the Trainer:** Schon zu Beginn des Pilotprojekts finden sich immer Mitarbeiter, die das Thema interessiert und die technologisch bewandert sind. Diese Personen sollten Sie früh mit der Technologie und ihrer Anwendung vertraut machen. Übertragen Sie ihnen die Rolle als Multiplikatoren und trainieren Sie sie darin.

5. **Enge Begleitung:** Unterstützen Sie das Pilotteam. Erfolgreich wird es nur dann sein, wenn Sie es besonders am Anfang eng begleiten. Eine gute Einführung in die neue Arbeitsumgebung gehört dazu. Auch regelmäßige Gesprächsrunden zur Frage, wie sich das Social Intranet am besten in die Arbeitsabläufe integrieren lässt, sind wich-

tig. Auch Phasen des Ausprobierens sind nötig, in denen Sie online Hilfestellungen geben können. Erforderlich sind auch regelmäßige Auswertungen, um festzustellen, wo das Pilotteam steht, ob die gesteckten Ziele erreicht sind und ob die Nutzergebnisse im Positiven oder Negativen Rückschlüsse auf den Umgang mit den neuen Arbeitsmedien zulassen.

6. **Reporting:** Das Pilotprojekt sollte regelmäßig im Management vorgestellt werden. Neben der Präsentation handfester Zwischenergebnisse zum Businessnutzen sollte hier auch anhand von Beispielen aus dem Arbeitsalltag beim Management die Lust geweckt werden, sich mit dem Thema zu beschäftigen.

7. **Learnings erfassen:** Machen Sie mit dem Pilotteam regelmäßig die Learnings sichtbar. Am einfachsten lassen sich die Lernerkenntnisse ermitteln, wenn Sie abgleichen, wann Erwartungen, die man im Vorfeld hatte, erfüllt wurden und wann nicht. Daraus können Sie einen kleinen Leitfaden nach dem Motto „Tipps & Tricks für die Einführung sozialer Technologien in meinem Team" entwickeln, den Sie zukünftigen Anwendern gleich zu Beginn bereitstellen können. Die Learnings und Empfehlungen können Sie darüber hinaus auch als Blog in einer Themen-Community pflegen.

Es lohnt sich, in die Pilotprojekte Zeit und Aufmerksamkeit zu stecken. Erfolgreiche Projekte und zufriedene Pilotteilnehmer sind die beste Werbung, die Sie für Ihr Intranet bekommen können, und die beste Möglichkeit, die Konzeption für den Gesamt-Rollout vorzubereiten. Wenn Sie sich mit den Veränderungen im Unternehmen befassen, können Sie davon profitieren (Kapitel 6.1).

Ich liebe es, wenn man das Praktische mit dem Nützlichen verbinden kann. Gilt es, einen Betriebsrat zu überzeugen? Setzen Sie doch einfach mit ihm eine Betriebsrat-Pilotgruppe auf. Sind die Führungskräfte noch zögerlich? Wickeln Sie mit ihnen ein bestehendes Projekt diesmal auf der neuen Plattform ab. Die Optimierung der Management Board Meetings kommt als Pilotprojekt immer besonders gut an. Und logisch, bevor Sie mit diesen beiden besonderen Zielgruppen starten, haben Sie schon ein paar Erfahrungen in anderen Pilotteams gesammelt und können genau einschätzen, wann die Zeit reif ist, sich diesen etwas anspruchsvolleren Zielgruppen zu stellen.

Netzwerk-Piloten bei einem Handelskonzern

Ein Netzwerk zu schaffen, in dem sich Kaufleute informieren und sich überregional austauschen können – das war das Ziel eines neuen Kommunikationsnetzwerks bei einem Handelskonzern. Es wurde im September 2014 auf Basis von Yammer eingeführt und war ein Wagnis von Beginn an. Denn wie fördert man bei Kaufleuten eine digitale Zusammenarbeit, wenn sie ganztags im Markt unterwegs sind und ihre Altersstruktur nicht eben eine Social-Media-Affinität voraussetzen lässt?

Deshalb wurden bereits ab dem Projektstart, also neun Monate vor der Einführung, Power User identifiziert und in Projektbesprechungen einbezogen. Schon im ersten Meeting stellte sich heraus, dass die Kaufleute von WhatsApp oder Facebook nur dann wegzulocken sind, wenn die neue Plattform einen deutlichen Mehrwert bietet, wie beispielsweise den Austausch mit Managern.

Es entstand der Plan: Communities gründen, hintereinander starten lassen und so nach und nach für immer mehr aktive Nutzer sorgen. Dazu wurden verschiedene Gruppen gebildet:

- Interessengruppen wie z.B. eine Gruppe zur Warenpräsentation
- Gruppen zum Abwickeln von Projekten wie das der Junior-Kaufleute
- Regionale Gruppen wie die „Region West"

Das Yammer-Projektteam mit den Power Usern war die erste Pilotgruppe, die vor dem Launch bereits Yammer zur Kommunikation nutzte und sich so mit der Technologie vertraut machen konnte. Jeder weiteren Community wurden ein Administrator und zwei Community Manager zur Seite gestellt. Durch Trainings wurden sie auf ihre Aufgabe vorbereitet.

Erste Erfolge gab es in den Pilotgruppen bereits im Juni 2014 zur Fußball-WM: Die Kaufleute tauschten untereinander Fotos zu speziellen Warenpräsentationen aus und diskutierten neue Ideen. In einer anderen Gruppe wurde von der jährlichen Bildungsreise per Smartphone berichtet. Die Pilotierungsphase hat Power Usern und Community Managern geholfen, sich langsam an ihr neues Aufgabengebiet heranzutasten und sich so auf den Launch vorzubereiten. Die Netzwerk-Piloten konnten ab dem offiziellen Start vor allem auch mit Kommentaren und Likes die Diskussionen bei den Netzwerk-Neulingen anregen, was die Plattform wesentlich spannender gestaltete und das Ziel des gemeinsamen Austauschs über Themen förderte. Das gesteckte Ziel, dass 40 Prozent der selbstständigen Kaufleute nach sechs Monaten Yammer nutzen, wurde bereits nach einem Monat erreicht. Nun heißt es für das Team, weiter am Ball bleiben.

ONBOARDING VON FÜHRUNGSKRÄFTEN UND MULTIPLIKATOREN

Führungskräfte – Schlüsselfiguren für ein lebendiges Social Intranet

Parallel zu den Pilotprojekten startet nun langsam die heiße Phase vor dem Rollout der neuen Plattform. Dafür müssen alle Personen, die für die Einführung wichtig sind, in Position gebracht werden. Sie alle müssen von dem bevorstehenden Wandel ein klares Bild vor Augen haben, sodass sie wissen, was auf sie zukommt und wie sie mit schwierigen Situationen umgehen können.

Anhand der Trainings, durch die die Pilotgruppen gegangen sind, wurden wichtige Erfahrungswerte gesammelt, welche Trainingsinhalte und -methoden besonders gut ankommen und an welchen Stellen die meisten Fragen entstehen. Mit diesen Erfahrungswerten können Sie die Trainings noch einmal anpassen, sodass nun beim Onboarding alles optimal vorbereitet ist.

Grundregeln für die Aktivierung von Führungskräften

Die Führungskräfte spielen bei der Einführung moderner Arbeitswelten eine ganz besondere Rolle. Vieles steht und fällt damit, ob eine Führungskraft die neuen Arbeitsweisen einfordert und vorlebt oder nicht. Auch wenn Sie im Vorfeld schon viele Angebote zur Beteiligung geschaffen haben, lassen Sie sich nicht täuschen: Nicht alle Führungskräfte sind zu diesem Zeitpunkt begeisterte Treiber. Wenn Sie mit dem viralen Change-Ansatz vorgegangen sind,

haben Sie bislang eher mit den Führungskräften gearbeitet, die motiviert und am Thema interessiert waren. Nun wird es Zeit, sich auch zu jenen Führungskräften vorzuarbeiten, die noch nicht überzeugt sind und viele Gründe anführen werden, warum es bei ihnen gerade nicht geht: keine Zeit, die Mitarbeiter wollen nicht, in der eigenen Abteilung wird es nichts bringen etc.

Auch wenn Sie vermutlich nie wirklich alle zu überzeugten Fans machen werden – tatsächlich liegt es an Ihnen, die sperrigsten Hürden zu überwinden, sodass die Führungskräfte zumindest ihre Unsicherheiten und Bedenken abbauen. Es lohnt sich dabei, folgende vier Grundregeln zu beherzigen:

❗ Praxistipps: Vier Tipps zur Aktivierung von Führungskräften

1. Sprechen Sie zunächst nur über solche Aktivitäten, welche die Führungskräfte wirklich benötigen und weiterbringen. Jede investierte Stunde sollte sich nach dem Eindruck der Führungskräfte lohnen.

2. Beachten Sie das Timing – wenn die Führungskräfte endlich starten wollen, sollten sie auch loslaufen können und nicht noch Tage oder Wochen warten, weil zum Beispiel die Technik noch hakt.

3. Bleiben Sie hartnäckig und lassen Sie sich nicht zu früh entmutigen. Manche Führungskräfte brauchen einfach länger. Die verschiedenen Geschwindigkei-

ten sind normal und machen das Projekt nicht kaputt.

4. Nutzen Sie die Multiplikatoren in den Abteilungen und andere Führungskräfte, um bei den sehr kritischen Führungskräften Überzeugungsarbeit zu leisten. Dabei dürfen Sie nie vergessen: Am

überzeugendsten sind Erfolge. Wenn ein Multiplikator aus der betreffenden Abteilung erste handfeste Ergebnisse aufzeigen kann, werden auch sehr kritisch eingestellte Führungskräfte schwach.

Doch wie genau bringt man Führungskräfte ins Intranet?

Gemeinsam das Projekt zum Erfolg führen – Führungskräfte-Onboarding bei einem Kunststoffhersteller

In Produktionsunternehmen muss alles meist ganz schnell gehen. In sehr kompakter Form wurden daher bei einem Kunststoffhersteller die Führungskräfte beim Start des neuen Intranets auf Basis von Office 365 vorbereitet. Am Beginn stand eine Schulung in kleinen Gruppen, bei denen auf spielerische Weise alle wichtigen Werkzeuge besprochen und ausprobiert wurden. Da diese Erfahrung für die meisten Führungskräfte die erste Berührung mit Office 365 war, konnten sie hier sehr gut erkennen, wo interessante Einsatzfelder für ihr eigenes Team liegen, wo aber auch mögliche Schwierigkeiten auftreten könnten.

Mit dieser klareren Vorstellung sind sie direkt in einen zweistündigen Onboarding-Workshop gegangen, wo sie nun auf die Stolpersteine bei der Einführung vorbereitet wurden. Hier wurden die Führungskräfte mit den Verhaltensweisen zweier typischer Charaktere konfrontiert – dem des hilfesuchenden Mitarbeiters und dem des Bedenkenträgers –, um zu diskutieren, was mit diesen Personen auf sie zukommen wird und wie sie mit diesen Situationen umgehen können. Aus diesem Diskurs entwickelten sie Guidelines für ihr Verhalten bei der Einführung und einen Fahrplan für die nächsten Schritte.

Während das Projekt vorher noch in weiter Ferne schien, konnten innerhalb eines halben Tages die Führungskräfte soweit geschult werden, dass sie mit sehr viel Engagement und Interesse die nächsten Schritte angingen.

Manchmal ist es zu zweit am schönsten... Sie wissen, wie ein Sprach-Tandem funktioniert? Dann können Sie sich sicher auch vorstellen, was ein Social-Media-Tandem ist. Manche verbinden es auch mit dem Begriff „Reverse Mentoring". In den meisten Unternehmen arbeiten heute drei Generationen zusammen. Daraus lässt sich ein Vorteil ziehen, nämlich dann, wenn nicht nur Jung von Alt lernt, sondern auch Alt von Jung – und zwar den Umgang mit Internet und Intranet 2.0. Es ist bestimmt nicht einfach, wenn sich die „alten Hasen" ausgerechnet von den jüngsten Mitarbeitern die Welt erklären lassen und die Jungen selbstbewusst die erfahrenen Kollegen unterrichten sollen. Der Versuch ist es wert. So manche Führungskraft ist froh zu erfahren, wie die neuen Medien für das Unternehmen nutzbar zu machen sind. Und auch bei meinen Trainings erfahre ich immer wieder: Einige Mitarbeiter, die auf das Ende ihrer Arbeitszeit zusteuern, freuen sich über eine neue Herausforderung, die sie auch im Privaten weiterbringt. Mehr dazu finden Sie in „Sag mal, wie geht das?" (Mühlberger, 2014).

❗ **Praxistipps:** In fünf Schritten Führungskräfte zum Mitmachen bewegen

1. Gute Einführungsschulungen sind das A und O für den Einstieg der Führungskräfte in die neue Arbeitswelt. Sie machen die Führungskräfte mit den vielen neuen Werkzeugen und Funktionen vertraut und regen erste Ideen an, wobei ihnen die neuen Werkzeuge nützlich sein können. Führungskräfte lassen sich übrigens von spielerischen Angeboten schnell begeistern: Ob Bundesliga-Tippspiel, Team-Challenge oder Notfallszenario im Unternehmen – beim Spielen werden alle wieder zu Kindern.

2. Damit die Führungskräfte die Einführung aktiv unterstützen, sollte man sie auf die wichtigsten Stolpersteine vorbereiten. Bewährt haben sich Workshops, bei denen sie anhand von Szenarien, die mit bestimmten Personentypen auftreten können, konkrete Handlungsoptionen erarbeiten. Ein solches gemeinsames Handeln schafft Sicherheit und zeigt den Führungskräften, dass sie sich im Zweifel auch gegenseitig mit Rat unterstützen können.

3. Einmal geschult und auf die bevorstehenden Aufgaben eingeschworen, sollten Führungskräfte schnell die Möglichkeit bekommen, auf der neuen Arbeitsplattform zu arbeiten. Ein eleganter Einstieg kann gelingen, wenn Abstimmungen und Informationen im Führungskreis auch über die neue Plattform laufen. Damit haben die Führungskräfte einen geschützten Raum, in dem sie unter sich noch „üben" können. Ein Teammitglied des Projekts sollte sie aber weiter unterstützen und beraten.

4. Beim Einführen der neuen Arbeitsweisen in der eigenen Abteilung hilft es manchen Führungskräften, wenn sie mit ihren Mitarbeitern in einem Workshop erarbeiten, bei welchen Abläufen die neue Plattform sie am besten unterstützen kann. Ist dies einmal gelernt, ist alles Weitere für sie klarer greifbar. Idealerweise ermitteln die Führungskräfte mit ihren Teams auch Messgrößen, anhand derer sie den Wert der neuen Plattform im Hinblick auf Effizienz, Ideen, Kundenerfolg etc. nachweisen können.

5. Wenn die Führungskräfte die ersten Erfahrungen mit der neuen Plattform gemacht haben, sollten sie darin unterstützt werden, ihre Führungsfähigkeiten im Intranet auszubauen. In Leadership-2.0-Workshops oder Lerngruppen finden sie die Möglichkeit zum Austausch von Erfahrungen und zum Erweitern ihrer Führungskompetenzen. Je praktischer die Themen, desto besser erreichen Sie in der Regel die Führungskräfte: Was gehört in einen Management-Blog und was muss ich beim Schreiben eines Beitrags beachten? Was mache ich, wenn ich den Eindruck habe, dass Mitarbeiter zu viel Zeit im Intranet verbringen? Wie gehe ich mit schwierigen Mitarbeitern um, die partout ihre Parallelsysteme pflegen?

FRAGE: Wie bekommt man die Führungskräfte an Bord eines Social-Intranet-Projekts?
http://bit.ly/1uM6sr

Dieser Abschnitt entstand in Zusammenarbeit mit Ragnar Heil, Customer Success Manager Office 365 Microsoft Deutschland GmbH

Führungskräfte verlassen ihre Komfortzone auf einem „etwas anderen Führungskräfte-Gipfel" bei Telefónica

Telefónica ist in 24 Ländern (vor allem in Europa und Südamerika) vertreten. Die Führungskräfte sollten vernetzt und offener für neue digitale Kommunikationswege gemacht werden.

Ein „etwas anderer Führungskräfte-Gipfel" sollte den Start für die Führungskräfte markieren, sich mit diesem Thema auseinander zu setzen. Der Marketing-Vorstand, HR, Strategieentwicklung, Marketing, Interne Kommunikation und Event Management arbeiteten gemeinsam an diesem Vorhaben mit dem griffigen Claim: #notjustanotherCumbre – „nicht nur ein weiterer Gipfel". Dieser Hashtag wurde bewusst zweisprachig gewählt, um die Internationalisierung und Globalisierung des spanischen Unternehmens auszudrücken. Ein Erfolgsfaktor bei der Nutzung und Akzeptanz von Yammer liegt sicherlich darin, dass der Zutritt exklusiv und geschlossen war – und vom Vorstandsvorsitzenden dazu eingeladen worden ist.

Später wurden sogenannte #YamJams vom Vorstand ins Leben gerufen. Hier konnte man in einer bestimmten Zeit konzentriert zu einem Thema Fragen stellen und die Dynamik dieses Netzwerks spüren. Inhaltlich wurde von den Managern reichlich diskutiert, auch Vorschläge und Ideen wurden ausgebreitet. Schließlich wurde abgestimmt, Entscheidungen und Ergebnisse wurden festgehalten, und alle Beschlüsse wurden immer wieder kommuniziert und wiederholt, sodass jedermann mit dem gewünschten neuen Verhalten vertraut gemacht wurde.

Die Vorbereitungszeit betrug acht Wochen und es wurde ein genauer Content-Plan erstellt, an welchem Tag welche Themen behandelt werden. Nicht jeder Manager ist von vornherein in Social Media geübt. Daher wurden Community Manager eingesetzt, um die Betreffenden zu führen, Konversationen zu taggen und das generierte Wissen aufzubereiten. Unstrukturierte Informationen wurden von den Community Managern aufbereitet und systematisiert. Heute wird ihre Arbeit als wesentlicher Beitrag für den Erfolg des ganzen Projekts angesehen. Die Profile der Community Manager erhielten die Bezeichnungen „Yamy" und „Sherpa". „Yamys" waren für die Debatten, für Strategieentwicklung, Einladungen und Statistiken zuständig, „Sherpas" arbeiteten an logistischen Themen wie der Registrierung beim Event, den Buchungen von Hotels und Flügen und dem Agendasetting. Persönliche Meinungen trugen sie niemals in die Diskussion, vielmehr hielten sie sich neutral zurück. Um Stimmungsbilder und Meinungen einzufangen, wurde intensiv auf Umfragen gesetzt, eine Funktionalität von Yammer. Es gab mehr als 3.300 Stimmabgaben bei 40 Umfragen. Die Anzahl der Postings im Zeitraum der Vorbereitung betrug mehr als 6.000. Durchgängig wurde der Wert einer aktiven Teilnahme bekräftigt. Es galt das Motto: „Wenn Du nicht auf Yammer bist, dann existierst Du nicht!"

Die Ziele des #notjustanotherCumbre-Gipfels lassen sich so zusammenfassen:
- **Führung**: Manager werden zu inspirierenden Vorbildern in der Organisation, die für die neuen 3D-Eigenschaften (Discover, Disrupt, Deliver), verbesserte Kollaboration und querverbindende Kooperation werben.
- **Telco Digital**: Sinnvoll ist ein kultureller Austausch, um das Interesse an Fragen der Technologie zu wecken, ohne zu überfordern. Der Gipfel hatte das Ziel, die Transformation zur Telco Digital zu forcieren.
- **Neue Formate**: Nach dem Gipfel wurde der Dialog online fortgesetzt.
- **Innovation**: Neue Formen des Arbeitens sollten ausprobiert werden.
- **Global**: Mehr Netzwerke, eine Verbindung und zwischenmenschliche Beziehungen ohne physische, geographische oder sprachliche Barrieren sollten entstehen. (Hinweis: Telefónica nutzt die Übersetzungsfunktion von Yammer, die auf BING Translator beruht.)

Dass die Direktoren- und Vorstandsebene aus ihrer Komfortzone geholt worden ist, muss als Erfolg gewertet werden. Manager, die sich vorher als Akteure entsprechend der Weisungen von oben sahen, wandelten sich zu aktiven Change Agents. Ein neues internes TV-Format, das von der Internen Kommunikationsabteilung gepflegt wird, ist ein weiteres wichtiges Ergebnis des Gipfels. Die Anmeldung ist nur über Yammer möglich. Aber seit der Einführung des TV-Kanals hat dieses soziale Netzwerk noch einmal einen bedeutenden Wachstumssprung an Mitgliedern erfahren. Darüber hinaus ist ein neues externes „Global Procurement Network" entstanden, um Einkaufsprozesse mobil zu organisieren und zu optimieren. Besonders Benachrichtigungen und Freigabeprozesse sind hier erwähnenswert. Die Neuerung wird von der Telefónica als Paradebeispiel dafür erwähnt, wie sich Social Media zu Social Business wandeln kann.

Multiplikatoren – Die rechte und linke Hand des Projektteams

Ein Projektteam ist in seinen Ressourcen immer beschränkt. Gerade in der Phase des Rollouts ist es sehr hilfreich, genügend Unterstützer zu haben – die Multiplikatoren.

Als eine Art erweitertes Projektteam sind Multiplikatoren dafür verantwortlich, die positive Stimmung für das Projekt im Unternehmen zu fördern. Sie haben das Ohr an der Basis, informieren das Projektteam, wenn bei den Mitarbeitern Bedenken, Widerstände oder Unsicherheiten entstehen oder räumen solche skeptischen Anflüge gleich direkt aus dem Weg. Sie sind auch Partner für die Führungskräfte, wenn in deren Bereich Schwierigkeiten auftreten.

Außerdem sind Multiplikatoren sehr hilfreiche Personen, wenn es um die Fähigkeiten im Umgang mit dem Intranet geht. Sie werden schon im Vorfeld geschult und übernehmen bei den Mitarbeiterschulungen und im Support Verantwortung.

Gute Multiplikatoren erkennt man anhand dreier charakteristischer Merkmale:

- Sie zeigen Interesse für das Thema, sehen die Chancen und wollen etwas bewegen.
- Das Arbeiten mit neuen Medien geht ihnen leicht von der Hand, in der Regel sind sie in privaten Netzwerken aktiv
- Sie haben einen guten Draht zu den Mitarbeitern, man hört auf sie.

Auch Multiplikatoren sollten gut auf ihre Rolle und Aufgabe vorbereitet werden. Hier sind dieselben fünf Schritte ratsam, die wir im vorhergehenden Abschnitt zum Onboarding der Führungskräfte beschrieben haben:

1. Einführungsschulung;
2. Auf Stolpersteine vorbereiten;
3. Reale erste Anwendungsfälle im neuen Intranet umsetzen lassen;
4. Aktive Rolle beim Vorbereiten der Abteilungen;
5. Regelmäßige Treffen zum Erfahrungsaustausch untereinander.

Ohne die Multiplikatoren geht oft nichts. Und doch wird eines oft vergessen: Sie arbeiten freiwillig am Projekt mit und das meist zusätzlich zu ihrer täglichen Arbeit. Sie brauchen das Gefühl, dass ihr Engagement etwas nützt und dass mit ihren Ideen und Rückmeldungen gearbeitet wird. Wir alle lieben Anerkennung: ein Schulterklopfen, ein lobendes Wort oder gar die öffentliche Belobigung zum Start der neuen Plattform wären deshalb gut. Bieten Sie attraktive Entwicklungsmöglichkeiten und Rahmenbedingungen – die Rolle des Multiplikators kann in die des Community Managers münden.

DAS INTRANET MIT INHALT BELEBEN

Dieser Abschnitt entstand in Zusammenarbeit mit Oliver Jorzik, PR-Berater Berlin PR

Das Intranet erlebt einen Paradigmenwechsel. Während im altbekannten „Intranet 1.0" die Inhalte von zentraler Stelle – aus der Unternehmenskommunikation oder der Intranet-Redaktion – zur Verfügung gestellt wurden, werden sie in modernen Social Intranets maßgeblich von den Nutzern mitgestaltet. User Generated Content im Intranet 2.0 wird von den Abteilungen direkt veröffentlicht und kann, sofern gewünscht, von Kollegen kommentiert oder ergänzt werden. Während die Kommunikationsprofis bislang vor allem klassische redaktionelle Aufgaben wahrnahmen, geht es heute vielfach um das Management von Kommunikation: nicht um das Schreiben selbst, sondern um die Förderung des Dialogs zwischen Kollegen, Mitarbeitern und Führungskräften oder um Anregungen für die Beschäftigten, sich aktiv zu beteiligen.

tion, um dialogfördernde Impulse und Reizpunkte zu setzen. Darüber hinaus gehört es weiterhin zu den Aufgaben der Internen Kommunikation, die Ziele des Unternehmens oder Veränderungsprozesse zu vermitteln und für die Imagepflege nach innen zu sorgen. Dies geschieht jedoch nicht mehr in Form einer Einweg-Kommunikation, sondern unter den veränderten Vorzeichen eines gestalteten Dialogs. Zwar ist noch immer in vielen Unternehmen der Verlautbarungsstil alter Prägung anzutreffen, mit dem vormals interne Informationen verbreitet wurden, aber er funktioniert nicht mehr. Gefordert ist ein Intranet-Management, das sich – ohne dabei die strategische Führungsaufgabe zu vernachlässigen – viel stärker auf den Nutzer einstellt, um eine bessere Akzeptanz und höhere interne Reichweitenzahlen zu erreichen.

Das Social Intranet verändert die Redaktionsarbeit

Die Nutzer von Web-2.0-Anwendungen werden durch die von ihnen gestalteten Inhalte, Kommentare oder Tags stärker in Wertschöpfungsprozesse einbezogen. Das Social Intranet trägt so zu einer höheren Aktualität, Interaktivität, Dezentralität und Dynamik bei. Aber: Auch wenn im Social Intranet Inhalte mit interaktiven Anwendungen verbunden sind und jeder Mitarbeiter Nachrichten eigenverantwortlich veröffentlichen kann, organisiert sich die Kommunikation nicht von selbst. Auch künftig bedarf es der Mitwirkung einer zentralen Unternehmenskommunika-

Erfolgsfaktor Intranet-Redaktion: Themen managen, über die gesprochen wird

Wenn das Intranet die Schaltstelle der Internen Kommunikation ist, dann ist die Intranet-Redaktion der Erfolgsmotor für qualitativ hochwertigen Content und seine Verteilung. Die zentrale Frage dabei ist: Wie schaffe ich mit meinem Social Intranet ein hinreichendes Maß an Relevanz und Aufmerksamkeit unter meinen Mitarbeitern? Wie sorge ich für Beachtung, sodass Nachschauen und Lesen zu einem unbedingten Muss werden und nicht zur ungeliebten Pflicht? Wie pflege ich meine Inhalte so, dass sie aktivieren und nicht verschrecken?

Häufig wird bei der Gestaltung von Inhalten und der Festlegung der internen Informations- und Dialogarchitektur übersehen, dass es „die Mitarbeiter" als eine einheitliche Zielgruppe genauso wenig gibt wie Kunden, Händler oder Lieferanten. Man denke nur an Geschlechterunterschiede, unterschiedliche Herkunft, kulturellen Background, religiöse Ausrichtung, Alter, Nutzungsgewohnheiten der Medien oder Informationsansprüche.

Hinzu kommt: Das Medienverhalten ändert sich gravierend. Gerade im Bereich der Internen Kommunikation ist heute ein professionell aufbereitetes Setting mit unterschiedlichen Inhalten gefragt, denn die Belegschaften sind heterogen. Eine Kommunikation, die Neugier weckt, emotionalisiert, mit starken Bildern arbeitet, Orientierung und Sicherheit gibt und manchmal auch nur unterhalten will, wäre auf dem richtigen Weg. Das Intranet soll also nicht mehr nur das Unternehmen mit seinen Geschäftszielen repräsentieren, sondern mit einem modernen Storytelling für die Mitarbeiter auch besonders attraktiv sein. Nur gut ausgebildete, fähige Redakteure mit dem Sensorium für die richtigen Themen können diese anspruchsvolle Aufgabe bewältigen. Eine gute Zusammenarbeit mit der Geschäftsleitung, eine dichtes Kommunikationsnetz nach außen und ein gut organisiertes Zusammenspiel im Redaktionsteam gehören dazu. Folgende Schritte helfen bei der Organisation der eigenen Intranet-Redaktion.

❗ Praxistipps: Sieben Schritte zur Intranet-Organisation

1. **Definieren Sie klare Verantwortlichkeiten:** Die wichtige Frage am Anfang lautet: Wer hat bei der Entscheidung über die Inhalte die oberste Verantwortung? Wer erteilt die Freigaben? Wer koordiniert die redaktionelle Mitarbeit? Aus welcher Mitgliedern setzt sich das Redaktionsteam zusammen?

2. **Bestimmen Sie klare Abläufe:** Gerade im Bereich der Internen Kommunikation muss man häufig mit längeren Vorlauffristen für Freigaben rechnen, die bei der Themenplanung berücksichtigt werden müssen. Richten Sie auf jeden Fall in Ihrem Intranet unterstützende Redaktions-Workflows ein.

3. **Lernen Sie Ihre Zielgruppen kennen:** Eine Befragung der Mitarbeiter nach Themenwünschen – beispielsweise in kleineren Gruppen aus unterschiedlichen Abteilungen und Standorten – schafft den nötigen Überblick, welche Themen und Inhalte interessieren und welche Erwartungen und Informationsbedürfnisse Ihre Mitarbeiter haben. Werten Sie auch das bisherige Intranet-Angebot auf Nutzungszahlen aus: Was lief gut, was schlecht? Wo war die Beteiligung besonders groß?

4. **Lassen Sie einen Redaktionsleitfaden zusammenstellen:** Jede Intranet-Redaktion sollte Klarheit darüber besitzen, welches Unternehmen sie vertritt und wie sich das Unternehmen am (Meinungs-)Markt positioniert. Je klarer, prägnanter und verständlicher die Positionierung und das Einverständnis über die Unternehmensziele ausfallen, desto mehr Orientierungssicherheit haben die Mitarbeiter im täglichen Geschehen. Der Redaktionsleitfaden ist beides: Er gibt Auskunft über den thematischen Überbau und ist wertvolles Hilfsmittel für den Arbeitsalltag. Der Redaktionsleitfaden ist mit seinen inhaltlichen und gestalterischen Vorgaben und mit seinen Verfahrensvorschriften für die Produktion von Content ein notwendiges Hilfsmittel der Qualitätssicherung.

So führt der Redaktionsleitfaden detailliert auf: ein thematisches Konzept des

Social Intranet; eine exakte Beschreibung der redaktionellen Formate (z.B. Textlängen); den Einsatz auf der Website; das Wording für redaktionelle Formate und Elemente; die Abläufe bei Text-, Bild-, Grafik- und Videoarbeiten inklusive der Freigabeprozesse. Hinzu kommen die genauen Beschreibungen des Dokumenten- und Ablagemanagements sowie technische Hinweise und Tipps zum Arbeiten im System: von der Textintegration über das Hochladen von Bildern und Grafiken bis hin zu rechtlichen Hinweisen etwa zur Verwendung von fremdem Bildmaterial, zu Quellenangaben sowie zu Ansprechpartnern bei technischen Problemen.

5. **Regelmäßige Redaktionsworkshops für die Themenfindung:** Für eine kreative Themenfindung empfehlen sich regelmäßig Themen- oder Redaktionsworkshops, an denen auch Mitarbeiter der Pressestelle und Vertreter aus dem Marketing, Vertrieb oder Forschung und Entwicklung teilnehmen können. In ihnen werden die Themen herausgefiltert, die aus Sicht des Unternehmens als Pflichtthemen „gesetzt" sind (siehe Infokasten) und als News zu neuen Produkten oder wichtigen Unternehmensentscheidungen zwingend bekannt gemacht werden müssen. Es werden darüber hinaus Themen gesammelt, die das Unternehmen in gewisser Weise markieren – beispielsweise Innovation, Qualität, Service, Kundenorientierung etc. Die Themen werden bewertet und mit entsprechenden journalistischen Formaten verbunden: News, Hintergrundgeschichte, Bericht, Reportage, Porträt, Interview, Blogbeitrag, Podcast, Videocast, Wiki u.a.

6. **Erarbeitung eines Themenkalenders:** Als wichtige Ergänzung für das Tagesgeschäft dient neben dem Redaktionsleitfaden der sogenannte Themenkalender. In ihm werden die gesammelten Themen festgehalten und der Zeitplan für die Bearbeitung fixiert. Auch die personellen Verantwortlichkeiten und mögliche Supports, etwa durch externe Fotografen oder Grafikdienstleister, werden festgehalten. Der Themenkalender ist kein statisches Produkt, sondern sollte permanent aktualisiert werden. Mit einer modernen Intranet-Software ist das kein Problem. In jedem Fall gilt: Je nach Größe des Unternehmens, laufenden Change-Management-Prozessen oder dynamischer Marktentwicklung kann sich die Themenlage eines Unternehmens schnell ändern und ein schlecht gepflegter Themenkalender rasch veralten.

7. **Prozess- und Erfolgskontrolle:** In regelmäßigen Abständen sollten die umgesetzten Maßnahmen evaluiert und dokumentiert werden: Welche Themen liefen gut und wurden oft abgerufen oder kommentiert? Wie war die Resonanz und Akzeptanz? Die quantitativen Ergebnisse, die sich aus Online-Zugriffszahlen ermitteln lassen, können wiederum durch Begleitinterviews vertieft werden, in denen die Mitarbeiter die Qualität der Informationen beurteilen und weitere Themenwünsche äußern. Auch das systematische Auswerten und Dokumentieren von Nutzer-Reaktionen auf Intranet-Inhalte gehört dazu. Wichtig zudem: Wenn es hakt oder Probleme im Workflow auftreten, sollte man genau und selbstkritisch hinschauen, um solche Stolpersteine in Zukunft nach Möglichkeit auszuschließen.

Ideen für den Themenplan

Eckpfeiler des Themenplans sind alle terminierten Jahresthemen:
Geschäfts- und Bilanzzahlen, strategische Entscheidungen, Investitionen, Produktneuheiten, Messeauf-tritte und Eventankündigungen, Hausmessen, Tage der offenen Tür, Produkt Kick-Offs, Schulungstermi-ne, Projektabschlüsse, interne Events, Verkaufsaktionen/Sonderaktionen, Jubiläen

Variable Themen für den Themenkalender:
Neue Standorte, spektakuläre Aufträge, wichtige Personalien, Kooperationen/Partnerschaften, Aus-zeichnungen und Preise, neue Standorte/Filialen, Porträts neuer/verdienter Mitarbeiter, zusätzliche Ar-beitsplätze, Produkt-News, Statusmeldungen von Projekten, Erfahrungsberichte aus cen Märkten, neue Forschungsergebnisse, Vorträge und Präsentationen

Hintergrundinformationen, die zusätzlich bespielt werden können:
Studien & Analysen, Erfolgsgeschichten, Use Cases, Anwenderberichte

Interne Themen/Human Resources als wichtige Service-Infos:
Schulungsprogramme, Incentives, Workshops, interne Events, betriebliches Gesundheitswesen

Soziale Themen/Engagement:
Geförderte Projekte und Initiativen, ehrenamtliches Engagement von Mitarbeitern bei Projekten

Spezielle Aktionen und Services für das Intranet:
Aktionen wie Gewinnspiele und Verlosungen, Würdigungen besonderer Inhalte im Intranet, INTRAviews (Interviews speziell für das Intranet), Würdigungen von ausgezeichneten Anwender-Stories oder Prä-sentationen, Vorstellen neuer Intranet-Inhalte, Serviceangebote und Funktionen, Umfragen zu neuen Tools, Werkzeugen und Intranet-Angeboten

Visualisierungen:
Fotos, (Anwender-)Videos, Infografiken, Illustrationen, interaktive Grafiken, Diagramme, technische Zeichnungen, 3-D-Animationen u.a.

Die Qualität von Beiträgen durch Schreibtrainings steigern

Die mangelnde Akzeptanz vieler Inhalte im Intranet rührt daher, dass sie sehr stark top-down bestimmt und nicht an den Informationsbedürfnissen und Rezeptionsgewohnheiten der Mitarbeiter ausgerichtet sind.

Ein einfaches Beispiel:

Inhalte anpassen statt kopieren

Ein Hersteller von 3D-Druckern plant im Rahmen eines Messeauftritts eine spektakuläre Produkteinführung. Das neue Produkt soll auf der Messe Technik- und Fachjournalisten vorgestellt werden. Dazu gibt es die passende Pressemitteilung mit dem für das Fachpublikum erarbeiteten Titel: „Leton (Name geändert) zeigt auf der EuroMold innovative Styrol-Block-Copolymer-Komponenten zur Verwendung in Fused Deposition Modeling". Die Pressemitteilung wurde von der Entwicklungsabteilung und der Abteilung Unternehmenskommunikation freigegeben und soll nun auch im Intranet des Unternehmens erscheinen. Konzentrieren wir uns nur auf die Headline. Kann ich mit ihr auch technisch weniger kundige Mitarbeiter erreichen?

Mit etwas sprachlichem Gespür lässt sich die trockene Technik-Mitteilung umwandeln in eine für einen breiteren Leserkreis durchaus spannende Meldung. Die neue Headline, die genau dasselbe aussagt, lautet nun: „100 Prozent Freiheit im Design, 100 Prozent recycelbar. Auf der EuroMold zeigt das Leton-Messeteam unsere völlig neue Kunststoff-Generation für 3D-Drucker." Die Aussage wirkt jetzt ansprechender, und auch Nicht-Techniker – beispielsweise aus der Verwaltung – können die Nachricht verstehen und sich damit identifizieren.

An dem Beispiel zeigt sich zudem, wie wichtig es ist, die eigene Firmen-Community zur Beurteilung von Texten heranzuziehen. Mit einem einfachen Pretest, in dem man einer kleinen Gruppe einen Beitrag in zwei Versionen vorlegt, kann man sehr schnell herausfinden, welche Variante besser ankommt und welche Tonlage und Sprachqualität für die Mitarbeiter wirklich attraktiv ist. Das Intranet lebt von guten, spannenden und abwechslungsreichen Inhalten und nicht von offiziellen Marketing- und PR-Sprechblasen. Mitarbeiter haben für abgedroschenes Firmen-Blabla nichts übrig.

Oft ist die Intranet-Redaktion bei der Abteilung Unternehmenskommunikation angebunden. Dadurch ergeben sich schnell unnötige Restriktionen, die eine journalistisch attraktive, professionelle Aufbereitung der Inhalte verhindern. Diese Inhalte sind jedoch für ein zeitgemäßes Intranet, das im Sinne eines fortschrittlichen Employer Brandings auch jüngere Mitarbeiter anspricht, unverzichtbar. Es lohnt sich daher, im Rahmen von Trainings und Schulungen in die journalistische Qualität der Intranet-Redakteure zu investieren und nicht nur in die technischen Systeme.

Grundsätzlich können die Kommunikationstrainings auf drei Ebenen stattfinden.

Die Redakteure als Content-Organisatoren

Die Inhalte im Intranet sollen Wissen, Interaktivität, Dialog und Aktualität miteinander verbinden. Das ist nicht einfach, zumal das Web 2.0 die klassische Intranet-Redaktion nicht nur entlastet, sondern auch ein konkurrierender Faktor ist. Damit wachsen die Herausforderungen an qualitativ guten Content. Gerade jüngere Mitarbeiter – häufig als Innovators oder Early Adopters bezeichnet – erwarten auch im Intranet eine professionelle journalistische Aufbe-

reitung von News, Beiträgen, Reportagen oder Porträts. Dazu gehören: gut lesbare Inhalte mit interessanten Informationen; spannende Magazinbeiträge, die sich hinter einem prominenten Medium wie „brand eins" nicht verstecken müssen und wirkliche Innenansichten zu neuen Unternehmensprojekten bieten; attraktive Serviceinformationen, die den eigenen Workflow erleichtern und Entscheidungssicherheit geben. Mit regelmäßigen Redaktionstrainings können neue Intranet-Mitarbeiter dem eigenen Intranet einen Kreativitätsschub geben, sodass Nutzerzahlen und Informationszufriedenheit spürbar steigen.

Redakteure überzeugen

Bei einem Energieerzeuger erschien es anfangs nicht einfach, die Redakteure des Intranets von den geplanten Neuerungen zu überzeugen, obwohl die Schwächen offenkundig waren. So stellte jede Abteilung für sich auf ihrer eigenen Abteilungsstartseite Mitarbeiter vor und informierte über Abteilungsneuigkeiten. Mit dem Relaunch sollte ihnen nichts „weggenommen werden", andererseits sollte aber das vorherrschende Abteilungsdenken aufgelöst werden. In einem ersten Schritt wurde den Redakteuren aufgezeigt, dass bestimmte Abteilungsseiten einfach zu wenig angeschaut wurden, weil sich kein Nutzer durch alle Abteilungen klickt. Beim neuen Redaktionssystem konnten die Redakteure ihre Abteilungsseiten weiter pflegen, aber gleichzeitig Inhalte daraus für die Startseite des kompletten Intranets und damit allen Nutzern vorschlagen. Der Chefredakteur der Startseite ging diese Vorschläge durch und gab die Freigabe zur Veröffentlichung. Ein Schreibtraining sorgte für gute Qualität.

Die Mitarbeiter als Top-Empfänger und Top-Beteiligte

Bei einem Social Intranet sollte der Kreis der schreibenden Mitarbeiter eigentlich wachsen, doch häufig grassiert die Angst, man könnte sich durch unprofessionelle Beiträge blamieren. Wenn in den Themen-Blogs Beitragsmangel herrscht, so liegt das meist an einer solchen bänglichen Einstellung. Die Blogs wurden zwar mit besten Absichten gestartet, doch werden sie von den Mitarbeitern nicht gefüllt. Auch hier können Schulungen und Trainings helfen, bestehende Befürchtungen abzubauen und den schreibwilligen Mitarbeitern die nötige Sicherheit für einen souveränen Umgang mit dem Social Intranet zu geben.

Führungskräfte als Vorbilder:

Management-Blog

Bei einem Folienhersteller sprachen zwei Gründe für einen Management-Blog auf der Startseite: Erstens wollte das Intranet-Team auf der Startseite die Präsenz der Führungskräfte mit ihrer Vorbildfunktion zeigen. Zweitens verfügte das Management über keinen geeigneten Kanal, um Mitarbeiter schnell über relevante Dinge zu informieren und mehr Nähe zur Basis aufzubauen.

Der Blogbereich auf der Startseite wies nach der Integration des Management-Blogs stets aktuelle Inhalte auf, weil von den 25 Führungskräften immer eine Person aktuell etwas berichtete. Für ein gutes Sicherheitsgefühl bei diesem neuen Informationskanal sorgte eine technische Schulung der Führungskräfte. Außerdem erhielt die bisherige Chefredakteurin des abgeschafften E-Mail-Newsletters eine neue verantwortungsvolle Aufgabe, nämlich das Checken und Optimieren der Beiträge vor der Veröffentlichung.

Management-Blogs und Namensbeiträge der Geschäftsleitung sind ein gutes Mittel für CEO-Positioning und Personal Branding im Innern – vorausgesetzt, die schreibenden Führungskräfte versuchen nicht, in gewohnter Hurra-Manier werblich ihre Unternehmenserfolge zu preisen. Vielmehr geht es auch hier darum, den Leser einzufangen, ihn zu interessieren. In speziellen Trainings wird das Themen- und Kompetenzprofil für bloggende Manager erarbeitet. Die Texte müssen punktgenau geschrieben werden. Sie müssen abwechslungsreich und authentisch sein und um spannende Geschichten aus dem persönlichen Umfeld oder dem Geschäftsgeschehen kreisen. All das lässt sich trainieren und mit jeder Veröffentlichung im Intranet sammelt man Erfahrungen, wie es beim nächsten Versuch noch besser gehen könnte. So erhöht sich das Vertrauen in die Unternehmensführung und der aktive Dialog stärkt die Bindung der Mitarbeiter an das Unternehmen. Positiver Nebeneffekt: Die Bedeutung des Social Intranet wird durch die regelmäßige Beteiligung der Geschäftsleitung erhöht. Zudem wird das Intranet, das nun zur Diskussion und Kommentierung einlädt, tatsächlich zu einem ‚must have' für gut informierte Mitarbeiter.

Liebe Intranet-Redakteure, wenn nun der Eindruck entstanden sein sollte, Sie werden „arbeitslos", weil jeder Mitarbeiter künftig selbst Beiträge verfasst – weit gefehlt! Redaktionell anspruchsvoll aufbereitete Texte auf Informationsseiten werden nach wie vor benötigt und neue spannende Herausforderungen warten bereits.

Als Berater unterstützen Redakteure insbesondere das mittlere Management und das Top-Management bei der Erarbeitung von Intranet-Beiträgen. In ihrer neuen Moderatoren-Rolle regen sie Diskussionen an, lenken sie und bewerten und kommentieren Beiträge. Sie schulen schreibinteressierte Mitarbeiter und kontrollieren die Einhaltung der Social-Media-Guidelines.

Nicht zu vergessen: Vor dem Start sind Kommunikationsmittel und Schulungsmaterialien erforderlich, ein inhaltsreiches Intranet mit aufbereiteten Erfolgsgeschichten aus den Pilotprojekten, einem Überblick über bestehende Inhalte vor der Migration und, und, und.

Liebe Redakteure, die neue Plattform braucht Sie in Ihrer interessantesten Rolle – als Intranet- und Kommunikationsmanager!

5.5 MIGRATIONSDURCHFÜHRUNG

Der technische und konzeptionelle Rahmen für das neue Intranet steht. Mithilfe von Tests wurden letzte Fehler beseitigt. Nun gilt es, die Inhalte dadurch attraktiv zu machen, dass Altbewährtes ins neue Intranet überführt wird und die Nutzer auf möglichst wenige Altanwendungen zurückgreifen müssen. Zu einer Migration gehört auch, dass die alten bzw. konsolidierten Systeme nach erfolgreicher Umstellung konsequent abgeschaltet werden.

Zwei Gründe dafür sollen hier behandelt werden.

Erstens ist dies die Voraussetzung für die Akzeptanz bei den Anwendern. Wenn nicht die Notwendigkeit besteht, sich auf das neue System einzulassen, weil die alte und gewohnte Umgebung immer noch zur Verfügung steht, werden zumindest einige Anwender weiterhin die bisherige Umgebung nutzen.

Der zweite Aspekt ist der Umgang mit Ressourcen wie Hardware und Lizenzen im Unternehmen. Eine Migration oder Umstellung sollte immer auch zum Ziel haben, die alten Systeme abzuschalten und dadurch Kosten, die durch die Migration entstehen, zumindest teilweise zu kompensieren.

Für eine erfolgreiche Migration ist eine Checkliste erforderlich, die in Tests bestätigt worden ist. Doch Achtung: Trotz bester Vorbereitung und ausführlicher Tests im Vorfeld kann es zu unvorhergesehenen Problemen kommen. Es ist daher wichtig, dass vor der Durchführung geklärt ist, wie mit Problemen umgegangen wird und wer entscheidet, welche Maßnahme einzuleiten ist. UND: Bevor Sie anfangen zu migrieren, stellen Sie sicher, dass Sie ein funktionierendes Backup angefertigt haben. Dann kann nichts mehr schiefgehen.

Migrationslotsen bei der Luzerner Kantonalbank

Bei der Migration des Intranets der Luzerner Kantonalbank wurden nur ca. 20 bis 30 Prozent der alten Daten übernommen. Rund 30 Mitarbeiter – sogenannte Migrationsautoren – aus verschiedenen Bereichen der Bank haben die für ihren Bereich relevanten Inhalte aufbereitet. Das heißt sie haben bestehende Inhalte überarbeitet, erweitert und häufig komplett neu erstellt. Die Migration der Inhalte fand innerhalb von rund drei Monaten statt. Diesen zum Teil sehr großen Arbeitsaufwand haben die Mitarbeiter zusätzlich zu ihrer regulären Tätigkeit erbracht. Der Mehrwert für die Bank? „Die Migrationsautoren waren Botschafter in Sachen Intranet und fungierten damit als wertvolle Multiplikatoren", sagt Roger Müller, der stellvertretende Kommunikationsleiter.

Dieser Abschnitt entstand in Zusammenarbeit mit Roger Müller, Stv. Leiter Kommunikation / Mediensprecher Luzerner Kantonalbank AG

Metadaten als Erfolgsfaktor

Metadaten – bei diesem Begriff ziehen viele die Köpfe ein. Nicht so bei der Luzerner Kantonalbank! Roger Müller hält sie sogar für einen wichtigen Erfolgsfaktor: „Unsere perfekten Metadaten und damit die konsequente Verschlagwortung unserer Dokumente und Intranet-Seiten sind zentrale Elemente für die hohe Qualität und den Erfolg unseres Intranets. Deshalb haben wir darauf von Anfang an großen Wert gelegt."

Auch hier haben die Migrationsautoren ganze Arbeit geleistet: Die angelegten Ordner wurden verschlagwortet. Beim Erstellen neuer Seiten werden diese Schlagworte automatisch „nach unten" vererbt. Die Redakteure wurden im Verschlagworten trainiert. Unterstützung erhalten Mitarbeiter auch durch das MatchPoint-Framework. Im Alltagsstress hilft das System, in dem neue Inhalte automatisch mit vererbten Metadaten versehen werden und sich die Datenqualität damit praktisch „ohne Aufwand" verbessert. Am Ende lohnt sich das für alle: Daten werden schnell gefunden, können strukturübergreifend angezeigt und effizient genutzt werden.

Die Produktseiten sind immer gleich aufgebaut (in-page TAB Navigation mit acht Laschen). Wie alle Intranet-Seiten zeigen sie jeweils einen Sachverständigen, der zum Inhalt dieser Seite Auskunft geben kann. Die Bereiche "Ergänzende Produkte" und "IDV Dokumente" auf den Produktseiten werden automatisch befüllt aufgrund der Metadaten.

Abbildung 5.5.1: Produktseite (Luzerner Kantonalbank)

5.6

AUF NEUN PUNKTE GEBRACHT

1 Die Phase des Testens wird oft unterschätzt. Geplantes und koordiniertes Testen ist jedoch die Grundlage für einen holperfreien Start. Definieren Sie die für Ihre Lösung relevanten Testfälle und führen Sie Tests und Auswertungen in Zusammenarbeit mit Nutzern und Entwicklern durch.

2 Fehler verzögern das Ausrollen der Lösung. Planen Sie neben der eigentlichen Testphase auch Zeiten für die Behebung der gefundenen Fehler oder Unstimmigkeiten ein.

3 Schon vor dem Rollout integrieren sorgfältig ausgewählte Pilotgruppen die neuen Arbeitsweisen in den Arbeitsalltag. Der Pilotansatz hilft, die Projekte klein zu halten und agil zu gestalten. Lernen Sie daraus für den großen Rollout!

4 Der Erfolg der Pilotprojekte kann auf das ganze Unternehmen ausstrahlen. Begleiten Sie Ihre Pilotteams eng und stellen Sie so sicher, dass aus den Piloten Leuchtturm-Projekte werden. So haben Sie Stoff für eine authentische Kommunikation.

5 Ohne aktive Führungskräfte läuft das Intranet nicht. Machen Sie den Mehrwert erlebbar und motivieren Sie die Führungskräfte, Verantwortung für eine erfolgreiche Intranet-Einführung zu übernehmen. Scheuen Sie dabei nicht den Diskurs über wichtige Themen wie Vertrauenskultur oder die Sorge vor Kontrollverlust.

6 Multiplikatoren haben oft ein gutes Standing. Nutzen Sie das!

7 Befürchtungen der Mitarbeiter sind ernst zu nehmen. Begleiten Sie die Einführung mit gezielten internen Kommunikations- und Motivationsmaßnahmen. Bauen Sie durch gezielte Schulungen Ängste im Umgang mit der neuen Plattform ab und stärken Sie die Beteiligung.

8 Ein gutes Intranet lässt Spaß beim Entdecken zu. Erklären Sie die Plattform und Tools auf spielerische Weise und wecken Sie so Lust auf's Intranet. Seien Sie dabei offen für neue Lernformate.

9 Gleich geht es los. Lassen Sie Ihr Intranet nicht „nackt" ins Unternehmen starten! Denken Sie an die Befüllung mit ersten Inhalten schon vor dem Start der Trainings.

Los geht`s!

1 TRÄUME 2 ANALYSIERE 3 PLANE 4 BAUE 5 ERPROBE 6 NUTZE

NUTZE

Mit einem würdigen Einführungsszenario wird das Social Intranet gestartet. Die Nutzer werden motiviert, aktiviert und mit zahlreichen Supportmaßnahmen in den Arbeitsalltag begleitet. Abschließende Evaluationsmaßnahmen lassen Verbesserungspotenzial erkennen.

Wenn das Intranet technisch einwandfrei läuft, von allen Anwendern aktiv genutzt wird und die Betreuung des Intranets etabliert ist, kann die sechste Phase und damit das Projekt abgeschlossen werden.

STARTSCHUSS FÜR
DAS INTRANET

Einführungsstrategie umsetzen

Welche Dramaturgie soll ich für die Einführung wählen? Eine inszenierte, etappenweise Lüftung des Intranet-Geheimnisses? Ein Launch mit Pauken und Trompeten? Oder doch lieber die sachliche Einführung nach und nach im laufenden Arbeitsprozess? Die Art der Einführung ist vor allem abhängig von der Unternehmenskultur, dem Zeitrahmen, den zur Verfügung stehenden Ressourcen und von der Kreativität der Intranet-Macher. Und natürlich von den geplanten Rollout-Etappen, über die Sie sich schon in Phase 3 Gedanken gemacht haben. Wir haben sie im Buch hier in Phase 6 beim Start verortet.

Big-Bang-Strategie

Der Name sagt es schon: Mit einem großen Schlag wird das gesamte Intranet auf einmal gelaunched und das alte System vollständig zum Stichtag abgelöst. Vor allem dann, wenn es im Unternehmen den Druck gibt, sofort zu starten, wird diese Variante häufig gewählt. Gibt es mehrere Standorte, erfolgt der lokale Big Bang ggf. an den einzelnen Standorten nacheinander. Theoretisch klingt das nach der besten Lösung, zumal alle sofort auf das neue System zugreifen können und es keine Parallelsysteme und keine Doppelarbeit in der Übergangsphase gibt. Überlegen Sie jedoch: Die Chance für einen Big Bang gibt es nur ein einziges Mal. Sollten sich Schwierigkeiten beim Einhalten des Veröffentlichungstermins ergeben, kann es zu unerfreulichen Reaktionen kommen. Weitere Risiken

entstehen durch die hohe Belastung aller Projektbeteiligten und durch die Gefahr zu vieler System-Bugs oder gar eines totalen Ausfalls des Intranets.

Um den notwendigen Hype für einen Big Bang aufzubauen, stellen Sie sicher, dass Sie für das neue Intranet bei jeder sich bietenden Gelegenheit werben. Dieser Weg sorgt auf jeden Fall für die notwendige Aufmerksamkeit.

Fokussierte Big-Bang-Strategie

Wem der Big Bang eine Nummer zu groß ist, der hat mit dem fokussierten Big Bang eine gute Alternative. Mit dieser iterativen Einführungsstrategie (iterativ als sich wiederholender Prozess) wird in einer Art Schleife zunächst das bisherige klassische Intranet einer strukturellen Neukonzeption unterzogen und auf eine zukunftsfähige technische Plattform gehoben. Dabei können erste einfache soziale Funktionen wie zum Beispiel Kommentare oder Bewertungen ermöglicht werden. Der Intranet-Nutzer bleibt vorwiegend Konsument im neu geordneten Intranet. Die gewohnte Push-Kommunikation (top-down) ins Unternehmen wird abgebildet, jedoch inklusive der neuen technischen Funktionen (Enterprise-Search, RSS, Benachrichtigungsfunktionen, mobile Ansichten etc.) In der nächsten Ausbaustufe (oder parallel/iterativ dazu) folgen dann diejenigen Funktionen die den Nutzer zum Produzenten von Inhalten machen. Er kann Netzwerke und Communities aufbauen und mit Kollegen zusammenarbeiten.

Ein neues Push-Intranet dieser Art erschließt sich dem Nutzer leicht. Die schnelle Akzeptanz der neuen technischen Plattform senkt die Eintrittsbarriere. Zusätzlich werden wertvolle Ressourcen geschont. Andererseits gilt: Mitarbeiter, die auf die einfachen Möglichkeiten zur internen Vernetzung und Zusammenarbeit schon lange warten, werden in der 1. Phase dieses Rollouts eher verprellt. Überhaupt ist das volle Programm der strategisch geplanten Plattform in dieser Phase noch nicht erkennbar. Die bevorstehenden Veränderungen müssen daher unbedingt kommuniziert werden, sodass sie in Umrissen sichtbar sind. Eine längere Laufzeit birgt zudem das Risiko eines vorzeitigen Abbruchs der Social-Collaboration-Einführung, da der Erfolg zu lange verborgen bleibt. Durch den Druck aus den Fachbereichen entstehen neue Insellösungen, die man eigentlich vermeiden wollte.

Funktions-Strategie

Sukzessive werden verschiedene Funktionalitäten freigeschaltet, beispielsweise zuerst die der Dokumentenbearbeitung und Aufgabenverteilung, später die Social-Elemente und die Echtzeit-Kommunikation. Das Projektrisiko ist gering und die Mitarbeiter werden nach und nach an die neuen Funktionalitäten herangeführt. Allerdings gibt es kein komplettes integriertes System während der Übergangsphase.

Prozess-Strategie

Bei der schrittweisen prozessorientierten Einführung beginnt man am besten mit den unkritischen Abläufen. Es besteht ein geringeres Risiko, wenn die Teilprozesse nicht miteinander verknüpft sind. Wie bei der Funktions-Strategie gibt es kein integriertes System während der Übergangsphase und meist tritt Doppelarbeit auf.

Abteilungs-Strategie

Einzelne Abteilungen erhalten nach und nach Zugriff auf die neue Plattform. Der Reiz wird erhöht, wenn die Abteilungen sich um den Start bewerben dürfen. Die Implementierung läuft getreu der Devise „Wettbewerb belebt das Intranet-Geschäft" oder „Wer zuerst kommt, teilt zuerst". Die Einzelprojekte sind überschaubar und die Abteilungen können voneinander lernen. Allerdings sollte der Gesamtzeitraum nicht unnötig ausgedehnt werden, weil sonst im Unternehmen zwei Geschwindigkeiten der Einführung entstehen. Es wird schwierig, wenn eine Abteilung mit dem neuen System und eine Abteilung mit dem alten System zusammenarbeiten müssen.

Pilot-Strategie

Bei der Pilot-Strategie bringt man nach und nach verschiedene Projekte zum Leuchten und verbreitet dann die frohe Kunde, welche die anderen Mitarbeiter im Unternehmen ansteckt. Die Erfahrungen der Teilprojekte können genutzt werden, so dass mit jedem Piloten die Erfolgsgarantie steigt. Eine wunderbare Strategie, die jedoch ein paar kleine Nachteile hat: Man durchlebt den Launch mit all seinen Risiken mehrmals und die Zusammenarbeit ist wie bei der Abteilungs-Strategie nicht konsistent. Die Erfolge sind aber wegen der gesammelten Erfahrungen, der Testschleifen und des Gesprächsstoffs viel wert.

Viral-Strategie

Die neue Plattform wird mit ein paar besonders engagierten Nutzern aufgebaut. Deren Zufriedenheit spricht sich sicher schnell in der Organisation herum, sodass weitere Nutzer mit dem neuen System unbedingt arbeiten wollen. Um mit dieser Strategie erfolgreich zu sein, sollten allerdings viel Geduld und ein Plan B vorhanden sein, falls die Mitarbeiter nicht mitziehen.

Viral ist chic. Das denkt heute jede zweite Kommunikationsabteilung. Deshalb erzähle ich auch so gern die Geschichte von den viralen Glückskeksen der ANWR GROUP.
Die hat kurz vor dem Start ihrer neuen Plattform „MY ANWR" Glückskekse statt mit den üblichen Weisheiten mit Links zu unterschiedlichen Intranet-Seiten, die vorher noch kein Mitarbeiter zu sehen bekommen hatte, gefüllt. Da jeder nun möglichst viele Seiten vorab sehen wollte, auch wenn man darauf noch nicht navigieren konnte, tauschten die Mitarbeiter die Links aus. Mit wenig Aufwand wurde das neue Intranet so zum Gesprächsthema Nr. 1.

Launch Event

Das Launch-Event kennzeichnet als Auftaktveranstaltung den offiziellen Start des neuen Intranets für alle Nutzergruppen. Ein Launch im Sinne einer Unternehmensveranstaltung ist natürlich kein Muss, jedoch sollte das Intranet einer würdigen Start bekommen. Nach meist einem Jahr Arbeit ist ein Launch-Event die entsprechende Würdigung aller Beteiligten und markiert sozusagen die Freigabe und den Startschuss für das Arbeiten in der neuen Arbeitswelt

Für das Launch-Event können verschiedene Vorgehensweisen gewählt werden:

- Ansprache der Geschäftsführung mit Übertragung in alle Bereiche und Standorte;
- Launch-Party mit allen Unterstützern;
- Verteilung von Starter-Kits;
- Feierliche „Übergabe" des Intranets an die Nutzer mit Durchschneiden eines Bandes;
- Town-Hall-Meeting: Präsentation und Beantwortung von Fragen;
- Emotionale Präsentation „What's new?", verknüpft mit der neuen Unternehmensvision;
- Lockere Expertendiskussion mit den Machern, von einem prominenten Moderator geführt.

Dass nicht in jedem Unternehmen ein Launch-Event im großen Stil möglich ist, sollte jedoch nicht dazu führen, dem Intranet-Start überhaupt keine Beachtung zu schenken. Eine offizielle „Eröffnung" sollte in jedem Falle stattfinden, denn sie bietet viele Vorteile:

- Umfassende Aufmerksamkeit für die neue Plattform;
- Sichtbare Unterstützung der Unternehmensführung;
- Eine positive Grundstimmung;
- Die Möglichkeit, die Neuerung als Besonderheit vorzustellen, und die Gründe noch einmal zu kommunizieren;
- Hinweise auf Support und Unterstützungsmöglichkeiten für die Teams;
- Beantwortung offener Fragen;
- „Starthilfe" für unerfahrene Nutzer.

Kommunikation zum Start und danach

So manches Intranet-Team lässt sich in der Startphase besondere Maßnahmen einfallen, um viel Aufmerksamkeit für die neue Plattform zu erlangen, mit den Nutzern in den Dialog zu treten oder die Mitarbeiter zu vernetzen.

! Praxistipps: Sechs Ideen für den Start des Intranets

1. **Botschafter ernennen:** Es ist beruhigend für Nutzer, wenn für den Fall der Fälle ein helfender Mensch in der Nähe ist. Statten Sie in der Startwoche Intranet-Botschafter mit T-Shirt oder Mützen aus, damit sie als Ansprechpartner erkennbar sind.

2. **Schatzsuche veranstalten:** Verstecken Sie im Intranet kleine Schätze, die gehoben werden müssen. Hat man die Seite X erreicht, findet man eine Belohnung und weiterführende Klick-Aufforderungen, um das Intranet kennenzulernen.

3. **Intranet-Get-Together organisieren:** Veranstalten Sie ein Frühstück oder Lunch mit gebrandeten Lebensmitteln (es eignet sich der Intranet-Name) oder auch ein Kuchenbuffet.

4. **Kantinen-Bündnisse schließen:** Die Cafeteria eignet sich ebenfalls als Ort, um Hinweise zu verteilen. Lassen Sie beispielsweise Servietten oder Tablettunterleger bedrucken. Noch besser: ein Intranet-Dessert in Intranet-Farben am Starttag.

5. **Erfolge präsentieren:** Stellen Sie Bildschirme bereit, beispielsweise im Eingangsbereich, um erste Erfolgsgeschichten zu präsentieren.

6. **Interaktive Führungen gestalten:** Schicken Sie die Nutzer mit einem Video vorab oder einem Demo/Klick-Dummy auf eine erste Entdeckungsreise durch das Intranet.

Welche Themen sollten beim Start eine Rolle spielen? Hier Anregungen dazu:

Themen zum Start

- Vision und Ziele;
- Neue Inhalte im Intranet;
- Bewerbung von Inhalten, die hohe Aufmerksamkeit auf sich ziehen, sich herumsprechen und zu schneller Beteiligung animieren;
- Quick-Wins, die schnell Nutzen stiften;
- Mehrwert für die Anwender: Was geht schneller, einfacher, besser?
- Würdigung des Projektteams;
- Vorstellung von verdienten Power Usern und Multiplikatoren.

Themen in der Phase nach dem Start

Auch nach dem gelungenen Launch sollte die Kommunikation weiterhin aufrechterhalten werden:

- Erwähnung von besonders engagierten Nutzern,
- Interviews,
- Best-Practice-Beispiele,
- Erfolgsgeschichten,
- Tipps und Tricks,
- Bewerbung Trainingsbereich und Hilfecenter im Intranet,
- Umfragen,
- Wettbewerbe,
- No-E-Mail-Tag.

MITARBEITERAKTIVIERUNG 6.2

Stellen Sie sich vor, das neue Intranet ist fertig und keiner geht hin. Bevor sich die Social-Technologien durchsetzten und viele Intranet-Projekte als reine IT-Projekte galten, waren viele Projektverantwortliche froh, wenn die Nutzerzahlen bei 45% lagen. Wir sind uns einig: Social Intranet gelingt nur mit nahezu hundertprozentiger Beteiligung. Doch wie schafft man das?

Wenn man die vorhergehenden Kapitel in einem Satz zusammenfassen wollte, mündete das in den Ratschlag: Wer motivierte Nutzer will, setzt auf sinnvolle Infos, interessante Inhalte, ansprechendes Design, hohen Bedienkomfort und eine ergiebige Antwort auf die Frage: Was habe ich davon? Je besser die Vorarbeit, desto weniger Arbeit bei der Mitarbeiteraktivierung in Phase 6.

Das Social Intranet bietet eine neue Technologie, die Nutzer und deren Aktivitäten sichtbar macht. Wenn Mitarbeiter spüren: Ja, sie werden wahrgenommen, sie werden als Kenner geschätzt, sie werden mit Anerkennungen in Form von Likes und Kommentaren bedacht, sie sind involviert, wenn entschieden wird, und sie können sich abseits von Hierarchien mit jedem im Unternehmen austauschen, dann entfaltet das eine enorme Kraft. Nutzen Sie die vorhandenen Möglichkeiten, den Umgang mit dem System auf aufregende Weise zu fördern und zu belohnen.

Doch müssen die neuen Arbeitsweisen erst beherrscht und die Vorteile der Social-Technologien erlebt werden. Wir schrieben vom Huhn-Ei-Problem. In Phase 6 werden besondere Maßnahmen zur Motivation und Aktivierung benötigt. Kleine Anreize und Belohnungen können dafür sorgen, dass die Bereitschaft der User zur Benutzung des Intranets steigt. Das sind jedoch allenfalls punktuelle Maßnahmen und ersetzen nicht die im Buch zuvor beschriebenen Vorbereitungen.

Entwickeln Sie Anreize und Belohnungen, die zu Ihrer Unternehmenskultur passen und möglichst langfristig einen Mehrwert erzielen. Hier ein Beispiel: Ein Softwarehersteller wollte mehr Videos in seinem Intranet. Ausgewählte Video-Redakteure erhielten dafür eine professionelle Kamera. Die Filme wurden dann von der Intranet-Community bewertet – durch Likes und Kommentare. Wer viel Resonanz in der Community fand, der durfte die Kamera auch privat nutzen.

Erste Hürde – das eigene Profil

Zu den ersten Nutzer-Schritten im Intranet gehört das Ausfüllen der Profilseite. Gleichzeitig scheint das aber aus Sicht des Projektteams auch die erste Hürde zu sein. Mitarbeiter müssen ihre Einwilligung zum Einstellen der Fotos geben, was auch mit dem Betriebsrat abgeklärt sein muss. Wie bekommen wir die User dazu, Ihre Profildaten zu vervollständigen?

! **Praxistipps:** Sieben Ideen, wie die Mitarbeiter motiviert werden, ihr Profil anzureichern

1. **Mitarbeiterbefragung:** Eine Vorab-Umfrage hilft herauszufinden, was die Mitarbeiter gerne von ihren Kollegen lesen möchten. Mit Sicherheit steigert die Neugier auf die Angaben der anderen die Bereitschaft, die eigene Profilseite auszufüllen.

2. **Überzeugen:** Die Vorteile der Profilseite liegen auf der Hand: Kollegen finden einander schneller, man lernt sich besser kennen und man kann sich mit seiner Expertise gut positionieren. Das sollte allen klar gemacht werden.

3. **Gutes Beispiel:** Toll, wenn die Geschäftsführung und das Management mit gutem Beispiel vorangehen und ihre Profilseite schon vor dem Launch ausfüllen.

4. **Automatik:** Bestimmte bereits vorhandene Daten wie Name, Position, Durchwahl und E-Mail-Adresse können schon vor dem offiziellen Start automatisch in der Profilseite eingetragen sein.

5. **Selbstauslöser:** Stellt ein Unternehmen eine Kamera (mit Selbstauslöser) zur Verfügung, können sich die Mitarbeiter selbst fotografieren. Diese Bilder werden dann direkt auf die Profilseite hochgeladen. Eine Fotosession mit Profi-Fotograf kann auch als „Event" in der Phase vor dem Launch die Aufmerksamkeit auf das Intranet lenken.

6. **Anreizerhöhung mit Belohnung:** „Die ersten 100 User, die bis Freitag ihre Profilseite ausgefüllt haben, erhalten eine kleine Überraschung."

7. **Gamification:** Ein Fortschrittsbalken (keine Standardfunktion) motiviert. Er zeigt an, wie viel Prozent der Angaben bereits erledigt sind. Das Ganze kann auch mit einem Belohnungssystem gekoppelt werden.

> ## „Bitte lächeln!" bei einem Kunststoffhersteller
>
> Das Thema Fotos für die Profilseiten erregt bei Mitarbeitern häufig Widerstände und wird daher von den Projektteams als problematisch eingeschätzt. Ein Kunststoffhersteller agierte nach dem Motto „Tatsachen schaffen". Innerhalb des Projektteams erinnerte man sich, dass im Unternehmen eine Kollegin für das Fotografieren von Produkten verantwortlich ist. Schnell waren die Genehmigungen (auch vom Betriebsrat!) eingeholt, dass diese Kollegin alle Profilseiten-Fotos der Intranet-Nutzer erstellt.
>
> Zuerst wurden die Multiplikatoren zum Fototermin geladen. In ihren Abteilungen konnten sich im Anschluss die Mitarbeiter in Terminlisten eintragen. Dass die Mitarbeiter beim Fototermin erstmals einen Blick auf die neue Startseite werfen durften, war ein kleiner Anreiz und erhöhte die Spannung.
>
> Beim Foto-Termin selbst gaben die Mitarbeiter ihre schriftliche Einwilligung für die Verwendung des Fotos auf der MySite. Kurz vor ihrer Einführungsschulung erhielten sie schließlich ihre Fotos per E-Mail; ihr Bild konnten sie dann im Laufe der Schulung direkt auf die eigene Profilseite hochladen. Damit bekam jeder Mitarbeiter von Anfang an ganz natürlich im Intranet ein Gesicht, was wesentlich dazu beitrug, dass der Austausch im Newsfeed so gut angenommen wurde und die Personal-News auf der Startseite ein echter Hingucker wurden. Übrigens: Die Mitarbeiter erhielten die Fotos auch für die private Nutzung – eine schöne Geste, die sehr positiv ankam.

Gamification – nicht ohne Strategie

KURZE EINFÜHRUNG

Ein Thema, das im Zusammenhang mit der Nutzeraktivierung oft genannt wird, ist Gamification. Damit meint man den Einsatz motivierender, spieltypischer Elemente und Prozesse im sonst vorwiegend spielfreien Kontext wie der Arbeit. Die Nutzer sollen angeregt werden, Dinge zu tun, die sie sonst ungern oder nicht so oft tun würden, weil sie sie als monoton oder langweilig empfinden, wie zum Beispiel das Erarbeiten von Berichten oder die Teilnahme an Befragungen. Durch Gamification-Elemente erhalten die Nutzer positive Rückmeldungen auf ihr Handeln, also Bestätigung und Motivation.

Der Marktforschungsspezialist Gartner (Goasduff & Pettey, 2014) identifizierte die vier wichtigsten Antriebe durch Gamification und unterstrich damit die Bedeutung von Spielen in Unternehmen:

- **Beschleunigte Feedback-Zyklen:** In der realen Welt erhält man häufig nur in sehr langen Zeitabständen Feedbacks, z.B. im Rahmen jährlicher Leistungsbeurteilungen. Gamification erhöht die Geschwindigkeit der Rückkopplungsschleifen, um das Engagement zu halten.

- **Klare Ziele und Spielregeln:** Im Gegensatz zur realen Welt, wo Ziele unscharf sind und Regeln selektiv angewandt werden, bietet Gamification klare Ziele und klar definierte Spielregeln, mit denen sich Spieler ermutigt fühlen, Ziele zu erreichen.

- **Eine fesselnde Geschichte:** Während in der realen Welt Tätigkeiten nicht immer fesselnd sind, baut Gamification eine Geschichte auf, die den Spieler zur Teilnahme motiviert und bis zur Erreichung der Ziele bindet.

- **Herausfordernde Aufgaben, die erfüllbar sind:** Zwar gibt es in der realen Welt keinen Mangel an Herausforderungen, doch sind diese Aufgaben oft zu groß und eher langfristig zu bewältigen. Gamification bietet viele kurzfristig erreichbare Ziele, um das Engagement zu halten.

Spiele liefern laut „Gamification fürs Geschäft" (Herzig & Ameling, 2012)
- Klares Feedback
- Ein Gefühl von Fortschritt/Entwicklung
- Die Möglichkeit erfolgreich zu sein
- Geistige Übung
- Eine Chance, die Neugierde zu befriedigen
- Chancen, Probleme zu lösen
- Ein Gefühl von Freiheit

Zu spieltypischen Elementen gehören unter anderem:

Fortschrittsanzeigen

Sie geben Auskunft darüber, wie weit man bei einer Aufgabe vorangeschritten ist. Das Ganze kann in Form von Balken, Kreisdiagrammen oder einer Prozentanzeige visuell aufbereitet sein. Gerade bei ungeliebten Aufgaben ist die Auskunft „Es sind bereits 75 Prozent geschafft" ein must-have, damit die Aufgabe auch wirklich zu Ende geführt wird. Praktisch angewendet kennen wir das Ganze in Form von Fortschrittsbalken beim Ausfüllen eines Umfrageformulars.

Quests

Um einfache oder Routine-Aufgaben mit einem kleinen Anreiz zu versehen, kann man auch den Faktor Zeit ins Spiel bringen: Die Aufgabe soll zügig erledigt werden. Mit einer kleinen Belohnung, z.B. in Form eines Abzeichens, erhöht man die Effektivität und sorgt für die Erinnerung, die ungeliebte Reisekostenabrechnung wirklich zeitnah fertig zu stellen.

Punktesysteme

Auch Punktesysteme, bei denen Mitarbeiter für ihre aktive Mitarbeit im Intranet belohnt werden, motivieren spielerisch. Für einen Post oder einen Blogbeitrag erhält man beispielsweise einen Punkt. Erhält ein Beitrag ein Rating von fünf Sternen, gibt es 20 Punkte zusätzlich. Dies kann individuell mit einem firmeninternen Anerkennungs- und Motivationssystem kombiniert werden. „Vielpunkter" werden mit Privilegien wie z.B. einem Expertenstatus belohnt: Für sie wird das Expertenlevel freigeschaltet, sie erhalten Zugriff auf Expertenwissen oder besondere Bereiche im Intranet.

Ranglisten

Ganz ähnlich funktionieren Ranglisten. Allerdings kann sich der Anwender hier mit anderen Mitarbeitern vergleichen. Dieser Vergleich fördert den Wettbewerb untereinander und verstärkt die Intensität der Nutzung. Bekannt ist diese Art von Motivation z.B. von Computerspielen. Und übrigens: Jedes Punkt-Spiel funktioniert letztlich nach demselben Prinzip.

Community Collaboration

Bei der Teamarbeit geht es oft darum, dass mehrere Anwender eine komplexe Aufgabe gemeinsam lösen müssen. Studien haben gezeigt, dass erfolgreiche Gruppen über einen starken Gruppenzusammenhalt und einen hohen Organisationsgrad verfügen. Genau das will auch Community Collaboration: die erkennbare Zusammenarbeit von mehreren Mitgliedern einer Gruppe. Das stärkt die Verantwortung des Einzelnen für die Gruppe und erhöht die Motivation der ganzen Gruppe.

Resultattransparenz

Frei nach dem Motto „WIIFM – What is in it for me" fußt dieses Spielprinzip darauf, dem Anwender das Ergebnis einer Handlung aufzuzeigen, bevor er eine bestimmte Aktion ausführt. Damit kann er selbst bewerten, was seine nächste Aktion für ihn selbst oder die Gruppe bringen kann. Praktisch können das Belobigungen, Preise oder z.B. der Status als Experte sein.

Quelle: (Wikipedia, 2015)

GAMIFICATION IN DER PRAXIS

Die Praxis hat gezeigt, dass der Einsatz von Gamification nicht die Probleme mit der Nutzerstatistik behebt, vor allem dann nicht, wenn bei der Konzeption und der technischen Umsetzung des Portals Fehler gemacht wurden. Im Gegenteil, schlecht konzipierte Gamification-Strategien können sogar unerwünschte Nebeneffekte haben. Im schlimmsten Fall den Abgang der Nutzer.

Eine falsch oder nicht konzipierte Gamification-Strategie zeichnet sich meist dadurch aus, dass:

- es an vielen Stellen Gamification-Elemente gibt, aber der Nutzer nicht weiß, warum es sie gibt;
- es an den falschen Stellen Gamification-Elemente gibt, die nicht zu den Zielen der Community passen (der Nutzer erhält eine Belohnung für Aktionen, die nicht zum Kern der Community passen);
- Gamification in übertriebenen Szenarien eingesetzt wird (wenn z.B. für einen kleinen Nutzerkreis zu viel Aufwand betrieben wird).

Egal ob Sie eine interne oder externe Community durch Gamification unterstützen wollen, beantworten Sie sich am besten folgende vier Fragen:

1. **Welche:** Welche Ziele existieren in der Community?
2. **Warum:** Warum soll Gamification eingesetzt werden?
3. **Wen:** Wen wollen wir mit diesem Gamification-Element ansprechen?
4. **Wie:** Wie kann Gamification unterstützen (Badges, Punkte,...)?

In der Praxis ist dies meist so noch nicht angekommen. Gamification wird entweder als Wunderwaffe oder Todbringer angesehen. Die meisten Unternehmen wollen daher entweder zu viel oder versuchen es erst gar nicht. Die Gründe dafür reichen von fehlendem Wissen bis hin zu schlechten Erfahrungen. Jedoch ist es meist nicht sinnvoll, Gamification im Übermaß und unüberlegt oder etwa aus Angst vor den Konsequenzen gar nicht im Unternehmen einzusetzen. Vielmehr kommt es darauf an, die beschriebenen Fragen objektiv für sich zu beantworten und eine zur Community passende Gamification-Strategie zu entwickeln.

Gamification im Einsatz muss zwingend als integraler Bestandteil der Community-Strategie angesehen werden. Nur so kann sichergestellt werden, dass ihre Elemente an der richtigen Stelle auch die Ziele unterstützen, die wichtig für die Community als Ganzes sind.

Eine gute Ausgangsbasis für eine passende Gamification-Kultur kann schon ab Phase 2 vorbereitet werden. Bei der Bedarfsabfrage der Nutzer können Kleinigkeiten eingebettet werden, wie die Nutzung von Kartenspielen oder Spielchips zur Priorisierung von Themen und Features. Auch bei den Führungskräften lässt sich Gamification antesten. Mit einer einfachen Methode lässt man den Mehrwert erleben, was sich hoffentlich auf ein Gamification-Budget niederschlägt. Etwas aufwendiger, aber sehr lohnenswert können Zusatzprogrammierungen sein, wie z.B. die im Intranet seit jeher beliebten Fußball-Tippspiele.

Dieser Abschnitt entstand in Zusammenarbeit mit Sandra Brückner, Social Business Consultant Pokeshot///SMZ

Gamification als strategischer Part der Community-Strategie bei einem Sportartikelhersteller

Bei einem Sportartikelhersteller wurde Gamification in der Sport-Community eher als Wunderwaffe denn als strategisches Element angesehen. So wurden an vielen Stellen Badges und Punkte vergeben, ohne dass man sie in eine Verbindung mit der Community-Strategie gebracht hätte. Deshalb liefen die Gamification-Maßnahmen bei den Nutzern weithin ins Leere (Elemente an der falschen Stelle). Daraufhin ging man einen Schritt zurück und schaute auf die Strategie der Sport-Community:

Frage 1: Welche Ziele? Ein Ziel ist es, die Mitglieder durch individuelle Sportpläne dazu zu motivieren, ihre Ergebnisse in die Community einzustellen und zu teilen. Jedoch sollten Gamification-Elemente nicht gleichzeitig bei allen Zielen Anwendung finden, da dies zu einer Überreizung und einem Interessenverlust der Nutzer führen kann (die Community wird langweilig).

Frage 2: Warum? Warum soll Gamification gerade dieses Ziel unterstützen? Warum wird dieses Ziel jetzt unterstützt? Wann folgen weitere Ziele? Es ist wichtig, die Mitglieder zu einem bestimmten Verhalten zu motivieren und dieses Verhalten mit Hilfe von Gamification zu fördern.

Frage Nr. 3: Wen? Dieser Aspekt ist von hoher Bedeutung, da nicht alle Personen durch die gleichen Anreize motiviert werden können. Es existieren verschiedene Typen von „Spielern" (Bartle, 1996): Achiever, Socializer, Explorer, Killer. Jeden Typ sprechen andere Anreize an: der Achiever möchte etwas erreichen (z.B. ein bestimmtes Level), der Socializer möchte mit möglichst vielen Personen in Kontakt treten, der Explorer ist immer auf der Suche nach neuen Herausforderungen und Entdeckungen und der Killer misst sich am liebsten mit anderen Nutzern (Challenges) (Bartle, 1996). Diese Typen sind zwar nicht exklusiv auf eine Person abbildbar, sagen jedoch einiges darüber aus, wer sich in der Community befindet und wie diese kategorisierten Personengruppen angesprochen werden können. Davon ausgehend, dass in einer Sport-Community mehr Achiever- und Killer-Typen sind, konzipierten wir die passenden Gamification-Elemente.

Frage Nr. 4: Wie? Heraus kam ein Gamification-Mix aus der Vergabe von Running-Levels, verschiedenen Challenges (Absolviere diese Woche Plan X), Badges (Runner of the week) und Teamaufgaben (Team A vs. Team B). All diese Elemente galt es im Anschluss aufzugreifen und zeitlich bzw. in Verbindung zueinander einzuordnen: Welche Elemente sind sofort sichtbar, welche Elemente werden erst nach einer bestimmten Zeit oder beim Erreichen eines bestimmten Levels sichtbar?

Dieses Muster muss für jedes Ziel der Community durchdacht werden. Wichtig dabei ist, die Ziele und die passenden Gamification-Maßnahmen zu verzahnen, damit sich verschiedene Elemente mit dem gleichen Ziel nicht überschneiden.

Mit Gamification die Motivation von Multiplikatoren ankurbeln

Eine besondere Bedeutung kam den Multiplikatoren bei Axel Springer zu. Versierte, neugierig-motivierte und aufgeschlossene Mitarbeiter aus den Einführungsteams unterstützten mit Tipps und Tricks die Herangehensweise an die Plattform und waren erste Anlaufstelle für Fragen und Anforderungen. Sie erhielten neben einem individuell auf sie zugeschnittenen Training eine eigene virtuelle Community und einen regelmäßig stattfindenden physischen Stammtisch als Austauschforum für Multiplikatoren-Themen.

Darüber hinaus wurden ihnen passend zur Rolle „Schulterstücke" für ihre wertvolle Aufgabe verliehen. Ein eigener Avatar auf T-Shirts und speziell entworfene Buttons fungierten hierbei als Erkennungszeichen. Das Multiplikatoren-Battle war ein spielerischer Wettbewerb, in dem verschiedene Level erreicht werden konnten. Je nach Aktivität der Pilotteams in CONNECT und dem Erfüllungsgrad der Kriterien pro Level konnten die Multiplikatoren vier Titel erhalten. Die Buttons kennzeichneten die Kompetenzstufen eins bis vier. Möglich waren die Stufen vom „Junior" bis zum „Guru". Level 3 und der Titel „Master Multiplikator" konnten erreicht werden, wenn beispielsweise ein Team insgesamt aktiv die Kollaborationsplattform nutzt, das Wiki strukturiert und lebendig verwendet oder die Anwendungsfälle im Stammtisch vorgestellt wurden. Den „Guru"-Status bekam ein Multiplikator im Level 4, wenn zusätzlich alle Aufgaben im Team über CONNECT verwaltet und umgesetzt waren oder Teammeetings bereits virtuell stattfanden. Sichtbar wurde der Rang durch den jeweiligen Button auf einem Jutebeutel, auf dem alle Stufen vorgeprägt waren. Zusätzlich wurde der Button digital vergeben, sodass er für alle im jeweiligen Teamraum sichtbar war.

Eine Besonderheit gab es. Die Multiplikatoren konnten die Level nur gemeinsam mit ihrem Team erreichen. So war es von Beginn an die Teamleistung, die honoriert wurde.

Dieser Abschnitt entstand in Zusammenarbeit mit Kati Sünderhauf, Referentin Change Management , Enterprise 2.0 Axel Springer SE

Abbildung 6.2.1: Gamification fördert das Engagement und Durchhaltevermögen der Multiplikatoren bei Axel Springer

Gewünschtes Verhalten belohnen: Teilen von Wissen

Die Vorteile eines Social Intranet sind u.a., dass das Wissen im Unternehmen bleibt und dass der Einzelne auf das Wissen vieler zugreifen kann. Doch teilen die Mitarbeiter einfach so ihr Wissen? Oft gilt vielerorts noch der Glaubenssatz „Wissen ist Macht!".

Für das Teilen von Wissen sind Denkanstöße durch kommunikative Unterstützung erforderlich. Kommunikationsthemen können sein: „Wie wir jetzt arbeiten", „Intelligenz der Masse" oder „Wie wir Wissen integrieren".

Damit sich eine Kultur des Wissenteilens entwickelt, kommt es stark auf das Verhalten der Führungskraft an. Inhalte, die informieren oder im Arbeitsalltag vieler Kollegen nützlich sind, sollten mit einem Lob für den Urheber einhergehen. Mitarbeiter müssen wissen, dass der Vorgesetzte das Erarbeiten qualifizierter Inhalte schätzt – ganz gleich, ob Texte, Fotos, Grafiken, Kommentare oder andere Materialien ins Intranet gestellt werden. Auch die Wiederverwendung von Inhalten ist wichtig. Nicht nur der Urheber einer Idee oder die Mitwirkenden an einem Dokument werden belohnt, sondern auch die „Wieder-Benutzer".

Vorsicht ist allerdings geboten bei speziellen Belohnungen für einzelne Mitarbeiter. Das Belohnen von Teamleistungen fördert den Austausch. In erster Linie geht es um ein Gefühl des Einbeziehens, des Teilens, des Miteinanders. Das sollte sich auch bei den Zielvereinbarungen in Mitarbeitergesprächen ausdrücken.

In einer Kultur des Teilens kommt die Anerkennung nicht nur vom Vorgesetzten. Mitarbeiter können Inhalte mitbewerten durch Abstimmungen, Liken, Kommentare oder Ratings. Wenn der Autor von Dokumenten, Best Practices und Präsentationen sichtbar ist, kann ein Kollege eine Verbindung zu ihm herstellen. Das bringt Anerkennung und Dank. Mitarbeiter belohnen sich damit gegenseitig.

Dieser Abschnitt entstand in Zusammenarbeit mit Florian Hoecherl, Manager Analytics & Tools Roland Berger Strategy Consulta Holding GmbH

Wissen teilen – bei Roland Berger erwünscht

Unternehmensberater teilen ihr Wissen grundsätzlich gern mit dem Kunden, doch unter Kollegen? Dafür muss es erkennbare Vorteile geben, sonst liegt die Motivation zur wissensbasierten Zusammenarbeit brach. Das wusste auch das Intranet-Projektteam von Roland Berger Strategy Consultants. „Wir wollten erreichen, dass das Teilen von Wissen für Mitarbeiter auf der neuen Plattform einfach und zielführend ist. Das Teilen sollte direkt verankert werden und den Arbeitsprozess sofort unterstützen", sagt Florian Hoecherl, technischer Projektleiter des Intranets im Unternehmen.

Hier drei Beispiele, wie diese Ziele bei Roland Berger umgesetzt werden:

1. **Expertise sichtbar machen:** Auf einer extra dafür eingerichteten Seite „My Publications" wird deutlich, wer Dokumente verfasst und für die Kollegen geteilt hat. Berater können so auf ihre Expertise aufmerksam machen, positionieren sich für attraktive Projekteinsätze und können über ihre Kenntnisse ein globales Netzwerk knüpfen.

2. **Belohnung durch grafische Badges:** Mit einem solchen Gamification-Ansatz wird Mehrwert stiftendes Verhalten im Netzwerk hervorgehoben. Der Teilen-Badge wird zum Beispiel vergeben, wenn Studien, Berichte oder Case Studies im Intranet zur Verfügung gestellt werden. Mitarbeiter, die Meilen und Hotelpunkte sammeln, streben auch nach diesen Abzeichen.

3. **Ambassadoren:** Für Botschafter einer vorbildlichen Nutzung des Intranets gibt es eine klare Rollenbeschreibung. Um den Status zu erhalten, muss der Ambassador regelmäßig Fragen beantworten, eigene Inhalte zur Verfügung stellen und neue Ambassadoren werben.

Mit diesen Maßnahmen wurde bereits einiges erreicht. Persönliches Wissen wird gut geteilt, nicht zuletzt weil es die Sichtbarkeit des Autors fördert. Das gleiche gilt für externes Wissen: Welche Trends gibt es? Was passiert mit der Energiewende? Studien, Reportagen oder Beiträge von Experten werden häufig weitergegeben. Zurückhaltend hingegen sind Mitarbeiter bei Posts zu Leads, Geschäftsanbahnungen und Kundenerfahrungen. Dort gelingt es noch nicht vollständig, die Silos zu durchbrechen.

„OFFLINE" DIE ONLINE-IDEE ERLEBBAR MACHEN

Das Arbeiten im Enterprise Social Network fordert und fördert neue Arbeitsweisen und eine veränderte Unternehmenskultur. Günstige Rahmenbedingungen dafür lassen sich nicht nur online herausbilden. Ganz im Gegenteil: Insbesondere, wenn es um eine intensive Zusammenarbeit zwischen den Teams und Abteilungen geht, wenn der Austausch unter Experten und das Teilen von Informationen unterstützt werden sollen, bedarf es ebenso des persönlichen Kontakts. In Anwender-Workshops wird immer wieder die Sorge beschrieben, dass das Miteinander in der Organisation 2.0 verloren geht und weniger persönlich miteinander gesprochen wird. Hier besteht Handlungsbedarf. Für eine ausgewogene Zusammenarbeit und den Austausch von Wissen ist Vertrauen nötig. Das aber entsteht seit jeher über persönliche Gespräche am besten. Aus den digitalen Berührungspunkten entstehen im Gespräch sofort Themen, die verbinden. Die direkte Begegnung macht es wiederum leichter, online den kurzen Weg zu suchen, wenn man in Kontakt treten will.

Passende Offline-Formate können für die bessere Vernetzung untereinander sorgen. Sie sollten auf spezielle Zielgruppen zugeschnitten werden und an verschiedenen Tageszeiten mit unterschiedlicher Längen stattfinden, damit viele Mitarbeiter erreicht werden. Mütter, die am Nachmittag zur Familie nach Hause eilen, Manager, die eher in den Abendstunden Ruhe finden und vielbeschäftigte Mitarbeiter, die sich teilweise nur eine halbe Stunde aus den Arbeitsabläufen ausklinken können. Für alle gilt: Oft lässt sich das Nützliche mit dem Angenehmen verbinden.

Beispiele könnten sein:
- Training für Frühaufsteher mit Croissants und Kaffee;
- Multiplikatoren-Picknick;
- Speed-Networking in der Kaffeepause;
- Best-Practice-Clubs;
- Community-Treffpunkte;
- Führungskräfte-Werkstätten;
- Abendtreff für Führungskräfte.

Dieser Abschnitt entstand in Zusammenarbeit mit Kati Sünderhauf, Referentin Change Management , Enterprise 2.0 Axel Springer SE

Wie bei Axel Spinger die Online-Kultur eine reale Note erhält

Eingebettet in die Initiative „move" geben die Projektverantwortlichen bei Axel Springer den Werten, die online gelten, in unterschiedlichster Weise ein Gesicht. Die neue Online-Welt soll kulturelle Veränderungen mit sich bringen, sodass es beispielsweise normal ist, Wissen zu teilen, sich zu vernetzen und eine stärkere bereichsübergreifende Zusammenarbeit zu wollen. Mehr Transparenz ist gefragt, und die soll auch physisch erlebbar sein.

Ein Format heißt „Pizza CONNECTion". In lockerer Talkshow-Atmosphäre diskutieren interne und externe Experten bei hauseigener Pizza über den Einfluss der Digitalisierung auf die verschiedensten Branchen und Lebensbereiche wie beispielsweise Musik, Fußball, Auto oder Bewegtbild. Beleuchtet wird, wie die entstandenen Herausforderungen und Chancen gemeistert werden. Die Talkgäste und Mitarbeiter wagen gemeinsam einen Ausblick in die Zukunft. Es geht um erfolgreiche Rezepte für die digitale Welt, von Insidern ergründet und beleuchtet. Die Mitarbeiter können während der Mittagspause diese Veranstaltung wahrnehmen.

Das Media Powerhouse repräsentiert das Forum der digitalen Expertise bei Axel Springer und ist ein neues und flexibles Lernformat für Menschen mit digitalem Wissensdurst. Im Rahmen der zweitägigen Veranstaltung teilen interne Referenten von Axel Springer und den digitalen Gesellschaften ihr digitales Know-how rund um innovative und zukunftsrelevante Themen aus Journalismus, Marketing und Gündertum u.v.m. Das Media Powerhouse bietet den perfekten Mix aus Wissens-Input der Top-Experten und aktiver Beteiligung des Publikums. Das Format zeichnet sich durch seine hohe Flexibilität aus, indem die Teilnehmer ihr Lernvolumen einschätzen und selbst entscheiden, ob sie zwei Tage mit der ganzen Themen-Palette oder modulartig 60-minütige Wissenspakete wahrnehmen wollen.

Das Netzwerken findet automatisch zwischen den einzelnen Sessions statt oder im Anschluss an die jeweiligen Veranstaltungstage. Parallel können alle Mitarbeiter online über Lync die Live-Übertragung mitverfolgen. Eine Teilnahme ist also in Präsenz und digital möglich. Zusätzlich werden alle Beiträge aufgenommen und im Anschluss on demand bereitgestellt. So geht Verbundenheit heute!

TECHNISCHER SUPPORT UND 6.3
MITARBEITERBEGLEITUNG

Das neue Intranet ist an den Start gegangen und muss sich nun im Unternehmensalltag bewähren. Das führt in der Übergangsphase vom Alten zum Neuen mitunter zu kleinen Turbulenzen. Fragen tauchen auf, trotz aller Trainings. Werden diese Fragen nicht sofort beantwortet und kommen die User in ihrem Arbeitsprozess nicht weiter, dann nutzen sie ganz schnell wieder alte Systeme und fallen in liebgewonnene Gewohnheiten zurück. Vor allem dann, wenn am Arbeitsplatz Hochbetrieb herrscht. Deshalb sollte gerade in den ersten vier Wochen nach dem Start ein umfassender Support gewährleistet werden.

! Praxistipps: Sechs Ideen für den Support

1. Intranet-Lotsen: Gerade am Tag des Starts vermitteln Intranet-Lotsen durch ihre Anwesenheit Sicherheit. Multiplikatoren oder Power User der Abteilung werden mit einem entsprechendem T-Shirt (z.B. Aufschrift: Hilfe in Person) ausgestattet. So weiß jeder, wen er schnell ansprechen kann, wenn Tipps benötigt werden.

2. Heißer Draht zur Support-Hotline: Über den klassischen Weg der Telefonhilfe können besonders die weniger erfahrenen Mitarbeiter schnell unterstützt werden. Statt dass sie lange herumprobieren oder gar aufgeben, lassen sich auf diesem Weg Probleme lösen, sobald sie auftreten. Die Hotline-Zeiten können nach und nach eingeschränkt werden.

3. Ansprechpartner für jede Portalseite: Einzelne Portalbereiche erhalten ein Gesicht, wenn persönliche Ansprechpartner für jede Portalseite präsentiert werden. Die Möglichkeit zur direkten und einfach gestalteten Ansprache schafft gerade in der Startphase das nötige Vertrauen und nimmt Mitarbeitern die Angst vor der neuen Technologie. Die Verantwortlichen sehen als Redakteure auch gleich nach dem Rechten und moderieren gegebenenfalls.

4. Community of Practice: Gemeinsam nach Lösungen suchen, Probleme besprechen, Hilfemöglichkeiten erarbeiten – und das am besten hierarchie- und fachbereichsübergreifend im neuen Portal. Redaktionell betreut wird der Bereich von den Power Usern, denn schließlich sollen sich nur die besten und einfachsten Lösungen verbreiten. Häufig auftretende Stolpersteine können wiederum als FAQs oder als „Tipp des Tages" aufbereitet werden.

5. Kleine Spickzettel: Was in der Schule verpönt war, darf im Intranet gern genutzt werden. Informationen zu den jeweiligen Funktionen und gut verständliche Anleitungen zu einzelnen Vorgängen auf jeder Intranet-Seite erleichtern das schnelle Zurechtfinden und sorgen an Ort und Stelle für Hilfe. Ein kurzer Blick auf den Spickzettel genügt, um im Arbeitsalltag kleine Handgriffe zufriedenstellend zu erledigen.

6. Kurze Screencasts: Manche Dinge versteht man am besten, wenn man sie sieht. Am Arbeitsplatz eignen sich dafür hervorragend Screencasts – kurze Videos, in denen Abläufe leicht verständlich erklärt und vorgeführt werden. In einer Mediathek lassen sich Videos zu zentralen Fragestellungen in der Anfangsphase zusammenfassen. Der Vorteil? Sie können bereits vor dem Launch produziert werden und sind jederzeit und immer wieder zugänglich – auch für später eingestellte Mitarbeiter. Verlinkungen an passenden Stellen sind hierbei sinnvoll.

6.4 MONITORING UND KONTINUIERLICHE VERBESSERUNG

Das neue Intranet ist live und füllt sich mit Inhalten? Das ist ein super Teilerfolg und darüber sollten Sie sich auch freuen! Denn es liegt viel Arbeit hinter Ihnen und es gibt nichts Schöneres, als wenn Sie damit belohnt werden, dass das System von den Nutzern wirklich angenommen wird. Aber Vorsicht: Wichtig ist gerade jetzt, dass keine Pause eintritt und das Intranet „am Leben gehalten" wird.

Natürlich läuft in dieser frühen Phase nach dem Rollout noch nicht alles perfekt. Die verschiedenen Abteilungen werden sehr unterschiedlich auf das neue Intranet reagieren. Einige können Sie allein laufen lassen, bei anderen müssen Sie stärker unterstützen und gegensteuern. Und auch technische Probleme werden Sie noch länger auf Trab halten.

Bei all der Flut an operativen Aufgaben verliert man nur zu leicht die großen Ziele aus dem Auge, die man sich einst in der „Träume"-Phase auf die Fahne geschrieben hat. Ein fehlender Erfolgsnachweis macht es aber ungemein schwer, auch langfristig die Aufmerksamkeit im Management und in den Gremien hochzuhalten. Es besteht die Gefahr, dass ein wichtiges Thema im Sande verläuft und die Leistungsfähigkeit des Systems nicht ausgeschöpft wird.

Ohne Ziele ist Monitoring nur die Hälfte wert

Wer keine Ziele hat, dem fällt es ungemein schwerer, den Überblick zu behalten und Wichtiges von Unwichtigem zu trennen. Schnell kommt man in einen Reaktionsmodus und arbeitet nur noch Anfragen ab, die auf einen einströmen. Ziele helfen Ihnen zu priorisieren und zu entscheiden, womit Sie sich sinnvoller Weise beschäftigen und womit nicht.

Ein gutes Monitoring-System ist gekennzeichnet durch:

- Ziele, sodass man Soll-Ist-Abweichungen frühzeitig erkennen kann;
- Reduzierung auf das Wesentliche, damit man den Überblick behält;
- ein Frühwarnsystem beim Auftreten von Abweichungen;
- einen guten Mix aus harten und weichen Zielen;
- regelmäßige Überprüfung, Auswertung und Anpassung durch die dafür verantwortlichen Gremien.

In der Phase „Träume" wurden bereits Intranet-Ziele definiert und vielleicht auch schon in Bezug zur Unternehmensstrategie gesetzt. Seither ist viel passiert und jeder Nutzer hat ein besseres Vorstellungsvermögen, was das Intranet leisten kann. Setzen Sie auf den damals definierten Zielen auf und entwickeln Sie ein Messgrößen-System, anhand dessen Sie den jeweiligen Status und die Weiterentwicklung mit vertretbarem Aufwand kontinuierlich monitoren können. Verlieren Sie auch die Ziele, die Sie im Rahmen der Anwendungsfälle (Use Cases) und der Pilotprojekte entwickelt haben, nicht aus dem Auge.

Sie werden sich erinnern, Ziele kann man in diesem Kontext auf drei Ebenen unterscheiden:

1. Nutzungsorientierte Ziele – um frühzeitig zu erkennen, wo es Bedarf zum Nachsteuern gibt;
2. Nutzenorientierte Ziele – um sichtbar zu machen, welchen Mehrwert die neue Plattform bringt;
3. Strategische Ziele – Einbettung in das Strategiehaus und das Zielvereinbarungs-System.

Intranet-Nutzung controllen, um agil gegenzusteuern

Nach der Einführung wollen Sie sicher relativ schnell ein Bild davon bekommen, welche Funktionen besonders stark genutzt werden und welche weniger, in welchen Abteilungen ein reger Austausch herrscht und wo nicht. Kennzahlen der Intranet-Nutzung helfen Ihnen bei der Einschätzung, wo Sie die Einführung laufen lassen können und wo Sie unterstützen oder gegensteuern sollten. Ganz im Sinne des agilen Change Managements.

Vieles lässt sich zählen und messen, beachten Sie aber: Weniger ist manchmal mehr! Konzentrieren Sie sich auf solche Werte, die wirklich aussagekräftig sind und bedenken Sie das Thema Datenschutz.

Hier eine Auflistung von ausgewählten Messgrößen, die sich für Nutzungsstatistiken eignen könnten:

- Anzahl ausgefüllter Personenprofile,
- abgeschlossene Aufgaben,
- Anzahl realisierter Workflows,
- Anzahl aktiver Nutzer,
- Anzahl an Beiträgen und Kommentaren,
- Klickraten,
- Welche Funktionen werden besonders genutzt, welche gar nicht?
- Anzahl mobiler Zugriffe,
- Verwendete Speicherkapazitäten im Intranet im Vergleich zu E-Mail-Servern.

Wählen Sie 3, 4 oder 5 Messgrößen aus, die Sie für geeignet halten, und monitoren Sie sie kontinuierlich im Wochen- oder Monatsrhythmus. Setzen Sie sich vorher Ziele, sodass Sie besser einschätzen können, ob Sie auf Zielkurs sind bzw. wie Sie ggf. nachsteuern müssen.

Architektur eines nutzenorientierten Monitorings für ein Social Intranet

Dieser Abschnitt entstand in Zusammenarbeit mit Jürgen Mirbach Social Business Consultant T-Systems Multimedia Solutions GmbH

Für Social Intranets sind wesentliche Instrumente des Monitorings die Auswertung von Logs und Nutzerbefragungen. Während die Auswertung von Logs in manchen Unternehmen aus datenschutzrechtlichen Erwägungen nur eingeschränkt möglich ist, bieten Nutzerbefragungen viele Möglichkeiten. Solche Befragungen können auf die Gesamtplattform bezogen werden oder auf spezifische Nutzenelemente, wie z.B. die vier von Fachbereichen priorisierten Handlungsfelder (siehe Abbildung 6.4.1). Den Handlungsfeldern lassen sich Use Cases oder Zielsetzungen zuordnen, die kontinuierlich nachverfolgt werden können. Denn die Antwort auf die Frage: „Beschleunigt Social Media den Zugriff auf Wissen im Unternehmen?" wird weniger konkret sein als die Einschätzung zur Aussage „In unserem Social Intranet werden Fragen immer schnell beantwortet". Die Zuordnung von Use Cases ermöglicht Abfragen

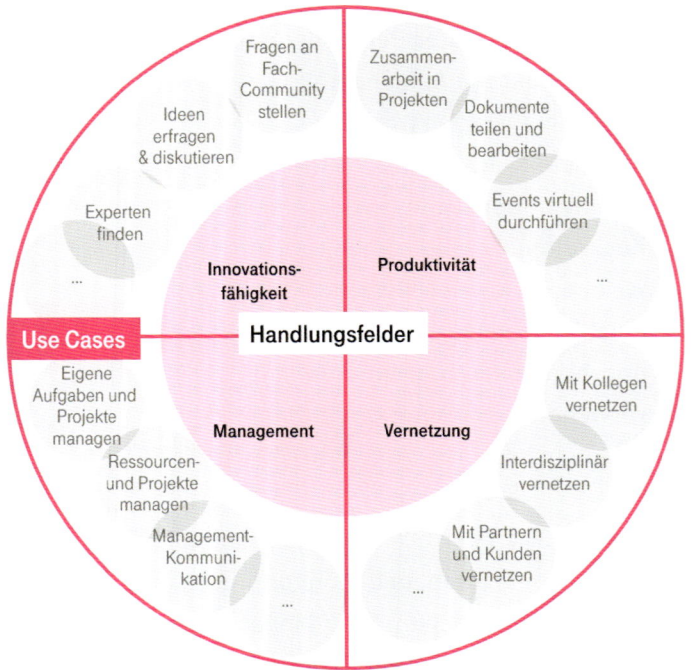

Abbildung 6.4.1: Handlungsfelder und zugeordnete Use Cases in Anlehnung an „Top 10 Handlungsfelder in D, FR und UK" (Pierre Audoin Consultants, 2013)

zu Handlungsbereichen auf konkretem, nachvollziehbarem Niveau. Zudem hilft die Zuordnung, den Schwerpunkt des Monitorings auf bestimmte Handlungsfelder zu fokussieren.

Die Systematik zur Ableitung von Befragungselementen, ausgehend von einem Handlungsfeld via Use Case zu Funktionen, zeigt Abbildung 6.4.2. Dabei gibt es in jedem Handlungsfeld in der Regel mehrere fachliche Use Cases. Meist bilden mehrere Funktionen einen fachlichen Use Case ab. Die Aggregation zur Nutzenaus-

sage erfolgt dann über Durchschnittsbildung oder Index-Funktionen. Zu beachten ist auch, dass Funktionen für mehrere Use Cases eine Rolle spielen können.

Monitoring auf den Reifegrad anpassen

Zuweilen kommt es vor, dass vom Management ein Nutzennachweis gefordert wird, obwohl die Social Collaboration Plattform erst seit Kurzem am Start ist und die Durchdringung im Unternehmen gemäß der gewählten Einführungsstrategie noch vergleichsweise gering ist. Eigentlich ist die Plattform noch nicht reif für eine Abfrage des Nutzens.

Hier könnten ein Stimmungsbild und die Erwartungshaltung der Nutzer bei der Nutzenargumentation helfen. Auf jeden Fall sollte die Chance genutzt werden, systematisch Key-Performance-Indikatoren zu erheben und sie für die Steuerung von Aktivitäten im Change Management und zur Befähigung der Mitarbeiter zu nutzen. Das Befragungsdesign wird in Abhängigkeit von der Reife der Plattform erstellt.

Grundlage bei der Nutzerbefragung kann ein Mapping zwischen Use Cases (z.B. Vernetzung mit Kollegen) und ausgewählten Dimensionen des Feedbacks sein. Dies wären etwa die Nutzererwartung, Bekanntheit, Nutzung, Zufrieden-

Abbildung 6.4.2: Ableitung von Abfrage-Elementen und Aggregation zur Nutzenaussage

heit und der Nutzen (siehe Abbildung 6.4.3). Die Antwort auf die Nutzenfrage wird systematisch erarbeitet, indem Fragestellungen zu den Use Cases an den Dimensionen des Feedbacks entlang entwickelt werden. So wird in einem Stimmungsbild die Nutzenerwartung beispielsweise mit einer Frage „Welche Aussagen spiegeln Ihre Erwartungen am besten wider?" erhoben.

In der Abbildung 6.4.3 sind Vorschläge für die Schwerpunkte der jeweiligen Erhebungen mit einem grünen Punkt gekennzeichnet. Der Vorschlag soll die Möglichkeit eröffnen, mit einem frühen Stimmungsbild in eine systematische Feedback-Erhebung einzusteigen. Mit der Fortführung der Systematik in späteren Befragungen ist die Argumentation bis hin zum Nutzen von Use Cases aus Sicht der Nutzer möglich. Der Reifegrad der Plattform wird also bei der Erstellung der Abfragen berücksichtigt. Je näher ein Use Case an der operativen Arbeit ist, desto näher ist diese Nutzenargumentation an einem echten Business Case.

Die Erhebung eines ersten Stimmungsbildes enthält andere Fragen als eine Nutzerbefragung zu einem späteren Zeitpunkt. Abbildung

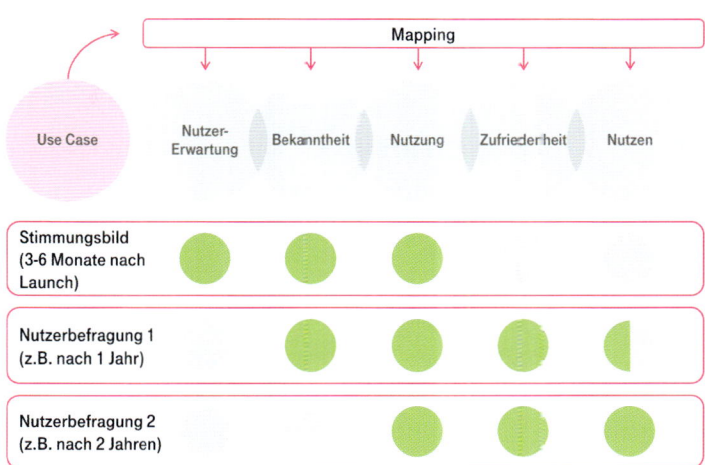

Abbildung 6.4.3: Mapping Use Case und Dimensionen des Feedbacks

6.4.4 enthält exemplarisch Fragestellungen für den Use Case „Vernetzung mit Kollegen" in der für das Stimmungsbild relevanten Dimensionen des Feedbacks.

In der Umsetzung kann ein Mapping von Use Cases auf Dimensionen des Feedbacks aufzeigen, auf welche Weise eine Nutzenargumentation weitergeführt werden kann. Es ist nicht erforderlich, vom ersten Tag an Anwenderaussagen zum Nutzen von Social Collaboration zu erheben. Nicht vom ersten Augenblick an wird das Nutzenpotenzial einer Social-Collabora-

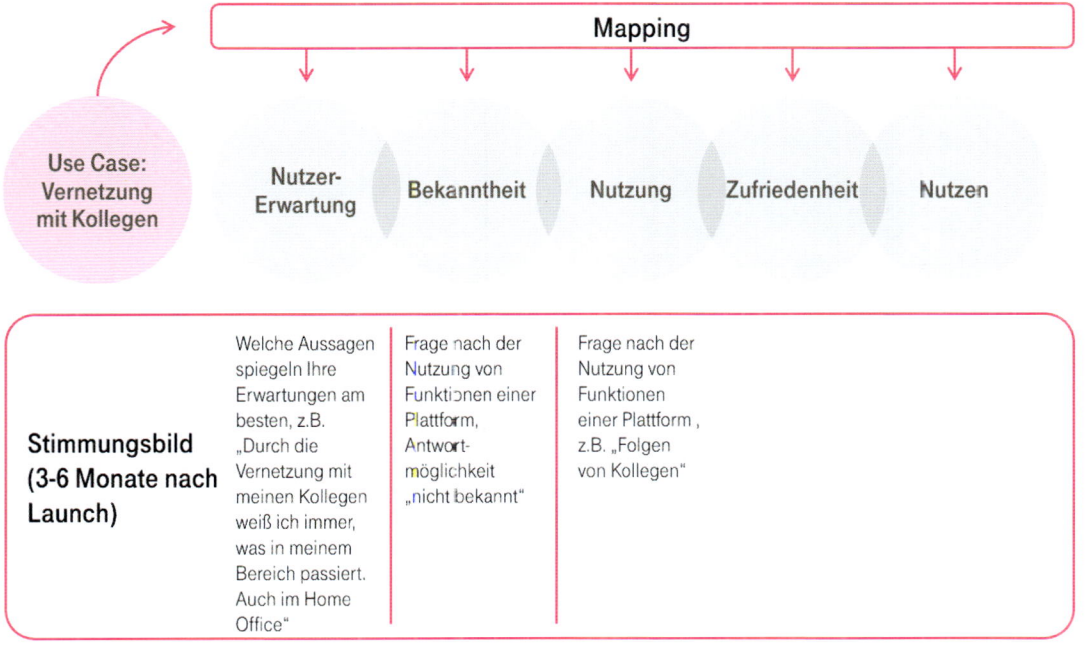

Abbildung 6.4.4: Exemplarische Fragestellungen zum Use Case „Vernetzung mit Kollegen" in einem ersten Stimmungsbild

tion-Plattform im Unternehmen vollständig erschlossen. Ein frühes Stimmungsbild kann Hinweise geben, an welchen Stellen das Enabling der Nutzer noch intensiver durchgeführt werden sollte oder welcher Use Case für das Unternehmen vielleicht auch gar nicht relevant ist. Im Sinne des Controllings eröffnet das Stimmungsbild die Möglichkeit, Steuerungsmaßnahmen zu ergreifen, damit Ziele erreicht werden können.

Bei regelmäßiger Anwendung des Instruments Nutzerbefragung komplettiert sich das Bild. Erwartungen der Nutzer können mit später geäußerten Nutzen-Bewertungen verglichen werden. Aussagen zu Bekanntheit, Nutzung und Zufriedenheit erklären den Status und geben vielfältige Ansätze zur Entwicklung von Maßnahmen als Follow-Up.

Die Diskussion um den Nachweis des Nutzens von Social Collaboration sollte eigentlich umgehend in folgende Fragen umgeleitet werden:

- In welchen Bereichen bestehen die größten Nutzenpotenziale von Social Collaboration im Unternehmen?
- Wie gut funktionieren die Use Cases und die Funktionen in der Social-Collaboration-Plattform im Unternehmen? Was bringt den Nutzern in ihrem Arbeitsalltag Vorteile, was nicht?
- Welche Maßnahmen werden umgesetzt, damit Social Collaboration noch besser funktioniert?
- Welche Ziele müssen angepasst werden und was wird getan, um diese Ziele zu erreichen?

Auf diese Weise wird die Diskussion produktiv auf das Ziel gelenkt, Social Collaboration im Unternehmen erfolgreich zu gestalten. Unternehmen, die diese Herausforderung annehmen, werden früher die Früchte von Social Collaboration ernten können.

Messbare Erfolge bei Robert Bosch

Auf dem Weg zum Enterprise 2.0 hat Bosch die Voraussetzung dafür geschaffen, dass aus einem hochvernetzten, gemeinschaftlichen „Social" Prozesse schlanker, transparenter, einfacher, besser und reichhaltiger werden. Um den Business-Nutzen sichtbar zu machen, wurden bei Bosch Social-Business-Prozesse identifiziert, die im Tagesgeschäft den Mehrwert einer Zusammenarbeit in Communities besonders gut sichtbar machen. Dazu gehören zum Beispiel die Meeting- oder Eventorganisation, der Prozess, um Experten zu finden, oder das Generieren neuer Ideen. Zudem wurden strategisch relevante interne Prozesse analysiert und in Communities ausgearbeitet. Ein Beispiel hierfür sind Kundenanfragen, die über mehrere Bereiche hinweg diskutiert werden müssen. Aus den gewählten Prozessen konnte Bosch Erfolge durch Social Collaboration messbar machen. So konnte u.a. aufgezeigt werden, dass unter völligem Verzicht auf E-Mails der komplexe Entscheidungsprozess „Customer Localization Request", bei dem sieben Abteilungen involviert waren, von vormals vier Wochen auf sechs Tage verkürzt werden konnte, sodass der Kunde wesentlich schneller als vorher eine belastbare Antwort bekam.

Quelle: (Göhring & Perschke, 2014)

Kritische Zwischenbilanz nach vier Jahren Social Collaboration mit IBM Connections bei der CONTAS KG

Als Beratungsunternehmen, welches von seinem Wissen und seiner Innovationsstärke lebt, hat die CONTAS KG bereits frühzeitig erkannt, dass Social Collaboration das Erreichen der strategischen Ziele sehr gut unterstützen kann. Im Jahr 2010 startete die Einführung von IBM Connections. Strategische Hintergründe für diese Entscheidung waren:

- höhere Mobilitätsanforderungen aufgrund der neuen Ausrichtung weg vom Regionalanbieter hin zum gesamtdeutschen Markt;
- das Bemühen um die Innovationsführerschaft im Bereich „integrierter Strategie- und Kulturwandel" in einem Arbeitsumfeld, in dem man immer seltener an einem Ort zusammenkommt;
- stärkeres vernetztes und verteiltes Arbeiten durch Partnerstrategie ohne Wissensverlust bei wechselnden Beratern;
- Home-Office-Arbeitsplätze, um die sehr verschiedenen Work-Life-Bedürfnisse zu erfüllen und dem Anspruch als attraktiver Arbeitgeber nachzukommen.

In einem Workshop erarbeiteten die Geschäftsführung und alle Mitarbeiter bereits ganz frühzeitig folgende drei Ziele im Zusammenhang mit der Einführung der Social Collaboration Software:

- Jeder kann jederzeit und von jedem Ort auf das Know-how des Unternehmens zugreifen.
- Die Arbeitszeit wird wertschöpfend genutzt und von Routineprozessen möglichst frei gehalten.
- Transparenz, Teilen von Wissen und gemeinsames Lernen sind fester Bestandteil der Unternehmenskultur. Wissen ist personenunabhängig für alle verfügbar.

Damit waren die Spiele eröffnet. Es folgte die Technologieauswahl, ihre Integration und die erste Test-Anwendung durch ein Pilotteam, bevor der schrittweise Rollout in alle Teams stattfand.

Dieser Abschnitt entstand in Zusammenarbeit mit Lydia Zillmann, Referentin Unternehmenskommunikat CONTAS KG

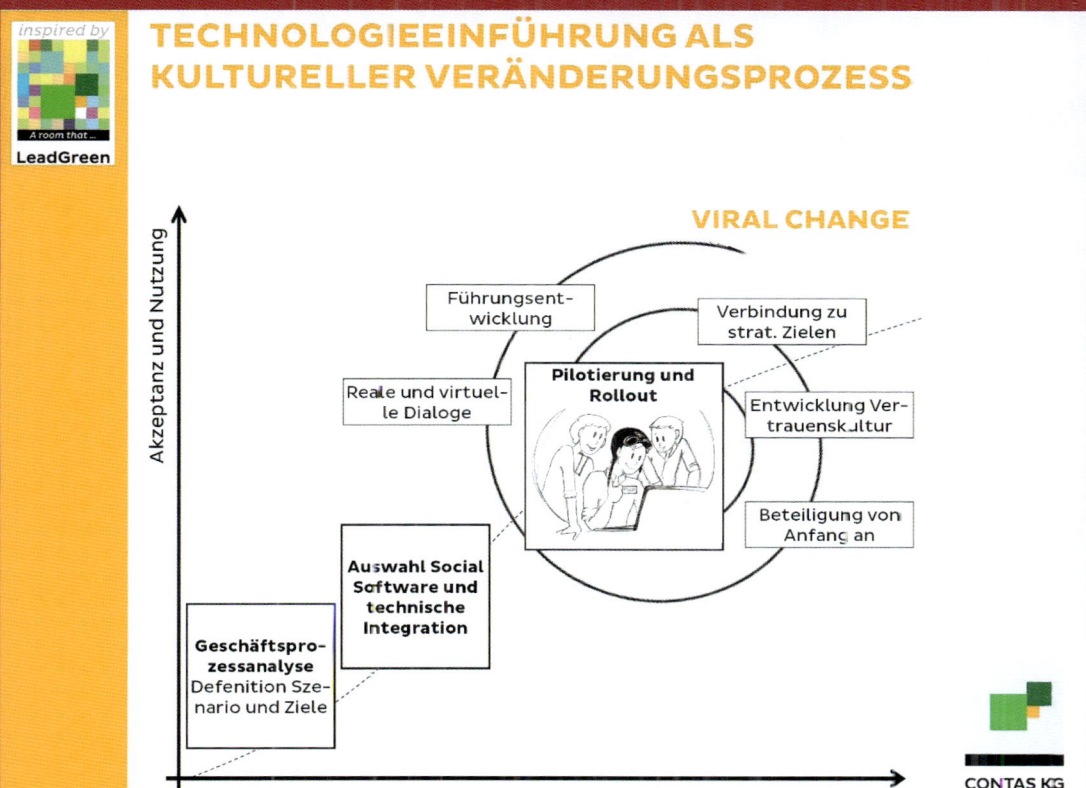

Abbildung 6.4.5: Einführung von Wissensmanagement als kultureller Veränderungsprozess bei der CONTAS KG

Soweit so gut. Aber...

Zurück in die Gegenwart und Hand auf´s Herz – wurden mit der Social Software die strategischen Ziele erreicht und ein echter Business Nutzen geschaffen?

Heute, vier Jahre später, zeigt eine Mitarbeiterbefragung ganz konkrete Vorteile einer inzwischen vernetzten Zusammenarbeit bei CONTAS auf:

1. weniger E-Mails (ca. 50 pro Tag und Person),
2. schnelleres Finden von Informationen (2h Zeitersparnis pro Woche und Person),
3. höherer Informationsgrad,
4. produktivere Meetings,
5. schnellere Übergaben und Einarbeitungen,
6. flexiblere Arbeitsmodelle,
7. schnellere Konzeptionsphasen,
8. produktiveres Teamwork in Projekten,
9. vernetzte Geschäftsprozesse und stärkeres unternehmerisches Denken, welches sich sowohl im Vertrieb als auch in der Kundenbetreuung auszahlt.

Für das Monitoring haben die Verantwortlichen der CONTAS KG bewusst auf abstrakte Kennzahlen verzichtet und sich darauf konzentriert, kontinuierlich in Gesprächen zu überprüfen, wie das System ankommt, an welchen Stellen Unzufriedenheit auftaucht und wo ein Mehrwert bei der Arbeit entsteht. Deshalb wurde ein Jour Fixe mit dem gesamten Team zur kontinuierlichen Verbesserung der Social Collaboration eingerichtet. Denn eines war klar – wenn der Nutzen gegeben ist, dann kommt die Nutzung automatisch. Und das Vorgehen brachte noch einen weiteren Vorteil: Im persönlichen Gespräch erfährt man wesentlich besser, was einen Mitarbeiter bewegt und was zu tun ist, damit die Ziele besser erreicht werden können. Im Vergleich dazu sind Kennzahlentabellen graue Materie ohne Effekt.

UND ES GEHT
WEITER

Auf das nächste Level bringen

Genau genommen ist die Einführung neuer Plattformen der Zusammenarbeit und Kommunikation gar kein Projekt, sondern ein Prozess. Was wie eine Nuance in der Formulierung klingt, macht in der Praxis einen Riesenunterschied: Ein Projekt ist definiert durch einen Anfang und ein Ende. Deshalb gilt das Projekt nach der Einführung von Social Intranet oft als abgeschlossen, sodass die Aufmerksamkeit deutlich sinkt.

Die Anwendungsfälle vor und während des Rollouts decken aber nur einen Teilausschnitt dessen ab, wie wertvoll das Social Intranet für das Unternehmen werden kann. Mit jeder Strategieanpassung und mit jedem neuen Zukunftsprojekt sind immer auch neue Anwendungsfälle für das Social Intranet verbunden. Wurde beispielsweise bei der Einführung besonders auf den Vertrieb geachtet, können nun auch andere Geschäftsbereiche in den Fokus gerückt werden. Wurde bislang nur auf die Vernetzung innerhalb des Unternehmens geschaut, kann nun auch geprüft werden, ob eine Anbindung externer Kunden oder Partner über ein Extranet Sinn machen könnte. Wird im nächsten Jahr die gesamte Personalentwicklung auf den Prüfstand gestellt, könnte auch eine Prüfung der Einsatzfelder von Social Learning erfolgen.

Das Social Intranet kann also auch strategische Zukunftsfelder unterstützen, die bisher unbeachtet geblieben sind. Damit solche Chancen erkannt werden, wurden schon zu einem früheren Zeitpunkt im Rahmen der Organisationsentwicklung entsprechende Verantwortlichkeiten festgelegt. Diese Verantwortlichkeiten können z.B. im Social Intranet Governance Board liegen oder im Steering Committee oder der Geschäftsleitung.

Im Idealfall sollten sich die Führungskräfte bei jeder Tagung oder Strategieanpassung die Frage stellen, wie eine stärkere Vernetzung und Nutzung helfen kann, die Ziele besser zu erreichen. Auch die Technologie ist in einem ständigen Wandel begriffen. Die Möglichkeiten, die dieser Wandel mit sich bringt, sollten kontinuierlich beobachtet und auf ihre Relevanz für das Unternehmen hin überprüft werden. Solche Maßnahmen gehören zur Routine in einem Enterprise 2.0.

Ein System ist nur so gut wie die Visionen, die damit verbunden sind. Wenn ich keine Visionen habe, dann wird das Social Intranet auch nur eines von vielen Werkzeugen sein.

Nie wieder ohne

Wir kennen es alle aus unserem Privatleben: Der Rückfall in alte Verhaltensmuster ist leichter als das konsequente Verändern langjähriger Gewohnheiten. Parallelsysteme sollte es möglichst nicht geben. Wer sich das Rauchen abgewöhnen will, wirft am besten seine Zigarettenschachtel weg.

Hier nun noch ein paar Tipps, damit Ihr Social Intranet eine blühende Wissens- und Austausch-Landschaft bleibt und nicht zu einer kümmerlichen Steppe verdorrt. Und das unabhängig von möglichen Personalwechseln in der Führungsebene.

❗ Praxistipps: Fünf Tipps für ein langlebiges Intranet

1. Schaffen Sie Parallelsysteme konsequent ab! Damit versperren Sie den Rückweg in alte Systeme.
2. Sorgen Sie dafür, dass neue Mitarbeiter sofort mit dem Social Intranet vertraut gemacht werden!
3. Machen Sie Leadership 2.0 zum festen Bestandteil der Aus- und Weiterbildung Ihrer Führungskräfte.
4. Schaffen Sie u.a. mit dem Community Manager feste Strukturen, die dazu beitragen, dass das Social Intranet lebt und Wert stiftet.
5. Werfen Sie jedes Jahr auf Ihrer Führungskräftetagung oder Strategieklausur die Frage auf, ob neue Technologien bei den anstehenden strategischen Themen hilfreich sein können. Fragen Sie auch anders herum, welche neuen strategischen Chancen durch die technologischen Entwicklungen entstehen.

6.6 AUF NEUN PUNKTE GEBRACHT

1 Es ist soweit – die neue Plattform startet. Überlegen Sie sich eine passende, auf Ihr Unternehmen und Ihre Ziele ausgerichtete Einführungsstrategie.

2 Es ist gut, nichts zu überstürzen und einen Schritt nach dem anderen zu machen. Führen Sie Funktionen nicht alle auf einmal ein und denken Sie bei einer so tiefgreifenden Veränderung auch an die Veränderung der Arbeitsweisen und der Unternehmenskultur.

3 Das neue Intranet hat nur dann eine Chance, wenn Parallelsysteme abgeschaltet werden. Schaffen Sie unvermeidliche Gründe zum Wechseln! Halten Sie die alten Systeme nur noch aus Gründen der Sicherheit aufrecht und keinesfalls länger als nötig. Service- und Verfügbarkeitsgarantien können Sie ohnehin nicht für zwei Systeme gleich hoch halten.

4 Der persönliche Austausch macht es leichter, online aufeinander zuzugehen. Vergessen Sie neben den Online-Einführungsmaßnahmen nicht die Offline-Formatideen für die Aktivierung und Vernetzung der Nutzer.

5 Das Projektteam und die IT-Abteilung werden entlastet, wenn die Nutzer Hilfe zur Selbsthilfe erhalten. Stellen Sie einen umfangreichen Support zur Verfügung, um besonders in der Anfangszeit Stolpersteine zu beseitigen und einem Rückfall in alte Arbeitsweisen zuvorzukommen. Begleiten Sie die Mitarbeiter im Arbeitsalltag.

6 Das neue Intranet braucht jetzt wahre Helden. Gehen Sie mit gutem Beispiel voran, zeigen Sie Präsenz, stellen Sie engagierte Nutzer vor und lassen Sie die Führungskräfte Gesicht zeigen, z.B. in einem Management-Blog.

7 Die ersten vier Wochen nach dem Start sind entscheidend! Halten Sie umfangreiche Aktivierungs-, Motivations- und Belohnungsmaßnahmen vor allem für diesen Zeitraum bereit. Immer neue Impulse sind wichtig. Gamification ist kein Allheilmittel, aber sinnvoll eingesetzt, kann es das Intranet beleben.

8 Der Glaubenssatz „Wissen ist Macht" gehört in die Mottenkiste. Geben Sie Denkanstöße und ermutigen Sie zu einer Kultur des Wissenteilens. Erwägen Sie ggf., die Zielvereinbarungen der Mitarbeiter an die neue Wissenskultur anzupassen.

9 Jetzt heißt es, am Ball bleiben! Social Intranet ist kein Projekt, sondern ein Prozess, der nur mit kontinuierlicher Aufmerksamkeit und Pflege sein volles Potenzial entfaltet. Halten Sie Ihr Intranet am Leben, evaluieren Sie Fortschritte und entwickeln Sie gemäß Ihrer Ziele fortlaufend Ausbaustufen.

So, nun haben Sie sich durch knapp 300 Seiten Text gekämpft. Respekt.
Ich denke: Jetzt übernehmen Sie – krempeln Sie die Ärmel hoch und dann los!
Viel Erfolg.

Herzlichst
Ihre Babett
mit Claudia Eichler-Liebenow, Regina Köhler und Steffi Gröscho

STEFFI GRÖSCHO

Die Marketing-Kommunikations-Ökonomin Steffi Gröscho gründete 2003 die Agentur perlrot. collaboration and communication. Zunächst widmete sie sich der Realisierung von Projekten in den Bereichen PR und Marketing, vor allem für Kunden aus den Bereichen Wissenschaft und IT. Mit ihrem Team und einem Netzwerk aus Beratern, Designern und Filmemachern begleitet sie seit 2011 große und mittelständische Unternehmen sowie Organisationen beim Wandel zur Arbeitswelt 2.0 und der erfolgreichen Einführung von Social Intranets in den Arbeitsalltag. Dafür entwickelte sie die perlrot-Einführungsmethode. Die passgenaue Umsetzung der Methodik, die begleitende Kommunikation und die Nutzeraktivierung stehen für sie dabei im Zentrum. Weitere Schwerpunkte ihrer Arbeit liegen in den Bereichen Wissensmanagement und Lernen 2.0. Zu diesem Themenspektrum hält sie Vorträge und veranstaltet Workshops. Die Agentur perlrot gehört zu den ersten elf in Deutschland zertifizieren Yammer-Partnern von Microsoft. Inspiration findet Steffi Gröscho bei ihren sportlichen Aktivitäten in der Natur und auf ihren Reisen in die ganze Welt.

XING:	https://xing.com/profile/Steffi_Groescho
BLOGS:	http://sharepointsocial.de/babetteria/
	http://social-intranet.net/author/intranet-babett/
FACEBOOK:	http://facebook.com/intranet.babett
TWITTER:	http://twitter.com/IntranetBabett
VIDEO:	http://diesharepointsendung.de

REGINA KÖHLER

Die Diplom-Psychologin Regina Köhler begleitet seit über zehn Jahren Veränderungsprozesse in mittleren und großen Unternehmen. Mit Gründung der Leipziger AviloX GmbH hat sie sich mit ihrem Team darauf spezialisiert, Organisationen auf dem Weg in die moderne vernetzte Arbeitswelt zu begleiten. Regina Köhlers persönlichen Schwerpunkt bilden die strategische Beratung und Begleitung von Entscheidern, Führungskräften aller Ebenen und Projektteams sowie die Gestaltung des gesamten Organisations- und Kulturentwicklungsprozesses rund um die Einführung neuer Arbeitswelten. Da der digitale Wandel Unternehmen vor sehr verschiedenartige Herausforderungen stellt, reicht ihr inhaltliches Spektrum von Social Collaboration und Wissensmanagement über moderne Personalentwicklung (Social Learning), moderne Mitarbeiterführung (Leadership 2.0), modernes Ideen- und Innovationsmanagement (Open Innovation) bis hin zur modernen Produktion von morgen (Industrie 4.0). Dazu hält sie Vorträge, Lehrveranstaltungen und Workshops. Zum Abschalten begibt sie sich gern zum Beachvolleyball in den Sand oder mit der Familie aufs Land.

WEBSITE:	http://AviloX.de
XING:	https://xing.com/profile/Regina_Koehler
BLOG:	http://AviloX.de/blog
FACEBOOK:	http://facebook.com/AviloX
TWITTER:	http://twitter.com/MyAviloX

DR. CLAUDIA EICHLER-LIEBENOW

Claudia Eichler-Liebenow hat 1999 auf dem Gebiet der numerischen Mathematik promoviert. Im Laufe ihrer Zeit an der Martin-Luther-Universität Halle-Wittenberg beschäftigte sie sich intensiv mit dem Aufbau von vernetzten Wissenschaftsinformationssystemen im Internet und entschied, sich beruflich weiter in diese Richtung zu entwickeln. Sie trat in die heutige T-Systems Multimedia Solutions GmbH als Entwicklerin für die Intranet- und Extranet-Portale ein. Ab 2004 begleitete sie als Projektmanagerin Kunden bei der Planung und -koordination von Projekten rund um Portale und Plattformen auf Basis von Microsoft Technologien. Ihre Erfahrungen bringt sie seit 2011 als Consultant im Team Social Business Technology ein, das die ganzheitliche Beratung rund um unterschiedliche Social Tools in der internen und externen Kommunikation von Unternehmen anbietet. Dr. Claudia Eichler-Liebenow unterstützt insbesondere bei der Initialisierung, Konzeption und im Projektmanagement in Projekten rund um moderne Intranets. Der technologische Schwerpunkt Microsoft SharePoint erweitert um Yammer und Office 365 blieb hierbei erhalten. Als Privatperson steht für sie die Familie im Mittelpunkt und das Streben, die Leidenschaften für Basketball, Volleyball und Radfahren nicht aus den Augen zu verlieren.

LINKEDIN:	http://de.linkedin.com/in/eichlerliebenow
XING:	https://xing.com/profile/Claudia_EichlerLiebenow
TWITTER:	http://twitter.com/ceitwitt
WEBSITE:	http://social-intranet.org
BLOG:	http://socialbusinessevolution.de/autoren/dr-claudia-eichler-liebenow

BABETT VON PERLROT

Babett ist virtuelle Mitarbeiterin der Agentur perlrot. Sie bringt sich dort ein, wo es etwas zum Thema Enterprise 2.0 zu sagen gibt. Babett ist Mitglied der SharePoint Community und bei allen wichtigen Community-Events vor Ort. Sie hat eine eigene Rubrik in der SharePoint Sendung und moderierte sogar live die Social Business Arena auf der CeBIT 2013. Babett versteht sich als Fürsprecherin der Interessen von Intranet-Nutzern. Ihr Wissen zum Thema Social Intranet teilt sie in ihrem Blog „Babetteria". An der „INTRAversität" lehrt Babett die Einführung neuer Formen der Kommunikation und Zusammenarbeit. Höhepunkt ihrer bisherigen Karriere: Sie ist weltweit die erste durch Microsoft zertifizierte virtuelle Yammer-Beraterin. Ihre Interessen in der Freizeit: Designer-Mode, Sport, ihr perlrotes Cabriolet und die e-Korrespondenz mit ihren Fans.

BLOG:	http://sharepointsocial.de/kolumnen/babetteria/
	http://social-intranet.net/author/intranet-babett/
FACEBOOK:	http://facebook.com/intranet.babett
TWITTER:	http://twitter.com/IntranetBabett
VIDEO:	http://diesharepointserdung.de

VINCENT U. AYDIN

Vincent U. Aydin ist Head of Business Development bei innosabi, einem führenden Anbieter von Open Innovation & Crowdsourcing Software. innosabi hilft Unternehmen dabei, Innovationsprozesse für interne und externe Stakeholder zu öffnen, um gemeinsam Produkte, Services oder gänzlich neue Geschäftsmodelle zu entwickeln. Vor innosabi war Vincent Aydin Consultant bei Bloom Partners. Er hat einen Master Abschluss der Queen Mary University of London in Management and Organisational Innovation und studierte zuvor BWL an der LMU München und an der University of California Riverside.

WEBSITE: http://innosabi.com
FACEBOOK: http://facebook.com/innosabi
TWITTER: http://twitter.com/innosabi

SANDRA BRÜCKNER

Sandra Brückner ist Social Business Expertin bei der Pokeshot///SMZ mit Sitz in Berlin. Spezialisiert hat sie sich auf die Themen Social Learning, Community Management und Gamification. Gemeinsam mit ihren Kunden aus unterschiedlichen Branchen (Telekommunikation, Versicherungen, Banking, Automotive) entwickelt sie innovative Konzepte für moderne Social-Business-Projekte und begleitet ihre Umsetzung bis in den operativen Betrieb hinein.

WEBSITE: http://www.smartsociallearning.com
LINKEDIN: http://de.linkedin.com/in/sandrabrueckner/
XING: https://xing.com/profile/Sandra_Brueckner12
TWITTER: http://twitter.com/SaBrueck

ANDREJ DOMS

Andrej Doms ist als Partner für den Bereich SharePoint bei der ConVista Consulting AG in Köln und seit 14 Jahren als Berater in der IT-Branche tätig. Seine Themengebiete umfassten Lotus Domino, Windows Server Systeme und Suse Linux Enterprise Systeme. Seit 2003 liegt sein Schwerpunkt auf dem SharePoint Server, insbesondere in den Bereichen Infrastruktur, Hochverfügbarkeit, Datensicherheit, Wissensmanagement und Collaboration. Die Erfahrungen, die er in vielen mittleren und großen SharePoint-Projekten sammeln konnte, gibt er in Workshops und Vorträgen an Interessierte weiter. Er leitet die SharePoint UserGroups in Düsseldorf und Köln, die sich regelmäßig zum Erfahrungsaustausch treffen und Teil der deutschen SharePoint Community sind. 2013 wurde er auf den vierten Platz des „European SharePoint Community Influencer"-Rankings gewählt.

LINKEDIN: http://de.linkedin.com/in/andrejdoms/
XING: https://xing.com/profile/Andrej_Doms
TWITTER: http://twitter.com/sprheinruhr
WEBSITE: http://sharepoint-rhein-ruhr.de
BLOG: http://sharepoint-rhein-ruhr.de/blog

ALEXANDER DÖHLING

Alexander Döhling arbeitet seit vielen Jahren als Berater und Software-Lösungsarchitekt im Umfeld von Microsoft Technologien. Er beschäftigte sich intensiv mit dem BizTalk Server und seit 2009 mit den Microsoft SharePoint Technologien. Seit 2013 arbeitet er als SharePoint Architekt bei der T-Systems Multimedia Solutions GmbH und arbeitet eng zusammen mit dem Social-Business-Consulting-Team an der Erstellung von modernen Intranetplattformen auf Basis von Microsoft SharePoint.

XING: https://xing.com/profile/Alexander_Doehling

STEFAN EHRLICH

Stefan Ehrlich ist Vorstand und Gründungsmitglied des Knowledge Research Center Dresden e.V. Er beschäftigt sich seit 2001 in verschiedenen Rollen in der T-Systems Multimedia Solutions GmbH, in Kundenprojekten, Forschungsvorhaben und als Vortragender mit den Themen Collaboration und Wissensmanagement. Seine Schwerpunkte l egen auf dem Menschen als Wissensträger und den Motivationsmechanismen für erfolgreiche Wissensarbeit.

XING: https://xing.com/profile/Stefan_Ehrlich
WEBSITE: http://krc-dresden.de

ERIK FRÖMDER

Erik Frömder ist digital Native und Themenexperte für Social Media und Social Bus ness mit dem Beratungsschwerpunkt, bestehende Unternehmensprozesse unter Einsatz von Social Software zu unterstützen. Aktuell in einer internen Support Community unterwegs und beteiligt an Konzepten für interne und externe Unternehmenscommunites. Erik Frömder arbeitet seit 2011 als Social Business Consultant bei der T-Systems Multimedia Solutions GmbH.

XING: https://xing.com/profile/Erik_Froemder
TWITTER: http://twitter.com/EFrmdr
LINKEDIN: http://de.linkedin.com/in/erikfroemder
BLOG: http://socialbusinessevolution.de/autoren/erik-froemder

EDGAR K. GEFFROY

Ihn faszinieren zwei Dinge: Alles was neu ist und alles was zur Nummer 1 führt. Edgar K. Geffroy ist Unternehmer, Wirtschaftsredner, Bestsellerautor und Business-Neudenker.

Mit 30 Jahren Berufserfahrung als Unternehmensberater zählt er heute zu den erfolgreichsten Referenten und Vordenkern in Deutschland. Der Erfinder des Clienting® setzte bereits in den 90er Jahren neue Maßstäbe im Bereich Kundenorientierung und Veränderung durch den digitalen Wandel. Als Business-Neudenker und Zukunftsmotivator zählt er zu den 10 wichtigsten Business-Motivatoren (Wirtschaftswoche) und zu den 25 führenden Wirtschaftsrednern Deutschlands (GQ). 2007 wurde er in die German Speakers Hall of Fame® aufgenommen.

WEBSITE: http://geffroy.com/
FACEBOOK: https://facebook.com/edgar.geffroy
TWITTER: https://twitter.com/edgargeffroy

CHRISTIAN GLESSNER

Christian Glessner ist Gründer und Geschäftsführer der Experts Inside GmbH Deutschland. Bei den Themen .NET und SharePoint ist er seit der ersten Stunde dabei und seit fünf Jahren Mitglied des Microsoft Most Valuable Professional (MVP) Programm für SharePoint. Von Beginn seiner Karriere an ist er Verfechter von agilen Vorgehensmodellen und Prozessen. Er ist ein Querdenker, der sich leiden-schaftlich mit innovativen Technologien beschäftigt. Aktuelle Schwerpunkthemen sind für Ihn Office 365 und Azure.

WEBSITE:	http://expertsinside.com
BLOG:	http://ilovesharepoint.com

STEPHAN GRABMEIER

Stephan Grabmeier ist Gründer und Geschäftsführer der Innovation Evangelists GmbH. Mit seinem Team berät er Unternehmen, coacht Vorstände zu Social Enterprise und hilft ihnen, schneller zu inno-vieren. Stephan Grabmeier war über vier Jahre Head of Culture Initiatives bei der Deutschen Telekom AG. Dort leitete er u.a. das Center of Excellence Enterprise 2.0 und trieb damit die Digitale Transfor-mation der Deutschen Telekom AG zu einer Enterprise 2.0. Er wurde im Juni 2011 als „Social Media Innovator" von der W&V gekürt und gab ebenfalls 2011 sein Buch „Auf dem Weg zur Organisation 2.0 – Mut zur Unsicherheit" heraus. Anfang 2012 hat er für seine Arbeit den „Corporate Web 2.0 Award" von IIR erhalten. Als Vorstand der Selbst-GmbH e.V. trägt er seit Jahren zur Stärkung der Innovationskraft innerhalb der Personalbranche bei.

WEBSITE:	http://innovation-evangelists.com
BLOG:	http://stephangrabmeier.de
XING:	https://xing.com/profile/Stephan_Grabmeier
FACEBOOK:	https://facebook.com/grabmeier
TWITTER:	https://twitter.com/trill_stephan
VIDEO:	https://youtube.com/user/Stephan1703/videos

MARTINA GROM

Martina Grom ist Geschäftsführerin von atwork information technology, einem auf Online und Cloud-Lösungen spezialisierten IT-Unternehmen in Wien. Sie hat Internationale BWL an der Univer-sität Wien studiert und ist die erste deutschsprachige Microsoft MVP für Office 365. Seit vielen Jahren beschäftigt sie sich intensiv mit den Microsoft-Online-Services sowie dem Thema Cloud Computing und berät kleine und große Unternehmen auf ihrem Weg in die Cloud. Martina Grom ist unter ande-rem Buchautorin und Autorin für das Microsoft TechNet Team Blog Austria und ist als Sprecherin auf internationalen Konferenzen aktiv.

WEBSITES:	http://atwork.at
	http://office365online.at
BLOG:	http://blog.atwork.at
XING:	https://xing.com/profile/Martina_Grom
TWITTER:	https://twitter.com/magrom
LINKEDIN:	http://at.linkedin.com/in/martinagrom

DANIEL HAMMER

Daniel Hammer ist seit 2002 Account Executive für Non-Government-Organisationen bei der Microsoft Deutschland GmbH. Er unterstützt diesen speziellen Kundenkreis bei allen Fragen rund um moderne IT-Lösungen. Seit seiner Wahl zum Betr ebsratsvorsitzenden der Niederlassung Berlin und in den Gesamtbetriebsrat 2010 und der Wiederwahl 2014 begleitet er intensiv den Wandel des Unternehmens zum modernen flexiblen Arbeiten.

XING: http://xing.com/profile/Daniel_Hammer6

FLORIAN HOECHERL

Florian Hoecherl ist IT Manager bei Roland Berger in München. Als technischer Projektleiter ist es seine Aufgabe, das soziale Intranet zu konzipieren, umzusetzen und zu betreiben. Dabei kann er seine Erfahrungen als IT Consultant einbringen: Mehr als 500 Kunden hat er zur Strukturierung und zum Einsatz eines SharePoint-gestützten Projektmanagement-Tools beraten. Er transformiert funktionale Anforderungen in technische Lösungen, bezeichnet sich dabei selbst gerne als „Übersetzer" und bevorzugt schnelles, pragmatisches Vorgehen gegenüber langwierigen Spezifikations-Prozessen.

WEBSITE: http://rolandberger.com
XING: https://xing.com/profile/Florian_Hoecherl
TWITTER: https://twitter.com/fhoecherl

RAGNAR HEIL

Ragnar Heil (M.A. in Sozialwissenschaften) betreut nach 15 Jahren im IT-Consulting nun als Customer Success Manager Office 365 Großkunden in Deutschland. Er berät sie, wie sie Cloud-Dienste wie Exchange, Lync/Skype, SharePoint und Yammer optimal einführen und nutzen können. Er ist vor allem daran interessiert, Kunden auf die Reise in neue Arbeitsstile mitzunehmen, die durch Enterprise Social geprägt sind. Er ist Senatsmitglied im Berufsverband Deutscher Soziologinnen und Soziologen e.V. und Teil des Social Media Councils der Microsoft Deutschland GmbH.

WEBSITE: http://about.me/ragnarh
XING: https://xing.com/profile/Ragnar_Heil
BLOG: http://ragnarheil.wordpress.com & blogs.msdn.com/b/ragnar
TWITTER: http://twitter.com/ragnarh

JOERG CH. JASPER

Joerg Ch. Jasper ist seit mehreren Jahren als Technologieberater bei der Microsoft Deutschland GmbH beschäftigt. Nach einem Studium der Wirtschaftsinformatik vertiefte er seine technische Expertise im Bereich der Microsoft Unternehmenssoftware im Bereich des SQL Servers und entsprechender Programmierung von Datenbankanwendungen. Mit der Zeit wanderte er über die Microsoft Office Suite zum SharePoint Server. Seit ca. drei Jahren konzentriert er sich auf Microsoft Dynamics CRM, die Einbindung in die Prozesse der Unternehmen und den Arbeitsplatz der Mitarbeiter im Vertrieb, Service und Marketing – und damit auf die enge Verzahnung von CRM mit Office, SharePoint und BackEnd ERP Systemen. Neben der Vermittlung von technischem Wissen sind ihm auch die Themen Change Management und UserJourneys wichtig.

OLIVER JORZIK

Oliver Jorzik ist Diplom-Politologe und Geprüfter PR-Berater (DAPR). Seit mehr als 10 Jahren unterstützt er Unternehmen und Non-Profit-Organisationen bei der Professionalisierung ihrer Kommunikationsarbeit: Dabei geht es um die Optimierung von Texten on- und offline, um strategische Medienarbeit und Kommunikationsplanung und eine wirksame Marken- und Produktkommunikation. Er engagiert sich seit 2004 als PR-Dozent bei verschiedenen Weiterbildungsinstitutionen wie der Deutschen Akademie für Public Relations (DAPR) oder der Steinbeis School of Management and Innovation (SMI). Zudem ist er Autor des Fachbuchs „Public Relations – Leitfaden für ein modernes Kommunikationsmanagement". Als Trainer ist er im Netzwerk der Agentur perlrot für die Qualifizierung von Redakteuren im Social Intranet verantwortlich.

WEBSITE:	http://berlin-pr.com
XING:	https://xing.com/profile/Oliver_Jorzik

SEBASTIAN KLENK

Sebastian Klenk ist Technical Evangelist bei der Microsoft Deutschland GmbH. Er schloss eine berufliche Ausbildung zum Fachinformatiker ab, ehe er sich für ein Studium der Wirtschaftsinformatik an der Hochschule München entschied. Unter anderem beschäftigte er sich umfassend mit dem Community Management sozialer Netzwerke. Seine Bachelorarbeit verfasste er zum Thema Lösungsvertrieb, in seiner Masterarbeit beschäftigte er sich mit der Einführung und Nutzung des Enterprise Social Networks Yammer.

BLOG:	http://blogs.technet.com/b/sebastianklenk/
TWITTER:	http://twitter.com/seklenk
XING:	https://xing.com/profile/Sebastian_Klenk3

ULF-JOST KOSSOL

Ulf-Jost Kossol leitet seit 2012 das Social Business Beratungs- und Implementierungsteam der T-Systems Multimedia Solutions. Zuvor war er selbst als Senior Berater für Collaboration und Social Media in der MMS tätig. Ihn treibt die Überzeugung an, dass Unternehmen von morgen im Umgang und Dialog mit Kunden, Mitarbeitern und Partnern immer mehr zusammenwachsen und moderne Technologien diese digitale Transformation positiv beeinflussen werden. Der studierte Diplomkaufmann ist das, was man als klassischen Quereinsteiger in der IT-Branche bezeichnen darf: Vor seiner Tätigkeit bei der MMS war Kossol Offizier der Bundeswehr und gründete 2007 nebenberuflich ein frühes web2.0-StartUp. Die Begeisterung für die neuen Möglichkeiten ebnete den Weg, diese Leidenschaft heute gewinnbringend für Kunden zu übersetzen.

XING:	https://xing.com/profile/Ulf_Kossol
LINKEDIN:	https://linkedin.com/in/ulfkossol
TWITTER:	http://twitter.com/manoeverkritik
WEBSITE:	http://social-intranet.org
BLOG:	http://socialbusinessevolution.de/autoren/ulf-jost-kossol
FACEBOOK:	http://facebook.com/socialbusinessevolution

GERNOT KÜHN

Gernot Kühn ist als Technologieberater für ausgewählte Lösungspartner bei der Microsoft Deutschland GmbH verantwortlich. Nach einem Wirtschaftsinformatik-Studium vertiefte er seine technische Expertise rund um Exchange sowie Office und seit dem SharePoint Server 2001 ist die Intranet-Beratung sein wesentliches Beschäftigungsfeld. Neben der Vermittlung von technischem Know-how sind ihm auch die Einführungsmethodiken und Anwendungsszenarien wichtig.

WEBSITE:	http://office.microsoft.com/de-de/business/
XING:	https://xing.com/profile/Gernot_Kuehn
YAMMER:	https://yammer.com/itpronetwork/users/gernotk
LINKEDIN:	http://de.linkedin.com/pub/gernot-kühn
TWITTER:	http://twitter.com/Gernotk
VIDEO:	http://diesharepointsendung.de

SVEN LINDENHAHN

Sven Lindenhahn ist Social Business Consultant bei der T-Systems Multimedia Solutions GmbH. Seine Aufgabenschwerpunkte liegen in der Beratung, Konzeption, Projektleitung und im Anforderungsmanagement bei Social-Intranet- und Social-Collaboration-Projekten. Seit knapp fünf Jahren berät er Kunden aus verschiedenen Branchen wie Gesundheit, Automobil, Telekommunikation etc. Die Beratung und Umsetzung von solchen Projekten basiert auf verschiedenen Technologien wie z.B. SharePoint, Jive, Connections, Confluence, Drupal etc. Daneben schreibt er für den Weblog www.besser20.de und www.socialbusiness evolution.de. Dem Berufsalltag entkommt er gerne auf Fernreisen, auf denen er auch die Unterwasserwelt beim Tauchen genießt.

XING:	https://xing.com/profile/Sven_Lindenhahn
LINKEDIN:	http://de.linkedin.com/pub/sven-lindenhahn/96/621/717
BLOG:	http://socialbusinessevolution.de/autoren/sven-lindenhahn
	http://besser20.de/author/sven-lindenhahn

JÜRGEN MIRBACH

Jürgen Mirbach arbeitet seit 2011 als Social Business Consultant für die T-Systems Multimedia Solutions GmbH. In den Beratungsfeldern Brand Communities und Social Collaboration liegen ihm die Themen Strategie, Erfolgssteuerung und User Experience besonders am Herzen. Im Blog www.socialbusinessevolution.de schreibt er von Zeit zu Zeit über Erlebnisse im Digitalen Wirtschaftsraum sowie Trends und Neuigkeiten im Markt.

XING:	https://xing.com/profile/Juergen_Mirbach
TWITTER:	http://twitter.com/jm_bonn
BLOG:	http://socialbusinessevolution.de/autoren/jurgen-mirbach

ROGER MÜLLER

Roger Müller ist seit 2008 stellvertretender Leiter Kommunikation/Mediensprecher der Luzerner Kantonalbank AG (LUKB). Davor arbeitete er zwei Jahre im internationalen Kommunikationsteam von SR Technics sowie mehrere Jahre für das Schweizer Radio DRS, davon rund zwei Jahre als stellvertretender Leiter Kommunikation. In allen drei Unternehmen war er u.a. bei der Umsetzung von neuen Intranet- und/oder Internet-Plattformen als (Teil-) Projektleiter tätig. Das neue Intranet der LUKB ist von der Nielsen Norman Group mit dem renommierten Award „Intranet Design Annual 2013: Year's Ten Best Intranets" ausgezeichnet worden.

WEBSITE: http://lukb.ch
XING: https://xing.com/profile/Roger_Mueller114

NADINE PACHALI

Nadine Pachali ist gelernte Werbekauffrau, Medienproduktionerin und staatlich geprüfte Kommunikationswirtin. Nach mehrjähriger Tätigkeit in einer PR- und Werbeagentur war sie im Marketing eines internationalen Pharmakonzerns tätig. Heute ist sie verantwortlich für den Bereich digitale Kommunikation bei der ANWR GROUP, ihre Tätigkeit als Intranet-Verantwortliche gehört dazu. 2012 ging das Intranet MY ANWR nach nur 7 Monaten Projektarbeit an den Start und belegte im gleichen Jahr direkt den 2. Platz beim IntraNET Award, der von der add-all AG vergeben wird.

WEBSITE: http://anwr-group.com
XING: https://xing.com/profile/Nadine_Pachali

MARKUS RAATZ

Markus Raatz ist Vorstandsvorsitzender der Ceteris AG, einem Microsoft Partnerunternehmen, das sich auf Business Intelligence spezialisiert hat. Er spricht regelmäßig auf deutschen und internationalen Konferenzen und ist Mitautor der Bücher zum SQL Server bei Microsoft Press. Zurzeit halten ihn hauptsächlich Data-Warehouse-Projekte mit den Analysis Services des SQL Server 2015 in Atem. Im Jahr 2014 erschienen von ihm zwei neue Video-Trainings zu SQL2014 und Power BI auf video2brain.

WEBSITE: http://ceteris.ag
XING: https://xing.com/profile/markus_raatz
BLOG: http://ceteris.ag/blog
VIDEO: http://ceteris.ag/akademie/ceteris-tv/

ANDREAS ROHR

Andreas Rohr ist als Software-Architekt ein Wandler zwischen den Welten. Sein Beratungsschwerpunkt liegt auf dem Gebiet der Interoperabilität und der Architektur von Schnittstellen. Dabei stehen Schnittstellen zwischen SAP und Microsoft-Produkten wie dem SharePoint-Server im Mittelpunkt. Er konnte seine Erfahrungen mit Lösungen wie Duet bzw. Duet Enterprise sammeln. Aber auch alternative Lösungen sind ihm vertraut. Neben seiner Tätigkeit als Software-Architekt und Berater hält Andreas Rohr Vorträge auf Entwicklerkonferenzen, ist Autor von Fachbüchern und Dozent an mehreren Hochschulen in Berlin.

WEBSITE: http://about.me/andreas.rohr
LINKEDIN: http://linkedin.com/in/andreasrohrberlin
XING: https://xing.com/profile/Andreas_Rohr

MICHAEL SCHOMISCH

Michael Schomisch ist "Head of Corporate ICT & Infrastructure" der Detecon International in Köln Er leitete u.a. das Knowledge Management Projekt „Merlin" und führte das Wissensmanagement in der Detecon als „Head of Knowledge Management" flächendeckend ein. Im Jahr 2012 übernahm er die Gesamtverantwortung für die Detecon interne ICT. Seit 2001 ist er aktives Mitglied des BITKOM Arbeitskreises Knowledge Engineering & Management, seit 2006 Mitglied im Programm-Komitee und Moderator der KnowTech und seit 2007 aktives Mitglied und Co-Moderator des Industriearbeitskreises WIMIP (Wissensmanagement in der Praxis).

XING: https://xing.com/profile/Michael_Schomisch
LINKEDIN: http://de.linkedin.com/pub/michael-schomisch/4/2aa/b34/de

KATHARINA SIMON

Katharina Simon ist Senior Social Business Consultant der T-Systems Multimedia Solutons GmbH. Sie berät Firmen im internen und externen Einsatz von Social Media und fokussiert dabei vor allem auf eine nutzerorientierte Konzeption durch den Einsatz von ethnographischen und Design-Thinking-Methoden.

XING: https://xing.com/profile/Katharina_Simon
LINKEDIN: http://uk.linkedin.com/in/katharinasimon
TWITTER: http://twitter.com/katharina01099
WEBSITE: http://social-intranet.org
BLOG: http://socialbusinessevolution.de/autoren/katharina-simon

ALEXANDER STRAHLECK

Alexander Strahleck ist Geschäftsbereichsleiter Banken und Versicherungen bei der Microsoft Deutschland GmbH. Er blickt auf eine langjährige Vertriebslaufbahn zurück. Vor seiner aktuellen Tätigkeit führte er vertrieblich und personell Vertriebsorganisationen in der IBM Deutschland GmbH sowie der EMC Deutschland GmbH. Hier verantwortete er Vertriebsorganisationen mit 50 bis 250 Vertriebs- und technischen Mitarbeitern. In seiner Laufbahn erlangte er tiefe Kenntnisse mit Schwerpunkten auf den Gebieten Mitarbeiterführung und Change Management in Vertriebsorganisationen.

KATI SÜNDERHAUF

Kati Sünderhauf ist seit 2009 in bei der Axel Springer SE mit wechselnden Verantwortungsbereichen in der Personalentwicklung im Change Management tätig und hat unterschiedliche digitale Einführungsprojekte geleitet. Seit Ende 2012 ist sie Teilprojektleiterin Change Management & Einführung E 2.0. Damit war sie verantwortlich für die stufenweise Implementierung von SharePoint 2013, und ist es zukünftig für Office 365 als unternehmensweites Enterprise Social Network. Dazu zählen insbesondere die strategische Konzeption des Vorgehens, der Kommunikation sowie der Change Management- und Qualifizierungsmaßnahmen. Kati Sünderhauf legt Wert darauf, zuerst den Anwender in den Fokus zu rücken und danach erst die Technologie. Kreative Lernformate zu entwickeln und zu etablieren gehört zu ihren zusätzlichen Kompetenzgebieten.

XING: https://xing.com/profile/Kati_Suenderhauf
LINKEDIN: http://de.linkedin.com/pub/kati-s%C3%BCnderhauf/83/348/263
TWITTER: https://twitter.com/KSuenderhauf
VIDEO: https://youtube.com/watch?v=FpUmFrD0KKE

STEFAN TRUTHÄN

Seit Januar 2002 arbeitet Stefan Truthän bei hhpberlin Ingenieure für Brandschutz. 2008 wurde er geschäftsführender Gesellschafter. Zur Kernaufgabe des studierten Wirtschaftsinformatikers gehört die operative und strategische Weiterentwicklung des Unternehmens. Zusätzlich zu den Tätigkeiten als kaufmännischer Leiter setzt sich Stefan Truthän stark für den effizienteren Einsatz von Informationstechnologie bei hhpberlin ein. Zudem ist er in unterschiedlichen Gremien u.a. als Arbeitsgruppenleiter der Gruppe „Development" im Microsoft Business User Forum (mbuf) zu verschiedenen IT Themen vertreten. In seiner Freizeit engagiert sich Stefan Truthän nicht nur in verschiedenen Vereinen und Organisationen, sondern ist auch aktives Mitglied der Feuerwehr Berlin-Friedrichshain.

XING: https://xing.com/profile/Stefan_Truthaen2
LINKEDIN: https://de.linkedin.com/pub/stefan-truthän/21/963/822
TWITTER: https://twitter.com/truthaen

UWE THUSS

Der Inhaber und Geschäftsführer der Firma Büroland GmbH beschäftigt sich seit mehr als 25 Jahren mit der Gestaltung und Einrichtung von Bürolandschaften. Seit nunmehr 7 Jahren umfasst dies auch die komplette Beschaffenheit der modernen Arbeitswelt und Arbeitsumgebung unter effektiverer Nutzung aller zur Verfügung stehender Ressourcen. In dem von ihm gegründeten Business Village Chemnitz kann man genau diese Arbeitswelt 2.0 sehen und durch vermietbare Arbeits- und Konferenzräume hautnah erleben. Ergänzend dazu berät er mit seiner 2014 gegründeten Firma VisioRealConsult interessierte Unternehmen dabei, durch den Aufbau und die Organisation der Arbeitswelt Mitarbeiter systematisch motivierter und produktiver werden zu lassen.

WEBSITE: http://business-village.de
XING: https://xing.com/profile/Uwe_Thuss

FRANK WOLF

Frank Wolf leitet als Geschäftsführer der EmployeeApp GmbH die Bereiche Marketing, Vertrieb und Beratung für die Eyo MitarbeiterApp. Zuvor war er Leiter des Bereiches Intranet und Social Business der T-Systems Multimedia Solutions GmbH. Er ist Autor und Herausgeber des Buches „Social Intranet", das 2011 im Hanser Verlag erschienen ist. Davor war er als Manager bei Accenture im Bereich eBusiness- und Prozessberatung tätig. Frank Wolf studierte Wirtschaftsingenieurwesen an der Technischen Universität Dresden.

WEBSITE: http://eyo.net
BLOG: http://eyo.net/blog
XING: https://xing.com/profile/Frank_Wolf3

REGINA WÜNSCH

Die Volljuristin Regina Wünsch (Weiterbildung u.a. in systemischem Coaching, ISB) verantwortet seit über 15 Jahren Führungspositionen im Bereich Human Resources u.a. in den Branchen Großhandel, Logistik und Medizintechnik. Bei der Lekkerland AG & Co. KG baute sie als Mitglied des internationalen Managementteams den Bereich Corporate HR mit auf und war Personalleiterin der Hauptverwaltung. Seit 2010 ist sie Director Human Resources & Legal Affairs bei der pfm medical ag, einem inhaberge-führten Handels- und Produktionsunternehmen (Medizintechnik). Der Schwerpunkt ihrer Tätigkeit ist die Organisationsentwicklung, Kulturwandel und Führungskräfteentwicklung.

XING: https://xing.com/profile/Regina_Wuensch

LYDIA ZILLMANN

Als Referentin für Unternehmenskommunikation war Lydia Zillmann sechs Jahre bei der CONTAS KG, einer Leipziger Beratungsgesellschaft für integrierten Strategie- und Kulturwandel, tätig. 2011 gestaltete sie hier als Projektverantwortliche die Einführung von Social Software als kulturellen Ver-änderungsprozess. Bis heute ist CONTAS dank dieses Prozesses Best Practice für den Kulturwandel und die Verbesserung der strategischen Zielerreichung durch vernetzte Zusammenarbeit im Unter-nehmen. Seit August 2014 berät sie als Projektmanagerin bei der AviloX GmbH Unternehmen auf dem Weg in moderne vernetzte Arbeitswelten. Ihre Schwerpunkte liegen dabei unter anderem in den The-men Social Collaboration und Change 2.0. Hierzu gibt sie Vorträge und Interviews unter anderem im BITKOM Arbeitskreis „Knowledge Management", auf der CeBIT oder bei der KnowTech.

XING: https://xing.com/profile/Lydia_Zillmann
TWITTER: https://twitter.com/zillmannly

ABBILDUNGS- UND TABELLENVERZEICHNIS

9 QUELLENVERZEICHNIS

agilemanifesto.org. (2001). Manifest für Agile Softwareentwicklung. Abgerufen am 09. 2014 von http://agilemanifesto.org

Andrews, W. (26. 09. 2013). Magic Quadrant for Enterprise Video Content Management. (Gartner) Abgerufen am 05. 08. 2014 von http://www.gartner.com/technology/reprints. do?id=1-1KWXTM2&ct=130927&st=sb

Aycin, G. (2012). Die Wiener Ausbildungsgarantie. Perspektiven von Jugendlichen mit Migrationshintergrund in Lehrwerkstätten. Diplomarbeit. Wien: Universität Wien.

Bartle, R. (June 1996). Hearts, Clubs, Diamonds, Spades: Players Who Suit MUDs. Journal of MUD Research. Vol. 1, Issue 1.

Dörfel, L. & Hirsch, L. (Hrsg.). (2012). Social Intranet 2012: Studienergebnisse, Fachbeiträge und Experteninterviews. prismus communications GmbH .

Drakos, N., Mann, J. & Gotta, M. (10. 09 2013). Magic Quadrant for Social Software in the Workplace. Abgerufen am 05. 09. 2013 von https://www.gartner.com/doc/2587020/magic-quadrant-social-software-workplace

Ganser, R. & Müller, C. (2012). Portale mit SharePoint 2010. O'Reilly.

Gloger, B. (2013). Scrum: Produkte zuverlässig und schnell entwickeln. Carl Hanser Verlag.

Goasduff, L. & Pettey, C. (12. 04. 2014). Gartner Says By 2015, More Than 50 Percent of Organizations That Manage Innovation Processes Will Gamify Those Processes. Abgerufen am 05. 09. 2014 von Gartner: http://www.gartner.com/newsroom/id/1629214

Göhring, M. & Perschke, K. (2014). Berufsbild Interner Community Manager: Triebkraft und Transformator im hochvernetzten Unternehmen. In 16. Kongress für Wissensmanagement, Social Media und Collaboration – „Zukunft der Wissensarbeit" (S. 70ff). Hanau: Bitkom.

Griffith, C. (24. 02. 2014). Predictions 2014: Smartphone penetration to beat computers („IDC says 83% of employees already use their personally purchased smartphone for work"). (The Australian) Abgerufen am 03. 06. 2014 von http://www.theaustralian.com.au/technology/predictions-2014-smartphone-penetration-to-beat-computers/story-e6fr-gakx-1226836221379%23

Grom, M. (2012). Office 365 in kleinen Unternehmen. Microsoft.

Hagen, S. (2014). Projektmanagement ≠ Agile. Eine Abgrenzung. Abgerufen am 09. 2014 von PM-Blog.com: http://pm-blog.com/2014/09/02/projektmanagement_agile_abgrenzung/

Herzig, P. & Ameling, M. (09. 2012). Gamification fürs Geschäft. iX, Magazin für professionelle Informationstechnik.

Hirsch, L. (25. 06. 2014). 5 Thesen zu Social Media in der Internen Kommunikation. Abgerufen am 04. 10. 2014 von http://social-intranet.net/thesen-social-media-und-interne-kommunikation/

Kada, M. (2010). ROI of Building a Company-wide, Video Podcasting Portal Using Microsoft® SharePoint® 2010. Microsoft Academy. Abgerufen am 02. 12. 2014 von http://download.microsoft.com/download/B/6/F/B6F226A3-91EB-4113-A92A-E37963AD6F0D/Microsoft%20Academy_Return%20on%20Investment%20(ROI)%20White%20Paper.pdf

Knoof, T. (24. 11. 2011). 21 verführerische Strategien, um hoch emotionale und spannungsgeladene Launches aufzubauen. Abgerufen am 06. 12. 2014 von http://www.digitale-infoprodukte.de/affiliate/21-verfuehrerische-strategien-um-hoch-emotionale-und-spannungsgeladene-launches-aufzubauen/

Kresse, A. (2011). Überholen ohne einzuholen – Das Paradoxon der Personalentwicklung. In A. Trost, & T. Jenewein, Personalentwicklung 2.0: Lernen, Wissensaustausch und Talentförderung der nächsten Generation (S. 88). Legewie, H. & Schervier-Legewie, B. (1995). Im Gespräch: Anselm Strauss. Journal für Psychologie 3 (1), 64-75.

McAfee, A. (2006). Enterprise 2.0: The Dawn of Emergent Collaboration. MIT Sloan Management Review, Jg. 47(H. 3), S. 20–28.

Microsoft. (2014). „Should I save my documents to OneDrive for Business or a team site?". Abgerufen am 30. 11. 2014. von https://support.office.com/en-us/article/Should-I-save-my-documents-to-OneDrive-for-Business-or-a-team-site-d18d21a0-1f9f-4f6c-ac45-d52afa0a4a2e?ui=en-US&rs=en-US&ad=US Microsoft. (2014). Low Enforcement Report.

Abgerufen am 05. 09. 2014 von http://www.microsoft.com/about/corporatecitizenship/en-us/reporting/transparency/

Mühlberger, S. (09. 2014). Sag mal, wie geht das? brand eins. Von http://www.brandeins.de/archiv/2014/arbeit/alt-lernt-vor-jung-viele-generationen-im-unternehmen-sag-mal-wie-geht-das abgerufen

Nonaka, I. & Takeuchi, H. (1995). The Knowledge-Creating Company: How Japanese Companies Create the Dynamics of Innovation. Oxford University Press.

Pappas, C. (16. 04. 2014). Top Learning Management System Trends for 2014. Abgerufen am 17. 09. 2014 von http://elearningindustry.com/top-learning-management-system-trends-for-2014

Pierre Audoin Consultants. (2013). Top 10 Handlungsfelder in D, FR und UK. In Social Collaboration in Deutschland, Frankreich und Großbritannien (S. 15).

Robertson, J. (21. 10. 2008) 25 reasons why saving time on your intranet is a bad metric. Abgerufen am 02. 12 2014 von http://www.steptwo.com.au/columntwo/25-reasons-why-saving-time-on-your-intranet-is-a-bad-metric/

Robes, J. (2011). Vom Personalentwickler zum Community Manager? Ein Rollenbild im Wandel. In A. Trost, & T. Jenewein, Personalentwicklung 2.0: Lernen, Wissensaustausch und Talentförderung der nächsten Generation (S. 65 ff.).

Rosenfeld, L. (23. 03. 2011). Adaptable Information Workshop slides. Vor Slideshare: http://de.slideshare.net/lrosenfeld/adaptable-ia-presentation abgerufen

Schneegans, M. (06. 2012). „Klassisches" versus agiles IT „Klassisches" versus agiles IT-Projektmanagement. amendos whitepaper. Abgerufen am 02. 12. 2012 von http://www.amendos.de/publikationen/fachartikel/Whitepaper_klassisch-vs-agil-PM.pdf

Three Motion. (04. 2013). The Power of Online Video – The Stats 2013. Von http://threemotion.co.uk/the-power-of-online-video-the-stats-2013/ abgerufen

Wegscheider, M. (22. 11 2012). Auf dem Weg zum Enterprise 2.0 (Allianz). Präsentation. Düsseldorf: K2-Tagung Interne Kommunikation.

Wikipedia. (10. 01. 2015). Gamification. Abgerufen am 30. 01. 2015 von http://de.wikipedia.org/wiki/Gamification

Wolf, F. (19. 10. 2010). Die drei wichtigsten Ziele eines Intranet 2.0 und wie man sie messen kann. Abgerufen am 02. 12. 2014 von http://besser20.de/die-drei-wichtigsten-ziele-eines-intranet-2-0-und-wie-man-sie-messen-kann/1472/

Wolf, F. (2011). Social Intranet – Kommunikation fördern – Wissen teilen – Effizient zusammenarbeiten. Carl Hanser Verlag.

Wolf, F. (14. 06. 2014). Der Enterprise 2.0 Irrtum: Wissensmanagement im Enterprise 2.0, Teil 4. Abgerufen am 14. 10. 2014 von http://de.slideshare.net/TSystemsMMS/der-enterprise-20-irrtum-wissensmanagement-im-enterprise-20

INDEX 10

DANKSAGUNGEN

Wir danken

… unseren Familien für ihr Verständnis und ihre Bereitschaft, uns während des 15-monatigen Buchprojekts bedingungslos den Rücken frei zu halten, auch wenn es ihnen viele Entbehrungen abverlangte.

… unseren Freunden für ihr Interesse, ihre Neugierde und ihre Vorfreude auf das Buch, welche uns sehr motiviert hat.

… unseren Mitarbeitern, Kollegen und Mitstreitern für die wertvollen fachlichen Anregungen, kritischen Hinweise und immer wieder neuen Blickwinkel, die unser Buch inhaltlich bereicherten.

… allen Gastautoren für den unkomplizierten produktiven Austausch und die vielen interessanten Einblicke, die sie uns und unseren Lesern mit so viel Freude geben sowie den Unterstützern Sabine Beck (VHV Gruppe), Nikolay Borisov (T-Systems MMS), Alexander Derno (Deutsche Telekom, TSN), Simone Happ (T-Systems MMS), Marie-Isabelle Fink (ifm electronic), Martina Garg (vitos), Oliver Jungmann (Ligatura), Barbara Koch (IBM), Christiane Kröhling (MAN Diesel & Turbo), Max Lund (Hamburg Süd), Caroline Ruenger (Microsoft), Fanny Schreiter (T-Systems MMS), Patrick Schwanebeck (Goethe-Institut), Jessica Staub (ifm electronic), Astrid Theis (Axel Springer), Michael Wegscheider (Allianz Deutschland) und Elmar Witte (Microsoft).

… unseren Kunden, die uns seit vielen Jahren vertrauen und maßgeblich dazu beigetragen haben, dass wir diese Fülle an Wissen weitergeben können.

… unserem Verlag SCM, insbesondere Theresa Schulz und Lars Dörfel für die Betreuung, dem Lektor Bernd Stadelmann sowie dem Grafiker Jens Guischard für die Formvollendung unseres Buches.

… Andreas Galling-Stiehler für seine kritischen Textbetrachtungen und neuen Buchstaben.

… zu guter Letzt auch unseren Marktbegleitern, die mit uns an die Vision moderner Arbeitswelten glauben und in ihren Veröffentlichungen mit uns dieses Thema immer wieder den Unternehmen und ihrer Aufmerksamkeit nahebringen.

Und speziell:

Steffi Gröscho

Claudia und Regina für die zusammengetrage-
ne Expertise und ganze Energie.

H. für´s Aushalten, die Inspiration, Bewegung,
Vernetzung und überhaupt.

Erika, Gabriele und Familie für den Schreib-
sommer im Garten.

Annemarie für Fragen nach den Buchfortschrit-
ten und Babett.

Dr. Claudia Eichler-Liebenow

Steffi, danke für Deine Einladung zu diesem
Buchabenteuer, was für eine Chance!

Regina, danke Dir für die neuen Blickwinkel und
vielen Diskussionen.

Kollegen, Ihr gabt mir den Mut mitzumachen,
danke für die tolle Unterstützung. N.

Stefan, Eric und Georg: Ihr bekommt mich nun
wieder „zurück" – danke für die Geduld.

Regina Köhler

Steffi für ein atemberaubendes 2014.

Lydia, Susanne und Claudia – ohne Eure Ablen-
kung, Aufmunterung und Aufheiterung wären
mir die nächtlichen Schreibstunden verdammt
lang vorgekommen.

Und André, Edgar und Frederik dafür, dass ihr
mir so viel gebt.

Babett

Bettina Lawrenz und Ulrike Petersen für die
Geburtshilfe, für ständig neue Schuhe und
Designerfummel.

SharOn für seine inspirierenden Mails, die stets
für das Training der Lachmuskeln sorgten.